SCOTT W. STARRATT

Special Publication reviewing procedures

The Society makes every effort to ensure that the scientific and production quality of its books matches that of its journals. Since 1997, all book proposals have been refereed by specialist reviewers as well as by the Society's Publications Committee. If the referees identify weaknesses in the proposal, these must be addressed before the proposal is accepted.

Once the book is accepted, the Society has a team of series editors (listed above) who ensure that the volume editors follow strict guidelines on refereeing and quality control. We insist that individual papers can only be accepted after satisfactory review by two independent referees. The questions on the review forms are similar to those for the *Journal of the Geological Society*. The referees' forms and comments must be available to the Society's series editors on request.

Although many of the books result from meetings, the editors are expected to commission papers that were not presented at the meeting to ensure that the book provides a balanced coverage of the subject. Being accepted for presentation at the meeting does not guarantee inclusion in the book.

Geological Society Special Publications are included in the ISI Science Citation Index, but they do not have an impact factor, the latter being applicable only to journals.

More information about submitting a proposal and producing a Special Publication can be found on the Society's web site: www.geolsoc.org.uk

It is recommended that reference to all or part of this book should be made in one of the following ways:

PYE, K. & ALLEN, J. R. L. (eds) 2000. *Coastal and Estuarine Environments: sedimentology, geomorphology and geoarchaeology*. Geological Society, London, Special Publications, **175**.

DUCK, R. W. & WEWETZER, S. F. K. 2000. Relationship between current measurements and sonographs of subtidal bedforms in the macrotidal Tay Estuary, Scotland. *In*: PYE, K. & ALLEN, J. R. L. (eds) 2000. *Coastal and Estuarine Environments: sedimentology, geomorphology and geoarchaeology*. Geological Society, London, Special Publications, **175**, 31–41.

GEOLOGICAL SOCIETY SPECIAL PUBLICATION NO. 175

Coastal and Estuarine Environments: sedimentology, geomorphology and geoarchaeology

EDITED BY

K. PYE
Royal Holloway, University of London, UK

and

J. R. L. ALLEN
Reading University, UK

2000

Published by

The Geological Society

London

THE GEOLOGICAL SOCIETY

The Geological Society of London was founded in 1807 and is the oldest geological society in the world. It received its Royal Charter in 1825 for the purpose of 'investigating the mineral structure of the Earth' and is now Britain's national society for geology.

Both a learned society and a professional body, the Geological Society is recognized by the Department of Trade and Industry (DTI) as the chartering authority for geoscience, able to award Chartered Geologist status upon appropriately qualified Fellows. The Society has a membership of 9099, of whom about 1500 live outside the UK.

Fellowship of the Society is open to persons holding a recognized honours degree in geology or cognate subject, or not less than six years' relevant experience in geology or a cognate subject. A Fellow with a minimum of five years' relevant postgraduate experience in the practice of geology may apply for chartered status. Successful applicants are entitled to use the designatory postnominal CGeol (Chartered Geologist). Fellows of the Society may use the letters FGS. Other grades of membership are available to members not yet qualifying for Fellowship.

The Society has its own publishing house based in Bath, UK. It produces the Society's international journals, books and maps, and is the European distributor for publications of the American Association of Petroleum Geologists, (AAPG), the Society for Sedimentary Geology (SEPM) and the Geological Society of America (GSA). Members of the Society can buy books at considerable discounts. The publishing House has an online bookshop (*http://bookshop.geolsoc.org.uk*).

Further information on Society membership may be obtained from the Membership Services Manager, The Geological Society, Burlington House, Piccadilly, London W1V 0JU, UK. (Email: *enquiries@geolsoc.org.uk*: tel: +44 (0)207 434 9944).

The Society's Web Site can be found at *http://www.geolsoc.org.uk/*. The Society is a Registered Charity, number 210161.

Published by The Geological Society from:
The Geological Society Publishing House
Unit 7, Brassmill Enterprise Centre
Brassmill Lane
Bath BA1 3JN, UK

(*Orders*: Tel. +44 (0)1225 445046
        Fax +44 (0)1225 442836)
Online bookshop: *http://bookshop.geolsoc.org.uk*

The publishers make no representation, express or implied, with regard to the accuracy of the information contained in this book and cannot accept any legal responsibility for any errors or omissions that may be made.

British Library Cataloguing in Publication Data
A catalogue record for this book is available from the British Library.

ISBN 1-86239-070-3

Typeset by Aarontype Ltd, Bristol, UK

Printed by The Alden Press, Oxford

Distributors

USA
   AAPG Bookstore
   PO Box 979
   Tulsa
   OK 74101-0979
   USA
Orders: Tel. +1 918 584-2555
        Fax +1 918 560-2652
        e-mail: *bookstore@aapg.org*

Australia
   Australian Mineral Foundation Bookshop
   63 Conyngham Street
   Glenside
   South Australia 5065
   Australia
Orders: Tel. +61 88 379-0444
        Fax +61 88 379-4634
        e-mail: *bookshop@amf.com.au*

India
   Affiliated East-West Press PVT Ltd
   G-1/16 Ansari Road, Daryaganj,
   New Delhi 110 002
   India
Orders: Tel. +91 11 327-9113
        Fax +91 11 326-0538
        e-mail: *affiliat@nda.vsnl.net.in*

Japan
   Kanda Book Trading Co.
   Cityhouse Tama 204
   Tsurumaki 1-3-10
   Tama-shi
   Tokyo 206-0034
   Japan
Orders: Tel. +81 (0)423 57-7650
        Fax +81 (0)423 57-7651

Contents

CONTENTS

Preface

This book arises from a two day international conference held at the Geological Society of London in November 1998. The meeting was organized with the purpose of bringing together sedimentologists, geomorphologists, archaeologists, environmental scientists and environmental managers to discuss recent research and topical issues relating to the interactions between natural processes, morphology and human activities in coastal and estuarine environments. More than 200 delegates, from 16 countries, attended the meeting over the course of the two days, stimulating lively discussion both about basic scientific issues and management implications. The meeting was sponsored by the British Sedimentological Research Group, the British Geomorphological Research Group, and English Heritage, and was also supported by the Environmental Sedimentology Committee of the International Association of Sedimentologists. The editors would like to thank these organizations, together with staff at the Geological Society and numerous daily helpers, especially postgraduate students and others from the University of Reading, for their generous assistance in making the meeting a great success.

The principal themes of this title are:

(1) The nature of basic processes affecting coasts and estuaries and their relationship to morphological and sedimentological changes on timescales ranging from months to millenia, and at spatial scales ranging from tens of metres to tens of kilometres;
(2) The effects of changes in the natural environmental forcing factors on coastal and estuarine morphology and sedimentary characteristics, and the implications for human activities and their record;
(3) The impacts of human activities and their record on coastal and estuarine processes and morphology;
(4) Issues relating to the future management and conservation of the natural and archaeological heritage, including outstanding problems and future research needs.

This publication contains 29 papers based on a selection of the 32 oral presentations and more than 30 poster presentations made at the conference, and draws on examples from all over the world. The ordering of chapters has been arranged broadly to follow the sequence of the four main themes, starting with the shorter term, smaller scale and moving to the longer term, larger scale and management issues. There is, naturally, considerable overlap between themes in many of the contributions.

We hope that this book will serve not only as a record of scientific knowledge and concerns at the end of the first millenium, but also as a stimulus for further research endeavour and a significant influence on thinking about the ways in which natural processes, historical changes and the record of human activities in coastal and estuarine environments need to be taken into account in their future management. The need for breadth of approach, and a willingness toward sympathetic communication between different specialists, has never been greater.

Ken Pye & John R. L. Allen

Past, present and future interactions, management challenges and research needs in coastal and estuarine environments

KENNETH PYE[1] & JOHN R. L. ALLEN[2]

[1] *Department of Geology, Royal Holloway, University of London, Egham, Surrey TW20 0EX, UK*
[2] *Postgraduate Research Institute for Sedimentology, University of Reading, Whiteknights, Reading RG6 6AB, UK*

Users, needs and research

There are many user interests on coasts and in estuaries, including economic activities (ports, harbours, navigation, fishing, mineral extraction), recreation (bathing, walking, sailing, fishing, birdwatching), flood defence, water quality, nature conservation, and conservation of the historical and archaeological heritage. Often these interests are conflicting, and managers frequently have to attempt a compromise or make hard decisions based on a prioritized course of action which reflects economic, political and legal constraints (see, for example, Barrett 1992; Kay & Alder 1999; Flemming 2000). Often the decisions are taken on the basis of inadequate background information and a poor understanding of the functioning of the invariably complex coastal system under consideration. In a world of increasingly rapid technological and economic development, sea-level rise, and possible global climate change, central tasks facing the coastal and estuarine manager are to predict and manage change, undertaken against a background of constantly moving goalposts. There is an urgent need for a much better framework of background environmental data and more effective and reliable management tools, founded on sound scientific understanding, which can provide the necessary guidance and basis for policy formulation. Although, these needs have been recognized, and some progress has been made in the past few years, an adequate suite of such tools and frameworks for environmental monitoring are still some way off.

Past and present interactions

Fundamental to a successful management strategy is an adequate understanding of the basic physical, chemical, biological and human properties and processes which affect coasts and estuaries, including their interactions and variability on different time and spatial scales. Much can be learned from the sedimentary and archaeological record about the way in which coasts and estuaries have varied in the past, the way in which man has responded to or caused such changes, and with what consequences, both for himself and for the 'natural' environment. Although the past may not always be the key to the future, it is the key to understanding the present, and an understanding of the causes and effects of past changes allow predictions of the impacts of possible future changes to be made with greater confidence.

Traditionally, research in coastal and estuarine environments has been undertaken by scientists in several different disciplines who have had a rather narrow focus and have often been quite unaware of what colleagues in other disciplines have been doing. Issues such as flood defence, navigation and water quality have traditionally been the preserve of engineers and mathematical modellers, concerned with (geologically) short time scales of hours to at most 50 years. At the other end of the spectrum, archaeologists, Quaternary scientists and geologists have been concerned with much longer timescales of centuries to millenia. Geomorphologists and ecologists have occupied something of a middle ground, concerned with a range of processes and effects ranging from small scale to large scale and short term to medium term, but often focusing on issues and techniques quite different to those concerning the engineer, geologist or archaeologist. There have, of course, always been exceptions to this generalization, but only in the past ten years or so has cross-disciplinary research – the holistic view – begun to emerge as a desirable

From: PYE, K. & ALLEN, J. R. L. (eds). *Coastal and Estuarine Environments: sedimentology, geomorphology and geoarchaeology*. Geological Society, London, Special Publications, **175**, 1–4. 0305-8719/00/$15.00 © The Geological Society of London 2000.

norm. There is now wider awareness both of the value of inter-disciplinary, integrated approaches to many scientific and practical management problems, including those relating to coasts and cstuaries, and of the need to adopt an integrated, strategic approach to the sustainable management of such environments, but there is still much progress to be made.

As noted by Pollard (1999), of all the sciences utilized in modern archaeological research, that of geology has the longest association with archaeology. However, many archaeologists, trained largely or wholly on 'dryland' sites, are still only dimly aware of the way in which geomorphological and sedimentary processes operate, and about how the properties of sedimentary materials influence the preservation potential and interpretation of archaeological remains in the geologically dynamic lowland coastal zone. Equally, geomorphologists and sedimentologists have not made full use of the information which archaeological records can provide about environmental conditions, ages of surfaces, rates of change, and the influence of man on the present coastal landscape. Many engineers, nature conservation bodies and coastal managers are still largely unaware of historical and archaeological heritage interests, and still think short term in relation to the timescales on which geomorphological processes and morphological changes operate. A report based on a survey commissioned by English Heritage and the Royal Commission on the Historical Monuments of England (Fulford et al. 1997) concluded that 'England's coastal zone contains an important legacy of historic assets which include a complex array of fragile and irreplacable archaeological remains' (Fulford et al. 1997, p. 16). Yet the existence of such assets, which range from prehistoric fishing engines, habitations and wharfage to monuments critical to landscape-transformation like redundant seabanks and outfalls (Allen 1997), has received scarcely a mention, let alone detailed consideration, in recent MAFF and Environment Agency-led debates about future flood defence and coast protection policy in England and Wales. While it is now widely acknowledged that a policy of managed realignment of sea defences in selected areas potentially offers many benefits in terms of maintenance costs and recreation of threatened wildlife habitats, such changes could inflict further damage and pose major conflicts with archaeological interests, which in general are likely to favour preservation (Horrocks 1995). The fact that government has traditionally separated archaeological and natural historical agencies concerned with conservation has perpetuated narrow outlooks and

created serious practical difficulties which have yet to be resolved (Bell 1995).

Comprehensive scientific studies of the linkages between the hydrodynamic, geomorphological, sedimentological, chemical and biological aspects of coasts and estuaries are also at a relatively early stage, although a detailed understanding of such linkages lies at the heart of sensible development, conservation and management strategies (Roman & Nordstrom 1996). In the UK, The Land-Ocean Interaction Study (LOIS), a seven year Community Research Project started in 1991 and funded by the Natural Environment Research Council (NERC), ostensibly had a better understanding of such interactions as part of its general scientific objective (LAND-OCEAN INTERACTION STUDY (LOIS) 1992). This multi-disciplinary study concentrated on the east coast of England between Berwick-upon-Tweed and Great Yarmouth, including the various river catchments, estuaries and adjoining area of the North Sea. Although much was achieved by LOIS and its consituent programmes, especially in terms of securing a better understanding of the Holocene evolution of the area and the contemporary fluxes of sediment, nutrients and contaminants (e.g. papers in Shennan & Andrews 2000), the linkages between meso-scale geomorphological processes, sediment properties morphological change and the longer term effects on water quality and ecology were largely ignored. Similarly, no significant consideration was given to geoarchaeological questions. The linkages between morphology, hydrodynamic processes, water quality and ecology are being addressed in Phase I of the UK Estuaries Research Programme currently funded by MAFF, The Environment Agency and English Nature, but geoarchaological interests are again not specifically included, and the timescales for the interactions under consideration are essentially limited to about 50 years.

Future interactions and research needs

It is against this background that we organized the conference on Coastal and Estuarine Environments: sedimentology, geomorphology and geoarchaeology in November 1998. The principal aims were to provide a forum in which sedimentologists, geomorphologists, archaeologists, engineers and others could present the results of their recent research, inform each other of their interests, methods and concerns, and identify further areas where future joint work might be fruitful.

The selection of papers included in this volume reflects the wide range of research currently being undertaken in coastal and estuarine environments, but underlines the fact that there are still significant gaps in understanding and major needs for further research which crosses traditional disciplinary boundaries. At the present, there remains a major gulf between those earth scientists and hydraulic engineers who focus primarily on short term hydrodynamics, sediment dynamics and small-scale bedform adjustments, and those who adopt a broader approach to large scale geomorphological relationships, average sediment properties and historical evolution. The one view affords a characterization at a single instant of a non-linear dynamical system which, in the other approach, is treated as having been at that instant powerfully influenced by its entire history up to that time. In simple terms, these approaches can be characterized as 'bottom-up' and 'top-down' approaches. What is needed in future is much more emphasis on 'hybrid' approaches, which may be interdisciplinary in character, and which combine conceptual elements of the top-down approach with the quantitative, predictive elements of the bottom up approach. As a first stage, formalized hybrid approach needs to be developed to provide an improved understanding of the interactions between changes in environmental forcing factors (sea-level, wind/wave climate, sediment supply), hydrodynamic processes, sediment transport processes, morphological changes and their feedbacks. At a later stage, the challenge is to broaden the interactions to include whole-system ecology, water quality and human activities.

A variety of options exist for the development of 'hybrid' approaches to coastal and estuarine investigation and prediction. Two of which we wish to emphasize here, specifically in the context of geomorphology, sedimentology and geoarchaeology, are 'historical trend analysis' and 'expert scientific assessment'.

Historical trend analysis (HTA) involves the interrogation of all available data about relevant changes affecting an area in the past, and may range from the timescale of the entire Holocene (10 ka) to periods as short as a few years. Those changes will not only include those of a wholly natural origin, but also those brought about by people, for example, changes in the land-use of catchments, which alter the sediment supply, or saltmarsh embanking, which reduce tidal prisms. Time series of recorded data (e.g. tide gauge, wind or wave records, topographic or sediment survey data) can be analysed statistically to identify shorter term trends, apparently random behaviour or cyclical fluctuations, while the morphological, sedimentary and geo-

archaeological record can be investigated to provide a longer term framework against which the shorter term changes can be interpreted. Extrapolations based on historical behaviour can be made, subject to the accuracy of assumptions about the nature of boundary conditions. Much of the data demanded by the HTA approach has yet to be acquired, for example, the behaviour of relative sea-level over the last few millennia, that period which is not covered by peat-based sea-level curves and during which people have most influenced the coastal zone.

Expert scientific assessment (ESA) involves a combination of historical trend analysis and an evaluation of the present functional dynamics of a system. The latter includes an assessment of the geological framework and geomorphological sensitivity of a system, based, for example, on an evaluation of the rock and sediment properties surrounding an estuary, rates of sediment supply, and the nature of the energy regime to which it is subjected. A conceptual model of the functioning of the system is developed, including an assessment of the sediment budget and the degree to which the system can be considered to be in equilibrium with the processes acting on it. Regime relationships can be determined, and compared with results from field process data collection and bottom-up type numerical modelling. The essential features of the ESA approach are data synthesis, integration, and cross-testing of different model outputs and hypotheses to arrive at semi-quantitative, best-estimate prediction of the likely response of a system or its components to an intrinsic or extrinsic change, or combination of changes. Consideration of a range of future change scenarios, from 'worst case' to 'best case', can provide the coastal manager with a means of assessing the degree of uncertainty and risk, from the perspective of various 'user' interests, including conservation, associated with any particular change.

The development of these and other possible approaches into practical management tools will require at least a decade of sustained research effort, with appropriate funding (the availability of which is, at present, uncertain). The challenge ahead lies as much with research funders and managers as with individual scientists to recognize and deliver what is needed.

References

ALLEN, J. R. L. 1997. The geoarchaeology of land-claim in coastal wetlands: a sketch from Britain and the north-west European Atlantic-North Sea coasts. *Archaeological Journal*, **154**, 1–54.

BARRETT, M. G. (ed.) 1992. *Coastal Zone Management and Planning*. Thomas Telford, London.

BELL, M. 1995. Archaeology and nature conservation in the Severn Estuary, England and Wales. *In*: COX, M., STRAKER, V. & TAYLOR, D. (eds) *Wetlands – Archaeology and Nature Conservation*. HMSO, London, 49–61.

FLEMMING, C. A. (ed.) 2000. *Coastal Management. Integrating Science, Engineering and Management*. Thomas Telford, London.

FULFORD, M., CHAMPION, T. & LONG, A. (eds) 1997. *England's Coastal Heritage*. English Heritage and the Royal Commission on the Historical Monuments of England, London.

HORROCKS, R. 1995. Managed retreat: The Devil or the Deep Blue Sea. *In*: COX, M., STRAKER, V. & TAYLOR, D. (eds) *Wetlands – Archaeology and Nature Conservation*. HMSO, London, 176–181.

KAY, R. & ALDER, J. 1999. *Coastal Planning and Management*. E. & F. N. Spon, London.

LAND-OCEAN INTERACTION STUDY (LOIS) 1992. *Science Plan for a Community Research Project*. Natural Environment Research Council, Swindon.

POLLARD, A. M. 1999. Geoarchaeology: an introduction. *In*: POLLARD, A. M. (ed.) *Geoarchaeology: exploration, environments, resources*. Geological Society, London, Special Publications, **165**, 7–14.

ROMAN, C. T. & NORDSTROM, K. F. 1996. Environments, processes and interactions of estuarine shores. *In*: NORDSTROM, K. F. & ROMAN, C. T. (eds) *Estuarine Shores: Environments and Human Alterations*. John Wiley & Sons, Chichester, 1–12.

SHENNAN, I. & ANDREWS, J. (eds) 2000. *Holocene Land-Ocean Interaction and Environmental Change around the North Sea*. The Geological Society, London, Special Publications **166**.

Sedimentation associated with estuarine frontal systems

JOHN McMANUS

School of Geography and Geosciences, University of St Andrews, Fife, KY16 9ST, Scotland

Abstract: Estuarine fronts may develop in several locations, across the water body as transverse, halocline-related features, as overbank spills, or where tidal flats release waters into principal tidal channels. In many estuaries longitudinal fronts originate at headlands or are associated with major sandbanks (Bowman 1988). Commonly a front separates a near-shore water mass from that of the main flow of tidal waters. In the marginal waters flows are slower than in the main channels, and suspended sediments and pollutants released to these marginal zones do not mix freely with the principal tidal waters entering and leaving the estuary. These nearshore waters also often differ in temperature from the channel waters (Anderson *et al.* 1992). It is suggested that the linear convergent frontal systems provide the ideal sites for the accumulation of sediment, and exert some control on the distribution of longitudinal estuarine sand banks. Some, but not all of these are associated with headlands. The geomorphological evolution of the sand bank systems within the upper and middle reaches of the Tay Estuary, Scotland, are discussed in relation to present and past locations of longitudinal fronts. The Middle Bank, off Dundee, is seen to occur between the lines of longitudinal fronts formed during the flood and ebb phases of the tide. The Naughton Bank, off Balmerino is related to an ebb phase headland-induced flow separation. In the seaward reaches longitudinal fronts locate the outer margins of the tidal flats and become axially convergent in the Tayport-Broughty Ferry narrows.

The long-held perception that fluvial and marine waters mix or form degrees of stratified systems in estuaries (Pritchard 1967) is satisfactory to explain overall estuarine circulation patterns in general terms, but does not provide adequate understanding of the patterns of water movement within individual reaches or at specific sites. In most estuaries foam bands on the water surface are manifestations of 'fronts', marking boundaries between more and less saline waters (Simpson & Nunes 1981; Simpson & Turrell 1986). However, measuring water profiles (McManus & Wakefield 1982; McManus 1984) shows that although some fronts may be related to sub-horizontal haloclines, many foam bands mark the intersections of the water surface with steeply inclined planes along which separate bodies flow past each other. Only limited lateral mixing occurs across such interfaces.

The classical approach to the analysis of water circulation patterns in estuaries is strongly based on the recognition of the presence or absence of density-induced stratification in the water column (McDowell & O'Connor 1977; Dyer 1986). Effectively this is controlled by the relative volumes of saline marine waters and fresh-waters discharged by the river system. The patterns recognized by Pritchard (1955, 1967) are essentially derived from averaging salinity data from sites within the principal channels to detect the degree of stratification present throughout the tide. Similarly, classifications such as that of Hansen & Rattray (1966) refer to the salinity variations within the main mass of the waters.

Frontal patterns

Transverse fronts

Since axially convergent frontal systems were first identified within the Seiont Estuary of North Wales by Simpson & Nunes (1981) their presence, marked at the surface by foam bands stretching across the principal channel, has been noted in many other narrow, channel-dominated systems. The transverse foam band has been interpreted as the surface manifestation of the top of the wedge of saline water penetrating up-estuary.

Lateral axially convergent fronts

Where rising tidal waters carry cool saline waters across estuary mouth sand bars to enter

From: PYE, K. & ALLEN, J. R. L. (eds). *Coastal and Estuarine Environments: sedimentology, geomorphology and geoarchaeology*. Geological Society, London, Special Publications, **175**, 5–11. 0305-8719/00/$15.00 © The Geological Society of London 2000.

channels bearing warm waters from the side the interfaces between the two water masses serve as fronts, complete with foam bands at the surface. As the tide advances such marginal V-shaped axially convergent fronts shear into single longitudinal features parallel to the channel margin, but separating water bodies which can be distinguished on the basis of their thermal and salinity characteristics (Anderson *et al.* 1992; McManus *et al.* 1998). In the Ria do Barqueiro, Galicia, NW Spain, where this form of frontal system was first recognized hand-held thermal radiometers were used to identify the different water bodies during much of the rising tide.

Tailed axially convergent fronts

Within the 50 km long macrotidal Tay Estuary, Scotland, the rising tide sweeps slowly across the northern and southern marginal tidal flats towards the topographic narrows between Tayport and Broughty Ferry (Fig. 2), at which sector they converge on the main influent waters which enter the estuary along the deep central channel. Marking the outer limit of the tidal flats on either shore a longitudinal front develops towards the narrows, and the marginal waters converge, over-riding the more saline channel waters and carrying their fronts with them. The foam bands are often observed to meet in the narrows, giving rise to the stem of a Y-shaped, or tailed axially convergent band, which migrates up estuary with the rising tide (Ferrier & Anderson 1997). This distinctive structure, which remains clear of the estuary margins, may be carried for over 3 km westward in the early part of the flood tide.

Longitudinal fronts

Further observations of foam bands in the Conwy Estuary of North Wales (Simpson & Turrell 1986) revealed that not all of the fronts are associated with such low angle halocline surfaces, but that they are commonly related to more steeply inclined surfaces aligned along the length of the estuary, and traceable for several kilometres. Measurement of salinity and temperature variations on profiles associated with such longitudinal surficial foam bands have confirmed that there are sharp contrasts across the steeply inclined surfaces (McManus & Wakefield 1982). Commonly the two water masses move at different speeds, so that across the front there is a change of velocity in currents at all depths (Fig. 1), as also illustrated by Bowman (1988). Important longitudinal frontal systems

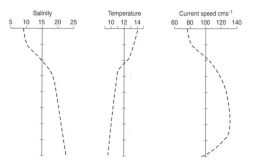

Fig. 1. Diagrammatic representation of the salinity, temperature, and current velocity variations on a line normal to a linear longitudinal front, measured 300 m west of the Tay railway bridge on the rising tide 1 June, 1978.

have been identified in the St Lawrence River of Canada, using thermal characterization from satellite imagery (Lavoie *et al.* 1985; El-Sabh 1988). In his review of the behaviour of estuarine fronts Bowman (1988), who stressed the importance of lateral shear in maintaining these longitudinal fronts, considered that they were best developed during the falling tide. Longitudinal frontal structures have been explored in some detail in the Tay Estuary of Scotland (Fig. 2) where, on the basis of airborne radiometric measurements Ferrier & Anderson (1997) demonstrated that they were also very well developed during the flooding tide. The reason for their formation is not always clear. Some form along the boundary between the deep channel and the marginal shallows, where fresher, warmer/colder, suspension and pollutant rich waters contrast sharply with those of the incoming tidal waters. Others are located upstream of shoals or islets. However, in many cases the associated foam bands may be seen to be carried along the margins of flow-parallel sandbanks. In the upper parts of the Tay Estuary longitudinal fronts are observed to form during the

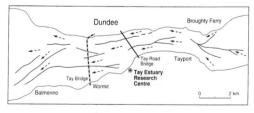

Fig. 2. Locations of commonly recognized fronts (continuous fine lines) at mid flood tide in the Tay Estuary, Scotland (after Ferrier & Anderson 1997). Arrows indicate directions of currents at this stage of the tide.

ebb below the mouths of influent creeks. The creeks drain large areas of tidal flats and carry the quite distinctive waters into the main tidal flows. Along the margins of visible plumes longitudinal fronts are formed as the adjacent water masses maintain separate identities during seaward motion.

Headland related fronts

According to Bowman (1988), when normal advective tidal flows on either the flood or the ebb phase of the tide encounter headlands, water may pass the headlands as gently moving streams. However, as current speeds increase in the channel the strongly moving waters may begin to behave as jet-like flows, to shoreward of which relatively slowly circulating eddies are formed. Thus, during the peak of current flows on the rising tide, to landward of headlands extending into the estuary, zones of sheltered water become established, past which the rising tidal flows travel up the estuary. The adjacent waters bodies function as distinct entities which shear past each other to create steeply dipping frontal boundaries trending parallel to the principal current direction and giving rise to a longitudinal front arranged along the channel margin. Beyond a certain distance from the headland, on each side of the front separating them the waters, which may have contrasting temperature, salinity and suspended sediment concentrations, flow in the same direction, albeit at different speeds. There is a convergence of the waters towards the top of the front and a foam band, often bearing flotsam is formed. The dynamic nature of these fronts is seen by eddies and swirls resembling Kelvin–Helmholtz instabilities at the surface.

Sedimentation related to frontal systems

Fronts which develop as a result of the presence of headlands may be followed for several kilometres beyond the feature, where they are frequently arranged along the margins of major sandbanks, or at the sharp boundary between muddy shoreward deposits and sandy channel-floor sediments.

It is suggested that the coincidence of the location of the fronts and the margins of the sandbanks is not accidental, but that the position of the sandbanks is partly controlled by the development of a separating boundary layer in the flow beyond the headland. The physical identities of the separate water masses become

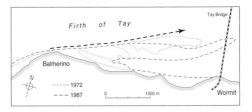

Fig. 3. Location of areas of sedimentation induced on one side of a headland at Balmerino on the Tay Estuary, presently dominated by ebb fronts. Continuous line-coast. Short light dashes – Low water mark, 1972–73 survey, Long dashes – Low water mark 1987 survey, Heavy broken line position of headland induced front line.

accentuated by the formation of a frontal system along the interface which divides the sheltered or entrapped body of water from the flows in the main channel. On the shoreward side of the separation the waters move relatively slowly, often generating an eddy with an upstream component immediately behind the headland. In such a location deposition of material from suspension will occur away from the channel, and sands moving with the bed load are deposited as they are carried out of the main flow in the channels. The sands may accrete to form tidally emergent sandbanks, whereas cohesive sediments form tidal flats.

Most commonly this phenomenon is seen on one side of a headland, as at Ribadeo and Castropol on the Ria de Ribadeo, NW Spain, and at Balblair on the Cromarty Firth, Scotland (Fig. 3), but at a suitable site it will develop on either side of a headland, as at Balmerino on the Tay Estuary, at Paimboeuf on the Loire, France, and Clashmore Links on the Dornoch Firth, Scotland (Fig. 4). Depending on the local

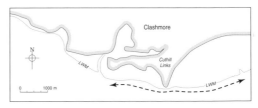

Fig. 4. Location of areas of frontally induced sedimentation beside headlands at Cuthill Links on the Dornoch Firth, Sutherland. Heavy broken lines mark position of the headland-induced fronts, with arrows indicating tidal sense. Flood tide flows to the west and ebb tide travels eastward. Map based on Ordnance Survey 1:50000 Sheet 22 of Dornoch.

sediment supply patterns sandbanks may form
on both sides of such a headland or a sandbank
on one side and muddy tidal flat on the other, as
at Balmerino.

Longitudinal frontal foam bands are often
situated directly along the margins of major
sand banks. In the Tay Estuary some of these
may be traced for over 6 km. Formed along the
outer margin of tidally exposed platforms within
the estuary the fronts mark zones of convergence

of the surface waters with components of the
currents directed downward. Near the bed there
is movement of the main flows towards the foot
of the front, and these flows may contribute to
deposition along the line of the front, for large
and very persistent sandbanks form on one side
of the fronts. One of the principal longitudinal
fronts of the Tay Estuary is associated with
Middle Bank, which has maintained its position, with slight variations since charting began

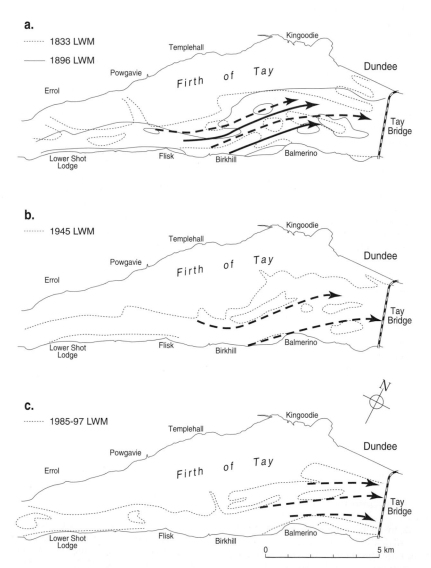

Fig. 5. Location of former positions of longitudinal sandbanks with probable positions of associated frontal
systems in the upper Tay Estuary. (**a**) Low Water Marks of 1833 and 1896. Ebb tidal fronts, broken line 1833,
solid line 1896. (**b**) Low Water Mark of 1945 survey, with ebb fronts marked by heavy broken line. (**c**) Low Water
Mark of survey of 1986–87 with fronts marked in heavy broken line.

in 1833 (Buller & McManus 1971). However, there has been a pattern of steady change of many sandbanks from further up estuary (Fig. 5). Such longitudinal fronts may provide deposition in areas inconvenient for navigation and introduce a need for long term maintenance dredging, e.g. Ria de Aveiro, Portugal (da Silva et al. 1999).

In recent studies of the Middle Bank reach of the Tay Estuary using side scan sonar techniques Duck & Wewetzer (2000) have recognized the presence of longitudinal fronts within the water column and shown them to separate sectors of the bed bearing dune bedforms of contrasting scale. Bed sampling has shown distinct linear patterns of sediment change along the northern margin of Middle Bank (Buller & McManus 1975), and this is supported by the sonar records.

Although the headland-related and longitudinal frontal systems are associated with sediment deposits there is no evidence that the cross-estuary fronts are directly linked to deposition. The cross-estuary front associated with the margin of the advancing saline wedge is a feature which has often been invoked as providing a mechanism for the enhancement of flocculation in the upper reaches of estuaries. In that the wedge migrates many kilometers up and down the estuary on each tide it is unlikely that it spends sufficient time at any single location to permit substantial sedimentation to occur, except in the uppermost sectors, where it will be static for an hour or so over high water.

The axially convergent front formed by overspilling waters entering the channel across marginal sandbanks, although well defined for short periods of the tide, is known to develop into a channel-parallel, longitudinal front, and no sediment deposition specifically related to the V front per se is envisaged.

The tailed axially-convergent front is associated with the formation of longitudinal fronts in the Tay Estuary, but the author does not know of its existence elsewhere. The tail of the front, formed by the coming together of the tidal-flat margin foam bands, forms where the water bodies cease to function as separate entities. The foam band degenerates with distance from the confluence and is not thought to be associated with sediment deposition.

Where a frontal system decays, perhaps due to water shoaling or to current speeds waning, the two adjacent water masses come into dynamic equilibrium and tidal currents may sweep across the line formerly taken by the front. At such sites no deposition will occur, but sediment transport may continue across the line as the currents establish fresh patterns.

Discussion

The presence of frontal systems which serve to subdivide the bodies of tidal marine and effluent river waters is recognized in estuaries from many parts of the world. The dynamics of essentially longitudinal fronts leads to local accumulations of sediment building up parallel to the steeply inclined frontal interface. Although a range of estuarine frontal types have been recognized on the basis of their modes of formation, not all are believed to be associated with active sediment deposition and accumulation. However, there are close correlations between the longitudinal fronts and the margins of sandbanks (Figs 3–5).

When examining the interrelationship between frontal systems and the deposition of sediments to form major sandbanks the question arises inevitably as to which came first, the frontal system or the sandbank. In that sediments respond to dynamic forces within the waters there can be little doubt that the deposition of sediment is a response to the presence of the fronts.

As tidal waters enter an estuary they follow the contours of the bed, often passing along neighbouring channels of differing depth and flow resistance, so that when the waters rejoin beyond the end of the split channel the adjacent water masses may differ in salinity, temperature and suspension concentration. Between the water bodies a frontal system will become established which migrates with the flow of the currents. In that as the waters converge at the surface and sink along the front, there is created a front-foot zone with waters and sediment passing down towards the bed. The overcharging of the bed in this area with sediment enhances the opportunity for sandy material to settle to the bed. Continued settling of material in this way permits build up of localized sandbanks along the front as it progresses up the estuary. During the ebb phase of the tide similar separations may occur within the body of effluent waters, with similar resultant deposits of material on the bed. The two sets of sandbanks so formed do not necessarily coincide in position and there will be reworking of one set of deposits during the opposite phase of the tide. On occasions the ground between two longitudinal fronts may serve as a zone of net accumulation.

The rise and fall of tide past a headland will cause flow separation in many instances. The flow separation enables the isolated water masses within the 'shelter zone' beside the headland to remain at least partly in place, so that the two water masses develop differing characteristics. Along the separated boundary layer which marks the interface between the water bodies and also serves as a front between the differing waters, sediment deposition is encouraged where flow speeds are checked.

Sedimentation in nearshore marginal shallow waters behind a frontally defined sandbank may lead to the formation or growth of tidal flats which extend from the shoreline towards the channel-parallel structure. Through time accretion of the tidal flat margin may reach forward to link with the sandbank, which becomes incorporated into the outer margin of the tidal flats, although totally different in structure and not related dynamically to the tidal flat in growth form or internal structure. Reference to maps of the evolution of the upper Tay Estuary tidal flat margins through time (McManus 1979, 1998) reveals that the outer margin of the flats has advanced discontinuously as a result of accretion of channel margin sandbanks. Today, and at least since the 1960s the sandbanks parallel to, but separated from, the outer margin of the upper estuarine tidal flats are closely associated with the presence of longitudinal ebb tide fronts, whose position is partly defined by the presence of major creek systems draining the surface of the tidal flats during the falling tide. When sedimentation of the intervening channel is completed the bank is accreted onto the flats, the outer margin of which then becomes effectively defined by the presence of the longitudinal front. Where this has happened in the Tay Estuary, as tidal flat consolidation occurs on the northern shore, so the channel migrates to the south, and banks previously associated with headland separation west of Balmerino have been eroded towards Flisk. A bank more than 2 km in length was lost between 1833 and 1896 (Fig. 5).

The condition in which we are able to observe estuarine sedimentation today is usually at a mature or, indeed, an advanced, stage of development. It is not during the early stages of evolution, so that the relationships between natural morphological features, frontal systems and sandbanks are several stages removed from their starting points. It is only where disturbances to flow patterns are introduced anthropogenically through harbour development, extended coastal protection schemes or pipeline installations that fresh impacts on flow and resultant sediment deposition can be observed.

Conclusions

Frontal systems separating water bodies with contrasting salinities, temperatures and suspension concentrations may form in several ways in estuaries. Along longitudinal fronts sediment deposition may occur to give rise to channel-parallel sandbanks. Associated with headlands, fronts form along separating boundary layers and deposition may again create sandbanks. However, the axially-convergent, cross-channel fronts associated with the migrating saline wedge are not believed to give rise to substantial deposits, except, perhaps at the extreme landward limit of the feature at high slack water, where fine cohesive sediments may settle to the bed and are not necessarily reentrained on subsequent ebb phases of the tide.

The author wishes to thank Mr Graeme Sandeman, Senior Cartographer, for drafting the diagrams for this contribution.

References

ANDERSON, J. M., DUCK, R. W., McMANUS, J. & DIEZ GONZALES, J. J. 1992. Recognition of an overspill-induced estuarine frontal system in the Ria do Barqueiro, NW Spain, using remote sensing techniques. *International Journal of Remote Sensing*, **13**, 1903–1911.

BOWMAN, M. J. 1988. Estuarine Fronts. *In*: KJERFVE, B. (ed.) *Hydrodynamics of Estuaries*, CRC Press, Boca Raton, 85–132.

BULLER, A. T. & McMANUS, J. 1971. Channel stability in the Tay estuary: controlled by bedrock and unconsolidated post-glacial sediment. *Engineering Geology*, **5**, 227–237.

—— & ——1975. Sediments of the Tay Estuary, 1 Bottom sediments of the Upper and Middle Reaches. *Proceedings of the Royal Society of Edinburgh*, **75**(13), 41–64.

DA SILVA, J. F., DUCK, R. W. ANDERSON, J. M., McMANUS, J. & MONK, J. G. C. 1999. *Observa, o remota aerea da pluma de 'gua turva na zona costiera da Barra da Ria de Aveiro*. Actas da 6a Conferincia Nacional Sobre a Qualidade do Ambiente, Lisboa, **3**, 709–716.

DUCK, R. W. & WEWETZER, S. K. 2000. Impact of frontal systems on estuarine sediment and pollutant dynamics. *The Science of the Total Environment*, in press.

DYER, K. R. 1986. *Coastal and Estuarine Sediment Dynamics*. John Wiley, Chichester.

EL-SABH, M. I. 1988. Physical oceanography of the St Lawrence Estuary, *In*: KJERFVE, B (ed.) *Hydrodynamics of Estuaries*, CRC Press, Boca Raton, 61–78.

FERRIER, G. & ANDERSON, J. M. 1997. The application of remotely sensed data in the study of frontal systems in the Tay Estuary, Scotland, UK. *International Journal of Remote Sensing*, **18**, 2035–2065.

HANSEN, D. V. & RATTRAY, M. JR 1966. New dimension in estuary classification. *Limnology and Oceanography*, **11**, 319–331.

LAVOIE, A., BONN, F., DUBOIS, J. M. & EL-SABH, M. I. 1985. Structure thermique et variabilite du courant de surface de l'estuaire maritime du Saint-Laurent a l'aide d'images du Satellite HCMM, *Canadian Journal of Remote Sensing*, **11**, 70–86.

MCDOWELL, D. M. & O'CONNOR, B. A. 1977. *Hydraulic behaviour of estuaries*, Macmillan, London.

MCMANUS, J. 1985. Gradients of change in the estuarine environments of the Tay. *In*: CRACKNELL, A. P. (ed.) *Remote Sensing Applications in Civil Engineering*, 143–149.

——1979. Sediments in estuaries. *In*: SEVERN, R. T., DINELEY, D. & HAWKES, L. E. (eds) *Tidal Power and Estuary Management*, Colston Papers No 30, Scientechnica, Bristol, 180–187.

——1998. Temporal and spatial variations in estuarine sedimentation. *Estuaries*, **21**, 622–634.

—— & WAKEFIELD, P. 1982. *Lateral transfer of water across the Middle Reaches of the Tay Estuary*. Sedimentological, Hydrological and Biological Papers, 7 Tay Estuary Research Centre, University of Dundee, Scotland, 25–38.

——, DUCK, R. W. & ANDERSON, J. M. 1998. The relative merits and limitations of thermal radiometric measurements in estuarine studies. *International Journal of Remote Sensing*, **19**, 53–64.

PRITCHARD, D. W. 1955. Estuarine circulation patterns. *Proceedings of the American Society of Civil Engineers*, **81**, 717–729.

——1967. Observations on circulation in coastal plains estuaries. *In*: LAUFF, G. E. (ed.) *Estuaries*. American Association for the Advancement of Science, Publication 93, 37–44.

SIMPSON, J. H. & NUNES, R. 1981. The tidal intrusion front: an estuarine convergence zone. *Estuarine and Coastal Marine Science*, **13**, 257–266.

—— & TURRELL, W. R. 1986. Convergent fronts in the circulation of tidal estuaries. *In*: WOLFE, D. A. (ed.) *Estuarine Variability*. Academic Press, New York, 139–152.

Processes controlling import of fine-grained sediment to tidal areas: a simulation model

JESPER BARTHOLDY

Institute of Geography, University of Copenhagen, Øster Voldgade 10, DK-1350, Copenhagen K., Denmark (e-mail: JB@geogr.ku.dk)

Abstract: Salt marsh and mud flat sedimentation in the Wadden Sea and in similar depositional regions is usually dependent on the net import of fine-grained sediments from adjacent marine environments. This net import takes place as a result of several processes such as settling lag and scour lag. This paper utilizes a database comprising time series of tidal velocity and turbidity in the Grådyb tidal area of western Denmark as the basis of a simple conceptual model which describes the transport, deposition and resuspension of fine-grained material in the area. The results demonstrate that: (a) grain sizes close to the sand/silt boundary are most sensitive to lag effects; (b) scour lag is much more important than settling lag; (c) raised temperatures enhance the net-lag effect for silt with increasing importance for finer grain sizes; (d) with increased suspended concentrations, the time it takes to resuspended the material deposited at slack water (the resuspension lag) is of increasing importance for the net-lag effect.

Understanding the import of fine-grained sediment to tidal areas has long been a key research task for sedimentologists (e.g. Nielsen 1935; Gry 1942; Postma 1954; Van Straten & Kuenen 1958; Jakobsen 1961; Groen 1967; Dronkers 1986; Allen & Pye 1992; Amos & Tee 1989; Ke *et al.* 1996; Flemming & Bartholoma 1997; Bartholdy & Anthony 1998). The fact that the majority of estuarine areas generally keep pace with rising sea level provokes a series of questions about the origin and transport of the supplied material. In some areas, it is possible to recognize local sources and gravitational circulation caused by fluvial fresh water input, but this is often not the case and the amount of sediment needed for the observed sedimentation rate is huge. In most cases, the only available answer implies that the sediment flux is able to work against a pronounced concentration gradient between relatively clean water in the adjacent sea to the tidal area, where the suspended sediment concentration level can be orders of magnitude higher. A qualitative description of transport phase lags between water and sediments in the Dutch Wadden Sea gave the first sound explanation for this apparent contradiction. Postma (1954) was the first to recognize the basic concept of the settling lag effect. He stated that because silt particles react slowly to velocity changes owing to their settling velocity, they will be transported further in the flood direction than would be the case if settling was instantaneous, and that the slow reaction of the silt to a decrease in current velocity during inward transport causes the silt to settle in places where the current is too weak to carry it away after the turn of the tide. Van Straten & Kuenen (1957, 1958) followed by Postma (1961, 1967) further developed these basic concepts, and identified formalized settling lag and scour lag mechanisms. These concepts were formulated in a mathematical way by Groen (1967) and Dronkers (1986). The latter concluded that only fine-grained material participates and that the magnitude and direction of the residual sediment flux is mainly determined by differences in the variation of current velocities around low water and high water. The mechanisms have since then been discussed and explained in detail, among others, by Dyer (1986, 1994).

In this paper, time series of suspended sediment concentrations and velocity variations measured in Grådyb tidal area, situated on the SW coast of Jutland (Denmark), form the basis for the formulation of a simple model to describe the size of the different lag effects and their relation to grain size, temperature and initial sediment concentrations.

From: PYE, K. & ALLEN, J. R. L. (eds). *Coastal and Estuarine Environments: sedimentology, geomorphology and geoarchaeology*. Geological Society, London, Special Publications, **175**, 13–29. 0305-8719/00/$15.00 © The Geological Society of London 2000.

Dynamics and fluxes of suspended sediment

Grådyb tidal inlet (Fig. 1) connects the North Sea with the northernmost part of the Wadden Sea. It forms a T-shaped tidal area behind the barrier spit of Skallingen and the barrier island of Fanø. The mean tidal range in the area is approximately 1.5 m producing a mean tidal prism which is in the order of $150 \times 10^6 \, \mathrm{m}^3$. The maximum tidal current in the 1000 m wide inlet is between 1.5 and $2 \, \mathrm{m \, s}^{-1}$ and the tidal excursion is 12–15 km (Bartholdy & Anthony 1998). The outer part of the tidal channel is ebb dominated. In the innermost part, there is a weak flood dominance. The fresh water input from the two small rivers in the area, Varde Å and Sneum Å is minor, usually less than 1% of the tidal prism. Consequently, the water

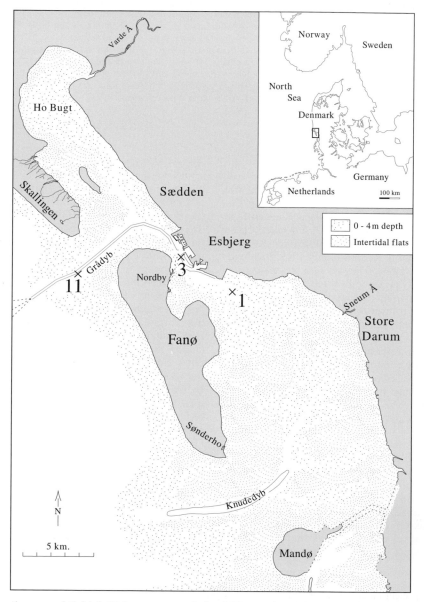

Fig. 1. Location map of Grådyb tidal area, western Jutland. The numbers 1, 3 and 11 refer to measuring stations in the main channel.

flowing in the tidal channel can be regarded as being extremely well mixed. The overall sediment budget shows that approximately $0.12 \times 10^6 \, t \, a^{-1}$, or 85% of the total deposited fine-grained sediment, is imported from the North Sea (Bartholdy & Madsen 1985). Analysing long time series of turbidity and velocity recordings from the central part of the tidal channel close to the harbour of Esbjerg, Bartholdy & Anthony (1998) concluded that, as a rule, the tidal area loses fine-grained sediment to the North Sea during storms, whereas the primary contribution to the sediment import from the North Sea is associated with windy events following long periods of calm weather, primarily concentrated in the summer period.

In Fig. 1 the numbers 1 3 and 11 refer to measuring stations where turbidity and velocity were recorded at 5 minute intervals over periods of 2–4 weeks, primarily in 1992 but also in 1993 and 1994. The stations were, as a rule, occupied two at a time. Details of the measurement procedures are given in Bartholdy & Anthony (1998). The two primary stations for the present study (1 and 11) are located in the accumulation area and in the tidal inlet respectively. There is approximately one tidal excursion between the two. Station 1 is located in the inner part of the tidal area close to the turbidity maximum associated with the watershed between Grådyb and the tidal area 'Knudedyb' to the south. In this area, the channel is wide and water depths around high water are about 5 m. Station 11 is located in the central part of ebb delta. Here, the navigation channel is dredged and the water depth close to low water is approximately 10 m.

The time series data shown in Fig. 2 show the dynamics during a typical calm summer situation, at Station 1 just before a spring tidal maximum. The prevailing wind speed was low, close to $5 \, m \, s^{-1}$, from the west. The typical tidal current asymmetry, with a quick shift around low water and a relatively slow shift around high water, is easily recognized, as are the higher flood current maxima, with more or less constant values around $0.8 \, m \, s^{-1}$ relative to the ebb current maxima of about $0.6 \, m \, s^{-1}$. The variation in the suspended sediment concentration

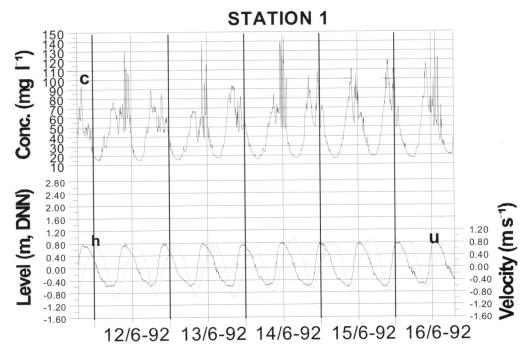

Fig. 2. Tidal dynamics at Station 1 (Fig. 1) in a typical calm summer situation from June 1992. The depth at the station at high water is c. 5 m. The current velocity (u) was measured 2 m above the bed with a self recording Niskin winged current meter. The concentration of suspended sediment (c) was measured 3 m above the bed with a self recording infrared light transmissiometer of the type GMI model TU-150IR. The water level (h) was measured at Esbjerg Harbour. The time series is from 11/6–16/6 1992.

showed the typical pattern of a station seaward
of, but close to, the turbidity maximum. The
concentrations are high, about 70–120 mg l⁻¹ in
the later part of the ebb period. During the low
water slack, the suspended sediment settles out
and the concentration drops to 30–70 mg l⁻¹.
In the subsequent accelerating part of the flood
period, a resuspension peak forms as a result
of the relatively rapid shift from $0 \, \mathrm{m \, s^{-1}}$ to 0.6–
$0.8 \, \mathrm{m \, s^{-1}}$ over less than one hour. Not all
concentration peaks during the flood period
are natural; some of the prominent daytime
peaks of up to 150 mg l⁻¹, with intervals of
about 1–1.5 hours, are most likely due to
fine-grained material dumped from the harbour basins. Towards high water, the concentration drops. This is in the beginning a result of
the generally lower sediment concentrations
in the water which originates further out in the
tidal area closer to the North Sea. Later, during
high water slack, the decreasing concentration
is due to the settling of the suspended sediments and, the concentration drops from a level
of $= 30 \, \mathrm{mg \, l^{-1}}$ to 15–20 mg l⁻¹ In the subsequent
ebb period, the velocity rises so gently that, as

a rule, resuspension of the settled sediment does
not generate a concentration peak, only a gentle
rise towards the next low water.

The time series chosen to illustrate the dynamics at Station 11 is shown in Fig. 3. The rapid
change from ebb to flood during low water slack
is very distinct, as is the low flood current
maximum of $0.4–0.5 \, \mathrm{m \, s^{-1}}$ relative to the ebb
current maximum of $1.0–1.3 \, \mathrm{m \, s^{-1}}$. In this remote
position, where the variations in concentration
of suspended sediment are controlled almost
solely by the North Sea and by occasional
outflows of turbid water from the inner part of
the tidal area, the concentration variations are
usually small. During storms, where the wind
induced set up increases the high water level,
sediment concentrations are only moderately
raised in the water being pumped into the tidal
area by the set up (in the case of Fig. 3 up
to 40 mg l⁻¹). After the storm, turbid water
(>100 mg l⁻¹) from the inner part of the tidal
area is flowing out to the North Sea as the wind
loses its grip on the inclined water level. The
overall pattern from this time series, therefore,
illustrates very well how the tidal area exports

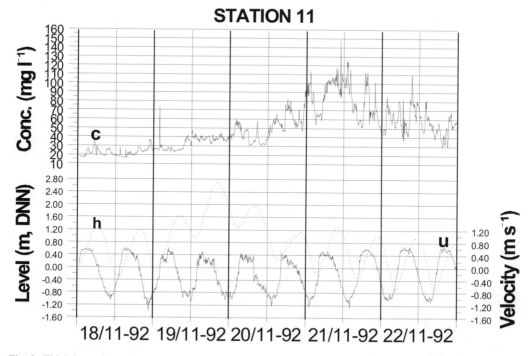

STATION 11

Fig. 3. Tidal dynamics at Station 11 (Fig. 1), November 1992. The depth at the station at low water is *c*. 10 m.
The current velocity (*u*) was measured 4 m above the bed with a self recording Nisking winged current meter. The
concentration of suspended sediment (*c*) was measured 5 m above the bed with a self recording infrared light
transmissionmeter of the type GMI model TU–150IR. The water level (*h*) was measured at Esbjerg Harbour.

fine-grained material during storms (Bartholdy & Anthony 1998).

Simulation of the lag effects

In order to examine the transport of suspended fine-grained sediment in the tidal prism, the conditions around high water at Station 1 and around low water at Station 11 are used as empirical background for the development of a simple conceptual model. It is assumed that suspended fine- grained material, outside the slack water periods, is transported in suspension with no lag between the water and sediment displacements, and that the velocity patterns in the vicinity of the two stations can be regarded as being represented by their records. Furthermore the simulations were restricted to calm weather situations, as these, after windy periods following long periods of calm weather, bear the primary potential for fine-grained import to the tidal area (Bartholdy & Anthony 1998). After selecting calm weather situations from both stations at the turn of the tide (Figs 4a & 4b), the typical shifts from flood to ebb at Station 1 and from ebb to flood at Station 11, are expressed by the simple mean of the current

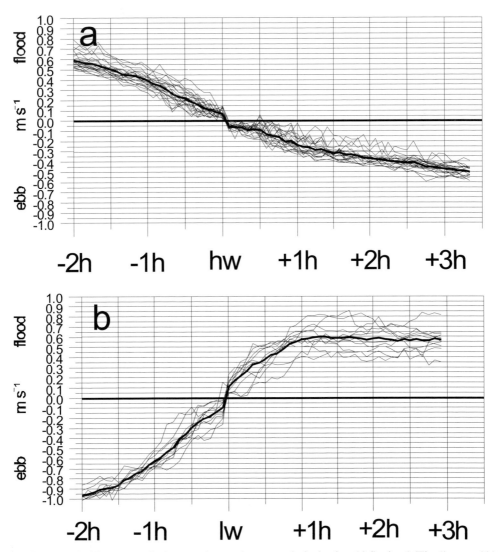

Fig. 4. Current velocities around slack water close to the mean velocity level at: (**a**) Station 1 (Fig. 1) around high water 2 m above the bed and (**b**) Station 11 (Fig. 1) around low water 4 m above the bed.

measurements. In spite of some variations, the main pattern of the mean current shift seems to be confirmed. Measurements at Station 11 were carried out during a period of mainly relatively rough weather, which is the reason for the fewer calm weather data sets from this location. Differences in the length of the slack water periods between the two stations are obvious. At Station 11 there are 1.5 hours between the current speeds $V = -0.5\,\mathrm{m\,s^{-1}}$ (ebb) and $V = +0.5\,\mathrm{m\,s^{-1}}$ (flood), whereas the corresponding period from flood to ebb at Station 1 is 4.75 hours. In addition, there is a marked asymmetry in the data from Station 1 which is absent at Station 11. At the latter station, the 1.5 hour period is symmetrically spaced with 0.75 hours on both sides of the low water slack, whereas the asymmetry of the velocity curve at Station 1 causes the period between $V = +0.5\,\mathrm{m\,s^{-1}}$ and high water slack to be significantly smaller (1.5 hours) than the corresponding period between high water slack and $V = -0.5\,\mathrm{m\,s^{-1}}$ (3.25 hours).

The following attempt to describe the path of sediment and water in the area includes theoretical assumptions that were deliberately made in order to keep the theory as simple and transparent as possible.

Velocity

The logarithmic velocity distribution is assumed to be valid and the bed roughness k_s was found in accordance with results from measurements carried out at Station 3 (Fig. 1). At this station the water surface slope was measured with pressure transducers (accuracy $\pm 8\,\mathrm{mm}$, 25 min. running mean) placed 2800 m apart. Three Niskin current meters were mounted on a moored steel wire lifted by buoyancy balls. The meters were located 1, 3 and 5 m above the bed. The level of the current meters was corrected for the influence of the shifting current on the wire by means of built-in pressure transducers (accuracy $\pm 6\,\mathrm{cm}$). The depth-average mean velocity was determined by integrating the measured velocity profile. Disregarding the convective acceleration term, which is assumed to be insignificant (e.g. McDowell & O'Connor 1977), the part of the slope related to the hydraulic friction (I_f) was found as:

$$I_f = I_o - \frac{1}{g}\frac{\delta V}{\delta t} \qquad (1)$$

where I_o is the slope of the water, g is the acceleration due to gravity and V is the mean

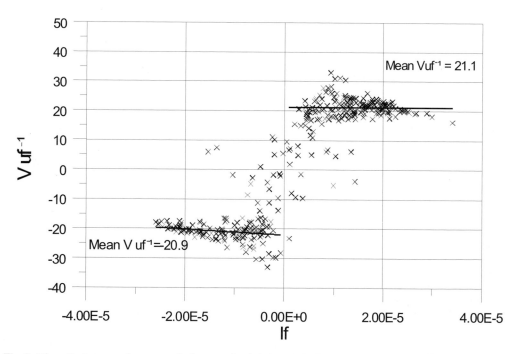

Fig. 5. The ratio between the mean velocity over depth (V) and the friction velocity (u_f) at Station 3 (Fig. 1), as a function of the part of the slope which is related to the hydraulic friction (I_f). The measurements were carried out in August 1994.

velocity over depth. The friction velocity:

$$u_f = (DI_f g)^{1/2} \qquad (2)$$

as well as the mean current velocity, V over the depth, D is used to calculate the hydraulic roughness determined as k_s in:

$$V/u_f = 6 + 2.5 \ln(D/k_s) \qquad (3)$$

Neglecting small values of abs(V/u_f) under 10, the mean value of this term was found to be 21 for both the flood and the ebb currents. With a water depth varying from 8 to 10 m at Station 3 this corresponds to a hydraulic roughness of 0.02 m.

The local friction velocity and the velocity variation over depth was determined by the equation:

$$u_z/u_f = 8.5 + 2.5 \ln(z/k_s) \qquad (4)$$

The velocity (u_z) was measured 2 m and 4 m above the bed at Station 1 and Station 11 respectively. For the smallest velocities $<0.08 \, \text{m s}^{-1}$, the hydraulic conditions enter the transition zone between rough and smooth currents. The errors introduced by using the rough current equations (eqs. 3 and 4) for all velocities, however, are marginal and can be neglected.

Sediment deposition and distribution

According to Yalin & Karahan (1979), the critical dimensionless erosional shear stress (Shields' parameter) for low values of the Particle Reynolds Number, $R_{*c} < 1$–2, under cohesionless conditions follows the equation

$$\Theta_c = 0.1 R_{*c}^{-0.3} \qquad (5)$$

In SI-units this can be rearranged to:

$$\tau_{cd} = \rho[0.1(s - 1)gv^{0.3}d^{0.7}]^{1/1.15} \qquad (6)$$

where τ_{cd} is the critical bed shear stress, ρ is the density of water, $s - 1$ is the submerged relative density of the sediment, g is acceleration due to gravity, v is the kinematic viscosity of water and d is the grain size.

The critical value of Shields' parameter under cohesionless conditions equals the critical values for deposition. Therefore, τ_{cd} is regarded as the lower limit over which the material is still transported and under which sedimentation will take place. Just before sedimentation starts, the suspended sediment is regarded as being distributed in the water column after the Rouse-equation:

$$C_z = C_a \left[\frac{D - z}{z} \frac{a}{D - a} \right]^{w_s/0.4u_f} \qquad (7)$$

where C_z and C_a are the concentrations at level z and a above the bed respectively, D is the water depth and w_s the settling velocity of the sediment. This procedure neglects the lag which is induced, before sedimentation starts, by the adjusting concentration profile under decelerating velocity. As discussed later this contribution is regarded as being negligible.

The settling velocity of the sediment is found by Stokes' Law:

$$w_s = \frac{(s - 1)gd^2}{18v} \qquad (8)$$

When sedimentation is initiated ($\tau_0 \le \tau_{cd}$), the decrease in concentration of the suspended sediment is calculated after an exponential function suggested by Krone (1962), cited in Amos & Mosher (1985):

$$C_t = C_0 \exp \frac{-Pw_s t}{D - z} \qquad (9)$$

C_t is the concentration at level z above the bottom at time t after the initiation of sedimentation. P is the probability of grain deposition, calculated as:

$$P = [1 - (\tau_0/\tau_{cd})] \qquad (10)$$

Where τ_0 is the bed shaear stress. In the original version, Krone (1962) used $\tau_{cd} = 0.121 \, \text{N m}^{-2}$. According to Equation 6 a critical shear stress of $0.12 \, \text{N m}^{-2}$ corresponds to a grain size close to 0.06 mm under normal temperature and salinity conditions. Thus, using the variable τ_{cd} instead of the constant value, the procedure takes into account a logical decrease in τ_{cd} with smaller grain sizes, but it does not change the conditions in relation to the original suggested procedure when calculating for grain sizes close to the sand/silt boundary.

In order to keep the simulation as simple as possible, it is assumed that the trajectory of a particle settling together with half of the settled material can be regarded as representing the mean conditions for fine-grained sediment participating in the deposition and resuspension process over slack water. The drawbacks induced by this approach will be discussed later. As a consequence of Equation 9 the actual mean settling velocity of a particle is calculated as

$$w_{sa} = Pw_s \qquad (11)$$

Erosion

After the turn of the tide, the current picks up speed and will eventually reach a value above which erosion can take place. The critical erosional bed-shear stress of newly deposited material is very hard to define exactly. In McDowell & O'Connor (1977), the values from laboratory experiments are stated to be in the range 0.3–0.6 N m^{-2}, whereas the values from 'the real world' (using American Geophysical Union data) are cited to range from 0.1 N m^{-2} to 1.3 N m^{-2}. In this study, a value of $\tau_c = 0.3$ N m^{-2} was chosen as the minimum value from the laboratory studies. After the followed particle is deposited together with half of the material, it is then buried by the other half during slack water. When the current gets strong enough to resuspend the deposited material, the material deposited over the particle has to be removed before it can be resuspended. Testing four algorithms of sea-bed erosion in fine grained-material, Amos et al. (1996) found the equation

$$E = M[(\tau_0/\tau_c) - 1] \tag{12}$$

with, $M = 4 \cdot 10^{-3}$ kg m^{-2} s^{-1} to yield the best results. This equation was chosen to simulate the erosion. When the material deposited on top of the followed particle is resuspended, the particle is released to further transport. As pointed out by Nichols (1986), there is also a lag stemming from the time it takes for the particle to reach higher levels in the flow. With the relatively low flow depths in this study, this delay is not expected to contribute significantly to the net sediment lag. In order to keep the calculations as simple as possible, but still give some kind of suggested particle trajectory after erosion, this particle lift is simulated based on the growth rate of turbulent eddies in the flow direction, as suggested by Yalin (1992):

$$D_e = (1/6)x \tag{13}$$

where D_e is the diameter of an eddy formed at $x = 0$, x being the distance in the current direction. A particle with no settling velocity would, according to the mixing caused by such a turbulent eddy, have a probable mean elevation above the bed defined by the eddy centre. The level of this centre will grow in the x direction with half of the eddy diameter growth, and the lift should, therefore, be expected to be equivalent to $[(1/12)x]$. A particle with the settling velocity of w_s will thus have a most probable lift in the x direction controlled by the vertical velocity:

$$w_{up} = (u_z/12) - w_s \tag{14}$$

Example of the calculation of lag effects

Based on the equations presented here, the sediment lags were calculated for different grain sizes, water temperatures and initial sediment concentrations by means of a Fortran computer program. With time steps of 100 s the program rearranges the concentration profile and follows the particle with calculated vertical positions expressed to the nearest 5 mm. The level above the bed where the particle starts (in order to settle with half of the deposited material) was found by trail and error.

The following example is given, with reference to Fig. 6a & 6b, where the results are visualized for a 50 μm particle in water with a temperature of 20°C and a salinity of 28‰. The initial mean sediment concentration in the water column is 30 mg l^{-1}.

At Station 1 (5 m water depth), the tracked particle starts to settle 1.80 m above the bed at a distance of +26 m on the x-axis. It reaches the bottom with half of the settled material at +188 m 162 m after sedimentation starts. By that time, the water mass from which the particle started to settle (tracked by the depth-average velocity) is only 18 m further inland. This supports the assumption that the lag introduced by the adjusting concentration profile under decelerating velocity is small. The water mass continues until +219 m before the current direction is reversed by the ebb tide. The sedimentation proceeds until the ebb current gets strong enough to prevent it. This happens when the limit for that particular grain size ($\tau_{cd} > 0.102$ N m^{-2}) is reached, at a distance of −36 m on the x-axis. The mean particle is deposited at +188 m whereas the centroid of the deposition has a slightly smaller displacement of +157 m. It is interesting that continued sedimentation after slack water in this way can decrease the mean settling lag. The decrease, however, is small and do not justify a deviation from the most simple definition of the lag, as that related to the displacement of the particle depositing with half of the deposited material.

It could be argued that the settling lag should include the lag introduced by the asymmetric slower start of the ebb current. However, since this displacement is in no way related to the settling conditions, it is more logical to include it in the displacement caused by the erosional delay, i.e. the scour lag. When the bed shear stress in the ebb current reaches 0.3 N m^{-2}, ($V_{5m} = 0.34$ m s^{-1}) the erosion of the deposited material starts. This happens when the water is at −1124 m relative to the deposition start. Half of the deposited material is removed when

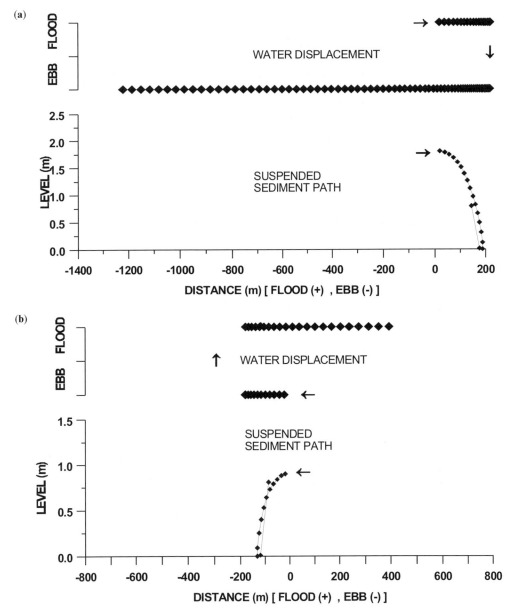

Fig. 6. Visualization of the predicted water and suspended sediment movement around slack water.
(a) at Station 1 (high water slack); (b) at Station 11 (low water slack). The example is based on a 50 μ particle in a typical summer situation with water temperature of 20°C , salinity of 28‰ and an initial suspended sediment concentration of 30 mg l^{-1}. The water displacement, based on the mean velocity over depth, is indicated above. The suspended sediment particle path, based on the velocity at the respective level of the depositing and resuspending particle, is shown beneath. All positions correspond to time increments of 100 s. The followed suspended particle is released at a level which allows it to settle with half of the suspended sediment depositing in the slack water period. The first data set is the first before sedimentation starts. Here the followed water mass and suspended particle are both at $X = 0$ m. The water mass continues its movement after the particle has settled. The last indication of the water mass position corresponds to the last indication of the suspended sediment particle, resuspended with half of the settled sediment over the slack water period.

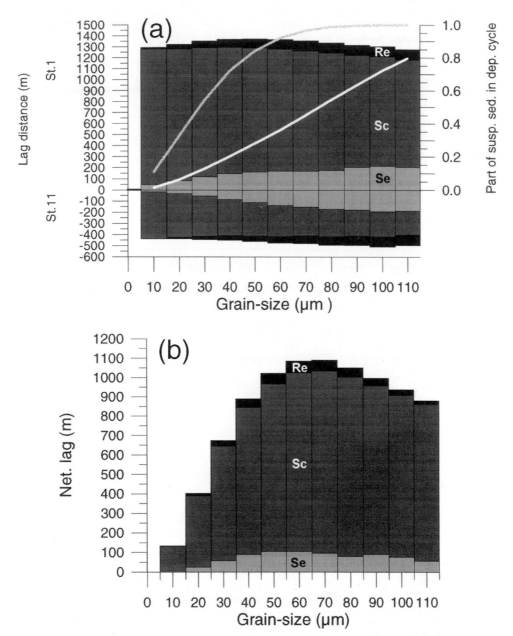

Fig. 7. The gross lag distance and the net lag as a function of grain-size. The simulation is carried out for a typical summer situation with water temperature of 20°C, salinity of 28‰ and an initial suspended sediment concentration of 30 mg l^{-1}. The lag is divided into *settling lag* (Se), *Scour lag* (Sc) and *Resuspension lag* (Re). In (**a**) the gross lag distance is displayed for Station 1 (positive values) and for Station 11 (negative values) together with an indication of the proportion (0–1) of the suspended sediment taking part in the deposition cycle (the part which reaches the bottom during slack water). The gray curve above indicates this proportion for Station 1 and the white curve beneath, the proportion for Station 11. In (**b**) the net lag is displayed after the correction for these proportions.

the water mass is at -1208 m relative to the deposition start. Thus, the total lag should be added a lag originating from resuspension of the deposited material on top of the particle, a *resuspension lag* of 84 m. Because of the small initial concentration, this contribution is also small but with higher concentrations the lag introduced in this way quickly exceeds the settling lag. After erosion, the lag introduced by the delayed uplift before the particle reaches the mean velocity level is about $+28$ m.

The corresponding process turning from ebb to flood at Station 11 (Fig. 6b; 10 m water depth) includes a settling lag of -112 m a scour lag of -299 m and a resuspension lag of -50 m. The lag caused by the delayed particle lift is here -35 m. Thus, the combined lag from the delayed particle lift at the two stations (-7 m) is directed outward, and so small that it can be neglected.

The combined lags according to the above stated figures, are: settling lag (162 m $-$ 112 m) 50 m scour lag (1124 m $-$ 299 m) 825 m and resuspension lag (84 m $-$ 50 m) 34 m. As only 84% and 28% of the initial suspended material are deposited during the respective slack water periods, the effective net lag is found by a correction based on these shares. The final results are: settling lag (136 m $-$ 31 m) 105 m scour lag (944 m $-$ 84 m) 860 m and resuspension lag (70 m $-$ 14 m) 56 m.

Variations in the size of the lag effects

If the mean hydrographic conditions are accepted as being representative, the other significant parameters which influence the lag effects are: grain size, temperature and initial suspended sediment concentration.

The effect of grain-size variations is demonstrated in Fig. 7. Water temperature (20°C), salinity (28‰) and initial suspended sediment concentration (30 mg l^{-1}) were selected as typical summer values, based on the time series shown in Fig. 2. The modelled grain sizes varied between 10 μm and 110 μm. The gross results (Fig. 7a) clearly demonstrate two basic properties:

(a) because coarser particles settle earlier in the depositional period than finer particles, a consequence of the constant critical condition for erosion ($\tau_c = 0.3$ N m^{-2}) is that the distance between the point where deposition starts and the point where erosion takes place again is smaller for coarser than for finer particles. Thus, the coarser the particle, the smaller the scour lag.

(b) there is a grain-size optimum for the settling lag which is controlled by the settling particles horizontal and vertical velocities.

For coarser particles in a waning flow, deposition takes place at higher velocities than those which allow finer particles to settle. This, other things being equal, brings a settling coarse particle forward with a higher speed than a settling fine particle. However, since coarse particles settle faster than finer particles, this reduces the time over which a coarse particle is transported before settling. For both stations, the resulting settling lag optimum is close to a grain size of 100 μm. Finer as well as coarser particles experience a smaller settling lag. Therefore, for particles finer than 100 μm, the coarser the particle, the larger the settling lag.

The different water depths and hydrographic conditions result in a smaller portion of the suspended sediment which participates in the deposition/resuspension process at Station 11 than at Station 1. For the coarsest particles, this proportion approaches 1 and, for the finest particles it becomes close to 0. It drops more rapidly with grain size at the outer station and the largest difference occurs in the central grain sizes close to 50 μm. In combination with the other two mentioned grain-size related properties, a combined net-lag optimum for grain sizes of 60–70 μm is produced, as shown in Fig. 7b, where the scour lag is also seen to be the dominating lag mechanism. For the central grain sizes, the settling lag is approximately 10% scour lag 85% and resuspension lag 5% of the total net lag which is of the order of 1000 m for this typical summer situation.

If particles between 60 μm and 110 μm were treated as particles that deposited in a matrix of similar grain sizes (coarser than the upper limit for cohesive behaviour), τ_c would be equal to τ_{cd}. Under these conditions, the net lag distance for that particular grain-size range would be of the order of 500 m. Thus, if sand-sized particles were assumed to settle with other particles of the same size, and not as particles incorporated in a fine-grained matrix with cohesive behaviour, the combined lag effect would be only about half of that predicted, and probably be small compared to other relevant mechanisms related to sand transport in the estuarine environment.

Variations caused by differences in the initial sediment concentration are demonstrated in Fig. 8. Here 60 μm particles are subject to the same temperature and salinity conditions as before. The resuspension lag is seen to exhibit a sharp rise with the initial concentration. From the referenced lag of 5% with an initial concentration of 30 mg l^{-1}, the resuspension lag is

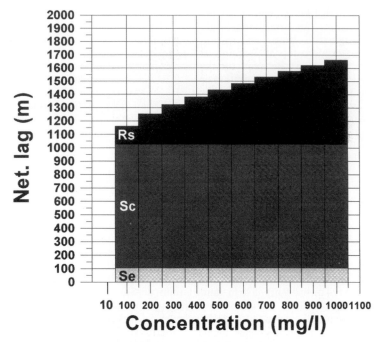

Fig. 8. The net. lag as a function of the initial concentration. The lag is divided into *settling lag* (Se), *Scour lag* (Sc) and *Resuspension lag* (Rs). The simulation is carried out for 60 μm particles in a typical summer situation with water temperature of 20°C and salinity of 28‰.

raised to 11% (136 m) at 100 mg l^{-1}, whereas the settling lag is only 9%. With an initial concentration of 1000 mg l^{-1}, the resuspension lag is 637 m or 38% of the total net lag. Very high concentrations of suspended sediment alter the hydraulic characteristics of the water which affect the validity of the equations used in the simulations. The greater significance of the resuspension lag with increased concentration, however, seems clear and it is evident that this type of lag plays an important role, especially in import situations, with raised initial concentrations in the water coming in from the North Sea (Bartholdy & Anthony 1998).

The effect of temperature on the net lag is demonstrated in Fig. 9 for 60 μm and 20 μm particles. The increased settling velocity with temperature, changes the net lag primarily as a result of a change in the settling velocity and thus is similar to the change induced by a change in grain-sizes. The larger net lag sensitivity in the finer grain-size ranges (Fig.7A), therefore, gives the 20 μm particles a larger net lag increase with temperature than the 60 μm particles. A change from 0°C to 10°C, 20°C and 30°C increases the net lag by 16%, 32%, and 45% respectively, whereas the same changes only lift the net lag for a 60 μm particle with 6%, 10% and 13%

respectively. Although these latter percentages are relatively small, it is interesting that 60 μm particles experience a larger net-lag lift than is possible with grain-size change alone (Fig. 7b). This is because warmer water has a lower viscosity and consequently, according to Equation 6, a lower τ_{cd}. A change from 0°C to 30°C causes τ_{cd} for a 60 μm particle to decrease from 0.132 N m^{-2} to 0.107 N m^{-2}. Consequently, even if the settling velocity in warm water is higher than in cold water, the sediment is carried further by the flood current before settling starts. This produces a larger scour lag because of the greater distance from the water mass at the sedimentation point to the water mass belonging to the point, where the outflowing water picks up the particle again. Hence, even if the settling proceeds more quickly in warm water (which produces slightly smaller settling lags) the raised scour lag, causes the overall lag to increase with temperature even for the coarse particles.

Model results compared with observations

Examples from the time series shown in Figs. 2 & 3 are illustrated in Fig. 10 in the form of a recalculation of the *Eulerian* observations, which

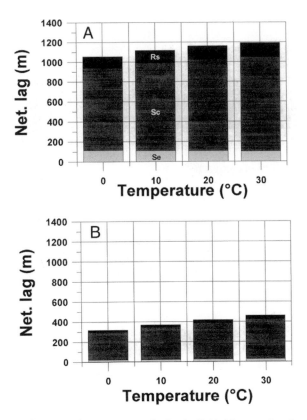

Fig. 9. The net. lag as a function of temperature. The lag is divided into *settling lag* (Se), *Scour lag* (Sc) and *Resuspension lag* (Rs). The simulation is carried out for 60 μm particles (**a**) and 20 μm particles (**b**). The initial suspended sediment concentration is 100 mg l^{-1} and the salinity is 28‰.

allows the data to be examined in a pseudo *Lagrangian* framework. The results from Station 1 (Figs. 10a & 10b) were plotted relative to the position of the water at the station at high water, as estimated by an integration of the measured Eulerian velocity over time. During the flood, the water passes the station before high water (the earlier, the more negative values) and vice-versa during the ebb. The results from Station 11 (Figs. 10c & 10d) were plotted in a similar way, relative to the water mass located at the station at low water.

The diagrams enable an examination of the local changes in the concentration of the water body close to slack water. Because of the limited distance, the changes induced by the horizontal concentration gradient are supposed to be of minor importance, and the diagrams can be used for an examination of lag distances produced by the displacements of 'the same concentration' before deposition starts and after resuspension has taken place.

Using the latter approach for all high water observations from Station 1 (Fig. 2), the mean displacement of the concentration levels 20 mg l^{-1} and 30 mg l^{-1}, are 1595 m and 1787 m with standard deviations of 330 m and 387 m respectively. This agrees relatively well, despite being a bit on the high side, with the model results shown in Fig. 7a. Attempts to do the same with data from Station 11 suffered from the fact that measurements from this station were carried out during relatively rough weather, and in the few situations when the weather was calm, the raised turbidity from inside the tidal area did not regularly reach the station at low water. Furthermore the directions of the tidal current in this exposed area were not always constant, especially around slack water. After the tide has turned, the character of the water being brought back can therefore change, compared to the water passing the station during the ebb. An example from the start of the time series shown in Fig. 3 (Fig. 10c) illustrates the small concentration variations and

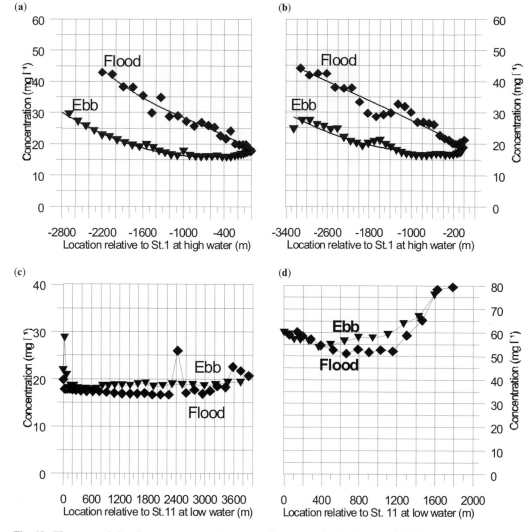

Fig. 10. The suspended sediment concentration versus distance at Station 1 around high water (**a** & **b**) and at Station 11 around low water (**c** & **d**). The suspended sediment concentration was measured when the water passed the station. The distance is calculated as the time integrated mean velocity measured at the station (positive in the flood direction). The water mass located at the station at the turn of the tide is in this context defined as being located at $x = 0$ m. Flood current measurements are indicated with *diamonds* and ebb current measurements with *triangles*.

thus the uncertainties of using this approach. The final example (Fig. 10d) is from a low-water situation after a storm (Fig. 3). Part of the fine-grained material that was removed from the tidal area by the storm was transported back, which raised the general concentration level at the station. The displacement of the lowest concentrations in the beginning of the flood period ($53-57$ mg l^{-1}) was between 400 m and 800 m. The higher concentrations later on in the flood period are interpreted as being the result of a

secondary turbidity maximum situated off-shore, formed by fine-grained sediment eroded from the Wadden Sea during the storm. The measured displacement agrees fairly well, although again rather on the high side, with the model.

Another way to compare measured data with the model is to use the model to calculate the concentration changes that take place over slack water, and to compare these results with the measurements. The primary drawback of using this approach with the present data is that even

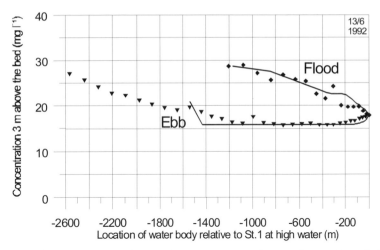

Fig. 11. Model simulation (full line) of the part of the concentration/distance-diagram shown in Figure 10a which is closest to slack water. The measurements are indicated with *diamonds* (flood) and *triangles* (ebb).

if the gross-lag distance is relatively insensitive to grain-size variations (Fig. 7a), the absolute values of concentration versus travelled distances are not, and the data contains no independent information about grain sizes. According to the results of Jago *et al.* (1994), typical seston in the North Sea (measured 1 m above the bed) consists of two modes with d_{50}-values of $\simeq0.075$ mm and $\simeq0.015$ mm respectively. In Fig. 11, a fifty-fifty mix of these two grain sizes ($d_{50} = 0.045$ mm) was used (based on the data shown in Fig. 10a) with the measured concentration 3 m above the bed at $x = -1200$ m taken as being the starting point ($C_{3m} = 28.7$ mg l^{-1} and $u_{2m} = 0.43$ m s^{-1}). The modelled concentrations coincide relatively well with the observed concentrations. During the part of the flood period when no sedimentation took place (until $x = -343$ m) the adjustments were based solely on the changed distribution caused by the velocity drop, and the corresponding adjustment of the concentration profile based on the Rouse Equation (Equation 7). The suspended material was subsequently deposited over slack water (Equation 9), until the returning water reached velocities high enough to prevent sedimentation but too low to cause erosion. Erosion started at $x = -1431$ m ($u_{2m} = 0.34$ m s^{-1}) and half of the deposited material was resuspended (Equation 12) at $x = -1540$ m ($u_{2m} = 0.35$ m s^{-1}). In this phase, the concentration at the measuring level was once again calculated by means of the Rouse Equation. It was this time adjusted so an integration over depth, gave the corresponding total suspended material in the water.

It is essential to stress that the relatively good agreement between the model and the observed data in Fig. 11 is totally dependent on the (not reported) grain-size distribution of the fine-grained sediment. The results of Fig. 11, therefore, can only be regarded as being an example of a possible good fit and not as a complete validation of the model. However, given the data available, no other tests of the model are possible.

Conclusions

The following main results were achieved by running the model with variations in the input values of grain size (10 μm–110 μm), initial concentration (30–1000 mg l^{-1}) and temperature (0°C–30°C).

(1) Considering the different lag effects that contribute to the import of fine-grained sediment, *scour lag* is by far the most important. For grain sizes in the range of 50 μm–80 μm and initial suspended sediment concentrations of $\simeq30$ mg l^{-1}, *settling lag* constitutes approximately 10% *scour lag* 85% and *resuspension lag* 5% of the total lag effect.

(2) There is a reverse proportionality between grain size and gross *scour lag*.

(3) There is a grain-size optimum, which is close to 100 μm, for the gross *settling lag*. Therefore, for particles finer than 100 μm, the coarser the particle the larger the gross *settling lag*.

(4) Because of the different water depths and hydrographical conditions, the share of the

suspended sediment which participates in the deposition/resuspension processes is smaller outside than inside in the tidal area. The largest difference occurs for grain-sizes close to 50 μm.

(5) Primarily as a result of a combination of points (2), (3) and (4), the net lag maximum ($\simeq$1050 m) occurs for grain sizes close to the sand/silt boundary (60–70 μm). For finer particles, the net lag quickly drops to a few hundred metres (10 μm–20 μm), whereas for coarser particles the drop is more gentle. This is a result of the assumption that sand settles together with cohesive material, with a constant τ_c of 0.3 N m^{-2}. If fine sand is considered to settle in a matrix of a similar grain size, the net lag is considerable smaller, in the order of 500 m.

(6) With raised initial sediment concentrations, the time it takes to resuspend deposited material becoms of increasing importance. The *resuspension lag* introduced in this way is more important than the *settling lag* for initial concentrations as low as 100 mg l^{-1}. From initial concentrations of 30 mg l^{-1}, over 100 mg l^{-1} to 1000 mg l^{-1}, it increases from 5% over 11% to 38% of the total net-lag effect.

(7) The net-lag effect increases with temperature for all grain sizes, mainly because of the raised settling velocity but also because the critical bed shear-stress for deposition increases with viscosity and thus decreases with temperature.

The field data precented in this paper were collected as part of an investigation carried out for the Harbour authorities in Esbjerg. I am thankful for the help and assistance I have achieved from Henning Nørgaard and Erik Brenneche at the administration and from Peter Kempf and his crew in the boat house. The field work and part of the data processing were carried out in corporation with Dennis Anthony and several other students at the Institute of Geography, University of Copenhagen and with Kirsten Simonsen & Heini Larsen at the Skalling Laboratory. I hereby wish to express my gratitude to all participants for good humour and labourious hours in boats and labs. The manuscript benefited from valuable comments and suggestions by J.R.L. Allen and K. Pye. The work was supported by The Danish Natural Science Foundation (#9701836).

References

ALLEN, J. R. L. & PYE, K. 1992. (eds) *Saltmarshes, Morphodynamics, Conservation and Engineering Significance*. Cambridge University Press, Cambridge.

AMOS, C. L. & MOSHER, D. C. 1985. Erosion and deposition of fine-grained sediemnts from the Bay of Fundy. *Sedimentology*, **32**, 815–832.

—— & TEE, K. T. 1989. Suspended sediment transport processes in Cumberland Basin, Bay of Fundy. *Journal of Geophysical Research*, **94**, 14 407–14 417.

——, SUTHERLAND, T. F. & ZEVENHUIZEN, J. 1996. The stability of sublittoral, fine-grained sediments in a subartic estuary. *Sedimentology*, **43**, 1–19.

BARTHOLDY, J. & MADSEN, P. P. 1985. Accumulation of fine-grained material in a Danish tidal area. *Marine Geology*, **67**, 121–137.

—— & ANTHONY, D. 1998. Tidal dynamics and seasonal dependent import and export of fine-grained sediment through a back barrier tidal channel of the Danish Wadden Sea. *In*: ALEXANDER, C., DAVIS, R. A. & HENRYM, V. J. (eds) *Tidalities: Processes and Products*, SEPM Special Publication No **61**, 43–52.

DRONKERS, J. 1986. Tide-induced residual transport of fine-grained sediment. *In*: VAN DEN KREEKE, J. (ed.) *Physics of shallow estuaries and bays*. Springer Verlag, New York, 228–244.

DYER, K. R. 1986. *Coastal and estuarine sediment dynamics*, John Wiley & Sons, New York.

——1994. Estuarine sediment transport and deposition. *In*: PYE, K. (ed.) *Sediment transport and depositional processes*. Blackwell Scientific Publications, Oxford, 193–218.

FLEMMING, B. W. & BARTHOLOMA, A. 1997. Responce of the Wadden Sea to a rising sea level: a predictive empirical model. *German Journal of Hydrography*, **49**, 1–11.

GROEN, P. 1967. On the residual transport of suspended matter by an alternating tidal current. *Netherlands Journal of Sea Research*, **3**, 564–574.

GRY, H. 1942. Das Wattenmeer bei Skallingen, physiographisch-biologishe untersursuchung eines Dänishen tidegebietes. Quantitative untersuchungen über den sinkstofftransport durch gezeitenströmungen. *Folia Geographica Danica*, **II**^{1}, 1–138.

JAGO, C. F., BALE, A. J., GREEN, O. M. *ET AL*. 1994. Resuspension processes and seston dynamics, southern North Sea. *In*: CHARNOCK, H., DYER, K. R., HUTHNANCE, J. M., LISS, P. S. SIMPSON, J. H. & TETT, P. B. (eds) *Understanding the North Sea System*. The Royal Society, Chapman & Hall, London, 97–110.

JAKOBSEN, B. 1961. Vadehavets sedimentomsætning belyst ved kvantitative målinger. *Geografisk Tidsskrift*, **60**, 87–103.

KE, X., EVANS, G. & COLLINS, M. B. 1996. Hydrodynamics and sediment dynamics of The Wash embayment, eastern England. *Sedimentology*, **43**, 157–174.

KRONE, R. B. 1962. *Flume studies of the transport of sediments in estuarial shoaling processes*: Hydraulic Engineering Laboratory and Sanitary Engineering Research Laboratory, University of California, Berkley.

MCDOWELL, D. M. & O'CONNOR, B. A. 1977. *Hydraulic behaviour of estuaries*. The Macmillian Press, London.

NICHOLS, M. M. 1986. Effects of fine sediment resuspension in estuaries. *In*: METHA, A. J. (ed.) *Estuarine cohesive sediment dynamics*. Springer Verlag, Berlin, 5–42.

NIELSEN, N. 1935. Eine Methoden zur exakten Sedimentationsmessung, Studien über die Marschbildung auf der Halbinsel Skalling. *Det Kongelige Danske Videnskabernes Selskab. Biologiske Meddelelser*, **XII⁴**, 97.

POSTMA, H. 1954. Hydrography of the Dutch Wadden Sea, a study of the relation between water movement, the transport of suspended materials and the production of organic matter. *Archives Néerlandaises de Zoologie*, **X**, 406–511.

——1961. Transport and accumulation of suspended matter in the Dutch Wadden Sea. *Netherlands Journal of Sea Research*, **1**, 148–190.

——1967. Sediment transport and sedimentation in the estuarine environment. *In*: LAUF, H. (ed.) *Estuaries*. American Association of Advanced Scientific Publications, No. **83**, 158–179.

VAN STRATEN, L. M. J. U. & KUENEN, P. H. H. 1957. Accumulation of fine-grained sediments in the Dutch Wadden Sea. *Geologie en Mijnbouw*, **19**, 329–354.

—— & ——1958. Tidal action as a cause of clay accumulation. *Journal of Sedimentary Petrology*, **28**, 406–413.

YALIN, M. S. 1992. *River Mechanics*. Pergamon Press, Oxford.

——& KARAHAN, E. 1979. Inception of sediment transport. *Journal of Hydraulic Div., ASCE*, **105**ᴴʸ¹¹, 1433–1443.

Relationship between current measurements and sonographs of subtidal bedforms in the macrotidal Tay Estuary, Scotland

ROBERT W. DUCK & SILKE F. K. WEWETZER

Department of Geography, University of Dundee, Dundee DD1 4HN, Scotland
(e-mail: r.w.duck@dundee.ac.uk)

Abstract: Near bottom current measurements have been compared with sonographs revealing a variety of subtidal dune geometries at eight stations in the middle reaches of the macrotidal Tay Estuary, Scotland. At six stations, dune asymmetries did not support the tidal dominance expressed in terms of maximum or average current speeds. Determination of bottom tidal current dominance according to the length of time during which a speed of $0.5\,\mathrm{ms^{-1}}$ was exceeded, as a proxy for the inequality of the total ebb and flood tide bedload sediment transports, provides a better, but not perfect, correlation with sonographs. Other controls on dune asymmetry and reversal are height, sediment discharge rate and bottom current velocity fluctuations. The study has shown that bedload transport processes and pathways in this relatively small ($c.\,8\,\mathrm{km^2}$), dynamic part of the estuary are far more complex than previously inferred and near bed flows do not simply correspond with the surface water circulation pattern. Neither sonographs nor current data alone are adequate to gain an understanding of subtidal bedforms in such an environment.

Estuaries are important, complex and highly variable geomorphological systems located at the interface between river-derived freshwaters and saline coastal waters. Such water bodies are therefore characterized by significant gradients in both physico-chemical and biological factors, in particular salinity and suspended sediment concentration. There have been countless investigations world-wide focusing on the understanding of suspended sediment circulation, transport, erosion/resuspension and deposition within estuarine systems (e.g. Allen *et al.* 1980; Dyer 1986, 1995; Hughes *et al.* 1998; Kirby & Parker 1983), together with many studies of emergent intertidal bedforms (e.g. Allen *et al.* 1994; Boersma & Terwindt 1981). However, there are considerable gaps in our knowledge of the sources, movement and transport pathways of coarser sediment at or near the bed, under the influence of the varying velocities of ebb and flood tidal currents and storm-related effects. This is particularly so in subtidal channels where direct observation of bedforms even at low water is either difficult or impossible. The study described in this paper was prompted by the discovery, using side-scan sonar, of a wide variety of subtidal bedform geometries, within a relatively small ($c.\,8\,\mathrm{km^2}$), geographically well defined reach of the Tay Estuary, Scotland, and forms an attempt to elucidate their relationship with water currents.

The study area

The Tay Estuary is a large embayment on the east coast of Scotland (Fig. 1) forming a linkage between the Tay drainage basin and the North Sea. It is of geomorphologically complex origin (Davidson *et al.* 1991; Paterson *et al.* 1981), arising from a number of geological constraints, Pleistocene glaciation, river erosion and sea-level fluctuation. One of the cleanest major estuaries in Europe (McManus 1986), this macrotidal (3.5/4–5.5/6 m) water body receives the drainage from a catchment area of $c.\,6500\,\mathrm{km^2}$. The principal influent is the River Tay, the foremost British river in terms of freshwater discharge, which, together with the subordinate River Earn, provides a long term mean inflow of $c.\,180\,\mathrm{m^3\,s^{-1}}$. The estuary has a tidal reach of 50 km, is, in general terms, partially mixed (McManus 1998), is up to 5 km in breadth and attains a maximum depth of $c.\,30\,\mathrm{m}$. Previous studies have shown that the bedrock channel in which the estuary is located is, to a large extent, infilled with a varied sequence of Late Glacial–Holocene deposits, into which estuarine channels are cut (Buller & McManus 1971), capped by a veneer of contemporary sediments (Buller & McManus 1975).

Delimited by two multi-pier bridges, the Tay Railway Bridge and the Tay Road Bridge, the

From: PYE, K. & ALLEN, J. R. L. (eds). *Coastal and Estuarine Environments: sedimentology, geomorphology and geoarchaeology*. Geological Society, London, Special Publications, **175**, 31–41. 0305-8719/00/$15.00 © The Geological Society of London 2000.

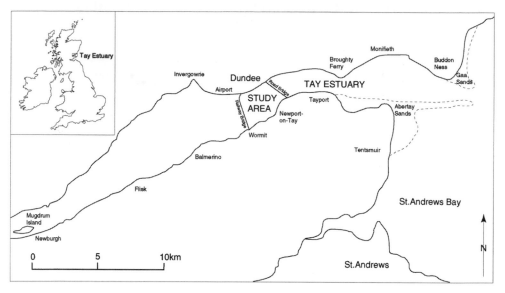

Fig. 1. Location of the Tay Estuary, eastern Scotland showing the study area between the Tay Railway Bridge and Tay Road Bridge.

area specifically chosen for this study (Fig. 1) forms part of the so-called middle reaches (Buller *et al.* 1971) of the Tay Estuary. Within this zone the estuary is highly dynamic, the bed being dominated by sand, migrating sand banks and shifting channels. Diver observations of bedform asymmetry indicative of flood tide orientation, reported by Buller & McManus (1975), supported by studies of heavy mineral populations in the modern sediments (Mishra 1969), suggest that some of the deposits of this region are of marine (North Sea) origin.

Within the study area, Middle Bank (Fig. 2) is the largest intertidal sand bank (over 1 km in length and 200 m in breadth). This feature creates a natural divide between Queen's Road Channel to the north and the main estuarine Navigation Channel to the south. The eastern end of Naughton–Wormit Bank, protruding beneath the Railway Bridge, separates the Southern Channel as it bifurcates from the Navigation Channel in the southwestern part of the study area (Fig. 2). At periods of low water on spring tides, water depths in the channels of this sector are of the order of 5 m (Fig. 2).

The dominant bottom sediment type between the Tay Bridges is slightly gravelly sand (nomenclature of Folk 1974) which veneers most of the central portion of the study area (Fig. 3) including Middle Bank (Buller & McManus 1975; Wewetzer 1997). Deeper waters of the Southern and Navigation Channels are characterized by a

bed of coarser deposits of gravelly sand incorporating pebbles and living colonies of mussels (mainly *Mytilus edulis*).

Side-scan sonar survey and observations

Side-scan sonar has been widely used to map the spatial distribution of coastal and estuarine sediment types (e.g. Hobbs 1986) and bedforms (e.g. Berné *et al.* 1993; Goedheer & Misdorp 1985; Milkert & Hühnerbach 1997). The first systematic side-scan sonar mapping of the study area defined in Fig. 1 was undertaken between August 1993 and March 1995. It achieved full spatial coverage, focusing on the morphology of subtidal bedforms during both ebb and flood tidal states (Wewetzer 1997). This survey was carried out principally using a Waverley Sonar 3000 system (operating frequency 100 kHz), deployed from *RV Mya* of the Tay Estuary Research Centre (University of Dundee), with sonographs recorded on a thermal linescan printer. Additional bathymetric data were acquired by vertical beam echo-sounding and sonographs were interpreted by the aid of correlation with 53 bottom sediment samples (Fig. 3) collected by a van Veen grab. A Magellan® NAV 1000 PLUS GPS receiver was used for position fixing (accuracy ±25 m or better). Sediment grain size analysis was carried out by a combination of dry sieving and Coulter Counter LS-100 (<63 μm size fractions).

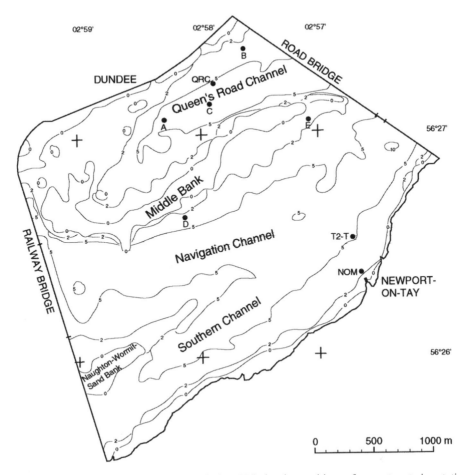

Fig. 2. Bathymetry of the study area (after Admiralty 1994) showing positions of current metering stations.

An important finding from the side-scan sonar observations in the Tay Estuary was the recognition of a wide range of bedform geometries, characteristically lacking bathymetric control (Wewetzer *et al.* 1999). In terms of the morphological classification of bedforms of Ashley (1990), as revised by Dalrymple and Rhodes (1995), those most abundant in the channels of the study area are small to medium dunes (wavelength 2–10 m; height up to 0.5 m). However, these were observed to display a variety of dune parameters, wavelength, height, forms of sinuosity and superposition, with often abrupt boundaries between dune types (Wewetzer *et al.* 1999). Although dune asymmetries indicative of the dominance of flood currents, thus supporting the marine provenance of sands, were frequently observed, they were by no means ubiquitous.

In order to gain a better understanding of the interactions between water movements

and the variety of subtidal bedform types recorded by side-scan sonar, a series of eight sites were chosen for the measurement of current velocities. The locations of these (Fig. 2) were determined on the basis of sonograph records and bottom sediment types, thereby affording current measurements coincident with the range of observed subtidal dune parameters (summarized in Table 1) characterizing the varying water depths of the study area.

As illustrative examples, sonographs are presented from three stations: (A) in Queen's Road Channel, T2-T, at the eastern end of the Navigation Channel and (D) in the centre of the study area, close to the southern edge of Middle Bank (Figs 4–6). The dunes imaged at Station A (Fig. 4) were observed to change in asymmetry according to tidal state (Wewetzer 1997). They were of small wavelength and small to medium height. Although sinuosity varied between straight during flood tidal conditions and sinuous

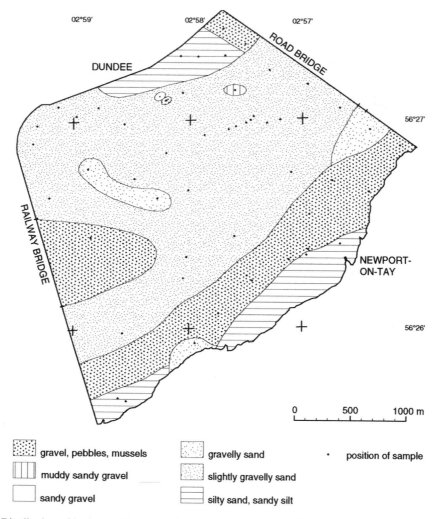

Fig. 3. Distribution of bottom sediments in the study area based on sediment samples in correlation with side-scan sonographs (textural classification after Folk 1974).

out of phase during ebb tidal conditions, dunes remained of compound superposition (superimposed dunes were of very small dimensions; wavelength <0.6 m, height < c. 0.05 m) during both tidal states. At Station T2-T, typical of many channel sectors in the south of the study area, sonographs revealed the presence of dunes characterized by a sinuosity described as 'patchy discontinuous' (Fig. 5) during both states of the tide. This acoustic signature has been attributed, with the aid of direct sampling, to the patchy colonization of mussels on the gentle stoss slopes of dunes, with resultant sediment stabilization, whilst uncolonized sediments are exposed on the steeper lee slopes (Wewetzer et al. 1999). At Station D (Fig. 6) sonographs revealed that

dune wavelengths were small and dune superposition was compound during both tidal states but dune height, sinuosity and asymmetry varied with the tidal condition. Ebb dominant dunes were recorded during the flood tide and dunes of mixed asymmetries during the ebb tide (Table 1). At each of the remaining five stations (B, C, E, QRC and NOM; Fig. 2) sonographs revealed dune asymmetry to be flood dominant, irrespective of the tidal state during which the side-scan sonar observations were made (Table 1).

Current measurements

Surface and bottom (1 m below the water surface and 1 m above the bed) currents were recorded

Table 1. *Variations of dune parameters (after Ashley 1990) as observed on sonographs recorded during ebb and flood tidal conditions at current meter stations shown in Fig. 2. Sediment textural classification after Folk (1974)*

Dune parameter	Tidal state	Station							
		A	B	C	D	E	QRC	T2-T	NOM
Wavelength	Ebb	Small	Medium	Medium	Small	Small	Small	Small	Small
	Flood	Small	Medium	Small	Small	Small	Medium	Small	Small
Height	Ebb	Medium	Medium	Medium	Medium	Small	Medium	Medium	Medium
	Flood	Small	Medium	Medium	Small	Medium	Medium	Medium	Medium
Sinuosity	Ebb	Sinuous out of phase	Sinuous out of phase	Sinuous out of phase	Sinuous out of phase	Sinuous in phase	Sinuous out of phase	Patchy, discontinuous	Patchy, discontinuous
	Flood	Straight	Sinuous out of phase	Sinuous out of phase	Catenary	Straight	Sinuous out of phase	Patchy, discontinuous	Patchy, discontinuous
Superposition	Ebb	Compound	Compound	Compound	Compound	Compound	Compound	Simple	Simple
	Flood	Compound	Simple	Simple	Compound	Simple	Simple	Simple	Simple
Asymmetry	Ebb	Ebb dominant	Flood dominant	Flood dominant	Mixed	Flood dominant	Flood dominant	Flood dominant	Flood dominant
	Flood	Flood dominant	Flood dominant	Flood dominant	Ebb dominant	Flood dominant	Flood dominant	Flood dominant	Flood dominant
Sediment type		Gravelly sand	Gravel, pebbles, mussels	Gravelly sand	Gravelly sand	Gravelly sand	Silty sand, sandy silt	Gravel, pebbles, mussels	Silty sand, sandy silt

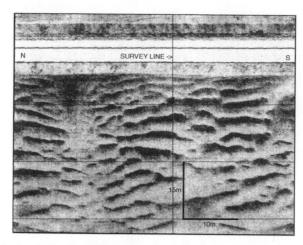

Fig. 4. Sonograph of the bed at Station A showing ebb dominant dunes of small wavelength and small to medium height (classification after Dalrymple & Rhodes 1995) recorded during ebb tidal conditions.

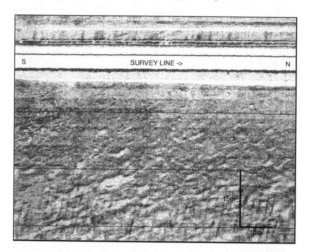

Fig. 5. Sonograph of the bed at Station T2-T showing 'patchy discontinuous' dunes (Wewetzer *et al.* 1999) which typify many channel areas. Note that the dark, parallel streaks towards the lower part of the sonograph are interference patterns.

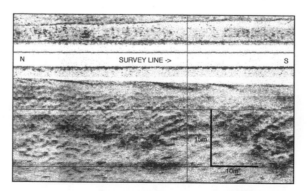

Fig. 6. Sonograph of the bed at Station D showing small and medium dunes of mixed asymmetries recorded during ebb tidal conditions.

simultaneously using two Braystoke MK 3 five inch diameter, impeller type current meters at each of the eight measuring stations (Fig. 2). Velocities were recorded for periods of 100 s at 20 minute intervals on complete tidal cycles (one at each station) with the days of current metering being selected, for optimum comparative purposes, to coincide with similar predicted tidal heights to those on which the side-scan sonographs had been previously recorded. These were on the falling tidal range, i.e. from spring to neap.

Results

In general, at each of the eight stations, maximum current speeds were recorded at approximately the mid-points of the ebb and flood tides with surface currents showing a higher speed, during both tidal states (e.g. Fig. 7a), than near bottom currents (e.g. Fig. 7b). For the purposes of this paper, only the latter will be considered further in the context of bedform generation and migration. Ebb bottom currents generally flow towards the NE quadrant (e.g. 050°–070°, average 057°, at Station A; Fig. 7b) whilst flood bottom currents flow towards the south west quadrant (e.g. 220°–270°, average 247°, at Station A; Fig. 7b). The durations of the flood and ebb components of the tidal cycle are approximately equal (e.g. Fig. 7a).

A summary of the maximum and average ebb and flood tidal bottom current speeds and directions, for each measuring station, is given in Table 2. These data reveal that ebb tidal flows dominate at six of the eight measuring stations (B, D, E, QRC, T2-T and NOM; Fig. 2), when analyzed in terms of both maximum and average bottom current speeds (cf. sonograph data of Table 1). By contrast, at the remaining two stations (A and C) flood tidal bottom currents dominate.

Comparison of current and sonograph data

Dunes with asymmetries indicative of the dominance of flood tidal bottom currents were recorded on both ebb and flood tides by side-scan sonar at five of the six current metering stations shown by the data of Table 2 to be ebb dominant (B, E and QRC in the north of the study area; T2-T and NOM in the south). At only two stations, one dominated by flood tidal bottom currents (C, in Queen's Road Channel, Fig. 2) and the other by ebb currents (D, in the centre of the study area, Fig. 2), were the current speed observations coincident with the sense of dune asymmetries recorded on sonographs. At the remaining station (A, centre north of the area in Queen's Road Channel, Fig. 2), flood dominant in terms of bottom current speeds, dune asymmetry, as referred to above, was observed to change according to the tidal state.

Broadly dunes may form in any sediment coarser than about the lower limit of fine sand (approximately 2.9∅; Dalrymple & Rhodes 1995). The minimum current speed at which dunes form is dependent on both sediment grain size and water depth (Southard & Boguchwal 1990), but is, according to Dalrymple & Rhodes (1995, p. 363), 'typically of the order of $0.5\,ms^{-1}$, rising as the depth and grain size increase'. If it is therefore assumed that a current speed of $0.5\,ms^{-1}$ may be considered as a threshold for dune formation and migration, the current data, when analyzed in terms of the time during which this speed is exceeded (Table 3), reveal a change in tidal dominance of bottom currents at two stations. At QRC and T2-T (Fig. 2), the lengths of time by which the $0.5\,ms^{-1}$ threshold were exceeded suggest that these stations are both, in fact, flood dominant. This indication of the marine derivation of bottom sediments at QRC and T2-T is thus in agreement with the side-scan sonar information (Table 1). Hence, using this

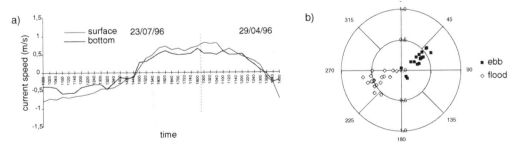

Fig. 7. (a) Time series plot of surface and bottom current speeds at Station A. **(b)** Speed and direction of near bottom currents at Station A. Radial velocity scale in ms^{-1}.

Table 2. *Average and maximum current speeds and directions recorded at current meter stations shown in Fig. 2*

Station	Tidal state	Average current		Maximum current	
		Speed (ms^{-1})	Direction	Speed (ms^{-1})	Direction
A	Ebb	0.40	057°	0.58	070°
	Flood	0.47	247	0.65	260
B	Ebb	0.60	058	0.93	060
	Flood	0.48	241	0.62	240
C	Ebb	0.31	070	0.47	060
	Flood	0.41	252	0.62	240
D	Ebb	0.61	072	0.95	070
	Flood	0.50	246	0.61	250
E	Ebb	0.63	043	0.86	040
	Flood	0.59	226	0.78	230
QRC	Ebb	0.50	058	0.70	040
	Flood	0.31	222	0.60	240
T2-T	Ebb	0.60	045	0.98	046
	Flood	0.45	238	0.60	227
NOM	Ebb	0.38	036	0.45	030
	Flood	0.28	269	0.45	260

form of data analysis, the bottom current and sonograph data are coincident at a total of four of the eight stations (C, D, QRC, T2-T).

At Station A, still flood dominant by this method of analysis (Table 3), sonographs reveal changing dune asymmetry according to tidal state, as referred to above. At Station NOM the 0.5 ms^{-1} threshold was never exceeded on either the ebb or flood tide yet dunes are recorded there. This suggests that the current speed required for dune occurrence is, in this shallow part of the area, less than 0.5 ms^{-1} or the currents can be >0.5 ms^{-1} on occasion. The 'patchy discontinuous' dunes in the region of Station NOM show flood dominant asymmetries according to sonographs (Table 1). That

the data of Table 2 are indicative of the ebb dominance of bottom currents may not be significant since these bedforms are believed to be at least partially stabilized, and therefore immobilized, by the colonization of mussels (Wewetzer *et al.* 1999). As such, Station NOM will be excluded from further discussion. There still remain two stations (B and E, Fig. 2) at which the bottom current data, when analyzed in terms of the length of time a speed of 0.5 ms^{-1} is exceeded, do not coincide with the side-scan sonar observations. At these two stations, the sonographs of bedforms show asymmetries indicative of flood tidal dominance at both states of the tide (Table 1) whereas the bottom current data indicate ebb dominance in the forms of data analysis employed (Tables 2 and 3).

Table 3. *Times for which the current speed exceeded the threshold for dune occurrence (0.5 ms^{-1}, Dalrymple & Rhodes 1995) at current meter stations shown in Fig. 2*

Station	Ebb tide (hours : minutes)	Flood tide (hours : minutes)
A	1:30	4:20
B	5:00	2:40
C	0:00	1:40
D	4:00	4:00
E	4:40	4:00
QRC	2:30	3:00
T2-T	3:30	4:00
NOM	0:00	0:00

Discussion and conclusions

It is almost inevitable that a study such as this should close with a statement that more data are required. However, this is indeed the case; more spatially coincident side-scan sonar and precision bottom current measurements are needed from both within and outside the study area. Nevertheless, some meaningful conclusions, both site-specific and generic, can be drawn from the investigation.

This study has shown that dune asymmetries revealed by sonographs were not, in the majority (six out of eight stations) of cases, supported by the measurements of maximum and average current speeds as an indicator of tidal dominance. It is to be anticipated that bedform asymmetry is best related of the inequality of the total sediment transports on the flood and ebb tides. This is, however, almost impossible to measure. As a proxy, albeit imperfect, determination of bottom tidal current dominance according to the length of time by which a bottom current speed of $0.5\,ms^{-1}$ is exceeded, as suggested by Dalrymple & Rhodes (1995) as the threshold for dune occurrence, was utilized. This provides a better correlation with sonograph observations than tidal dominance expressed in terms of either maximum or average current speed. The observations thus suggest that the length of time during which the above bottom current speed is exceeded has a greater effect on the asymmetry of dunes than the maximum and average bottom current velocities recorded during tidal cycles. However, this is not the sole control on bedform asymmetry.

The observed reversal of dune asymmetry at Station A according to tidal state is believed to be related to dune height. The dunes imaged at this station are among the smallest in height in the study area. The time required to reverse the asymmetry of a dune is a function of dune height and sediment discharge rate (Bokuniewicz et al. 1977). Thus, it is suggested that dune reversal at Station A is favoured as less sediment is required

to be moved from the surficial caps of the dunes (Bokuniewicz et al. 1977) to effect reversal than for the generally higher bedforms characterizing the other stations. Berné et al. (1993) suggested that, in the macrotidal Gironde Estuary, France, it should take 19 tidal cycles for spring tide currents to reverse flood dominated large dunes and 185 cycles for neap tide currents to reverse ebb dominated large dunes. However, fortnightly oscillation or even semi-diurnal reversal of the tidal current during spring tides could cause reversal of small dunes.

Salsman et al. (1966), on the basis of diver observations in St Andrew Bay, Florida, reported that:

$$C \propto V^5 \qquad (1)$$

where, C = bedform migration rate (quoted in $cm\,day^{-1}$) and V = mean flow velocity (quoted in $cm\,s^{-1}$). Other researchers (see Dalrymple & Rhodes 1995 for details) have suggested that, in unidirectional flows:

$$U_B \propto q_S \propto U_D^3 \qquad (2)$$

5pt > where, U_B = dune migration rate; q_S = net sediment discharge; U_D = maximum or modal speed of the dominant current. Thus, on the basis of equation 2 and, to an even greater extent equation 1, dune migration rates, and therefore asymmetries, are extremely sensitive to changes or fluctuations in current speeds, depending on the

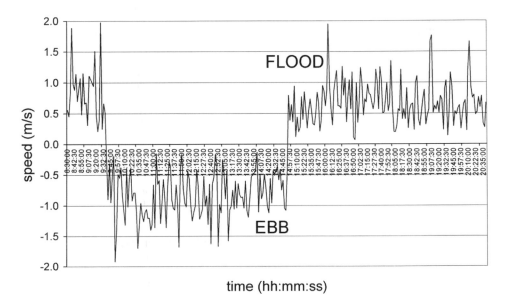

Fig. 8. Time series plot of bottom current (0.5 m above the bed) speeds recorded at Station A by means of an Acoustic Doppler Current Profiler (ADCP).

magnitude of the constant in equation 1 and the q_S relative to the bedform mass in equation 2.

In order to improve on the precision and sensitivity of current velocities in the study area, the acquisition of Acoustic Doppler Current Profiler (ADCP) data from the eight stations of Fig. 2 is in progress. ADCPs measure water currents throughout the water column (e.g. Swift et al. 1996) by means of the Doppler shift of acoustic pulses emitted from four directional transducers and backscattered from suspended particles, such as plankton, in the water column. Importantly, current velocity data may be obtained at time intervals of less than or equal to the time period typically required (100 s) to record a significant number of impeller revolutions by a conventional current meter. For example, the ADCP record of near bottom currents at 2.5 minute intervals at Station A (Fig. 8) demonstrates a much greater complexity of fluctuation in speed than shown in Fig. 7 with instantaneous speeds being up to 1 ms^{-1} greater on both the flood and ebb tides than those recorded by impeller current metering. However, the flood dominance of the station, in terms of the length of time the bottom current speed of 0.5 ms^{-1} is exceeded, remains the same.

Float tracking of *surface* currents (Charlton et al. 1975) and measurements of salinity variations (McManus & Wakefield 1982) indicate that the flood tide tends to be dominant in Queen's Road Channel. When the tide turns, the waters flow southwards and then ebb along the Navigation Channel, resulting in a counter-clockwise circulation pattern in the study area. The bottom current measurements of this study do not fully conform to this pattern. Although the data of Stations A C and QRC suggest a flood dominance, Station B appears to be characterized by ebb dominant currents (Table 3). Data from three stations south of Middle Bank (D, E and NOM) are, however, generally indicative of ebb dominant bottom currents (Tables 2 and 3), and so support the counter-clockwise circulation pattern observed for surface currents, whilst T2-T, in the Navigation Channel, is flood dominant. It is suggested that the flood dominant dune asymmetries recorded by side-scan sonar at Stations B and E during both tidal states are relict asymmetries from a previous, higher tidal current flow. The current measurements at both of these stations were recorded during a sequence of tides moving from springs to neaps in which current speeds would be expected to decay. Such bedform lag effects, as the tides shift from springs to neaps and back, are common in estuaries (e.g. the Gironde Estuary, Berné et al. 1993).

What is clear from this study, however, is that the bedload transport processes and pathways in this highly dynamic part of the Tay Estuary are far more complex than previously inferred (Buller & McManus 1975) and near bed flows do not simply correspond with the surface water circulation pattern described by Charlton et al. (1975). Furthermore, it has been shown that neither sonographs nor current data alone are adequate to gain an understanding of subtidal bedforms in such an environment. There is a need for more data from the Tay and similar estuaries world-wide to gain a better understanding of subtidal bedforms and bedload transport processes. The findings of this study suggest that ideally an integrated programme of acoustic remote sensing coupled with precision current velocity data, (e.g. acquired by ADCP) are required to investigate the complexities of subtidal bedform occurrence, migration and asymmetry in sandy-gravelly estuaries.

We thank Ian Lorimer of the Tay Estuary Research Centre, for his invaluable help during the field work. The financial support of the Commission of the European Communities (Human Capital and Mobility Fund) and the Durham Bequest is gratefully acknowledged.

References

ADMIRALTY. 1994. *River Tay*, Chart No. **1481**.

ALLEN, G. P., SALOMON, J. C., BASSOULET, P., DU PENHOAT, Y. & DE GRANDPRE, C. 1980. Effects of tides on mixing and suspended sediment transport in macrotidal estuaries. *Sedimentary Geology*, **26**, 69–90.

ALLEN, J. R. L., FRIEND, P. F., LLOYD, A. & WELLS, H. 1994. Morphodynamics of intertidal dunes: a year long study at Lifeboat Station Bank, Wells-next-the Sea, eastern England. *Philosophical Transactions of the Royal Society*, **A347**, 291–345.

ASHLEY, G. 1990. Classification of large-scale subaqueous bedforms: a new look at an old problem. *Journal of Sedimentary Petrology*, **60**, 160–172.

BERNÉ, S., CASTAING, P., LE DREZEN, E. & LERICOLAIS, G. 1993. Morphology, internal structure and reversal of asymmetry of large subtidal dunes in the entrance of the Gironde Estuary (France). *Journal of Sedimentary Petrology*, **63**, 780–793.

BOERSMA, J. R. & TERWINDT, J. H. J. 1981. Neap-spring tide sequences of intertidal shoal deposits in a mesotidal estuary. *Sedimentology*, **28**, 151–170.

BOKUNIEWICZ, H. J., GORDON, R. B. & KASTENS, K. A. 1977. Form and migration of sand waves in a large estuary, Long Island Sound. *Marine Geology*, **24**, 185–199.

BULLER, A. T. & MCMANUS, J. 1971. Channel stability in the Tay Estuary: controls by bedrock and unconsolidated post-glacial sediment. *Engineering Geology*, **5**, 227–237.

—— & ——1975. Sediments of the Tay Estuary. I. Bottom sediments of the upper and upper middle reaches. *Proceedings of the Royal Society of Edinburgh* (B), **75**, 41–64.

——, —— & WILLIAMS, D. J. A. 1971. *Investigations in the Estuarine Environments of the Tay*. Tay Estuary Research Centre Research Report, University of Dundee, **1**.

CHARLTON, J. A., MCNICOLL, W. & WEST, J. R. 1975. Tidal and freshwater induced circulation in the Tay Estuary. *Proceedings of the Royal Society of Edinburgh* (B), **75**, 11–27.

DALRYMPLE, R. W. & RHODES, R. N. 1995. Estuarine dunes and bars. *In*: PERILLO, G. M. E. (ed.) *Geomorphology and Sedimentology of Estuaries*, Elsevier Science, Amsterdam, 359–422.

DAVIDSON, N. C., LAFFOLEY, D. d'A., DOODY, J. P. *ET AL.* 1991. *Nature Conservation in Estuaries in Great Britain*. Nature Conservancy Council, Peterborough.

DYER, K. R. 1986. *Coastal and Estuarine Sediment Dynamics*. Wiley, Chichester.

——1995. Sediment transport processes in estuaries. *In*: PERILLO, G. M. E. (ed.) *Geomorphology and Sedimentology of Estuaries*, Elsevier Science, Amsterdam, 423–449.

FOLK, R. L. 1974. *Petrology of Sedimentary Rocks*. Hemphill, Austin, Texas.

GOEDHEER, G. J. & MISDORP, R. 1985. Spatial variability and variations in bedload transport in a subtidal channel as indicated by sonographs. *Earth Surface Processes and Landforms*, **10**, 375–386.

HOBBS, C. H. 1986. Side-scan sonar as a tool for mapping spatial variations in sediment type. *Geo-Marine Letters*, **5**, 241–245.

HUGHES, M. G., HARRIS, P. T. & HUBBLE, T. C. T. 1998. Dynamics of the turbidity maximum zone in a micro-tidal estuary: Hawkesbury River, Australia. *Sedimentology*, **45**, 397–410.

KIRBY, R. & PARKER, R. W. 1983. The distribution and behaviour of fine sediment in the Severn Estuary and inner Bristol Channel. *Canadian Journal of Fisheries and Aquatic Sciences*, **40**, 83–95.

MCMANUS, J. 1986. Sediment transport patterns in the Tay Estuary, Scotland. *In*: WANG, S. Y., SHEN, H. W. & DING, L. Z. (eds) *Proceeding of the Third International Symposium on River Sedimentation*, University of Mississippi, 517–524.

——1998. Mixing of sediments in estuaries. *In*: CRACKNELL, A. P. & ROWAN, E. S. (eds) *Physical Processes in the Coastal Zone: Computer Modelling and Remote Sensing*, SUSSP Publications and Institute of Physics, 281–293.

—— & WAKEFIELD, P. 1982. Lateral transfer of water across the middle reaches of the Tay Estuary. *In*: MCMANUS, J. (ed.) *Sedimentological, Hydrological and Biological Papers*, Tay Estuary Research Centre Report, University of Dundee **7**, 25–37.

MILKERT, D. & HÜHNERBACH, V. 1997. Coastal environments. *In*: BLONDEL, P. & MURTON, B. J. (eds) *Handbook of Seafloor Sonar Imagery*, Wiley/Praxis, Chichester 193–221.

MISHRA, S. K. 1969. Heavy mineral studies in the Firth of Tay region, Scotland. *Journal of the Geological Society of the University of Saugar* (Pakistan), **5**, 37–49.

PATERSON, I. B., ARMSTRONG, M. & BROWNE, M. A. E. 1981. *Quaternary Estuarine Deposits in the Tay-Earn Area, Scotland*. Institute of Geological Sciences Report, **81/7**.

SALSMAN, G. G., TOLBERT, W. H. & VILLARS, R. G. 1966. Sand-ridge migration in St. Andrew Bay, Florida. *Marine Geology*, **4**, 11–19.

SOUTHARD, J. B. & BOGUCHWAL, L. A. 1990. Bed configurations in steady unidirectional water flows. Part 2. Synthesis of flume data. *Journal of Sedimentary Petrology*, **60**, 658–679.

SWIFT, M. R., FREDRIKSSON, D. W. & CELIKKOL, B. 1996. Structure of an axial convergence zone from Acoustic Doppler Current Profiler measurements. *Estuarine, Coastal and Shelf Science*, **43**, 109–122.

WEWETZER, S. F. K. 1997. *Bedforms and Sediment Transport in the Middle Tay Estuary, Scotland: A Side-scan Sonar Investigation*. Unpublished PhD thesis, University of St. Andrews.

——, DUCK, R. W. & MCMANUS, J. 1999. Side-scan sonar mapping of bedforms in the middle Tay Estuary, Scotland. *International Journal of Remote Sensing*, **20**, 511–522.

Controls on suspended sediment deposition over single tidal cycles in a macrotidal saltmarsh, Bay of Fundy, Canada

DANIKA VAN PROOSDIJ[1,3], JEFF OLLERHEAD[2]
& ROBIN G. D. DAVIDSON-ARNOTT[1]

[1] *Department of Geography, University of Guelph, Guelph, Ontario, Canada N1G 2W1*
[2] *Department of Geography, Mount Allison University, Sackville, New Brunswick, Canada E4L 1A7*
[3] *Present address: Department of Geography, Saint Mary's University, Halifax, Nova Scotia, Canada B3H 3C3*

Abstract: A field study was conducted on a section of Allen Creek marsh in the Bay of Fundy to examine changes in suspended sediment circulation and deposition over single tidal cycles. Net flow velocity, suspended sediment concentration and sediment deposition were measured over 13 individual tidal cycles during the summer of 1998. A vertical array was deployed in the low marsh region, consisting of three pairs of electromagnetic current meters, OBS[tm] probes and one pressure transducer. Sediment deposition was measured using full-cycle sediment traps. The temporal distribution of sediment deposition was monitored using sequential sediment traps exposed at different tidal stages. The data suggest that sediment deposition on the marsh surface is primarily controlled by the interaction of water flow, marsh morphology and vegetation. The highest amounts of sediment are deposited during conditions of high suspended sediment concentration and low wave activity, particularly when the relative roughness of the vegetation is the highest. Loss of suspended sediment from the water column was shown to be correlated with the sediment trap data; however, predictions of sediment deposition based on the variation in suspended sediment concentration were found to be valid only for conditions with less than 0.15 m high waves. For higher wave conditions, the use of suspended sediment loss calculations should be used primarily for estimating the relative rather than absolute values of deposition on the marsh surface.

Over the past decade, there have been a number of studies of short-term saltmarsh sediment dynamics and their incorporation into models of saltmarsh morphodynamics (Allen 1990; French 1993; French *et al.* 1995; Woolnough *et al.* 1995; Callaway *et al.* 1996; Allen 1997). A number of biophysical variables affecting sedimentation have been postulated such as wind-wave stress, water depth, vegetation, biological activity, proximity to sediment source and micro-topography (Stevenson *et al.* 1985; Allen & Pye 1992; French & Stoddart 1992; Cahoon & Reed 1995; French *et al.* 1995; Leonard *et al.* 1995; Luternauer *et al.* 1995; Shi *et al.* 1995; Woolnough *et al.* 1995; Leonard 1997; Yang 1998). In addition, the relationship between these biophysical variables and flow characteristics in tidal creek channels and over the marsh surface, particularly as they relate to tidal stage, have been explored (Pethick 1981; Reed 1989; French & Stoddart 1992; French & Spencer 1993; Leonard *et al.* 1995).

A general hypothesis derived from these studies is that net deposition on marsh surfaces is a function of the availability of sediment and the opportunity for deposition. Despite these studies, however, the spatial and temporal relationships between wave activity, water depth, vegetation and suspended sediment supply within the time span of a single tidal cycle remain unclear. Hence the purpose of this study was to examine the controls on sediment deposition on a marsh surface over single tidal cycles. Four objectives were identified:

(1) To measure the temporal and vertical change in suspended sediment concentration under varying conditions of wave activity, suspended sediment concentration and tidal height.

From: PYE, K. & ALLEN, J. R. L. (eds). *Coastal and Estuarine Environments: sedimentology, geomorphology and geoarchaeology.* Geological Society, London, Special Publications, **175**, 43–57. 0305-8719/00/$15.00 © The Geological Society of London 2000.

(2) To measure the temporal variation in the amount of sediment deposited on the marsh surface over a tidal cycle.

(3) To measure the total amount of sediment deposited on the marsh surface.

(4) To determine the relationship between measured suspended sediment inputs and factors controlling deposition and measured deposition from sediment trap data.

Study site

The research was conducted within a 200 m × 300 m section of Allen Creek marsh, situated on the NW shore of the Cumberland Basin in the Bay of Fundy. The Bay of Fundy is a large, macrotidal embayment on the east coast of Canada; it is the NE extension of the Gulf of Maine, between the provinces of New Brunswick and Nova Scotia (Fig. 1). The Bay is characterized by high suspended sediment concentrations ($\simeq 0.3\,\mathrm{g\,l^{-1}}$) which vary seasonally and are derived from erosion of the bordering Paleozoic sandstone, siltstone and shale cliffs (Amos 1987; Amos et al. 1991). The Cumberland Basin is an 118 km^2 turbid estuary at the head of the Bay of Fundy with a tidal range of approximately 14 m. A shallow subtidal zone occupies approximately one third of the basin (Amos et al. 1991) while the remainder consists of mud and sandflats with saltmarshes occupying the upper intertidal zone (Fig. 1). Allen Creek marsh is one of the few remaining tracts of saltmarsh, which have not been dyked.

Saltmarshes in the Bay of Fundy are characterized by exposure to a high suspended sediment concentration, a tidal range in excess of 12 m and the influence of ice and snow for at least 3 months of the year. During this period, much of the marsh vegetation is either sheared off, exposing base sediment or buried under snow

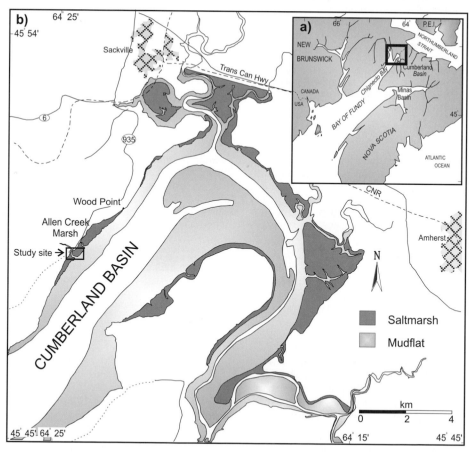

Fig. 1. (a) Map of the Bay of Fundy and regional setting; (b) Map of the Cumberland Basin showing the location of major marshes and mudflats.

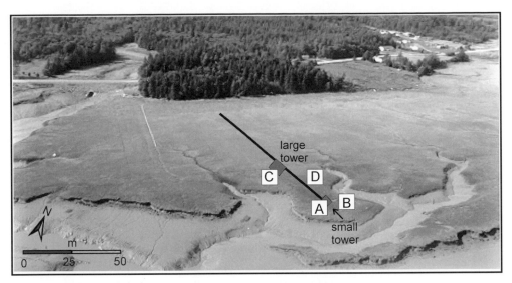

Fig. 2. Oblique aerial photograph of Allen Creek marsh taken July 1996. Vertical instrument array moved between sampling locations A to D. Two towers and a boardwalk were built to facilitate data collection over the marsh surface.

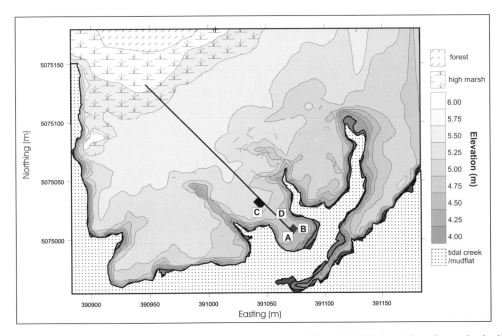

Fig. 3. Topographic map of Allen Creek marsh constructed from differential GPS data. Note the gently sloping marsh surface towards the creeks and margin cliffs.

and ice. Sediment in suspension is composed of 95% silt, with lesser amount of clay (2.5%) and sand (1.5%) and has a mean grain size of 4.8 phi (36 μm) (van Proosdij *et al.* 1999). The study site itself occupies a section of shoreline which is narrow (0.2–0.3 km) and consists of a gently sloping vegetated surface which grades abruptly into cliffs 1–2 m in height at the marsh/mudflat transition (Figs 2 & 3). The landward end of the marsh grades abruptly into woodland behind a steep, 1.5 m slope cliffed by wave activity during high spring tides. Allen Creek occupies the western boundary of the site. The marsh surface is dissected by 3 tidal creek networks in the mid to low marsh region which exhibit a simple dendritic pattern and drain into a main channel oriented parallel to the shoreline (Fig. 2). The SW (offshore) side of this main channel consists of a narrow strip of marsh surface which is lower in elevation than the main marsh surface and is eroding at a rate of approximately $1.2 \, \mathrm{m \, yr}^{-1}$ (van Proosdij *et al.* 1999). High marsh vegetation, dominated by *Spartina patens,* occupies the upper 40 m of the marsh surface with low marsh species, dominated by *Spartina alterniflora,* covering the remainder.

Research design and methodology

The study was conducted as a component of a larger research project on saltmarsh sediment dynamics. It was carried out during a five week period between June 22 and July 23, 1998. In order to measure variations in flow velocity and suspended sediment concentration over a tidal cycle, a vertical array, consisting of three pairs of Marsh McBirney model 512 bi-directional electromagnetic current meters (EMCM) and OBS[tm] probes, was deployed in the low/mid marsh region. The current meter probes were oriented in the horizontal plane and instrument pairs located at 0.15, 0.35 and 0.5 m above the bed (Fig. 4). The X axis of the EMCM was oriented perpendicular to the marsh margin which also coincided with the direction of dominant wave advance. A pressure transducer and an additional OBS[tm] probe were located at 0.3 m and 1 m above the bed respectively. Throughout the study period, the array was moved between the four topographic locations (A to D) illustrated in Figs 2 and 3.

Instruments were hardwired to an instrument platform located in the mid marsh region. A smaller tower was built in the low marsh region for suction sampling and operating sequential sediment traps (Fig. 2). Time series data were recorded at 4 Hz for 8.5 minutes every 20 minutes over thirteen individual tidal cycles. The OBS[tm] probes and electromagnetic flow meters were calibrated at laboratory facilities at the University of Toronto and the University of Guelph.

Fig. 4. Typical vertical instrument array. EMCM and OBS probes are at 0.15, 0.35 and 0.5 m above the bed. An additional OBS probe is located at 1 m above the bed. A pressure transducer is located at 0.03 m above the bed.

Flow velocities were derived from the resultant vector velocities of both X and Y nodes. A measure of the relative wave activity for each day was derived from the root-mean-square of the wave-induced velocity measured at a water depth of 0.8 m on the rising tide. The root-mean-square of wave-induced velocity is equal to $(\sigma_u^2 + \sigma_v^2)^{1/2}$, where σ_u and σ_v are the standard deviations of X and Y node velocities respectively.

Sediment deposition was measured as the amount of sediment, which settled out of the water column after one tidal cycle, onto surface mounted sediment traps. Traps were designed to operate on the same principle as Reed's (1989) petri dish traps but were modified for use in a macro-tidal environment. The weight of material directly deposited on filter papers was recorded then converted to a gm^{-2} estimate. These full-cycle sediment traps consisted of three glass fiber 9 cm diameter filter papers, placed on a 0.5 cm thick woven mesh for drainage and then sandwiched between two 15×30 cm aluminum plates with 8 cm diameter holes cut into them. These were secured approximately 1 cm above the bed by four brass rods. A total of 8 traps was laid out in a grid format around the vertical array. Traps and filters were removed after each tide, oven dried at 60°C and sediment deposited weighed to the nearest 1×10^{-4} g.

In order to examine the timing of sediment deposition over a tidal cycle, a series of 6 sequential sediment traps was deployed. Each sequential trap consisted of a full-cycle sediment trap with an aluminum plate covering the filter paper section and sealed along the edges with petroleum jelly. A thin wire was attached to each lid and connected to the small tower platform. Traps were labeled T_1 through to T_6. The lid of T_1 was removed when the water depth was 0.2 m T_2 at 0.6 m, T_3 at the beginning of high tide, T_4 as the tide was observed to begin to fall, T_5 at 0.6 m and T_6 at 0.2 m. Removal times were recorded. Two additional full-cycle sediment traps were deployed to provide a measure of the total amount of sediment deposited over the tidal cycle. The amount of sediment deposited (dp_i) during each depth interval (P_i) was calculated by the equation:

$$dp_i = \frac{(T_{i-1} - T_i)}{A} \quad \text{if } i \neq 1 \qquad (1)$$

$$dp_i = \frac{(T_T - T_i)}{A} \quad \text{if } i = 1 \qquad (2)$$

Where: dp_i = amount of sediment deposition during depth interval Pi (gm^{-2})
T_i = mean mass of sediment deposited on trap i (gm^{-2})

T_T = mean mass of sediment deposited over entire tidal cycle on full-cycle traps
A = area of filter paper (63.62 cm^2)

A rate of sediment deposition during each stage interval can then be determined by:

$$qp_i = \frac{dp_i}{t_i} \qquad (3)$$

qp_i = rate of sediment deposition during depth interval Pi (gm^{-2} min^{-1})
t_i = length of time exposed between intervals (minutes)

Results

Temporal and vertical variations in flow velocity and suspended sediment concentration

Three representative days were chosen to illustrate the variability over a tidal cycle in flow velocity, suspended sediment concentration and wave activity, with height above the bed and differing wave conditions: calm on July 23, moderate on July 15 (waves 0.1–0.15 m) and high on June 24 (waves 0.2–0.3 m). Unfortunately, EMCM data 0.35 m will not be included due to a potential electrical malfunction. In all cases, mean flow velocity was low, less than 0.2 m s^{-1}, and remained fairly constant throughout the tidal cycle with slight increases during the initial and latter portions of the tide (Fig. 5a). In the vertical plane, however, a definite difference between near-bed and surface flow magnitude and wave activity was observed during calm and moderate wave conditions. The lowest flows (0.06 m s^{-1}) were observed, as expected, at 0.15 m above the bed in the canopy. The highest flows (0.18 m s^{-1}) were observed 0.5 m above the bed during all conditions including periods of calm (Fig. 5a). This suggests that the increased velocities may be attributed to conditions external to the marsh system such as tidal currents and wave conditions in the Cumberland Basin.

Variations in suspended sediment concentration were measured at 0.15, 0.35, 0.5 and 1 m above the bed over a tidal cycle. In general there was a decreasing trend in the suspended sediment concentration over the tidal cycle as illustrated in Fig. 5b. Under all conditions, the highest rate of decrease in suspended sediment concentration occurred during the initial 40 minutes of the flood tide (Fig. 5b). The OBS^{tm} records for both calm and moderate wave conditions

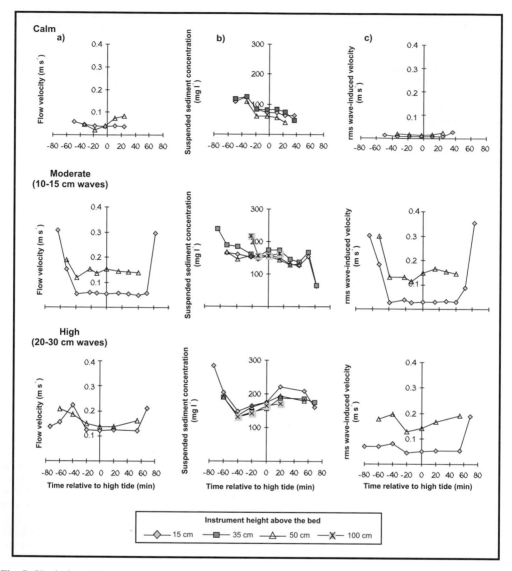

Fig. 5. Vertical variation in: (**a**) net flow velocity; (**b**) suspended sediment concentration [SS]; (**c**) root-mean-square (rms) of wave-induced velocity over a tidal cycle at 0.15, 0.35, 0.5 and 1 m above the bed for calm (July 23), moderate (July 15) and wavy (June 24) conditions.

demonstrated an approximate $100\,mg\,l^{-1}$ loss of suspended sediment from the water column, whereas during periods of high wave activity, such as on June 24, much of the sediment remained in suspension. The June 24 data did demonstrate an initial decrease in suspended sediment concentration during the initial stages of the flood tide; however this was followed by a subsequent increase during the latter stages of the ebb (Fig. 5b). Overall, there was an increase in the mean amount of sediment in

suspension with increasing wave activity. The highest values of suspended sediment concentration ($280\,mg\,l^{-1}$) were found on June 24, coincident with the highest fluctuations in wave-induced velocity (Fig. 5c). The lowest suspended sediment concentrations ($38\,mg\,l^{-1}$) were observed to be at the end of the tidal cycle during calm conditions, when the root-mean-square of wave-induced velocity was below $0.025\,m\,s^{-1}$. During all conditions, variation in suspended sediment concentration with height was generally less than $30 \, \text{mg} \, \text{l}^{-1}$. This minimal change in suspended sediment concentration with height suggests that the water column is well mixed. The highest suspended sediment concentrations were recorded at 0.35 m above the bed.

In order to explore the hypothesis that the interaction between wave activity, topography and vegetation height exerts an important control on variations in velocity and suspended sediment concentrations over a tidal cycle, the vertical variation in the root-mean-square of wave-induced velocity was examined (Fig. 5c). The root-mean-square values of wave-induced velocity exhibited some variation in both temporal and vertical fields (Fig. 5c). As expected, the root-mean-square values were lowest at 0.15 m above the bed, due to the location of this instrument within the vegetated canopy. However, sharp increases in velocity fluctuations were observed during the initial and final stages of the tidal cycle when water depths were less than 0.4 m during moderate and high wave conditions. Conversely, root-mean-square values were less than $0.025 \, \text{m} \, \text{s}^{-1}$ at all elevations during calm conditions. The highest velocity fluctuations were observed at 0.5 m above the bed, which is not surprising, given that most of the wave activity is near the water surface.

Temporal variations in sediment deposition over a tidal cycle

A series of sequential sediment traps were deployed to measure the distribution of sediment deposition over a tidal cycle for 8 of the 13 tides. Figure 6a illustrates the change in rate of sediment deposition over a tidal cycle. The amount of sediment deposited during each water depth interval was determined using equations 1 & 2 and normalized for the amount of time each trap was uncovered (equation 3). Data are shown for calm (July 23) and moderate (July 15) wave conditions as well as for the mean of all 8 sequential trap experiments. The data collected for high wave conditions (June 24) could not be used since all of the filter papers were ripped off the sequential traps due to wave action.

The mean data demonstrated that, in general, the highest rates of sediment deposition ($1.8 \, \text{gm}^{-2} \, \text{min}^{-1}$ and $3.8 \, \text{gm}^{-2} \, \text{min}^{-1}$ respectively) were experienced during the initial (P_1) and latter (P_2) 0.2 m of the tide (Fig. 6a). Suspended material did settle out of the water column at a rate between 0.1 and $0.4 \, \text{gm}^{-2} \, \text{min}^{-1}$ over the entire tidal cycle; however this was not restricted to the 'slack water' period (P_4) (Fig. 6a). For all

conditions, the highest rates of sediment deposition ($>3.0 \, \text{gm}^{-2} \, \text{min}^{-1}$) took place during the latter 0.2 m (P_7) of the ebb tide. Surprisingly however, during calm conditions, a peak in the suspended sediment deposition rate was not observed during P_1 as was seen during higher wave conditions (Fig. 6a). Rather, the second highest rates observed during calm conditions ($0.6 \, \text{gm}^{-2} \, \text{min}^{-1}$) arose during interval P3 and P5 when water depths were between 0.6 m and high tide. This may be attributed to the fact that a larger volume of water, and hence suspended sediment was influenced by the vegetation canopy (Fig. 6a). Given that for a $36 \, \mu\text{m}$ particle of quartz, the settling velocity, based on Stokes Law and not including the effects of flocculation, would be approximately $9.19 \times 10^{-4} \, \text{m} \, \text{s}^{-1}$, it is anticipated that most of the suspended material in the upper portion of the water column would never reach the bed. The inset of water depth in Fig. 6a illustrates that the marsh surface was covered with higher depths of water during moderate wave conditions for a longer period of time than during calm conditions. In conjunction with the higher wave activity, this restricted deposition to the initial 0–0.6 m (P_1–P_2) of the flood tide and latter 0.2 m (P_7) of the ebb. Minimal amounts were deposited ($0.05 \, \text{gm}^{-2} \, \text{min}^{-1}$) between P3 and P6 (Fig. 6a).

The use of sedimentation rate, however, may not be an adequate indicator of the distribution of sediment being deposited over a tidal cycle since it does not account for differences in the initial or input suspended sediment concentration. As a result, Fig. 6b was derived to show the percent distribution of total sediment deposited over a tidal cycle. In general, in terms of the percent of total sediment deposited, there was a relatively even distribution (between 8 and 18%) over the entire tidal cycle, apart from during the P_7 period. Approximately 50% of the total amount of sediment was deposited during this period (Fig. 6b). During calm conditions a similar pattern to Fig. 6a was evident. However, the percentage of material deposited during P3 (35%) was equal to the percentage of material deposited in P_7. The contributions during P1, P2, P4 and P6 were all less than 10%. For moderate waves (between 0.1–0.15 m), Fig. 6b illustrates that a larger contribution of sediment was deposited during the last 0.2 m (P_7) of the tide rather than the initial 0.2 m (P_1). The percentage of sediment deposited appeared to decrease from 32% to 2% on the flood tide as the water depth increased (Fig. 6b). Moreover, minimal amounts of material were deposited during the ebb tide, except during the final 0.2 m.

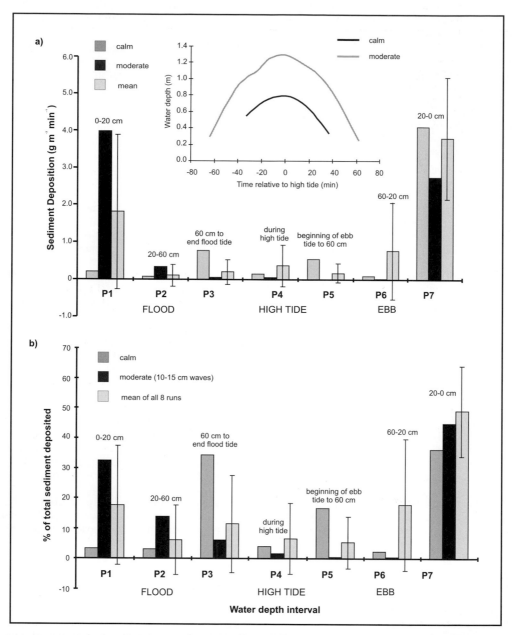

Fig. 6. Variations in the temporal distribution of sediment deposited on sequential sediment traps under conditions of increasing wave height. The amount of sediment deposited during each tide stage interval (0.2 and 0.6 m on flood and ebb, pre/post high tide) is represented as: (**a**) total sediment deposition during each stage interval; and (**b**) a percentage of the total amount of sediment recorded on the associated full cycle sediment trap. Both calm (July 23) and moderate (10–15 cm wave; July 15) conditions are illustrated along with the mean of eight sequential trap experiments.

Factors affecting sediment deposition

Sediment deposition is hypothesized to be a complex function of the availability of sediment and the opportunity for this sediment to be deposited. As a result, three main factors which influence these conditions were measured: the depth of water over the marsh surface, the length of time that the marsh surface is inundated and the amount of wave activity on a given sampling date. These are summarized in Fig. 7. The influence of topography and vegetation are examined indirectly through water depth and wave activity data.

Depth of inundation

There was no significant relationship at the 90% confidence level, between the amount of sediment deposited on the marsh surface and water depth (Fig. 7a). The mean amount of sediment trapped over a tidal cycle was $38 \pm 14\,\text{gm}^{-2}$. The highest amount recorded was $64.8 \pm 12.3\,\text{gm}^{-2}$ on June 26 when the maximum water depth was 0.94 m and the lowest was $13 \pm 8.2\,\text{gm}^{-2}$ recorded on June 24 in 1.29 m of water.

Inundation time

There was no significant relationship, at the 90% confidence level, between inundation time and the amount of sediment deposited on the marsh surface (Fig. 7b).

Wave activity

A significant negative relationship at the 95% confidence level was observed between sediment deposited and the root-mean-square of wave-induced velocity (Fig. 7c). Sediment deposition decreased from approximately $60\,\text{gm}^{-2}$ to $20\,\text{gm}^{-2}$ with increasing wave activity.

Estimated versus actual deposition

Since sediment deposition on the marsh surface requires a source of suspended sediment, one would expect that a rough prediction of the

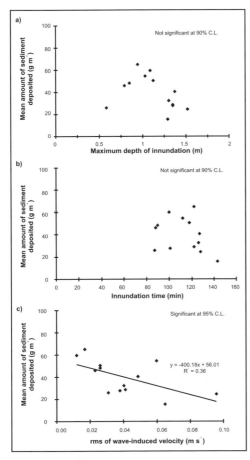

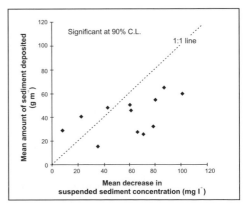

Fig. 7. The influence of the following variables on the amount of sediment deposited on the marsh surface over a tidal cycle: (**a**) water depth (not significant at 90% C.L., F = 0.18); (**b**) length of time depth of water is greater than 15 cm (not significant at 90% C.L., F = 0.32) ; and (**c**) the root-mean-square of wave-induced velocity (significant at 90% C.L., F = 0.07).

Fig. 8. Correlation between the mean amount of sediment deposited on full cycle sediment traps and the difference between initial flood and final suspended sediment concentrations from the OBS record of all instruments submerged (Prob > F = 0.07).

amount of material deposited should be able to be determined based on variations in the suspended sediment concentration. In addition, since sampling techniques of different temporal scales were being employed, it was important to decide if the amount of sediment deposited on the marsh surface on sediment traps correlated with the amount of suspended material lost from the water column. Each method can provide important information regarding controls on sediment deposition. First, data were plotted in order to determine if the decrease in the amount of suspended sediment in the water column over the period of time that the marsh surface was inundated was reflected in the amount of material collected on sediment traps on the marsh surface (Fig. 8). The decrease in the amount of suspended sediment was measured as the difference between the mean of the initial (early flood) two OBS records and the final (late ebb) two OBS records for all instruments covered during that time. The mean of all instruments covered, rather than solely the lowermost OBS probe was

employed, since it was felt to better reflect the amount of sediment in the entire water column. Particularly since the lowest instrument often displayed very high suspended sediment concentration values when water depths were less than 0.2 m. Correlation between sediment deposition and the mean decrease in suspended sediment was significant at the 95% confidence level, indicating that the trap data were representative of the amount of suspended sediment which was apparently lost from the water column as reflected in the OBS^{tm} data. Figure 8 also suggests that use of the decrease in suspended sediment concentration alone to predict sediment deposition may result in an overestimation.

Figure 9 illustrates the variation in input and output suspended sediment concentrations for all sampling dates, arranged in order of increasing wave activity. In general, input (early flood) suspended sediment concentrations exceeded $150 \, mg \, l^{-1}$ and output (late ebb) suspended sediment concentrations were less than $125 \, mg \, l^{-1}$. Both input and output concentrations increased

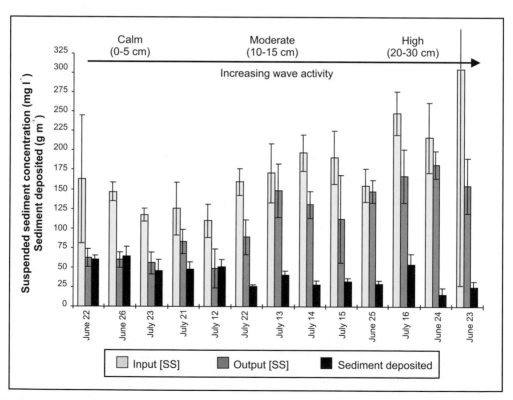

Fig. 9. Variations in mean suspended sediment concentration, and sediment deposited on the marsh surface during 13 days in order of increasing wave height. Both input (early flood) and output (late ebb) measurements of suspended sediment concentration were derived from the mean of the first two and last two records respectively for all the OBS instruments submerged.

Table 1. *Environmental conditions during the sampling periods. Spring and neap tides are identified based on two days pre and post full/new and half moons respectively. All other tides are termed 'transitional'. For locations of the vertical instrument array (A–D) refer to Fig. 2*

Sampling date	Maximum water depth at array (m)	Tide	Sea conditions	Location on marsh	Mean vegetation height (m)
June 22	1.09	spring	waves 2–5 cm	A	0.15
June 23	1.52	spring	waves 15–25 cm	A	0.15
June 24	1.29	spring	waves 20–30 cm	A	0.17
June 25	1.35	spring	waves 15–20 cm	A	0.18
June 26	0.94	transitional	calm and fog	A	0.18
July 12	1.12	transitional	waves 2–5 cm	B	0.23
July 13	1.37	transitional	waves 10–12 cm	B	0.24
July 14	1.35	neap	waves 10–15 cm	B	0.25
July 15	1.30	neap	waves 10–15 cm	B	0.26
July 16	1.03	neap	waves 20–30 cm	B	0.28
July 21	0.85	spring	calm	C	0.33
July 22	0.58	spring	waves 5–10 cm	D	0.49
July 23	0.79	spring	calm	D	0.49

with increasing wave activity and this relationship did not appear to be related to spring or neap cycles (Table 1). Figure 9 also illustrates the variation in the amount of sediment deposited on the marsh surface based on full-cycle sediment trap data, over the range of experimental conditions. In general, sediment deposition ranged between 15 to 60 gm^{-2}. The highest recorded amounts of sediment collected on the traps were found during periods of low wave activity. The least amount of sediment was deposited during periods of high wave activity (wave height >0.2 m).

To pursue this further, OBS^{tm} data were used to derive estimates of sediment deposition using two methods to be discussed in relation to Fig. 10. The first (I) estimate was derived entirely from the difference in mean input (early flood) and output (late ebb) suspended sediment concentrations along with the mean water depth of the entire tidal cycle. The second (II), incorporated the change in suspended sediment concentration with the mean depth of the water column for each sampling interval. Full-cycle sediment trap data were plotted for comparison.

In general, the highest estimates of sediment deposition occurred while using data based on the loss of suspended sediment; the lowest while employing the full-cycle sediment traps alone. Figure 10a illustrates that there was little or no difference between predictions of sediment deposition derived from method I or II. The difference in estimated deposition between methods I and II rarely exceeded 30 gm^{-2}. However, the difference between estimated and measured deposition at times exceeded 60 gm^{-2}. It appears that for waves greater than 0.15 m predictions of sediment deposition based on variations in suspended sediment concentration lead to an overestimation of sediment deposited on the marsh surface. In order to examine this more closely, correlations between predicted and actual deposition were derived for all experiments and then data for wave conditions less than 0.15 m (Fig. 10b & c). No significant correlation was found between predicted and actual values if all data were used. However, for data for periods of waves less than 0.15 m the relationship became significant at the 95% confidence level for both methods I and II.

Discussion

On the order of a tidal cycle, the rate and amount of sediment deposited on the marsh surface may be viewed as a function of both the availability of sediment in suspension and the opportunity for this material to be deposited. The availability of sediment in suspension is dictated primarily by conditions within the Cumberland Basin, external to the Allen Creek marsh system. The mean suspended sediment concentration of tidal waters entering the system during the study period was approximately 150 mg l^{-1}. However, Fig. 5 illustrates that during periods of high wave activity when the root-mean-square of wave-induced velocity is greater than 0.2 m s^{-1}, mean suspended sediment concentrations may exceed 250 mg l^{-1}. These higher waves and suspended

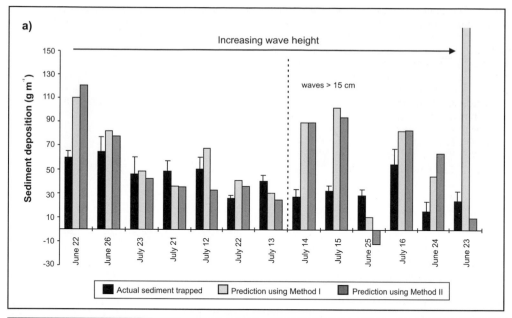

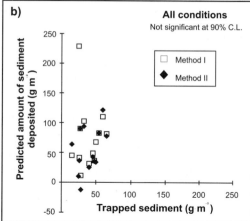

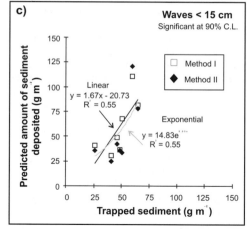

Fig. 10. (**a**) Predicted amount of sediment which would be deposited over a tidal cycle based on suspended sediment and average water depth data. Expressed either as: (method I) the difference between initial and final mean suspended sediment concentrations and mean water depth or (method II) the sum of changes in sediment volume for each tidal stage interval; (**b**) correlation between the predicted amount of sediment deposited and the actual amount of sediment deposited on full-cycle sediment traps for all records; and (**c**) same as (**b**) but for waves less than 15 cm in height (methods I and II both significant at 90% C.L., linear $r^2 = 0.55$, exponential (method I) $r^2 = 0.55$).

sediment concentrations affect sediment deposition during the tidal cycle in which they occur as well as the situation over the next few days. For example, the suspended sediment concentration on June 26 (Fig. 9) was higher than would be expected given the calm conditions. However, the period between June 23 and 25 saw considerable wave activity and subsequent high sus-

pended sediment concentrations ($>200 \, \mathrm{mg} \, l^{-1}$; Fig. 9). Figure 5 illustrates that during higher wave conditions, sediment may be re-suspended from the marsh or tidal creek system due to increased wave activity during the initial and final stages of the tide. During these portions of the tide, water depths are low and considerable wave breaking takes place, particularly at the marsh margin. The data suggest that within the Allen Creek marsh system, there is always enough sediment available in suspension for deposition on the marsh surface. However, the percentage of this available sediment that actually gets deposited is a function of the opportunity for this sediment to settle out of the water column.

The ability of the suspended sediment to settle out of the water column is a function of conditions both external and internal to the marsh system. External controls include tidal stage and wave activity while internal controls include topography and vegetation. The tidal stage of the spring/neap tidal cycle dictates the depth of the water column and hence the impacts of the incoming wave energy. The amount of wave energy that can penetrate into the marsh system is dependent on the interaction between the external tidal waters and internal controls such as marsh morphology and vegetation. Together, these conditions determine the proportion of material available in suspension that will be deposited on the marsh surface. In a macro-tidal environment such as the Allen Creek marsh system, the majority of incoming tidal waters enter the marsh across the marsh edge rather than being confined within the creek system for the duration of the tide. As a result, the surface of Allen Creek marsh is directly exposed to conditions operating within the Cumberland Basin. Therefore, flow vectors may be quite complex since these are dictated by wind direction and the tidal circulation patterns of the Basin itself during high tide, rather than local topography.

Previous studies (Fonesca & Fisher 1986; Stevenson *et al.* 1988; Pethick *et al.* 1990; French 1993; Woolnough *et al.* 1995; Shi *et al.* 1995) have suggested that important controls on sediment deposition within a saltmarsh are the inundation time and the height of the vegetation relative to the water depth. Inundation time is directly related to the tidal stage and marsh topography. During all conditions, the marsh surface is inundated for a period of time between 80 and 140 minutes (Fig. 7b). In this study, however, no significant correlation was found between the mean amount of sediment deposited on full-cycle sediment traps and inundation time (Fig. 7b) indicating that inundation time is not an important control on deposition at this study site. The data presented in Fig. 7a suggest that water depth is probably an important control only as it affects wave penetration. When waves over the marsh surface are higher, so are the shear stresses at the bed, thereby restricting deposition on the marsh surface. Figure 7c demonstrates this significant negative correlation between sediment deposition and

root-mean-square of wave-induced velocity. The opportunity for deposition is further explored by examining the temporal distribution over the tidal cycle.

Data in Fig. 5 suggest that given the high suspended sediment concentrations and flow velocities less than $0.2 \, \text{m s}^{-1}$ over the marsh surface, sediment may be deposited over the entire tidal cycle and is not restricted to the slack water period. Figure 6b supports this observation by illustrating that, on average, the percent of the total amount of sediment available for deposition was spread over the tidal cycle. However, in terms of the rate of sediment deposition (Fig. 6a), the majority of sediment deposition during these conditions occurred between the initial 0.2 m water depth on the flood and the latter 0.2 m of the ebb tide, particularly during moderate wave conditions (Fig. 6a). During these conditions, the relative roughness of the marsh vegetation was at its maximum and may potentially account for increased deposition during this time. Examination of the vertical variation in suspended sediment and flow properties in Fig. 5 reveal that within the canopy, even during periods of moderate wave heights between 0.15 to 0.2 m flow velocities and root-mean-square wave-induced velocity values were less than $0.06 \, \text{m s}^{-1}$ and $0.04 \, \text{m s}^{-1}$ respectively. These observations support previous studies which indicate that marsh vegetation can dampen flow velocity and dissipate wave energy (Shi *et al.* 1995; Nepf *et al.* 1997; Yang 1998). A relative roughness index, ratio of vegetation height to water depth, has been employed to describe the influence of vegetation as a roughness element to a flow (Fonesca & Fisher 1986; Shi *et al.* 1995). In order to illustrate this, two sampling dates were chosen: July 13 and July 22 (Table 2). Both had input suspended sediment concentration of approximately $150 \, \text{mg l}^{-1}$ and measured deposition of $40.5 \, \text{g m}^{-2}$ and $39.0 \, \text{g m}^{-2}$ respectively. On July 13, the height of the vegetation was 0.24 m relative to a maximum water depth of 1.37 m producing a relative roughness index of 0.17. By July 22, the vegetation had grown and with a lower maximum water level, the relative roughness index was 0.84, over four times greater than on July 13. Since the marsh surface had been inundated for almost twice as long on July 13 (128 min) than on July 22 (87 min) and there were similar amounts of deposition, this suggests that a high relative roughness index may increase the efficiency of sedimentation during a particular tide. This has important implications for the sediment dynamics within a macrotidal system where vegetation may only occupy a very small proportion of the water column.

Table 2. *Example of the influence of vegetation on sediment deposition using July 13 and July 22 as representative conditions*

		July 13	July 22
Maximum water depth at array (m)		1.37	0.58
Vegetation height (m)		0.24	0.49
Relative roughness		0.17	0.84
	15 cm	0.118 ± 0.024	0.042 ± 0.019
Average flow velocity (m s^{-1})	**50 cm**	0.118 ± 0.031	0.112 ± 0.025
Duration (min) marsh surface inundated		128 min	87 min

Lastly, the significant correlation between sediment trap data and the decrease in suspended sediment concentration suggests that the decrease in the amount of suspended sediment in the water column over the time that the marsh surface is inundated is reflected in the amount of material collected on sediment traps on the marsh surface. This has important implications for the use of sediment traps in the estimation of the sediment budget of marsh systems. Based on this relationship, Fig. 10 explores two preliminary methods for predicting sediment deposition using variations in the OBS^{tm} record. For wave conditions less than 0.15 m in height, the proposed predictions of deposition appear to be valid (Fig. 10c). However, there appears to be some threshold in the predictive capabilities which develops as wave height increases (Fig. 10a & b). Rough predictions of sediment deposition based solely on the loss of suspended sediment and water depth appear to overestimate the amount of deposition on the marsh surface when waves exceed 0.15 m (Fig. 10a), suggesting that other variables are important under those conditions. As a result, these data suggest that estimating the amount of sediment which will be deposited on the marsh surface over a particular time period from the suspended sediment record may only provide a measure of the relative amount of sediment deposited on the marsh surface and not an absolute value.

Conclusions

This study suggests that in order for the highest amount of sediment to be deposited on a marsh surface, both high suspended sediment concentration and low wave activity are required. A high suspended sediment concentration in itself does not guarantee high deposition rates. Low wave energy and a high relative roughness index enhance the depositional process. Both the

sequential trap data and the OBS record support this conclusion.

In this macrotidal environment, it appears that the dominant control on sediment deposition is wave activity, both in terms of increased suspended sediment concentrations within the water column and interaction with the marsh surface. Sediment deposition has been shown to be a complex interaction between marsh morphology, vegetation and tidal stage. Water depth is an important control only as it relates to wave penetration onto the marsh surface. Furthermore, since some sediment is still being deposited during periods of high wave activity and minimal vegetation cover, such as during the early spring, other factors such as flocculation need to be examined.

We thank J. Dawson, R. Rush, L. Schostak, J. Doucette and L. Borse for their help in the field. Don Forbes of the Atlantic Geoscience Centre is thanked for assistance with the field survey. B. Greenwood of the University of Toronto is thanked for the use of his re-circulating fall column for calibration of the OBS probes. Both M. Finoro of the Department of Geography, University of Guelph and W. Anderson of the Biology Department, Mount Allison University provided considerable technical support. Mount Allison University and the Sackville office of Environment Canada provided logistical support. The study was supported by research grants from the Natural Sciences and Engineering Research Council of Canada (NSERC) to RDA and JO and by post-graduate scholarships to DVP and LS.

References

ALLEN, J. R. L. 1990. Salt marsh growth and stratification: A numerical model with special reference to the Severn Estuary, southwest Britain. *Marine Geology*, **95**, 77–96.
——1997. Simulation models of salt marsh morphodynamics: Some implications for high-intertidal sediment couplets related to sea-level change. *Sedimentary Geology*, **113**, 211–223.

—— & PYE, K. 1992. *Saltmarshes: Morphodynamics, Conservation and Engineering Significance*. Cambridge University Press, Cambridge.

AMOS, C. L. 1987. Fine-grained sediment transport in Chignecto Bay, Bay of Fundy, Canada. *Continental Shelf Research*, **7**, 1295–1300.

AMOS, C. L., TEE, K. T. & ZAITLIN, B. A. 1991. The post-glacial evolution of Chignecto Bay, Bay of Fundy, and its modern environment of deposition. *In*: SMITH, D. G., REINSON, G. E., ZAITLIN, B. A. & RAHMANI, R. A. (eds) *Clastic Tidal Sedimentology*, Canadian Society of Petroleum Geologists Memoir, 16. Geological Survey of Canada Contribution number 26390, 59–90.

CALLAWAY, J. C., NYMAN, J. A. & DELAUNE, R. D. 1996. Sediment accretion in coastal wetlands: a review and simulation model of processes. *Current Topics in Wetland Bio-geochemistry*, **2**, 2–23.

CAHOON, D. R. & REED, D. J. 1995. Relationships among marsh surface topography, hydroperiod, and soil accretion in a deteriorating Louisiana salt marsh. *Journal of Coastal Research*, **11**, 357–369.

FONESCA, M. A. & FISHER, J. S. 1986. A comparison of canopy friction and sediment movement between four species of seagrass with reference to their ecology and restoration. *Marine Ecology-Progress Series*, **29**, 15–22.

FRENCH, J. R. 1993. Numerical simulation of vertical marsh growth and adjustment to accelerated sea-level rise, North Norfolk, U.K. *Earth Surface Processes and Landforms*, **18**, 63–81.

—— & SPENCER, T. 1993. Dynamics of sedimentation in a tide dominated backbarrier salt marsh, Norfolk, United Kingdom. *Marine Geology*, **110**, 315–331.

FRENCH, J. R. & STODDART, D. R. 1992. Hydrodynamics of salt marsh creek systems: implications for marsh morphodynamic development and matter exchange. *Earth Surface Processes and Landforms*, **17**, 235–252.

FRENCH, J. R., SPENCER, T., MURRAY, A. L. & ARNOLD, N. S. 1995. Geostatistical analysis of sediment deposition in two small tidal wetlands, Norfolk, U.K. *Journal of Coastal Research*, **11**, 308–321.

LEONARD, L. A. 1997. Controls on sediment transport and deposition in an incised mainland marsh basin, southeastern North Carolina. *Wetlands*, **17**, 263–274.

——, HINE, A. C. & LUTHER, M. E. 1995. Surficial sediment transport and deposition processes in a *Juncus roemerianus* marsh, west-central Florida. *Journal of Coastal Research*, **11**, 322–336.

LUTERNAUER, J. L., ATKINS, R. J., MOODY, A. I., WILLIAMS, H. F. L. & GIBSON, J. W. 1995. Salt Marshes. *In*: PERILLO, G. M. E. (ed.) *Geomorphology and Sedimentology of Estuaries*, Developments in Sedimentology, 53, Elsevier, Amsterdam, 307–332.

NEPF, H. M., MUGNIER, C. G. & ZAVISTOSKI, R. A. 1997. The effects of vegetation on longitudinal dispersion. *Estuarine, Coastal and Shelf Science*, **44**, 675–684.

PETHICK, J. S. 1981. Long term accretion rates on tidal salt marshes. *Journal of Sedimentary Petrology*, **5**, 571–577.

——, LEGGET, D. & HUSAIN, L. 1990. Boundary layers under salt marsh vegetation developed in tidal currents. *In*: THORNES, J. B. (ed.) *Vegetation and Erosion*. Wiley Publishers, 113–123.

REED, D. J. 1989. Patterns of sediment deposition in subsiding coastal salt marshes, Terreborne Bay, Louisiana: the role of winter storms. *Estuaries*, **12**, 222–227.

SHI, Z., PETHICK, J. S. & PYE, K. 1995. Flow structure in and above the various heights of a salt marsh canopy: A laboratory flume study. *Journal of Coastal Research*, **11**, 1204–1209.

STEVENSON, J. C., KEARNEY, M. S. & PENDLETON, E. C. 1985. Sedimentation and erosion in a Chesapeake Bay brackish marsh system. *Marine Geology*, **67**, 213–235.

——, WARD, L. G. & KEARNEY, M. S. 1988. Sediment transport and trapping in marsh systems: implications of tidal flux studies. *Marine Geology*, **80**, 37–59.

VAN PROOSDIJ, D., OLLERHEAD, J., DAVIDSON-ARNOTT, R. G. D. & SCHOSTAK, L. 1999. Allen Creek marsh, Bay of Fundy: a macro-tidal coastal saltmarsh. *The Canadian Geographer*, **43**, 316–322.

WOOLNOUGH, S. J., ALLEN, J. R. L. & WOOD, W. L. 1995. An exploratory numerical model of sediment deposition over tidal salt marshes. *Estuarine, Coastal and Shelf Science*, **41**, 515–543.

YANG, S. L. 1998. The role of *Scriptus* marsh in attenuation of hydrodynamics and retention of fine sediment in the Yangtze estuary. *Estuarine, Coastal and Shelf Science*, **47**, 227–233.

Patterns of flow and suspended sediment concentration in a macrotidal saltmarsh creek, Bay of Fundy, Canada.

LAURA E. SCHOSTAK[1], ROBIN G. D. DAVIDSON-ARNOTT[1],
JEFF OLLERHEAD[2] & RAY A. KOSTASCHUK[1]

[1] *Department of Geography, University of Guelph, Guelph, ON, CANADA, N1G 2W1*
(e-mail: rdarnott@.uoguelph.ca)
[2] *Department of Geography, Mount Allison University, Sackville, NB, CANADA, E4L 1A7*

Abstract: Measurements of velocity and suspended sediment concentration were carried out in a saltmarsh tidal creek network in the Cumberland Basin, Bay of Fundy, Canada. The study area was located on the NW shore of the basin in part of an undyked marsh that is about 200 m wide with a simple reticulate creek network. The area is macrotidal with spring tides greater than 12 m and suspended sediment concentrations in the basin characteristically range from 150–300 mg l^{-1}. The purpose of the study was to determine vertical and along channel variations in these two parameters over individual tidal cycles and to use these data to assess the role of the tidal creeks in the import and export of water and sediment from the marsh surface.

Measurements using a vertical array of co-located electromagnetic current meters and OBS probes for measuring suspended sediment concentration were carried out over four spring tides at a cross section in the lower part of Middle Creek. Six sets of measurments were carried out at four locations along the length of the creek, a distance of about 200 m over six tides ranging from spring to neap. Maximum mean velocities measured over sampling times of eight minutes did not exceed 0.1 m sec^{-1} in Middle Creek and 0.15 m sec^{-1} in Main Creek. Transient high velocities associated with the overbank flows were weakly developed as a result of the absence of significant levees or embankments on the marsh surface. Suspended sediment concentrations in the creek generally decreased steadily over the period of inundation. Flow across the marsh margin occurred simultaneously with the achievement of bankful conditions and the creeks themselves appear to play a relatively minor role in the movement of water and sediment onto and out of the marsh. Despite the fact that the marsh surface is still low in the tidal frame and active sedimentation is still occurring, the low flow velocities and observations in the field suggest that the tidal creek network is unable to flush itself and that it is contracting.

Tidal saltmarshes in temperate regions are characterized by the presence of a branching network of tidal creeks which are similar in form to those of terrestrial river systems (Myrick & Leopold 1963; Pestrong 1965; Shi *et al.* 1995; Steel & Pye 1997). Saltmarsh creeks are often extensions of systems that occur on the intertidal mud and sand flats that exist seaward of the marsh and, while most terminate on the marsh, some may extend beyond the landward margin. The creek networks have been characterized as providing a significant pathway for the flow of water, sediment and nutrients into and out of the saltmarsh (Boon 1974, 1975; Settlemeyr & Gardner 1977; Nixon 1980; Ward 1981; French & Stoddart 1992; Gordon & Cranford 1994;

Hemminga *et al.* 1996). The hydrodynamics of flows in tidal creeks are complex (Boon 1975; Bayliss-Smith *et al.* 1979; French & Stoddart 1992), as is the transport of sediment (Pestrong 1965; Ashley & Zeff 1988; Leonard *et al.* 1995b). Nevertheless, an understanding of the behaviour of flows and sediment transport in tidal creeks is an important component of studies of the morphodynamics and sediment budgets of saltmarshes (Reed *et al.* 1985; Stevenson *et al.* 1988; Leonard *et al.* 1995a).

Among the factors controlling marsh and tidal creek morphodynamics is tidal range. There have been a number of studies of hydrodynamics and sediment transport processes on microtidal and mesotidal marshes but relatively few

From: PYE, K. & ALLEN, J. R. L. (eds). *Coastal and Estuarine Environments: sedimentology, geomorphology and geoarchaeology*. Geological Society, London, Special Publications, **175**, 59–73. 0305-8719/00/$15.00 © The Geological Society of London 2000.

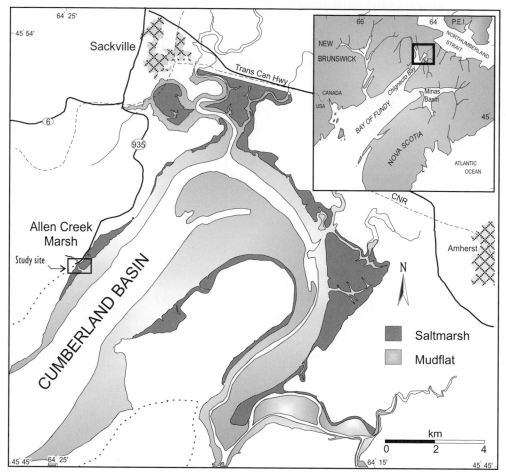

Fig. 1. (a) Bay of Fundy showing location of the Cumberland Basin; (b) location map of Cumberland Basin and Allen Creek Marsh.

have been carried out on macrotidal coasts, and most of those have been on low macrotidal saltmarshes (Bayliss-Smith *et al.* 1979; Green *et al.* 1986; Stoddart *et al.* 1989; French & Stoddart 1992). The work reported here was carried out in a tidal creek network of Allen Creek marsh, a high macrotidal (spring tidal range >12 m) saltmarsh in the Cumberland Basin, Bay of Fundy (Fig. 1). The purpose of the study was to determine vertical and along channel variations in flow and suspended sediment concentration over individual tidal cycles and to use these data to assess the role of the tidal creeks in the import and export of water and sediment from the marsh surface. The work is part of a larger study of the morphodynamics of Allen Creek marsh (Van Proosdij *et al.* 1999; van Proosdij *et al. this volume*).

Study area

The Bay of Fundy is located on the east coast of Canada between New Brunswick and Nova Scotia and forms the NE extension of the Gulf of Maine (Fig. 1a). The Cumberland Basin is the eastern extremity of Chignecto Bay, which in turn forms the northwestern extension of the upper Bay of Fundy (Fig. 1a & b). The basin is a 45 km long estuary with a maximum width at the entrance of about 3 km and a total area of 118 km^2 (Amos & Tee 1989). Amplification of the tidal oscillation of about 4 m near the entrance to the Bay of Fundy results in some of the largest tides in the world within the Cumberland Basin, with tidal range generally greater than 12 m and exceeding 16 m in places during spring high tides. The basin has a tidal prism of about 1 km³ and about two-thirds of it is exposed during spring low tide (Gordon *et al.* 1985). The tides are semi-diurnal with only relatively small differences between the two tides, though the absolute difference can be nearly 1 m at spring tide. While the lower portions of the Bay of Fundy are characterized by the presence of sandy material (Amos 1987; Amos *et al.* 1991), considerable accumulations of fine sediment occur in the Cumberland Basin and extensive marshes have formed (Fig. 1b). Sediment concentrations in the waters of the main basin are generally in the range of 0.05–0.2 g l⁻¹ (Gordon & Cranford 1994), with measurements of up to 6–7 g l⁻¹ during fall storms (Amos & Tee 1989). Saltmarshes are found in the upper part of the intertidal zone around the level of mean high water and do not extend appreciably below the high water level of neap tides (Gordon *et al.* 1985), thus occurring over a range in elevation of 4–5 m.

Saltmarshes in the basin vary considerably in their width and exposure (Gordon *et al.* 1985). They are bordered offshore by extensive mudflats, and ultimately grade into sand and gravels near the low water level. Over the past four centuries much of the marsh has been dyked and drained, leaving about 65 km² of natural,

tidally flooded marsh today (Gordon & Cranford 1994). Estuarine studies (Amos & Tee 1989) suggest that reclamation for development and cultivation has reduced the marsh area available for deposition by approximately 70%.

The NW shore of the Cumberland Basin is a fairly steeply sloping rocky shoreline with a number of relatively narrow (<300 m wide) marshes which have developed at the upper end of extensive tidal mudflats, particularly in areas which are sheltered from exposure to waves coming into the basin from the larger Chignecto Bay (Fig. 1b). Allen Creek marsh is about 3 km long stretching SW from a bedrock outcrop at Wood Point and it is undyked except for a small section at the NE end (van Proosdij *et al.* 1999, Fig. 1b). The marsh itself is about 200 m wide and is dissected by small tidal creek networks. The majority of the marsh surface consists of gently sloping low marsh with a cliffed margin 1–2 m in height at the marsh–mudflat transition in the central area. The cliff is absent at the eastern and western ends of the marsh and there is no evidence of erosion in these locations.

The study was carried out in the central portion of the Allen Creek marsh along a 200 m long stretch bounded on the west by Allen

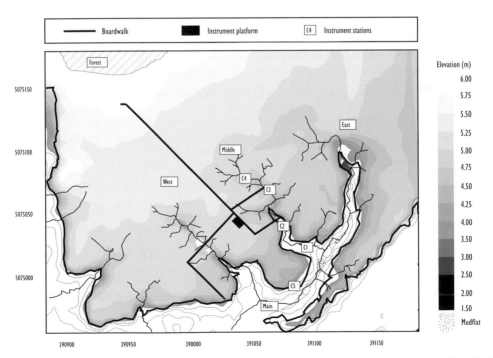

Fig. 2. Topographic map of the study area in Allen Creek Marsh showing the creek network, access boardwalks, instrumentation platform and location of instrument stations used in this study.

Creek, a small river which is tidal for about 1 km upstream (Figs 1b & 2). The river provides very little in the way of fresh water and sediment inputs. The marsh can be divided into the traditional low and high marsh zones identified in New England marshes on the basis of vegetation characteristics (Redfield 1972). The low marsh zone is flooded frequently and is composed almost entirely of *Spartina alterniflora*, with *Salicornia sp.* in the sub-canopy. The high marsh zone is only about 30 m wide and is flooded less frequently. It is dominated by *Spartina patens,* although it has a much higher species diversity than the low marsh. Landward, there is an abrupt transition from marsh to woodland along a steep slope.

Within the primary study area the tidal creek network consists of three channel systems (informally termed East, Middle and West creeks) which are oriented roughly perpendicular to the shoreline and join to form a single channel (Main Creek) which is oriented nearly parallel to the shoreline and empties into Allen Creek just at the point where it leaves the saltmarsh (Fig. 2). At their lower ends, the creek channels are entrenched 2.5–3 m below the marsh surface and have steep V-shaped banks which are muddy and bare of vegetation. In the mid-marsh areas the channels are <0.3 m deep and have gently sloping sides that are covered by vegetation. The channel network itself extends only about two-thirds of the width of the marsh (Fig. 2). The SW (offshore) side of Main Creek consists of a narrow strip of marsh surface that is lower in elevation than the main marsh surface and consequently is overtopped during the rising tide before the rest of the low marsh.

Tidal range at spring high tide is 12–13 m. There is, however, considerable variation in the depth and duration of flooding over the neap–spring cycle because of both astronomical variations over the year, and meteorological events. At neap high tides, water may flood only the tidal creek channels and the margins of the low marsh surface. At normal spring high tides, water depth over the low marsh surface may exceed 2 m. The landward edge of the high marsh zone may be inundated only once or twice a month during spring high tides and/or conditions of strong onshore winds. In the summer months the night spring tides are typically 0.4–0.5 m higher than those during the day.

Methodology

A boardwalk made of planks 0.25 m wide and raised 0.5 m above the surface of the marsh was

used to provide access to various parts of the marsh surface, tidal creek channels and the seaward edge of the marsh (Fig. 2). A 9 m bridge was used to span Middle Creek to provide a site for observations and sampling (Figs 2 & 4). A platform roughly 3.5×3.5 m and raised 3.5 m above the marsh surface was constructed between Middle and West creeks (Fig. 2). A small instrumentation hut, occupying about one half of the platform surface, was used to house the electronics.

A local triangulation network of control points was established on the marsh surface in 1996 using a theodolite and EDM (electronic distance measurement) unit, and elevation tied to a NB Department of Highways benchmark (#9648). Surveys of the marsh surface, tidal creek thalwegs and cross-profiles were made using these instruments or an automatic level. A detailed survey of the marsh surface and marsh margin was carried out at the beginning of December, 1997 using a Geotracer 2000 differential GPS system with the base station established over the benchmark. Operating in this mode the system has a positional accuracy of 0.01 m and an elevation accuracy of 0.02 m. All control points from the triangulation network were tied to the GPS survey and the combined elevation and location data were used to construct a topographic map (Fig. 2).

Flows were measured using four model 512 and one model 555 bi-directional Marsh-McBirney electromagnetic current meters. The model 512 meters were paired at the same elevation with optical backscatter (OBS) probes used for measuring suspended sediment concentration. The current meters were calibrated following the field experiment in a small towing tank at the University of Guelph, and the OBS probes were calibrated at the University of Toronto using sediment from the study site. Tidal stage was

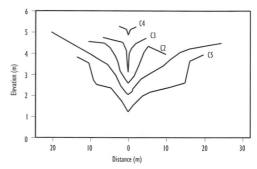

Fig. 3. Cross sections on Middle (study) Creek and Main Creek. Location of the cross sections is shown on Fig. 2.

monitored at two locations using Shaevitz pressure transducers.

One instrument array consisting of the 555 current meter, one OBS probe and one pressure transducer, mounted 0.3 m above the bed, was deployed in Main Creek at C5 (Figs 2 & 3). The array remained at this location throughout the experiment and served as a reference station. Two instrument configurations were used within Middle Creek. In one set of experiments, four 512 current meters, four OBS probes and the pressure transducer were mounted on a vertical array at C2 in the lower portion of Middle Creek (Figs 2 & 3). Current meters were paired with OBS probes at elevations of 0.15 m, 0.75 m, 1.5 m and 2.63 m above the bed and the instruments in each pair were separated horizontally by 0.4 m. The pressure transducer was mounted 0.15 m above the bed. In the second set of experiments, pairs of current meters and OBS probes were mounted 0.15 m above the bed at locations C1 through C4 along the length of Middle Creek from the upper tributaries on the marsh surface to the confluence with Main Creek (Figs 2 & 4). The pressure transducer remained at C2.

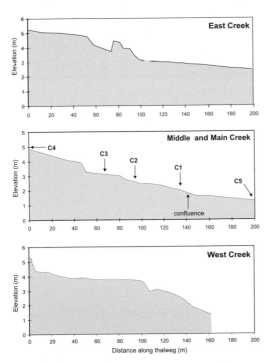

Fig. 4. Long profiles of East, West and Middle Creeks, and Main Creek below the confluence with Middle Creek.

All the instruments were hard wired to a computer data logger located in the instrumentation hut on the platform. Power for the instrumentation was supplied by a generator on the platform. Sampling runs were made over individual tidal cycles during the period when the tidal creeks and marsh surface were inundated. The instruments were sampled at 2 Hz for 8.5 minutes during each run. Sampling runs were separated by about ten minutes resulting in about 10 to 12 runs over the period during which the marsh and creeks were flooded.

Point measurements of flow speed were made in Middle and West creeks at bridge locations with a hand-held, single-axis Marsh McBirney Model 2000 electromagnetic current meter mounted on a 4 m wading rod. Data were recorded as 30 second averages of 0.2 Hz readings. Water samples were obtained at point locations during most runs using 0.5 l plastic bottles fixed to the end of a 3 m pole. Suspended sediment concentrations were determined by filtration using a 8 μm Magna nylon 47 mm filter. These samples served as indicators of average suspended sediment concentration in the water column and were also used as a check of the calibration of the OBS probes. An anemometer and wind vane were mounted on the platform approximately 5 m above the marsh surface with data recorded once a minute on separate StowAway™ data loggers. These instruments operated continuously over the whole field season.

A variety of small problems resulted in malfunctioning of some instruments for individual runs and the OBS probe at the reference station (C5) could not be properly calibrated at the end of the season. One axis on a 512 probe did not function and data for this instrument are reported for the X axis only.

Results

Tidal creek geometry and morphology

The cross-sections where instrumentation arrays were located and creek long profiles are shown in Figs 3 & 4 and morphological data for the creek network are summarized in Table 1. Creek channel patterns on the marsh generally are reticulate in the lower portions and dendritic on the upper marsh (Fig. 2). Three basic channel cross-sectional forms can be recognized corresponding roughly to the lower, middle and upper sections of the creeks (Figs 3, 5a & b). In the lower sections of the three tributary creeks and all of Main Creek, the channel bottom is incised more than 2 m below the marsh surface and the

Table 1. *Morphometric properties of the tidal creek system*

Creek	Length (m)	Confluence Width	Upper Slope	Lower Slope
West	160	36	0.008	0.047
Middle (Study)	225	15	0.021	0.016
East	125	13	0.008	0.007
Main	140	30		0.024

Fig. 5. Photographs of the tidal creek system and marsh: (**a**) view of the lower section of Middle Creek looking up-channel from the confluence with Main Creek. Note mud covered banks and bottom of channel. Cross section 1 is located in the mid foreground. The platform and instrumentation hut, part of the boardwalk network and the bridge over the creek at cross section 2 are visible in the background; (**b**) View looking landward of the middle and upper sections of Middle Creek taken in early spring. Note deposition of mud on banks and leaves of vegetation and the blocking of the channel evident in the lower left and middle right of the photograph. (**c**) View of the bridge at C2 from the platform during a spring tide showing measurements with hand-held current meter and collection of suspended sediment samples. The arrow points to the H frame used for the vertical array at C2. The tidal stage is about 1 m below high tide; (**d**) View offshore during rising spring tide showing complete inundation of the tidal creek network. At this stage water floods the marsh surface across the entire length of the marsh front and advances across the marsh as a sheet.

channel is greater than 10 m wide at the level of the marsh surface (Fig. 5a). The banks are steep and linear with slopes of 10–20° and are bare of vegetation. There is often a small cliffed section near the top that appears to coincide with the root base of the *Spartina alterniflora*. Soft mud overlies the substrate of consolidated marsh sediments or sandstone bedrock and covers the bottom and lower portions of the slopes to a depth of 0.5 m or more. A small notch at the bottom of the channel serves to carry a very small amount of

drainage from the marsh surface and groundwater table during low tide (Fig. 5a).

The middle section of the channel is transitional from lower to upper sections (Fig. 5b). The channel is <1 m wide, and may be as much as 1 m deep. The bottom of the channel is flat and cut in marsh sediments, and the sides are nearly vertical and grass covered. Portions of the channel are often blocked by mud which slumped into the channel (Fig. 4 East Creek & Fig. 5b). Water may flow beneath the slumped material for sometime but over a few months it becomes consolidated, thus raising the channel elevation at this point.

The upper section of the channels are shallow, vegetated indentations on the upper marsh surface with gently sloping sides (Fig. 5b). The channel slope here is not much greater than that of the marsh surface itself.

Both the middle and upper sections of the channels appear to be aggrading as a result of deposition of mud on the vegetation on the sides and bottom of the channels. In the case of the middle section, aggradation takes place mainly through deposition on the grass along the channel edge and sides which is then bent over to obstruct the channel. On the upper section where the bottom of the channels are grassed, sediment is deposited directly on the surface around the stems of the grass.

Vertical variations in flow and suspended sediment concentration

Measurements of flow and suspended sediment concentration were carried out over four spring tides on June 5 and 6 1997 using a vertical array located at C2 in Middle Creek. The objectives of this set of experiments were to:

- determine the nature of the vertical velocity profile;
- to estimate variations in bed shear stress over the tidal cycle;
- to estimates net sediment flux through the cross section over the tidal cycle from simultaneous measurements of velocity and suspended sediment concentration.

Problems were experienced with the lowermost current meter at V1 and the instruments at the top of the array were only submerged briefly during the higher night tides so that data are not reported for them.

Variations in tidal stage, mean suspended sediment concentration and mean flow velocity recorded over one tidal cycle on June 6 night are shown in Fig. 6. Data for mean flow and suspended sediment concentration for all four experiments are summarized in Fig. 7. The data in both figures have been plotted relative to high tide as determined from pressure transducer records. Velocities are for the resolved vector magnitude, with positive flows being onshore. The data show that flows generally coincide closely with the channel axis when water elevations are below bankfull. Once the whole marsh surface is inundated the flow is usually eastward (i.e. at right angles to the channel axis at this

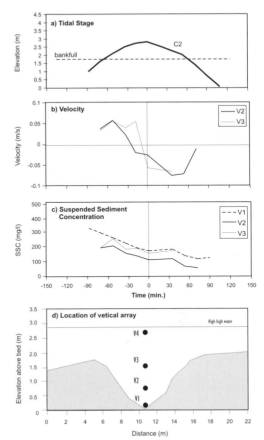

Fig. 6. Measurements of flow magnitude and suspended sediment concentration on the night of June 6 1997 at cross section C2 using a vertical array: (**a**) tidal stage; (**b**) mean velocity magnitude; (**c**) mean suspended sediment concentration; and (**d**) location of the instruments in the vertical array.

location) towards the entrance of the Cumberland basin, reflecting the general pattern of circulation within the basin. However, this pattern can be altered by the effects of strong winds.

Flow magnitude and variation over the tidal cycle on the night of June 6th at V2 and V3 are similar (Fig. 6). Flow velocities are low, reaching a maximum on the flood of about $0.05 \, \text{m sec}^{-1}$ about half an hour before high tide, and a maximum of about $0.08 \, \text{m s}^{-1}$ on the ebb about 45 minutes after high tide. Current velocities during the rising tide were generally higher closer to the bed at V2 than at V3, while the flow was confined to the channel. However, around high tide higher velocities were recorded at V3, probably because water near the bottom of the tidal creek channel becomes sheltered from the general flow over the whole marsh.

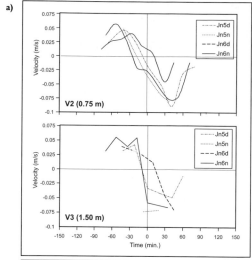

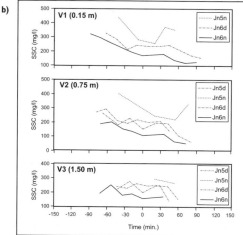

Fig. 7. Mean velocity (**a**) and mean suspended sediment concentration (**b**) recorded over four experiments carried out on June 5 and 6 1997 at the vertical array at C2.

three experiments generally show the same patterns as those for the night of June 6 (Fig. 7a). Mean flows are low and do not exceed $0.1 \, \mathrm{m \, s^{-1}}$. Maximum velocities usually occur within 30 minutes of high tide and there is often a marked asymmetry, with maximum ebb velocity being higher than the maximum flood velocity. However, flows at V3 are nearly as high at high tide as they are later, reflecting the general easterly flow over the marsh at this stage that was noted above.

Suspended sediment concentrations over all four experiments are highest at the start of the flood and concentrations decrease to a minimum near the end of the ebb (Fig. 7b). The rate of decrease in suspended sediment concentration slows somewhat around high tide and this is evident in the difference in the pattern between the sensor at V3 (1.5 m above the bed) compared to the two lower locations. At V3 the period during which the sensor is covered is shorter and the decreasing trend is not as apparent. Suspended sediment concentration measured at V1 range from a maximum of about $450 \, \mathrm{mg \, l^{-1}}$ to a minimum of about $100 \, \mathrm{mg \, l^{-1}}$. The highest suspended sediment concentrations were recorded on the night of June 5th after a day with moderate winds and considerable wave action in the basin, while the lowest concentrations occurred on the night of June 6th under relatively calm conditions. The pattern of variations in suspended sediment concentration recorded at all three elevations was similar over the four experiments and the absolute magnitudes were similar at V1 and V3. As noted earlier, the magnitudes recorded at V2 were about $50 \, \mathrm{mg \, l^{-1}}$ lower than those recorded at the other two probes because of a calibration problem. However, this difference was essentially constant during all four experiments, thus supporting the proposition that there is little vertical variation in suspended sediment concentration within the tidal creek.

Spatial variations in flow and suspended sediment concentration

Variation in flow and suspended sediment concentration along the length of Middle Creek were measured over six tidal cycles covering the full neap to spring range. At spring tides the water depth over the low marsh was about 1 m while at neap tide the water level did not exceed bankfull in the channel and the upper marsh was not inundated. Attention is focused on the four stations located on Middle Creek because no suspended sediment data are available for the

The pattern of suspended sediment concentration is also similar at all three locations above the bed, with highest concentrations at the beginning of the flood as water enters the channel, and then decreasing throughout the tidal cycle. The magnitude of suspended sediment concentration at V1 and V3 is similar, but is lower at V2. This pattern held during all four runs and probably reflects a problem with calibration of this instrument rather than a real difference in vertical concentration.

Data for mean flow and suspended sediment concentration for all four experiments are summarized in Fig. 7. Flow velocities for the other reference station at C5 and because the current meter at this location is fixed at 0.3 m above the bed compared to 0.15 m for the other stations. However, flow dynamics at C5 are described at the end of the section.

Tidal stage, velocity magnitude and suspended sediment concentration recorded for a spring tide and a neap tide are shown in Fig. 8. On the spring tide (Fig. 8a) the whole marsh surface is covered for a period of about 0.5 hours either side of high water. The highest velocities occurred at C4 on the mid-marsh surface and at C1 near the confluence with Main Creek. Flow velocity at the mouth of the creek is highest at the beginning of the flood when the water advances up the lower portion of the channel which has a relatively gentle gradient and large channel width. Velocities are lower over the middle part of the flood, when the tide is still confined to the channel, and the decreasing channel width and increased slope in the middle portion of the channel of the channel mean that the area flooded by the rising tide decreases in each time increment. There is a small velocity pulse evident near the end of the rise when flow expands rapidly over the mid and high marsh and a similar pulse on the ebb as water drains from the upper marsh. Flow speeds measured parallel to the channel at C3 remain very low throughout the inundation period. This reflects in part the effect of the very narrow channel and small area flooded during the first part of the flood. When flow expands rapidly across the upper marsh observations and measurements with the hand held current meter show flow velocities in the surface flow at C3 to be similar to those recorded at other stations, but within the channel itself flow is obviously greatly retarded by the small channel width and the roughness effect of dense vegetation. Measured velocities on the neap tide (Fig. 8b) are considerably lower than for the spring tide. Velocity at C1 is again highest during the initial period of flooding but there is little evidence of a velocity pulse around high tide because overbank flooding is confined to a small area near the marsh margin.

Mean suspended sediment concentrations measured at C1, C2 and C4 have similar patterns and magnitudes on both days (Fig. 8a, b). As was the case for the vertical array, concentrations tend to decrease over the tidal cycle but the decrease is more pronounced on June 13th than on June 8th.

Variations in velocity magnitude and suspended sediment concentration at each station are summarized for all six experiments in Fig. 9. Flow magnitude (Fig. 9a) tends to increase from neap to spring tides associated with the increase in area of marsh flooded, though the velocities are still generally $<0.1\,\mathrm{m\,s}^{-1}$, the highest velocities are recorded at C1 near the mouth of the creek and at station C4 on the marsh surface. Flows at C4 on the marsh surface are lowest around high tide, but at C1 and C2 flows show a pulse around the time that overbank flow occurs over much of the low marsh and relatively high velocities are experienced over high tide reflecting general circulation in the bay over the flooded marsh. The significance of control by flow over the marsh surface is brought out by the early flow reversal and high speed recorded at C2 on June 9 (Fig. 9a). The actual velocity vector at this time is directed primarily alongshore and slightly offshore under the influence of the general tidal circulation in the basin and strong northerly winds blowing over the marsh.

The pattern for suspended sediment concentration is similar to that noted earlier for the vertical array. Concentrations tend to decrease over the tidal cycle as sediment is deposited on the marsh surface, but the extent of this depends on wind and wave conditions (van Proosdij *et al.* *this volume*). At station C1 several runs show an increase at the end of the ebb and observations show that this results from re-suspension of sediment by small amounts of water draining down the sides of the channel in the lower portion of the creek.

The flow pattern at station C5 in Main Creek is more complex than those recorded at the stations in Middle Creek and the velocity magnitude is higher (Fig. 9a). Observations and an analysis of the vector directions showed that water on the flood tide enters the channel from Allen Creek and flows into the lower channels of the three tributary creeks so that the flow is parallel to the thalweg. As the tide rises, the arm which forms the seaward bank of the channel (Fig. 2) is overtopped and this is followed shortly by overtopping of the landward bank onto the main marsh about 60–80 minutes before high tide. At this point, water reaching the tributary creeks and the marsh surface switches direction from the thalwegs of the creek channels to directly onshore across the marsh margin. At station C5 the shift in direction of flow was recorded as offshore flows because of the orientation of the channel at C5 relative to the marsh surface (Fig. 9a). Maximum velocities were recorded around the time of high tide as the flow here reflects the onset of strong flows out of the Cumberland Basin along the NW shore. As water depth over the marsh decreases the flow magnitudes also decrease and there is a period of low velocities as the water level drops below bankfull. Finally, flow velocities increase

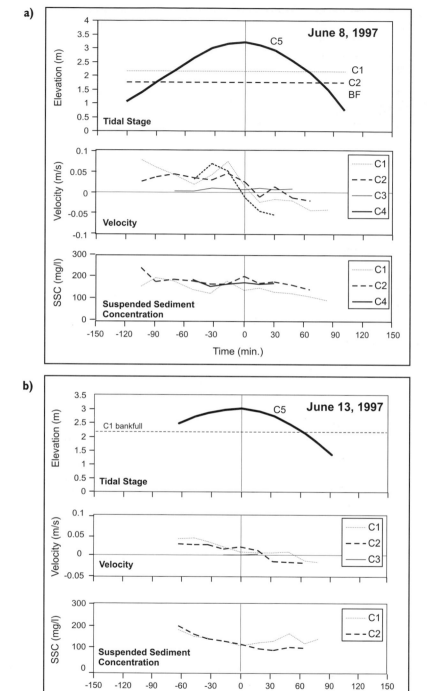

Fig. 8. Tidal stage, mean velocity magnitude and mean suspended sediment concentration recorded at stations C1-C4 along the tidal creek for (**a**) spring tide on June 8 1997; and (**b**) neap tide on June 13. The OBS probe at C3 was not functioning during these experiments and the tide did not reach as far as C4 during the neap tide run on June 13.

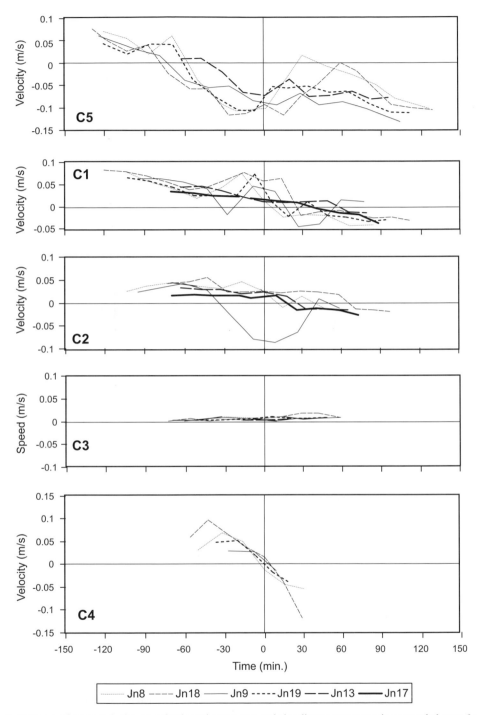

Fig. 9. Patterns of mean velocity magnitude and mean suspended sediment concentration recorded over 6 tidal cycles at C5 on Main Creek and at the four stations along Middle Creek. Tidal range increases from the lowest neap tide on 17/06, through 13/06, 9/06/, 19/06, 08/06 and the highest spring tide on 18/06. Note that no measurements of suspended sediment concentration were obtained at C3 and only the × axis, aligned parallel to the channel was functioning at this station. There are no suspended sediment concentration measurements for 19/06 and on 17/06 the tide only reached as far as stations C1 and C2.

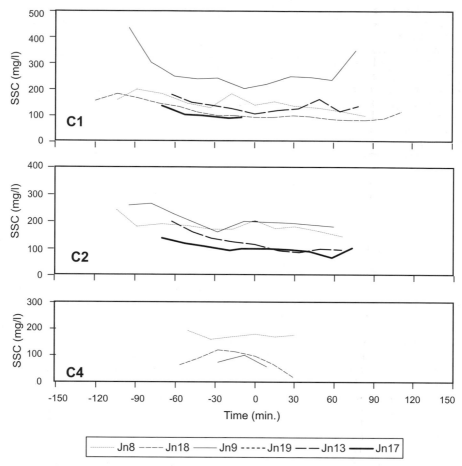

Fig. 9. (*continued*)

again as drainage is re-established down the creek system.

Discussion

Given the very high tidal range in the study area and the cross sectional dimensions of the tidal creeks (Figs 3 & 5a), an interesting feature of this study was the very low mean flow velocities measured in the tidal creeks. Maximum velocities recorded in Middle Creek never exceeded $0.1 \, \mathrm{m\,s^{-1}}$ and were $<0.2 \, \mathrm{m\,s^{-1}}$ in Main Creek. These values are thus below the threshold for transport of sand and for erosion of mud, except immediately after deposition. They are also much lower than those recorded in a number of other field studies of micro-tidal, meso-tidal and macro-tidal marshes (e.g. Green *et al.* 1986; Reed 1988; French & Stoddart 1992; Wang *et al.* 1993; Leonard *et al.* 1995*a, b*). These low

velocities occur because, despite the large tidal range, the tidal prism of the creek is small. This is a reflection of the short total channel length, steep gradient and simple pattern of the creek network. The low velocities also reflect the lack of levee development along the creek channels and of an embankment or elevated ridge separating the low and high marsh areas. There are few areas on the marsh surface with elevations below that of the creek banks which could increase the area flooded by waters originating directly from the creek, and much of the gently sloping mid- and upper marsh surface lies beyond the limits of the creek network (Fig. 5d) so that it is flooded by water coming directly over the marsh margin. These characteristics also explain the lack of well-defined transient high velocities associated with overtopping of the channel banks which have been described in a number of other marshes (e.g. Pestrong 1965; Bayliss-Smith *et al.* 1979; French & Stoddart

1992). Slightly higher velocities do occur within the Main Creek channel and can be expected near the mouths of the larger creek systems on the marsh, but in general tidal flows sufficiently strong to entrain sand and erode muds are confined to channels such as Allen Creek which extend well beyond the marsh, and which have gentler gradients and more extensive flats. However, it should be noted that residual drainage from the marsh surface after the tide has fallen does produce flows in the bottom of the channel which are sufficiently strong to erode a small notch (Fig. 5a).

During transitional and spring tides, when the marsh surface is inundated, flow over the marsh margin occurs essentially simultaneously with bankfull in the creeks. From this point in the tidal cycle, inundation of the marsh surface occurs more or less uniformly along the margin and the tidal creeks cease to play a distinct role in water and sediment transport to the marsh surface. Subsequent flow over the marsh is controlled by tidal stage and the tidal circulation within the Cumberland Basin as a whole, as well as by wind and wave action. A number of studies have shown that wind and wave action are important controls on the amount of suspended sediment in water reaching the marsh and on flow speeds and shear stresses exerted on the marsh surface (Ward 1979; Wang et al. 1993; Leonard et al. 1995a), and this has been demonstrated for flows on the marsh surface at Allen Creek (van Proosdij et al. 2000). At tidal stages above bankfull when the whole marsh surface becomes inundated waves generated within Chignecto Bay and the Cumberland Basin can reach the marsh surface directly and have an effect on the bed of the channels on the upper marsh and the upper sides of the lower channels which are unvegetated. However, because of the short period and relatively low wave heights, their effect on the bed of the lower reaches of the channel is small because water depth at this time exceeds 2.5 m.

Processes within the tidal creek channels themselves do not appear to have much influence on suspended sediment concentrations. As would be expected in a system which is dominated by such a large background suspended sediment load, there is little correlation between flow velocity at station cross sections and total suspended sediment concentrations (e.g. French & Stoddart 1992; French et al. 1993). Variations in the input concentrations appear to be controlled primarily by wind and wave action in the Cumberland Basin and upper Bay of Fundy, and there is little contribution from erosion or re-suspension within the creeks in contrast to

some other studies where much of the sediment in suspension is derived from the tidal creek channels themselves (Wang et al. 1993; Leonard et al. 1995b).

There is a tendency for measured suspended sediment concentrations to decrease through the tidal cycle. However, unlike the marsh surface where highest values are found during the initial flooding of the surface (van Proosdij et al. 2000), most stations in the creek show higher readings occurring a bit later in the flood. This may reflect the deposition of some sediment as the flood initially advances up the channel and subsequent influx of suspended sediment from the basin waters. The high initial values on the marsh can be attributed to re-suspension of sediment from the surface and from vegetation resulting from wind and wave action in shallow flows over the surface of the marsh while shallow flows in the channel tend to be protected from wind and wave action. Much of the later decrease through time probably results from deposition on the marsh surface (van Proosdij et al. 2000) and, to a lesser extent, in the creeks.

No attempt has been made here to compute discharges of flow and sediment through the tidal channel cross sections or to calculate a sediment budget based on these. During neap tide conditions, where flow is confined to the channel system, flows are so low that velocity variations are small compared to the precision of the current meter and particularly to current meter calibration. During tides where the marsh surface is flooded, it is evident that the dominant transfer of water and sediment occurs across the marsh margin rather than through the creek network (e.g. French & Stoddart 1992). In addition, the presence of a strong alongshore movement of water across the marsh surface on many days means that there is considerable movement of water and sediment across the tidal creek topographic watersheds, so that water leaving the tidal creek may have entered the marsh system hundreds of metres away.

The low measured velocities in the tidal creeks suggest that shear stresses are generally too low to result in vertical incision or headward extension of the creek network as is often the case during the early stages of marsh development (Pestrong 1965; Collins et al. 1987; Steel & Pye 1997). Indeed, the velocities are generally so low that net deposition should occur in the channels under most conditions and the network should be contracting. There is evidence of this from clogging of the upper channels by vegetation and by slumping of silt deposited along the banks (Fig. 5b), and the lower portions of the channels are characterized by mud deposits

0.5 m or more in thickness. Steel & Pye (1997) found that contraction of the drainage network occurred once the marsh surface had grown to the point where the annual frequency of flooding, which produces strong flows in the creeks, fell below 280. At Allen Creek annual frequency of flooding of the marsh surface is >400, but the key determinant of the ability to generate flows strong enough to erode the channels here may be the narrow marsh width, rather than the effect of increasing elevation of the surface on flooding frequency. The tendency towards siltation of the creek channels may also be increased by the ongoing reduction in drainage area due to recession of the marsh margin which is occurring at >1 m yr^{-1}.

In the middle and upper portions of the creek network it may continue to function because, as a result of the high frequency of inundation, accretion of the marsh surface is nearly as great as in the creek channels. In the lower reaches, where the channel sides are unvegetated, deposition may be inhibited by wave action during storms. In addition, Schostak (1998) found that all episodes of erosion of the banks of the lower channel sections were associated with rainfall. It is also possible that processes associated with ice movement during winter months, coupled with reduced vegetation cover can lead to some flushing of sediment from the channels.

Finally, the apparent inactivity of the tidal creek network suggests that it may be inherited from the system developed initially on the mudflats. On other marshes along the coast which are in an earlier stage of development, the creek network extends to the spring high tide limit (Dawson *et al.* 1999). The drainage density is greater and the creek networks are more complex than those on the Allen Creek marsh, suggesting that contraction of the network may begin very early in marsh growth. The system may be maintained for some time because deposition rates in the channels are only a bit higher than those on the developing marsh surface.

Conclusions

Velocities measured in the tidal creek network on Allen Creek marsh are much lower than those reported in many other marsh systems, despite the extremely high tidal range. The small marsh width, limited network development and the steep channel gradients all act to limit the tidal prism and produce low flow velocities. The absence of significant levee development along the creek channels and the relatively simple topography of the marsh surface also inhibit high

transient currents associated with overbank flows. Instead, flooding of the marsh surface across the marsh margin occurs simultaneously with the achievement of bankfull conditions in the creeks. As a result, the tidal creek network plays a limited role in the transfer of water and sediment into and out of the marsh, and the bulk of these transfers take place across the marsh margin. Flows in the creeks appear to be too low to flush the system, leading to contraction of the drainage network while the marsh surface is still relatively low in the tidal frame.

We thank D. van Proosdij, J. Dawson and B. Rush for assistance with the fieldwork for this study and D. Forbes of the Canadian Geological Survey for assistance with mapping of the site. B. Greenwood of the University of Toronto kindly made available his facilities for calibration of the OBS probes. We thank M. Finoro and M. Puddister of the Department of Geography, University of Guelph for their respective technical and cartographic assistance. D. van Proosdij commented on a draft of the paper. The study was supported by research grants from the Natural Sciences and Engineering Research Council of Canada to RD-A, JO and RK, and by a Postgraduate Scholarship to LS.

References

Amos, C. L. 1987. Fine-grained sediment transport in Chignecto Bay, Bay of Fundy, Canada. *Continental Shelf Research*, **7**, 1295–1300.

—— & Tee, K. T. 1989. Suspended sediment transport processes in Cumberland Basin, Bay of Fundy. *Journal of Geophysical Research*, 94(C10), 14407–14417.

——, —— & Zaitlin, B. A. 1991. The post-glacial evolution of Chignecto Bay, Bay of Fundy, and its modern environment of deposition. *In*: Smith, D. G., Reinson, G. E., Zaitlin, B. A. & Rahmani, R. A. (eds) *Clastic Tidal Sedimentology*. Canadian Society of Petroleum Geologists Memoir 16, 59–90.

Ashley, G. M. & Zeff, M. L. 1988. Tidal channel classification of a low-mesotidal salt marsh. *Marine Geology*, **82**, 17–32.

Bayliss-Smith, T. P., Healey, R., Lailley, R., Spenser, T. & Stoddart, D. R. 1979. Tidal flows in salt marsh creeks. *Estuarine Coastal and Shelf Science*, **9**, 235–255.

Boon, J. D. 1974. Suspended sediment transporting a salt marsh creek – an analysis of errors. *In*: Kjerfve, B. (ed.) *Estuarine Transport Processes*, Columbia, University of South Carolina Press, 147–159.

——1975. Tidal discharge asymmetry in a salt marsh drainage system. *Limnology and Oceanography*, **20**, 71–80.

Collins, L. M., Collins, J. L. & Leopold, L. B. 1987. Geomorphic processes of an estuarine marsh: preliminary results and hypotheses. *International*

Geomorphology (Proceedings International Geographical Union Meeting) **1**, 1049–1072.

DAWSON, J., VAN PROOSDIJ, D., DAVIDSON-ARNOTT, R. & OLLERHEAD, J. 1999. *Characteristics of saltmarshes in the Cumberland Basin, Bay of Fundy.* Proc. Canadian Coastal Conference, Canadian Coastal Science and Engineering Association, Ottawa, Canada, 267–280.

FRENCH, J. R. & STODDART, D. R. 1992. Hydrodynamics of salt marsh creek systems: implications for marsh morphodynamic development and matter exchange. *Earth Surface Processes and Landforms*, **17**, 235–252.

——, CLIFFORD, N. J. & SPENSER, T. 1993. High frequency flow and suspended sediment measurements in a tidal wetland channel. *In*: CLIFFORD, N. J, FRENCH, J. R. & HARDISTY, J. (eds) *Turbulence: Perspectives on flow and sediment transport.* Wiley, Chichester, 249–277.

GORDON, D. C. & CRANFORD, P. J. 1994. Export of organic matter from macrotidal saltmarshes in the upper Bay of Fundy, Canada. *In*: MITSCH, W. J. (ed.) *Global Wetlands: Old World and New.* Van Nostrand Reinhold Company, New York, 257–264.

——, CRANFORD, P. J. &. DESPLANQUE, C. 1985. Observations on the ecological importance of salt marshes in the Cumberland Basin, a macrotidal estuary in the Bay of Fundy. *Estuarine, Coastal and Shelf Science*, **20**, 205–227.

GREEN, H. M., STODDART, D. R., REED, D. J. & BAYLISS-SMITH, T. P. 1986. Saltmarsh tidal creek dynamics, Scolt Head Island, Norfolk, England. *In*: SIGBJARNARSON, G. (ed.) *Iceland Coastal and River Symposium Proceedings*, 93–103.

HEMMINGA, M. A., CATTRIJSSE, A. & WIELMAKER, W. 1996. Bedload and nearbed detritus transport in a tidal saltmarsh creek. *Estuarine, Coastal and Shelf Science*, **42**, 55–62.

LEONARD, L. A., HINE, A. C., LUTHER, M. E., STUMPF, R. P. & WRIGHT, E. E. 1995a. Sediment transport processes in a west-central Florida open marine marsh tidal creek; the role of tides and extra-tropical storms. *Estuarine, Coastal and Shelf Science*, **41**, 225–248.

——, —— & ——1995b. Surficial sediment transport and deposition processes in a Juncus roemerianus marsh, West-central Florida. *Journal of Coastal Research*, **11**, 322–336.

MYRICK, R. M. & LEOPOLD, L. B. 1963. *Hydraulic Geometry of a small tidal estuary.* US Geological Survey. Professional Paper 422B, 1–18.

NIXON, S. W. 1980. Between coastal marshes and coastal waters – a review of twenty years of speculation and research in the role of salt marshes in estuarine productivity and water chemistry. *In*: HAMILTON, R. & MCDONALD, K. B. (eds) *Estuarine and Wetland Processes.* Plenum, New York, 437–525.

PESTRONG, R. 1965. *The development of drainage patterns on tidal marshes.* Stanford University Publications in Geological Sciences, **10**.

PETHICK, J. S. 1980. Velocity surges and asymmetry in tidal channels. *Estuarine, Coastal and Marine Sciences*, **11**, 331–345.

REDFIELD, A. C. 1972. Development of a New England salt marsh. *Ecological Monographes*, **42**, 201–237.

REED, D. J. 1988. Sediment dynamics and deposition in retreating coastal salt marsh. *Estuarine, Coastal and Shelf Science*, **26**, 67–79.

——, STODDART, D. R. & BAYLISS-SMITH, T. P. 1985. Tidal flows and sediment budgets for a salt-marsh system, Essex, England. *Vegetatio*, **62**, 375–380

SCHOSTAK, L. E. 1998. *Dynamics of a High-macrotidal Saltmarsh Tidal Creek.* MSc Thesis, University of Guelph.

SETTLEMYRE, J. L. & GARDNER, L. R. 1977. Suspended sediment flux through a salt marsh drainage basin. *Estuarine, Coastal and Shelf Science*, **5**, 653–663.

SHI, Z., LAMB, H. F. & COLLIN, R. L. 1995. Geomorphic changes of saltmarsh tidal creek networks in the Dyfi Estuary, Wales. *Marine Geology*, **128**, 73–83.

STEEL, T. J. & PYE, K. 1997. *The development of saltmarsh tidal creek networks:evidence from the UK.* Proc. 1997 Canadian Coastal Conference. Canadian Coastal Science and Engineering Association, Ottawa, Canada, 267–280

STEVENSON, J. C., WARD, L. G. & KEARNEY, M. S. 1988. Sediment transport and trapping in marsh systems: implications of tidal flux studies. *Marine Geology*, **80**, 37–59.

STODDART, D. R., REED, D. J. & FRENCH, J. R. 1989. Understanding salt-marsh accretion, Scolt Head Island, Norfolk, England. *Estuaries*, **12**, 228–236.

VAN PROOSDIJ, D., OLLERHEAD, J. & DAVIDSON-ARNOTT, R. G. D. 2000. Controls on suspended sediment deposition over single tidal cycles in a macrotidal saltmarsh, Bay of Fundy, Canada. *This volume.*

——, ——, —— & SCHOSTAK, L. E. 1999. Allen Creek marsh, Bay of Fundy: a macro-tidal coastal saltmarsh. *Canadian Geographer*, **43**, 316–322.

WANG, F. C., LU, T. & SIKORA, W. B. 1993. Intertidal marsh suspended sediment transport processes, Terrebone Bay, LA, USA *Journal of Coastal Research*, **9**, 209–220.

WARD, L. G. 1979. *Hydrodynamics and sediment transport in a saltmarsh tidal channel.* Proc. 16th Confernece on Coastal Engineering. American Society of Civil Engineers, New York 1953–1970.

——1981. Suspended-material transport in marsh tidal channels, Kiwah Island, South Carolina. *Marine Geology*, **40**, 139–154.

A diagnostic tool to study long-term changes in estuary morphology

IAN TOWNEND[1] & RICHARD DUN[2]

[1] *ABP Research & Consultancy, Pathfinder House, Maritime Way, Southampton,*
SO14 3AE, UK (e-mail: iht@research.abports.co.uk)
[2] *W S Atkins, West Glamorgan House, 12 Orchard Street, Swansea, SA1 5AD, UK*
(e-mail: Rwdun@WSAtkins.co.uk)

Abstract: One method of studying the functional morphology of estuaries and the potential implications of developments is presented. The approach makes use of a hybrid modelling approach to predict the state of the estuary relative to its present day target steady state. The technique has now been applied to a number of UK estuaries, which allows the variability between systems to be illustrated. For one of the estuaries a range of modifications has been examined to try and identify how the functional behaviour of the system might be affected (e.g. remove flood banks) and these are discussed. Experience to-date has shown that this approach helps to develop an understanding of gross system behaviour and how this might change in the future. It does not provide detailed predictions for specific locations within the estuary, although the role of particular components in the system is highlighted.

Estuaries are important economically and socially as prominent locations for ports, industry, agriculture, recreation and urban development. Their natural resources also make them important ecologically and hence they tend to have a high nature conservation value. The many and varied activities that take place within an estuary can often give rise to conflicting interests, which in some cases may constrain the dynamic response of the estuary system (HR Wallingford *et al.* 1996).

Estuaries are complex interfaces between the fluvial upland systems and the wave and tidally dominated regimes of the open coast. This gives rise to energy and sediment inputs, predominantly, at landward and seaward ends of the system. An estuary is subject to a wide range of natural variability, including changing climate (storminess, rainfall, waves, surges, etc), fluctuations in relative sea level and variations in sediment supply and demand. In addition, an estuary may be subject to a variety of constraints that limit the way in which the form can adjust to change. Typically these include the catchment characteristics, the underlying geology, the surficial sediments, the historical response time of the estuary (notably over the Holocene) and human developments (such as sea walls, urban and industrial conurbations, navigation channels and aggregate extraction).

Previous approaches to the study of long-term morphological change in estuaries have been categorized into two groups; top-down and bottom-up models (HR Wallingford *et al.* 1996). The former seeks to characterize the system as a whole in some way. Typically such models assume a steady state and parameterize the discharge-form relationships, referred to as regime models, or seek to determine a steady state, based on assumptions about the relationship between inputs (O'Brien 1931), outputs and energy distribution (Leopold & Langbein 1962; Pethick 1994). In contrast, bottom-up models seek to represent the detailed processes of hydraulics, sediment transport, erosion and deposition to compute the changes to the seabed over time. To allow for the variability in input parameters, a probabilistic approach can be adopted. This approach remains particularly sensitive to the errors in predicting sediment transport. As a consequence, medium or long-term predictions (greater than about one year) are not, as yet, feasible.

To illustrate the recently developed approach, and role it can play in developing a better understanding of the controls which influence the long-term response of an estuary, case studies from three estuaries are presented; namely the Humber, Southampton Water and the Bristol Channel (Fig. 1).

From: PYE, K. & ALLEN, J. R. L. (eds). *Coastal and Estuarine Environments: sedimentology, geomorphology and geoarchaeology.* Geological Society, London, Special Publications, **175**, 75–86. 0305-8719/00/$15.00 © The Geological Society of London 2000.

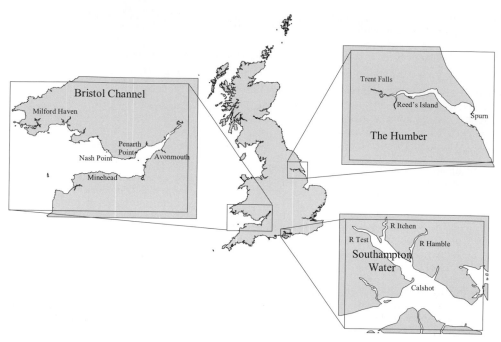

Fig. 1. Location map for the Humber, Southampton Water and the Bristol Channel.

Tools to investigate long-term morphological evolution of estuaries

The late nineteen fifties and early nineteen sixties saw a substantial advance in the generalization and application of the Second Law of Thermodynamics, particularly in the context of irreversible processes (Prigogine 1955). Leopold & Langbein (1962) applied this to the problem of river hydraulics and morphology. A subsequent paper by Langbein (1963) considered the application of the same approach to shallow estuaries. This however deals with an 'ideal' estuary (Pillsbury 1956) and therefore is constrained by the assumption that the amplitude of the tidal elevation and velocity are constant throughout the system. The influence of the frictional terms (Lamb 1932; Dronkers 1986) and the interaction of M_2 and M_4 tidal constituents, referred to as the *overtide* (Friedrichs & Aubrey 1988), further limit the validity of Langbein's application of this approach to the case of an estuary.

In order to develop a more rigorous approach, the derivation of minimum entropy production in a river system was re-examined. This was found to be a special instance of the more general case of a reach with bi-directional and variable discharge. The generalized formulation applies to the estuary case and can be used to investigate the relationship between morphology and tidal energy distribution.

For the evolution to a probable state in a system near to equilibrium, it has been suggested that the entropy production per unit volume will tend to evolve to a minimum compatible with the conditions imposed on the system (Prigogine 1955). Relating this to an estuary suggests that, in the long term, a natural system will tend to evolve in an attempt to achieve the most probable distribution of tidal energy. However, the time taken to evolve to this state will be dependent on constraints imposed upon the system (such as geological constraints and supply of sediments). Such constraints may be significant enough to prevent the evolution to the most probable state in which entropy is maximized, or may induce a switch to some other steady state. Another complication is that the energy available to the system varies temporally over the evolutionary timescale, due to climatic changes, sea level rise, etc.

The concept of minimum entropy production per unit discharge has been derived for the more general case of a bi-directional variable discharge along a channel reach. This suggests that the longitudinal energy distribution along an estuary may be represented as:

$$\rho g \int HQ \, dt = \exp(Cx + D) \qquad (1)$$

where C and D are constants, and $\rho g \int HQ \, dt$ is the sum of the energy passing through a section at a distance x from the mouth of the estuary over a complete tide, with ρ being density of water, g the acceleration due to gravity, H is the specific energy head and Q is the discharge.

Equation 1 represents the most probable distribution of tidal energy within an estuary and states that this will occur when there is an exponential decay of tidal energy upstream. This theory suggests that the estuary morphology will evolve in an attempt to achieve this steady minimal production of entropy. This may be achieved via mutual co-adjustment of channel morphology and tidal characteristics. However, this distribution may not be a single exponential for the system as a whole, due to internal natural or anthropogenic constraints.

The equation of minimum entropy production is solved with the aid of a hydrodynamic numerical model of the estuary. Discharges and elevations from the model are used to compute the longitudinal tidal energy distribution for the estuary and to generate boundary conditions for the solution of Equation 1.

Case study – The Humber Estuary

Characterization of the estuary

The Humber Estuary (Fig. 1) is located on the NE coast of England and drains a catchment area of some $23\,690\,km^2$ (Law *et al.* 1997). Fresh water enters the estuary through many rivers and tributaries, the largest of which are the Ouse, Don, Aire and Trent. Although the fresh water flows do not significantly influence water levels in the estuary, they are sufficient to give rise to density currents, which are particularly important in the outer region of the estuary. At the seaward end there is a tidal range of about 6 metres, due to the position of the mouth within the North Sea basin. This tide is further amplified as it propagates up the estuary and the overtide causes significant asymmetry, particularly upstream of Trent Falls. Substantial reclamation and dredging has taken place in the past (Dun & Townend 1997). One of the benefits of this activity is that there is a good historic record of bathymetry. Changes since about 1850

have been studied in some detail and suggest that, overall, the estuary has been accreting, although there has been a switch to a more erosional phase in the period 1950 to the present (Dun & Townend 1997; Wilkinson *et al.* 1973).

Long-term morphological evolution of the estuary

The existing tidal energy distribution along the longitudinal axis of the Humber Estuary and the combined major tributaries, for the mean of a spring-neap tidal cycle, is illustrated in Fig. 2. The solution to Equation 1 for the energy supplied during a tide, is also illustrated in Fig. 2 as the 'Theoretical' distribution. It is apparent that the actual distribution of tidal energy along the Humber system generally decays exponentially in the upstream direction. This result is in general agreement with the model of minimum entropy production; however, some areas deviate from the most probable state. For instance, the major tributary channels and the area close to Trent Falls (at a chainage of 80 km on the figures) have a lower fraction of tidal energy transmission than is predicted from the most probable state model. Such areas would be expected to attempt to achieve an increase in channel capacity. This would have been the situation prior to the historical programme of land reclamation along the tributaries, and to a lesser degree prior to the training wall construction, when these channels would have had a far greater capacity. Further downstream the model suggests that much of the middle Humber (Immingham to Reed's Island) would tend to accrete.

The historical trend for deposition of sediments in the inter-tidal and the subsequent land reclamation supports the inference that the Humber Estuary has generally acted as a sink for sediments during the recorded past. Furthermore, volumetric analysis of the estuary (from Trent Falls to Spurn Head) for the period from 1851 to 1993 (Dun & Townend 1997) suggests that the estuary as a whole has generally accreted during this time.

In order to investigate the variation in the energy distribution along the estuary during this period, the 1851, 1920 and 1946 bathymetries were generated and the 1D model re-run. For this analysis, tidal range was assumed constant over time but mean sea level was varied based on a rate of 2 mm/year (derived from records taken at 3 stations along the estuary). The energy distribution for the 1851 bathymetry is shown on Fig. 2 for comparison with the 1993 case. Each year will have its own most probable curve

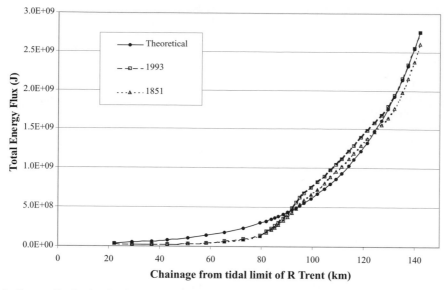

Fig. 2. Energy distribution in the Humber for historic and present day bathymetry.

based on the boundary conditions. Differences from the respective 'most probable' state for each year are illustrated in Fig. 3. This suggests that from the head to about chainage 90 km and from 130 km to the mouth, the energy transmission has moved towards the most probable state over time. For the interval from 90 km to 130 km, a more complex variation has taken place, with the system initially moving towards (1851–1920) and subsequently moving away from the most probable state. However integrating the differences over the length of the system reveals a progressive reduction in the total difference. This implies that the system as a whole has progressively moved towards a more probable state.

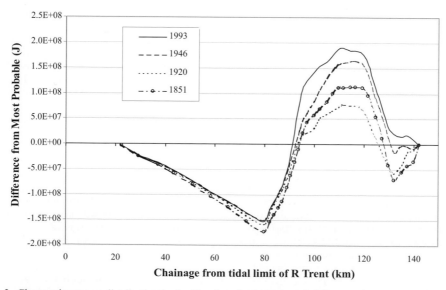

Fig. 3. Changes in energy distribution in the Humber, from most probable, over time.

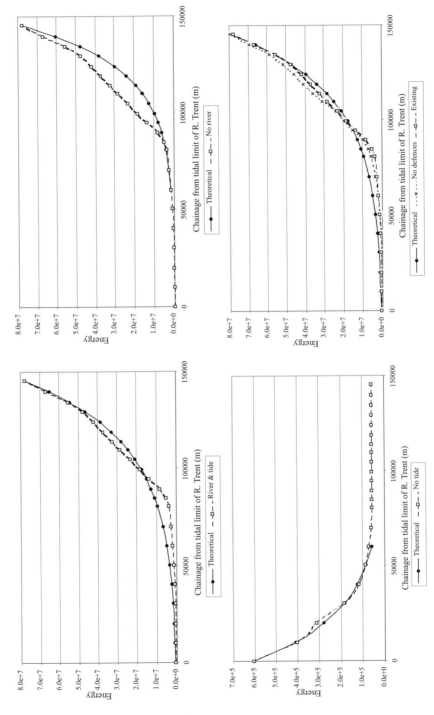

Fig. 4. Energy distribution in the Humber for the existing, no river, no tide and no defences scenarios.

In the period 1851–1920 this was achieved by a move towards the 'most probable' state throughout. This corresponds to the period over which the estuary underwent a significant reduction in volume (6% in both the inter- and subtidal). Between 1920 and 1946 the estuary lost subtidal volume (7%) while the intertidal did not change. The channel then enlarged from 1946 to 1993 (2% in both inter- and subtidal). The reversal in trend within the middle section during the period 1920–1946 may be a consequence of a perturbation to the system caused by the construction of the training works at Trent Falls in 1936. Whatever the cause, the move away from the 'most probable' in the middle Humber has served to achieve a better balance with the inner and riverine sections of the system and so move the system as a whole towards a more probable state.

To examine the relative influence of fluvial and tidal flows on the development of the system morphology, the model was run for the 'no river' and 'no tide' cases (Fig. 4). For the case of a river only (bottom left plot) the energy decays from the head to an approximately constant level at a chainage of about 60 km from the tidal limit. As can be seen, the curve compares well with the theoretical most probable state for the river on its own. The small deviations are thought to be a consequence of the way in which the energy from the different tributaries has been summed together. The case with a tide only decays in the opposite direction and only deviates from the river and tide case for the inner reaches of the estuary (above the 60 km chainage). Fitting the most probable curve to the outer portion of the estuary (60 km+) suggests a more marked gap between actual and most probable states over the length from 80–130 km (i.e. Trent Falls to Hawkins Point).

Considering the two cases together, there would appear to be a transition from fluvial to tidal dominance at about the 60 km chainage. This is supported by examination of the energy head and discharge parameters, which also indicate a transition at around this location. Upstream the energy head dominates the energy term, whereas downstream the discharge makes the major contribution. This in turn is reflected in the morphology. As one would expect, river bed elevation governs energy for the fluvial section. In contrast, in the tidal reach there is an almost constant energy head and discharge decays exponentially. Given velocities throughout are of approximately the same magnitude ($1–2\,\mathrm{m\,s^{-1}}$), this can only be achieved by the cross sectional area varying exponentially.

This only approximately translates into an exponential decay in width. An examination of width and hydraulic depth variations along the length of the estuary reveals a strong negative correlation, particularly in the vicinity of the major bends in the system. This appears to reflect a degree of redundancy in the system which allows the width and depth to adjust to accommodate local asymmetries but maintain the longitudinal variation in cross sectional area.

Human influence on the estuary system has been briefly examined to assess the potential sensitivity of the system. The estuary sections within the 1D model were modified to remove the flood banks and include a floodplain approximately out to the 5 m ODN contour. The resulting energy transmission is also shown on Fig. 4 (bottom right plot). When compared with the existing and theoretical cases, this appears to indicate that the system would move closer to the most probable state in the vicinity of Trent Falls (80 km) and further away downstream. The implication of this result is that the removal of flood defences to re-introduce or extend intertidal wetland area, needs to be considered with some care. It is also important to recognize that the most probable state may be changing with time (e.g. due to sea level rise).

Case Study – Southampton Water

Characterization of the estuary

Southampton Water (Fig. 1) is a mesotidal estuary with a spring range of 3.9 metres. Fresh water is supplied by the rivers Test, Itchen and Hamble and at times gives rise to density driven currents. These are not however accompanied by significant sediment inputs (largely due to the chalk stratigraphy, which forms most of the catchment), and the marine supply is also limited. The estuary has a unique tidal curve, which exhibits both a double high water and a stand on the flood tide. This is a consequence of tidal interactions in the English Channel, with the Solent amplifying the effect as the tide propagates through and into Southampton Water (Price & Townend 2000). The unique nature of the tidal wave affects the sediment transport in a complex way and provides a mechanism for the landward transport and deposition of fine suspended sediment into the estuary. The length of the slack water period, which occurs prior to the ebb phase of the tide, is longer than before the flood phase because of the double high water. This means that fine sediment which enters the estuary has longer to settle out of suspension before, potentially, being transported down river on the ebb.

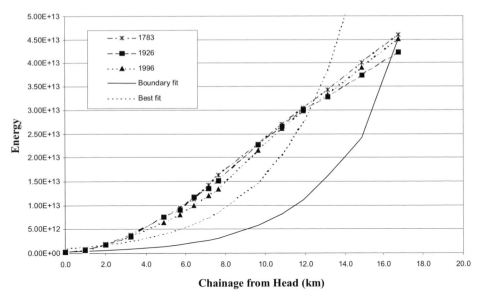

Fig. 5. Energy distribution in Southampton Water as a whole.

Long-term morphological evolution of the estuary

To establish any changes over time, a 1D hydraulic model was established for the 1783, 1926 and 1996 bathymetry. Water elevations and discharges were extracted from the model at intervals along the length of the estuary and used to derive the energy transmission over a tidal cycle. When compared with the most probable state for the system as a whole (derived using the 1996 boundary conditions and Equation 1), it is seen that the energy distribution varies almost linearly rather than exponentially (Fig. 5.).

Furthermore it is notable that there is little change over time. In order to move towards the most probable state, the energy distribution needs to either reduce over extensive lengths, or

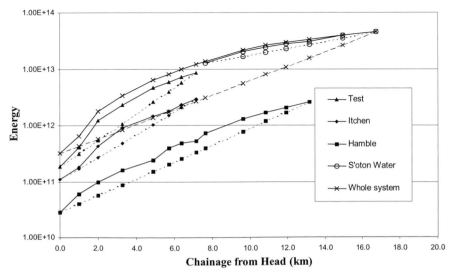

Fig. 6. Energy distribution in Southampton Water and the rivers Test, Itchen and Hamble.

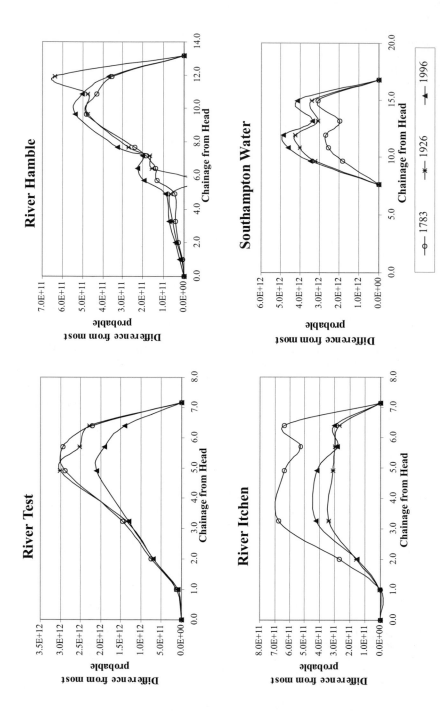

Fig. 7. Changes in energy distribution in Southampton Water and the rivers Test, Itchen and Hamble.

increase through the mouth. This might suggest that the system could either accrete within, or widen at the mouth, in order to move towards a more probable state. The linear distribution is indicative of a system doing uniform work rather than minimum work and is characteristic of canal or linear channel like systems.

An alternative to fitting Equation 1 using the model boundary conditions is to fit an exponential curve to the model data using least squares regression. The differences between the model data and the resulting curve can be interpreted as excess entropy production in the existing system. This curve is also included on Fig. 5 and, whilst still suggesting that the system as a whole is a long way from the most probable state, suggests that the inner portion is perhaps closer than the outer. To examine this further a number of internal constraints were introduced. These exist at the mouth of the three rivers due largely to structures such as sea walls and docks. The energy curves for each individual river and the associated boundary fitted most probable state (dashed lines with similar symbols) are shown in Fig. 6. In this figure Southampton Water is taken to be the reach which connects the confluence of the rivers Test and Itchen, at Dock Head, to the Solent. It should be noted that, in order to highlight the rivers, a log scale has been used for the y-axis. Consequently, the most probable state – an exponential – is a straight line. The differences from the most probable curves suggest that the component rivers are in fact much closer to the most probable state than the system as a whole. This highlights the importance of incorporating the constraints, as stressed by Prigogine (1955).

Looking again at the historical changes, we can now see a clearer pattern of change. Figure 7 shows the differences from the most probable state for each of the component rivers as it has changed over time. In the River Test there appears to have been little change between 1783 and 1926, followed by a substantial move towards the most probable state in the period to 1996. This is probably a consequence of the reduction in tidal volume caused by the construction of Western Docks in Southampton during this time. The differences in the Itchen are an order of magnitude smaller and suggest a much earlier move towards the most probable state, followed by a localized move away in the reach 3 to 5 km from the head. Differences in the Hamble are again an order of magnitude smaller and show a small move away from the most probable state over time. This may be due to dredging associated with leisure developments in the river (the Hamble is a major yacht haven).

Finally, the connecting reach shows a marked move away from the most probable state, most likely due to the channel deepening that has taken place in stages over the time interval studied (although notably not at the mouth, such that the boundary conditions used remain valid).

Case Study – Bristol Channel

Characterisation of the estuary

The Bristol Channel (Fig. 1) represents the seaward extension of the macrotidal Severn Estuary in SW Britain. As a result of reductions in the channel width and depth, the tidal wave is amplified in the up-channel direction. The mean spring tidal range at Lundy is some 5.0 m, increasing to 8.6 m at Swansea and to 12.3 m at Avonmouth, within the Severn Estuary (Admiralty 1993). Generally, freshwater discharges into the Bristol Channel are small when compared to the tidal flows. They give rise to very localized effects close to the river entrances, where salinity gradients can influence sediment movements (Heathershaw et al. 1981)

The Channel consists of a series of embayments, separated by sections of cliffed coastline enclosing a submarine valley, which links the Outer Severn Estuary and the Irish Sea. The locations of embayments along the northern coastline of the Central Bristol Channel (such as those at Swansea and Carmarthen) are related to the onshore geology. In many cases, a hard, erosion resistant, Carboniferous limestone headland on the most westward edge of the embayment, provides protection from the prevailing southwesterly wave climate. Sandy beaches within these embayments are generally aligned parallel to the oncoming south to southwesterly wave fronts (King 1972). Large volumes of sand are present within the Channel, although largely confined to a series of sand bank systems. More widely there is relatively little sediment on the bed of the Channel and bare rock is exposed over extensive areas.

Long-term morphological evolution of the Bristol Channel

Tidal elevations and velocities from a 2D numerical model were used to compute variations in energy at sections along the Bristol Channel. In this case there was no historical bathymetry available. The results presented are for the contemporary case only and as a consequence it is not possible to give any indication of

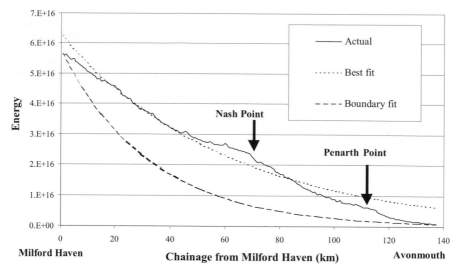

Fig. 8. Energy distribution for the Bristol Channel as a whole.

the timescale of change. As with Southampton Water, the most probable state has been examined by both boundary fitting Equation 1 and by determining the excess entropy production based on a 'best fit' exponential curve.

The broad exponential energy distribution, predicted by the entropy model, is again present within the Bristol Channel (Fig. 8). For the 'boundary fitted' case the model suggests that large scale accretion is needed throughout the system to achieve the most probable state. How-

ever, this is highly unlikely because of the limited sediment supply in the system. In effect this restriction on the supply of sediments is one of many constraints on the system. The 'best fit' case suggests that areas within the Severn Estuary will tend to erode to accommodate increased volumes of tidal energy, whilst other areas will accrete. This may not be achievable because of constraints on the system. As before, sediment supply is limited but in addition the opportunity for the system to widen is restricted by cliffed and

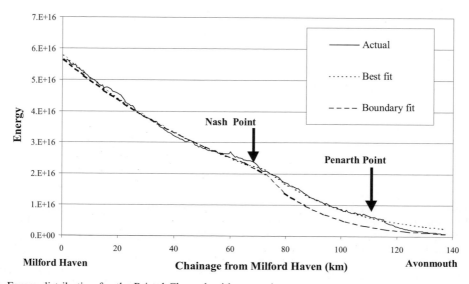

Fig. 9. Energy distribution for the Bristol Channel, with constraints.

bedrock controlled sections, limiting the energy that can be transmitted further upstream. In the long term it may be that erosion of the cliffed sections between Nash Point and Penarth will gradually lead to increased upstream tidal energy propagation and this, in turn, will lead to continued expansion of the Severn Estuary.

The hard sections between Nash Point and Minehead thus constrain the tidal energy which can enter the Severn Estuary. Assuming that in the medium term this acts as a hard spot, the entropy model may be re-evaluated incorporating this constraint. Introducing a constraint at Nash Point results in a very good fit downstream of Nash point for both methods (Fig. 9). Upstream, the 'best fit' method provides a good representation to Penarth Point and then overshoots. The 'boundary fitted' method continues to show lower energy transmission. Given that the length between Nash Point and Penarth Point is hard rock, it would be reasonable to introduce either a continuous constraint between the two points, or a further constraint at Penarth Point. The latter option results in a good fit along the whole length, using either fitting method, and provides an appropriate starting constraint for the Severn Estuary. It is interesting to note that even along the hard rock length the variation in energy transmission is exponential. Given the range of sedimentary and lithological environments within the estuaries examined, it appears that the concept may be widely applicable and not unduly sensitive to the detailed mechanisms of adjustment that takes place within the estuary.

Conclusions

The concepts outlined above have been found to be useful in developing a better understanding of the functioning of estuary systems. They enable potential long-term evolution to be considered using readily available hydraulic modelling techniques to derive the necessary estimates of energy transmission. The approach of gathering as complete as possible a description of the estuary characteristics in conjunction with the 'top down' entropy modelling, provides for a heuristic approach to developing an understanding of how the systems function. Until a more rigorous theoretical basis for functional form has been developed, this provides a practical way forward. Used in conjunction with 'bottom up' deterministic hydraulic/sediment transport/morphological models to examine more detailed short-term changes (up to about one year), the approach provides a means of assessing the potential impacts of changes to the system.

There remains much to be done to develop the approach. Ongoing work is looking at how to incorporate time varying constraints and in particular the significance of a moving frame of reference as a result of landward transgression in response to sea level rise.

The work on the Humber and Southampton Water was funded by the ABP ports of Goole, Grimsby, Hull, Immingham, and Southampton, whose support is gratefully acknowledged. Tracy Somerville and Tim Wells at ABP Research carried out the model simulations of energy for these estuaries.

References

ADMIRALTY 1993. *Tide Tables: European Waters.* Hydrographic Office, Taunton.

DRONKERS, J. 1986. Tidal asymmetry and estuarine morphology. *Netherlands Journal of Sea Research*, **20**, 117–131.

DUN, R. & TOWNEND, I. H. 1997. *Studies to examine the contemporary morphological evolution of the Humber Estuary.* 32nd MAFF Conference of River and Coastal Engineers, F1.1–F1.11, Ministry of Agriculture, Fisheries and Food, UK.

FRIEDRICHS, C. T. & AUBREY, D. G. 1988. Non-linear tidal distortion in shallow well-mixed estuaries: a synthesis. *Estuarine Coastal and Shelf Science*, **27**, 521–546.

HEATHERSHAW, A. D., CARR, A. P. & BLAKLEY, M. W. L. 1981. *Final Report: Coastal erosion and Nearshore Sedimentation Processes.* Institution of Oceanographic Sciences, Taunton.

HR WALLINGFORD, INSTITUTE OF ESTUARINE AND COASTAL STUDIES, ABP RESEARCH & CONSULTANCY, SOUTHAMPTON UNIVERSITY DEPARTMENT OF OCEANOGRAPHY, MAFF DIRECTORATE OF FISHERIES RESEARCH & OWEN, M. 1996. *Estuary Processes and Morphology Scoping Study.* Report SR 446, 1–104, HR Wallingford.

KING, C. A. M. 1972. *Beaches and Coasts.* Edward Arnold, London.

LANGBEIN, W. B. 1963. The hydraulic geometry of a shallow estuary. *International Association of Scientific Hydrologists Publication*, **8**, 84–94.

LAMB, H. 1932. *Hydrodynamics.* Cambridge University Press, Cambridge.

LAW, M., WASS, P. & GRIMSHAW, D. 1997. The hydrology of the Humber catchment. *Science of the Total Environment*, **194/195**, 119–128.

LEOPOLD, L. B. & LANGBEIN, W. B. 1962. *The concept of entropy in landscape evolution.* United States Geological Survey Professional Paper, 500-A, A1–A20.

O'BRIEN, M. P. 1931. Estuary tidal prism related to entrance areas. *Civil Engineering*, **1**, 738–739.

PETHICK, J. S. 1994. *The Humber Estuary Coastal Processes and Conservation.* Institute of Estuarine and Coastal Studies, University of Hull.

PILLSBURY, G. B. 1956. *Tidal Hydraulics.* US Army Corps of Engineers, Vicksburg, Mississippi.

PRICE, D. M. & TOWNEND, I. H. 2000. Hydrodynamic, Sediment Process and Morphological Modelling. *In*: COLLINS, M. B. & ANSELL, K. (eds) *Solent Science: A review*, Elsevier, Amsterdam.

PRIGOGINE, I. 1955. *Introduction to Thermodynamics of Irreversible Processes*. John Wiley & Sons, London.

WILKINSON, H. R., DE BOER, G. & THUNDER, A. 1973. *A cartographic analysis of changes in the bed of the Humber*, Miscellaneous Series No 14 (2 volumes), University of Hull.

Marine sand supply and Holocene coastal sedimentation in northern France between the Somme estuary and Belgium

EDWARD J. ANTHONY

Coastal Geomorphology and Shoreline Management Unit JE2208, Université du Littoral Côte d'Opale, 32, Avenue Foch, F-62930 Wimereux, FRANCE (e-mail: anthony@univ-littoral.fr)

Abstract: From the Somme estuary to Belgium, much of the French coast is characterized by aeolian dunes, sand-choked estuaries and nearshore sand banks. The lack of sand-bearing rivers in this area and the abundance of sand in the English Channel point to the latter as the source of this important sandy accumulation. A comparison of patterns of nearshore and coastal accumulation with results from studies of the hydrodynamics and marine sand transport pathways suggests long-term drift of sand towards the French coast and the North Sea in response to tidal flows and meteorological forcing. This has occurred through sand bank migration onshore, and sand transport alongshore in a pathway hugging the French coast. From this tide-driven 'conveyor belt', fine sand moved onshore to form aeolian dunes, while sand of all sizes has accumulated as thick estuarine fill. This mode of Holocene coastal development emphasizes the joint action of tidal currents, storm waves and wind activity, within an overall framework of tidal dominance in this macrotidal setting.

The most remarkable geomorphic feature of the north coast of France (Fig. 1) is the substantial amount of sand that has accumulated as aeolian dune systems and in estuaries during the Holocene. These onshore deposits are associated with offshore sand banks in the eastern English Channel, and especially in the southern North Sea (Fig. 1). Although numerous studies have been carried out on the dunes and estuarine systems of northern France since the work of Briquet (1930), these efforts have been either site-specific, or highly discipline-oriented, essentially from geological or geomorphic standpoints, and very little attention has been paid to the long-term dynamic relationship between marine sand supply and sandy coastal sedimentation. The highly dynamic marine environment of the eastern English Channel and the southern North Sea have been investigated in recent years in terms of the large-scale tide-dominated hydrodynamic circulations (Salomon & Breton 1993; Salomon *et al.* 1993) and sand transport patterns (Grochowski *et al.* 1993*a* & 1993*b*). As more specifically regards the French coast, a narrow coastal pathway of sand transport from the English Channel to the North Sea was identified by Dewez *et al.* (1989) and Beck *et al.* (1991). Mapping of this coastal zone shows that it is characterized by numerous sand waves migrating northward over a substrate of relict gravel or stranded sand banks (Augris *et al.* 1995).

The specific hydrodynamic and sand transport patterns highlighted by these studies are valuable in understanding and explaining spatial and temporal patterns of onshore sand accumulation in this area of northern France, which lacks major sand-bearing rivers. From a confrontation of miscellaneous hydrodynamic, sedimentological and geomorphic data covering the coastal and nearshore environments, a holistic view of sandy coastal sedimentation is proposed. It highlights a relayed pattern of sand transport between the bed of the eastern English Channel and this coast, involving large-scale long-term tidal, storm wave and wind activity, modulated by sea-level change.

Coastal sandy sedimentation

Aeolian dunes

Two different dune morphological types have developed on the north coast of France from the Somme estuary to the Belgian border (Fig. 2), depending essentially on antecedent coastal morphology. Between the Somme estuary and the bedrock headland of Cape Gris Nez south of

From: PYE, K. & ALLEN, J. R. L. (eds). *Coastal and Estuarine Environments: sedimentology, geomorphology and geoarchaeology.* Geological Society, London, Special Publications, **175**, 87–97. 0305-8719/00/$15.00 © The Geological Society of London 2000.

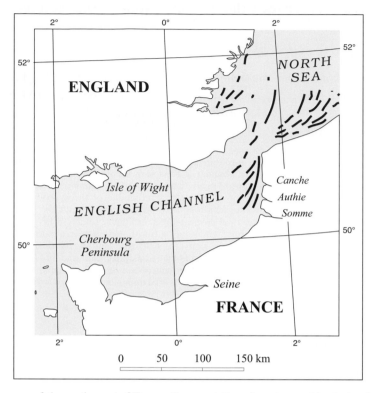

Fig. 1. Location map of the north coast of France. Representation of marine sand banks is schematic.

the Straits of Dover, dunes have accumulated in former coastal embayments between headlands bounded by cliffs. The dune type in this zone is predominantly transgressive. Thick sand sheets associated with parabolic dune formation, and stabilized by vegetation, have moved several kilometers inland in places. This mode of dune formation has left hardly any backbarrier wetlands (Fig. 2). The most important dune fields have fossilized coastal cliffs and even form cliff-top dunes above 150 m. Between the Canche and Authie estuaries, the transgressive trend is less pronounced and the thick dune fields are separated from the abandoned cliffs inland by now largely reclaimed lagoonal and estu-arine wetlands.

Between Cape Gris Nez and the North Sea, dune fields are less massive but still form sig-nificant coastal accumulations up to 25 m high. The predominant dune type on this coast is the shore-parallel, barrier type (Fig. 2). Two or three generations of sub-shore-parallel dunes form a single barrier hinged on bedrock in the west. Two barriers of this type have developed, respectively between Capes Gris Nez and Blanc Nez, and

from Cape Blanc Nez along the southern North Sea as far as the Netherlands. The dunes in this North Sea sector of the French coast have been massively transformed or obliterated by urban and port development (Fig. 2). This dune barrier type has impounded marshland comprising orga-nic mud and isolated patches of sand represent-ing tidal channel fill (Houthuys *et al.* 1993). The back-barrier marshlands have been largely reclaimed since the 11th century.

Estuaries

The three main estuaries in northern France (the Somme, Authie and Canche) north of the Seine River (Fig. 1) are associated with short coastal rivers (100 to 250 km long) that drain Jurassic–Cretaceous limestone catchments. Their liquid discharges are relatively moderate (the mean discharge of the Somme which drains the biggest catchment is only $35 \, \text{m}^3 \, \text{s}^{-1}$), but constant throughout the year. The transport loads brought down by the rivers are solution or suspension loads. Estuaries show a characteristic

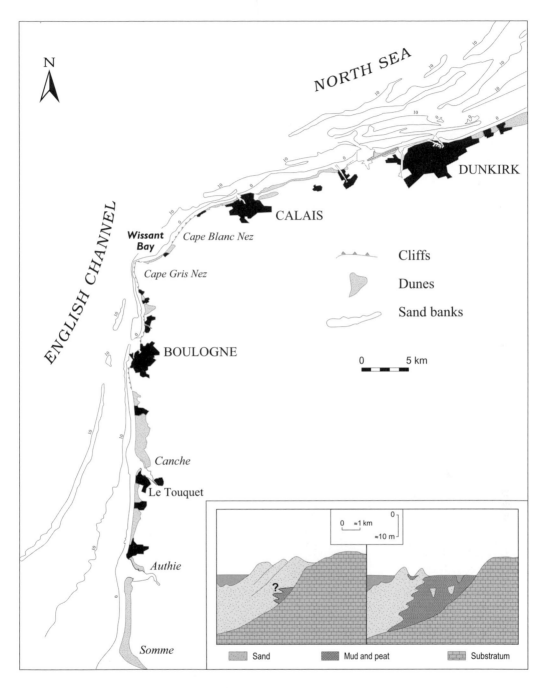

Fig. 2. Dune distribution and sketch of simplified dune and backbarrier morphostratigraphy.

massive south bank sand platform that extends northwards across their mouths (Fig. 3), under the influence of longshore sand transport due to tides and waves. Historical reconstructions of estuary mouth evolution over the last two to three centuries (Briquet 1930; Dallery 1955) show significant northward extension of the dune-bound south bank sand platforms and concomitant erosion of the north bank dunes, the sand being recycled into the estuarine sinks.

Fig. 3. 1994 aerial photographs of the Canche and Authie estuaries showing advanced sandy infill (Courtesy of IGN).

In all cases, massive accretion is resulting in active infill of these estuaries.

This advanced accretion is matched by thick sandy infill. Borehole data from the Canche estuary (Fig. 4) show a tripartite sediment stacking pattern. The Mesozoic limestone basement is overlain by up to 10 m of fluvial deposits. These are overlain by a 15 m thick intermediate unit of grey estuarine sand with occasional mud layers. This unit is bounded at its base and top by peat.

The surficial overlying unit consists of yellow beach and aeolian dune sands up to 30 m thick in places. A similar stacking pattern has been described by Sommé *et al.* (1994) from an estuarine backbarrier environment between Calais and Dunkirk.

The marine environment

Regional hydrodynamic conditions

The eastern English Channel and southern North Sea are influenced by tidal circulations, storm wave activity and aeolian processes. Water movement and hydrodynamic conditions are largely dominated by tides. The main water movements are due to the lunar semi-diurnal M_2 (12.4 hours) and solar semi-diurnal, S_2 tidal constituents (Pingree 1980). Tides in the eastern English Channel and southern North Sea show elements of both standing and progressive motions. Both marine environments are macrotidal. Spring tidal ranges along the French coast reach 10 m in the eastern English Channel, but diminish to around 5.5 m in the southern North Sea. The tidal currents are strong, with surface velocities ranging between 0.5 and 2.0 m s^{-1} (SHOM, 1968). Current strength is strongest in the central Channel and decreases eastward towards the Straits of Dover where velocities increase once more, before decreasing once again in the southern North Sea (SHOM, 1968).

Both the English Channel and the southern North Sea are storm wave environments characterized by episodic high-energy wind waves (peak periods of 4 to 7 s) between more or less long intervening periods (order of days in winter to several weeks in summer) of low energy wind waves. The North Sea is characterized by dominantly northerly wind waves (Bonnefille *et al.* 1971). South of the Straits of Dover, swell working its way in from the Atlantic occasionally complements the locally generated wind waves. Waves in this area are essentially from the west to southwesterly directions (Despeyroux 1985), in response to the prevailing synoptic wind flows in this region. Analyses of long-term (1–24 yr) wave measurement records from the English Channel by Grochowski & Collins (1994) show that the significant wave height (Hs) diminishes from 1.3 m at the western approaches to the Channel to 0.75 m in the Straits of Dover.

The hydrodynamic circulation close to the French coast shows interesting characteristics that are important in understanding patterns of coastal sediment transport and sedimentation. Overall, Salomon & Breton (1993) and Salomon

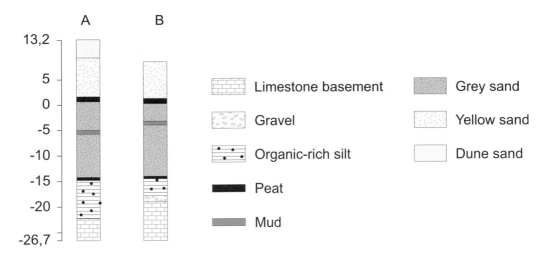

Fig. 4. Stratigraphy of the south bank of the Canche estuary showing the important sandy infill.

et al. (1993) have shown, following earlier flow volume computations by Prandle (1978) and Maddock & Pingree (1982), that there is a net North Sea directed residual flow of water from the eastern English Channel through the Straits of Dover, essentially as a result of meteorological forcing by the dominant southwesterly winds. There is, however, a lateral variation of ebb and flood-dominant flow across the Straits and the extreme eastern English Channel (Dewez *et al.* 1989; Beck *et al.* 1991). Adjacent to the rectlinear north–south oriented French coast in the eastern English Channel, the conjunction of progressive tidal motion, meteorological forcing from the SW and rectification processes related to Coriolis forcing, pressure gradient balancing, and Ekman pumping result in net northward propagation of coastal water (Aelbrecht *et al.* 1993). This coastal zone of flood-dominated North Sea directed flow, whose width decreases from over 30 km south of the Authie estuary to only a few kilometers in the narrow Straits area, is characterized by strong flood currents of up to 1.4 to 1.7 m s^{-1} (SHOM, 1968; Beck *et al.* 1991). This concentration of North Sea directed flow along the French coast is important in terms of net long-term residual sand transport. Further offshore, there is an ebb-dominated flow directed towards the English Channel (Dewez *et al.* 1989; Beck *et al.* 1991).

As far as wave action goes, Grochowski & Collins (1994) have inferred that this process is only intensive along the coast at shallow depths of less than 10–20 m. This is a reasonable 'depth of closure' given the short period waves. Along the English Channel coast of France, these depths correspond to a 20% sediment disturbance level by waves, a value that drops to 5% along the North Sea coast of France (Grochowski & Collins 1994). These workers have identified the central axis of the Channel as being the least wave-affected part, with wave disturbance occurring less than 1–2% of the time.

Marine bedload and sand banks

The sea floor in both the English Channel and the North Sea is considered as a Pleistocene submarine erosion surface bevelled by successive marine transgressions and regressions (Sommé 1979; Larsonneur *et al.* 1982; Curry 1989). The surficial sediments consist essentially of a veneer of gravel and cobbles up to 1 m thick, overlying bedrock or channel fill deposits throughout much of the Channel and southern North Sea floor (Larsonneur *et al.* 1982; Hamblin *et al.* 1992; Augris *et al.* 1995). This coarse fraction is overlain by large areas of sand that are particularly abundant along the French coast from the Somme estuary to Belgium (Augris *et al.* 1995). Sand represents generally less than 50% of the surficial bedload cover south of Cape Gris Nez, increasing northwards, except in the Straits of Dover, and becoming almost continuous off Dunkirk (Fig. 2), where it forms the western part of the Flemish bank system (Beck *et al.* 1991; Augris *et al.* 1995). Large portions of bedrock crop out in the Straits (Augris *et al.* 1995).

It is important to distinguish between 'young' and 'old' sand banks (Tessier 1997). The old sand banks generally occur in deep water (<20 m) where they show aspects of being both 'allocyclic' and 'autocyclic' features, i.e., comprising facies inherited respectively from sea-level changes and modern hydrodynamic processes. South of the Straits of Dover, the sand banks are essentially old and allocyclic banks, according to high resolution seismic stratigraphy of one of the most important banks near the coast (De Batist *et al.* 1993). These authors identified three seismic units: a basal unit interpreted as heterogeneous fluvial channel fill offshore of the Authie and Canche estuaries, an intermediate unit comprising landward-dipping reflectors, interpreted as representing a phase of shoreward sand bank migration during the Holocene sea-level rise, and an upper unit comprising northward dipping reflectors that indicate active longshore migration of surficial sandy meso-scale bedforms. The old sand banks in this area are therefore essentially draped with different mobile sand ribbons, sand waves and megaripples that have been mapped by Beck *et al.* (1991) and Augris *et al.* (1995). The more abundant loose sand in the southern North Sea includes both old allocyclic banks (Berné *et al.* 1994) and young to modern autocyclic banks (Tessier 1997). Between the two coastal sectors, the narrow, largely bedrock-exposed, Straits of Dover are swept clean of sands by the strong tidal currents (Dewez *et al.* 1989; Beck *et al.* 1991).

Marine sand dynamics

The present marine sedimentary cover in the eastern English Channel shows a spatial arrangement that reflects the overriding influence of tidal currents (Kenyon & Stride 1970; Stride *et al.* 1972; Johnson *et al.* 1982). There is an overall fining trend towards the Straits of Dover (Larsonneur *et al.* 1982), schematically presented in Fig. 5. An interesting feature of the loose sediment cover is the existence of a zone of bedload parting in the central Channel zone (Fig. 5), from where loose sediment, essentially sand, has moved both to the east and to the west, leaving a lag of very coarse sediment (Kenyon & Stride 1970; Grochowski *et al.* 1993a). This bedload parting zone has been identified from bedform asymmetry and from the presence of very coarse lag deposits coupled with hydrodynamic observations. It corresponds to the area of highest current velocities associated with an amphidromic point situated on land in southern England. The recent sediment modelling studies by Grochowski *et al.* (1993a,b) confirm a pathway of long-term sand transport (Fig. 5), initially identified along the French coast by Dewez *et al.*

(1989) and Beck *et al.* (1991). These studies also identified a present belt of sand convergence between Hastings and the French coast due to the convergence of the flood and ebb flows respectively from the central Channel and the North Sea. The modelling study by Grochowski *et al.* (1993a) suggests the Somme estuary as the French coast location of this sand convergence belt. This Hastings–Somme sand convergence zone is bypassed by the active sand transport pathway towards the North Sea (Fig. 5).

The pathway perfectly reflects the concentration of North Sea directed residual flows that hug this part of the northern French coast and the sand transport processes towards the North Sea described by Beck *et al.* (1991). These workers have attributed the sand transport processes in this pathway almost exclusively to flood tidal dominance. They also deduced from their radioactive tracer experiments that the mean regional sand transport rate northwards was of the order of $0.2\,\mathrm{m}^3$ per linear meter per day, the rate being the volume of sand crossing a 1 m long line perpendicular to transport direction. These experiments, which included wave and current measurements, led them to conclude that waves did not play a significant role in horizontal sand movement. This conclusion is in agreement with that of Grochowski & Collins (1994).

In the southern North Sea, longshore sand transport patterns are similarly directed northeastwards towards Belgium in the shallow subtidal zone (Vicaire 1991; Corbau 1995), due to flood tidal dominance, but the sand movement patterns are more complex further offshore in this area than in the eastern English Channel corridor. There is some evidence of interfingering of ebb and flood channels, especially near the shear zone between eastward-directed flood-dominant flow and Channelward-directed ebb dominant flow (Beck *et al.* 1991).

Sand transfer from the nearshore banks to the coast in this area has been a long recognized feature of accretion on the French North Sea coast and has been recently reiterated by Corbau (1995) and Tessier (1997). This process was probably known to the local Flemish populations who used dykes built out into the sea to intercept nearshore sand banks migrating shoreward in the Dunkirk area. Historical records and ancient maps suggest that the coastward sand transfer mechanism involves the attachment to the shoreline of shallow linear coastal bodies. Garlan (1990) has documented from bathymetry chart differencing between 1911 and 1988 the rapid coastward migration of the landward flank of a sand bank just east of Calais. Supply of sand from this bank to the coast may

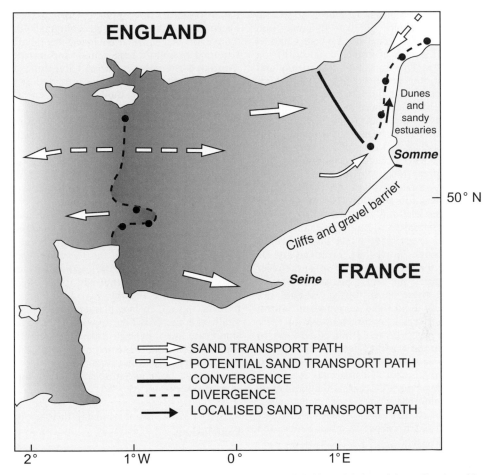

Fig. 5. Sand transport patterns and pathways in the eastern English Channel (adapted from Grochowski *et al.* 1993*a*). Shading schematically depicts the overall eastward fining of the sea bed sediments mapped by Larsonneur *et al.* (1982).

explain localized but massive coastal accretion observed in this area from topographic surveys. These sand bodies are thus presumably shed off progressively from the shoreface which acts as a storage zone for the sand transferred by tidal currents from the deeper Channel bed. Historical records and the ancient maps show welding of these coastal banks onto the wide, dissipative ridge and runnel beaches that provide very low gradient surfaces conducive to aeolian sand transfer inland onto dunes.

Marine sand supply and coastal sedimentation: a long-term perspective

Much of the loose sediment in the English Channel and southern North Sea originally accumulated in a subaerial environment as het-erogeneous periglacial outwash and terrestrial runoff deposits (Larsonneur *et al.* 1982). These were derived from England, France, and the North Sea countries and were emplaced during the Late Pleistocene eustatic lowstand. These sediments progressively assumed their present distribution during and subsequent to the Holocene sea-level rise. Austin (1991) suggested the development of strong tidal currents following the opening up of the Straits of Dover. It is believed that the sand banks adjacent to the French coast were formed during this phase by combined tidal and wave action (Tessier 1997).

The lack of major sand-bearing rivers between the Somme estuary and Belgium, and the abundance of sand on the bed of the English Channel, point to the latter as the source of the important Holocene coastal sandy accumulation in northern France. This thesis is supported by a comparison of the coastal geomorphology with the foregoing results of hydrodynamic and sediment studies covering the English Channel and the short stretch of French coast bordering the North Sea. However, the mechanisms and time frame of the relationship between long-term marine sand supply and coastal dune formation and estuarine infill still need to be clarified.

A two-stage time framework is tentatively proposed, as a simple basis for discussion. This time framework is based on the history of the Holocene sea level from the neighbouring Belgian coastal plain (Denys & Baeteman 1995). The first stage essentially involved sand bank formation and migration towards the coast in response to Holocene sea-level rise, up to around 4000 yr BP. The eastward-dipping seismic reflectors from the deeper sand banks off the French coast and in the North Sea, identified by De Batist et al. (1993), Berné et al. (1994) and Tessier (1997), suggest that early active coastward migration of these banks during sea-level rise was driven by both tidal currents and storm waves. The allocyclic nature of some of these banks shows that they were stranded offshore, as the late Holocene sea-level rise outstripped their rate of coastward migration (Tessier 1997). The shoreward attachment of banks may have contributed at this stage to estuarine infill and early sandy sedimentation in the coastal embayments.

The coexistence of both modern shoreface-attached and older, deeper stranded banks, and the historical evidence for shoreward sand bank migration and welding in the southern North Sea, attest to the continuity of sand transfer processes towards the French coast following the Holocene marine transgression. This second, essentially stillstand, phase has thus involved sand bank migration and welding to the coast, as well as the establishment of the long-term sand transport pathways identified in the eastern English Channel (Fig. 5).

The coastal sand transport pathway in northern France identified by Dewez et al. (1989), Beck et al. (1991) and Grochowski et al. (1993a, b) has, as these various workers have suggested, served to transfer sand from the eastern English Channel to the North Sea. A strong assumption here is that this sediment circulation system has been in operation over the last few thousand years as sea-level stabilization allowed long-term organization of the loose sand stocks by the regional tidally-dominated hydrodynamic circulation and by North Sea-directed residual water flow along the French coast. South of the Straits of Dover, this transport system was fed by long-term sand drifting from the central English Channel under a combination of tidal stirring,

meteorological forcing and Coriolis forcing. From this tide- and meteorologically-driven 'conveyor belt', which included the shallower stranded nearshore banks, fine sand moved onshore to form embayment infill and dunes while sand fractions of all sizes accumulated as thick estuarine fill. The relationship between coastal and nearshore facies, their stacking pattern and the large-scale hydrodynamic circulations involved in long-term coastal sand transfers is schematically depicted in Fig. 6.

Depending on the relationship between coastal orientation, impinging storm waves and winds, tidal current orientation, and inherited coastal morphology (notably the presence of embayments and estuaries), the dunes accumulated either as thick transgressive sand sheets or as shore-parallel dune barriers (Fig. 2). These dune systems have regularized the shoreline from the Somme estuary to Belgium, sealing off embayments that initially perturbed both the tidal current structure and the wave field. The initial morphology of an irregular embayed shoreline south of Cape Gris Nez appears to have been a significant factor in large-scale dune formation in this area by disrupting the longshore sand transport. Additionally, the impinging southwesterly winds have been favourable to direct onshore sand transport.

Conclusions

Unlike open ocean coasts where long period swell may drive in sand from the nearshore shelf, the waves in the fetch-limited environments of the eastern English Channel and southern North Sea have been shown to be active in sand transport only in the shallow coastal zone. Because of the marine origin of the substantial volumes of sand that have accumulated both in the nearshore zone and onshore in northern France, the overriding influence of long-term residual tidal circulations is emphasized by this mode of coastal accretion.

The specific hydrodynamic circulation patterns characterizing the north coast of France are embedded within the large-scale regional circulation patterns controlled by the tides, aided by meteorological forcing. At the regional scale, recent studies have highlighted the potential for net eastward drift of the lighter, sandy fraction from the heterogeneous central Channel sediment reservoir towards France, in response to variations in overall current strength (Grochowski et al. 1993a & b). Given the relative depletion of sand observed in the central bedload parting zone between the Isle of Wight and

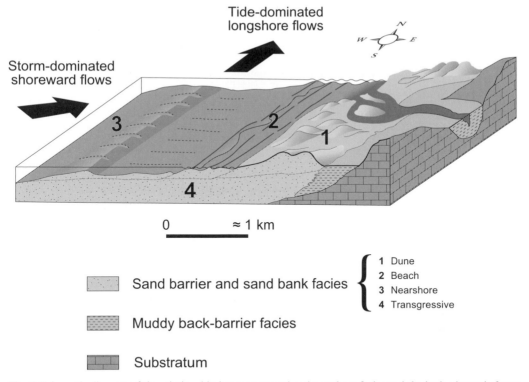

Fig. 6. Schematic diagram of the relationship between coastal and nearshore facies and the hydrodynamic forces involved in sand transport in the coastal zone. Arrows show net sand transport directions.

the Cherbourg Peninsula, and the enrichment of the eastern Channel and North Sea in sand, hydrodynamic sorting related to this bedload parting may have been operating over the last few thousand years. However, the sand transfer mode suggested by the architecture of offshore sand banks near France appears to have included storm wave influence in the onshore migratory phase of these sand banks (Tessier 1997), at a time when their crests were close to the then prevailing sea-level.

The longshore distribution of sandy coastal sediments in northern France fits perfectly with the sand transport pathway identified along this coast. The Somme estuary, identified by Grochowski *et al.* (1993a) as the southern limit of the sand transport pathway hugging the coast of France (Fig. 5), is in fact the most significant coastal sand sink on the north coast of France. It also marks the starting point of important northward accumulation of both nearshore sand banks and coastal sand dunes which extends to the southern North Sea.

A number of areas require future research. These include:

(1) the time frame of aeolian dune accumulation and estuarine infill and its correlation with that of marine sand bank development and Holocene sea-level rise;

(2) the respective roles of storms and tidal currents, in both the English Channel and the North Sea, in the critical inshore zone where sand is transferred from the sea to the coast; and

(3) finer resolution of sand transport rates and sand budgets, and their correlation with the present status of dunes and estuaries.

References

AELBRECHT, D., CHABERT D'HIÈRES, G. & ZHANG, X. 1993. Generation of a residual current by interaction between the coastal boundary layer and the Ekman layer in a tidal motion. *Oceanologica Acta*, **16**, 479–487.

AUGRIS, C., CLABAUT, P. & TESSIER, B. 1995. *Le domaine marin côtier du Nord-Pas de Calais : Carte des formations superficielles au 1:100 000.* IFREMER/Région Nord-Pas de Calais/Université de Lille I.

AUSTIN, R. M. 1991. Modelling Holocene tides on the NW European continental shelf. *Terra Nova*, **3**, 276–288.

BECK, C., CLABAUT, P., DEWEZ, S., VICAIRE, O., CHAMLEY, H., AUGRIS, C., HOSLIN, R. & CAILLOT, A. 1991. Sand bodies and sand transport paths at the English Channel-North Sea border: morphology, dynamics and radioactive tracing. *Oceanologica Acta*, **11**, 111–121.

BERNE, S., TRENTESAUX, A., MISSIAEN, T & DE BATIST, M. 1994. Architecture and long term evolution of a tidal sand bank: the Middelkerke Bank (Southern North Sea). *Marine Geology*, **121**, 57–72.

BONNEFILLE, R., LEPETIT, J. P., GRAF, M. & LEROY, J. 1971. *Nouvel avant-port de Dunkerque*. Mesures en nature. Report, Laboratoire National d'Hydraulique, HC042/05.

BRIQUET, A. 1930. *Le littoral du Nord de la France et son évolution morphologique*. Thèse de Doctorat ès Sciences, Université d'Orléans.

CORBAU, C. 1995. *Dynamique sédimentaire en domaine macrotidal: exemple du littoral du Nord de la France (Dunkerque)*. Thèse de Doctorat, Université des Sciences et Technologies, Lille.

CURRY, D. 1989. The rock floor of the English Channel and its significance for the interpretation of marine unconformities. *Proceedings of the Geological Association, London*, **100**, 339–352.

DALLERY, F. 1955. *Les rivages de la Somme, autrefois, aujourd'hui et demain*. Mémoires de la Société d'Emulation Historique et Littéraire d'Abbeville, Editions A. & J. Picard et Cie, Paris.

DENYS, L. & BAETEMAN, C. 1995. Holocene evolution of relative sea level and local mean high water spring tides in Belgium – a first assessment. *Marine Geology*, **124**, 1–19.

DESPEYROUX, Y. 1985. *Etude hydrosédimentaire de l'estuaire de la Canche*. Thèse de Doctorat, Université des Sciences et Technologies, Lille.

DE BATIST, M., MARSSET, T., MISSIAN, T., REYNAUD, J., TESSIER, B. & CHAMLEY, H. 1993. *Large- and small-scale internal structures of the Bassure de Baas Bank: recording by high resolution seismics and sub-bottom profiling*. Annual Report Project MAST-Starfish MAS-CT92-0029, 77–83.

DEWEZ, S., CLABAUT, P., VICAIRE, O., BECK, C., CHAMLEY, H. & AUGRIS, C. 1989. Transits sédimentaires résultants aux confins Manche-Mer du Nord. *Bulletin de la Société Géologique de France*, **5**, 1043–1053.

GARLAN, T. 1990. L'apport des levés bathymétriques pour la connaissance de la dynamique sédimentaire. L'exemple des Ridens de la Rade aux abords de Calais. *Littoral '90, Eurocoast Symposium*, 71–75.

GROCHOWSKI, N. T. L. & COLLINS, M. B. 1994. Wave activity on the sea-bed of the English Channel. *Journal of the Marine Biological Association of the, U.K.*, **74**, 739–742.

——, ——, BOXALL, S. R. & SALOMON, J. C. 1993a. Sediment transport predictions for the English Channel, using numerical models. *Journal of the Geological Society, London*, **150**, 683–695.

——, ——, ——, ——, BRETON, M. & LAFITE, R. 1993b. Sediment transport pathways in the eastern English Channel. *Oceanologica Acta*, **16**, 531–537.

HAMBLIN, R. J. O., CROSBY, A., BALSON, P. S., JONES, S. M., CHADWICK, R. A., PENN, I. E. & ARTHUR, M. J. 1992. *The Geology of the English Channel*. British Geological Survey, Her Majesty's Stationery Office, London.

HOUTHUYS, R., DE MOOR, G. & SOMMÉ, J. 1993. The shaping of the French-Belgian coast throughout recent geology and history. *In*: HILLEN, R. & VERHAGEN, H. J. (eds) *Coastlines of the southern North Sea*. American Society of Civil Engineers, New York, 27–40.

JOHNSON, M. A., KENYON, N. H., BELDERSON, R. H. & STRIDE, A. H. 1982. Sand transport. *In*: STRIDE, A. H. (ed.) *Offshore tidal sands. Processes and deposits*. Chapman & Hall, London, 58–94.

KENYON, N. H. & STRIDE, A. H. 1970. The tide-swept continental shelf sediments between the Shetland Isles and France. *Sedimentology*, **14**, 159–173.

LARSONNEUR, C., BOUYSSE, P. & AUFFRET, J. P. 1982. The surficial sediments of the English Channel and its western approaches. *Sedimentology*, **29**, 851–864.

MADDOCK, L. & PINGREE, R. D. 1982. Mean heat and salt budgets for the eastern English Channel and the southern bight of the North Sea. *Journal of the Marine Biological Association of the, U.K.*, **62**, 559–575.

PINGREE, R. D. 1980. Physical oceanography of the Celtic Sea and English Channel. *In*: BANNER, F. T., COLLINS, M. B. & MASSIE, K. S. (eds) *The North-West European Shelf Seas: the Seabed and the Sea in Motion, II. Physical and Chemical Oceanography and Physical Resources*. Oceanography series 24B, Elsevier, Amsterdam, 415–465.

PRANDLE, D. 1978. Monthly-mean residual flows through the Dover strait 1949–1972. *Journal of the Marine Biological Association of the, U.K.*, **58**, 965–973.

SALOMON, J. C. & BRETON, M. 1993. An atlas of long-term currents in the Channel. *Oceanologica Acta*, **16**, 439–448.

——, —— & GUEGUENIAT, P. 1993. Computed residual flow through the Dover Strait. *Oceanologica Acta*, **16**, 449–455.

SHOM 1968. *Les courants de marée dans la mer de la Manche et sur les côtes françaises de l'Atlantique*. Service Hydrographique Océanographique et de la Marine, 550, Paris.

SOMME, J. 1979. Quaternary coastlines in northern France. *Acta Universita Upsala*, **2**, 147–158.

——, MUNAUT, A. V, EMONTSPOHL, A. F., LIMONDIN, N., LEFEVRE, D., CUNAT-BOGE, N., MOUTHON, J. & GILOT, E. 1994. The Watten boring – an Early Weichselian and Holocene climatic and palaeoecological record from the French North Sea coastal plain. *Boreas*, **23**, 231–243.

STRIDE, A. H., BELDERSON, R. H. & KENYON, N. H. 1972. Longitudinal furrows and depositional sand bodies of the English Channel. *In*: *Colloque sur la géologie de la Manche*. Mémoires du Bureau de Recherches Géologiques et Minières, **79**, 233–240.

TESSIER, B. 1997. *Expressions sédimentaires de la dynamique tidale*. Mémoire d'Habilitation à Diriger des Recherches. Sciences Naturelles, Université des Sciences et Technologies, Lille.

VICAIRE, O. 1991. *Dynamique hydrosédimentaire en Mer du Nord méridionale (Du Cap Blanc Nez à la frontière belge)*. Thèse de Doctorat, Université des Sciences et Technologies, Lille.

Storm surges and erosion of coastal dunes between 1957 and 1988 near Dunkerque (France), southwestern North Sea

BRUNO VASSEUR & ARNAUD HEQUETTE

Coastal Geomorphology and Shoreline Management Unit JE 2208,
Université du Littoral Côte d'Opale, 32, Avenue Foch, F-62930 Wimereux, France
(e-mail: hequette@univ-littoral.fr)

Abstract: The comparison of aerial photographs of eroding coastal dunes located between Dunkerque (Northern France) and the Belgium border revealed that the retreat rate of the dune front increased between 1957 and 1988. Analyses of hourly water levels from the Dunkerque Harbour tide gauge showed an increase in the frequency of high water levels associated with storm surges during the same period. Significant wave heights that could be generated during these high water level events were computed according to a wave hindcast model and using wind data collected at Dunkerque. These analyses show an increase in storm magnitude and frequency during the last two decades of the study period, and suggest a strong relationship between dune front erosion and frequency of storm surge conditions. Since relative sea-level is rising in the southern North Sea , coastal dunes will probably be more frequently reached by storm waves in the future. Consequently, more severe coastal dune erosion may take place during the next decades, increasing the risk of flooding of coastal lowlands.

Coastal dunes commonly play a major role in the sediment budget of sandy coastal environments (Pye 1983; Psuty 1988; Davidson-Arnott & Law 1996). Several studies showed that coastal stability is strongly influenced by the sediment exchanges occurring between beaches and dunes (Short & Hesp 1982; Kriebel & Dean 1985; Nordstrom *et al.* 1990). Among a series of complex interactions that link beaches and dunes, coastal dunes act as sand reservoirs which may episodically supply sediment to adjacent beaches (Psuty 1988; Sherman & Bauer 1993).

Dunes also constitute an important barrier protecting low-lying areas in the backshore of many coastlines of the world. This is particularly the case along the southwestern coast of the North Sea where a large proportion of the coastal plain consists of reclaimed land (Baeteman *et al.* 1992; Verger & Goeldner 1995). In the Netherlands, for example, up to 80% of the country's coastline is protected by coastal dunes (Van der Meulen *et al.* 1989). In such context, coastal erosion may result in the breaching of coastal dunes and eventually in the inundation of the low-lying coastal areas. For example, in 1953 a major storm surge striking the Dutch coast was responsible for the flooding of 130 000 hectares of cultivated land and 1772 fatalities in Holland (Pollard 1978). The low-lying coastal lands of northern France have also been flooded

by storm surges on several occasions during the last decades (Deboudt 1997).

The aim of this study was to evaluate the effects of storm-induced episodic high water levels on the erosion of coastal dunes along the coastline of northern France. A coastal site at Leffrinckoucke, near Dunkerque (Fig. 1), was chosen to carry out analyses of coastal dune erosion between 1957 and 1988 and to look at the history of the storms that may have caused the observed erosion.

Regional setting

The northern coast of France consists mainly of wide dissipative macrotidal beaches commonly associated to coastal dunes in the backshore. Dune stability or even progradation may locally occur, especially near the mouth of small estuaries, due to the redistribution of sand transported by the littoral drift from adjacent eroding shorelines (Dobroniak & Anthony 1999). Most of the coastal dunes within the region, however, show signs of erosion either in the form of erosional scarps (Fig. 2) on their seaward side or breaches resulting from the local incursion of storm waves through the dune crest (Fig. 3). Extensive coastal retreat since at least the middle of the 19th century has been documented in

From: PYE, K. & ALLEN, J. R. L. (eds). *Coastal and Estuarine Environments: sedimentology, geomorphology and geoarchaeology*. Geological Society, London, Special Publications, **175**, 99–107. 0305-8719/00/$15.00 © The Geological Society of London 2000.

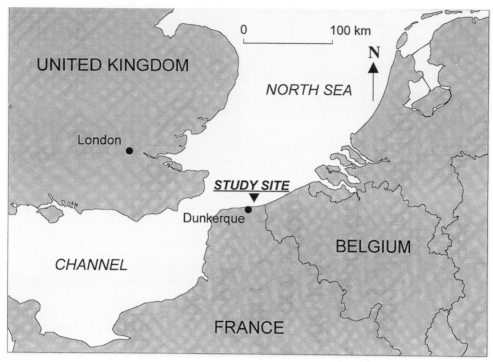

Fig. 1. Location map of the study site at Leffrinckoucke.

several studies (Briquet 1930; Corbau *et al.* 1993; Deboudt 1997).

The region is macrotidal, the mean tidal range at Dunkerque being 5.4 m for spring tides and 3.5 m for neap tides (SHOM 1997). Winds at Dunkerque mainly come from the SW, west and NE, but storm winds mostly originate form the west and NW directions (Corbau 1995). Such winds, combined with the effects of Coriolis force, may induce storm surges along the coast of northern France by causing an onshore transport of surface water. According to a 21 year study carried out by Clique & Lepetit (1986), the mean annual storm surge at Dunkerque is 1.04 m. The directional distribution of deep-water waves, offshore of Dunkerque, show that the most frequent waves come from the north–NE to north, generated in the North Sea, followed by waves from the SW, originating from the English Channel (Clabaut *et al.* 1996). Most waves (60%) have a period and a significant height of less than 5 s

Fig. 2. Erosional scarp on the seaward side of a coastal dune near Dunkerque, September 1998. The presence of a blockhouse on the beach indicates that the coastline has retreated by several tens of metres at this site since World War II.

Fig. 3. Breached coastal dune, east of Leffrinckoucke, near Dunkerque, October 1998.

and 1.5 m respectively, but long period waves can reach a period of 14–15 s and exceed heights of 7 m. Due to the orientation of the coastline at the study site (Fig. 1), the coastal dunes are mostly exposed to waves from the NW, north and NE.

Coastal dune erosion at Leffrinckoucke between 1957 and 1988

The study site, at Leffrinckoucke, consists of a seaward dune ridge and several inner dunes (Fig. 4). This site is located in an area between the city of Dunkerque and the Belgium border where coastal retreat from 1872 to 1977 was estimated at 1.3 m/yr (Corbau *et al.* 1993). This rate does not reflect, however, the large inter-annual variability in coastal erosion due to the effects of individual storms that can cause a retreat of several metres.

Changes in the position of the dune front were evaluated from the comparison of aerial photographs taken in 1957, 1967, and 1988 at scales of 1 : 20 000 (1957, 1967) and 1 : 25 000 (1988). The photographs were scanned and integrated at the same scale with a mapping software. Although parts of the dune front showed only minor changes during the complete period of this study, significant erosion occurred at several locations. These sites were selected for computing mean retreat rates for the periods 1957–1967, 1967–1977, and 1977–1988. Erosion mainly occurred during the 1977–1988 period, averaging 3.0 m/yr, while the periods 1967–1977 and 1957–1967 were characterized by retreat rates of 1.0 m/yr and 0.8 m/yr respectively.

Water level analyses

Hourly water levels from the Dunkerque tide gauge, 9 km SW of the study site, were analysed for the 1957–1988 period. The study was limited to the 1957–1988 period because too many gaps exist in the data set prior to 1957 and during 1989 and 1992. Topographic surveys at Leffrinckoucke showed that the dune toe is at approximately 6.5 m above the Hydrographic Datum (HD). In order to consider only storms that may have caused dune erosion, only water levels of 6.5 m or more above HD were taken into account.

The return period of water levels above the dune toe was computed according to the method defined by Gumbel (1958) which is commonly used for analysing extreme water levels in the coastal zone (Pirazzoli 1991). This method enabled us to estimate the frequency of extreme water levels using the highest annual water levels recorded between 1957 and 1988. According to this method, the probability F that a water level of height x will not be exceeded is related to the return period T by the equations:

$$F(x) = e^{-e^{-y}} \tag{1}$$

$$T(x) = 1/1 - F \tag{2}$$

where y is a reduced variate linear function of x. The thin lines on each side of the thick straight line (Fig. 5) define a confidence interval of 0.8 probability.

Between 1957 and 1988, sea-level reached the dune toe at least once every year, and exceeded that level by several tens of cm several times. Not only was the dune toe reached by the sea at least once a year on average, but water levels with a characteristic return period of about 50 years occurred 2 times during that 30 years period (Fig. 5). On these occasions, water level reached an elevation of 0.78 m and 0.8 m above the base of the dune during storms that occurred on February 2, 1983 and January 12, 1978 respectively.

The number of occasions where the water level was above the dune toe was also calculated for each period corresponding to the coastal change measurements made from aerial photographs (Fig. 6). The water level reached or exceeded the base of the dune on 35 occasions during the 1957–1967 period. This level was exceeded on 53 and 90 occasions during the 1967–1977 and

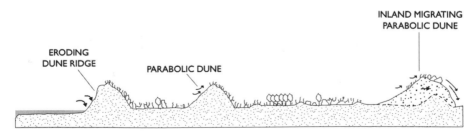

Fig. 4. Schematic profile of the coastal dune system at Leffrinckoucke (modified from Fauchois 1998).

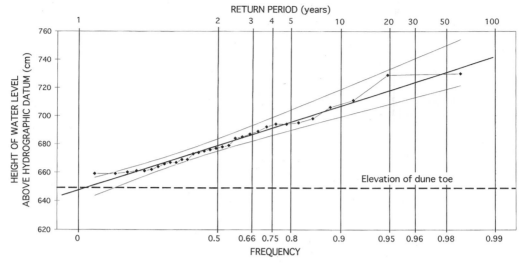

Fig. 5. Frequency and return period of extreme water levels at Dunkerque between 1957 and 1988. Water level data are maximum annual water levels collected at the Dunkerque Harbour tide gauge, 9 km SW of Leffrinckoucke.

1977–1988 periods respectively. Our results show that high water levels were much more frequent during the latter period, which was also characterized by the highest water level observations.

Comparison of predicted tidal elevations and observed water levels showed that the observed high water levels were not only due to astro-

nomical tides, but to other forcing mechanisms. Observed water levels at about 1.0 m above the predicted tide level are common in our data set, and water levels exceeding 1.3 m above the predicted tide occurred several times. Wind data collected at the Dunkerque Harbour during these events show that virtually all high water levels

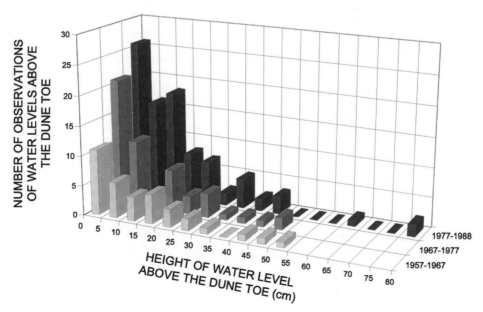

Fig. 6. Distribution of water levels above the base of the coastal dune at Leffrinckoucke between 1957 and 1988 (base of coastal dune is at 6.5 m above Hydrographic Datum).

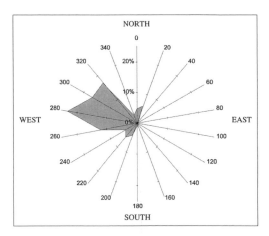

Fig. 7. Directional wind distribution during storm surges that exceeded 6.5 m above Hydrographic Datum (wind data from Dunkerque Harbour).

were the result of combined tidal- and wind-forcing. Analysis of hourly mean wind velocities and directions showed that the distribution of wind directions was dominated by onshore-blowing winds from the west and NW when high water levels occurred (Fig. 7). Most winds had a velocity of 10 m/s or more (up to 29 m/s) and were responsible for an onshore-directed wind stress inducing a shoreward transport of surface water and a set-up of sea-level against the coast. On some rare occasions, however, the observed water levels above the predicted tide were probably due to changes in barometric pressure rather than wind-forcing, since the wind was blowing from the south to SW, directions that would not result in a transport of surface waters against the coast.

The magnitude of a storm surge above the predicted tide level does not necessarily reflect the potential erosion that may affect the coastline. The maximum storm surge for the study period was recorded on November 2, 1986, reaching 1.38 m above the predicted tide level, but the water level reached only 0.17 m above the dune toe (6.67 m above HD). A similar water level (6.72 m above HD) was reached on October 25, 1980, while the surge was only 0.31 m above the predicted tide level. Conversely, even a moderate storm surge could result in a water level largely above the dune toe, like on December 10, 1965, when a surge of 0.96 m induced a water level set-up of 7.01 m above HD.

We, therefore, used actual measurements of water levels rather than storm surge elevations (i.e. elevation above predicted tide) for analysing the potential effects of these events on coastal dunes. Only observations characterized by onshore-blowing winds (including obliquely onshore-blowing winds) were considered for subsequent analyses, because winds from other directions would not result in the generation of incident surface gravity waves. These events were deleted from the following analyses because they would not result in eroding processes at the coast.

Wave conditions during storm surges and potential erosion events

Wave conditions associated with high water levels were investigated in order to distinguish potentially eroding events and to get a better insight of the potential effects of the storm surges on coastal erosion during each 10-year period. Because there is no continuous wave record for the period of this study, a hindcast of significant wave heights, based on hourly mean wind data collected at Dunkerque and fetch length, was carried out. Deep-water significant wave heights (H_0) were obtained according to the following empirical equation (CERC 1984) which is a simplification of the parametric wave prediction model developed by Hasselman *et al.* (1976):

$$H_0 = 5.112 \times 10^{-4} U_A F^{1/2} \qquad (3)$$

where U_A is a wind-stress-factor (which corresponds to adjusted wind speed over water) and F is the length of fetch (relative to the shoreline orientation at the study site). Fetch length was calculated for each 20° sector facing the coastline.

The distribution of hindcasted wave heights (Fig. 8) show that most waves during storm surges had a height of 1 to 2.5 m in deep-water. There are considerable variations, however, between the different periods. The 1957–1967 period corresponds to a low number of moderate wave events, wave heights ranging mostly from 1.0 to 1.5 m. The 1967–1977 period shows an increase of both the frequency of wave events and wave heights, the modal wave height corresponding to the 2.0–2.5 m interval. An increase in storminess is more pronounced during the following period (1977–1988) which was characterized by a significant increase in the frequency of waves with heights of more than 1.0 m and especially by the occurrence of high-amplitude waves that exceeded 5.0 m on several occasions. These waves were generated during a major storm on January 11 and 12, 1978, when wind speeds of more than 100 km/hr were recorded.

When only potentially eroding events are considered (i.e. water level ≥ 6.5 m above HD and incident waves), our analyses show that the study site was affected by 13 storm surges during the

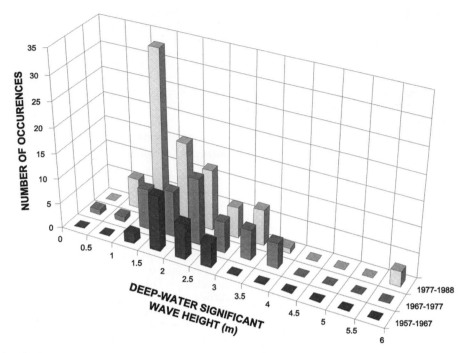

Fig. 8. Distribution of deep-water significant wave heights during storm surges that exceeded 6.5 m above Hydrographic Datum. Waves heights were estimated according to a wave hindcast model (see text for explanation).

1957–1967 period, which is rather low compared to the number of surges that characterized the following periods, with 25 and 23 storm surges during the 1967–1977 and 1977–1988 periods respectively (Table 1). Although storm frequency is similar for the last two periods, the number of observations of high water levels accompanied by potentially eroding wave conditions may be different from one storm to another, and is variable for each period. For the complete study period, most storm surges resulted in 1 or 2 hourly observations of potentially eroding high water levels (Table 1). These results do not mean that these storm events were limited to a duration of 1 or 2 hours; they can be explained by the large tidal range that restricted the time during which the base of the coastal dunes could be reached dur-

ing a storm. Differences in storm duration are obvious, however, for the 1977–1988 period during which 3 significant long-lasting storms occurred. Waves could reach the base of the coastal dunes during 5, 8 and 12 hours during each of these storm surges (Table 1).

Our analyses of storm surge conditions based on water level and wave hindcast data indicate an increase in frequency with time of high water levels associated with potentially eroding conditions between 1957 and 1988 (Fig. 9). Storm surges were responsible for 25 occurrences of high water level that could induce coastal dune erosion between 1957 and 1967. The number of observations of such conditions increased to 48 between 1967 and 1977, and reached 75 for the 1977–1988 period.

Table 1. *Number of storms per period and number of observations of high water levels per storm*

Number of observations of potentially erosive high water levels per storm	1	2	3	4	5	8	12	Total
Number of storms (1957–1967)	6	3	3	1				13
Number of storms (1967–1977)	12	6	4	3				25
Number of storms (1977–1988)	12	6	2	5	1	1	1	23
Total	30	15	9	9	1	1	1	61

Discussion and conclusion

The results of these analyses show that high water levels were more frequent during the 1977–1988 period compared to the 2 preceding 10-year periods (Fig. 9). Our calculations show that the coastal dunes at the study site were potentially reached by storm waves more than 1.5 times more frequently during the 1977–1988 period than during the 1967–1977 period and 3 times more frequently compared to the 1957–1967 period. Such differences can be partly explained by the longer duration of storm surges during the most recent period. These results suggest a possible increase in storminess during the last two decades of the study period, with more frequent storms and storms lasting longer (Table 1).

Our results are consistent with other studies carried out on storm surge frequency and wind/wave regime in nearby areas. An increase in the magnitude and frequency of storms (WASA 1995) and an increase in wave heights (Bouws et al. 1996) have been documented for the NE Atlantic Ocean and North Sea between 1960 and 1990. Increasing storm surge frequency during the last decades was also reported by Costa (1997) who analysed wind data and water levels at several sites on the French coast of the English Channel. This author found that northwesterly winds associated with North Atlantic depressions occurred more frequently between 1975 and 1990 compared to the rest of the 20th century, resulting in more frequent sea-level set-up along the northwestern coast of France. Although coastline orientation is different at Leffrinckoucke, which is more exposed to winds from the North Sea, it is noteworthy that most storm surges recorded in the present study were also caused by westerly and northwesterly winds (Fig. 7). Our results of variations in storminess and storm surge frequency between 1957 and 1988 are not necessarily indicative of a new trend that may be projected in the future, but may be due to cyclic fluctuations of storm conditions in the North Atlantic, possibly related to the low-frequency cycles of the North Atlantic Oscillation (Sutton & Allen 1997).

This study also suggests that a strong relationship exists between dune front erosion and the frequency of storm surge conditions (Fig. 10). The significant coastal dune erosion between 1977 and 1988 was probably also favoured by the action of high-amplitude waves that occurred during that period (Fig. 8). Such rapid geomorphic response of coastal dunes to low-frequency, high-magnitude, storm surges represents a major concern for the coastal lowlands of Northern France that are threatened by flooding. The risk of coastal erosion and flooding is aggravated along the coast of the southern North Sea where rising sea-level during the 20th century is well documented (Houthuys et al. 1993; Jensen et al. 1993). Although water level observations from different tide gauges along the southern North Sea reflect distinct relative sea-level histories, all tide gauge records show a clear trend of relative sea-level rise estimated at approximately 1.5 mm/yr since the end of the 19th century by Jensen et al. (1993). According to these authors, these changes in sea-level were mainly controlled by thermal eustatic processes.

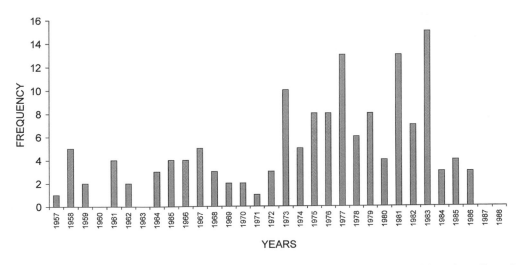

Fig. 9. Annual frequency of water levels higher than 6.5 m above Hydrographic Datum, with onshore-directed deep-water waves (relative to the coastline at Leffrinckoucke).

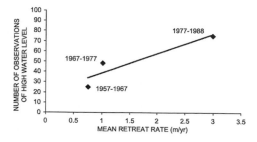

Fig. 10. Relationship between mean retreat rate of eroding coastal dunes at Leffrinckoucke between 1957 and 1988 and frequency of high water levels with wave activity. Values correspond to periods 1957–1967, 1967–1977 and 1977–1988.

Tide gauges and other evidence suggest that world sea-level is presently rising at a rate of about 1 mm/yr (Milliman & Haq 1996; Zerbini et al. 1996), and most models predict that sea-level may continue to rise by several tens of centimetres during the next century as a result of global warming (Wigley & Raper 1992; Warrick et al. 1993; Titus & Narayanan 1995). If the projected estimations of sea-level rise prove to be correct, high water levels will reach coastal dunes more frequently in the future, and more severe coastal dune erosion will probably take place, increasing the risk of flooding of coastal lowlands. Rising sea-level may also result in an increase of the tidal range, a phenomenon that would also favour higher water levels at the coast. Increased tidal range with rising sea level has already occurred in the North Sea during the Holocene transgression due to increasing water depths (Hinton 1995) and more recently during the 20th century along the Belgian (Houthuys et al. 1993) and Dutch coasts (Jensen et al. 1993). In addition, recent models of the possible effects of global warming on the wind regime of the North Sea suggest an increase of 0.1 m of storm wave heights (Bijl 1995). All these projections raise the question of the vulnerability of the coastal lowlands of Northern France to future climatic and environmental changes, and call for the need for continuing precise monitoring programs of coastline changes and water level variations.

The authors would like to thank S. E. Saye who critically reviewed the manuscript and made useful suggestions that contributed to improve the quality of the paper.

References

BAETEMAN, C., DE LANNOY, W., PAEPE, R. & VAN CAUWENBERGHE, C. 1992. Vulnerability of the Belgian coastal lowlands to future sea-level rise. *In*: TOOLEY, M. J. & JELGERSMA, S. (eds) *Impacts of Sea-Level Rise on European Coastal Lowlands*, Blackwell, Oxford, 56–71.

BIJL, A. 1995. *Impact of a wind climate change on storm surge in the Southern Part of the North Sea*. National Institute for Coastal Marine Management, Report RIKZ-95.016, The Hague.

BOUWS, E., JANNINCK, D. & KOMEN, J. 1996. The increasing wave height in the North Atlantic Ocean. *Bulletin of the American Meteorological Society*, **77**, 2275–2277.

BRIQUET, A. 1930. *Le littoral du Nord de la France et son évolution morphologique*. Armand Colin, Orléans.

CERC 1984. *Shore Protection Manual*, vol. 1., U.S. Army Corps of Engineers, Coastal Engineering Research Center, Washington DC.

CLABAUT, J. P., CHAMLEY, H., CORBAU, C. & TESSIER, B. 1996. *Etude de l'érosion du littoral Est-dunkerquois*. Projet, S.I.L.E.-L.N.H. 2ème phase, Rapport Final, Université des Sciences et Technologies de Lille, Lille.

CLIQUE, P. M & LEPETIT, J. M. 1986. *Catalogue sédimentologique des côtes de France. Côtes de la Manche et de la Mer du Nord*. Direction d'Etudes et Recherche d'EDF. Laboratoire National d'Hydraulique.-Laboratoire Central d'Hydraulique de France, Paris.

CORBAU, C. 1995. *Dynamique sédimentaire en milieu macrotidal: exemple du littoral du Nord de la France (Dunkerque)*. Doctoral Thesis, Université des Sciences et Technologies de Lille, Lille.

——, CLABAUT, J. P., TESSIER, B. & CHAMLEY, H. 1993. *Modifications morphosédimentaires histori-ques et récentes du domaine côtier dunkerquois* (France). Comptes Rendus de l'Académie des Sciences, Paris, Série II, **316**, 1573–1580.

COSTA, S. 1997. *Dynamique littorale et risques naturels: l'impact des aménagements, des variations du niveau marin et des modifications climatiques entre la Baie de Seine et la Baie de Somme*. Doctoral Thesis, Universite de Paris I, Paris.

DAVIDSON-ARNOTT, R. G. D. & LAW, M. N. 1996. Measurement and prediction of long-term sediment supply to coastal foredunes. *Journal of Coastal Research*, **12**, 654–663.

DEBOUDT, P. 1997. *Etude de géomorphologie historique des littoraux dunaires du Pas-de-Calais et du nord-est de la Manche*. Doctoral Thesis, Université des Sciences et Technologies de Lille, Lille.

DOBRONIAK, C. & ANTHONY, E. J. 1999. Recent patterns of accretion and erosion in a macrotidal estuary mouth in northern France. *Journal de Recherche Océanographique*, **25**, 69–76.

FAUCHOIS, J. 1998. *L'intérêt de la cartographie à grande échelle dans l'étude géomorphologique du Littoral du Nord-Pas-de-Calais*. Doctoral Thesis, Université des Sciences et Technologies de Lille, Lille.

GUMBEL, E. J. 1958. *Statistics of Extremes*. Columbia University Press, New York.

HASSELMAN, K., ROSS, D. B., MULLER, P. & SELL, W. 1976. A parametric wave prediction model. *Journal of Physical Oceanography*, **6**, 200–228.

HINTON, A. C. 1995. Holocene tides of The Wash, U.K.: the influence of water-depth and coastline shape changes on the record of sea-level change. *Marine Geology*, **124**, 87–111.

HOUTHUYS, R., DE MOOR, G. & SOMME, J. 1993. The shaping of the French-Belgium North Sea coast throughout recent geology and history. *In*: HILLEN, R. & VERHAGEN, H. J. (eds) *Coastlines of the Southern North Sea, Coastal Zone 93*, New York, 27–40.

JENSEN, J., HOFSTEDE, J. L. A., KUNZ, H., DE RONDE J., HEINEN, P. F. & SIEFERT, W. 1993. Long term water level observations and variations. *In*: HILLEN, R. & VERHAGEN, H. J. (eds) *Coastlines of the Southern North Sea, Coastal Zone 93*, New York, 110–130.

KRIEBEL, D. L. & DEAN, R. G. 1985. Beach and dune response to severe storms. *Proceedings of the 19th Conference on Coastal Engineering*, ASCE, 1584–1599.

MILLIMAN, J. D. & HAQ, B. U. (eds) 1996. *Sea-level Rise and Coastal Subsidence: Causes, Consequences, and Strategies*. Coastal Systems and Continental Margins, v. 2 Kluwer Academic Press, Dordrecht.

NORDSTROM, K. F., PSUTY, N. P. & CARTER, R. W. G. (eds) 1990. *Coastal Dunes: Forms and Processes*. John Wiley, Chichester.

PIRAZZOLI, P. A. 1991. Possible defenses against a sea-level rise in the Venice area, Italy. *Journal of Coastal Research*, **7**, 231–248.

POLLARD, M. 1978. *North Sea Surge: The story of the East Coast Floods of 1953*. Dalton, Lavenham.

PSUTY, N. P. 1988. Sediment budget and dune/beach interaction. *Journal of Coastal Research*, Special Issue **3**, 1–4.

PYE, K. 1983. Coastal dunes. *Progress in Physical Geography*, **7**, 531–557.

SHERMAN, J. D. & BAUER, B. O. 1993. Dynamics of beach-dune systems. *Progress in Physical Geography*, **17**, 413–447.

SHOM 1997. *Annuaire des ports de France, Tome 1*. Imprimerie de l'établissement principal du Service Hydrographique et Océanographique de la Marine, Brest.

SHORT, A. D. & HESP, P. A. 1982. Wave, beach and dune interactions in southeast Australia. *Marine Geology*, **48**, 258–284.

SUTTON, R. T. & ALLEN, M. R. 1997. Decadal predictability in Gulf Stream sea surface temperature. *Nature*, **388**, 563–567.

TITUS, J. G. & NARAYANAN, V. K. 1995. *The probability of sea level rise*. US Environmental Protection Agency, Report 230-R-95–008, Washington DC.

VAN DER MEULEN, F., JUNGERIUS, P. D. & VISSER, J. (eds) 1989. *Perspectives in coastal dune management*. SPB Academic, The Hague.

VERGER, F. & GOELDNER, L. 1995. Endiguements littoraux et conservation des marais et vasières dans le nord-ouest de l'Europe. *Cahiers du Conservatoire du Littoral*, **7**, 75–91.

WARRICK, R. A., BARROW, E. M. & WIGLEY, T. M. L. 1993. *Climate and sea level change: observations, projections and implications*. Cambridge University Press, Cambridge.

WASA 1995. T*he WASA project: changing storm and wave climate in the northeast Atlantic and adjacent seas?* 4th International Workshop on Wave Hindcasting and Forecasting, Banff, Canada.

WIGLEY, T. M. L. & RAPER, S. C. 1992. Implications for climate and sea level of revised, I.P.C.C. emissions scenarios. *Nature*, **357**, 293–300.

ZERBINI, S., PLAG, H.-P., BAKER, T. *ET AL.* 1996. Sea level in the Mediterranean: a first step towards separating crustal movements and absolute sea-level variations. *Global and Planetary Change*, **14**, 1–48.

Erosion and recycling of aeolian dunes in a rapidly infilling macrotidal estuary: the Authie, Picardy, northern France

EDWARD J. ANTHONY & CHRISTINE DOBRONIAK

Coastal Geomorphology and Shoreline Management Unit JE 2208, Université du Littoral Côte d'Opale, 32, Avenue Foch, F-62930 Wimereux, France
(e-mail: anthony@univ-littoral.fr)

Abstract: The Authie is a rapidly infilling macrotidal (mean estuary-mouth spring tidal range = 8.5 m) estuary in Picardy, northern France, whose mouth is affected by strong tidal currents and wind waves generated in the English Channel. The estuary cuts across a major sand dune barrier and has been sourced by sand derived from offshore and alongshore, as well as from recycling of the aeolian dunes lining its north bank. Sand released by the severe erosion of these north bank dunes is temporarily stored on the beaches. A small fraction of the sand is back-cycled into the dunes via blowouts. The rest is transported towards the inner estuary where it forms longitudinal aeolian dune ridges and sand sheets that are ultimately recycled into sandy-muddy intertidal flats that develop into salt marshes. The erosion of the dunes lining the north bank of the estuary represents a morphodynamic adjustment to concentration of the tidal flux against this north bank by massive accretion and progradation of a south-bank sand platform. This erosion contributes in giving a funnel-shaped estuary mouth and probably in accommodating the tidal prism following large-scale reclamation of the inner estuary. The estuary-ward recycling of aeolian dune sand enhances overall accretion of the estuary whose ultimate fate is complete silting up in the decades to come.

Mid- to high-latitude coasts commonly show estuaries associated with aeolian dunes. While, in exceptional circumstances of massive aeolian sand supply, this situation may lead to dunes overwhelming small estuaries (e.g. Carter 1990), in other, more common cases, such dunes serve as sand reservoirs for estuarine infill, either through sand inputs by longshore drift following updrift erosion of open-coast dunes, or through inlet reworking of estuary-mouth dunes. These are fairly common processes and have been widely documented in the literature. A third source of dune sand for estuarine infill is where dunes lining the banks of an estuary, and whose formation was entirely extraneous to estuarine development, are eroded and their sand recycled into the intertidal estuarine sink. This is a rarer process. The Authie is one of a few small estuaries in northern France (Fig. 1) that cut across the massive dune barrier bounding this coast. Like the neighbouring Somme and Canche estuaries (Fig. 1), it is a good example of an estuary whose advanced sandy infill has been due to sand supply directly from the sea, from updrift erosion of the coastal dune barrier and from recycling of the dunes lining its northern shore-

line. A significant part of the sand accumulating within the inner estuary is derived from this process. The paper focuses on this mechanism of

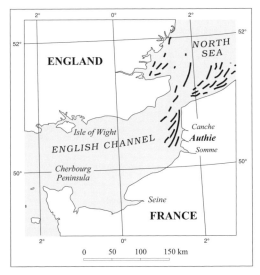

Fig. 1. Location map of the Authie estuary.

From: PYE, K. & ALLEN, J. R. L. (eds). *Coastal and Estuarine Environments: sedimentology, geomorphology and geoarchaeology*. Geological Society, London, Special Publications, **175**, 109–121. 0305-8719/$15.00 © The Geological Society of London 2000.

estuarine infill which appears to reflect morpho-dynamic adjustment to pressure due to massive accretion of the south bank and mouth of the estuary, as well as to changes in tidal flux due to large-scale reclamation of the estuary. Under-standing such patterns of erosion and sedimen-tation and their driving mechanisms is impor-tant to a variety of estuarine management issues such as conservation, shoreline protection, navi-gation, dredging and embanking, especially when decisions need to be made concerning the most appropriate management options or strategies.

Methods

The medium-term (10–100 yrs) evolution of the dune-bound north shoreline of the Authie estuary has been determined from the analysis of a fairly dense time series of aerial photo-graphs edited by the French Institut Géographi-que National, and covering the years 1947, 1961, 1977, 1981, 1987, 1994 and 1997. Short-term topographic surveys of the dune front and the adjacent beach were carried out from November 1997 to June 1998 using a LEICA TC600 Elec-tronic Total Station whose errors are within ±3 mm for distance and ±0.0015° for direction. Surveys were carried out along a total of seven profiles tied to a benchmark of the French National Geodesic Service (IGN 69). Over 100 sediment samples were collected from various locations and analysed for sand content and grain size characteristics using standard sieving procedures. A self-recording S4ADW Interocean electromagnetic current meter with a built-in pressure sensor was deployed at various locations along the dune-bound northern shoreline of the estuary in order to determine current and water level characteristics. The instrument was fixed

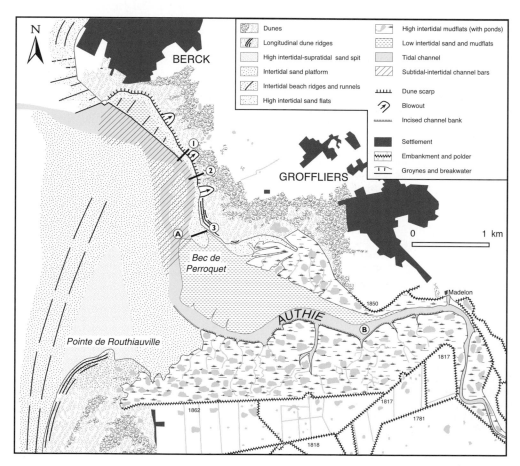

Fig. 2. Morphology of the Authie estuary mouth, and topographic profile locations (circled numbers) and current meter deployment sites (circled letters).

40 cm above the beach surface on a stainless steel frame whose mountings were buried in the sand and was exposed at low tide. It recorded flow velocities and water pressure at a burst duration of 9 minutes every 15 minutes and at a frequency of acquisition of 2 Hz. The recorded data were processed by InterOcean Systems wave and current software packages supplied with the S4ADW current meter. They provided tabular and graphic displays of the Fourier-transformed raw data. Results included burst-averaged mean current velocities and the angles of these steady currents. The locations of three profile and two current meter deployments whose results are presented here are shown in Fig. 2.

Estuary-mouth morphology and sediments

The Authie estuary is located on a low-lying dune coast in the extreme north of France (Fig. 1). Briquet (1930), Dallery (1955) and Verger (1968) provide a useful introduction to the general morphology and historic evolution of the three main estuaries on this coast. The Authie estuary forms the terminus of a relatively short (98 km long), straight coastal river whose valley is cut into a Mesozoic limestone plateau. This plateau is bounded seaward by largely reclaimed lagoonal wetlands impounded by a 1–5 km wide dune barrier cut by the Authie and other estuaries. The Authie is a shallow estuary and shows advanced sandy infill. Nothing is known of this sedimentary infill for lack of boreholes, although the better known, morphologically similar, Canche estuary (Fig. 1) may serve as an example of the expected stratigraphic succession. Unpublished boreholes logs from the Canche show a thick fining-upward sandy fill of marine origin comprising superficial peat layers. This sand body represents much of the transgressive and highstand sediments.

The most significant feature of the Authie estuary is the presence of a massive sand platform (Fig. 2), comprising a spit and its sandy base, that stretches across the shallow estuary mouth, confining the main Authie channel towards the north bank. This platform is part of the dune barrier that bounds the coast of Picardy down to the Somme estuary (Fig. 1). The platform grades seaward into shallow linear coastal sand banks. The north bank of the estuary is similarly bounded by a dune barrier that extends northwards up the coast. On the north bank, the downdrift continuation of the dune barrier lines the inner estuary for 4 km (Fig. 2). The dunes have been urbanized in places, especially with the estuary-ward extension of Berck (Fig. 2), a tourist resort and sanatorium that

developed in the 19th century from a small port founded in the 12th century (Briquet 1930; Dallery 1955).

The Authie estuary exhibits a single 10 to 200 m wide main channel whose present position is controlled by the major estuarine accumulation features, notably the south bank sand platform and the north bank intertidal flats of Bec de Perroquet (Fig. 2). Near the mouth, the channel evolves into a 0.2 to 0.5 km wide feature comprising a deeper narrow subtidal channel flanked by lower intertidal sand flats and sand bars. Channel depths in this deeper section are less than 3 m below mean spring low water. This narrower and deeper channel is quite mobile in this sector but stays confined within the wider intertidal channel zone constrained between the south bank spit platform and the north bank dunes.

Sands throughout the estuary are dominantly very fine to medium ($D_{50} = 0.1–0.5$ mm) quartz grains with shelly debris, except in parts of the main Authie channel where coarse sand and gravelly lag deposits rich in shelly debris are present. The finest sands are associated with the dunes. Sands are generally clean on the estuary-mouth sand platform but are less well sorted and mixed with silt-sized materials on exposed intertidal sand flats on both banks of the estuary. The sediment suite gradually merges inland into mudflats and saltmarshes (Fig. 2).

Estuary-mouth hydrodynamics

The Authie river drains a low-gradient catchment covering an area of 989 km^2. River discharge data are relatively sparse, and cover the years 1983–1985, which showed mean liquid discharges ranging from 10.4 to 14.1 m^3 s^{-1} (IFREMER 1989). The Authie is a macrotidal estuary subject to semi-diurnal tides. The mean spring and mean neap tide ranges at Berck are respectively 8.54 m and 4.89 m (Service Hydrographique et Océanographique de la Marine Tide Data). These ranges increase slightly inside the estuary mouth before decreasing rapidly to around 4 m and 1.8 m respectively, at the small fishing port of Madelon just 7 km up the estuary (Fig. 2). The spring tidal influence goes up to 16 km inland. Because of the important tidal range and the weak river discharge, much of the Authie estuary is largely dominated by tides, while wave-induced longshore drift and storm waves play a major role in sediment supply and redistribution at the mouth. Calculation of the mean tidal prism based on an average estuary-mouth cross sectional area of around 1500 m^2, an average flood current velocity of 0.40 m s^{-1}, and a 3 hr duration of the flood, shows a volume of around $6.5 \times 10^6 \, \mathrm{m}^3$, so that the river discharge is only around 8% of the combined estuarine discharge. This, together with salinity measurements, suggests a well mixed estuary controlled by the tidal current circulation.

Residual circulation patterns identified from miscellaneous sources such as current measurements, monitoring of surface drifters, macroscale bedform orientations and sand transport patterns from engineering structures are depicted in Fig. 3. Monitoring of surface drifters at the mouth of the Authie has shown that the northward propagating progressive flood tidal wave pivots around the massive intertidal to supratidal sand accumulation at the estuary mouth to enter the estuary along the north bank (Bonnefille

& Allen 1967). Current measurements carried out by these workers during this study at the mouth showed that the flood tides were much stronger and of shorter duration than the ebb. Peak flood current velocities of up to $2.5 \, \mathrm{m \, s^{-1}}$ were recorded during a spring tide cycle with a very large range (9.4 m), while peak ebb current velocities were no more than $1.3 \, \mathrm{m \, s^{-1}}$. The results from another set of stations 2 km further inside the estuary along this north bank show less marked flood dominance and lower peak current velocities. Current velocities during both flood and ebb remained high however, peaking respectively at $1.5 \, \mathrm{m \, s^{-1}}$ and $1 \, \mathrm{m \, s^{-1}}$. All the current data show peak velocities at mid-tide stage, thus suggesting a dominantly standing tidal wave.

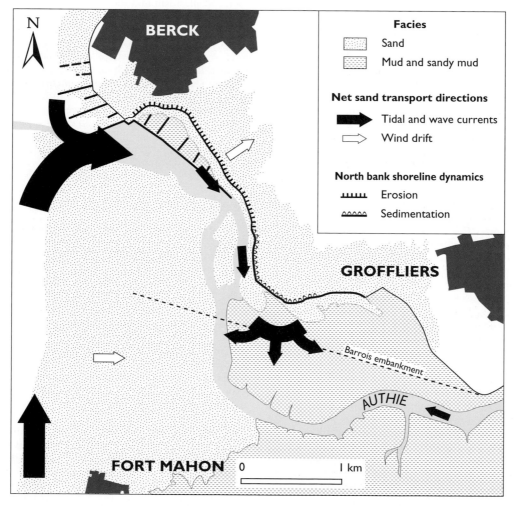

Fig. 3. Sketch of sedimentary facies and schematic residual sand transport patterns in the Authie estuary. Arrow size indicates relative importance of sand transport mechanisms. The Barrois embankment is no longer visible as it had been completely buried by sand by the 1940s.

At the mouth of the estuary, the highest predicted tides have a range of 9.99 m and are expected at the time of the spring and autumn equinoxes. Storm surges associated with low pressure zones in the western English Channel in winter can lead to rises of predicted water levels by over 1 m. The strong waves often associated with such storm surges can have a dramatic impact on sediment transport at the mouth of the Authie. The most important recent storm surge occurred in February, 1990.

The estuary mouth of the Authie is affected by short, dominantly westerly wind waves generated in the English Channel. Wave rider bouy records (Bonnefille & Allen 1967) between the Canche and Authie estuaries (Fig. 1) show that waves offshore are from SW to west. Closer inshore, the wave approach direction, recorded at the south bank approaches to the neighbouring Canche estuary, narrows down to west–SW to west (Despeyroux 1985) as a result of refraction. These records show wave periods ranging from 3 to 6 s and offshore wave heights from 0.25 to 1.5, exceptionally reaching 2 to 3 m during storms. Similar results on this fetch-limited wind wave environment were obtained from the records of several pressure sensors deployed for two weeks on a beach 8 km to the north of Berck (Sipka 1998).

Evidence from the morphology and from beach macro-scale bedforms on the coast adjacent to the estuary shows that the Authie is affected by two opposed sediment drift directions that converge within the estuary mouth (Fig. 3). On this coast, current meter records from the beach 8 km to the north of Berck and from another beach 25 km to the south of the Authie estuary highlight a strong northward longshore current component attributed to combined tidal and wave currents (Dolique 1998; Sipka 1998). Counteractive drift from the north towards the inner estuary is a classic situation that arises from differential wave refraction and energy dissipation at the mouths of estuaries and inlets (Carter 1988). At the mouth of the Authie, this counteractive drift to the south (Fig. 3) is confirmed by preferential entrapment of sand on the northern updrift sides of groynes on the Berck seafront and by the orientation of small dune spits along the inner reaches of the north bank. In addition to wave-driven longshore drift, our observations show that impinging storm waves, most frequent in winter, introduce massive sand packets, in the form of sand bars, within the estuary mouth. These are progressively driven within the Authie channel by the flood-dominant tidal currents, forcing seasonal changes in the position of the subtidal channel

within the estuary. While wave activity is most pronounced at the mouth of the estuary, storm wave effects are felt well within the estuary. Waves from the westerly direction, the one with the biggest fetch and from which come the largest waves, can be particularly effective against the north bank of the estuary. Because of the exposure, waves generated outside the estuary affect the north bank shoreline up to 1.5 km inland.

Offshore of the estuary, results of hydrodynamic studies, including modelling studies of the circulation patterns, show a progressive tidal wave and net flood-dominated coast-parallel flow towards the North Sea (SHOM, 1968), aided by meteorological forcing by the dominant southwesterly winds (Salomon & Breton 1991). Ten kilometers offshore of the Authie estuary, flood tides attain maximum velocities at high water of up to 1.5 m s^{-1}, while maximum ebb tide velocities are around 0.5 to 1 m s^{-1} at low water (SHOM, 1968). Numerical modelling studies of offshore and coastal sediment transport in this area show a net concentration of sand, derived from the English Channel, along a coastal transport corridor between the Somme estuary (Fig. 1), and Belgium, under the influence of the residual flood-dominant tidal and meteorologically forced circulation (Grochowski et al. 1993).

Dune erosion and sand recycling

The advanced infill of the Authie estuary (Fig. 2) reflects both wave- and tide-induced longshore transport towards the estuary mouth and flood-dominant tidal activity along the axis of the estuary (Fig. 3). These processes have been responsible for introducing, within the estuary, sand advected alongshore from the south, and from offshore by storm waves, wave-generated longshore currents and tidal currents. Globally, the estuary shows the wide funnel shape typical of macrotidal estuaries. Historically documented work by Briquet (1930) and Dallery (1955) shows that the spit platform on the south bank of the estuary-mouth has progressively extended northwards over the last three centuries, diverting the Authie channel towards the north bank where it is constrained against the thick dune fields along this bank. Overall, the south bank encroachment has tended to mask the original funnel shape of the estuary, and has been accompanied by northward retreat of the north bank. Dallery (1955) also showed that the width of the estuary mouth between the tip of the south bank spit platform, the Pointe de Routhiauville and Bec de Perroquet (Fig. 2), decreased from an initial 3.5 km in 1671 to 1.8 km in 1953, which is the same width as it is today. The decrease in width over the last centuries suggests that the rate of south bank spit progradation exceeds the rate of erosion and retreat of the north bank dunes. The progressive northward progradation of the south bank sand platform has been matched by reclamation of the backbarrier lagoon. Reclamation started as early

as the 12th century but accelerated in the 18th century (Dallery 1955).

Erosion of the north bank has posed a thorny problem to the resort of Berck and to the dunes and polders within the estuary. Since 1868, various attempts to protect the dune front have, at best, only been variably successful. Works have

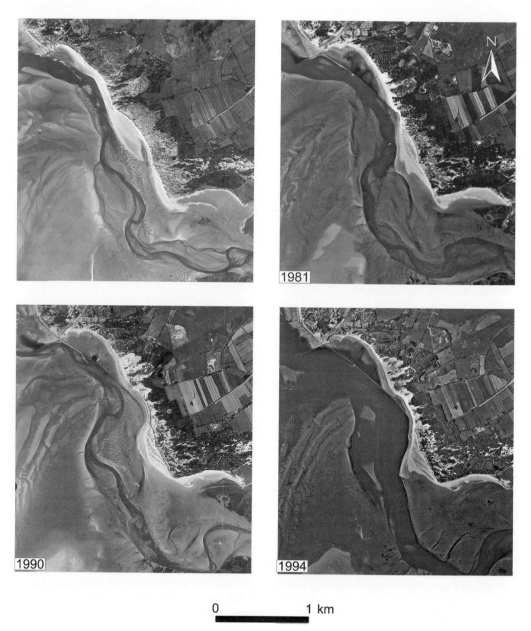

Fig. 4. Aerial photographs showing progressive erosion of north bank dunes and downdrift migration of this erosional sector (courtesy of Institut Géographique National). Much of the eroded sand has been incorporated into mudflats forming the accumulation of Bec de Perroquet.

included an embankment, the Barrois embankment (Fig. 3), constructed in 1868 in the axis of the estuary in order to prevent the Authie channel from attaining the north bank dunes and polders of Groffliers, and several groynes, in the Berck area, associated with a low-tide breakwater (Fig. 2) whose effects will be discussed below. The Barrois embankment had been completely buried by sandy estuarine accretion by the 1940s.

Interpretation of aerial photographs covering the last half century shows that the erosion of the north bank dunes is an important process in feeding inner estuarine accretion. Figure 4 is an assemblage of photographs covering the years 1965 to 1994. They highlight the marked changes that have affected this north bank shoreline. These changes have basically involved updrift reworking and downdrift migration of the zone of dune erosion. The medium term average annual retreat rate since 1947 has been estimated at about $4.5\,\mathrm{m\,a^{-1}}$. This rate is lower than that deduced from maps covering the period 1671 to 1936, which is about $8\,\mathrm{m\,a^{-1}}$, keeping in mind the limitations of accuracy of the older maps. In the early 1960s, the erosion near Berck prompted a defence programme comprising a submerged breakwater, dune front armouring and groynes. The programme was completed in 1989.

Fig. 5. Extract of 1994 aerial photograph depicting sand recycling processes along the north bank of the Authie estuary (courtesy of Institut Géographique National). Arrow 1: Wind blowout. Arrow 2: Erosion and southward transport of sand temporarily stored on the beach, and reworking of longitudinal dune ridges by the Authie as a result of downdrift migration of the erosional zone. Arrow 3. Sand transport towards Bec de Perroquet. Note the mesoscale bedforms (compound dunes) due to large current velocities over the shallow sandy bed.

These works have succeeded in slowing down erosion, and could explain the lower annual retreat rate for the more recent period estimated from the aerial photographs. Comparison of these photographs (Fig. 4) shows that large quantities of sand have been transported alongshore towards the inner estuary. This reworked dune sand forms distinct longitudinal dune ridges and mobile sand sheets, both of which are subsequently reworked by the Authie (Fig. 5). The current data from this sector obtained at spring tide in October, 1998 (Julian days 279–280) show flood-dominant tidal flows well within the nearby Authie channel (Fig. 6a & b). Field observations show however that some sand may be recycled directly back into the eroding dunes (see below).

The short-term beach and dune front profiles obtained during the winter and spring of 1997/98 (Fig. 7) and observations of erosional and depositional patterns confirm the longer term changes while highlighting the role of the estuarine beach in the sand recycling process. Profiles

from a transect in the former erosional zone updrift (Transect 1 Fig. 2) show relative stability compared to the now actively eroding zone further downdrift (Transect 2). The defence structures (Fig. 2) in the former area apparently slow down tidal currents and dissipate waves. Current measurements carried out in April, 1998 (Julian days 104–106) during moderate to large tidal range conditions at the mouth of the estuary (tidal range at Berck = 8.02 to 7.22 m) yielded much lower peak flood and ebb velocities ($<0.75\,\mathrm{m\,s^{-1}}$) than those recorded by Bonnefille & Allen (1967) at a time when the defence programme was just getting underway.

Dune retreat results from hydraulic sapping of the dune toe during high spring tide stages, even under mild weather conditions. Such scarping is encouraged by the steep unconsolidated dune cliff faces (Fig. 8a & b), and dramatically increases at such tidal stages when large waves and surge conditions occur. While being highly variable alongshore, rates of dune cliff retreat are

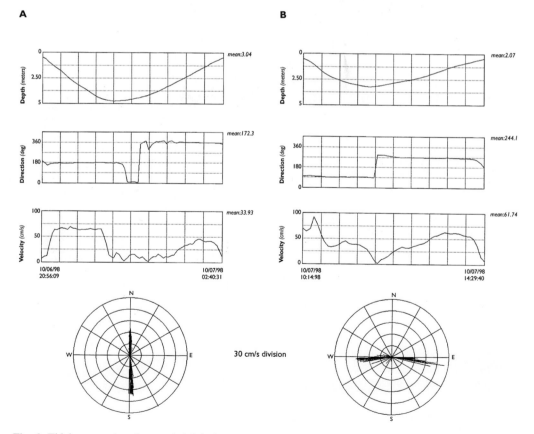

Fig. 6. Tidal current data for two brief deployments near the north bank of the inner estuary (see **Fig. 2** for deployment sites). The flood currents are of shorter duration and have higher peak velocities than the ebb currents.

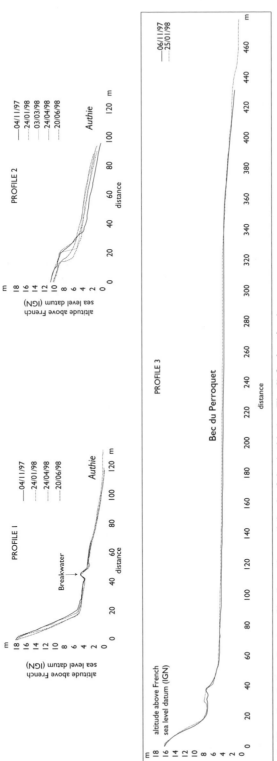

Fig. 7. Three beach-dune front profiles from the north bank of the Authie (see **Fig. 2**) for locations).

Fig. 8. Photographs of dune erosion and sand recycling: (**a**) sand collapse from the steep eroding dune face occurs during high spring tide stages and does not require storm surge conditions; note the wind blowout accumulation in the foreground; (**b**) erosion of longitudinal dune ridges by the Authie to the left; note the downdrift (flood-oriented direction indicated by arrow) migrating channel bedforms in the lower left corner.

quite high, and may attain several meters over periods of several weeks. Profiles from transect 2 clearly show that the beach fronting the dunes in the erosional sector serves as a temporary storage zone for sand released by the dunes. The beach shows substantial short-term accretion, sometimes punctuated by erosion, in sharp contrast to the retreating dune front. Transect 3 shows the generalized accretion characterizing the wide flat downdrift accumulation sector of the Bec de Perroquet (Fig. 7).

In this sector, the depositional sand bodies derived from dune erosion and tidal channel reworking are progressively incorporated into sandy-muddy intertidal deposits. Shallow cores (<0.5 m) in the transitional zones between sandy and muddy sedimentation show interstratification of sand and mud. The incoming sand deposits, interstratified with the fine-grained sediments brought from upstream by the river, provide a shallow substrate for saltmarsh development. The recycled dune sand thus ends up feeding accretion of the tidal flats in the Bec de Perroquet area.

This estuary-ward recycling of the dune sands and downdrift intertidal aggradation are also confirmed by a comparison, realized by the Institut Géographique National of an as yet unpublished 1997 chart of the northern half of the estuary with an earlier 1965 chart from the Service Hydrographique de la Marine (Dobroniak 1998). The 1997 chart shows overall accretion of up to 2.5 m over large parts of the mud flats south of Bec de Perroquet, bringing the surface of these flats close to mean high spring tide level in places. This is permitting widespread colonization by halophytes and the development of saltmarshes.

The longer-term trends from the aerial photographs (Fig. 4) suggest that the sand temporarily stored on the beach is evacuated through net shoreline retreat as the Authie channel moves close inshore (Fig. 5). This is happening under pressure from accretion of the Bec de Perroquet and from generalized accretion of the estuary mouth and the south bank sand platform. On-going work on dune-beach sand exchanges show that there is some sand reinjection into the dunes by onshore winds, especially in zones where blowouts have developed (Figs. 5 & 8a). There is thus some back-cycling of sand towards the dunes. However, our field observations suggest that the sand fraction involved in this landward flux is very small (<10%).

The sand recycled by the Authie forms intertidal bars comprising compound mesoscale bedforms, notably hydraulic dunes. These well developed forms (Figs. 6 & 8b) constantly change and reflect the active sand migration processes related to the large current speeds (Fig. 6) over the shallow channel bed. With such channel changes, sand on the shallow intertidal zones flanking the deeper subtidal channel is also blown onshore by winds towards the dune ridges landward of the Bec de Perroquet. Over the last century, the Authie channel has become narrower and shallower as a result of estuarine accretion. Reports by boat owners show that bed level changes in the lower estuary over the last thirty years exceed 2 m in places, considerably affecting navigation within the estuary.

Discussion

The foregoing sections have shown that the Authie estuary is now in an advanced state of infill. This is an outgrowth of both its very low river discharge compared to its tidal prism, and its location on a sand-rich coast where massive amounts of sand have been reworked from offshore and nearshore banks, essentially by tidal currents, aided by storm waves and longshore drift. The observations presented above show two significant features:

(1) northward sand transport along the coast due to combined tidal currents, wave-induced drift and wind stress, and
(2) large-scale accretion of the entire estuary.

Apart from south bank accretion and extension of this south bank platform towards the north bank, there are suggestions of general net sand transport up the estuary (Fig.3), attested by bedform orientations and the observation of sand bank migration estuary-ward, forcing shifts in the Authie channel at the mouth. This inward sand migration is occurring in response to 'flood-dominant' tidal current asymmetry (Dronkers 1986; Van der Spek 1997). Ebb dominance prevails in the channel up the estuary upstream of Madelon (Fig. 2) where our ongoing current meter recordings highlight stronger ebb currents near the bed, and and our observations of bedforms show downstream orientations. Observations of the net sand transport directions suggest that much of this transport is occurring near the north bank (Fig. 3) where the tidal flux is concentrated as a result of massive accretion of the south bank platform. This accretion has diverted the Authie channel northwards and has brought portions of the platform above mean high tide level.

Erosion of the north bank aeolian dunes and estuary-ward recycling of the eroded dune sand is thus largely a reflection of estuarine morphodynamic adjustment to topographic forcing of the tidal flux towards the north bank. Such erosion is aided by a favourable exposure to storm waves and to wind stress. These combine to enhance a flood-dominant estuarine circulation that transports some of the eroded sand towards the inner estuary. Because short-term rates of sand release from dune cliffs outstrip rates of downdrift evacuation towards the inner estuary, substantial intervening storage occurs on the beaches, enabling back-cycling of sand onto the dunes, especially where blowouts have developed.

These adjustments appear to have been intensified by human intervention. A good example is that of the marked downdrift shift in the erosional zone and intensification of dune erosion along the north bank downdrift of the submerged dyke constructed in the 1960s. No less important but less clear however has been the role of reclamation and embankment. Natural accretion and embankment have been shown to induce changes in tidal prism (Pethick 1996; Van den Berg et al. 1996; Van der Spek 1997). One significant difference between these two processes is that estuarine systems progressively adapt, over time, to subtle changes in accretion, through, for instance, changes in flood or ebb asymmetry or variations in tidal prism. Reclamation is sometimes a dramatic operation that excludes over a very short time large portions of a small estuary from tidal influence. This has been the case of the Authie where such operations were carried out on a significant scale in the 19th century (Fig. 2), leaving the estuary little time to adjust. The average rate of empoldering of the Authie in the 19th century exceeded $3 \, \text{ha} \, \text{a}^{-1}$, a rather aggressive rate for the small size of this estuary. Such emploldering must have forced rapid changes in estuarine morphodynamics. Unfortunately, the historical documents do not shed much light on reclamation practice. Pethick (1996) has suggested that the reclamation of intertidal mudflats and saltmarshes has a similar effect to that of sea level, by resulting in an increase in mean water depth. Adjustment may occur by estuarine lengthening or widening, both of which are ways of accomodating a relative increase in tidal prism. We do not have any data on changes in water level within the Authie estuary or on shifts in tidal limits. As a result, any link of massive reclamation with a relative increase in tidal level due to short term confinement of the tidal prism within a smaller intertidal accommodation space must remain speculative. However, with little time to adjust to reclamation, and assuming no lengthening of the estuary, a decrease in tidal accomodation space would imply an increase in relative tidal prism. Enhanced north bank ero-

sion may be one adjustment to this increase, through both water level increase and concentration of the tidal flux along the deeper north bank. Such retreat and the attendant estuary widening enable the establishment of a more funnel-shaped estuary and better accommodation of any relative increase in tidal prism. This process may also enhance flood-tide asymmetry, except where protective structures lead to accretion and tidal dissipation, resulting in more active sedimentation towards the inner estuary.

In further adjustment to this inner estuarine sedimentation, the Authie channel is progressively getting longer, through both southward progradation of the Bec de Perroquet and northward retreat of the north bank dunes near the estuary mouth. The channel also shows evidence of shallowing over the past decades as a result of sand inputs from outside the estuary, as well as from estuarine retention of sand eroded from the north bank dunes. It is therefore progressively becoming underfit. Its ultimate fate is complete silting up, ending up as a narrow, weakly tidal channel. Other, much smaller estuaries have simply disappeared on this sand-rich coast. The Arche, a small estuary just north of the Authie, reached this evolutionary stage in the 19th century, and has now been completely overwhelmed by dunes.

Conclusions

The Authie is an example of a small temperate estuary undergoing rapid sandy infill. This sand is derived directly from offshore as well as from both coastal dune erosion updrift of the estuary-mouth and from erosion of the dune barrier along the north shoreline of the estuary. Sand is released by the erosion of these north bank dunes during spring high tidal stages. The sand is temporarily stored on the beaches. A small fraction of sand is back-cycled into the dunes via blowouts. The rest is transported towards the inner estuary where it forms longitudinal dune ridges and sand sheets that are ultimately recycled into sandy-muddy intertidal flats that develop into salt marshes. This last sand source is thus particularly important in supply sand to the intertidal zone within the inner estuary. Estuarine dune erosion represents a morphodynamic adjustment to concentration of the asymmetric flood tidal flow against the north bank by massive accretion and progradation of a south-bank sand platform. This erosion contributes in giving a funnel-shaped estuary mouth and probably in accommodating the important tidal prism following large-scale reclamation of the inner estuary in the 19th century. The estuary-ward recycling of dune sand enhances overall accretion of the estuary which is characterized by low river discharge relative to the tidal prism. The ultimate fate of the Authie estuary will be complete silting up in the decades to come.

References

BONNEFILLE, R. & ALLEN, H. 1967. *Etude de la Baie d'Authie et des moyens de défense contre la mer*. Report, Laboratoire National d'Hydraulique, Electricite de France, Chatou.

BRIQUET, A. 1930. *Le littoral du Nord de la France et son évolution morphologique*. Thèse de Doctorat ès Sciences, Université d'Orléans.

CARTER, R. W. G. 1988. *Coastal environments*. Academic Press, London.

——1990. The geomorphology of coastal dunes in Ireland. *Catena Supplement*, **18**, 31–40.

DALLERY, F. 1955. *Les rivages de la Somme, autrefois, aujourd'hui et demain*. Mémoires de la Société d'Emulation Historique et Littéraire d'Abbeville, Editions A. & J. Picard et Cie, Paris.

DESPEYROUX, Y. 1985. *Etude hydrosédimentaire de l'estuaire de la Canche*. Thèse de Doctorat, Université de Lille I.

DOBRONIAK, C. 1998. *L'estuaire de l'Authie: dynamiques naturelles et anthropiques*. Report, Conservatoire de l'Espace Littoral et des Rivages Lacustres, Observatoire de l'Environnement Littoral et Marin Manche et Sud Mer du Nord, Wimereux.

DOLIQUE, F. 1998. *Dynamique morphosédimentaire et aménagements induits du littoral picard au Sud de la Baie de Somme*. Thèse de Doctorat, Université du Littoral Côte d'Opale, Dunkirk.

DRONKERS, J. 1986. Tidal asymmetry and estuarine morphology. *Netherlands Journal of Sea Research*, **20**, 117–131.

GROCHOWSKI, N. T. L., COLLINS, M. B., BOXALL, S. R. & SALOMON, J. C. 1993. Sediment transport predictions for the English Channel, using numerical models. *Journal of the Geological Society, London*, **150**, 683–695.

IFREMER 1989. *Le littoral de la Région Nord-Pas de Calais. Apports à la Mer*. IFREMER Scientific and Technical Report 15, Brest.

PETHICK, J. S. 1996. The geomorphology of mudflats. *In*: NORDSTROM, K. F. & ROMAN, C. T. (eds) *Estuarine Shores: Evolution, Environments and Human Alterations*, Wiley & Sons, Chichester, 185–211.

SALOMON, J. C. & BRETON, M. 1991. Courants résiduels de marée dans la Manche. *Oceanologica Acta*, **11**, 47–53.

SHOM 1968. *Les courants de marée dans la mer de la Manche et sur les côtes françaises de l'Atlantique*. Service Hydrographique Océanographique et de la Marine, 550, Paris.

SIPKA, V. 1998. *Les plages macrotidales du Nord-Pas de Calais: contexte environnemental et caractérisation morphodynamique*. Thèse de Doctorat, Université du Littoral Côte d'Opale, Dunkirk.

VAN DER SPEK, A. J. F. 1997. Tidal asymmetry and long-term evolution of Holocene tidal basins in The Netherlands: simulation of palaeo-tides in the Schelde estuary. *Marine Geology*, **141**, 71–90.

VAN DEN BERG, J. H., JEUKEN, C. J. L. & VAN DER SPEK, A. J. F. 1996. Hydraulic processes affecting the morphology and evolution of the Westerschelde estuary. *In*: NORDSTROM, K. F. & ROMAN, C. T. (eds) *Estuarine Shores: Evolution, Environments and Human Alterations*, Wiley & Sons, Chichester, 157–184.

VERGER, F. 1968. *Marais et waddens du littoral français*. Caen, Paradigme.

Lake gravel beach sedimentological variability, Milarrochy Bay, Loch Lomond, Scotland

LYDIA R. PIERCE

*Surface Processes and Modern Environments Research Group, Department of Geology,
Royal Holloway, University of London, Egham, Surrey TW20 0EX, UK
(e-mail: l.pierce@gl.rhul.ac.uk)*

Abstract: The nature and environmental significance of variations in sedimentological parameters of a restricted-fetch lake coastal system (Milarrochy, Loch Lomond) are described in the context of climate change. Grain size characteristics of the beach, streams, cliffs and nearshore/offshore sedimentary environments are distinct, with variability being related to sediment supply, beach altitude and process conditions. Beach grain sizes range from silt to cobble, and are predominantly rounded discs and blades. There is an overall trend of offshore fining with increasing depth, beyond the mixed surf zone and clear limit of coarse sediment (coarser than -1 phi), resulting from dominant shore-normal process trends. Seasonal trends of water level fluctuation, sediment discharge and transfer from river to beach are important controls on local scale variability. The broader significance is that local physiography, sediment characteristics and supply strongly influence beach sedimentology and morphological response, even in the context of larger scale climate change. The record of sedimentological variability detailed here is significant for beach management projects and a better understanding of lake sedimentary facies within the Quaternary.

The influence of changing environmental conditions on beach behaviour is of increasing significance in the light of changing water levels, increased storminess and variable coastal land-use. Within low energy systems, such as lakes, lagoons, and some estuaries, scales and types of response to energy processes are different from the open coast (e.g. Sly 1994; Gracia Prieto 1995; Jackson 1995; Perillo 1995; Seymour 1997). These responses are distinctive in terms of morphological and sedimentological change leading to shore erosion and sediment redistribution within relatively short time periods (Makaske & Augustinus 1998). Within the UK, lake shore zones in particular are under ever increasing pressure from natural environmental change as well as multiple land-uses resulting in extensive alteration of beach geomorphology and sedimentology. Relatively little is known of low-energy, sediment-poor, gravel beach morphology, dynamic behaviour and sedimentary characteristics. Recent studies have documented gravel beach behaviour in high energy marine settings (e.g. Carter & Orford 1984; Orford 1987; Forbes *et al.* 1995), and large lakes such as the USA/Canadian Great Lakes (e.g. Hands 1979, 1983, Davidson-Arnott, 1989), but low energy regimes are frequently neglected.

The purpose of this paper is to discuss the significance of the changes in sedimentological characteristics of a low-energy, lake gravel beach at Loch Lomond, Scotland, at the meso-time-scale of 1 year, set within the context of longer term coastal change. The findings have wider implications for the understanding of low-energy beach systems and coastal zone management in lakes, coastal lagoons, estuaries and restricted-fetch coastal environments.

Context and study area

Increased westerly air circulation and higher precipitation levels over Scotland in recent decades (Black 1995; Houghton *et al.* 1996), have led to higher water levels, flooding, increased wave activity and shore erosion in many Scottish lochs, including Loch Lomond, (Pender *et al.* 1993). Loch Lomond (Fig. 1) is Britain's largest lake, being 33 km long, up to 7 km wide and a maximum of 192 m deep. The climate is cool and wet, with a mean annual precipitation greater than 1500 mm, increasing to over 2000 mm per annum in the northern catchment. Mean temperature in January is 4°C and in July is 14°C (Meteorological Office 1989). Between 1969 and 1988, precipitation increased by over 30%,

From: PYE, K. & ALLEN, J. R. L. (eds). *Coastal and Estuarine Environments: sedimentology, geomorphology and geoarchaeology*. Geological Society, London, Special Publications, **175**, 123–138. 0305-8719/00/$15.00 © The Geological Society of London 2000.

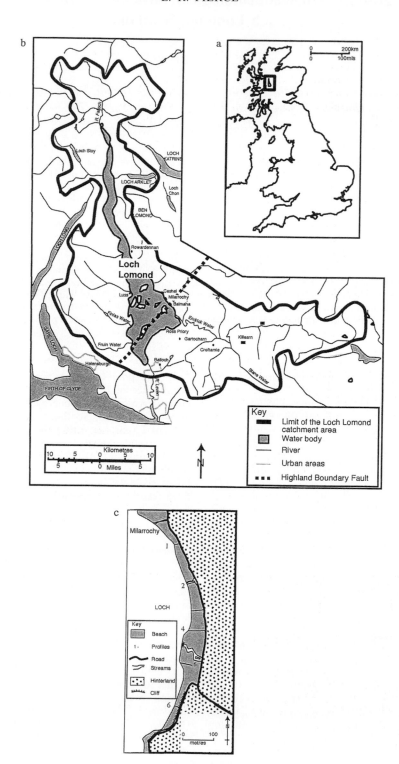

Fig. 1. Location map of Milarrochy Bay and Loch Lomond, Scotland.

a trend which has largely continued. River inflow records from the River Endrick (1969–1990) show a 36% (±11%) increase (Curran & Poodle 1994) leading to increased water levels. Contemporary land-use, economic and recreational pressures mean that even small fluctuations in lake level can have significant consequences for human activity (Fig. 2).

Loch Lomond drains an upland (>900 m OD) catchment which has been extensively modified by ice during the Quaternary. The Loch occupies an overdeepened basin, trending N–S, which traverses the structural geology of the Highland Boundary Fault (Pierce 1999). The Loch shore comprises numerous small bays enclosed by headlands with gravel or mixed sand and gravel beaches and some marshland in the south. Sediment reworked by ice during the Pleistocene, particularly during the Loch Lomond Stadial, is the predominant source of beach material.

Milarrochy (NS 411924; Fig. 1b & c) has been identified as a particularly significant area of shore erosion, flooding and environmental degradation (e.g. Tivy 1980; Pender 1991). No quantification of change had been made prior to the study reported here, although, map evidence shows a general trend of shore retreat. Milarrochy beach is 1.2 km long and is located on the SE shore of the Loch (Fig. 1c). It is a steep (6 to 12°), narrow, gravel beach, constrained at the landward edge by a road and to the north and south by headlands formed in rocks of Dalradian age. Glaciogenic sediments are exposed as small cliffs (maximum height 2.0 m) behind the southern end of the beach. Three steep gravel bedded streams (slope gradient ≃0.11) entering the Loch at Milarrochy provide the primary sediment supply for the beach. Deltas occur at the stream exits.

The beach is exposed to waves from the NW, west and SW with the longest fetches from the SW (7.5 km). The nearshore bathymetry shows generally shore-parallel isobaths with a relatively steep gradient away from the water's edge. Deep water (25 m) is found offshore to the south of the bay, beyond the line of the headlands. Diving surveys identified a bathymetric trough approximately 40 m offshore in the northern part of the bay. The nearshore throughout the Loch is characterized by deep water and incident waves become modified by shallow water bottom effects only very close to the shore limiting wave refraction.

Wave recording during 1994 (Pierce 1997; Pierce in press) identified a wave regime of small amplitude, steep, high frequency waves interspersed with periods of calm. Mean significant wave height (Hs) was 0.08 m (excluding calms) and mean frequency (Tc) was 0.92 seconds. Modal frequency throughout the year was between 1 and 2 seconds, which is high compared to the open coast. The highest wave heights recorded (peak to trough) were 0.64 m (Hs). Wind recording identified highly variable wind velocities and directions. Wind recordings over the entire year showed the modal wind direction as westerly (42%) followed by northeasterly (19%). Dominant wind-wave activity coincided with the longest fetches affecting the SE Loch shore, in particular Milarrochy.

Sediment sampling and survey methods

The grain size characteristics of the beach, streams, cliffs and nearshore/offshore sedimentary environments were investigated to identify sediment supply and transfer through the beach to the nearshore and offshore.

Beach samples were systematically collected from the upper beach, the beach face (mid beach) and the Loch edge along 6 profiles normal to the shore, at a mean distance of 87 m apart. Profile locations were chosen to represent the morphological characteristics of the adjacent beach area and at sites where a Temporary Bench Mark could be set up with lasting back markers. At each sampling point on the profile, samples were collected from an area of one square metre. The top layer of sediment, determined by the vertical dimension of the largest particle in the sampling area, was collected for each surface sample (Kellerhals & Bray 1971). Sub-surface samples were also taken to a maximum depth of 0.2 m over the same square metre as the surface samples. Theoretically, the largest clast in the sample should be less than 0.1% of the total mass of the sample (Gale & Hoare 1981), although for very coarse material this limitation was relaxed to 1%.

Fig. 2. High loch levels at Balmaha, Loch Lomond, during Winter 1990/91 (photo: T. Darke).

Nearshore and offshore sediments were sampled using an Ekman grab sampler, giving bulk samples, and an echo-sounder (Fuso-10) was used to record depth (Buller & McManus 1979). A shore based Total Station (Leica T1010) was used to monitor boat location, with a tracking reflective prism mounted on the boat.

Investigation of sediment supply from the 3 streams at the beach focused on bedload, (Gomez & Church 1989; Harvey 1991), defined as 'fluid transported sediment which moves along or in close proximity to the bed of the flow,' Goudie et al. (1990). Bedload generally constitutes the coarser fraction of fluvial sediment which was needed for calculation of supply to the gravel beach sediment budget. At each stream, on the reaches adjacent to the beach, 6 cross sections were set up. From each of these 100 random river-bed particles were sampled using procedures detailed by Kellerhals & Bray (1971) and Church et al. (1987). The majority of these samples were analysed in the field using 0.5ϕ size templates, 3ϕ (8 mm) to -8.5ϕ (362 mm) as described by Wolman (1954), those sampled from nearest the beach were also weighed.

Cliff samples were taken from the exposed cliff face at profile 6 and at 2 additional sites, two metres either side of profile 6 at heights of 0.5, 1 and 1.5 m above the back beach altitude. Templates of 0.5ϕ were used in the field to record the coarsest particle sizes.

Various techniques were used for particle size analysis to encompass the wide variation of size fractions and available equipment: dry-sieving; hydrometry and laser granulometry (Goudie et al. 1990; Agrawal et al. 1991). Given this variation, comparative analysis and interpretations were made with caution (e.g. Sytvitski 1991; Nathier Dufuour et al. 1993). For example in experiments by Shi (1995), dry-sieving gave finer values than laser granulometry, but the latter produced significant fine tails. Shi found the difference to be consistent and therefore could be mathematically modelled. In this research however, the dominant beach sediment is gravel and therefore particle size analysis was predominantly by dry-sieving.

The coarse sediment samples were dried and split where necessary and dry-sieved at 0.5ϕ intervals from -5.0ϕ (32 mm) to 4.0ϕ (0.063 mm) using a mechanical shaker. Most fine particle samples were analysed by hydrometry, using the dispersant sodium hexa-metaphosphate, and the fine cliff samples by laser granulometry. From these data phi median, mean, sorting and skewness was determined. The parameters and formulae after Folk & Ward (1957), were used for convenience of calculation, and comparison of descriptive parameters (Davis & Erlich 1970; Warren 1974; Pye 1982; Agrawal 1991). Percentage values e.g. D16 and D84, calculated from the cumulative frequency graphs, were also used to describe sediment populations. For example, D84 is the grain size diameter of the 84th percentile. This means 84% of the sample is finer than this value on the graph.

Particle shape was also investigated as an aid to identification of sediment provenance, and to help reconstruct palaeo-environments. Comparisons were made of the less than -1ϕ fraction from the mid-beach surface samples from profiles 1, 3 and 6. The three principle axes of each particle (long (a), intermediate (b) and short (c), defined at $90°$ to each other) were measured and plotted as a graph comparing the b/a axis with the c/b axis ratio (after Zingg 1935). The system divides particle shape into four descriptive categories based on axial ratios being greater or less than 0.667. These are: Bladed, where both axial ratios are less than 0.667; Tabular or Discoid, for which the b/a ration is greater than 0.667; Equant or Spherical where both axial ratios are greater than 0.667 and Prolate or Roller, where the c/b ratio is greater than 0.667. For this classification, the a b, and c axes of 50 particles from a selection of samples used in the sieving and template size analysis were used.

The second descriptor of particle shape was a two-dimensional visual comparator of roundness described by Powers (1953). Classes of 'very angular', 'angular', 'sub-angular', 'sub-rounded', 'rounded' and 'well rounded', corresponding to Wadell's grain roundness (1933) were used. The degree of particle roundness infers the degree of abrasion, which is an indicator of palaeo-environmental conditions. For example, heavily rounded clasts are more likely to have been subject to high energy conditions such as wave action.

To monitor sub-aerial beach sedimentological variation, both temporally and spatially, a repeatable systematic point sampling strategy was used to identify the morphological and sedimentological changes that occurred simultaneously. A technique of photo-sieving, modified from Ibbeken & Schleyer (1986), using black and white vertical photographs, recorded surface sub-aerial beach sediment characteristics. This gave a rapid, permanent and non-extractive and widely applicable method, suitable for large datasets. Field and laboratory visual analysis identified frequently occurring and recognizable 'sedimentological types' (Fig. 3). This classification began with a visual comparator of these types, which was extended quantitatively. To do this, on each photograph, axes of uniform length were drawn parallel and perpendicular to the water's edge at

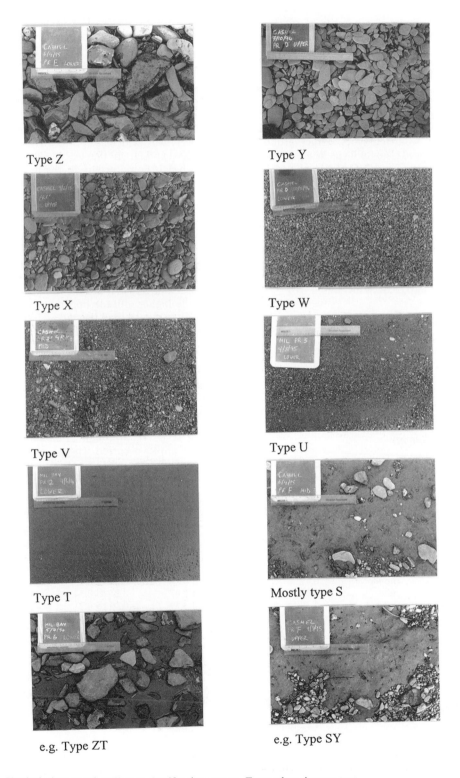

Type Z

Type Y

Type X

Type W

Type V

Type U

Type T

Mostly type S

e.g. Type ZT

e.g. Type SY

Fig. 3. Vertical photograph sediment classification system. For explanation see text.

a random point. The number of grains along each axis was counted and recorded and an average taken. Where 2 or more sediment types were visible these were considered separately. Where between 1 and 10 clasts occurred on the 30 cm long axis, the type was designated Z; where between 11 and 20 clasts occurred the Type was designated Y and 21–30 clasts designated Type X. For the smaller sediment sizes and less frequently occurring types, larger group sizes were used e.g. 31–60 for Type W 61–80 for Type V 81–100 for Type U. Type T comprised sand, Type S clays and silt and further types were mixed (Fig. 3). Any distortion associated with the angle of the beach face and camera position was obvious and gave only a small error (less than 1 mm at the corners). The photographic record provided valuable information which could be compared with antecedent wave conditions, cliff failure and fluvial discharge estimates (cf. Parker & Sutherland 1990).

Results

A summary of grain size parameters of the beach, streams, river and nearshore/offshore environments at Milarrochy is given in Table 1 and typical examples of grain size frequency histograms are shown in Fig. 4.

Beach sediments

The beach sediments showed considerable variability ranging from sands to cobbles. The median surface size varied both alongshore and cross-beach (Fig. 5a). The upper beach sediments showed a general trend of southwards coarsening, suggesting a directional drift at higher water levels (Komar 1987). The mid and lower beach results showed no consistent alongshore trends in median size. Sub-surface sediments tended to be finer or mirror the surface characteristics. Cross-beach coarsening (upper to lower) was evident at profiles 1 and 6 which are less exposed in the lee of the headlands. Cross-beach fining occurs in the most exposed areas of beach (profiles 2 and 3). Profile 5 did not show a pattern but this may have been affected by artificial sources of sediment supplied to this area (discussed later).

Sorting was moderate and reasonably uniform on the upper beach (Fig. 5b). The mid beach ranged from poorly sorted in the northern profiles (profiles 1, 2) and by the stream (profile 5) to good, mid way between the headlands. In general, the higher altitude upper beach sediments were better sorted than the mid and lower beach.

Skewness (Fig. 5c) at Milarrochy showed considerable variability both alongshore and cross-shore. Interpretation was not straightforward as fluvially derived sediment tended to complicate pre-existing trends, making statistical description difficult (Smith *et al.* 1997). Individual samples showed considerable variability in their grain size distributions. Most samples were unimodal (Fig. 4), although bi-modal and poly-modal samples occurred. These complex samples represented fluvially transported sediment from different sources, such as from bank falls, or

Table 1. *Ranges of summary statistics of grain size parameters in sub-aerial beach, cliff, river and nearshore/offshore environments at Milarrochy Bay, Loch Lomond*

Sedimentary environment	Sample location	Mean phi range	Sorting phi range	Skewness phi range	Median phi range
Beach surface ($n = 18$)	upper	0.49 to 5.13	0.44 to 0.8	−0.26 to 0.22	−5.27 to 0.57
	mid	−5.66 to −1.98	0.45 to 2.07	−0.24 to 0.54	−5.7 to −1.47
	lower	−6.39 to −0.66	0.32 to 2.39	−0.19 to 0.2	−6.55 to −0.22
Beach sub-surface ($n = 18$)	upper	−2.47 to 0.89	0.94 to 2.04	−0.67 to 0.5	−2.22 to 1.41
	mid	−3.45 to −0.36	0.63 to 2.53	−0.45 to 0.25	−3.75 to 2.6
	lower	−2.85 to 0.5	1.11 to 2.73	−0.35 to 0.55	−4.29 to 1.05
Cliff ($n = 6$)	matrix	5.22 to 5.49	1.8 to 2.6	0.05 to 0.39	3.74 to 3.94
	clasts	−1.75 to −9.0	–	–	−6.5 to −6.75
Streams ($n = 25$)	bedload ($< −1\phi$)	−5.63 to −5.77	0.08 to 1.25	−0.04 to −0.37	−5.64 to −5.95
Nearshore/ Offshore ($n = 18$)		1.52 to 6.39	0.08 to 1.9	−0.19 to 0.1	0.32 to 6.47

(Statistical measures after Folk and Ward 1957).
Total mean grain size values for each environment are not included because of the wide ranges of grain sizes.

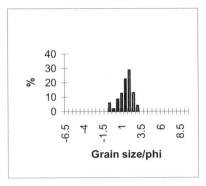

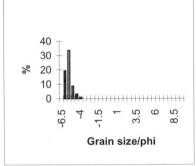

a) Beach sub-surface sediment, profile 1, mid beach

b) Beach surface sediment, profile 6, mid beach

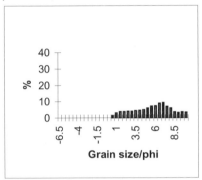

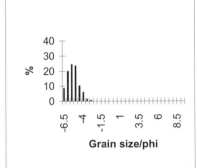

c) Cliff sediment (at profile 6)

d) Stream bedload (close to profile 5)

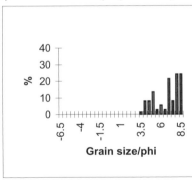

e) Offshore sediment S6

Fig. 4. Grain size frequency histograms of typical sediment samples from (**a**) sub-surface beach environment, (**b**) surface beach environment, (**c**) cliff matrix (**d**) stream bedload, and (**e**) offshore bulk sediment. NB Figs 4a, b & d show % mass in class sizes (from dry-sieving analysis and hydrometry) and Figs 4c & e show % volume (from laser granulometry).

upland glacial diamicts. Overall, skewness was towards the coarser grain sizes in most samples, with the exception of Profile 1 where medium grained ($D84 = -0.36\phi$) were found on the upper beach. Coarse skewness (0.11) may indi-cate winnowing away of finer sediment in the more exposed profiles. The anomaly of the upper beach sands at Profile 1 may result from depo-sition of near/offshore sands at exceptionally high water levels.

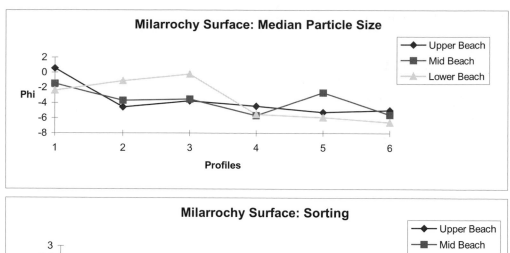

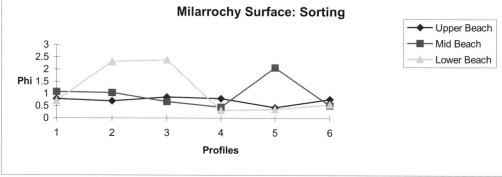

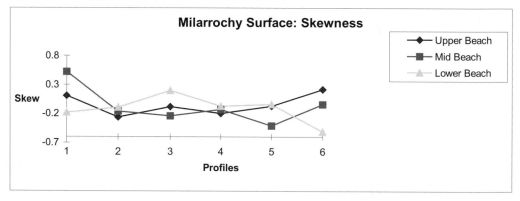

Fig. 5. Summary of Milarrochy beach surface median particle size, sorting and skewness.

The findings from the particle shape analysis are presented in a series of Zingg plots and Powers Roundness tables (Fig. 6). Profiles 1, 3 and 6 showed consisted of predominantly discs and blades, although the spread of b/a to c/b ratios at profile 6 is more centralized, showing particle forms closer to the spherical and roller shapes. This could be attributable to the higher percentage of more resistant quartz clasts occurring in this location. Between 48 and 52% were rounded, and 15–24% sub-rounded. Overall there were approximately equal proportions of discs and blades, but the dominant shape is rounded. These results are consistent with marine beach sediments (Bluck 1967)

Pebble imbriccation was frequently observed on the beach, with long axes normal to the shore suggesting shore-normal dominant fluid flow (Allen 1982) consistent with dominant on-shore wave trends. Again, trends were similar to those described by Bluck (1967) on marine beaches. Imbriccation was also observed in the stream-channels, normal to flow direction (cf. Johansson 1976).

a) Zingg shape diagrams from beach surface samples

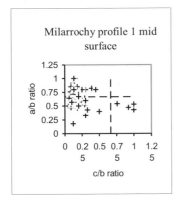

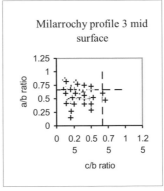

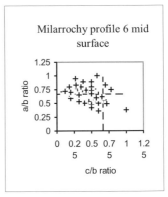

b) Powers' Roundness results: VA = very angular; A = angular; SA = sub-angular;
Sr = sub-rounded; R = rounded; WR = well rounded

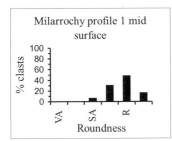

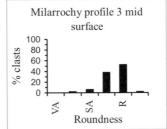

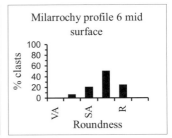

Fig. 6. Particle shape and roundness, Milarrochy, Loch Lomond; using classifications by (**a**) Zingg 1935 and (**b**) Powers 1935. For further explanation, see text.

The sub-aqueous beach was characterized by very mixed sediment sizes (Fig. 7), with an abrupt limit to the coarse sediment (-1ϕ) at approximately 2.5 m depth. This transition can be said to mark the limit of the high energy regime (e.g. Hakanson 1977; Sly 1994). Since sediment size is broadly associated with energy available for entrainment and transport (e.g. Komar 1987), the limit of coarse sediment is associated with a decrease in hydraulic energy available for sediment transport.

Beach sediment temporal and spatial sedimentological change

The vertical photographs taken of the sub-aerial beach showed considerable grain size variation with some complex depositional patterns. Types W X, Y and Z and mixed sediment types occured most frequently (Table 2). Field observation and photographic analysis showed the upper beach (at higher altitudes) to be the most stable. The mid beach results showed more complex sedimentation patterns with several sediment 'types' in one location, frequently occurring in 'sediment stripes' parallel to the water's edge extending for up to several hundred metres. These comprised of gravel ridges with fining down-slope on either side of the ridge crest. The location and altitude on the beach of these forms reflected changing water levels and wave breaking position. Thus they would be preserved for time periods of hours to days/weeks depending on precipitation and water levels. The lower beach close to the stream exits showed the coarsest sediments (Type Z) which appear to be less mobile, with infills of different sediment grades. The section of beach which exhibited the most variation in mixed sediment types occurred

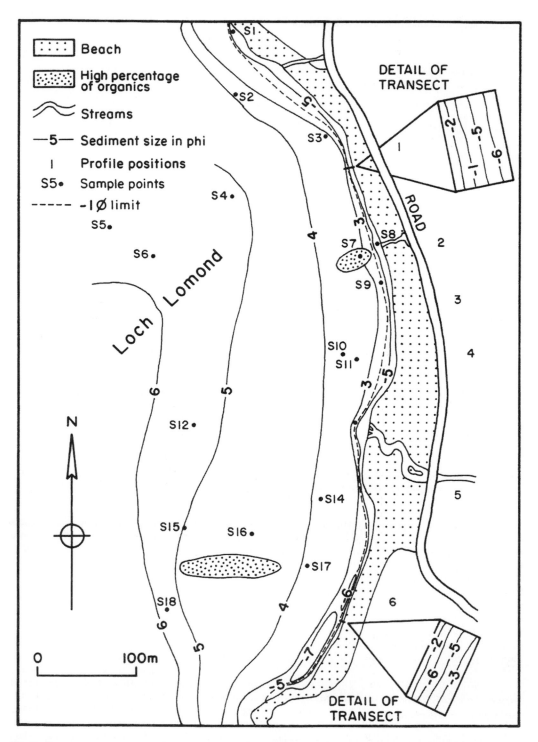

Fig. 7. Summary contour map of nearshore and offshore mean particle sizes, Milarrochy, Loch Lomond. Numbered samples were taken on 07/09/94. Eight offshore surveys were carried out between 1993 and 1996.

Table 2. *Sub-aerial beach surface sediment types, Milarrochy, Loch Lomond. (Refer to Fig. 3 for photograph type classification)*

Profile	1994	Jan	Feb	Mar	Apr	May	Jun	Jul	Aug	Sep	Oct	Nov	Dec
1	upper	W		WT	X	XT	W	W	WT	W	W	W	W
	mid	W		XT	W	W	U	V	W	W	W	XT	W
	lower	Z		ZT	U	VW	ZT	Y	WT	VY	Y	WV	X
2	upper	X		X	X	X	X	X	X	X	X	X	X
	mid	X		X	X	UZT	UZT	UZT	W	X	W	X	W
	lower	U		ZT	U	U	T	WT	ZT	YT	Y	UT	Y
3	upper	Y		Y	Y	Y	Y	Y	Y	Y	Y	Y	Y
	mid	V		V	T	W	W	W	W	X	W	W	W
	lower	T		TZ	T	Y	SZ	YZ	W	WV	YW	TV	Z
4	upper	Y		Y	Y	Y	Y	Y	Y	Y	Y	Y	Y
	mid	Y		WT	W	Y	Y	X	Y	Y	X	Y	Y
	lower	Y		ZT	U	Y	Z	Y	Y	Y	Y	Y	Y
5	upper	Y		Y	Y	Y	Y	Y	Y	Y	Y	Y	X
	mid	Z		Z	U	ZUS	Z	Y	Y	Y	Z	Y	Y
	lower	Z		Z	Z	Z	Z	Z	Z	Z	Z	ZT	Z
6	upper	YS		W	X	Y	Y	Y	Z	Y	Y	Y	Y
	mid	Y		Y	Y	ZS	ZS	Z	Z	YS	ZS	Z	Y
	lower	Z		Z	Y	ZT	ZT	T	TS	ZT	ZT	T	YT

adjacent to profile 6. This variation was due to the supply of fines from the cliff (e.g. upper beach D84 = −6.06ϕ).

When the sedimentological trends were compared with other variables such as wave heights, storm incidence, profile type and sediment supply volumes there were no clear controls on sedimentological patterns at the monthly scale (Pierce 1997).

Beach armouring occurred where coarse sediment provided a relatively immobile surface for extended periods of time (>2 years). Parker & Sutherland (1990) have described mobile and static armour layers of bedload in fluvial environments. Whilst there is no precedent for beach armouring, the temporal series photographs obtained in the present study suggested sedimentary stability, because of static armour in some areas of the beach.

Nearshore/Offshore sediments

Lake-ward of the mixed 'surf zone' and the coarse sediment limit (−1ϕ; Fig. 7), the nearshore and offshore sediments were fine grained (range = −0.33 to 7.54ϕ) a trend generally increasing with depth. Overall, individual samples were less well sorted than many of the beach sediment samples, but this may be a function of sampling in the nearshore/offshore zone. Skewness ranged from −0.81 to 0.65, reflecting significant tails of both coarse and fine particles.

Deposits of organic material (primarily leaf litter from the deciduous woodlands fringing the Loch) were located in the nearshore/offshore zone. Organics were mostly deposited close to stream exits beyond the deltas.

Fluvial sediments

Sampling of fluvial sediments focused on the coarse fraction (for calculation of the gravel beach sediment budget). Samples of the coarse fraction showed median particle size range of −5.05 to −5.64ϕ, and were moderately to poorly sorted (Fig. 4c). Most bedload samples were unimodal and skewed towards the coarse fraction. Winnowing of finer particles from the streambed leaves a tail of coarser grains. Additional bulk sampling identified bi-modal, tri-modal and polymodal particle size distributions with a dominance of very coarse particles.

Cliff sediments

The cliff sediments comprised a fine matrix which included sub-rounded and sub-angular clasts of cobble to boulder size, the latter constituting approximately 7–10% of the exposed cliff face. Analyses of the matrix showed uni-modal particle size distribution with mean particle size of 5.49ϕ and modal particle size of 6.4ϕ. Sorting was very poor, indicating little selection has taken place during transport or deposition and vice versa. Skewness was near-symmetrical and these sediments were interpreted as tills (Rose 1981; Pierce 1999)

Environmental significance of sedimentological parameters

Although the sedimentological signature of this lake beach (and others, e.g. Norrman 1964; Davidson-Arnott 1989) is complicated, trends can be interpreted in the light of water level change, wave activity, sediment supply and human influence.

Water levels and waves

Water levels have a critical influence on beach sedimentology, are a primary control on the effects of wave activity, and are an underlying determinant of sediment entrainment and transport. Sediment sorting is better on the higher altitude areas of beach. These areas of beach are less frequently affected by water level and wave action, but when they are it tends to be on occasions of winter storms, therefore producing significant changes (Pender et al. 1993; Pierce 1996). Landward roll-over of gravel occurred each winter between 1992 and 1997 (the study period) as the beach responded to higher water levels and increased storm frequency. Under lower energy conditions, the frequently occurring beach-parallel 'stripes' of graded sediment indicate wave breaking deposition, at the elevation of former water levels. Grain size sorting on the ridge slopes was influenced by sediment availability and wave energy affecting sediment transport and deposition. Water level and beach altitude were important controls on sediment deposition. During 1994 the mean daily water level varied from 7.49 to 9.25 m OD, with a rapid fall in May and a rapid rise in September, a pattern observed in most years (Clyde River Purification Board 1995, pers comm.) which relates to precipitation variation. The rapid water level fall in May was associated with changes in surface sediment patterns (Table 2).

The high frequency waves (mean frequency = 0.92 s), characteristic of restricted-fetch conditions, influence sedimentation patterns. At the shore, the rapid succession of breaking waves means that backwash is frequently interrupted by incoming swash, limiting the depositional area. This resulted in some complicated sedimentation patterns exhibited by the photographic evidence. Wind and wave records during 1994 highlighted the rapid variability of wave direction, amplitude

and frequency. The Loch location (Fig. 1), in particular proximity to the coast and the surrounding mountainous terrain, contributes to high variability in weather conditions, particularly wind direction and velocity. High precipitation in this area leads to flashy stream drainage and high run-off (factors between 60 and 80%), (Tippett 1994). The dominance of westerly winds affects Milarrochy in particular because of the beach orientation. Limited wave refraction means shore-normal processes dominate. This is demonstrated by the overall trend of cross-beach fining into the nearshore and offshore zone, apart from the very mixed surf zone (Table 1 & Fig. 7). The down-beach coarsening at the headland profiles (1 & 6) occurred where process energies were lower. Several authors have identified cross-beach sorting trends (Ingle 1966; Jago & Barrusseau 1981; Shipp 1984; Horn 1992). Where swash backwash processes dominate, the observed sediment size variation depends on the beach composition (e.g. Swift et al. 1971; Horn 1992, 1997).

The shore-parallel limit of the coarse grain sizes in the nearshore delimits beach closure depth, and indicates the relatively low energy wave climate. As coarse sediment was not found offshore from the headlands, or within the offshore area, this confirms that coarse sediment is land derived and transport is limited to within the bay under contemporary process conditions. Thus beach and delta residence time of coarse sediment is likely to be long-term (decades) unless the wave regime should increase sufficiently to entrain the coarser size fractions and transport them alongshore, or if the macro-scale geology should change.

When compared to other beaches on the same shore (Pierce 1997), different depositional trends under similar conditions were observed, although nearshore limit of coarse sediment occurred throughout the Loch and at other UK lakes (Pierce in press). Variations in beach particle size and shape can be explained by the differing land-derived sediment sources and local sheltering effects. Because of the relatively low wave energy, sediment supply pathways show a dominance rarely observed on open marine coasts. Thus Milarrochy and other lake beaches at Loch Lomond and elsewhere show considerable sedimentological variation which is a function of local conditions (geology, sediment supply, beach elevation etc.) which prevail in spite of the larger scale environmental change such as increasing water levels or a change in wind-wave climate.

Role of sediment supply

The characteristic poor sorting of the Milarrochy (and other lake) beach sediments may be explained by supply from sedimentologically distinct units, namely cliff and fluvial sediments, themselves poorly sorted. With low wave energy to bring about beach sorting, the role of sediment supply is more critical than on higher energy coasts. Thus individual areas of beach closely reflect the character of the source material. Beach areas subject to cliff falls (e.g. Profile 6) show the greatest variability in sediment populations. The sub-surface sedimentology (Table 1) reveals potential sources of fine sediment within 0.1 m of ground level. The cliff at Milarrochy is eroding at an average rate of $0.54\,\mathrm{m\,a^{-1}}$. From survey measurements the total cliff sediment contribution to the beach sediment budget was estimated to be $77\,\mathrm{m^3}$ during 1994, with approximately $7\,\mathrm{m^3}$ of that being coarse sediment (coarser than -1ϕ). Re-working of fine cliff sediment within the beach increased the spread of finer particles, although over time these are lost offshore or settle in the beach sub-surface. On the basis of the results from the sampling programme, and field observations, the majority of the finer sediment was transported offshore. In sediment-rich areas of beach at Milarrochy and other lake beaches (Pierce 1997), landward gravel roll-over was observed. Gravel roll-over of up to 2 m horizontal distance occurred after the New Year 1992/93 storms.

At Milarrochy the location of the three streams affects the distribution of more mixed size particles at the surface more than on some other Loch beaches. This is illustrated by sediment types at profiles 1 lower beach, and 2 mid beach, (Table 2). A mixed sediment composition (gravel/sand) can increase beach instability (Kirk 1980; Allen 1981), especially as the stream channels are mobile, therefore affecting a greater beach area. Overall the fluvial influence on the Loch beaches is strong, transferring large amounts of sediment to deltas at the point where the streams enter the lake. The formation and persistence of small scale spits at stream mouths indicate the dominance of fluvial hydraulic energy under relatively calm lake conditions. As the stream hydrological regimes are flashy, sediment delivery is intermittent. Such pulses of sediment delivered by gravel-bedded streams were recognized by Hoey (1992), and are significant in understanding sediment supply to the beach.

Human influence

The main human influence has been to alter the sedimentological composition of the beach by beach feeding. As part of shore protection measures, $111\,\mathrm{m^3}$ of poorly sorted coarse sediment (Coarser than -1ϕ) during 1994 together with $11\,\mathrm{m^3}$ of fine sediment (finer than -1ϕ) were added to the Milarrochy beach by mechanical digger. The sediment comprised mostly builders' gravel, sand and rubble deposited in mounds up to 1.3 m high on the mid beach. A further $75\,\mathrm{m^3}$ of mixed grade sediment (rubble) was introduced adjacent to profile 5 in March 1995. Photographic surveys (1994–95) indicated dispersal of sediment alongshore from the injection point. Over a period of approximately three months, most of the finer particles (finer than -1ϕ) moved to the beach sub-surface or were transferred offshore. The coarser particles (coarser than -1ϕ) were dispersed into the beach fabric and the nearshore by stream and wave processes. Such management practice where mixed sediment grades are added to the beach is likely to increase beach instability which may contribute to the more rapid erosion occurring at Milarrochy. The beach feeding does not however, greatly change the overall trends observed at this beach as other beaches studied show similar sedimentological trends (Pierce 1997).

Compaction of beach material, lessening its ability to respond to waves, has occurred from car-parking (mostly adjacent to profile 5). With the construction of artificial car-parking areas this problem has eased, but the line of the back berm and upper beach is now further constrained as alongshore sediment transport is interrupted. The effects of this may be apparent in the longer-term. Channelization of the largest stream entering the Loch at Milarrochy (in 1997, N. of profile 5) affects fluvial-beach sediment transfer. To date this has resulted in an increase of fine material on the foreshore adjacent to the stream mouth. Further modification has included the emplacement around tree roots of imported cobble-boulder sized clasts during 1997–8). Longer-term it is likely there will be a net loss of sediment feeding the upper beach, leading to a less responsive, sediment-poor area, which will provide limited shore defence. With continued landward beach recession, the back beach now lies directly adjacent to the road.

Varied riparian interests on the Loch shores (private and commercial) have been responsible for numerous ad hoc shore protection attempts including deployment of rip-rap, gabion boxes, walls, beach feeding and replanting of backshore vegetation, as at Milarrochy. There has been no overall strategy for shoreline management although Scottish Natural Heritage is currently addressing this. Of significance is the fact that artificially introduced (coarse) sediment is likely to stay within the beach system. The broader importance is that local hard-engineering shore protection schemes deployed world-wide may have much more serious implications for low energy beaches than for high energy beaches. This is because of the reliance on land-derived sediment, rather than alongshore or offshore supplies. Even small variations in sediment availability can lessen the beach's ability to function as the buffer between water and land. At any given site, a specific analysis of sediment sources, characteristics and supply rates in the context of geomorphological conditions is the first step in beach management protocol. An awareness of sediment re-circulation in low energy beaches and the importance of relatively 'minor' changes to sediment supply is therefore a pre-requisite for management initiatives in the coastal zone.

Conclusions

Several general conclusions can be drawn from this work:

(1) The high degree of sedimentological variability reflects the nature of variable sediment supply, predominantly low energy wave conditions and temporal changes in wind-wave conditions. Seasonal trends of water level fluctuation and sediment discharge and transfer from river to beach are important controls on local scale variability. The dominance of fluvial cycles at low energy beaches is important for understanding low energy coastal responses. Sediment-rich areas of beach show greater variability than sediment-poor areas. Dominant process trends (in this case, shore-normal waves) are reflected by the overall trend of cross-beach fining into the offshore.

(2) Variations in particle size and shape distributions reflect the character of the source material and sediment transfer processes within the beach. There is a tendency for beach sediments to be negatively skewed reflecting coarse grained sediment delivery from streams and a selective transport of fine material into the offshore. This is directly related to the low energy conditions. Some areas of beach are more stable because of a gravel lag or armoured layer. The clear nearshore limit to the coarse sediment and the presence of lags indicate overall low-energy conditions and the re-circulation of coarse sediment within the bay.

(3) Under restricted-fetch conditions, local wind-wave climate and sediment supply assume a much greater importance than in higher energy environments. Sediment transfer within the beach system and off-shore is strongly controlled by particle size, dominant wind-wave conditions and water levels. Different sections of beach and adjacent beaches experiencing the same macro-scale environmental conditions may show different trends depending on the local conditions. This has important implications for lake and low energy marine coastal management in that specific local conditions are major controls on beach response.

(4) The lack of a comprehensive strategy for coastal management at Loch Lomond, and indeed the failure to recognize lake beach environments as dynamic 'coasts,' has resulted in inappropriate coastal defence structures and an exacerbation of existing erosion problems. The location of the road behind the back berm further constrains an already 'squeezed' coastal system.

Financial support for this study was provided by a University of Glasgow New Initiatives Award. Thanks to the landowners for granting permission to work at the site; to T. Hoey and J. Hansom for discussion during the fieldwork period and to the Universities of Glasgow and Reading who provided laboratory facilities.

References

AGRAWAL, Y. C., McCAVE, I. N. & RILEY, J. B. 1991. Laser diffraction size analysis. *In*: SYVITSKI, J. P. M. (ed.) *Principles, methods and application of particle size analysis*. Cambridge University Press, 119–128.

ALLEN, J. R. L. 1982. *Sedimentary structures, their character and physical basis*, v 1–2, Elsevier, Amsterdam.

ALLEN, P. A. 1981. Wave-generated structures in the Devonian lacustrine sediments of southeastern Shetland and ancient wave conditions. *Sedimentology*, **28**, 369–379.

BLACK, A. R. 1995. Flood seasonality and physical controls on flood risk estimation. *Scottish Geographical Magazine*, **111**, 187–190.

BLUCK, B. J. 1967. Sedimentation of beach gravels: examples from South Wales. *Journal of Sedimentary Petrology*, **37**, 128–156.

BULLER, A. T. & McMANUS, J. 1979. Sediment sampling and analysis. *In*: DYER, K. R. (ed.) *Estuarine Hydrography and Sedimentation*. Cambridge University Press, Cambridge, UK, 87–130.

CARTER, R. W. G. & ORFORD, J. D. 1984. Coarse clastic beaches: a discussion of their distinctive morphosedimentary characteristics. *Marine Geology*, **60**, 377–389.

CHURCH, M. A., McLEAN, D. G. & WOLCOTT, J. F. 1987. River bed gravels: Sampling and analysis. *In*: THORNE, C. R., BATHURST, J. C. & HEY, R. D. (eds) *Sediment transport in Gravel-bed rivers*. John Wiley and Sons Ltd., 43–79.

CURRAN, J. C. & POODLE, T. 1994. Aspects of the hydrology and hydrography of Loch Lomond. *Hydrolobiologia*, **290**, 21–28.

DAVIDSON-ARNOTT, R. G. D. 1989. The effect of water level variation on coastal erosion in the Great Lakes. *Ontario Geography*, **33**, 23–39.

DAVIS, J. H. & ERLICH, R. 1970. Relationships between measures of sediment size frequency and the nature of the sediments. *Geological Society of America Bulletin*, **81**, 3537–3548.

FOLK, R. L. & WARD, W. C. 1957. Brazos River bar: a study in the significance of grain size parameters. *Journal of Sedimentary Petrology*, **27**, 3–26.

FORBES, D. L., ORFORD, J. D. CARTER, R. W. G., SHAW, J., & JENNINGS, S. C. 1995. Morphodynamic evolution, self-organisation, and instability of coarse-clastic barriers on paraglacial coasts. *Marine Geology*, **126**, 63–85.

GALE, S. J. & HOARE, P. G. 1981. *Quaternary Sediments: Petrographic methods for the study of un-lithified rocks*. Belhaven Press, Wiley, New York.

—— & ——1991. *Quaternary Sediments: Petrographic methods for the study of unlithified rocks*. Belhaven Press, Wiley, New York.

GOMEZ, B. & CHURCH, M. 1989. An assessment of bed load sediment transport formulae for gravel bed rivers. *Water Resources Research*, **25**, 1161–1186.

GOUDIE, A. (ed.) & ANDERSON, M. BURT, T. LEWIS, J. RICHARDS, K. WHALLEY, B. WORSLEY, P. 1990. *Geomorphological Techniques*. 2nd edn, Unwin Hyman.

GRACIA PRIETO, F. J. 1995 Shoreline forms and deposits in Gallocanta Lake (NE Spain). *Geomorphology*, **11**, 323–335.

HAKANSON, L. 1977. The influence of wind, fetch and water depth on the distribution of sediments in Lake Vanern, Sweden. *Canadian Journal of Earth Science*, **14**, 397–412.

HANDS, E. B. 1979. *Changes in rates of shore retreat, Lake Michigan, 1967–76*. US Army Coastal Engineers Research Centre Technical Paper.

——1983. The Great Lakes as a test model for profile response to sea level changes. *In*: KOMAR, P. D. (ed.) *Handbook of coastal processes and erosion*. CERC Press, Florida, 167–189.

HARVEY, A. M. 1991. The influence of sediment supply on the channel morphology of upland streams: Howgill Fells, Northwest England. *Earth Surface Processes and Landforms*, **16**, 675–684.

HOEY, T. B. 1992. Temporal variation in bedload transport rates and sediment storage in gravel river beds. *Progress in Physical Geography*, **16**, 319–338.

HORN, D. P. 1992. A review and experimental assessment of equilibrium grain size and the ideal wave-graded profile. *Marine Geology*, **108**, 161–74.

——1997 Beach research in the 1990s. *Progress in Physical Geography*, **21**, 454–470.

HOUGHTON, J. T., MEIRA FILLO, L. G., CALLANDER, B. A., HARRIS, N. KATTENBERG, A. & MASKELL, K. (eds) 1996. *Climate change 1995: The science of climate change*. Report of the Intergovernmental Panel on Climate Change. Cambridge University Press, Cambridge.

IBBEKEN, H. & SCHLEYER, R. 1986. Photosieving: A method for grain size analysis of coarse grained unconsolidated bedding surfaces. *Earth Surface Processes and Landforms*, **11**, 59–78.

INGLE, J. C. 1966. The movement of beach sand: an analysis using fluorescent grains. *Developments in Sedimentology*, vol. 5. Elsevier, Amsterdam.

JACKSON, N. L. 1995. Wind and waves: influence of local and non-local waves on mesoscale beach behaviour in estuarine environments. *Annals of the Association of American Geographers*, **85**, 21–37.

JAGO, C. F. & BARUSSEAU, J. P. 1981. Sediment entrainment on a wave-graded shelf, Roussilion, France. *Marine Geology*, **42**, 279–299.

JOHANSSON, I. 1976. Structural studies of frictional sediments. *Geografiska Annaler*, **58A**, 200–300.

KELLERHALS, R. & BRAY, D. I. 1971. Sampling procedures for coarse fluvial sediments. *Journal of the Hydraulics Division*, Proceedings of the American Society of Civil Engineers, 97(HY8), 1165–1180.

KIRK, R. M. 1980. Mixed sand and gravel beaches: morphology, processses and sediments. *Progress in Physical Geography*, **4**, 189–210.

KOMAR, P. D. 1987. Selective grain entrainment by a current from a bed of mixed sizes. *Journal of Sedimentary Petrology*, **57**, 203–211.

MAKASKE, B. & AUGUSTINUS, P. G. E. F. 1998. Morphological changes of a micro-tidal, low wave energy beach face during a spring-neap tidal cycle. *Journal of Coastal Research*, **14**(2), 632–645.

METEOROLOGICAL OFFICE 1989. *The Climate of Scotland*. HMSO.

NATHIER-DUFUOUR, N., BOUGEARD, L., DEVEAUX, M-F., BERTRAND, D. & LE DESCHAULT DE MONREDON, F. 1993. Comparison of sieving and laser diffraction for the particle size measurements of raw materials used in foodstuff. *Powder Technology*, **76**, 191–200.

NORRMAN, J. O. 1964. Lake Vattern. Investigations on shore and bottom morphology. *Geographiska Annaler*, **46**, 1–238.

ORFORD, J. D. 1987. Coastal Processes: the coastal response to sea level variation. *In*: DEVOY, R. J. M. (ed.) *Sea-surface studies: A global view*. Croom Helm, London.

PARKER, G. & SUTHERLAND, A. J. 1990. Fluvial Armor. *Journal of Hydraulic Research*, **28**, 529–544.

PENDER, G. 1991. Wave generated shore erosion in Loch Lomond. *In*: *Loch Lomond 1991. A symposium on environmental conditions in the Loch Lomond basin and their implications for resource management and development*. University of Glasgow & University of Strathclyde Conference Proceedings, 31–34.

——, DICKINSON, G. & HERBERTSON, J. G. 1993. Flooding and shore damage at Loch Lomond January to March 1990. *Weather*, **48**, 8–15.

PERILLO, G. M. E. 1995. *Geomorphology and sedimentology of estuaries*. Elsevier, Oxford, Amsterdam.

PIERCE, L. R. 1996. Loch Lomond: A challenge for environmental management, *Geography Review*, **9**, 11–14.

——1997. *Lake waves and gravel beach variation, Loch Lomond, Scotland.* PhD thesis, University of Glasgow.

——1999. Loch Lomond: An example of Quaternary megageomorphology. *Scottish Geographical Journal*, **115**, 71–80.

—— in press. Restricted-fetch lake waves, water levels and gravel beach variation, Loch Lomond, Scotland. *Journal of Coastal Research*.

POWERS, M. C. 1953. A new roundness scale for sedimentary particles. *Journal of Sedimentary Petrology*, **23**, 117–119.

PYE, K. 1982. Negatively skewed aeolian sands from a humid tropical coastal dunefield, Northern Australia. *Sedimentary Geology*, **31**, 249–266.

ROSE, J. 1981. *Field guide to the Quaternary Geology of the southeastern part of the Loch Lomond Basin.* Proceedings of the Geological Society of Glasgow for 1980/81.

SEYMOUR, R. J. 1977. Estimating wave generation on restricted fetchen. *Journal of Waterway Port Coastal and Ocean Division*, **103**, 251–264.

SHI, S. 1995. *Observational and theoretical aspects of tsunami sedimentation.* PhD Thesis, Coventry University, Coventry.

SHIPP, R. C. 1984. Bedforms and depositional sedimentary structures of a barred nearshore system, eastern Long Island. *Marine Geology*, **60**, 235–259.

SLY, P. G. 1994. Sedimentary processes in lakes. *In*: PYE, K. (ed.) *Sediment Transport and Deposi-* tional Processes. Blackwell Scientific Publications, Oxford, 157–191.

SMITH, G. H. S., NICHOLAS, A. P. & FERGUSON, R. I. 1977. Defining bimodal sediments: problems and implications. *Water Resources Research*, **33**, 1179–1185.

SYVITSKI, J. P. M. 1991. (ed.) *Principles, methods and application of particle size analysis.* Cambridge University Press, Cambridge.

SWIFT, D. J. P., SANDFORD, R. E., DILL, C. E. JR & AVIGNONE, N. F. 1971. Textural differentiation on the shoreface during erosional retreat of an unconsolidated coast, Cape Henry to Cape Hatteras, Western North Atlantic Shelf. *Sedimentology*, **16**, 221–250.

TIPPETT, R. 1994. An Introduction to Loch Lomond. *Hydrobiologia*, **290**, xi–xv.

TIVY, J. 1980. *The effect of recreation on freshwater lochs and reservoirs in Scotland.* Countryside Commission for Scotland.

WADELL, H. 1933. Sphericity and roundness of rock particles. *Journal of Geology*, **41**, 310–331.

WARREN, G. 1974. Simplified form of the Folk-Ward skewness parameter. *Journal of Sedimentary Petrology*, **44**, 259.

WOLMAN, M. G. 1954. A method of sampling coarse bed material. *Transactions of the American Geophysical Union*, **35**, 951–956.

ZINGG, T. 1935. *Beiträge zur Schotteranalyse Schweizer mineralogische und Mitteilungen petrographische*, **15**, 39–140.

Applications of ground-penetrating radar (GPR) to sedimentological, geomorphological and geoarchaeological studies in coastal environments

ADRIAN NEAL & CLIVE L. ROBERTS

School of Applied Sciences, University of Wolverhampton, Wulfruna Street, Wolverhampton WV1 1SB, UK (e-mail: cs1815@wlv.ac.uk)

Abstract: Acquisition of high resolution data regarding the stratigraphy and internal structure of coastal sedimentary sequences is becoming increasingly important in many sedimentological, geomorphological and geoarchaeological studies. Such information is usually obtained from the logging of field exposures, shallow trenches and cores. However, ground-penetrating radar (GPR), a relatively new and rapidly developing non-invasive geophysical technique, may also aid such investigations in certain coastal settings, providing additional, complimentary and often unique data sets. The technique is based on the transmission, reflection and reception of high frequency electromagnetic (radar) waves, with reflections occurring in the subsurface due to the varying electrical properties of the sediments. Such reflections can occur due the presence of primary sedimentary structures, lithological/material changes or water content changes. Examples presented from the UK indicate that the technique can accurately delineate the stratigraphy and internal sedimentary structure of coastal barriers, spits and strandplains, both above and below a fresh groundwater table. Sand and/or gravel-dominated beach-dune systems on moderate to high wave energy, macrotidal coasts appear to provide optimum settings for GPR deployment. In addition, the technique also has the potential to locate, map and provide stratigraphic context for a wide range of archaeological features that are commonly found in such coastal environments.

Until recently it has generally been necessary to rely on the logging of field exposures, shallow cores and surface excavations to determine the detailed stratigraphy, internal sedimentary structure and archaeology of unconsolidated coastal sedimentary sequences. However, such an approach has a number of associated problems:

(1) good field exposures are often scarce and limited to the zone above the groundwater table. For example, many UK coastal dune systems are heavily stabilized by vegetation; suitable and extensive exposures are typically only revealed in frontal dunes that have been eroded during significant storms.

(2) extensive shallow coring or excavation work is often time consuming and expensive. Consequently, cores and trenches are usually limited in number and/or have considerable spacing, making correlation between them difficult. The restricted nature of borehole sampling also ensures that only limited information regarding the internal sedimentary structure of the deposits can be obtained. In addition, the application of such invasive techniques may be undesirable or unfeasible due to important conservation considerations at the site.

During the last decade, however, rapid developments in the field of environmental geophysics have begun to allow the non-invasive acquisition of a wide range of shallow subsurface data (Reynolds 1997). In particular, ground-penetrating radar (GPR, also referred to as impulse radar, ground-probing radar or georadar) has found a wide range of applications in this field. GPR has proven valuable in many glaciological, hydrogeological, environmental, engineering and forensic investigations (see examples in Reynolds (1997)). It also has the potential to aid future planetary exploration programmes (Ori & Ogliani 1996; Herique & Kofman 1997). However, with respect to coastal studies it is recent developments in geological and archaeological applications that are of particular interest. GPR has successfully been used to determine the extent, thickness, stratigraphy and internal sedimentary structure of a wide range of unconsolidated sediments. These have included aeolian, fluvial, glacial, lacustrine,

From: PYE, K. & ALLEN, J. R. L. (eds). *Coastal and Estuarine Environments: sedimentology, geomorphology and geoarchaeology*. Geological Society, London, Special Publications, **175**, 139–171. 0305-8719/00/$15.00 © The Geological Society of London 2000.

deltaic and freshwater peat deposits (for example, Jol & Smith 1991; Smith & Jol 1992, 1997; Gawthorpe *et al.* 1993; Huggenberger 1993; Schenk *et al.* 1993; Theimer *et al.* 1994; Bridge *et al.* 1995, 1998; Mellet 1995; Olsen & Andreasen 1995; Bristow *et al.* 1996; Harari 1996; Lønne & Lauritsen 1996; Busby 1997; Leclerc & Hickin 1997; Roberts *et al.* 1997; Vandenberghe & van Overmeeren 1999). In tandem with the growth in geological applications there has been an increasing use of GPR in archaeological investigations. GPR can quickly and accurately locate and define many buried archaeological features and, in many cases, determine their stratigraphic context (Vaughan 1986; Sternberg & McGill 1995; Arnold *et al.* 1997; Conyers & Goodman 1997; Reynolds 1997). Consequently GPR is a geophysical technique that has recently gained wide acceptance within the archaeological community (Conyers & Goodman 1997). However, few of the archaeological investigations reported in the literature have utilized GPR in truly coastal settings.

A preliminary investigation into the likely coastal geomorphological and sedimentological applications of GPR was first undertaken by Leatherman (1987). Subsequent studies have confirmed its potential, particularly in North America (Fitzgerald *et al.* 1992; Dott & Mickelson 1995; Jol *et al.* 1996; Meyers *et al.* 1996; van Heteren *et al.* 1996; van Heteren & van de Plassche 1997; van Heteren *et al.* 1998; Smith *et al.* 1999), but also in Europe (Strand Petersen & Andreasen 1989; van Overmeeren 1994, 1998; Clemmensen *et al.* 1996) and elsewhere (Baker 1991; Roy *et al.* 1994; Harari 1996). However, despite this research GPR studies in coastal environments are still very much in their infancy. This is due, at least in part, to the fact that many coastal scientists who may wish to utilize GPR in their studies do not have a sufficiently detailed knowledge of geophysical surveying and interpretation to use the technique with confidence. The limited number of studies undertaken so far, combined with the need to examine both the relevant geological/archaeological and geophysical literature, means that it is often difficult for the non-specialist to easily ascertain whether the technique will provide the required information at a particular study site. With these problems in mind, the aims of this paper are as follows: (a) to introduce the GPR technique, explaining how, why and where it is most likely to work; (b) to examine some of the important issues surrounding survey design, data processing and interpretation; (c) to illustrate a range of coastal geomorphological and sedimentological applications by presenting examples from a series of

studies recently undertaken in the UK; (d) to discuss the potential geoarchaeological applications of GPR in coastal environments through a qualitative evaluation of archaeological targets in the coastal dunefields of South Wales.

The GPR technique

In many respects GPR is analogous to the perhaps more familiar reflection seismic and sonar techniques (McCann *et al.* 1988). At an individual survey point the GPR system emits a short pulse of high frequency electromagnetic energy in the MHz range (Davis & Annan 1989; Reynolds 1997). This is transmitted into the ground, where it encounters materials of differing electrical properties. Variations in these properties lead to changes in the velocity of the propagating electromagnetic wave. Where velocity changes are abrupt, with respect to the dominant wavelength of the radar wave, a proportion of the energy will be reflected. This will then be transmitted back to the surface, where it can be received by the GPR system (Fig.1). The time taken for the signal to be transmitted, reflected and then received is a function of the depth of the reflecting horizon and the average velocity of the electromagnetic wave. This is referred to as the two-way travel time and is measured in nanoseconds (10^{-9} seconds). In modern GPR systems the received signal is digitized and stored on a lap-top computer, which also allows real-time data display and simple processing. Where standard radar reflection profiling is being undertaken, the data collection process is repeated at sequential survey points. The resulting traces are then placed next to each other to build up the radar reflection profile of the subsurface (Fig. 1).

GPR systems operate either in monostatic mode, with a single antenna or bistatic mode with separate transmitting and receiving antennae. Monostatic systems tend to be towed along the ground and the horizontal axis is recorded on a time-base. Conversion to a distance-base is then required. Bistatic systems are usually operated in a step-wise manner and the horizontal axis is recorded on a distance-base.

Theoretical background

In the MHz frequency range and at low conductivities (<100 mS/m) and low relative magnetic permeabilities ($=1$ for non-magnetic materials), it is the dielectric properties of materials that determines their response to propagating electromagnetic energy (Davis & Annan 1989;

a)

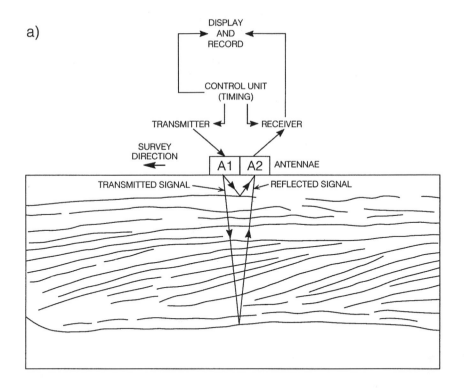

b)

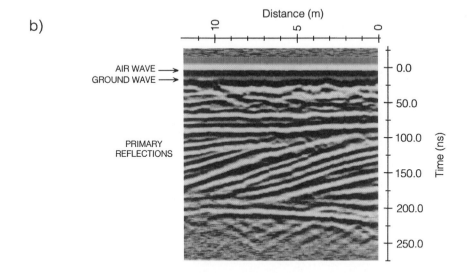

Fig. 1. Ground penetrating radar data acquisition and the resulting radar reflection profile. (**a**) GPR data acquisition at an individual survey point showing the GPR system components and the subsurface reflector configuration (as defined by the presence of primary sedimentary structures, water content variations and lithology changes). (**b**) Radar reflection profile resulting from the sequential plotting of individual traces from adjacent survey points. The air wave is the first arrival and results from part of the electromagnetic pulse generated at the transmitting antenna traveling directly through the air to the receiving antenna. The ground wave is the second arrival and results from part of the electromagnetic wave initiated at the transmitting antenna being strongly refracted within the uppermost part of the subsurface. The air and ground wave are followed by a series of primary reflections resulting from the changing dielectric properties of the subsurface.

Table 1. *Typical electrical properties of some common geological materials at 80–120 MHz (based primarily on van Heteren et al. 1998, but with additional data from Davis & Annan 1989; Theimer et al. 1994; van Overmeeren 1994)*

Medium	Relative Dielectric Permittivity	Electromagnetic wave velocity (m/ns)	Conductivity (mS/m)	Attenuation (dB/m)
Air	1	0.3	0	0
Fresh water	80	0.03	0.5	0.1
Sea water	80	0.01	30 000	1000
Unsaturated sand	2.55–7.5	0.1–0.2	0.01	0.01–0.14
Saturated sand	20–31.6	0.05–0.08	0.1–1	0.03–0.5
Unsaturated sand and gravel	3.5–6.5	0.09–0.13	0.007–0.06	0.01–0.1
Saturated sand and gravel	15.5–17.5	0.06	0.7–9	0.03–0.5
Unsaturated silt	2.5–5	0.09–0.12	1–100	1–300*
Saturated silt	22–30	0.05–0.07	≤100	1–300*
Unsaturated clay	2.5–5	0.09–0.12	2–20	0.28–300*
Saturated clay	15–40	0.05–0.07	20–1000	0.28–300*
Unsaturated till	7.4–21.1	0.1–0.12*	2.5–10	†
Saturated till	24–34	0.1–0.12*	2–5	†
Freshwater peat	57–80	0.03–0.06	<40	0.3
Bedrock	4–6	0.12–0.13	10^{-5}–40	7×10^{-6}–24

* Unsaturated and saturated values not differentiated (van Heteren *et al.* 1998).
† Values not available.

Reynolds 1997). These high frequency electrical properties are measured as the Relative Dielectric Permittivity (RDP) of a material (also referred to as the dielectric constant). RDP is calculated as the ratio of a material's electrical permittivity to the electrical permittivity of a vacuum, which is one (Conyers & Goodman 1997). In physical terms it can be thought of as the degree to which a material within an electromagnetic field becomes polarized and, therefore, responds to propagating electromagnetic waves (Olehoft 1981; Conyers & Goodman 1997). For a given frequency and at low conductivities, the lower the RDP then the higher the radar wave

Table 2. *Modelled reflection coefficients for typical changes in water content, porosity, lithology, grain shape and grain orientation in coastal barrier settings. The reflection coefficients indicate the proportion of energy that would theoretically be reflected from a particular interface. Values lie in the range +1 to −1, the sign indicating the polarity of the reflected wave. Modified from Baker (1991)*

Layer 1 Layer 2	Porosity (%)	Relative Dielectric Permittivity	Reflection coefficient (+1 to −1)	Geological significance
Dry sand	35	3.1		
Saturated sand	35	20.7	−0.44	Water table
Dry sand	35	3.1		5% porosity change
Dry sand	30	3.27	−0.013	in dry sand
Saturated sand	35	20.7		5% porosity change
Saturated sand	30	17.7	+0.04	in saturated sand
Saturated sand	35	20.7		Lithology change to
Peat	70	46.5	−0.2	high porosity peat
Dry sand	35	3.1		Dry heavy mineral
Dry heavy mineral sand	35	19.9	−0.43	placer deposit
Saturated sand	35	20.7		Saturated heavy mineral
Saturated heavy mineral sand	35	53	−0.23	placer deposit
Round grains	33	23.5		
Platy grains	33	16.9	+0.08	Grain shape change
Isotropic grain packing	33	22.5		Orientation change for
Anisotropy grain packing	33	16.9	+0.7	platey grains

velocity and the lower the attenuation (Table 1). As freshwater has a high RDP compared to air and the common rock-forming minerals (Olehoft 1981), the dielectric properties of common geologic materials are primarily controlled by water content (Topp *et al.* 1980; Davis & Annan 1989). Hence in unconsolidated sediments radar is sensitive to variations in the sediment : air : freshwater ratio. Consequently, changes in the fluid occupying the pore space (e.g. air to freshwater) or variations in the porosity itself lead to significant changes in the RDP and corresponding radar wave velocity, thus causing reflections. In addition, radar is also sensitive to changes in sediment composition and grain shape, orientation and packing (Davis & Annan 1989; Baker 1991). As a result of these relationships, features such as the water table, sedimentary structures and lithological boundaries all give significant reflections (Table 2). However, these seemingly simple relationships can be complicated by the introduction of significant amounts of high conductivity pore water (e.g. sea water) or sediment (e.g. saturated clay). These will often provide strong reflections when encountered, but also rapidly attenuate the signal, preventing any further significant penetration.

For any given frequency and RDP, the propagating electromagnetic wave has a specific wavelength and this limits the horizontal and vertical resolution that can be achieved (Jol 1995; Smith & Jol 1995; Reynolds 1997). With respect to vertical resolution, wave theory indicates that the best that can be achieved is one-quarter of the dominant wavelength (Sheriff 1977). All reflections that occur within that vertical distance will interfere constructively to a greater or lesser extent and form the final observed single reflection (Fig. 2). Horizontal resolution is determined by the size of the first Fresnel zone, which itself is a function of wavelength and depth of the reflector (Sheriff 1977; Reynolds 1997). Depth to the reflector is significant because the down going signal travels in an ever-expanding elliptical cone. Consequently for a given wavelength, as the depth increases the size of the first Fresnel zone also increases, leading to lower horizontal resolution.

In all GPR surveys there is a trade off between depth of penetration and resolution (Davis & Annan 1989; Jol 1995; Smith & Jol 1995). For any given earth material, as the antennae frequency is increased there is an increase in resolution but a decrease in the depth of penetration (Fig. 3). However, this relationship can be complicated by significant changes in the dielectric properties of the subsurface with depth.

As a consequence of the technical limitations placed on the vertical and horizontal resolution

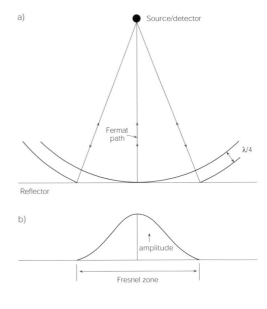

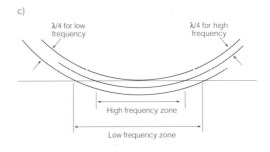

Fig. 2. The horizontal resolution of unmigrated radar data is given by the width of the Fresnel zone. (**a**) Electromagnetic waves propogate through the ground in an ever-expanding elliptical cone, with the apex of the cone at the centre of the transmitting antenna. All reflections within one-quarter of the dominant wavelength will interfere constructively to form a single reflection (as observed by the receiving antenna). (**b**) Waves closest to the Fermat path contribute most to the amplitude of the reflection. (**c**) The width of the Fresnel zone at any particular depth is a function of the depth to the reflector and the wavelength of the electomagnetic wave, which is in turn frequency dependent. The higher the frequency (and the shorter the wavelength) the higher the horizontal resolution. Modified from Emery & Myers (1996).

of a radar reflection profile, it must be viewed as some form of average or approximation of the true subsurface structure. The degree of approximation depends on the radar wavelength (which in itself is a function of the centre frequency of the

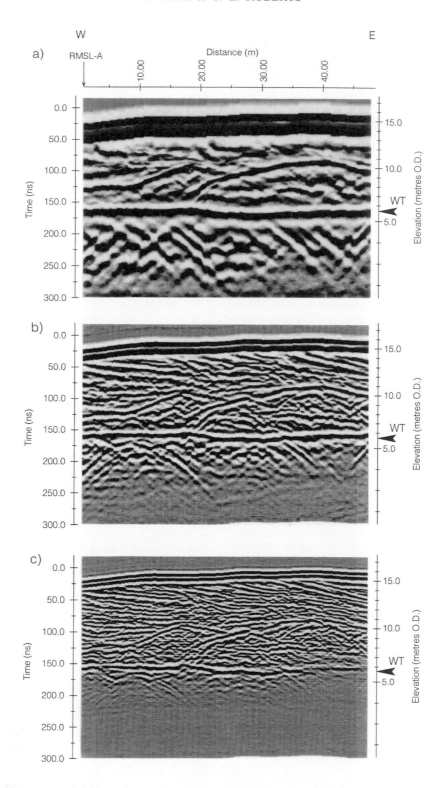

returning radar waves and the dielectric properties of the subsurface) and depth in the profile. This is an important point to consider when attempting to interpret radar reflection profiles.

System set-up and survey design

Prior to undertaking a full GPR survey a number of critical decisions regarding system set-up and survey design must be made. These will be guided primarily by the nature and scale of the features of potential interest and the electrical properties of the geological and/or archaeological material. It should be noted that with respect to system set-up the considerations outlined below apply to the more recent digital GPR systems.

(1) *Antennae frequency.* This will be guided by the resolution and depth of penetration required or predicted (see preceding discussion).

(2) *Time window.* This is the amount of time over which the system is to record data being received. The size of window required can be predicted based on the estimated radar wave velocity and depth of penetration. A window larger than that actually required is usually desirable, in case the electrical properties of the subsurface change along the survey line, allowing greater depth of penetration and hence the detection of reflectors with longer travel times.

(3) *Trace stacking.* The stacking of individual traces is a means of increasing the signal to noise ratio by arithmetically averaging out the random and variable portions of the reflected wave (Fisher *et al.* 1992; Conyers & Goodman 1997). Digital GPR systems allow this to be performed in the field, but it should be borne in mind that the greater the number of stacks the longer it takes to acquire data at an individual survey point.

(4) *Gains.* As radar waves pass down through the ground, energy is lost due to conical spreading and attenuation. Consequently, later arrivals on a reflection trace will generally have lower amplitudes than earlier arrivals. In order to enhance these later arrivals gains are applied that amplify the weaker signal. Unlike the system parameters outlined so far, the application of gains to the data is not always fixed once the survey has begun. In digital GPR systems gains can be applied to the real-time data display without affecting the raw data. A sensible gain must be applied at this point in order to ensure that all significant reflections are being observed.

(5) *Survey line orientation and length.* With respect to geomorphological and sedimentological features, e.g. bedforms, survey lines should ideally be aligned either parallel or normal to the assumed depositional strike. They should also be longer than one bedform wavelength. Rectangular grids or regularly spaced parallel survey lines allow the acquisition of pseudo-3D data. Where linear archaeological features are the target, for example walls and ditches, survey lines should ideally be normal to their strike and extend well beyond their horizontal limits. However, for most archaeological applications a rectangular survey grid is required (Conyers & Goodman 1997). For routine reconnaissance work the individual grid squares must be smaller than the smallest realistic target. For detailed subsurface mapping care must be taken to ensure that survey lines are sufficiently close to avoid spatial aliasing. In reality survey line orientation and length are usually a compromise between what is ideal and what is feasible given the ground conditions at the site.

(6) *Horizontal sampling interval.* In order to construct an image of the subsurface sequential traces from individual survey points are placed next to each other to provide a continuous profile (Fig. 1). The horizontal sampling interval must be smaller than the feature of interest, ideally ensuring that its full characteristics in the plane of the survey are represented on the radar image. Where data are being recorded by a continuously moving antenna, the horizontal sampling interval is a function of the

Fig. 3. The relationship between resolution and depth of penetration, as demonstrated by radar reflection profiles obtained at three different antennae frequencies along survey line B (see Fig.7) at Raven Meols blowout on the Sefton coast. (**a**) 50 MHz profile. Vertical resolution = 0.89 m, horizontal resolution at 5 m depth = 3.41 m (**b**) 100 MHz profile. Vertical resolution = 0.38 m, horizontal resolution at 5 m depth = 2.9 m (**c**) 200 MHz profile. Vertical resolution = 0.3 m, horizontal resolution at 5 m depth = 2.8 m. The survey line was orientated roughly parallel to the axis of the depositional lobe of the blowout. The strong horizontal reflection at 5.5 m OD is the water table (WT). The intersection with Raven Meols survey line A (RMSL-A) is indicated (see Fig. 8). Further details regarding the radar stratigraphy of the profiles can be found by reference to Figs 8 & 9 and Table 3.

rate of movement and the transmission and recording rates. Where data are being recorded in a step-wise manner, the horizontal sampling interval is merely a function of the distance between individual survey points.

(7) *Topographic survey*. As a GPR system measures only two-way travel time to reflectors it does not take into account the effect of changing topography on the relative position of adjacent traces. Consequently, where significant topography is encountered a static correction must be applied i.e. individual traces must be moved up or down to take into account changes in elevation along the survey line. In order to do this effectively, and to avoid distortions of the radar image, a topographic survey must be undertaken. The sampling interval will be a function of the terrain encountered. All breaks of slope should be accounted for.

(8) *Velocity surveys*. Where transmitter and receiver are independent, it is possible to carry out CMP (Common Mid-Point) surveys to estimate subsurface radar wave velocities (Annan & Davis 1976; Reynolds 1997). In order to obtain the most reliable results, reflections that appear horizontal on the standard radar reflection profiles should be used for the velocity analysis. The velocities are derived from the CMP profiles in exactly the same way as in reflection seismics (Robinson & Çoruh 1988, p. 88–90). Once obtained, the velocities can be used to convert two-way travel time to estimated depth on the radar reflection profiles. Where the subsurface radar response is seen to vary significantly along a survey line, a series of CMP surveys should be undertaken to determine the nature and magnitude of any velocity variations. Any significant changes will have considerable bearing on subsequent interpretation. If transmitter and receiver are not independent (e.g. monostatic systems), subsurface velocities must be estimated in another manner. This is usually best achieved by carrying out radar reflection profiling over objects or stratigraphic horizons of known depth, allowing direct measurement of radar wave travel times. This can also provide verification of velocities obtained from CMP surveys.

Data editing and processing

Once GPR survey data have been acquired in the field a certain amount of data editing and processing is required. This should be done in a systematic manner, in order to ensure comparability between individual survey lines. All data presented in this paper were collected using a Sensors and Software PulseEKKO[TM] 100 GPR system and edited and processed using version 4.2 of the system software. A flow diagram of the editing and processing procedure applied to the data is shown in Fig. 4. The need for certain, particularly important, operations is more fully explained below.

It is essential that time zero, which effectively marks the position of the ground surface on the radar reflection profile, is located in the correct position i.e. at the zero offset time. The spacing between the transmitter and the receiver means that the first signal (the direct air wave) is received at a small, but finite, time after the pulse was initiated. As a result, the zero offset time lies just above the air wave, by an amount of time determined by the velocity of the air wave and the antennae separation (Conyers & Goodman 1997). In towed systems antenna separation will be determined by the rate of movement and the transmission and recording rates.

It is usually desirable to estimate the return centre frequency for the primary reflections in a standard radar reflection profile. This is because as an electromagnetic wave propagates through the ground the higher frequencies are attenuated preferentially. Consequently, the returning electromagnetic wave has a lower centre frequency than the initial pulse generated by the transmitting antenna. The use of the return centre frequency, in conjunction with the relevant velocity estimates, leads to a more accurate estimate of radar wavelength and hence vertical and horizontal resolution.

If there are significant changes in the radar wave velocity with depth, it is not appropriate to plot the radar reflection profiles with elevation/depth scales derived from an average velocity for the whole sequence. This would lead to inaccurate depth estimates for most of the profile and distortion of the image due to an inappropriate degree of topographic correction. Instead velocities for individual layers within the profile must be derived. For example, where a water table is encountered in an otherwise uniform sequence of sandy sediments a two-layer velocity model is required, as the radar wave velocity in unsaturated sand is typically over twice that in saturated sand. Consequently, split elevation/depth scales are required (e.g. Fig. 3).

Various filters can be applied to radar data, but this must be done with caution. With respect to PulseEKKO[TM] GPR systems the only filter that tends to be universally applied is 'Dewow'

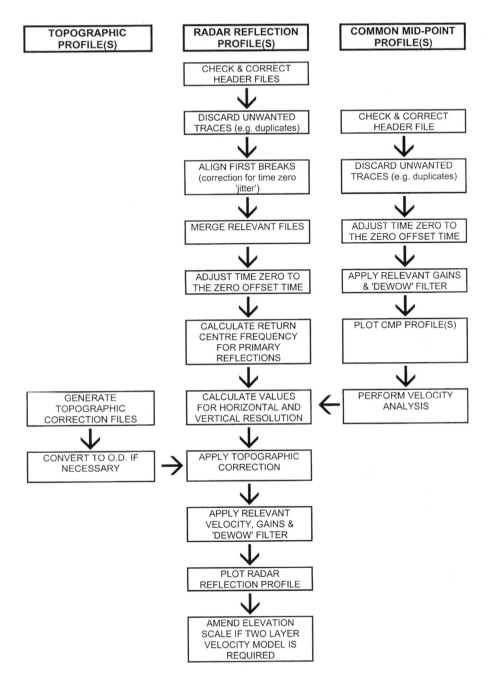

TOPOGRAPHIC PROFILE(S)

RADAR REFLECTION PROFILE(S)

CHECK & CORRECT HEADER FILES

DISCARD UNWANTED TRACES (e.g. duplicates)

ALIGN FIRST BREAKS (correction for time zero 'jitter')

MERGE RELEVANT FILES

ADJUST TIME ZERO TO THE ZERO OFFSET TIME

CALCULATE RETURN CENTRE FREQUENCY FOR PRIMARY REFLECTIONS

COMMON MID-POINT PROFILE(S)

CHECK & CORRECT HEADER FILE

DISCARD UNWANTED TRACES (e.g. duplicates)

ADJUST TIME ZERO TO THE ZERO OFFSET TIME

APPLY RELEVANT GAINS & 'DEWOW' FILTER

PLOT CMP PROFILE(S)

GENERATE TOPOGRAPHIC CORRECTION FILES

CALCULATE VALUES FOR HORIZONTAL AND VERTICAL RESOLUTION

PERFORM VELOCITY ANALYSIS

CONVERT TO O.D. IF NECESSARY

APPLY TOPOGRAPHIC CORRECTION

APPLY RELEVANT VELOCITY, GAINS & 'DEWOW' FILTER

PLOT RADAR REFLECTION PROFILE

AMEND ELEVATION SCALE IF TWO LAYER VELOCITY MODEL IS REQUIRED

Fig. 4. Flow diagram of the editing and processing procedure applied to the data in this paper using Sensors and Software Pulse EKKO[TM] 100 system software.

or 'Signal Saturation Correction'. This is a time filter that removes the slowly decaying low frequency noise which may be generated by the large transmit pulse of the GPR system. Beyond this, perhaps the simplest and most widely applied

filters to GPR data are trace-to-trace and down-the-trace averaging. Both help to reduce random noise by averaging it out. Trace-to trace averaging, which is one of a suite of spatial filters, also emphasizes horizontal or gently dipping features and suppresses rapidly changing ones. However, any form of averaging, especially when heavily applied, effectively reduces the resolution that can be achieved and subtle features are often lost from the data set. Often it is more appropriate to use one of a series of more complex time filters. These selectively remove certain frequencies from the data set, trace by trace. They include bandpass filtering, which removes high and low frequency noise outside the portion of spectrum of interest, lowpass filtering, which removes high frequency noise above a specified cut-off point, and highpass filtering, which removes the low frequency signal below a specified cut-off point.

Of the various filters outlined above, only 'Dewow' filtering has been routinely applied to the data presented in this paper. An extensive series of experiments indicated that further filtering did not significantly enhance the features of interest and that when heavy filtering was applied features were lost or distorted. Where subsequent filtering is deemed to be desirable it is best performed with reference to hard-copies of the essentially unfiltered reflection profiles, thus ensuring that features observed are 'real' and not artifacts of the filtering process.

More complex processing procedures, such as migration and deconvolution, are not as yet routinely applied to radar data, unlike in reflection seismics. This reflects the relative infancy of GPR studies, the rather crude nature of such processing in much of the available radar software and the different survey techniques and demands of the end users. However, even relatively simple migration routines can enhance radar data significantly in some instances. As in seismic reflection studies, the effects of migration are three-fold: (a) dipping reflections are returned to, or nearer to, their true horizontal and vertical position; (b) structural distortions on steeply undulating reflections are partially or wholly removed; (c) diffraction patterns generated from point reflectors and strongly curved reflectors are partially or wholly removed. In addition to using processing software supplied by GPR manufacturers, radar data can also be converted to formats that are compatible with more complex reflection seismic packages. Research to date suggests that this approach may provide an effective means of performing more advanced processing (Fisher *et al.* 1992; Todoeschuck *et al.* 1992; Fisher *et al.* 1996). However, it should not be forgotten that although there are many obvious similarities between the radar reflection and seismic reflection techniques, the physical basis for the generation, propogation and reflection of energy is fundamentally different.

Interpretation of radar reflection profiles: radar stratigraphy

Although a reasonably significant number of GPR studies have now been carried out, a means for the systematic interpretation of radar reflection profiles for geological applications is only just being developed. Researchers have begun to apply seismic stratigraphic techniques (Mitchum *et al.* 1977) to the interpretation of radar reflection profiles (Beres & Haeni 1991; Jol & Smith 1991). The development of 'radar stratigraphy' has allowed the delineation and mapping of genetically related stratigraphic units within sedimentary deposits (Gawthorpe *et al.* 1993; Huggenberger 1993; van Overmeeren 1994, 1998; Bridge *et al.* 1995; Bristow 1995; Leclerc & Hickin 1997; Roberts *et al.* 1997; Smith & Jol 1997; van Heteren *et al.* 1998).

As in seismic stratigraphy (Mitchum *et al.* 1977; Emery & Meyers 1996), radar stratigraphy relies on the identification of systematic reflection terminations (Fig. 5). These terminations define *radar sequence boundaries*. Geologically these are believed to represent significant non-depositional or erosional hiatuses (Gawthorpe *et al.* 1993). Radar sequence boundaries define genetically related packages of reflections termed *radar sequences*. Gawthorpe *et al.* (1993) define these as the 'fundamental stratigraphic units' that can be identified on radar reflection profiles. Working within the framework of radar sequences it is then possible to define various *radar facies*. These are mappable three-dimensional packages of reflections with distinctive configurations, continuity, frequency, amplitude, velocity characteristics and external form (Jol & Smith 1991; Gawthorpe *et al.* 1993; Huggenberger 1993).

Despite the obvious appeal of such a systematic approach to the interpretation of radar reflection profiles, a number of problems remain. Firstly, various type of electromagnetic 'noise' are commonly seen on many radar reflection profiles and care must be taken to avoid mis-identifying apparent reflection terminations associated with the resulting interference patterns. Sources of noise include the GPR equipment itself, the ambient environment (e.g. radio and television signals) and, where unshielded antennae are deployed, scattering due to surface objects in close proximity to the survey line (Sun & Young 1995). In addition, secondary reflections, analogous to those seen on seismic profiles, can also occur. These include reflection hyperbolae caused by point sources or major lateral discontinuities in the subsurface, although in both cases these can be removed by migration. It should be

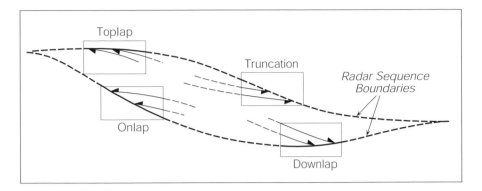

Fig. 5. The basic descriptive terminology associated with the definition of radar sequences and their boundaries. Modified from Gawthorpe *et al.* (1993).

noted that in many archaeological applications the identification of such point sources is fundamental to the location of potential targets.

Secondly, not all of the primary reflections are the result of the presence of geologically significant units or sedimentary structures. A common example is the presence of a fresh groundwater table. The top of this feature gives a particularly strong reflection which often cross-cuts radar sequence boundaries and radar facies (e.g. Fig. 3).

Thirdly, the primary geological reflection patterns observed are to some degree dependent upon the return centre frequency of the signal and the dielectric properties of the earth materials (Jol & Smith 1991; Huggenberger 1993). It has already been noted that resolution is a function of these two parameters and this will clearly affect the scale of geological feature that can be detected and the resulting reflection configurations. For example, lateral variations in bed thickness can lead to apparent reflection terminations where values fall below the level of resolution. As a result, terminations may be present where the return centre frequency is low (e.g. 50 MHz antennae) and/or the RDP of the material is low (e.g. unsaturated sand above a water table), but absent on an equivalent profile where the frequencies are higher (e.g. 200 MHz antennae) or on the same profile where the RDP is higher (e.g. saturated sands below a water table). Consequently, in addition to the radar sequence and radar facies characteristics, the resolution and the scale of reflections are also important considerations when interpreting radar reflection profiles geologically (Bristow 1995; van Heteren *et al.* 1998). It is in this way that radar stratigraphy differs significantly from seismic stratigraphy. Reflection seismics can at best resolve sequences and facies that are 'equal

in size to or larger than complete macroforms in major elements of depositional systems' (van Heteren *et al.* 1998). By contrast GPR has the resolution to image the internal structure of a range of sedimentary units from individual bedforms (e.g. aeolian dunes) up to complete macroforms (e.g. a barrier island).

A more qualitative approach of radar facies description and interpretation has been adopted in some instances. This is because in many instances: (a) non-geological primary reflectors such as the water table can be of considerable importance; (b) secondary interference patterns such as reflection hyperbolae can aid geological (or archaeological) interpretation and (c) modern high resolution surveys generate very complex profiles with high numbers of reflection terminations (Bristow 1995; van Overmeeren 1998; van Heteren *et al.* 1998). As a consequence, a number of attempts have been made to attach definitive interpretations to various radar facies in specific depositional settings (Beres & Haeni 1991; Huggenberger 1993; van Overmeeren 1994, 1998; Busby 1997; van Heteren *et al.* 1998). However, although this is probably useful on a local or regional scale, the application of these to data from new study sites is somewhat difficult. This situation may improve as the total data set increases.

Geomorphological and sedimentological applications in coastal environments.

Theory and practical experience suggest that GPR surveying is likely to be most successful where ground conductivities and resulting attenuation are low (cf. Table 1), thus allowing significant penetration of the radar signal.

Consequently, coastal deposits dominated by sands, gravels and peats, that are either unsaturated or below a fresh groundwater table, are likely to be the most amenable to radar reflection profiling (Leatherman 1987; Baker 1991; Clemmensen *et al.* 1996; Meyers *et al.* 1996; van Heteren *et al.* 1996; van Heteren & van de Plassche 1997; van Heteren *et al.* 1998; van Overmeeren 1998). Deposits dominated by significant amounts of fine grained sediment (e.g. saltmarshes) or areas with a brackish to saline groundwater are usually far less suitable, due to considerable attenuation of the electromagnetic signal (Leatherman 1987; Jol *et al.* 1996; van Heteren *et al.* 1996; van Heteren *et al.* 1998).

In order to demonstrate the types of geomorphological and sedimentological data that can be obtained from GPR surveys in suitable coastal settings, examples from a series of recently completed UK based studies will be presented. The aim is not to introduce complete data sets and furnish full interpretations, but to indicate the nature and range of information that can be obtained and its potential contribution to future coastal research.

Sefton coast, NW England

The Sefton coastal dune barrier system in NW England (Fig. 6) consists of a series of unconsolidated Holocene sediments, often over 30 m thick. The shoreface, foreshore and dune deposits of the barrier consist predominantly of fine-grained and well-sorted sand (Pye 1991; Neal 1993; Pye & Neal 1993). The sediments of the former backbarrier area consist of freshwater and estuarine peats, clays and silts and are partially overlain by at least 12 m of dune sand on their western (seaward) margin (Neal 1993; Pye & Neal 1993). Several periods of dune activity, separated by phases of dune stabilization and soil formation, have taken place up to the present day (Pye 1990; Neal 1993; Pye & Neal 1993, 1994; Pye *et al.* 1995). As a consequence the barrier system consists of a thick and extensive suite of coastal sediments that are suitable for radar profiling. In particular, there exists a wide range of deposits associated with active and recently active coastal dunes, in addition to the extensive mid- to late-Holocene aeolian sequences.

(1) Raven Meols blowout

At Raven Meols, in the southern part of the coastal dune system (Fig. 6), a large active trough

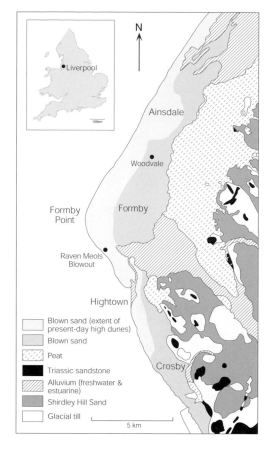

Fig. 6. Location and surficial geology of the Sefton coast, immediately to the north of Liverpool in NW England. Locations of the two study sites at Raven Meols and Woodvale are also indicated. Modified from Pye *et al.* (1995).

blowout is developed. The blowout has formed during approximately the last 100 years. It lies landwards of a broad belt of parallel foredunes that have been developing since at least 1880 (Pye 1990). The blowout is recorded on the first aerial photographs taken of the area in 1945, when it was approximately 60 m long and 30 m wide. It is now around 300 m long and 100 m wide, with a major depositional lobe at its downwind (northeastern) end (Fig. 7).

A series of intersecting radar reflection profiles were collected at the site at various antennae frequencies. CMP surveys indicated that radar wave velocities above and below the water table were significantly different and that a two-layer velocity model should be employed. As a consequence, elevation scales on the profiles presented are different above and below the ground

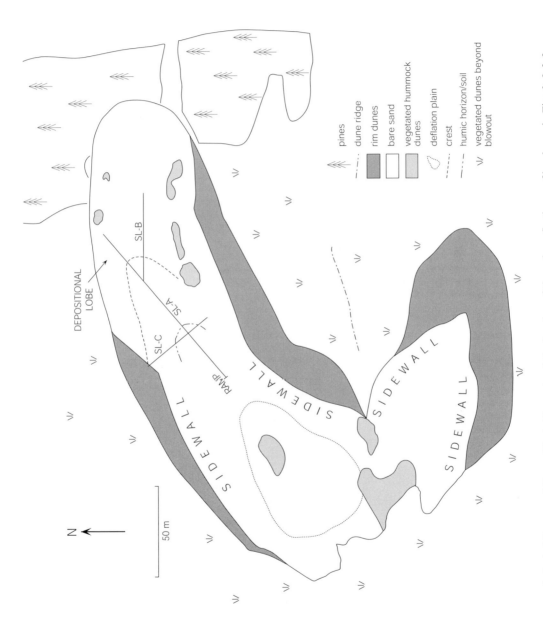

Fig. 7. The main geomorphological features of Raven Meols blowout and the location of the radar reflection profiles shown in Figs 3, 8 & 9.

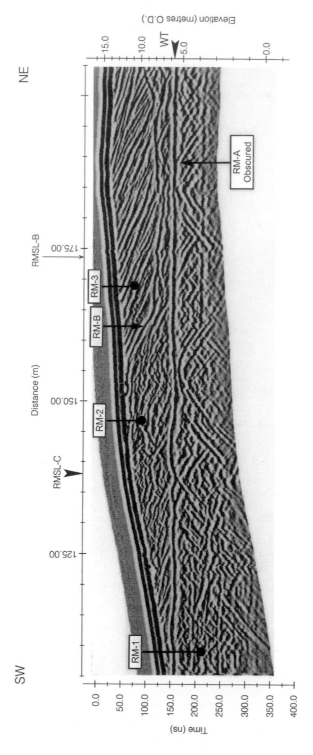

Fig. 8. 100 MHz radar reflection profile from Raven Meols blowout survey line A. The survey line was orientated parallel to the axis of the blowout throat (Fig. 7), running across the blowout ramp (105–150 m) and the depositional lobe (150–205 m). Radar sequence boundaries (RM-A, B), radar facies (RM-1, 2, 3) and the location of the water table (WT) are indicated, as are the intersections with survey lines B (RMSL-B) and C (RMSL-C). A full description of the radar stratigraphy of the profile and its geological interpretation can be found in Table 3.

water table (e.g. Fig. 3). Ground truthing from hand auger holes indicated that the elevation/depth estimates were remarkably accurate, lying within the likely errors associated with augering (e.g. ±0.1 m at 8 m depth). This probably reflects the highly uniform nature of the dune sands at the study site. Results from three intersecting survey lines that traverse a number of the main geomorphological features of the blowout (Fig. 7) are presented here (Lines A, B and C; Figs 8, 3 & 9).

Distinct radar sequence boundaries and facies can be identified on all the reflection profiles obtained, allowing the construction of a radar stratigraphy for the blowout. This stratigraphy can be interpreted geologically with the aid of field observations, auger holes and aerial photograph analysis (Table 3). The thin dune soil forming radar sequence boundary RM-B provides a distinct and laterally continuous reflection that can easily be traced in the subsurface. The radar facies identified have reflection characteristics that clearly indicate they represent packets of primary sedimentary structures. This is confirmed by field observations. Furthermore, the nature of the various radar facies can be related to the formation of sedimentary structures under differing depositional conditions. In particular, the dune internal structure represented by radar facies RM-3 can be clearly related to the geomorphological development of the depositional lobe, as identified on recent aerial photographs.

The strong reflection from the water table is the most important non-geological feature that can be identified on the radar reflection profiles. It forms a near horizontal and laterally continuous reflection that can be traced across the study site. Associated with this reflection are a complex series of interfering hyperbolae, whose apex appear to lie at the water table and obscure many of the primary sedimentary structures beneath. The cause of these hyperbolae is unclear, but may be related to discontinuities on the water table surface and the large size of the Fresnel zone at depths of up to 10 m. However, whatever their origin, they prevent detailed geological interpretation beneath the water table.

(2) Woodvale, Ainsdale Hills

The Ainsdale Hills lie in the central part of the Sefton coastal dune barrier complex (Fig. 6). At this point the dune belt is approximately 3 km wide, although the Woodvale area has been levelled for cultivation or housing. Boreholes indicate that the main body of the dune complex, both at Ainsdale and elsewhere, consists of a

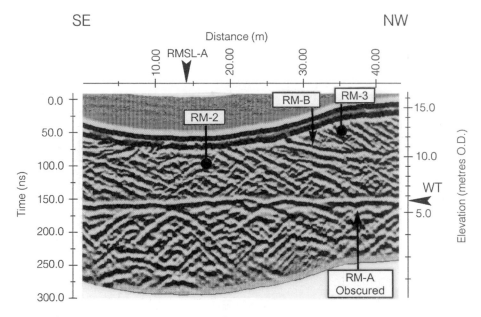

Fig. 9. 100 MHz radar reflection profile from Raven Meols blowout survey line C. The survey line was orientated normal to the axis of the blowout (Fig. 7), cross-cutting the ramp (10–25 m) and the depositional lobe (0–10 m and 25–43 m). Radar sequence boundaries (RM-B), radar facies (RM-2, 3) and the location of the water table (WT) are indicated, as is the intersection with survey line A (RMSL-A). A full description of the radar stratigraphy of the profile and its geological interpretation can be found in Table 3.

Table 3. *Description and interpretation of the radar stratigraphy from Raven Meols blowout, as shown in Figs 3, 8 & 9. The geological interpretation was aided by the analysis of hand auger hole logs, field exposures and aerial photographs*

	Radar Wave Velocity	Vertical Resolution	Description	Interpretation
Radar Facies RM-1	0.06 m/ns	0.2 m	Series of sub-horizontal, laterally continuous, sub-parallel reflections. Partially obscured by a series of complex interfering hyperbolae developed below the top of the water table	Upper foreshore sediments, deposited as part of a progradational beach-dune complex. Now lying below a fresh ground water table
Sequence Boundary RM-A			Obscured by complex series of interfering hyperbolae developed below the top of the water table	Contact between the underlying beach deposits of RM-1 and overlying dune deposits of RM-2
Radar Facies RM-2	0.135 m/ns	0.4 m	Series of cross-cutting reflections with limited lateral continuity. Reflections have low to moderate apparent dips and downlap onto RM-A and toplap onto RM-B	Complex series of aeolian cross-strata separated by cross-cutting bounding surfaces. Indicative of dune development in the presence of at least a partial vegetation cover
Sequence Boundary RM-B			Laterally continuous, undulating reflection	Thin humic horizon representing a dune stabilisation surface which has been buried by the recently deposited aeolian sediments of RM-3
Radar Facies RM-3	0.135 m/ns	0.4 m	Laterally continuous, sub-parallel, generally moderate to high angle reflections. Occasionally display low-angle cross-cutting relationships. All reflections downlap onto RM-B	Packets of cross-strata deposited as the vegetation free depositional lobe of the blowout has extended progressively north-eastwards. Low-angle third order bounding surfaces occasionally seen representing minor reactivation surfaces

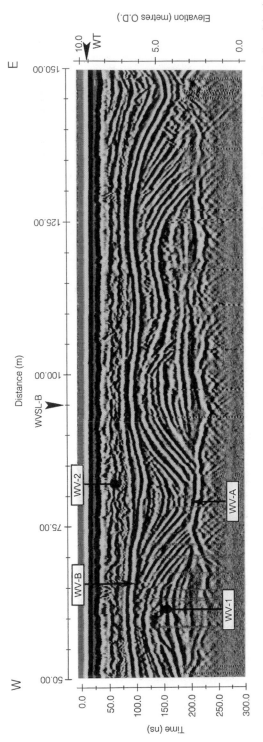

Fig. 10. 100 MHz radar reflection profile from Woodvale survey line A. The profile is orientated west to east, normal to the presumed gross depositional strike of the dune system. Radar sequence boundaries (WV-A, B), radar facies (WV-1, 2) and the location of the water table (WT) are indicated, as is the intersection with survey line B (WVSL-B). A full description of the profile's radar stratigraphy and its geological interpretation can be found in Table 4.

series of aeolian sediments at least 12 m thick and extending well below the current ground water level (Neal 1993; Pye & Neal 1993). Several boreholes also indicate that parts of the aeolian sequence contain a series of peats and humic horizons, the oldest of which can be dated to approximately 5100 ^{14}C years BP (Neal 1993; Pye & Neal 1993). However, correlation of these peats and humic horizons is extremely difficult due to the limited number and wide spacing of the boreholes and the small number of samples suitable for radiocarbon dating. In order to try and overcome these difficulties, a series of radar reflection and CMP profiles were collected along a number of survey lines across the Ainsdale Hills, including Woodvale. The survey lines were designed so as to run approximately parallel or normal to the presumed gross depositional strike of the dune system, based on the orientation of surficial bedforms.

At Woodvale the fresh ground water table was generally within less than 1 m of the surface along all of the survey lines. At an antennae frequency of 100 MHz the radar signal was able to penetrate the full dune sequence to depths of at least 8 m (Figs 10 & 11). CMP surveys again indicated that radar wave velocities above and below the water table were significantly different and that a two-layer velocity model should be employed. The complex interference hyperbolae associated with the water table at Raven Meols blowout were not observed on the profiles from Woodvale. This allowed a detailed radar stratigraphic and geological interpretation for the aeolian sedimentary sequence beneath the water table (Table 4).

The lack of radar wave penetration beneath the aeolian sequence (i.e. below sequence boundary WV-A) and evidence from a number of nearby boreholes indicates that the dune sediments overlie a peat, which is in turn underlain by thicker sequences of either silts or muddy sands. Within the aeolian sequence a distinct sequence boundary (WV-B) can be identified and is interpreted as a bounding surface marking a significant hiatus in dune sand deposition. Shallow boreholes at the study site were unable to locate any major lithological change at this boundary (e.g. a humic horizon or peat). Consequently, it can be assumed that the break in deposition was not sufficiently long to allow significant soil formation.

The bounding surface defined by WV-B separates two major phases of aeolian activity, represented by radar facies WV-1 and WV-2. Reflection configurations within both radar facies are interpreted as being the product of primary sedimentary structures within the dune sediments. Interpretation of these structures indicates that in both phases of dune activity deposition was rapid, with little or no vegetation cover. During the first phase of aeolian activity (WV-1), a series of broad, low, undulating dunes developed immediately on top of the underlying peat. The lack of evidence for bounding surfaces within this sequence and the apparent preservation of topsets, foresets and bottomsets suggests that sedimentation rates were very high. The dune topography associated with the end of this phase of dune activity appears to have been preserved during the second phase of activity, represented by WV-2. The very low angle, subparallel nature of the reflections in radar facies WV-2 suggests that the second phase of dune formation was probably associated with extensive sand sheet development. Rapid burial of the palaeo-dune topography is indicated by the divergent fill present in the topographic depressions associated with WV-B. Levelling of the area for agricultural purposes, during the latter part of the nineteenth century and early part of the twentieth century, is likely to have removed any small dunes that were present during the final phase of sand sheet stabilization.

The Ayres foreland, Isle of Man

The Ayres coastal foreland lies at the northern tip of the Isle of Man (Fig. 12). It is over 7 km long and widens progressively from west to east. At its eastern margin it is over 2.5 km wide. The landward margin of the Ayres is marked by a cliff cut into till. This cliff is noticeably degraded along its central and eastern portions. Seaward of this cliff are a series of Holocene deposits, principally of coastal or coastal-margin origin. Field sections, exposed along the eroding eastern edge of the foreland, suggest that the inner part of the Ayres consists of a series of shallow basins (Fig. 12) containing a complex sequence of fine-grained clastic and organic deposits (Phillips 1967, 1969; Ward 1970; Dackombe & Thomas 1985; Gonzales et al. 2000). These basins are separated either by till or beachface sands and gravels. The most southerly of these basins, at Phurt, is also an important geoarchaeological site (Dackombe & Thomas 1985; Gonzales et al. 2000). By contrast, the outer part of the foreland consists entirely of sands and gravels with distinct sets of beach ridges (Dackombe & Thomas 1985). Discontinuous and thin (<3 m, Lamplugh 1903) coastal dune sand deposits form the top of the sedimentary sequence, both on the inner and outer Ayres.

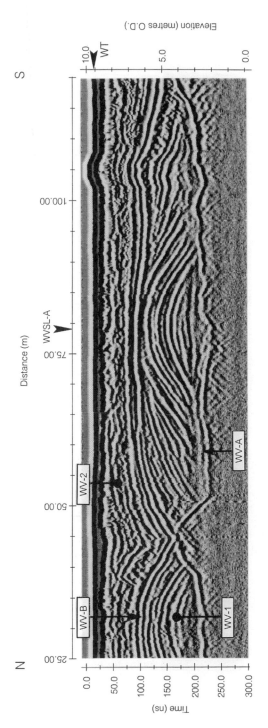

Fig. 11. 100 MHz radar reflection profile from Woodvale survey line B. The profile is orientated north to south, parallel to the presumed gross depositional strike of the dune system. Radar sequence boundaries (WV-A, B), radar facies (WV-1, 2) and the location of the water table (WT) are indicated, as is the intersection with survey line A (WVSL-A). A full description of the profile's radar stratigraphy and its geological interpretation can be found in Table 4.

A. NEAL & C. L. ROBERTS

Table 4. *Description and interpretation of the radar stratigraphy from Woodvale, Ainsdale Hills, as shown in Figs 10 & 11. The geological interpretation was aided by the analysis of published and unpublished borehole logs for the area*

	Radar Wave Velocity	Vertical Resolution	Description	Geological interpretation
Sequence Boundary WV-A			Laterally continuous, undulating reflection. Associated small interference hyperbolae	Base of the dune sequence. Underlain by peat and then either muddy or silty sediments, primarily of intertidal origin
Radar Facies WV-1	0.065 m/ns	0.22 m	Laterally continuous, wavy parallel reflections. Sometimes divergent. Multi-directional apparent dips of 0 to 24°. Concordant with or downlapping onto WV-A. Toplap relationship with WV-B. Maximum thickness 4.5 m, but generally ≤4m	Predominantly parallel sets of aeolian cross-strata with widely varying orientations. Often display a complete series of topsets, foresets and bottomsets. Bounding surfaces are not present. Suggests rapid deposition and multi-directional dune growth in a setting dominated by a series of broad, low undulating dunes with little or no vegetation cover
Sequence Boundary WV-B			Laterally continuous, undulating reflection with topography of up to 2.5 m	Bounding surface marking a distinct hiatus in dune sand deposition. No evidence for soil formation
Radar Facies WV-2	0.065 m/ns	0.22 m	Laterally sub-continuous, wavy parallel reflections. Divergent fill within depressions associated with undulating WV-B. Apparent dips of 0 to 20°. Dips of reflections controlled by concordant relationship with WV-B beneath. Maximum thickness 5 m, but generally ≤3 m	Parallel sets of aeolian cross-strata draping the underlying dune stabilisation surface. Suggests rapid deposition as part of a large sand sheet with little or no vegetation cover

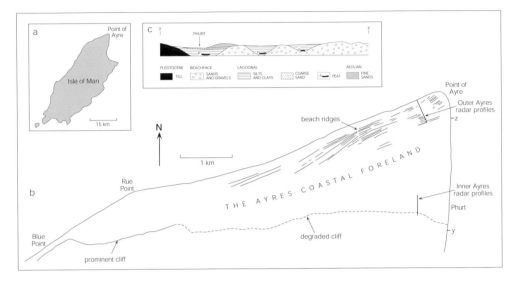

Fig. 12. (**a**) Location and (**b**) main geomorphological features of the Ayres foreland, Isle of Man. Location of the GPR transects on the eastern part of inner (southern) and outer (northern) Ayres are indicated. (**c**) Schematic geological cross section along the eastern shoreline of the Ayres (based on Ward 1970).

A series of radar reflection and CMP surveys were completed along transects on both the inner and outer Ayres (Fig. 12). The surveys were performed to test the feasibility of using GPR to provide information on the nature of the broader depositional setting at Phurt, primarily through an examination of the large-scale sedimentary architecture of the foreland.

(1) Outer Ayres

On the outer Ayres, surveys were run approximately normal and parallel to the beach ridges (Figs 13 & 14). In both profiles the water table forms an excellent horizontal reflection and consequently a two-layer velocity model is employed. The estimated depth to the water table, derived from the velocities obtained from a CMP survey, is consistent with water table elevations in an adjacent sand and gravel pit (± 0.1 m). The beach ridge deposits themselves are dominated by a single radar facies. It consists of concave-up, seaward dipping, oblique tangential clinoforms normal to the beach ridges (Fig. 13) and even parallel reflection configurations parallel to the ridges (Fig. 14). This radar facies is interpreted as representing the primary internal sedimentary structure produced by a series of dominantly seaward prograding sand and gravel beachface deposits. In the upper part of the profile, normal to the beach ridges (Fig. 13), occasional low-angle landward dipping reflections are observed

between the major clinoforms. These are interpreted as representing the foresets of berm ridge deposits that have welded onto the upper foreshore during beachface progradation. Based on their internal structure, it is suggested that the deposits of this portion of the outer Ayres are equivalent to the progradational gravel beach sequences of Massari & Parea (1988), Bluck (1999) and Bluck *et al.* (2000).

(2) Inner Ayres

On the inner Ayres, radar reflection and CMP profiles were run approximately normal to the degraded till margin (Fig. 12). In addition to the distinct reflection from the water table, two main radar facies can be identified in the radar reflection profiles, separated by a well-defined radar sequence boundary (Fig. 15a, b). CMP surveys indicate that not only are there vertical variations in radar wave velocity above and below the groundwater table, but also significant lateral variations, associated with the different radar facies units (Table 5). Radar facies unit AY-2 has a significantly higher average radar wave velocity above the water table (0.12 m/ns) than AY-3 (0.077 m/ns). In addition, AY-3 is of variable thickness and is not always present. Such variations lead to significant lateral distortion of the radar reflection profile. For example, the fresh ground water table, which would normally appear near horizontal if the lateral radar

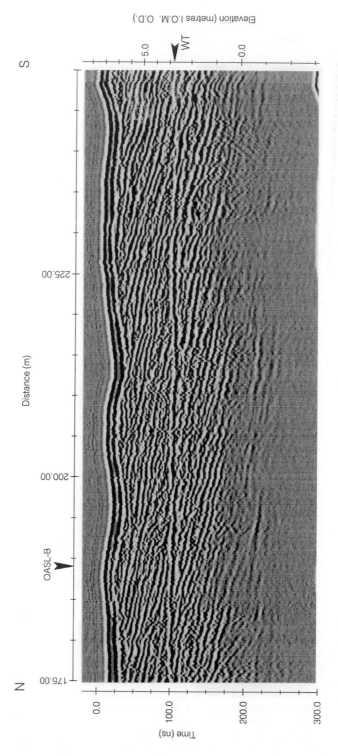

Fig. 13. 200 MHz radar reflection profile from Outer Ayres survey line A. The profile is orientated normal to a complex series of beach ridges (Fig. 12b). The location of the water table is indicated (WT), as is the intersection with survey line B (OASL-B).

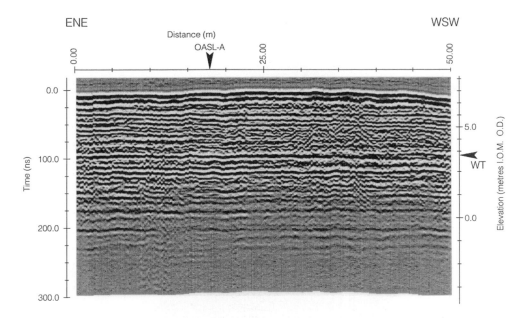

Fig. 14. 200 MHz radar reflection profile from Outer Ayres survey line B. The profile is orientated parallel to one of a complex series of beach ridges that characterize this part of the Ayres (Fig. 12b). The location of the water table is indicated (WT), as is the intersection with survey line A (OASL-A).

wave velocity variation was minimal (e.g. Fig. 13), appears deeper when AY-3 is present. Moreover, the degree of distortion is greater the thicker the AY-3 unit. This is because it is two-way travel time of the radar wave, rather than depth, that is actually being measured during data collection. The two-way travel time to the water table is a function of the average radar wave velocity of the material above it. As AY-3 thickens along a section of profile, the average radar wave velocity becomes lower as the lower velocity material of AY-3 assumes greater importance. Consequently, the two-way travel time to the water table lengthens and the water table appears deeper in the reflection profile. More importantly, however, in addition to the distortion of the water table, there are also distortions in the dip and configuration of the reflections from radar sequence boundaries and radar facies units. As these cannot easily be corrected, they must be compensated for in a qualitative manner during the interpretation of the radar stratigraphy.

Interpretation of the radar reflection profiles obtained (Table 5), supplemented by a series of commercial boreholes and trial holes, suggests the presence of a complex sequence of beach ridge deposits of different internal character and sedimentary facies associations to those of the outer Ayres. The base of the sequence, where reached, is characterized by sequence boundary

AY-A, which dips gently to the north and possibly west. Boreholes indicate that this is the till surface. Above this till base a distinct cross sectional beach ridge morphology is observed, delineated by radar sequence boundary AY-B. Boreholes indicate that radar facies AY-2, which lies between these two radar sequence boundaries, is characterized by medium to coarse sands and sub-rounded to rounded gravel. Its reflection configuration is interpreted as representing the presence of a complex series of primary sedimentary structures within coarse beach ridge deposits. Such structures suggest significant spatial and temporal variation in bedform type and migration direction during beach ridge emplacement.

Lying above radar sequence boundary AY-B is a complex trough fill defined by radar facies AY-3. Boreholes and trial holes indicate that this fill is a complex mix of sandy and silty clays, sands and sands and gravels. These deposits are interpreted as inter-beach ridge fill and may include estuarine, freshwater and aeolian deposits. A more detailed interpretation of similar trough fill sequences in this area can be found in Neal *et al.* (2000).

The overall radar and sedimentological characteristics of these deposits are clearly very different to those of the younger, outer Ayres, but have at least some similarities to the sections described to the east at Phurt. However, radar

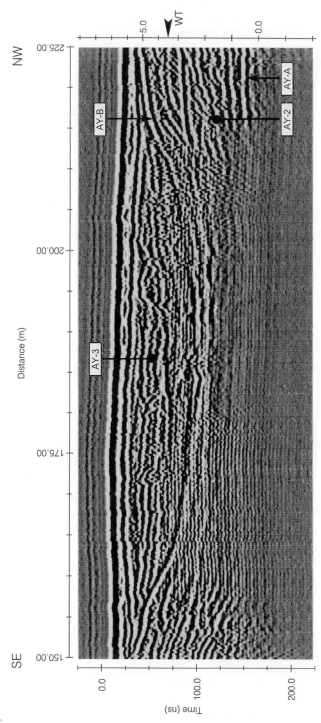

(a)

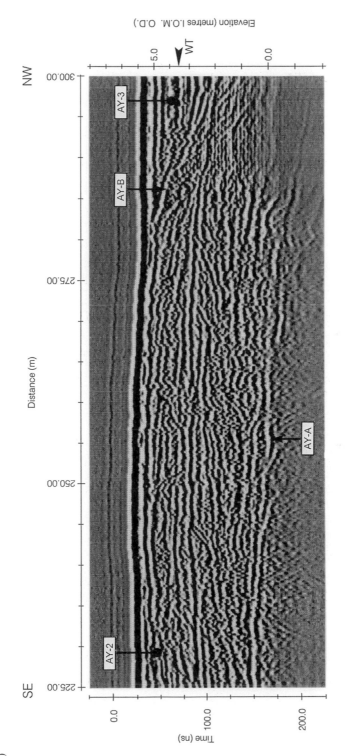

Fig. 15. 200 MHz radar reflection profiles from the Inner Ayres. The profiles are orientated approximately normal to the cliff cut into till immediately to the south (Fig. 12b), with (**b**) a continuation of (**a**). Radar sequence boundaries (AY-A, B), radar facies (AY-2, 3) and the location of the water table (WT) are indicated. A full description of the radar stratigraphy of the profiles and their geological interpretation can be found in Table 4.

Table 5. *Description and interpretation of the radar stratigraphy from the inner Ayres, as shown in Fig. 15a & b. The geological interpretation was aided by the analysis of unpublished borehole and trial hole logs located on or near the survey lines*

	Radar wave velocity	Vertical resolution	Description	Geological interpretation
Sequence Boundary AY-A			Distinct, laterally continuous reflection dipping gently to the north and possibly west	Contact between the overlying Holocene sediments and the underlying till surface
Radar Facies AY-2	0.120 m/ns (above WT) 0.071 m/ns (below WT)	0.24 m 0.14 m	Hummocky reflection configuration up to 7 m thick. Complex arrangement with different groups of reflections varying in both dip direction and angle, irrespective of transect orientation. Dips typically <5°, but with some packets of higher angle reflections up to 15° (typically 5–10°). Baselap relationship with AY-A, toplap relationship with AY-B	Beach ridge deposits, with individual ridges around 150 m wide. Reflections represent complex packets of primary sedimentary structures, suggesting spatial and temporal variation in bedform type and migration direction during beach-ridge emplacement
Sequence Boundary AY-B			Distinct, laterally continuous trough-shaped reflection.	Contact between the top of the underlying beach-ridge deposits and the base of the overlying inter-beach ridge fill
Radar Facies AY-3	0.077 m/ns (above WT)	0.15m	Complex trough fill 0–4 m thick. Typically low-angle (<3°), wavy sub-parallel reflections. Onlap AY-A. Associated high frequency noise (closely spaced horizontal banding) and reflection free zone immediately beneath the trough fill	Complex fill of inter-beach ridge area by sandy and silty clays, sands and sands and gravels of potentially intertidal/subtidal, aeolian and freshwater origin

reflection profiles collected on adjacent transects (Neal *et al.* 2000) suggest that the beach ridges and inter-beach ridge areas have a complex form and internal structure and are not simple linear features. Consequently, simple correlations or comparisons cannot be made. Evidence from other coarse clastic beach systems indicates that extensive, geometrically complex lagoonal deposits are associated with areas of former spit development (Bluck *et al.* 2000). In addition, similar beach ridge and inter-beach ridge morphologies, primary sedimentary structures and sedimentary facies associations have been described from an active, rapidly prograding and strongly recurved sand-dominated spit on Cape Cod, USA (Hine 1979). This suggests that the deposits of the inner Ayres represent a similar type of depositional environment, although more research is required to determine their detailed sedimentology and geomorphology and how this might relate to the rich archaeological finds in the area.

Potential geoarchaeological applications in coastal environments

The primary role of GPR in archaeological studies has been the location and mapping of potential targets (see comprehensive review in Conyer & Goodman (1997) and examples in Reynolds (1997)). This usually involves the detection of subsurface anomalies, e.g. reflection hyperbolae, on closely spaced parallel or gridded traverses over the area of potential interest. However, some of the more recent studies have attempted to relate archaeological targets to their stratigraphic setting (Conyers & Goodman 1997). In addition, attempts have also been made to combine archaeological data with GPR derived stratigraphic and sedimentological data as part of larger palaeoenvironmental reconstruction projects (e.g. Taylor & Macklin 1997 and the results presented here from the Ayres, Isle of Man).

The studies presented in this paper clearly demonstrate that sand and/or gravel dominated coastal systems provide ideal settings for GPR deployment. Horizontal and vertical resolutions are high, depth of penetration is large and reflections from primary sedimentary structures are clear and often have significant lateral continuity. Consequently, these would provide ideal ground conditions for the identification of subsurface anomalies. However, only one published archaeological study has utilized GPR in such coastal settings. Vaughan (1986) was able to locate artifacts and archaeological features buried by up to two metres of gravel beach

deposits and peat at Red Bay, Canada. These included buried walls and the disturbed ground associated with graves. However, individual large cobbles and boulders within the beach material also produced anomalies and these complicated interpretation of the radar reflection profiles. It should be noted that such anomalies are also commonly seen in the radar reflection profiles from the sand and gravel deposits of the Ayres, Isle of Man (Figs 13, 14, 15a & b).

The lack of geoarchaeological studies utilizing GPR surveys in sand and/or gravel dominated coastal settings does not reflect their potential. For example, the coastal dunefields of South Wales are rich in archaeological sites that have been excavated and recorded throughout this century (Fox 1927; Higgins 1933; Lees 1982; Lees & Sell 1983; Cole 1986; Davidson *et al.* 1987; Benson *et al.* 1990). Higgins (1933) and Benson *et al.* (1990) relied heavily on this archaeological evidence to construct a broad chronology for coastal sand dune activity in South Wales. Both studies suggest that there have been three major phases of dune activity, in the Bronze Age (2500–600 BC), Iron Age (600 BC–1st century AD) and Medieval (14th to 16th century AD) periods. However, for a number of reasons such a simplistic chronology should be treated with some caution. Firstly, many of the early excavations were poorly recorded and the stratigraphic context of the archaeological evidence is often unclear. Secondly, evidence for each of the phases is not known to be present at all of the dune sites. Thirdly, the role of human activity in the local reactivation of the coastal dune sands is uncertain, especially on the thin deposits of the dunefield margins e.g. Stackpole Warren (Benson *et al.* 1990).

The broad problems outlined above are common to many previous studies, especially where attempts have been made to synthesize archaeological and geological data from investigations carried out separately. Clearly more work is required to resolve them and GPR is one tool that could potentially be employed in future investigations. The archaeological and stratigraphic evidence present in the South Wales coastal dunefields is particularly suitable for location and mapping by GPR (Table 6). Large features such as walls, ditches and compacted mud floors have distinctly different electrical properties to dune sands. This means they should be easily identified as anomalies on radar reflection profiles. Problems are likely to arise, however, where the targets are small i.e. below the horizontal and vertical resolution of the method as dictated by the antennae frequency, electrical properties of the subsurface and depth of the

Table 6. *Feasibility of using GPR to locate, map and provide the stratigraphic context for a variety of archaeological targets in the coastal dunefields of South Wales. Feasibility analysis based on the general principles outlined in Conyers & Goodman (1997)*

Archaeological Target	Depth and location(s) of potential targets in the coastal dunefields of South Wales	Feasibility of detection by GPR	Reason for assessment
Pit dwelling with foreign fill	1–2 m, Stackpole Warren (Benson et al. 1990)	Good	Significant velocity contrast between base and matrix will produce strong reflections
Trenches	1–2 m, Stackpole Warren (Benson et al. 1990)	Good	Significant velocity contrast between fill and surrounding matrix producing strong reflections
Stone foundations and walls	<5 m?, Rhossili (Davidson et al. 1987); 0–2 m, Stackpole Warren (Benson et al. 1990); 0–5 m, St. Ishmael (James 1991)	Good	Strong velocity contrast with vertical features creating reflection hyperbolae from their tops and sides
Stone and mud hearths	0.2–1.5 m, Merthyr Mawr Warren (Fox 1927); 0.5–2.5 m, Pennard Burrows (Lees & Sell 1983; Cole 1986); <1 m, Stackpole Warren (Benson et al. 1990)	Moderate to Good	Firing can create baked surfaces which produce strong reflections. However, small hearths (<1 m diameter) may be difficult to detect unless at shallow depth and high frequency radar is employed
Compacted mud floor and walls	0.1–2.5 m, Pennard Burrows (Lees & Sell 1983; Cole 1986); <5 m?, Rhossili (Davidson et al. 1987)	Good	Significant velocity contrast from spatially extensive surfaces producing a significant reflection
Cremation and burial pits with foreign fill	1–2 m, Stackpole Warren (Benson et al. 1990)	Good	Providing a strong velocity contrast exists, these features are usually large enough to be visible at most radar frequencies

Small, dispersed artifacts	0.1–2.5 m, Pennard Burrows (Lees & Sell 1983; Cole 1986) 0–2m, Stackpole Warren (Benson et al. 1990)	Poor	Target objects too small to reflect enough radar energy to be visible
Occupation horizons with spatially extensive concentrations of artifacts	0.2–1.5 m, Merthyr Mawr Warren (Fox 1927) 0.3–2.9m, Broughton Burrows (Lees 1982; Cole 1986) 0–0.5 m, Stackpole Warren (Benson et al. 1990)	Moderate to Good	Although individual artifacts cannot be located, as a whole they may have a sufficient velocity contrast and thickness to produce noticeable reflections which appear as one layer
Soil horizons	0.3–2.9 m, Broughton Burrows (Lees 1982; Cole 1986) 0–3.5m, Pennard Burrows (Lees & Sell 1983; Cole 1986) 0–2m, Stackpole Warren (Benson et al. 1990)	Poor	Where thickness of stratigraphic layers is less than one-quarter of the received radar wavelength
		Good	Where thickness of stratigraphic layers is greater than one-quarter of the received radar wavelength
Bedrock/till	0.9–2 m, Merthyr Mawr Warren (Fox 1927) 0.8–6 m, Broughton Burrows (Lees 1982; Cole 1986) 1.5–5 m, Pennard Burrows (Lees & Sell 1983; Cole 1986) 1–2m, Stackpole Warren (Benson et al. 1990) 0–5 m, St. Ishmael (James 1991)	Good	Significant velocity contrast producing strong reflections

target. Consequently, the location of small constructions (e.g. fire pits <1 m in diameter) or scattered artifacts is likely to be difficult (Conyers & Goodman 1997). In addition to locating subsurface anomalies, however, the studies presented from the Sefton coastal dunes in NW England have clearly demonstrated that peat and soil horizons can easily be delineated by GPR. Such soils not only provide an important stratigraphic framework for coastal dune deposits, but are also often associated with occupation horizons (e.g. Benson et al. 1990; Gonzalez et al. 2000). Consequently, their initial identification and subsurface mapping may greatly aid the formulation of later excavation strategies.

Suitable archaeological targets for GPR are present in many suitable coastal locations, both in Europe and elsewhere. As a result, it is anticipated that there will be a significant increase in the number of coastal geoarchaeological studies utilizing GPR in the coming decade.

Conclusions

GPR works most effectively in coastal deposits dominated by clean sand and/or gravel sediments and a fresh groundwater table. When fine grained sediments are present there is often significant signal attenuation and depth of penetration is limited, although useful data can still be obtained. The presence of saline groundwater tends to preclude the use of GPR due to its very high conductivity and associated high attenuation.

An understanding of how a GPR system works, the electrical properties of earth materials and the issues surrounding horizontal and vertical resolution are required in order to collect, process, display and begin to interpret radar data effectively. Good survey design is fundamental to obtaining meaningful results, even in relatively simple and favourable settings. Although this can largely be achieved by detailed surveys of the proposed study site and some forward modelling, there is still an element of trial and error in choosing the optimum system set-up and survey parameters. Data processing should be undertaken with caution, in order to avoid creating 'artifacts' in the reflection profiles that are purely the result of the processing algorithms employed. At present, more complex processing, such as that normally applied to reflection seismic data (e.g. migration), is not routinely carried out on radar data. This largely reflects the relatively simple nature of the standard GPR processing packages and the different aims and subject base of the two user groups.

However, the rapidly developing nature of GPR technique and current experiments with seismic processing packages means that this situation is likely to improve in the future.

The stratigraphic and sedimentological interpretation of radar reflection profiles has been greatly aided by the broad adoption of radar stratigraphy, as first proposed by Beres & Haeni (1991) and Jol & Smith (1991). However, different authors have so far adopted radar stratigraphy to a greater or lesser extent, depending upon personal preference and individual site characteristics. This reflects the difficulty in trying to apply a system of interpretation originally designed for geological features on a significantly larger scale than those seen in radar reflection profiles. There is clearly a need to further formalize the approach to the interpretation of radar data for geological applications. However, this is only likely to occur after the completion of a significant number of additional studies.

Despite the limitations outlined above, the careful interpretation of radar reflection profiles from coastal environments dominated by coarse grained, unconsolidated sediments can provide high resolution stratigraphic, sedimentological, geomorphological and archaeological information to depths well in excess of 10 m. At present, the range of information that can be acquired is not available through the application of any other technique. Furthermore, GPR is non-invasive and data collection is relatively rapid and inexpensive. Initial GPR surveys can allow boreholes and excavations to be located in optimum positions for subsequent subsurface sample collection and provide a detailed stratigraphic context for their interpretation. In most instances radar facies can be directly related to discrete sedimentary environments and facies, potentially allowing detailed large-scale subsurface mapping of their distribution and the development of three-dimensional models for entire depositional systems (e.g. van Heteren et al. 1998). In addition, the primary reflections within individual radar facies are usually generated by collections of primary sedimentary structures and their interpretation allows the reconstruction of bedform type and the nature of bedform growth and migration. With suitably detailed three-dimensional surveys, such data could be used to reconstruct palaeocurrent directions. As GPR technology, data processing software and data interpretation techniques continue to develop, the technique is likely to become a routine reconnaissance and primary data collection tool in many sedimentary, geomorphological and geoarchaeological studies.

Assistance provided by the Sefton Coastal Ranger Service, the Sefton Coast Life Project, the Isle of Man government and the Centre for Manx Studies is gratefully acknowledged. Field assistance was provided by Robert Arklay, Martin Fenn, Dr Craig Reuben Smith and Jane Washington-Evans. We are particularly grateful to Dr Roger Dackombe for field assistance and in-depth discussion regarding the data from the Isle of Man. Andy Brown and Peter Fenning of Earth Science Systems Ltd., Kimpton are thanked for their logistical and technical support. Kay Lancaster prepared the illustrations. The research was supported by NERC Geophysical Equipment Pool Loans 555 and 556 and the School of Applied Sciences, University of Wolverhampton.

References

ANNAN, A. P. & DAVIS, J. L. 1976. Impulse radar sounding in permafrost. *Radio Science*, **11**, 383–394.

ARNOLD, J. E., AMBOS, E. L. & LARSON, D. O. 1997. Geophysical surveys of stratigraphically complex Island California sites: new implications for household archaeology. *Antiquity*, **71**, 157–168.

BAKER, P. L. 1991. Response of ground-penetrating radar to bounding surfaces and lithofacies variations in sand barrier sequences. *Exploration Geophysics*, **22** 19–22.

BENSON, D. G., EVANS, J. G., WILLIAMS, G. H., DARVILL, T. & DAVID, A. 1990. Excavations at Stackpole Warren, Dyfed. *Proceedings of the Prehistoric Society*, **56**, 179–245.

BERES, M. & HAENI, F. P. 1991. Application of ground-penetrating-radar methods in hydrogeologic studies. *Groundwater*, **29**, 375–386.

BLUCK, B. J. 1999. Clast assembling, bed-forms and structure in gravel beaches. *Transactions of the Royal Society of Edinburgh: Earth Sciences*, **89**, 291–323.

——, WARD, J. D. & SPAGGIARI, R. 2000. Gravel beaches of southern Namibia. *In*: PACKHAM, J. R., RANDALL, R. E., BARNES, R. S. K. & NEAL, A. (eds) *Ecology and Geomorphology of Coastal Shingle*. Westbury Academic & Scientific, Yorkshire, 56–76.

BRIDGE, J. S., ALEXANDER, J., COLLIER, R. E. L. L., GAWTHORPE, R. L. & JARVIS, J. 1995. Ground-penetrating radar and coring used to study the large-scale structure of point-bar deposits in three dimensions. *Sedimentology*, **42**, 839–852.

——, COLLIER, R. & ALEXANDER, J. 1998. Large-scale structure of Calamus River deposits (Nebraska, USA) revealed using ground-penetrating radar. *Sedimentology*, **45**, 977–986.

BRISTOW, C. 1995. Facies analysis in the Lower Greensand using ground-penetrating radar. *Journal of the Geological Society, London*, **152**, 591–598.

——, PUGH, J. & GOODALL, T. 1996. Internal structure of aeolian dunes in Abu Dhabi determined using ground-penetrating radar. *Sedimentology*, **43**, 995–1003.

BUSBY, J. P. 1997. Calibration and interpretation of ground penetrating radar data from around Sellafield, West Cumbria, UK. *European Journal of Environmental and Engineering Geophysics*, **2**, 137–152.

CLEMMENSEN, L. B., ANDREASEN, F., NIELSEN, S. T. & STEN, E. 1996. The late Holocene coastal dune-field at Vejers, Denmark: characteristics, sand budget and depositional dynamics. *Geomorphology*, **17**, 79–98.

COLE, D. J. 1986. *The coastal dunes of Broughton and Pennard Burrows on Gower, South Wales: their origin, growth and resulting landscape changes.* PhD thesis, University College, Swansea.

CONYERS, L. B. & GOODMAN, D. 1997. *Ground-Penetrating Radar: An Introduction for Archaeologists*. Altamira Press, London.

DACKOMBE, R. V. & THOMAS, G. S. P. (eds) 1985. *Field Guide to the Quaternary of the Isle of Man.* Quaternary Research Association, Cambridge.

DAVIES, J. L. & ANNAN, A. P. 1989. Ground-penetrating radar for high-resolution mapping of soil and rock stratigraphy. *Geophysical Prospecting*, **3**, 531–551.

DAVIDSON, A. F., DAVIDSON, J. E., OWEN-JOHNS, H. S. & TOFT, L. A. 1987. Excavations at the sand covered Medieval settlement at Rhossili, West Glamorgan. *Bulletin of the Board of Celtic Studies*, **34**, 244–269.

DOTT, E. R. & MICKELSON, D. 1995. Lake Michigan water levels and the development of Holocene beach-ridge complexes at Two Rivers, Wisconsin: stratigraphic, geomorphic and radiocarbon evidence. *Geological Society of America Bulletin*, **107**, 286–296.

EMERY, D. & MYERS, K. J. (eds) 1996. *Sequence Stratigraphy*. Blackwell Science, Oxford.

FISHER, E., MCMECHAN, G. A. & ANNAN, A. P. 1992. Acquisition and processing of wide-aperture ground-penetrating radar data. *Geophysics*, **57**, 495–504.

FISHER, S. C., STEWART, R. R. & JOL, H. M. 1996. Ground penetrating radar (GPR) data enhancement using seismic techniques. *Journal of Engineering and Environmental Geophysics*, **1**, 88–96.

FITZGERALD, D. M., BALDWIN, C. T., IBRAHIM, N. A. & HUMPHRIES, S. M. 1992. Sedimentologic and morphologic evolution of a beach-ridge barrier along an indented coast: Buzzard Bay, Massachusetts. *In*: FLETCHER, C. H. & WEHMILLER, J. F. (eds) *Quaternary Coasts of the United States: Marine and Lacustrine Systems*. Special Publication of the Society of Economic Palaeontologists and Mineralogists, **48**, 64–75.

FOX, C. 1927. A settlement of the Early Iron Age (La Tene I Sub Period) on Merthyr Mawr Warren, Glamorgan. *Archaeologia Cambrensis*, **82**, 44–66.

GAWTHORPE, R. L., COLLIER, R. E. L., ALEXANDER, J., LEEDER, M. & BRIDGE, J. S. 1993. Ground penetrating radar: application to sandbody geometry and heterogeneity studies. *In*: NORTH, C. P. & PROSSER, D. J. (eds) *Characterization of Fluvial and Aeolian Reservoirs*. Geological Society, London, Special Publications, **73**, 421–432.

GONZALEZ, S., INNES, J., HUDDART, D., DAVEY, P. & PLATER, A. 2000. Holocene coastal change in the north Isle of Man: Stratigraphy, palaeoenvironment and archaeological evidence. *This volume.*

HARARI, Z. 1996. Ground-penetrating radar (GPR) for imaging stratigraphic features and groundwater in sand dunes. *Journal of Applied Geophysics,* **36**, 43–52.

HERIQUE, A. & KOFMAN, W. 1997. Determination of the ice dielectric permittivity using the data of the test in Antarctica of the ground-penetrating radar for Mars '98 Mission. *IEEE Transactions of Geoscience and Remote Sensing,* **35**, 1338–1349.

HIGGINS, L. S. 1933. An investigation into the problem of the sand dune areas of the South Wales coast. *Archaeologia Cambrensis,* **88**, 26–67.

HINE, A. C. 1979. Mechanisms of berm development and resulting beach growth along a barrier spit complex. *Sedimentology,* **26**, 333–351.

HUGGENBERGER, P. 1993. Radar facies: recognition of facies patterns and heterogeneities within Pleistocene Rhine gravels, NE Switzerland. *In*: BEST, J. L. & BRISTOW, C. S. (eds) *Braided Rivers.* Geological Society, London, Special Publications, **75**, 163–176.

JAMES, T. 1991. Where sea meets land: the changing Carmarthenshire coastline. *In*: JAMES, H. (ed.) *Sir Gar, Studies in Carmarthenshire History.* Carmarthenshire Antiquarian Society Monograph Series, **4**, 143–166.

JOL, H. M. 1995. Ground penetrating radar antennae frequencies and transmitter powers compared for penetration depth, resolution and reflection continuity. *Geophysical Prospecting,* **43**, 693–709.

—— & SMITH, D. G. 1991. Ground penetrating radar of northern lacustrine deltas. *Canadian Journal of Earth Sciences,* **28** 1939–1947.

——, —— & MEYERS, R. A. 1996. Digital Ground Penetrating Radar (GPR): A new geophysical tool for coastal barrier research (examples from the Atlantic, Gulf and Pacific coasts, USA). *Journal of Coastal Research,* **12**, 960–968.

LAMPLUGH, G. W. 1903. *The Geology of the Isle of Man.* Memoir of the Geological Survey of Great Britain, London.

LEATHERMAN, S. P. 1987. Coastal geomorphological applications of ground-penetrating radar. *Journal of Coastal Research,* **3**, 397–399.

LEES, D. J. 1982. The sand dunes of Gower as potential indicators of climatic change in historical time. *Cambria,* **9**, 25–35.

—— & SELL, S. 1983. Excavation of a medieval dwelling at Pennard. *Gower,* **34**, 44–52.

LECLERC, R. F. & HICKIN, E. J. 1997. The internal structure of scrolled floodplain deposits based on ground-penetrating radar, North Thompson River, British Columbia. *Geomorphology,* **21**, 17–38.

LØNNE, I. & LAURITSEN, T. 1996. The architecture of a modern push-moraine at Svalbard as inferred from ground-penetrating radar measurements. *Arctic and Alpine Research,* **28**, 488–495.

MASSARI, F. & PAREA, G. C. 1988. Progradational gravel beach sequences in a moderate- to high-

energy, microtidal marine environment. *Sedimentology,* **35**, 881–913.

McCANN, D. M., JACKSON, P. D. & FENNING, P. J. 1988. Comparison of the seismic and ground probing radar methods in geological surveying. *Proceedings of the Institute of Electrical Engineers,* **135**, 380–390.

MELLET, J. S. 1995. Profiling of ponds and bogs using ground-penetrating radar. *Journal of Palaeolimnology,* **14**, 233–240.

MEYERS, R. A., SMITH, D. G., JOL, H. M. & PETERSON, C. D. 1996. Evidence for eight great earthquake-subsidence events detected with ground-penetrating radar, Willapa barrier, Washington. *Geology,* **24**, 99–102.

MITCHUM, R. M., VAIL, P. R. & SANGREE, J. B. 1977. Stratigraphic interpretation of seismic reflection patterns in depositional sequences. *In*: PAYTON, C. E. (ed.) *Seismic Stratigraphy – Applications to Hydrocarbon Exploration.* Memoirs of the American Association of Petroleum Geologists, **16**, 117–133.

NEAL, A. 1993. *Sedimentology and morphodynamics of a Holocene coastal dune barrier complex, northwest England.* PhD Thesis, University of Reading.

——, DACKOMBE, R. V. & ROBERTS, C. L. 2000. Applications of ground-penetrating radar (GPR) to the study of coarse clastic (shingle) coastal structures. *In*: PACKHAM, J. R., RANDALL, R. E., BARNES, R. S. K. & NEAL, A. (eds) *Ecology and Geomorphology of Coastal Shingle.* Westbury Academic & Scientific, Yorkshire, 77–106.

OLEHOFT, G. R. 1981. Electrical properties of rocks. *In*: TOULOUKIAN, Y. S., JUDD, W. R. & ROY, R. F. (eds) *Physical Properties of Rocks and Minerals.* McGraw-Hill, New York, 257–330.

OLSEN, H. & ANDREASEN, F. 1995. Sedimentology and ground-penetrating radar characteristics of a Pleistocene sandur deposit. *Sedimentary Geology,* **99**, 1–15.

ORI, G. G. & OGLIANI, F. 1996. Potentiality of ground-penetrating radar for the analysis of the stratigraphy and sedimentology of Mars. *Planetary and Space Science,* **44**, 1303–1315.

PHILLIPS, B. A. M. 1967. The post-glacial raised shoreline around the northern plain, Isle of Man. *Northern Universities Geographical Journal,* **8**, 43–50.

——1969. *Cliff and shore platform development on the Isle of Man.* PhD thesis, University of Aberystwyth.

PYE, K. 1990. Physical and human influences on coastal dune development between the Ribble and Mersey estuaries, northwest England. *In*: NORDSTROM, K. F., PSUTY, N. P. & CARTER, R. W. G. (eds) *Coastal Dunes: Form and Process.* Wiley, Chichester, 339–359.

——1991. Beach deflation and backshore dune formation following erosion under storm surge conditions: an example from northwest England. *Acta Mechanica Supplementum,* **2**, Springer Verlag, Berlin, 171–181.

—— & NEAL, A. 1993. Late Holocene dune formation on the Sefton coast, northwest England. *In*: PYE, K. (ed.) *The Dynamics and Environmental Context of*

Aeolian Sedimentary Systems. Geological Society, London, Special Publications, **72**, 201–217.

—— & ——1994. Coastal dune erosion at Formby Point, north Merseyside, England: causes and mechanisms. *Marine Geology*, **119**, 39–56.

——, STOKES, S. & NEAL, A. 1995. Optical dating of aeolian sediments from the Sefton coast, northwest England. *Proceedings of the Geologists' Association*, **106**, 281–292.

REYNOLDS, J. M. 1997. *An Introduction to Applied and Environmental Geophysics*. Wiley, Chichester.

ROBERTS, M. C., BRAVARD, J. P. & JOL, H. M. 1997. Radar signatures and structure of an avulsed channel, Rhone River, Aoste, France. *Journal of Quaternary Science*, **12**, 35–42.

ROBINSON, E. S. & ÇORUH, C. 1988. *Basic Exploration Geophysics*. Wiley, Chichester.

ROY, P. S., COWELL, P. J., FERLAND, M. A. & THOM, B. G. 1994. Wave-dominated coasts. *In*: CARTER, R. W. G. & WOODROFFE, C. D. (eds) *Coastal Evolution – Late Quaternary Shoreline Morphodynamics*. University Press, Cambridge, 121–186.

SCHENK, C. J., GAUTIER, D. L., OLHOEFT., G. R. & LUCIUS, J. E. 1993. Internal structure of an aeolian dune using ground-penetrating radar. *In*: Pye, K. & LANCASTER, N. (eds) *Aeolian Sediments Ancient and Modern*. Special Publication of the International Association of Sedimentologists, **16**, 61–69.

SHERIFF, R. E. 1977. Limitations on resolution of seismic reflections and geologic detail derivable from them. *In*: PAYTON, C. E. (ed.) *Seismic Stratigraphy – Applications to Hydrocarbon Exploration*. Memoirs of the American Association of Petroleum Geologists, **16**, 3–14.

SMITH, D. G. & JOL, H. M. 1992. Ground-penetrating radar investigation of a Lake Bonneville delta, Provo level, Bingham City, Utah. *Geology*, **20**, 1083–1086.

—— & ——1995. Ground-penetrating radar: antenna frequencies and maximum probable depths of penetration in Quaternary sediments. *Journal of Applied Geophysics*, **33**, 93–100.

—— & ——1997. Radar structure of a Gilbert-type delta, Peyto Lake, Banff National Park, Canada. *Sedimentary Geology*, **113**, 195–209.

——, MEYERS, R. A. & JOL, H. M. 1999. Sedimentology of an upper-mesotidal (3.7 m) Holocene barrier, Willapa Bay, SW Washington, USA. *Journal of Sedimentary Research*, **69**, 1290–1296.

STERNBERG, B. K. & McGILL, J. W. 1995. Archaeology studies in southern Arizona using ground penetrating radar. *Journal of Applied Geophysics*, **33**, 209–225.

STRAND PETERSEN, K. & ANDREASEN, F. 1989. Holocene coastal development reflecting sea-level rise and isostatic movement in NW Jutland, Denmark. *Geologiska Föreningens i Stockholm Förhandlingar*, **111**, 287–303.

SUN, J. & YOUNG, R. A. 1995. Recognising surface scattering in ground-penetrating radar data. *Geophysics*, **60**, 1378–1385.

TAYLOR, M. P. & MACKLIN, M. G. 1997. Holocene alluvial sedimentation and valley floor development: the River Swale, Catterick, North Yorkshire, UK. *Proceedings of the Yorkshire Geological Society*, **51**, 317–327.

THEIMER, B. D., NOBES, D. C. & WARNER, B. G. 1994. A study of the geoelectrical properties of peatlands and their influence on ground-penetrating radar surveying. *Geophysical Prospecting*, **42**, 179–209.

TODOSCHUCK, J. P., LaFLÈCHE, P. T., JENSEN, O. G., JUDGE, A. S. & PILON, J. A. 1992. Deconvolution of ground probing radar data. *In*: PILON, J. A. (ed.) *Ground Penetrating Radar*. Geological Survey of Canada Paper **90-4**, 227–230.

TOPP, G. C., DAVIS, J. L. & ANNAN, A. P. 1980. Electromagnetic determination of soil water content: measurements in coaxial transmission lines. *Water Resources Research*, **16**, 574–582.

VANDENBERGHE, J. & VAN OVERMEEREN, R. A. 1999. Ground penetrating radar images of selected fluvial deposits in the Netherlands. *Sedimentary Geology*, **128**, 245–270.

VAN HETEREN, S. & VAN DE PLASSCHE, O. 1997. Influence of relative sea-level change and tidal-inlet development on barrier-spit stratigraphy, Sandy Neck, Massachusetts. *Journal of Sedimentary Research*, **67**, 350–363.

——, FITZGERALD, D. M., BARBER, D. C., KELLEY, J. T. & BELKNAP, D. F. 1996. Volumetric analysis of a New England barrier system using ground-penetrating radar and coring techniques. *Journal of Geology*, **104**, 471–483.

——, ——, McKINLAY, P. A. & BUYNEVICH, I. V. 1998. Radar facies of paraglacial barrier systems: coastal New England, USA. *Sedimentology*, **45**, 181–200.

VAN OVERMEEREN, R. A. 1994. Georadar for hydrogeology. *First Break*, **12**, 401–408.

——1998. Radar facies of unconsolidated sediments in The Netherlands: a radar stratigraphy interpretation method for hydrogeology. *Journal of Applied Geophysics*, **40**, 1–18.

VAUGHAN, C. J. 1986. Ground-penetrating radar surveys used in archaeological investigations. *Geophysics*, **51**, 595–604.

WARD, C. 1970. The Ayre raised beach. *Geological Journal*, **7**, 217–220.

Textural and geochemical evidence for the provenance of aeolian sand deposits on the Aquitaine coast, SW France

SAMANTHA E. SAYE & KENNETH PYE

Surface Processes and Modern Environments Group, Department of Geology, Royal Holloway, University of London, Egham, Surrey, TW20 0EX, UK

Abstract: The coastal dune system of the Aquitaine region, SW France, is the largest in Europe. At the present time the dunes are mostly stabilized by forest vegetation which is largely the product of dune stabilization schemes undertaken since the late 18th century. Much of the shoreline is currently eroding at rates of $1–2\,\mathrm{ma}^{-1}$, which are likely to increase if predictions of accelerated sea-level rise and increased storminess are correct. The sources of the beach and dune are poorly understood, and need to be identified in order to assess the sand budgets and likely dynamic response of the dune systems to changes in environmental forcing factors. This paper presents the results of an investigation to characterize the beach and aeolian sand in the region, and to identify its origin. The dune sands were found to be texturally and compositionally similar to the Quaternary Sable de Landes which occurs landward of, and partially beneath, the coastal dune belt. The results suggest that marine, aeolian and local fluvial reworking of the Sable de Landes has provided the main source of coastal dune sand, although marine erosion of Pleistocene deposits exposed in the coastal cliffs of the Medoc has made a secondary contribution.

The Aquitaine coast in SW France consists of a 250 km long, almost straight and continuous sandy beach interrupted only in its middle by Arcachon Bay which is partially closed by the Cap Ferret spit (Fig. 1). The coast is dominated by the largest coastal dune complex in Europe, ranging in width from 0.2–10 km, that encloses several large lakes. The dune system consists of foredunes and older inland dunes which have previously been mapped separately by the French Geological Survey, largely on the basis of morphology, as 'modern' and 'primary' dunes.

The predominant wind direction on the coast is essentially westerly (N 280°) and the consistent orientation of the dune axes parallel to the coast suggests that the wind climate has remained largely unchanged in the Aquitaine region during the last 3500 years (Froidefond & Prud'homme 1991).

In the northern part of the region, on the Medoc Peninsula, the dunes rest upon Holocene estuarine sediments associated with tributary valleys and terraces of the Gironde estuary. Further south the dunes overlie Pleistocene sand sheet sediments (the Sable de Landes) which form a generally flat, triangular area extending up to 100 km inland. These deposits are mainly fluvio-aeolian in origin, with discontinuous areas

of low relief continental dunes and aeolian sand sheets separated by, and interbedded with, fluvial deposits. These sediments are believed to have been transported to the area by rivers flowing from the Pyrenees under periglacial conditions during the late Pleistocene (Legigan 1979).

The coastal dunes are largely stabilized by coniferous forests at the present day, the result of dune stabilization schemes undertaken since the late 18th century (Barrère 1992; Favennec 1996). Parabolic and barchanoid dune forms are both well represented. Parallel with the shore in many areas is a foredune ridge or regressive foredune platform which is also heavily managed at the present time (Fig. 2). The beaches and frontal dunes have experienced significant net erosion during the last 50 years, as indicated by the presence of fallen Second World War German military blockhouses which are now situated on the beach in many places (Fig. 3). Average historical erosion rates vary spatially from $1–2\,\mathrm{ma}^{-1}$, with coastal progradation limited only to a relatively small number of areas (Froidefond & Prud'homme 1991; Aubié & Tastet 2000). Large transgressive dunes occur in only one or two places such as the famous Dune du Pyla situated at the entrance to the Arcachon basin (Fig. 4; Froidefond & Legigan 1985).

From: PYE, K. & ALLEN, J. R. L. (eds). *Coastal and Estuarine Environments: sedimentology, geomorphology and geoarchaeology*. Geological Society, London, Special Publications, **175**, 173–186. 0305-8719/00/$15.00 © The Geological Society of London 2000.

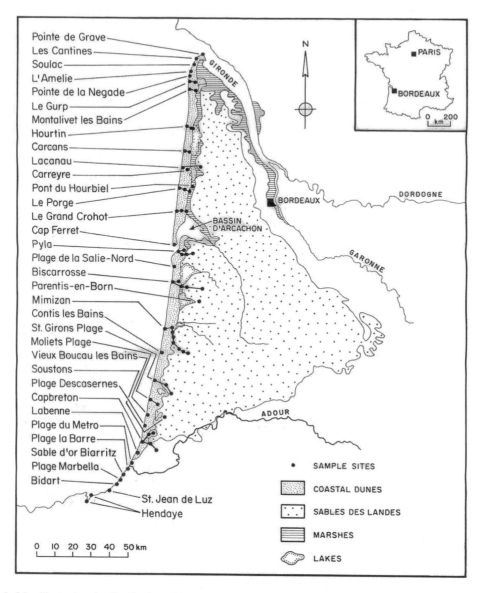

Fig. 1. Map illustrating the distribution of the morphological units in the Aquitaine region and the location of the samples collected.

A number of previous studies have examined the morphostratigraphy and chronology of the dunes and associated deposits (Bressolier *et al.* 1990; Tastet & Pontee 1998; Clarke *et al.* 1999), but the sedimentary characteristics and provenance of the coastal sands remain poorly documented. In this study the textural and geochemical characteristics of the aeolian sediments was investigated in order to provide information regarding sediment provenance,

and in particular to test the hypothesis that the fluvio-aeolian sand sheet (the Sable de Landes) is the main source of the dune sands.

Sampling rationale and methods

Sediment samples weighing 200–400 g were collected at regular intervals along transects perpendicular to the coastline between Pointe de Grave at the mouth of the Gironde Estuary

Fig. 2. Highly managed foredune platform north of Cap Ferret.

and Hendaye near the French/Spanish border (Fig. 1). The sampling sites were located using a global positioning system (GPS) with a spatial resolution of approximately 50 m.

The mid-beach, upper beach and foredune sediments were sampled from the surface to a depth of 15 cm using a bulb planter. Only the beach was sampled south of the Adour River as the coastline is cliffed and dunes are largely absent. Further inland, shallow pits were dug to obtain samples from the modern and primary dunes, the Sable de Landes and the fluvially reworked Sable de Landes up to 16 km east of the coastline. These units were identified with the aid of topographic maps (Institut Geogra-

phique National, Paris 1:25 000) and geological maps prepared by the BRGM, the Bureau de Recherches Geologiques et Minieres (Marionnaud 1972, Carte Geologique de la France 1:50 000). Samples were generally collected from a depth of 25 cm below the surface in the modern and primary dune units but samples were taken at variable depths from the sand sheet depending on evidence of horizonation due to pedogenesis. The depth profiles were obtained to test a subsidiary hypothesis that surface area, geochemistry and surface texture features of the sand is influenced by weathering.

The modern and primary dunes were considered as one morpho-sedimentary unit for the

Fig. 3. Coastal dune erosion at Cap Ferret, SW France illustrated by the distance between the shoreline and fallen German Second World War blockhouses now located on the beach.

Fig. 4. Dune du Pyla a large transgressive dune encroaching upon forested modern/primary dunes.

purposes of sampling in this study since existing maps which distinguish the two units on the basis of morphology are almost certainly inaccurate (Tastet & Pontee 1998; Clarke *et al.* 1999). The fluvially reworked Sable de Landes and aeolian reworked Sable de Landes deposits were differentiated though not on the location map due to the dispersed and less extensive coverage of the former morphological unit. A sixth sampling category, 'other', used in this study included samples from the Pleistocene cliff exposure beneath the foredunes in the Medoc region.

Laboratory analytical methods

The grain size distributions of 98 samples were determined by dry sieving at 0.25ϕ intervals. The mean, standard deviation (sorting) and skewness for each sample were obtained from the resulting particle size distribution data by the method of moments using a computer programme.

Textural and chemical fingerprinting of the aeolian sands and potential source sediments was undertaken using a standardized grain size fraction. This procedure was adopted primarily to minimize variation in these properties due to grain size. The size fraction chosen for analysis was $1.5–2.0\phi$ as this is the predominant modal fraction present in most of the samples. The separated grains in this size fraction were cleaned by boiling in 18% hydrochloric acid for 30 minutes to remove carbonates, oxides, alumino-silicate and organic coatings.

X-ray fluorescence (XRF) spectrometry was used to determine the major oxide and trace element composition of 66 selected grain size

fractions. Approximately 5 g of each sample was ground using an agate mill and made into a pressed powder pellet with lithium borate backing. In order for the particles to bind together to form a pressed powder pellet it was necessary to add approximately 8 drops of 2% Moviol glue solution comprising polyvinyl acetate.

A Coulter SA 3100 BET instrument, which uses the nitrogen gas adsorption method, was used to measure the surface area of c. 10 g subsamples from the unground size fraction used for the geochemical analyses. This instrument can measure surface area in the range 0.01 to $>2000 \, m^2 \, g^{-1}$. The precision (relative error) of the technique was ascertained by running four samples twice and was found to range from 0–1.25%. The accuracy of the technique, established by running certified standards of known surface area, was better than 5%.

Scanning electron microscopy (SEM) was used to examine the shapes and surface textures of the grains and to assist in interpretation of the surface area results. The samples were examined using the secondary electron mode on a JSM 5300 SEM with a Link Systems AN 10085 energy dispersive X-ray (EDX) analyser. The EDX was used to determine the composition of individual grains and to distinguish between quartz and feldspar grains which can appear very similar when the quartz is weathered. The EDX was also used on surface features to aid the visual differentiation between secondary silica and remains of clays that had not been removed during the cleaning process. Selected grains were embedded in epoxy resin, sectioned and polished to allow backscattered electron mode SEM examination of the grain outlines and internal structure in plan view.

Table 1. *Mean textural values of the sample populations, determined by the processing of 0.25φ interval dry sieving data*

Sample population	N_S	Mean grain size (ϕ)	Description	Standard deviation	Description	Skewness	Description
Beach	29	1.39 ± 0.63	Medium sand	0.52 ± 0.26	Moderately well sorted	-0.44 ± 0.69	Very negatively skewed
Foredune	13	1.71 ± 0.08	Medium sand	0.37 ± 0.07	Well sorted	-0.13 ± 0.25	Negatively skewed
Modern/primary dunes	18	1.65 ± 0.14	Medium sand	0.35 ± 0.06	Well sorted	-0.03 ± 0.31	Symmetrical
<0.3 m depth	15	1.63 ± 0.16	Medium sand	0.35 ± 0.07	Well sorted	0.04 ± 0.27	Symmetrical
>0.3 m depth	3	1.75 ± 0.07	Medium sand	0.33 ± 0.03	Well sorted	-0.46 ± 0.41	Very negatively skewed
Sable de Landes	21	1.73 ± 0.17	Medium sand	0.58 ± 0.15	Moderately well sorted	-0.36 ± 0.52	Very negatively skewed
<0.3 m depth	8	1.74 ± 0.22	Medium sand	0.68 ± 0.11	Moderately well sorted	-0.49 ± 0.61	Very negatively skewed
>0.3 m depth	13	1.72 ± 0.14	Medium sand	0.52 ± 0.14	Well sorted to moderately well sorted	-0.29 ± 0.46	Negatively skewed
Sable de Landes fluvially reworked	12	1.64 ± 0.19	Medium sand	0.61 ± 0.17	Moderately well sorted	-0.22 ± 0.52	Negatively skewed
<0.3m depth	5	1.65 ± 0.19	Medium sand	0.58 ± 0.17	Moderately well sorted	0.05 ± 0.59	Symmetrical
>0.3m depth	7	1.63 ± 0.20	Medium sand	0.64 ± 0.20	Moderately well sorted	-0.41 ± 0.40	Very negatively skewed
Other	5	1.79 ± 0.29	Medium sand	0.61 ± 0.15	Moderately well sorted	-0.39 ± 0.93	Very negatively skewed
<0.3m depth	2	1.89 ± 0.40	Medium sand	0.64 ± 0.05	Moderately well sorted	-1.12 ± 1.26	Very negatively skewed
>0.3m depth	3	1.72 ± 0.28	Medium sand	0.59 ± 0.20	Moderately well sorted	0.10 ± 0.23	Symmetrical to positively skewed

The data refer to the -2.0 to 4.0ϕ grain size fraction. N_S is the number of samples used in dry sieving analysis. ($\pm$) denotes the population standard deviation (σ_n). (Description classification system according to Folk & Ward 1957).

Results

Grain size

The mean grain of all the sampling units was found to lie within the range of medium sands (Table 1). The beach sediments show a wide range of mean grain sizes but on average are slightly coarser, less well sorted and more negatively skewed than the aeolian sediments. The examples of coarser beach sediments also show a tendency to be more poorly sorted and less negatively skewed than the finer beach sediments (Fig. 5).

The foredunes and modern/primary dune samples are both predominantly well sorted to very well sorted with near-symmetrical to negatively skewed grain size distributions, while the Sable de Landes and fluvially reworked Sable de Landes are moderately well sorted to poorly sorted with skewness values ranging from slightly positively skewed to very negatively skewed. The negative skewness values obtained for the dunes are in agreement with previous grain size analysis at Dune du Pyla by Vincent (1996).

The average mean grain size of the foredunes ($1.71 \pm 0.08\phi$) is relatively coarse in comparison with foredunes found in many other parts of Europe, and is in part a reflection of the coarse nature of the source material on the beach from which the fines have probably been winnowed by marine processes.

The modern and primary dune sands are slightly coarser but have similar average sorting to the foredune sands. They have a slightly wider range of skewness values and are intermediate between the foredunes and Sable de Landes samples in this respect. The Sable de Landes and reworked Sable de Landes samples have a broadly similar average mean size to the foredune and primary/modern dune samples but show poorer sorting.

Figure 6 shows the variation in mean size of the different sampling units as a function of geographical position between the northern Medoc (top of columns) and the Spanish border (bottom of columns). Although there are two or three localized areas of exceptionally coarse beach sediments, the mean size shows only limited longshore variation between Point de Grave and the Adour River Mouth. South of the Adour there is a marked fining trend towards the Spanish border. Very little alongshore variation in mean size is evident amongst the foredune, modern/primary dune and Sables de Landes samples.

Statistical analysis using the Mann-Whitney U-test indicated that the beach and foredune samples are texturally similar to the Sable de Landes samples, differing only in terms of mean size and sorting, respectively, at the 95% confidence level (Table 5). The mean size of the modern/primary dunes is not significantly different from that of the Sable de Landes at the 95%

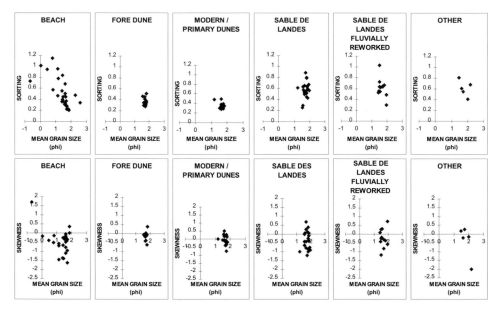

Fig. 5. Bivariate plot of statistical parameters for samples from different morphological units in the Aquitaine region.

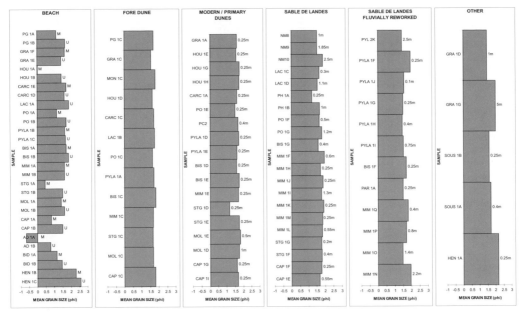

Fig. 6. Mean grain size of samples from different morphological units in the Aquitaine region.
NB The values are ordered north to south with samples from the same profile in depth sequence. The beach and the foredunes were sampled from the surface to a depth of 0.15 m and the sample depths of the other units are given to the right of the mean grain size bars. The mid and upper beach were sampled denoted by M and U respectively.

confidence level, although there are significant differences in sorting and skewness between the two groups. Values of the mean, sorting and skewness for the Sables de Landes and fluvially reworked Sable de Landes are not statistically different.

Chemical composition of the sands

All the morphological units have very low calcium carbonate and heavy mineral contents and are very siliceous, containing greater than 90% silica. The percentage of the major oxides of aluminium, sodium, potassium and calcium are similar in foredunes, modern/primary dunes and the Sable de Landes sands (Table 2).

Figure 7 shows the silica to potassium oxide ratio for the samples from each morphological unit, plotted from north to south down the coast. Potassium oxide concentration is related to the presence of potassium feldspar, and thus the ratio can be used as a proxy to indicate the quartz:feldspar ratio and degree of weathering (Krauskopf & Bird 1995). It can be seen from Fig. 7 that values of the ratio are slightly higher in the foredunes than in the modern and primary dunes, and are slightly higher in the foredunes on the central sections of the coast than in the northern and southern sections. Within the Sable de Landes, very high values of the ratio

are found in the highly weathered and podsolized surface sand layers, with lower values at depth. Values within the fluvially reworked Sable de Landes deposits are broadly similar to those in the foredunes, while those in the 'Other' sampling category show a systematic increase towards the south.

Values for the average concentrations of selected trace elements in the different sampling units are shown in Table 3. There are no statistically significant differences in chemical composition between the Sable de Landes and the reworked Sable de Landes. The foredune sands have significantly different (at the 95% confidence level) concentrations of aluminium oxide, strontium and zirconium compared with the Sables de Landes, whilst the modern/primary dunes differ significantly from the Sables de Landes in terms of aluminium oxide, potassium oxide, rubidium, strontium and zirconium (Table 5). As mentioned above, these differences may reflect a lower content of feldspars in the more weathered and podsolized Sable de Landes near-surface sediments. Careful examination of the data for individual samples indicates that there is a higher degree of similarity between the near surface samples from the foredunes and modern/primary dunes with the B horizons of the more pedogenetically modified Sable de Landes sediments.

Table 2. *Mean oxide compositions for the sample populations, determined by XRF analysis of pressed powder pellets*

Sample population	N_S	Na_2O %	MgO %	Al_2O_3 %	SiO_2 %	P_2O_5 %	K_2O %	CaO %	TiO_2 %	MnO %	Fe_2O_3 %	Total %
Foredune	12	0.14 ± 0.03	<0.01	0.94 ± 0.29	93.64 ± 3.06	<0.01	0.40 ± 0.11	<0.01	0.02 ± 0.01	0.01 ± 0.00	0.05 ± 0.06	95.00 ± 3.33
Modern/primary dunes	17	0.17 ± 0.03	<0.01	0.92 ± 0.17	93.49 ± 3.42	<0.01	0.49 ± 0.09	<0.01	0.02 ± 0.01	0.01 ± 0.00	0.02 ± 0.05	94.88 ± 3.45
Mean <0.3m	14	0.16 ± 0.02	<0.01	0.92 ± 0.18	94.02 ± 3.09	<0.01	0.48 ± 0.09	<0.01	0.02 ± 0.01	0.01 ± 0.00	0.03 ± 0.05	95.41 ± 3.08
Mean >0.3m	3	0.18 ± 0.06	<0.01	0.92 ± 0.19	90.99 ± 4.46	<0.01	0.57 ± 0.04	<0.01	0.01 ± 0.01	<0.01	<0.01	92.42 ± 4.73
Sable de Landes	21	0.08 ± 0.06	<0.01	0.59 ± 0.34	94.79 ± 2.16	<0.01	0.37 ± 0.17	<0.01	0.01 ± 0.01	<0.01	0.01 ± 0.04	95.58 ± 2.58
Mean <0.3m	8	0.04 ± 0.04	<0.01	0.40 ± 0.27	94.18 ± 2.37	<0.01	0.31 ± 0.20	<0.01	0.01 ± 0.00	<0.01	<0.01	94.62 ± 2.61
Mean >0.3m	13	0.10 ± 0.05	0.07 ± 0.24	1.34 ± 2.25	94.46 ± 3.28	<0.01	0.40 ± 0.14	0.07 ± 0.21	0.04 ± 0.01	0.04 ± 0.13	0.53 ± 1.82	96.81 ± 3.15
Sable de Landes fluvially reworked	12	0.09 ± 0.05	<0.01	0.67 ± 0.25	94.49 ± 2.77	<0.01	0.47 ± 0.16	<0.01	0.01 ± 0.00	<0.01	<0.01	95.48 ± 2.66
Mean <0.3m	5	0.08 ± 0.07	<0.01	0.59 ± 0.25	94.19 ± 3.18	<0.01	0.37 ± 0.08	<0.01	0.01 ± 0.00	<0.01	<0.01	94.99 ± 3.21
Mean >0.3m	7	0.10 ± 0.05	<0.01	0.73 ± 0.24	94.71 ± 2.69	<0.01	0.55 ± 0.16	<0.01	0.01 ± 0.00	<0.01	<0.01	95.83 ± 2.40
Other	4	0.13 ± 0.16	<0.01	1.29 ± 1.26	94.28 ± 3.48	<0.01	0.73 ± 0.69	<0.01	0.03 ± 0.02	<0.01	0.05 ± 0.06	96.37 ± 2.00
Mean <0.3m	1	<0.01	<0.01	0.25 ± 0.00	97.30 ± 0.00	<0.01	0.19 ± 0.00	<0.01	0.02 ± 0.00	<0.01	<0.01	97.89 ± 0.00
Mean >0.3m	3	0.16 ± 0.16	<0.01	1.63 ± 1.29	93.27 ± 3.48	<0.01	0.92 ± 0.71	<0.01	0.04 ± 0.02	0.01 ± 0.01	0.60 ± 0.07	95.87 ± 2.12

Data refer to the 1.50–2.00ϕ grain size fraction. N_S is the number of samples used in XRF analysis. (±) denotes the population standard deviation (σ_n).

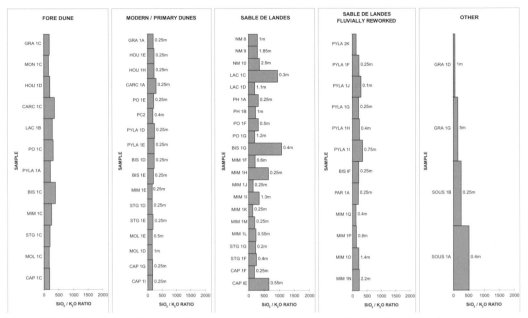

Fig. 7. SiO$_2$/K$_2$O ratio for the 1.5–2 phi grain size fraction of sand samples from the different morphological units in the Aquitaine region.
NB The values are ordered north to south with samples from the same profile in depth sequence. The foredunes were sampled from the surface down to a depth of 0.15 m and the sample depths for the other units are given to the right of the ratio bar.

The trace element yttrium is present in low concentrations in the foredune, the modern/primary dune unit and the Sable de Landes to the north of Pyla and generally absent in the south. This corresponds with the presence of yttrium in the Pleistocene cliff at Le Gurp in the Medoc region, possibly indicating that erosion of these cliffs has locally contributed to the sediment supply. The chromium and zinc concentrations demonstrate almost identical spatial distributions. The opposite trend was displayed by the copper concentrations with low concentrations present in the samples situated from Pyla moving southwards and a general absence to the north of Pyla with the exception of the Pleistocene cliff at Le Gurp (GRA 1G) and the corresponding foredune sample (GRA 1C), supporting a localized sediment source. The signature of the Pleistocene cliff in the samples from the dune system in the north is also observed in the zirconium concentrations.

Surface area

The BET surface area values generally vary between 0.1 and 1.0 m^2 g^{-1} (Table 4). The foredune and modern/primary dunes are uniform and similar with mean values of 0.496 m^2 g^{-1} and 0.439 m^2 g^{-1} respectively. At any one sampling site on the sand sheet the surface area increases with depth. The mean values of the surface horizons are 0.188 m^2 g^{-1} and 0.315 m^2 g^{-1} for the Sable de Landes and fluvially reworked Sable de Landes, respectively, and at depths below 0.3 m the average values are 0.526 m^2 g^{-1} and 0.630 m^2 g^{-1} respectively. The values for the foredune and modern/primary dunes are intermediate between these values. At the 95% significance level there are no statistically significant differences between the Sable de Landes sands and the other sampling units in terms of surface area values. However, the P-values obtained from the Mann-Whitney U-test indicate that the highest degree of similarity is between the Sable de Landes sands and the fluvially reworked Sable de Landes, and the lowest level of similarity is between the Sable de Landes sands and the foredune sands (Table 5).

There is little longshore variation in the surface area values for the foredune sands, suggesting homogeneity due to well-mixing by marine and aeolian processes (Fig. 8). Similarly, there is no systematic longshore variation in the values for the modern/primary dunes, Sable de Landes and reworked Sable de Landes sediments. Variations in these units are evidently more related to depth of sampling, and thereby to degree of weathering and pedogenesis.

Table 3. *Mean trace element compositions of the sample populations, determined by XRF analysis of pressed powder pellets*

Sample population	N_S	V ppm	Cr ppm	Co ppm	Ni ppm	Cu ppm	Zn ppm	Pb ppm	Rb ppm	Sr ppm	Y ppm	Zr ppm
Foredune	12	2.25 ± 1.82	8.75 ± 9.36	2.83 ± 0.58	0.25 ± 0.45	0.42 ± 0.67	2.17 ± 2.86	1.17 ± 1.11	15.42 ± 3.50	15.00 ± 2.59	0.67 ± 0.78	15.58 ± 4.27
Modern/primary dunes	17	1.82 ± 1.33	5.76 ± 11.66	3.06 ± 1.09	0.76 ± 1.03	1.82 ± 2.96	0.76 ± 1.71	1.76 ± 1.20	17.71 ± 2.91	16.00 ± 2.21	0.59 ± 0.62	15.12 ± 3.60
Mean <0.3 m	14	1.93 ± 1.38	7.00 ± 12.57	3.21 ± 1.05	0.79 ± 1.12	1.86 ± 3.23	0.93 ± 1.86	1.57 ± 1.22	17.14 ± 2.85	15.86 ± 2.21	0.57 ± 0.65	14.79 ± 3.91
Mean >0.3 m	3	1.33 ± 1.15	<0.10	2.33 ± 1.15	0.67 ± 0.58	1.67 ± 1.53	<0.10	2.67 ± 0.58	20.33 ± 1.53	16.67 ± 2.52	0.67 ± 0.58	16.67 ± 0.58
Sable de Landes	21	2.45 ± 2.28	3.70 ± 5.54	3.05 ± 0.69	0.65 ± 1.04	1.00 ± 2.13	0.55 ± 1.39	1.60 ± 1.54	14.20 ± 5.01	9.45 ± 4.91	0.20 ± 0.52	11.90 ± 3.68
Mean <0.3 m	8	1.75 ± 2.87	3.00 ± 4.69	3.00 ± 0.76	0.75 ± 1.16	1.25 ± 2.38	0.25 ± 0.46	1.00 ± 1.20	12.25 ± 5.87	6.63 ± 3.85	<0.10	12.13 ± 3.94
Mean >0.3 m	13	2.92 ± 1.78	4.17 ± 6.19	3.08 ± 0.67	0.58 ± 1.00	0.83 ± 2.04	0.75 ± 1.76	2.00 ± 1.65	15.50 ± 4.10	11.33 ± 4.75	0.33 ± 0.65	11.75 ± 3.67
Sable de Landes fluvially reworked	12	1.92 ± 2.68	6.83 ± 9.46	3.00 ± 0.74	1.83 ± 2.37	1.58 ± 1.38	0.25 ± 0.87	2.00 ± 1.81	17.08 ± 5.00	11.42 ± 4.48	<0.10	11.00 ± 4.16
Mean <0.3 m	5	2.20 ± 3.49	10.80 ± 12.07	3.40 ± 0.55	2.80 ± 3.27	2.60 ± 1.14	0.60 ± 1.34	2.20 ± 2.49	14.00 ± 2.55	10.40 ± 5.59	<0.10	12.40 ± 1.82
Mean >0.3 m	7	2.00 ± 2.28	4.50 ± 7.15	2.67 ± 0.82	1.17 ± 1.47	1.00 ± 1.20	<0.10	1.50 ± 1.05	18.67 ± 5.50	11.50 ± 3.73	<0.10	9.17 ± 5.12
Other	4	4.00 ± 5.66	7.75 ± 11.15	3.25 ± 0.50	0.75 ± 0.96	0.25 ± 0.50	6.75 ± 11.00	3.25 ± 3.86	25.50 ± 21.38	17.50 ± 14.27	0.75 ± 0.96	16.25 ± 8.26
Mean <0.3 m	1	<0.10	<0.10	4.00 ± 0.00	<0.10	<0.10	23.00 ± 0.00	1.00 ± 0.00	8.00 ± 0.00	5.00 ± 0.00	<0.10	8.00 ± 0.00
Mean >0.3 m	3	5.33 ± 6.11	10.33 ± 12.10	3.00 ± 0.00	1.00 ± 1.00	0.33 ± 0.58	1.33 ± 2.31	4.00 ± 4.36	31.33 ± 21.94	21.67 ± 14.19	1.00 ± 1.00	19.00 ± 7.55

Data refer to the 1.50–2.00ϕ grain size fraction. N_S is the number of samples used in XRF analysis. (±) denotes the population standard deviation (σ_n).

Table 4. *Mean surface area values of the sample populations, determined by the nitrogen gas adsorption technique*

Sample population	N_S	Mean surface area (m^2 g^{-1})
Foredune	12	0.496 ± 0.071
Modern/primary dunes	17	0.439 ± 0.170
Mean <0.3m	14	0.456 ± 0.170
Mean >0.3m	3	0.363 ± 0.177
Sable de Landes	21	0.383 ± 0.388
Mean <0.3m	8	0.188 ± 0.236
Mean >0.3m	13	0.526 ± 0.465
Sable de Landes fluvially reworked	12	0.512 ± 0.381
Mean <0.3m	5	0.315 ± 0.246
Mean >0.3m	7	0.630 ± 0.448
Other	4	1.545 ± 2.484
Mean <0.3m	1	0.111 ± 0.000
Mean >0.3m	3	2.023 ± 2.808

Data refer to the 1.50–2.00ϕ grain size fraction. N_S is the number of samples used in surface area analysis. (±) denotes the population standard deviation (σ_n).

Surface texture

SEM examination revealed the samples are very largely composed of subangular to subrounded quartz grains, defined according to the visual comparative scheme of Powers (1953), with only a few percent of feldspar grains, regardless of the morphological environment. The Sable de Landes and the fluvially reworked Sable de Landes were petrographically very similar but significant differences in the surface texture were observed between samples from the pedogenic A and B horizons. The majority of the quartz grains within the A horizon of the Sable de Landes possess smooth surfaces with chemical etch pits which is indicative of a leached horizon in a podzolic soil profile (Figs 9A & B). Leaching (eluviation) of the A horizon causes dissolution of mineral grains, including quartz. Fine,

granular secondary silica, arising from the reprecipitation of the mineral material lost from the A horizon, is easily identifiable on the quartz grains from the B horizon samples (Figs 9C, D). These changes in grain surface texture probably explain the lowering of the surface area values in the A horizon and the observed increase in the B horizon.

In the foredune samples the quartz grains displayed evidence of either secondary silica preservation within depressions on smooth grain surfaces with chemical etch pits (Fig. 9E) or freshly fractured surfaces (Fig. 9F). The chemical etch pits and the freshly fractured grains are indicative of recent marine reworking and exposure to mechanical abrasion/breakage processes. Fresh, angular quartz and feldspar grains, possibly indicative of an additional source of sediment supply, were found to be rare.

Table 5. *P-values derived from the Mann-Whitney U-test during significance testing of the textural and geochemical data between the Sable de Landes and the other morphological units in the Aquitaine region*

	Beach	Foredune	Modern/primary dunes	Sable de Landes fluvially reworked
Mean grain size	0.003*	0.368	0.089	0.089
Sorting	0.089	0.000*	0.000*	0.841
Skewness	0.484	0.193	0.028*	0.424
Surface area	–	0.110	0.134	0.271
Aluminium	–	0.016*	0.016*	0.689
Potassium	–	0.424	0.007*	0.134
Rubidium	–	0.271	0.007*	0.110
Strontium	–	0.007*	0.000*	0.368
Zirconium	–	0.046*	0.021*	0.424

NB * Indicates that a difference exists between the sample populations at the 95% confidence level.

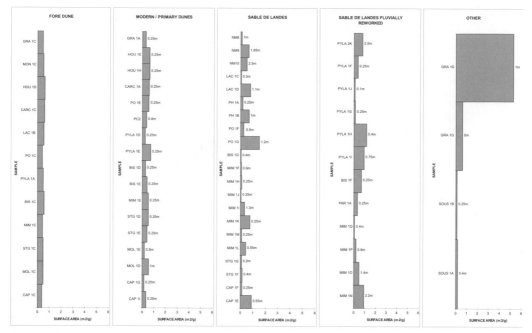

Fig. 8. Surface area of the 1.5–2.0 phi grain size fraction of sand samples from different morphological units in the Aquitaine region

NB The values are ordered north to south with samples from the same profile in depth sequence. The foredunes were sampled from the surface to a depth of 0.15 m and the sample depths of the other units are given to the right of the surface area bars.

Discussion

The grain size, surface textural and chemical compositional data obtained in this study are consistent with the hypothesis that the main source of the coastal dune sands on the Aquitaine coast is fluvial, marine and aeolian reworking of the Pleistocene Sable de Landes deposits. These sediments were ultimately derived from the Pyrenees but have experienced significant post-depositional weathering prior to reworking.

Reworking of the Sable de Landes sand sheet probably began while sea-level was over 100 m below its present level during the last glacial maximum (Lambeck 1997). Pedogenesis of the Sable de Landes probably continued during its partial submergence due to sea-level rise, between 15 000 and 6000 years ago (Lambeck 1997). Parts of the sand sheet were probably reworked during the Holocene transgression, with sand being pushed landwards as a transgressive marine-aeolian wedge in the manner originally proposed by Cooper (1958) for the Oregon coast.

Sea-level has been relatively stable at or near to the present level in this area since 5000 years ago. During the last few thousand years episodic aeolian activity is more likely to have reflected variations in storminess. The Little Ice Age of the 17th to 18th centuries (cf. Lamb 1995) appears to correlate well with widespread aeolian activity in the Aquitaine region which is known to have occurred from historical accounts and maps (Tastet & Pontee 1998).

Although coastal erosion of the Pleistoene cliffs in the Medoc region has locally contributed to the sediment supply in recent centuries, there appears to be very limited supply of new sediment to the Aquitaine coast at the present day. Most of the shoreline is eroding, with landward transfer of sediment by aeolian processes and some infilling of embayments and estuaries. Beach and dune erosion is likely to continue for the foreseeable future, and may accelerate if the rate of sea-level rise increases or there is a significant increase in storminess. Such changes will bring increased pressure on the dunes and favour instability of the type which was widespread prior to stabilization measures in the late 18th and early 19th centuries.

Conclusions

• The morpho-sedimentary units sampled in this study are texturally and geochemically similar, supporting the hypothesis that the

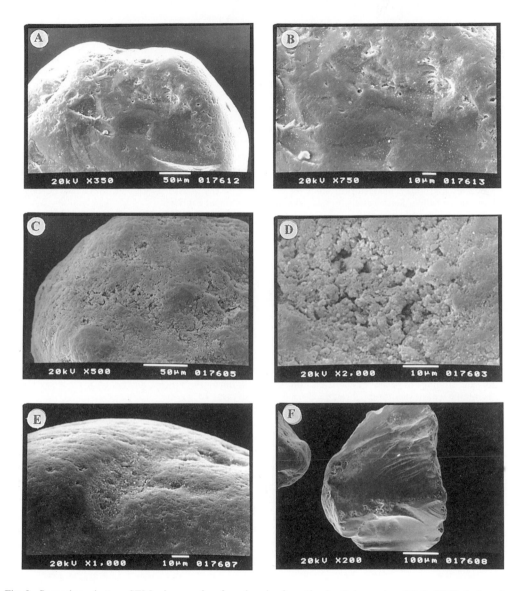

Fig. 9. Secondary electron SEM micrographs of sand grains from the Aquitaine region: (**A**) & (**B**) Etched surface texture of quartz grain from a depth of 0.1 m in the A horizon of profile PYLA 1J, Fluvially Reworked Sable de Landes; (**C**) & (**D**) Secondary silica on quartz grain from a depth of 0.4 m in the B_{IR} horizon of PYLA 1H, Fluvially Reworked Sable de Landes; (**E**) Secondary silica preserved in a depression on the surface of a quartz grain with smooth surface texture and chemical etch pits from PYLA 1A, foredune; (**F**) Freshly fractured quartz grain from PYLA 1A, foredune.

dune sand was derived from reworking of the Sable de Landes.
- Reworking was probably initiated by sea-level rise in the early Holocene and continued to the present day.
- Erosion of the Pleistocene sedimentary cliffs in the Medoc region has provided an additional localized source of sand.

- Variations in the chemical and surface area data sets obtained in this study appear to be due mainly to differences in weathering and pedogenesis with depth in deposits of varying age.
- The BET surface area method provides a useful tool for quantitative comparison of the 3D surface textures of bulk sand samples.

This work was partially supported by a NERC MRes Studentship to S. E. Saye and a Leverhulme Trust Grant to Professor K. Pye. The assistance of Professor J-P. Tastet of the Department of Geology and Oceanography at the University of Bordeaux I and of technical support staff at the Postgraduate Research Institute for Sedimentology, University of Reading, is also gratefully acknowledged.

References

AUBIÉ, S. & TASTET, J-P. 2000. Coastal erosion, processes and rates: an historical study of the Gironde coastline, Southwestern France. *Journal of Coastal Research*, in press.

BARRÈRE, P. 1992. Dynamics and management of the coastal dunes of the Landes, Gascony, France. *In*: CARTER, R. W. G., CURTIS, T. G. F. & SHEEHY-SKEFFINGTON, M. J. (eds) *Coastal Dunes: Geomorphology, Ecology and Management for Conservation*. Proceedings of the Third European Dune Congress, Galway, Ireland, 17–21; Balkema, Rotterdam, 25–32.

BRESSOLIER, C., FROIDEFOND, J. M. & THOMAS, Y. F. 1990. Chronology of coastal dunes in the southwest France. *Catena Supplement*, **18**, 101–107.

CLARKE, M. L., RENDELL, H. M., PYE, K., TASTET, J-P., PONTEE, N. I. & MASSE, L. 1999. Evidence for the timing of dune development on the Aquitaine coast, Southwest France. *Zeitschrift fur Geomorphologie NF Supplement Band*, **116**, 147–163.

COOPER, W. S. 1958. *Coastal sand dunes of Oregon and Washington*. Memoirs of the Geological Society of America, **104**.

FAVENNEC, J. 1996. Coastal management by the French National Forestry Service in Aquitaine, France. *In*: JONES, P. S., HEALY, M. G. & WILLIAMS, A. T. (eds) *Studies in European Coastal Management*. Samara Publishing Limited, Cardigan, UK 191–196.

FOLK, R. L. & WARD, W. C. 1957. Brazos River bar: a study in the significance of grain size parameters. *Journal of Sedimentary Petrology*, **37**, 327–354.

FROIDEFOND, J. M. & LEGIGAN, P. 1985. La Grande Dune du Pilatet la progression des dunes sur le littoral Aquitaine. *Bulletin Institut de Géologie du Bassin d'Aquitaine*, **38**, 69–79.

—— & PRUD'HOMME, R. 1991. Coastal erosion and aeolian sand transport on the Aquitaine coast, France. *Acta Mechanica Supplement*, **2**, 147–159.

KRAUSKOPF, K. B. & BIRD, D. K. 1995. *Introduction to Geochemistry*, 3rd edn, McGraw-Hill International Editions.

LAMB, H. H. 1995. *Climate, history and the modern world*. 2nd edn, Routledge, London.

LAMBECK, K. 1997. Sea-level change along the French Atlantic and Channel coasts since the time of the last glacial maximum. *Palaeogeography, Palaeoclimatology, Palaeoecology*, **129**, 1–22.

LEGIGAN, P. 1979. *L'elaboration de la formation Sable de Landes, le residual de l'environment sedimentaire Pliocene Pleistocene centre Aquitaine*. Memoire Institut Geologique du Bassin d'Aquitaine, **18**.

MARIONNAUD, J. M. 1972. *Carte geologique de la France* (1/50 000), Feuille St. Vincents de-Medoc-Soulac-sur-Mer, Orleans, 729–730.

POWERS, M. C. 1953. A new roundness scale for sedimentary particles. *Journal of Sedimentary Petrology*, **23**, 117–119.

TASTET, J-P. & PONTEE, N. I. 1998. Morpho-chronology of coastal dunes in Medoc. A new interpretation of Holocene dunes in Southwestern France. *Geomorphology*, **677**, 1–17.

VINCENT, P. 1996. Variation in particle size distribution on the beach and windward side of a large coastal dune, southwest France. *Sedimentary Geology*, **103**, 273–280.

Post-reclamation changes in estuarine mudflat sediments at Bothkennar, Grangemouth, Scotland

BEVERLEY F. BARRAS & MICHAEL A. PAUL

*Department of Civil and Offshore Engineering, Heriot-Watt University,
Edinburgh EH14 4AS, Scotland (e-mail: B.F.Barras@hw.ac.uk)*

Abstract: The Engineering & Physical Sciences Research Council research site at Both-kennar is located on former intertidal mudflats adjacent to the Forth estuary, which were reclaimed for agricultural use around the year 1784. A desiccated surface crust has developed in the 200 years following the reclamation, largely in response to the introduction of artificial drainage. Its formation has involved both compaction and material translocation, due to effective stress changes and to infiltration and geochemical alteration respectively. At first, new deposits accumulated in an artificial tidal lagoon and underwent autocompaction under saturated conditions. The subsequent introduction of field drains and cultivation then induced suction stresses due to evapotranspiration, leading to overconsolidation by around 150–200 kPa. These processes have also been associated with the development of an immature soil profile to a depth of around 0.7 m. The infiltration of fresh water has caused both desalination and the eluviation of clay particles. There is also a general rise in pH and fall in Eh with depth, which is associated with leaching and the downward translocation of DCB (dithionate-citrate-bicarbonate) soluble iron compounds. We conclude that the physical development of the crust was rapid and is now largely completed, whereas the chemical development is not yet completed and thus the soil profile remains immature.

In this paper we describe the desiccated crust that has developed at the EPSRC Bothkennar Soft Clay Research Site, which lies on land reclaimed from estuarine tidal flats in the late eighteenth century. Under temperate climates, such estuarine clays often possess an oxidized surface crust of lowered water content, increased strength and altered geochemistry, which develops in response to partial saturation and changes in the near-surface redox environment. The time required for this crust to develop and the relative rates of the processes involved can, however, be difficult to assess, although analogous work on the development of soil profiles on alluvial river terraces (Robertson-Rintoul 1986) indicates that the development of a recognizable soil profile can commence in less than a hundred years.

Our work at the Bothkennar research site has provided an opportunity to determine the time-scales and relative chronology of the processes involved over the 200 year period since the reclamation. These can be related to well-documented historical accounts of the reclamation process itself. We argue that the effective stress changes caused by autocompaction (selfweight compression), partial saturation and soil suction have been primarily responsible for the present-day density profile of the deposit. The development of the crust by these processes has been rapid and is now largely completed. Within this crust, above the groundwater table, there is a further textural and geochemical stratification due to the development of an immature soil profile over the two centuries since the completion of the reclamation works. This has largely formed by chemical processes, such as iron release, oxidation and desalination, although it has also involved the lessivation of clay-sized particles, probably under the action of percolating water, which have moved only a limited distance in the time so far available.

Geological setting

The site is adjacent to the Forth estuary in central Scotland [NS 921859], about 1 km south of the Kincardine Bridge, and has an elevation of between 2.45 m and 3.1 m AOD. It lies within the outcrop of the Holocene raised estuarine deposits, locally termed 'carse clays', which occur widely at the head of the Forth estuary (Fig. 1). This Holocene sequence overlies the Late-glacial

From: PYE, K. & ALLEN, J. R. L. (eds). *Coastal and Estuarine Environments: sedimentology, geomorphology and geoarchaeology*. Geological Society, London, Special Publications, **175**, 187–199. 0305-8719/00/$15.00 © The Geological Society of London 2000.

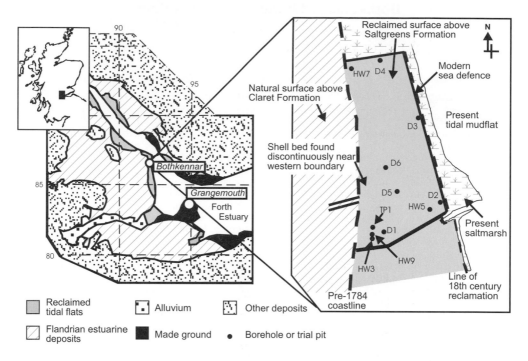

Fig. 1. Outline geological map of the Bothkennar area and detailed geological plan of the EPSRC Soft Clay Research Site showing the positions of the boreholes mentioned in the text.

Bothkennar Gravel Formation (BGF), which is present throughout this area (Sissons 1969; Browne *et al.* 1984; Peacock 1998), and at the site occurs as a gravelly sand at an elevation around −13 m to −19 m OD. At Bothkennar the BGF is succeeded by 14 m to 20 m of micaceous silty-clays which extend nearly to ground surface. They are placed stratigraphically within the Claret Formation (Browne *et al.* 1993; Barras & Paul 1999) on the basis of lithology, radiocarbon age and stratigraphical position relative to the BGF. These sediments can mostly be divided into a bedded and a mottled facies (Fig. 2) on the basis of their primary fabric and the extent and nature of subsequent bioturbation. In the Bothkennar area they accumulated between about 5000 and 3000 ^{14}C yrs BP, during a period of coastal regression when the local palaeo-environment changed from subtidal (up to 20 m water depth at LWOST) to intertidal.

In the uppermost part of the Claret Formation, individual beds within the bedded facies are frequently separated by strongly erosional contacts and, locally, by horizons of mudflakes or mud pellets. They also contain numerous macroscopic burrows, believed by comparison with the modern fauna (McLusky 1987; Kingston pers. comm.) to be largely the traces of *Corophium*,

Hydrobia and bivalves such as *Macoma*. This part of the sequence is interpreted as the product of an intertidal to immediately subtidal environment. At greater depths below ground surface the sediments become mottled, macroscopic burrows appear to be less frequent and bed contacts show fewer erosional features, a combination which agrees with the deeper subtidal setting deduced from their decompacted elevations and radiocarbon ages (Paul *et al.* 1995; Paul & Barras 1998). The sediments have a total organic content of 2% to 4% by weight (dichromate oxidation method [BS 1377 1990]), much of which is believed to have been derived from polysaccharides and lipids associated with the estuarine flora and fauna (Paul & Barras 1999).

The Claret Formation is terminated upwards by an erosion surface which is believed to represent a former intertidal surface. Upon this surface there is a discontinuous shell bed, dated to around 3000 ^{14}C yrs BP, which principally contains *Cerastoderma edule*, together with *Hydrobia ulvae* and *Retusa obtusa*. This bed occurs fairly widely at this level over much of the carseland in the Grangemouth area (Robinson 1993). Above this surface lies a thin unit of clayey-silt, containing lenses of detrital shell material and disseminated shell debris, which is

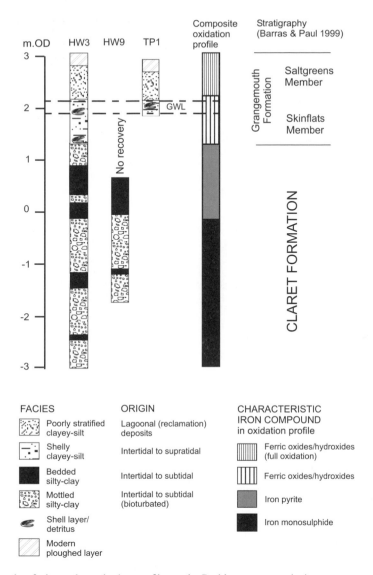

Fig. 2. Stratigraphy, facies and weathering profiles at the Bothkennar research site.

assigned to the Skinflats Member of the Grangemouth Formation (Barras & Paul 1999). We consider that it represents an intertidal deposit which formed under limited wave action above the erosion surface and so is similar to that seen at the back of the intertidal flats at the present day.

Above the Skinflats Member lie further clayey-silts, termed the Saltgreens Member of the Grangemouth Formation (Barras & Paul 1999), which extend from around 2 m AOD to the modern ground surface at around 3 m AOD. This unit has been the focus of our present work, since we believe it to have accumulated in an artificial

tidal lagoon during the late 18th century reclamation work. Its present-day thickness is around one metre or less, although contemporary records (Udney 1831) suggest that the *maximum* initial thickness could have been as great as nine feet (2.7 m) at the eastern margin of the reclamation. If so, it has thus suffered substantial post-depositional compaction, probably due in large part to the introduction of the artificial drainage, which maintains the present groundwater level at a relatively constant elevation of 2.0 m to 2.2 m AOD (0.7 m to 1.1 m below local ground surface level across the site). Following the reclamation, desiccation and oxidation have formed a weathered, hardened crust that now extends almost to the depth of the shell bed and so involves both the Saltgreens and Skinflats members.

Reclamation history

An account of the process of land reclamation was published in 1831 by Joseph Udney, the original land surveyor, and was later quoted by Cadell (1929) in his survey of land reclamation in the Forth estuary. Udney explains that the area to be reclaimed was first impounded by wattle fences, each three feet (0.9 m) high, which were closed after each high tide, causing deposits of clayey-silt to accumulate up to about the level of the highest spring tides (at the present day the highest astronomical tide at Kincardine, the nearest (1.6 km) secondary port to Bothkennar, is ≃3.5 m AOD, based on data from the primary port of Rosyth (Hydrographer of the Navy 1999). The work was carried out in three stages (termed warps), each lasting one year: during each stage the surface of the reclaimed deposit could thus have been raised by a maximum of 0.9 m. Immediately on completion of the reclamation, the thickness of these deposits at the outer (eastern) margin of the area would thus have been between two and three warps (1.8 m to 2.7 m): the third warp may not have reached the full 0.9 m, since the highest spring tides are relatively infrequent over one year). From this maximum thickness at the eastern margin of the site the deposits would have feathered out westwards.

After the third warp the area was completely closed to the sea and artifical drainage introduced. The consequent lowering of the water table would have caused compaction of the lagoonal sediments, desalination (due to rainfall and inflow of adjacent fresh water) and oxidation to form the characteristic brown to greyish brown surface crust. This is effectively the condition seen today. This compaction, together with some additional consolidation of the underlying deposits of the Claret Formation due to the weight of the lagoonal sediments, probably accounts for a slight change of level (≃1 m) between the site and the adjacent natural carseland surface to the west of the site, from which it is separated by a minor (≃0.5 m to 1 m) cliffline. Udney records that the land was able to be ploughed and sown with rape in the year following the final warp and was let to tenants in the year following that (1789), which suggests that desalination was rapid, at least at shallow depth. Udney's report

also accords with the presence, adjacent to the reclaimed land at Bothkennar, of the aptly named 'Saltgreen Cottage', a renovated farm building whose lintel bears the date 1791.

Field and laboratory methods

The present investigations have been based on the examination of continuous, 100 mm diameter, thin-walled piston core samples from boreholes HW3, HW5, HW7 and HW9 (Fig. 1) together with block samples from a shallow trial pit (TP1, Fig. 1). We have also re-examined borehole records and certain cores from the 1986 site selection exercise conducted by Bristol University (Fig. 1, D series; Hawkins *et al.* 1989). Selected geotechnical properties of samples from the HW boreholes and trial pit were measured in standard tests, described in BS 1377 (1990) and Head (1982). Measurements of pH, Eh and chloride were made using a bench meter with suitable selective electrodes. Dithionate-citrate-bicarbonate (DCB) digestion was used to extract sesquioxides and hydroxides (Mehra & Jackson 1960) and the more aggressive nitric acid-hydrogen peroxide digestion (Krishnamurtly *et al.* 1976) was used for comparison as a measure of total inorganic iron, including that contained within free oxides and clay colloids. The digested extracts were assayed for iron by atomic absorption spectrophotometry.

Geochemical profiles

The principal geochemical changes associated with the reclamation have been desalination, oxidation and acidification. The crust itself represents the uppermost part of an oxidation profile that extends for at least 3 m to 4 m from the ground surface down into the Claret Formation (Fig. 2). At depth the sediments are mainly black (5Y2.5/1) due to the presence of finely disseminated iron monosulphide, with occasional very dark grey (5Y3/1) and dark grey (5Y4/1) horizons. Above about 4 m below surface, the sediments are lighter in colour (very dark grey to dark grey: 5Y3/1 to 5Y4/1) due to the diagenetic alteration of the monosulphide to the disulphide (pyrite). This colour difference allows the recognition of the two common oxidation zones based on the species of iron sulphide: the monosulphide zone and the pyrite zone. This distinction is the consequence of the diagenetic alteration of iron minerals such as Mackinawite ('iron monosulphide') to pyrite (Berner 1971). The persistence of the monosulphide at depth may be associated with the relatively high percentage of organic material (Paul & Barras 1999) and possibly with high levels of sulphate-reducing microbial activity (Pye *et al.* 1997).

The pyrite zone extends upwards to about the water table, normally about 1 m below ground surface, at which depth it is replaced by a further, limited zone of irregular iron-staining that takes the form of yellowish-red (5YR4/6) streaks and rings, the latter with light grey (10YR7/1) cores, developed against a grey to greyish brown (10YR5/1 to 10YR5/2) background. This zone is clearly developed as a result of the formation of iron oxides and hydroxides and is associated with a local increase in the proportion of DCB-extractable iron (below). The boundary between this zone and the underlying pyrite zone is not always well defined, particularly if the sediments contain shell debris. From around 0.6 m depth upwards to the ground surface, the irregular zone is replaced by a zone of full oxidation to ferric iron upon which an immature soil profile has developed.

The salinity profile (Fig. 3a) shows three distinct zones. Previous work (Paul *et al.* 1992)

has shown that at depth the groundwater salinity is close to the tidal average in the adjacent estuary ($\simeq$12 ppt). The top of this zone is seen in Fig. 3a as a sharp change in salinity at about 6 m depth. Above this level there is a steady decrease to around 2 m depth, which we interpret as a zone of infusion of fresh water, probably from the adjacent, slightly higher, carselands to the west. This zone of infusion is broadly coincident with the pyrite zone and may reflect the input of oxygenated waters from the surface. The highest zone, from 2 m depth to surface, contains almost no sodium chloride and is interpreted as a fully desalinated zone, developed largely by vertical leaching in response to precipitation and improved soil drainage.

Below about 2 m depth, the groundwater alkalinity (Fig. 3b) is constant at around pH 8, probably due to the presence of buffered, saline water infused from the estuary and possibly also to the presence of shell debris. The redox potential (Fig. 3c) is around zero volts, which may be a result of the organic content, whose decomposition has created an oxygen deficiency. Above the water table, in the unsaturated, aerated percolation zone, the acidity falls to around pH 6 and the redox potential rises to around 0.6 V.

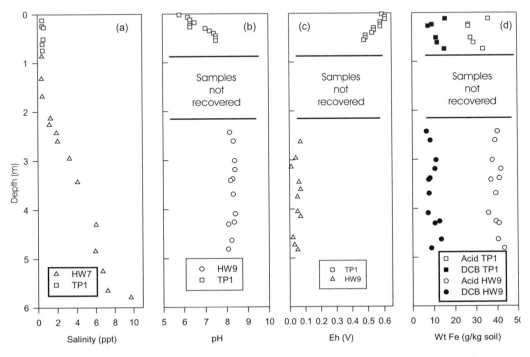

Fig. 3. Geochemical profiles from the Bothkennar research site (boreholes as noted). (**a**) salinity; (**b**) pH; (**c**) redox potential; (**d**) extractable iron.

Below the crust (Fig. 3d), acid-extractable iron comprises $3.96 \pm 0.21\%$ of the dry soil weight. The DCB-extractable iron is relatively more variable at around $0.94 \pm 0.22\%$. Comparison of Fig. 3d with Fig. 3b indicates that below the crust both the total weight and relative proportion of DCB-extractable iron are positively correlated with the soil pH, which we attribute to the increased precipitation of iron compounds such as goethite and ferrihydrite as the pH rises. Within the crust itself (below the cultivated horizon), the formation of the soil profile has involved iron translocation and the consequent formation of horizons both of depletion and of enrichment (cf. below and Fig. 4).

The desiccated crust

Above the groundwater table the sediments are partially to fully oxidized and an immature soil profile has developed. Four principal lithological units can be distinguished (Fig. 4: units L1–L4), both on the basis of their initial lithology and granulometry and from their colour, which largely reflects the subsequent translocation of clays and iron compounds. Units L4 to L2 are developed on the lagoonal deposits of the Saltgreens Member, and correspond in part to the A and B horizons of the soil profile, whereas Unit L1 represents the top of the Skinflats Formation, which here comprises an intertidal shell horizon

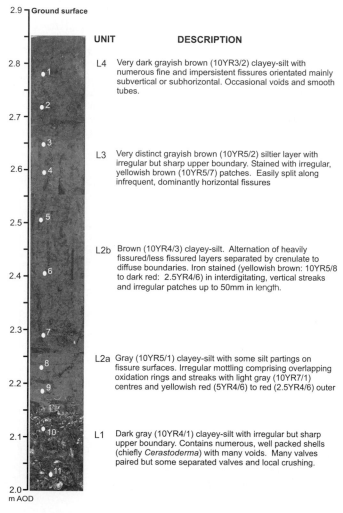

UNIT   **DESCRIPTION**

L4   Very dark grayish brown (10YR3/2) clayey-silt with numerous fine and impersistent fissures orientated mainly subvertical or subhorizontal. Occasional voids and smooth tubes.

L3   Very distinct grayish brown (10YR5/2) siltier layer with irregular but sharp upper boundary. Stained with irregular, yellowish brown (10YR5/7) patches. Easily split along infrequent, dominantly horizontal fissures

L2b Brown (10YR4/3) clayey-silt. Alternation of heavily fissured/less fissured layers separated by crenulate to diffuse boundaries. Iron stained (yellowish brown: 10YR5/8 to dark red: 2.5YR4/6) in interdigitating, vertical streaks and irregular patches up to 50mm in length.

L2a Gray (10YR5/1) clayey-silt with some silt partings on fissure surfaces. Irregular mottling comprising overlapping oxidation rings and streaks with light gray (10YR7/1) centres and yellowish red (5YR4/6) to red (2.5YR4/6) outer

L1   Dark gray (10YR4/1) clayey-silt with irregular but sharp upper boundary. Contains numerous, well packed shells (chiefly *Cerastoderma*) with many voids. Many valves paired but some separated valves and local crushing.

Fig. 4. Detailed soil profile log from trial pit TP1. Points 1 to 11 are the locations of particle size analyses. The nomenclature of the units should not be confused with that provisionally adopted for the stratigraphical units within the Claret Formation by Paul *et al.* (1992) and later superseded (Barras & Paul 1999).

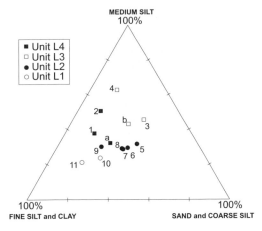

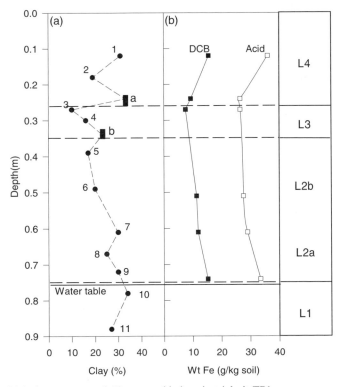

Fig. 5. Ternary composition diagram for units L1 to L4 (sample positions shown in Fig. 4). The upper size boundaries used are: clay 2 μm; fine silt 6 μm; medium silt 20 μm; coarse silt 63 μm.

interbedded with clayey-silts derived from the underlying Claret Formation.

In the trial pit TP1 (Fig. 4) the highest unit (L4) is a uniformly oxidized clayey-silt, 0.21 m to

0.26 m thick, penetrated by numerous fissures (subvertical and subhorizontal) and rootlets. We consider that it is the modern ploughed horizon, on the basis of its uniform appearance and sharp base. It rests with a sharp contact upon a paler, silty, faintly iron-stained unit (L3), 0.09 m to 0.10 m thick, which possesses a pronounced horizontal fissility. L3 rests with an irregular, diffuse contact upon a heavily iron-stained unit (L2), 0.40 m to 0.44 m thick, and itself divisible into two subunits: the upper (L2b) shows crude stratification based on the frequency of horizontal fissuring and has a vertical pattern of iron staining, which largely follows rootlet holes or vertical fissures. The lower subunit (L2a) has a complex, ring-like pattern of iron staining and contains occasional shell fragments. The base of L2a rests sharply on a grey coloured, clayey-silt unit (L1) that is packed with shells (not *in situ*) and shell fragments and extends below the water table at the base of the section (≃0.75 m bgl in TP1).

The units exhibit major variations in the grading of their silt fraction (Fig. 5). A profile through the lower units L1 and L2 (points 11 to 5) shows a consistent coarsening upwards trend from a fine

Fig. 6. Profiles of (**a**) clay content and (**b**) extractable iron in trial pit TP1.

silt and clay (<6 μm) content of >60% to ≃30%. Unit L3 is further depleted in this fraction (<30%) and also shows some translocation of medium silt (6 μm to 20 μm) from its top (point 3) to its base (point 4). This pattern is consistent with the early development of a soil profile by the loss of fines from an upper A horizon (the top of L3) and their accumulation lower in the sequence (the base of L3), together with a more general coarsening upwards trend within the lagoonal Saltgreens Member, due perhaps to increasing periods of exposure or surface winnowing as the level of the deposits rose towards the maximum tidal height. Such a profile might have developed from a material of initially homogeneous composition, perhaps indicated by the composition of unit L4.

The development of the soil profile can be further seen in the profiles of clay and iron content (Fig. 6). Within unit L3, there is a clear downward migration of clay particles which appear to have accumulated near its base. In the underlying unit L2b the downward fining trend seen in Fig. 5 is again apparent, although this is less rapid than in L3. The downward movement of clay in L3 is accompanied by depletion of both acid-extractable and DCB-extractable iron. The underlying unit L2 shows a corresponding downward enrichment (Fig. 6b). This iron translocation is also indicated by the change in colour from L3 (10YR5/23, greyish brown with occasional 10YR5/6 yellowish brown iron staining) to unit L2 (10YR4/3, brown, with frequent 10YR5/8 to 2.5YR4/6 yellowish brown to red iron staining).

This pattern provides further evidence that units L3 and L2 represent an immature soil profile that has developed by eluviation, which has caused clay migration (lessivation) and iron translocation. L3 is the (upwardly incomplete) eluviated A horizon and has suffered a relative loss of clay and iron in its upper part. These components have migrated downwards to unit L2, which is thus an illuvial B horizon. This horizon appears to be composite: unit L2b (the higher subunit) shows a streak-like oxidation pattern, probably associated with rootlet holes, whereas in L2a (the lower subunit) a ring-like pattern of oxidation is predominant (with minor vertical streaking) and is probably attributable to gleying immediately adjacent to the water table. Unit L1 is stratigraphically distinct from those above it and its grading appears instead to be largely controlled by the underlying Claret Formation from which it was derived. Although it is formally a C horizon in the soil profile, this attribution does not seem helpful in this case since it does not represent the substrate from which the soil profile has developed.

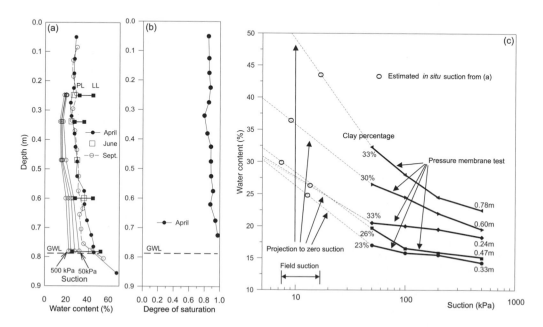

Fig. 7. Trial pit TP1 (**a**) Profiles of field water content during the summer months and at various laboratory suctions; (**b**) saturation; (**c**) laboratory drying curves.

Water content and soil suction

Throughout most of its thickness the crust is not fully saturated and so is subject to suction stresses. Their likely value is central to its development and can be estimated from the *in situ* water content and from laboratory suction curves. In the top 0.55 m of the crust the water content (Fig. 7a) lay consistently in the range 24%–30% at various times of measurement between the months of April and September. It is probable that this represents the field capacity of the soil. Comparison with profiles of the water contents at fixed suctions over the range 50 kPa to 500 kPa (Fig. 7a) suggest that at these water contents the suction stress is fairly low (5–20 kPa). This is consistent with the relatively high degree of saturation (0.78 to 0.87: Fig. 7b). Below this depth the water content rises to $\simeq$50% as the water table is approached.

Above $\simeq$0.55 m the water content shows little variability, but the liquidity index is more variable (Fig. 7a). I_P has a minimum value in L3 ($I_P = 9\%$) and reaches a maximum in L1 ($I_P = 27\%$), which allows the liquidity index to rise from a minimum value of -0.84 in L3 (0.34 m bgl) to 0.43 in L1 (0.79 m bgl). In consequence, the undrained shear strength varies strongly with depth. Previous work (Paul *et al.* 1992; Paul & Barras 1993) has shown that the undrained (laboratory vane) strength increases from around 31 kPa to 89 kPa between the depths of 0.85 m and 0.28 m below surface. In unit L2 the undrained strength agrees with the liquidity index and follows the general relationship applicable to many normally consolidated clays (Skempton & Northey 1953). However, in L3 and L4 the relationship breaks down and the undrained shear strength of the soil mass may be as little as about one-half to one-third of the expected value. This is probably a result of the lower clay content and extensive fissuring seen in these units. We have not found direct evidence that interparticle cementation (due to translocated iron compounds, for example) is a factor in the undrained strength of the crust at Bothkennar, as has been suggested for the crust on other estuarine clays (Hawkins 1984). However, it may well be that, even if cementation were effective at small scales, fissuring would mask its effects at the larger scale of the soil mass.

Drying curves from each of the lithological units L1 to L4 (Fig. 7c) were obtained by the pressure membrane method over the suction range 50 kPa to 500 kPa. The results are typical of those from other fine-grained soils (e.g. Croney 1953). The water content held at a given suction increases with increasing clay content, probably as a consequence of the distribution of pore sizes, the higher water retention being associated with a higher proportion of smaller pores. If this is the case then L3 and, to a lesser extent, L2b, appear to have a more open structure than unit L1, which agrees with their proposed origin as eluvial and illuvial soil horizons. Unit L4, the uppermost horizon, has relatively low water retention despite a high clay content which possibly arises from the effects of cultivation and artificially induced pedogenesis.

Discussion: development of the crust

The compression history of the lagoonal deposits can be reconstructed from a comparison of their present-day thickness with their initial thickness. The latter can be deduced from the account given by Udney (1831), together with a knowledge of the tidal level to which they accumulated, which we have assumed to be similar to the modern high water spring tidal level at Kincardine (1.6 km distant from Bothkennar). Implicit in our method is the assumption, supported by numerical modelling (Wallis & Brockie 1997), that the tidal frame is horizontal in the upper Forth estuary. The central problem is to reconstruct the initial thickness and water content of the lagoonal sediments by estimating the key levels of their surface at various stages (Fig. 8) using geotechnical theory to model their likely compression.

We illustrate the approach using data from trial pit TP1 (Fig. 1). This pit is located on the western part of the site and so exhibits less than the maximal thickness of the lagoonal deposits (Saltgreens Member). Here we can identify about 0.7 m of probable lagoonal sediments (cf. Fig. 4), resting at a present-day elevation of 2.2 m AOD on a detrital shell layer, which is believed closely to represent the surface of the intertidal deposits which rest upon the sediments of the Claret Formation. This surface is today lower than when it was exposed, owing to additional compression of the underlying Claret Formation, here 18 m thick, caused by the weight of the lagoonal deposits themselves (interval A in Fig. 8). The application of a decompaction model to the Claret Formation (Paul & Barras 1998) based on its known geotechnical properties (Nash *et al.* 1992*b*) indicates that this compression would have been around 0.9 m and thus that the original elevation of the tidal flat surface prior to reclamation would have been $\simeq$3.1 m AOD.

The maximum depositional level of the lagoonal sediments in TP1 cannot have exceeded the height of the highest spring tides ($\simeq$3.5 m AOD

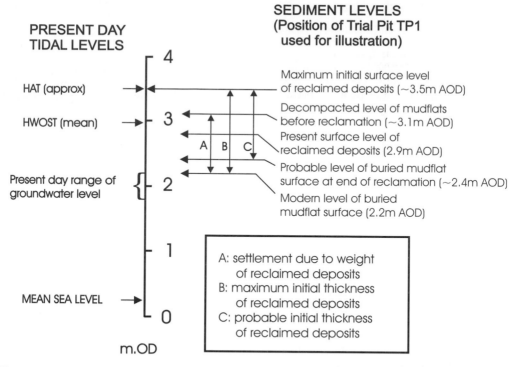

Fig. 8. Key levels during the accumulation and dewatering of the lagoonal sediments, based on the stratigraphy in TP1. See text for details of the reconstruction of the original depositional levels.

at present day: Hydrographer of the Navy 1999) and thus their initial thickness lay between a maximum of 1.3 m (interval B in Fig. 8) and a minimum of 0.7 m (their present-day thickness). Their actual initial thickness would have been determined by the extent to which compression of the underlying Claret Formation had kept pace with their deposition (and thus created an accommodation space). Calculations based on standard Terzaghi consolidation theory (as described in e.g. Smith & Smith 1998, using data from Nash *et al.* 1992*a*) suggest that consolidation would probably have been relatively rapid and that after three years (the three warps) about 75% ($\simeq$0.7 m) of the final settlement (0.9 m) would have already occurred. Thus our best estimate of the initial thickness of the lagoonal deposits at TP1 is $\simeq$1.1 m (interval C in Fig. 8).

From this initial thickness and the present-day water content (Fig. 7a), we calculate that the initial water content, when averaged over the whole profile, would have been $\simeq$42% and the corresponding average initial void ratio would have been 1.12. This uniform void ratio is an idealization. In reality, the void ratio would have varied

with depth, following a profile determined by the compression model applicable to the newly deposited sediment and by its stress history of incremental loading and periodic phases of syn-depositional drying. Although this history is not known with certainty, our reconstruction (below) suggests that the conventional Terzaghi model may be applicable to this early phase. This seems reasonable, since the sediment has a substantial silt content, is thus of low plasticity ($W_L = 45\%$, $W_P = 28\%$) and had a relatively low initial water content. It is also possible to show, using the methods of Gibson (1958), that the accumulating lagoonal sediments would have been fully consolidated throughout the period of their deposition. These factors together imply that a relatively dense particle skeleton could have formed at an early stage in the history of the deposit.

The subsequent compression history of the deposits is illustrated in Fig. 9, which shows the stress history of one soil element (0.60 m depth) from TP1. Two possible initial conditions are shown: the uniform profile (point A) and the Terzaghi profile (point B). A conventional oedometer test was then used to model the main

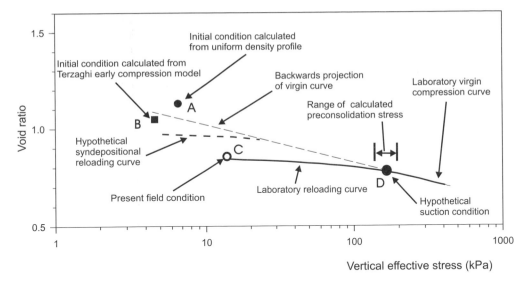

Fig. 9. Schematic compression history of a soil element in the crust at 0.60 m depth.

phase of compression. The backward projection of the virgin line passes close to the calculated Terzaghi initial condition, which suggests that a Terzaghi compression model can be applied over most of the stress range since initial deposition. However, the present field condition (point C: Fig. 9) clearly lies on a reloading line and the sample has a preconsolidation stress of around 150–200 kPa. If we presume this to be the result of soil suction (shown hypothetically at D in Fig. 9) it would (from Fig. 7c) imply a fall in water content to around 23% at some time since the installation of soil drainage.

The relatively invariant water content profiles reported above (Fig. 7a) probably represent the normal field capacity of the soil and projection of the drying curve back to full saturation (zero suction) suggests that they correspond to low field suctions around 5–20 kPa. The observed preconsolidation stress is thus an order of magnitude greater than this and requires a fall in water content by $\simeq 13\%$ from the present field value. Such a fall could possibly be due to evapotranspiration by vegetation during a prolonged dry period and it is known that under such conditions plant roots can locally exert suctions $\simeq 1000$ kPa or greater. Long term climatic records (e.g. Smith 1995; Jones *et al.* 1997) indicate several significant drought periods since 1784, the most severe of which have occurred in recent years (e.g. 1976 and 1990), although direct evidence, such as relict desiccation cracks, is not visible at surface due to recent annual ploughing.

Conclusions

The desiccated surface crust at Bothkennar has developed during the past 200 years by three sets of processes. The sediments of the Saltgreens Member accumulated over a three year period (c.1784–87) by artificially induced settling. They consolidated under their own weight and also induced an additional, slower, consolidation of the underlying sediments of the Claret Formation. During this stage they probably remained fully saturated, except perhaps in their uppermost few centimetres, and so their water content was controlled by selfweight compression. Following this stage, the introduction of artificial drainage created an upper, partially saturated zone in which the effective stress was thus increased by soil suction, probably in particular by plant evapotranspiration during periods of drought. This resulted in an additional volume reduction and a moderate (150–200 kPa) degree of overconsolidation. Concurrently with these stages, the profile became desalinated, acidified and oxidized to an extent controlled by depth, fresh water inflow and aeration. We conclude that the physical development of the crust was rapid and is now largely completed, whereas its chemical development is not yet completed, as shown by the soil profile which remains immature.

Field and laboratory assistance was given by H. Barras and A. Heron to whom we express our thanks. J. D. Peacock offered much helpful information and advice throughout the work. We thank J. J. M. Powell and the staff of the Building Research Establishment for advice and sample collection and thank C. Cameron of the University of St Andrews for the use of the Sedi-Graph. We thank D. F. T. Nash for access to the Delft cores at Bristol University. We gratefully acknowledge the financial support of the former SERC (Grant GR/H/14151) and also thank the EPSRC for allowing continued access to the Bothkennar research site for subsequent work. We thank the referees for their constructive comments on an earlier draft of this paper.

References

BARRAS, B. F. & PAUL, M. A. 1999. Sedimentology and depositional history of the Claret Formation ('carse clay') at Bothkennar, near Grangemouth. *Scottish Journal of Geology*, **35**(2), 131–144.

BERNER, R. A. 1971. *Principals of chemical sedimentology*. McGraw-Hill, New York.

BRITISH STANDARDS INSTITUTION 1990. *Methods of test for soils for Civil Engineering purposes*. British Standard BS1377. British Standards Institution, London.

BROWNE, M. A. E., GRAHAM, D. K. & GREGORY, D. M. 1984. *Quaternary deposits in the Grangemouth area, Scotland*. British Geological Survey Report 16/3. HMSO, Edinburgh.

——, MENDUM, J. R. & MONRO, S. K. 1993. *Geology. In:* CORBETT, L. & DIX, N. J. (eds) *Central Scotland*. Forth Naturalist and Historian. Stirling University. 1–17.

CADELL, H. M. 1929. Land reclamation in the Forth Valley. *Scottish Geographical Magazine*, **45**, 7–22.

CRONEY, D. 1953. The movement and distribution of water in soils. *Géotechnique*, **3**(1), 1–16.

GIBSON, R. E. 1958. The progress of consolidation in a clay layer increasing in thickness with time. *Géotechnique*, **8**, 171–82.

HAWKINS, A. B. 1984. Depositional characteristics of estuarine alluvium: some engineering implications. *Quarterly Journal of Engineering Geology*, **17**, 219–34.

——, LARNACH, W. J., LLOYD, I. M. & NASH, D. F. T. 1989. Selecting the location and the initial investigation of the SERC soft clay test bed site. *Quarterly Journal of Engineering Geology*, **22**, 281–316.

HEAD, K. H. 1982. *Manual of soil laboratory testing. Vol 2: Permeability, shear strength and compressibility tests*. Pentech Press, London.

HYDROGRAPHER OF THE NAVY 1999. *Admiralty Tide Tables. Volume 1. European Waters*. Hydrographic Office, Taunton.

JONES, P. D., CONWAY, D. & BRIFFA, K. R. 1997. Precipation variability and drought. *In:* HULME, M. & BARROW, E. (eds) *Climates of the British Isles*. Routledge, London. 197–219.

KRISHNAMURTY, K. V., SHPIRT, E. & REDDY, M. 1976. Trace metal extraction of soils and sediments by nitric acid – hydrogen peroxide. *Atomic Absorption Newsletter*, **15**(3), 68–70.

MEHRA, O. P. & JACKSON, M. L. 1960. Iron oxide removal from soils and clays by a dithionite-citrate system buffered with sodium bicarbonate. *Clays and Clay Minerals*, **7**, 317–27.

MCLUSKY, D. S. 1987. Intertidal habitats and benthic macrofauna of the Forth estuary, Scotland. *Proceedings of the Royal Society of Edinburgh*, **93B**, 389–99.

NASH, D. F. T. & LLOYD, I. M. 1988. *Soft Clay Test Bed Site, Bothkennar. Survey Grid and deep benchmark*. Report UBCE-SM-88-3. University of Bristol.

——, POWELL, J. J. M. & LLOYD, I. M. 1992a. Initial investigations of the soft clay test site at Bothkennar. *Géotechnique*, **42**(2), 163–181.

——, SILLS, G. C. & DAVISON, L. R. 1992b. One dimensional consolidation testing of soft clay from Bothkennar. *Géotechnique*, **42**(2), 241–56.

PAUL, M. A. & BARRAS, B. F. 1993. *The Engineering Geology of the surface crust at the SERC Soft Clay Research Site, Bothkennar*. Bothkennar Research Report, Heriot-Watt University, Edinburgh

—— & ——1998. A geotechnical correction for post-depositional sediment compression: examples from the Forth valley, Scotland. *Journal of Quaternary Science*, **13**, 171–6.

—— & ——1999. The role of organic material in the plasticity of Bothkennar clay. *Géotechnique*, **49**(4), 529–35.

——, PEACOCK, J. D. & BARRAS, B. F. 1995. Flandrian stratigraphy and sedimentation in the Bothkennar–Grangemouth area, Scotland. *Quaternary Newsletter*, **75**, 22–35.

——, —— & WOOD, B. F. 1992. The engineering geology of the carse clay at the National Soft Clay Research Site, Bothkennar. *Géotechnique*, **42**(2), 183–98.

——, WOOD, B. F. & PEACOCK, J. D. 1992. *An Illustrated Guide to the Engineering Geology at the SERC Soft Clay Research Site, Bothkennar*. (2 Vols). Swindon: SERC.

PEACOCK, J. D. 1998. The Bothkennar Gravel Formation ('buried gravel layer') of the Forth Estuary. *Scottish Journal of Geology*, **34**, 1–5.

PYE, K., COLEMAN, M. L. & DUAN, W. M. 1997. Microbial activity and diagenesis in saltmarsh sediments, North Norfolk, England. *In:* JICKELLS, T. D. & RAE, J. E. (eds) *Biogeochemistry of intertidal sediments*. Cambridge University Press. 119–151.

ROBERTSON-RINTOUL, M. S. E. 1986. A quantitative soil-stratigraphic approach to the correlation and dating of post-glacial river terraces in Glen Feshie, western Cairngorms. *Earth Surface Processes and Landforms*, **11**, 605–17.

ROBINSON, M. 1993. Microfossil analyses and radiocarbon dating of depositional sequences related to Holocene sea-level change in the Forth valley, Scotland. *Transactions of the Royal Society of Edinburgh: Earth Sciences*, **84**, 1–60.

SISSONS, J. B. 1969. Drift stratigraphy and buried morphological features in the Grangemouth-Falkirk-Airth area, central Scotland. *Transactions of the Institution of British Geographers*, **48**, 19–50.

SKEMPTON, A. W. & NORTHEY, R. D. 1953. The sensitivity of clays. *Géotechnique*, **3**, 30–53.

SMITH, G. N. & SMITH, I. G. N. 1998. *Elements of Soil Mechanics*. 7th Edition. Blackwell Science, Oxford.

SMITH, K. 1995. Precipitation over Scotland, 1757–1992: some aspects of temporal variability. *International Journal of Climatology*, **15**, 543–56.

UDNEY, J. 1831. Essay III: Embankments. *Transactions of the Highland Agricultural Society*, **13**, 100–3.

WALLIS, S. G. & BROCKIE, N. J. W. 1997. Modelling the Forth Estuary with MIKE11. *Coastal Zone Topics*, **3**, 1–10.

The use of Nuclear Magnetic Resonance Imaging (MRI) to assess impact of oil-related waste on estuarine sediments and sediment dynamics

ALISON D. REEVES[1] & JOHN A. CHUDEK[2]

[1] Geography Department, University of Dundee, Dundee DD1 4HN
(e-mail: a.d.reeves@dundee.ac.uk)
[2] Chemistry Department, University of Dundee, Dundee DD1 4HN

Abstract: The Marine Pollution Control Unit of the Department of Transport are at present testing the suitability of burial and landfarming of oily residues in sandy coastal environments as an alternative to landfill sites. The tendency for oil related compounds to sorb to sediments (and hence to affect their cohesiveness) has been extensively investigated, but this has not involved or permitted the 'observation' or measurement of advection/diffusion processes or the breakdown of these residues within sediments.

MRI, which is a multidimensional technique allowing the position of nuclei (most commonly protons) to be located within a known volume of substrate, for example sediment, provides a means of monitoring the change in position and the eventual breakdown of oil within sediments, thus offering a method of assessing the harming potential of oils in near-shore environments. Two dimensional (2D) and three dimensional (3D) MRI analysis of the movement of oil in estuarine sediments show that, using appropriate parameters, movement of the oil can be both observed and quantified. To aid quantification a sample holder fabricated from polyvinylsiloxane, an inert material visible in magnetic resonance images has been used as an internal intensity standard. The results show the great potential of MRI in studying protonated contaminants in these materials, notwithstanding the presence of paramagnetic species in estuarine sediments, which might distort the image. Sediments studied thus far have been collected from the Tay Estuary, NE Scotland.

Magnetic resonance imaging (MRI) is a development of nuclear magnetic resonance spectroscopy (NMR). Unlike the MRI used in hospitals the data for the images shown here were collected using a magnet of considerably greater field strength and smaller bore, thus MRI is potentially capable of producing images at a much higher resolution, 10^{-5} mm^3, compared with 5 mm^3 typically attained by medical imagers. MRI is non-invasive and non-destructive. Its use allows specimens to be re-examined over a time course or after treatment (for example, in the course of this work addition of contaminants). As its name implies, NMR spectroscopy measures the interactions of atomic nuclei with magnetic fields. Different atomic nuclei have different nuclear spins and when a powerful magnetic field is applied these nuclear spins align themselves to the field in a finite number of allowed orientations. These orientations can be perturbed by applying a force, for example from a burst of radio frequency (rf) energy, after initial absorption of the energy it is re-transmitted again as rf.

It is this re-transmitted rf which is detected. Although the nuclei of many isotopes can theoretically be imaged, sensitivity restraints limit the range to a select few of which the hydrogen nucleus (^{1}H) is by far the most commonly observed. Intra- and intermolecular interactions, along with the strength of the applied magnetic field, determine the frequency at which energy is absorbed. In a uniform field, therefore, moieties of the same type, in equivalent environments, will absorb energy (or resonate) at the same frequency. The superimposition of a linear magnetic field gradient on the original field introduces a spatial dimension and nuclei (here ^{1}H) chemically equivalent, but physically separated along the gradient, will resonate at a frequency governed by the strength of the gradient and their respective positions. By applying three orthogonal field gradients it is possible to generate a three dimensional map of the distribution of the protons. The density of ^{1}H's, moderated by restraints imposed by their physical and chemical environment, dictates the intensity of the signal (Chudek

From: PYE, K. & ALLEN, J. R. L. (eds). *Coastal and Estuarine Environments: sedimentology, geomorphology and geoarchaeology*. Geological Society, London, Special Publications, **175**, 201–206. 0305-8719/00/$15.00 © The Geological Society of London 2000.

& Hunter 1997). Image intensity and contrast are further dependent on image acquisition parameters which can be varied to highlight different features within the sample.

MRI data may be viewed in a number of ways; initially they may be viewed along any of the three main axes as a series of slices through the sample. Often gross changes are better viewed using one of the pseudo-3D projections available in the data manipulation software. Two are shown here. The first, *a maximum intensity projection*, replaces the grey levels of the slices by a range of translucencies, opaque white representing maximum voxel intensity, through a range of reducing white translucency to transparent for the darkest grey level. These images can be manipulated spatially at will. A second projection, using *surface reconstruction*, or *rendering*, involves selecting a range of grey levels, for example, those associated with the sample container or those associated with a certain level of contamination. The software sorts through the data and where voxels within the subset are contiguous they are clustered together. A 'skin' is placed round each cluster to give the surface rendering and like the maximum intensity projection this can be viewed from any angle. Surfaces can be electronically sliced to allow further clusters, of the same grey level range or of another grey level range, inside the first to be viewed. The images can, if required, be given a 'cosmetic' treatment to enhance their 3D nature.

MRI has been shown to be an ideal method for the analysis of fluid flow in a variety of environmental substrates. Borgia (1994) reviews the 'explosive growth' in MRI techniques which are being applied to a diverse range of studies involving fluids in heterogeneous or model systems. More specifically MRI has been used to obtain porosity distributions and fluid flow velocities by measuring localized porosity values inside natural porous rocks (Williams & Taylor 1994; Fordham *et al.* 1994; Amin *et al.* 1994, 1996; McDonald *et al.* 1996; McDonald 1996).

MRI is at present being used to map the position of oil in rock cores and it can also be used to approximate the relative concentrations of oil and water (Davies *et al.* 1994). Related work is being carried out in the field of *in situ* oil well logging (Goelman & Prammer 1995). Technological advances have meant a move towards examining reservoir properties, especially those not measured in a continuous log for example, producibility, irreducible water saturation and residual water saturation (Martin 1995). A novel, geological application is the imaging of the Lake Agassiz-Lake Winnipeg transition in Section 4 of Core Namao 94-900-122a (313–465 cm), using a newly developed MRI technique called Single-Point, Ramped Imaging with T_1 enhancement (SPRITE). Contrast between sediment layers is best observed from regions of the core with high magnetic susceptibility (Rack *et al.* 1998).

The ability of 'conventional' MRI to image oil in the various rock cores show that susceptibility effects in the sediment need not necessarily be a major problem. The presence of paramagnetic materials, air spaces, liquid/air and liquid/liquid interfaces can all potentially wipe out MRI images by perturbing the linear magnetic field gradients used in imaging, to an extent that the images become meaningless. Appropriate choice of acquisition parameters and the acquisition sequence, means that these effects can be largely discounted.

While it is difficult to quantitatively extract petroleum from environmental samples and analyse by chromatographic means (GC/MS), this is recognized as the best and most widely used methodology for the purpose (e.g. Killops & Readman 1985; Davies & Wolff 1990). Conventional oil analysis gives detailed information on oil composition. MRI can provide complimentary information if used in conjunction with these traditional analytical techniques and exceeds these methods in the examination of diffusion patterns of petroleum residues in sediment samples. The tendency for selected organic compounds to sorb to sediments has also been extensively investigated (Means *et al.* 1980). The diffusion/advection of oil within sediments of differing characteristics (organic carbon content and grain size) naturally varies. In the vacinity of an oil discharge or spill, organics of limited water solubility are expected to rapidly associate with suspended and bedded sediment particles. In areas where sediments have high binding capacities i.e., are organic rich and fine grained, then hydrocarbons may concentrate to levels far exceeding those of the polluted water column. Such studies have not permitted the measurement of movement of oil residues or their breakdown in sediment.

Allied NMR spectroscopic studies have given direct evidence as to the composition of petroleum fractions, through identification and quantification of different structural units in the spectra produced (Schmitquiles *et al.* 1994; Frometa 1994; Christopher *et al.* 1996; Michon *et al.* 1997). More importantly here, spectroscopy has also been used to follow the degradation of organic materials (Dosseh *et al.* 1992; Matlengiewicz *et al.* 1992). There are very few reported applications for examination of organic material in sediments. An example of this type of study is the employment of ^{13}C Cross Polarization Magic

Angle Spinning to characterize the diagenesis of organic material in 'organic rich' Black Sea Sediments (Ergin *et al.* 1996; sediments previously described by Yucesoy & Ergin 1992).

Imaging liquids in sediments has, until recently, been thought to be very difficult if not impossible. It has now been shown (Chudek & Reeves 1998; Reeves & Chudek 1998) that with suitable parameters both the presence of protic impurities and their movement in sediments can be observed. In order to make this method quantitative it is necessary to include a reference in close proximity to the sample being measured, the image intensity of which will act as a standard against which the intensity of the image of the contaminated material might be measured and quantified.

In the series of experiments reported here, 3D images of samples of sediment, contaminated and uncontaminated, were obtained. The samples were held in a container made of polyvinylsiloxane. Polyvinylsiloxane is visible using MRI and thus fulfils a dual role as holder and reference.

Under normal conditions the main requirement of MRI is to produce an image of the best resolution achievable. This can be time consuming. In these experiments quantification of contaminant distribution, measured in the shortest possible time, was considered more important than resolution, consequently parameters were chosen which gave the best resolution along the vertical axis, with a lower resolution in the horizontal plane, this reduced imaging time by a factor of 12.

Methods

Sample collection and handling

Sediment was collected from a site in Invergowrie Bay, near Dundee on the north side of the Tay estuary [OS 357 297] using a grab sampler, of modified van Veen design (0.25 m³ volume), with added teeth to collect material more effectively (commissioned by the Tay Estuary Research Center). The grab penetrates bottom sediments to a depth of 10 cm. Samples were collected, returned to the laboratory and air dried for immediate use. The sediment characteristics, determined in the laboratory, were as follows: Loss on ignition 2.05%; 75.2% sand, 23.3% silt, 1.5% clay (determined by laser granulometry).

Sub-samples were examined in the MR imager with no pre-preparation. An inert polyvinylsiloxane sample holder (Coltene President Impression Material; 23 mm × 17 mm ID) was filled with artificially contaminated sediment (Granville diesel oil 15W/40). Amounts added are indicated in the results section. The sample holder was subsequently placed in a 25 mm OD glass tube and inserted into the magnet. Image data collection was started immediately.

NMR Imaging Experiments

Nuclear magnetic resonance images were accumulated using a Bruker AM300/WB FT NMR spectrometer fitted with a Bruker Microimaging probe using a 25 mm saddle resonator. A standard Bruker 3D spin-echo sequence (XYSE3D) was used. By keeping the time to echo (TE) to <4 ms it is possible to image oil in marine sediments containing 3% Fe.

Acquisition Parameters were as follows:

Sweep width	:	125 000 Hz
Pulse width	:	10 μs (90°)
Repetition time	:	1 s
Echo time	:	2.35 μs
Field of view	:	(30 mm)³

Sample AR31
Matrix size	:	128 × 32 × 32
Voxel size	:	240 μm × 980 μm × 980 μm

Sample AR35
Matrix size	:	(128)³
Voxel size	:	(240 μm)³

Discussion

Figure 1 shows a transverse slice out of a 128 voxel³ image (interpolated to 192 voxel³) of the polyvinylsiloxane container with a sample of air dried sediment saturated with diesel oil. Both the container and the diesel oil in the sediment can be seen in the image, the slight distortions in the intensity of the container are almost certainly

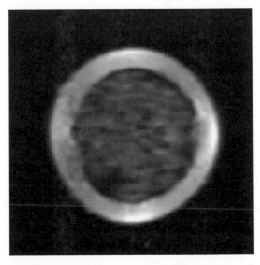

Fig. 1. Transverse slice; Air dried sediment saturated with diesel oil.

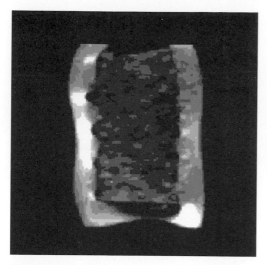

Fig. 2. Longitudinal view of maximum intensity projection of Fig. 1.

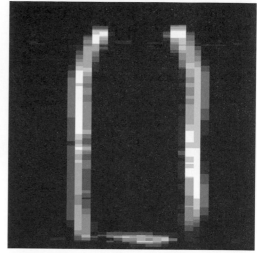

Fig. 4. Air dried sediment with 800 µl diesel oil added.

due to the effects of paramagnetic materials in the sediment. However, this would appear to indicate that the paramagnetic effects of the sediment are minimal. Figures 2 & 3 show a longitudinal view of a maximum intensity projection through the full 3D data set from which the slice shown in Fig. 1 was extracted, and a longitudinal view of a electronically sliced surface rendered reconstruction from the same data set respectively. In the case of the latter, a range of grey levels representing the container and a range representing higher levels of con-

tamination were selected. Figure 2 again shows signs of the effects of paramagnetism. This highlights a secondary role of the reference material, in that the effects of the paramagnetic materials in the sediment are observable and serve as an indicator of their strength. In Fig. 3 the distribution of oil density is instantly observable. As can be seen oil has concentrated near the top, the bottom and down one side. The oil was originally evenly distributed through the sample and this shows the position after 36 hours. The image shown in Fig. 4 is of sediment containing

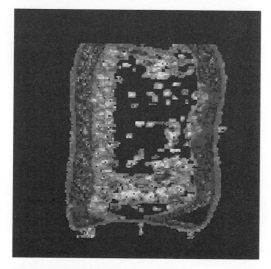

Fig. 3. Longitudinal view of surface rendered projection of Fig. 1.

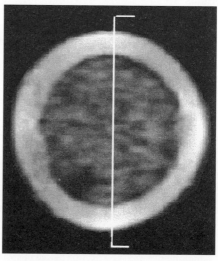

Fig. 5. Image showing position of section used to calculate variations in pixel intensity across a sample.

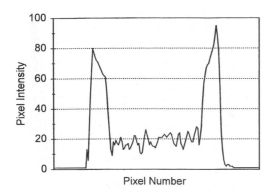

Fig. 6. Graph to show variation in pixel intensity through a contaminated sediment. Pixel numbers range from 0 to 192.

800 μl diesel oil, this data was collected as an 128 × 32 × 32 matrix which gives maximum resolution along the longitudinal axis only. This data set was collected in only 1 hour. It allows sufficient information on concentration and movement to be collected in a short time. The 128 voxel[3] images shown in the other figures took 36 hours to collect.

As an indication of the ability to quantify intensities, Fig. 6 shows an intensity profile through the slice in Fig. 5. Modern software also allows integration of intensities over variable areas of the image (not shown). Using the aquisition parameters for images such as that in Fig. 4 a series of samples with different concentrations of oil were imaged. The area of the sediment was integrated for each image and the intensity, if plotted, gave a linear calibration curve (see data provided in Table 1). This again demonstrates the quantitative nature of these experiments.

Conclusion

By combining sample container with reference material, it has been demonstrated that MRI offers a new and important method for quantitatively assessing concentration (and potential movement) of oil in marine sediments hence offering a method of determining the harming potential, in terms of the spread, of pollutant oils in the coastal marine environment. Sacrifice of resolution in the transverse plane with maximum resolution in the longitudinal axis allows relatively rapid sample accumulation allowing dynamic changes to be followed. Such an analytical protocol could be used for calculating the extent to which longer term remedial action is required when oil residues reach coastal areas, by allowing the effects of pollution incidents to be understood in greater detail. Over succeeding years, improvements in environmental quality could be monitored allowing recovery rates to be calculated. This is of particular relevance when bioremediation rates need to be monitored *in situ*. The importance of microbial biochemical transformation of toxic organic pollutants into harmless inorganic species is highlighted in the work of Atlas (1996); Al-Hadhrami *et al.* (1996); Braddock *et al.* (1995). Biodegradation by indigenous organisms is the principal mechanism for the removal of petroleum from the environment. The MR technique is non-destructive and samples can be used for further analysis.

References

AMIN, M. H. G., HALL, L. D., CHORELY, R. J., CARPENTER, T. A., RICHARDS, K. S. & BACHE, B. W. 1994. Magnetic resonance imaging of soil-water phenomena. *Magnetic Resonance Imaging*, **12**(2), 319–321.

AMIN, M. H. G., RICHARDS, K. S., CHORELY, R. J., GIBBS, S. G., CARPENTER, T. A. & HALL, L. D. 1996. Studies of soil-water transport by MRI. *Magnetic Resonance Imaging*, **14**(7–8), 879–882.

AL-HADHRAMI, M. N., LAPPIN-SCOTT, H. M. & FISHER, P. J. 1996. Effects of the addition of organic carbon sources on bacterial respiration and n-alkane biodegradation of Omani crude oil. *Marine Pollution Bulletin*, **32**(4), 351–357.

Table 1

		Intensity
Amount of oil added:	Dry	3.39×10^4 (background noise level)
	400 μl	3.53×10^4
	800 μl	3.61×10^4
	1600 μl	3.85×10^4

Intensities are averages of duplicate samples.

ATLAS, R. M. 1996. Slick solutions. *Chemistry in Britain*, 42–45.

BRADDOCK, J. F., LINDSTROM, J. E. & BROWN, E. J. 1995. Distribution of hydrocarbon-degrading microorganisms in sediments from Prince William Sound, Alaska, following the Exxon Valdez oil spill. *Marine Pollution Bulletin*, **30**(2), 125–132.

BORGIA, G. C. 1994. The many facets of current work in nuclear magnetic resonance for fluids in heterogeneous systems. *Magnetic Resonance Imaging*, **12**(2), 163–165.

CHRISTOPHER, J., SARPAL, A. S., KAPUR, G. S., KRISHNA, A., TYAGI, B. R., JAIN, M. C., JAIN, S. K. & BHATNAGAR, A. K. 1996. Chemical stucture of bitumen-derived asphaltenes by nuclear magnetic resonance spectroscopy and x-ray diffractometry. *Fuel*, **75**(8), 999–1008.

CHUDEK, J. A. & HUNTER, G. 1997. Magnetic resonance imaging in plants. *In*: EMSLEY, J. W. & FEENEY, J. (eds) *Progress in NMR spectroscopy*. Pergamon, Oxford, 43–63.

—— & REEVES, A. D. 1998. An application of Nuclear Magnetic Resonance Imaging to study migration rates of oil-related residues in estuarine sediments. *Biodegradation*, **9**, 443–449

DAVIES, N. J. & WOLFF, G. A. 1990. The Mersey Oil Spill, August 1989: a case of sediments contaminating the oil? *Marine Pollution Bulletin*, **21**(10), 481–484.

DAVIES, S., HARWICK, A., ROBERTS, D., SPOWAGE, K. & PACKER, J. 1994. Quantification of oil and water in preserved reservoir rock by NMR spectroscopy and imaging. *Magnetic Resonance Imaging*, **12**, 394–353.

DOSSEH, G., ROUSSEAU, B. & FUCHS, A. H. 1992. Structural characterization of a crude-oil by one and 2-dimensional Nuclear magnetic resonance spectroscopy. *Journal De Chimiee Physique et de Physico-Chimie Biologique*, **89**(2), 533–539.

ERGIN, M., GAINES, A., GALLETTI, G. C., CHIAVARI, G., FABBRI, D. & YUCESOYERYILMAZ, F. 1996. Early diagenesis of organic matter in recent Black Sea sediments: characterization and source assessment. *Applied Geochemistry*, **11**(5), 711–720.

FORDHAM, E. J., GIBBS, S. J. & HALL, L. D. 1994. Partially restricted diffusion in a permeable sandstone: observations by stimulated echo PFG NMR. *Magnetic Resonance Imaging*, **12**(2), 279–284.

FROMETA, A. E. N. 1994. Improvement in the determination of aromatic carbons in petroleum fractions by proton nuclear magnetic resonance spectroscopy. *Analyst*, **119**(5), 987–989.

GOELMAN, G. & PRAMMER, M. G. 1995. The CPMG pulse sequence in strong magnetic field gradients with application to oil-well logging. *Journal of Magnetic Resonance Series A*, **113**(1), 11–18.

KILLOPS, S. D. & READMAN, J. W. 1985. HPLC fractionation and GC-MS determination of aromatic hydrocarbons from oils and sediments. *Organic Geochemistry*, **8**(4), 247–257.

MARTIN, A. 1995. Nuclear magnetic resonance imaging: technology for the 21st Century. *Oil Review*, **7**(3), 19–33.

MATLENGIEWICZ, M., HENZEL, N., LAUER, J. C., LAURENS, T., NICOLE, D. & RUBINI, P. 1992. Computer-aided analysis of ^{13}C nuclear magnetic resonance spectra of multicomponent mixtures 2: Determination of the content of alkadienes in a light gasoline. *Analyst*, **117**(3), 387–393.

MEANS, J. C., WOOD, S. G., HASSET, J. J. & BANWART, W. L. 1980. Sorption of PAHs by sediments and soils. *Environmental Science Technology*, **16**, 93–98.

MCDONALD, P. J. 1996. The application of broad-line MRI to the study of porous media. *Magnetic Resonance Imaging*, **14**(7–8), 807–810.

——, PRITCHARD, T. & ROBERTS, S. P. 1996. Diffusion of water at low saturation into sandstone rock plugs measured by broad-line magnetic-resonance profiling. *Journal of Colloid and Interface Science*, **177**(2), 439–445.

MICHON, L., MARTIN, D., PLANCHE, J. P. & HANQUET, B. 1997. Estimation of average structural parameters of bitumens by C-13 nuclear magnetic resonance spectroscopy. *Fuel*, **76**(1), 9–15.

RACK, F. R., BALCOM, B. J. MACGREGOR, R. P. & ARMSTRONG, R. L. 1998. Magnetic resonance imaging of the Lake Agassiz-Lake Winnipeg transition. *Journal of Paleolimnology*, **19**(3), 255–264.

REEVES, A. D. & CHUDEK, J. A. 1998. Application of Nuclear Magnetic Resonance Imaging (MRI) to migration studies of oil residues in estuarine sediments (Tay Estuary). *Water Science and Technology*, **38**(11), 187–192.

SCHMITQUILES, F., NICOLE, D., MATLENGIEWICZ, M. & HENZLE, N. 1994. Computer aided analysis of C-13 NMR-spectra of multicomponent mixtures. 4. Structural analysis of a heavy gasoline from liquefaction of Polish coal. *Fuel*, **73**(6), 980–983.

WILLIAMS, J. L. A. & TAYLOR, D. G. 1994. Measurements of viscosity and permeability of 2-phase miscible fluid-flow in rock cores. *Magnetic Resonance Imaging*, **12**(2), 317–318.

YUCESOY, F. & ERGIN, M. 1992. Heavy metal geochemistry of surface sediments from the southern Black Sea shelf and upper slope. *Chemical Geology*, **99**, 265–287.

Sedimentological controls on the erosion and morphology of saltmarshes: implications for flood defence and habitat recreation

STEPHEN CROOKS[1,2,3] & KENNETH PYE[4]

[1] *Department of Marine Science and Coastal Management, University of Newcastle, Newcastle Upon Tyne NE1 7RU, UK*
[2] *Jackson Environment Institute, University of East Anglia, Norwich NR4 7TJ, UK*
[3] *Centre for Social and Economic Research on the Global Environment (CSERGE), University of East Anglia, Norwich NR4 7TJ, UK*
[4] *Department of Geology, Royal Holloway, University of London, Egham, Surrey TW20 0EX, UK*

Abstract: The factors which influence the morphology, drainage characteristics and erosion resistance of saltmarshes are of major interest from the standpoint of flood defence and habitat recreation. Sedimentological characteristics, including grain size distribution, mineral composition and pore fluid chemistry are all highly important. Of particular importance in muddy marshes is the nature of the clay mineral assemblage and dissolved cations present in the pore fluids. In marshes which are deficient in detrital calcium carbonate, such as those in Essex, UK, sodium ions dominate the exchange sites on clays, leading to the formation of thick water films around the clay particles and slow rates of sediment consolidation. This, in turn, causes low erosion resistance and a tendency for the development of highly dissected marsh morphology. Calcium and magnesium-rich marsh sediments, on the other hand, allow these ions to replace sodium in exchange sites, leading to more rapid dewatering and consolidation. Erosion resistance is thereby enhanced and such marshes tend to be characterized by low drainage densities and a low ratio of bare mud to vegetated surface area. The possibilty of engineering the erosion resistance and morphology of marshes through chemical treatments requires further investigation.

Within the UK, there is currently considerable interest in the factors that govern the stability and morphology of saltmarshes in the context flood defence and habitat conservation. A number of studies in southern Britain, in particular SE England, have demonstrated saltmarshes have experienced serious erosion in recent decades (Burd 1992; Pye & French 1992, 1993; Carpenter & Pye 1997), increasing the pressure on estuarine flood-defences and raising concerns about ecological effects of serious habitat loss.

Saltmarsh erosion takes place by a number of mechanisms, including

(1) retreat of near-vertical, clifflets at the marsh edge;
(2) stripping of a root-bound turf immediately landward of the clifflet top;
(3) retreat of the degraded ramp, which may be incised by a series of shore-normal erosional furrows at the seaward marsh edge;
(4) incision of the natural marsh creek system, with associated back collapse and headward erosion;
(5) vegetation die-back and erosion of the surface mud over large areas of the interior of the marsh; and
(6) incision coalescence of drainage ditches or agricultural ridge and furrow systems.

In the majority of saltmarshes along the coast of western and NE England erosional modes (1), (2) and (3) and locally (4) are prevalent, but in SE England modes (5) and (6) are also widespread (Pye & French 1993).

Several factors have been suggested to explain the observed differences in the rates and mechanism of saltmarsh erosion, including: higher rates of mean sea-level rise, changes in tidal range and asymmetry, increased mean wave height and storm surge frequency, the effects of dredging, embankment and navigation, reduced sediment supply from coastal cliffs and pollution induced

From: PYE, K. & ALLEN, J. R. L. (eds). *Coastal and Estuarine Environments: sedimentology, geomorphology and geoarchaeology*. Geological Society, London, Special Publications, **175**, 207–222. 0305-8719/00/$15.00 © The Geological Society of London 2000.

vegetation die-back (Pye & French 1993; Carpenter & Pye 1997). However, analysis of the available data suggests that these factors cannot fully explain the observed variations in the rates and modes of erosion, or the significant morphological differences which exist among marshes.

A further factor which acts as an important control on sediment erosion resistance and hence, through interactions with the physical environment, the morphology of a marsh, is the regional and inter-regional variation in the geotechnical behaviour of saltmarsh deposits.

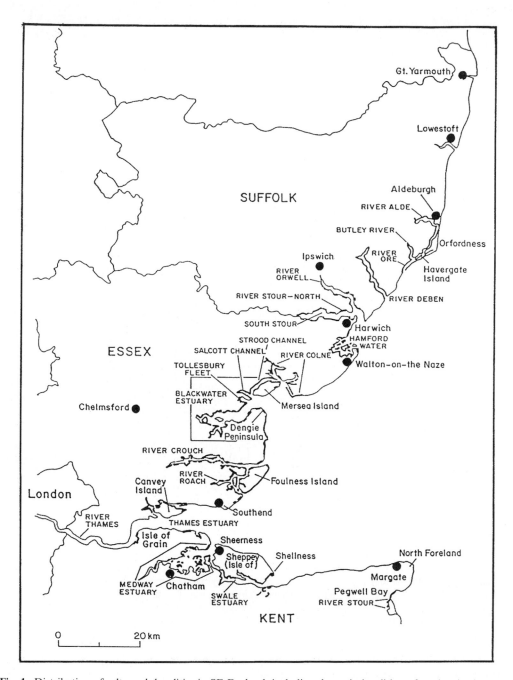

Fig. 1. Distribution of saltmarsh localities in SE England, including the main localities referred to in the text.

These geotechnical properties are, in turn, strongly influenced by the textural, mineralogical and geochemical nature of the accumulating sediments. This paper illustrates these points by reference to examples from Essex, SE England.

Study areas

As part of a wider investigation (Crooks 1996), several active and reclaimed marsh sites in England and northern France were investigated in order to determine the effects of such factors as parent sediment type, tidal range, vegetation type, and reclamation/reactivation history of marsh sediment properties and marsh morphology. Attention was focused mainly on the surface 1 m of sediment since this is the part

mostly affected by wave and tidal current action, and has the most direct influence on vegetation growth and biota. Where possible, marshes of differing ages were sampled to determine changes in sediment properties associated with vertical accretion of the marsh surface and associated reduction in tidal flooding frequency. Full results will be presented elsewhere; in this paper we refer mainly to examples from the Blackwater and Crouch estuaries, Essex (Fig. 1).

Most of the active marshes in SE England are of the 'estuarine fringing' type (terminology of Pye & French 1993), lying seaward of sea-embankments. Other types are locally represented, with 'mid-estuarine island' marshes having formed around the low-lying islands of London Clay in the Blackwater estuary and

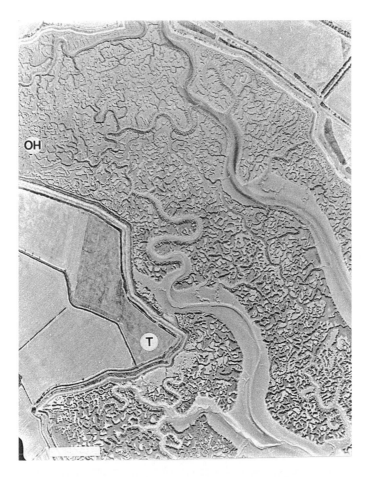

Fig. 2. Aerial photograph of Old Hall Marsh, Tollesbury Fleet, taken in October 1988 (scale bar = 100 m). Note the heavily dissected nature of the marsh surface with a high density of sinuous creeks which often terminate in sub-circular basins or coil back upon themselves. The reclaimed land to the left of the photograph is the site of the MAFF managed retreat experiment which commenced in 1995. (OH) and (T) mark sampling locations on the active and reclaimed marshes respectively. (Source: Cambridge University Committee for Air Photography.)

Medway, 'back-barrier' marshes behind large shingle or shell spit complexes, as at Colne Point and Shell Ness on the Isle of Sheppey, and 'open coast' marshes on the Dengie Peninsula.

Unlike NW England and the Severn estuary, saltmarshes in SE England do not display clear series of marsh terrace formations and it is uncommon to find more than two marsh levels juxtaposed. By further contrast, most of the marshes are highly incised by creek systems and have a much higher proportion of bare mud relative to vegetated surface. Many individual creeks terminate in sub-circular basins or coil back on themselves, for example on Old Hall Marsh, Tollesbury (Fig. 2) and Northey Island in the Blackwater estuary (Fig. 3). Elsewhere, anastomsing and complex, superimposed channel systems are developed, as at North and South Fambridge in the Crouch estuary (Fig. 4), and on many of the marsh islands within the Medway estuary. Open coast and outer estuarine marshes at Dengie and Foulness are exceptions to this regional morphological generalization. Dengie marsh in particular is characterized by a lower density of linear creeks which often extend the full width of the marsh (Fig. 5).

In recent decades many of the marshes in SE England have experienced significant erosional loss, both through lateral retreat and internal dissection. Using aerial photographs taken in 1973 and 1988, Burd (1992) determined that marshes in different estuaries lost 9–44% of their 1973 area. Several factors have contributed to this loss, but the most important short-term factor appears to have been an increase in wave energy (Carpenter & Pye 1997; Pye 2000).

Fig. 3. Aerial photograph of the NE region of Northey Island taken in 1988 (area: 860×600 m). Note the two morphologicaly distinct drainage networks which have developed on this reactivated marsh since a storm breached the sea wall in 1897. The reticulate drainage network (centre-top) has formed on a ridge of London Clay whereas the surrounding sinuous dendritic network, in which cross-linking between creeks is common, has developed at lower elevation on a relatively thick sequence of former reclaimed marsh muds. (N) marks the sampling location. (Source: Cambridge University Committee for Air Photography.)

Fig. 4. Aerial photograph of the regenerated marsh at North Fambridge taken in 1988 (area: 885 × 685 m). (R) and (D) represent the sampling sites within regions dominated by reticulate and dendritic creek networks, respectively cf. Steel & Pye (1997). (Source: Cambridge University Committee for Air Photography.)

As in the Severn estuary, larger areas of former saltmarsh have been reclaimed during past centuries, mainly for use as grazing marsh but more recently for arable agriculture, industry and port development. Much of the reclaimed land is protected by earth embankments, which total more than 800 km length in Essex alone. Increasingly, these flood defences have been placed under pressure as a result of marsh erosion and higher extreme water levels. Breaches in the defences have, in fact occurred at various times in the past, usually during storm surges such as those of 1897, 1938, 1953 and 1978. Where the defences have not subsequently been repaired, the reclaimed land has reverted to active saltmarsh or tidal mudflat. These sites provide useful historical analogues which can provide a guide to the likely future development of marshes which are now being created deliberately through managed realignment schemes.

The first experimental managed retreat and marsh creation scheme was begun on a small site on Northey Island, located in the Blackwater estuary, in 1991. Subsequently, further experimental sites were established in 1995 at Old Hall in Tollesbury Fleet and in 1996 at Orplands on the south side of the Blackwater estuary. A further, large-scale marsh recreation scheme is currently being planned for 2001 at Abbots Hall, adjacent to Salcott Channel in the Blackwater estuary.

Many of the saltmarshes which have been reactivated following storm surge breaching of the sea defences in Essex and Kent show high degrees of dissection and a very high ratio of bare mud to vegetated surface, even after 100 years (Figs 3 & 4). While this is not necessarily a problem from the viewpoint of habitat recreation and nature conservation, it does reduce the efficiency of the marshes as natural flood defences. Dissipation of wave and tidal energy is, in general,

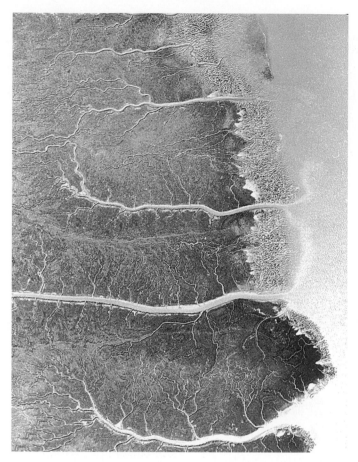

Fig. 5. Aerial photograph showing active saltmarshes on a section of the Dengie Peninsula (area: 890 × 690 m). Note the linear dendritic nature of the drainage system and the erosional mud mound topography along the retreating marsh edge. (Source: Cambridge University Committee for Air Photography.)

favoured by a high, wide and largely 'intact' saltmarsh platform; areas of low ground and wide, deep channels allow waves to penetrate and reform, increasing the energy expended on the flood defence embankments themselves.

On several of the 'natural set-back' marshes in the Crouch, Blackwater and Medway estuaries, creeks and mud basins occupy a larger area than the vegetated marsh surface, resulting in isolated saltmarsh islands and eroded mudmound topography (Fig. 6). This is particulary common on the lower parts of the reactivated areas. On higher areas, a regenerated rectilinear creek network has formed in many places, inherited from the 'drain and grip' features of the former agricultural surface (Figs 4 & 7). Following the reintroduction of tidal waters, vegetation has preferentially colonized the topographical highs,

and flow has been concentrated in the intervening troughs. Over time, and as vertical accretion has proceeded, these rectilinear tidal creek networks have begun to break down to form more sinuous, braided and dendritic type creek systems (Figs 3, 4). Many of the former reclaimed surfaces in this region were initially (at the time of reactivation) low in the tidal frame, owing to the combined effects of sea-level rise and compaction/settlement of the reclaimed land. Consequently, rates of vertical sediment accumulation have been high, with as much as 80 cm of mud having acumulated since 1897. An understanding of the properties and evolution of these sediments can therefore provide important insight into the future behaviour and development of large scale managed realignment and habitat recreation schemes.

Fig. 6. Internal dissection associated with dendritic drainage channels on the lower part of the reactivated marsh at North Fambridge.

Fig. 7. Reticulate drainage pattern on the upper, higher part of the reactivated marsh at North Fambridge.

Field and laboratory methods

Cores were collected from the mature active marsh at Old Hall, the adjacent reclaimed Tollesbury marsh (now reflooded as part of the MAFF Tollesbury experimental managed retreat site), from a naturally reactivated marsh at Northey Island in the Blackwater estuary, and from two areas with contrasting drainage pattern on a naturally reactivated marsh at North Fambridge in the Crouch estuary. At both Northey Island and North Fambridge the reactivated marshes began to form after the enclosing seabanks were breached during a storm surge in November 1897. The exact locations of the coring sites are shown on Figs 2, 3 & 4. Additionally, short core samples and *in situ* shear-strength measurements were taken at other points on Mersea Island, in the Colne estuary, Strood, Blackwater estuary and Crouch estuary to further examine the relationship between marsh sediment composition, geotechnical properties, erosion resistance and morphology.

Undisturbed sediment cores were collected for laboratory analysis and *in situ* undisturbed undrained shear strength measurements were made in the field. Cores were obtained by hand-driving short lengths of plastic pipe (250 mm length; 100 mm diameter), with a bevelled leading edge, vertically into the marsh surface. Because of the large diameter of the cores and because the cores were collected in short lengths, compaction was avoided. After insertion of the first core tube, a pit was dug to allow gentle removal of the core which was sealed with water-tight end-caps and stored upright. A second core tube was then placed in the exact location from which the previous tube had been removed and driven into the marsh in a similar manner. This procedure was repeated to a give total core length of 1 m. This method of sampling, although laborious, was found to be most effective in providing undisturbed samples with minimal compaction. At each stage of core extraction five undisturbed undrained shear strength measurements were made using an ELE Field Inspection Vane (range 0–200 kPa).

In the laboratory the sediment was extruded in short, measured lengths (generally 3–4 cm; accurate to ±0.5 mm) and the colour recorded. A section from the centre of each sediment segment was removed using a square cutter (area 36 cm^2) and used to determine bulk density and moisture content according to the methods described in BS 1377 (British Standards Institution 1990).

Sub-samples from the sediment slices were prepared for microfabric analysis by scanning electron microscopy (SEM), determination of clay mineralogy by x-ray powder diffraction (XRD), grain size analysis by laser granulometry (Coulter LS130; range 0.1–900 μm), determination of Atterberg limits (according to BS 1377, British Standards Institution 1990), and chemical analysis (notably sodium adsorption ratio).

At depth intervals of approximately 15 cm, 100–150 g of sediment was collected from the excess cutting, dried at 45°C for three weeks and ground in an agate mill for 10 minutes to a particle size of 5 μm. These powdered sub-samples were used to determine the whole-rock mineralogy by XRD, carbonate content by calcimetry, organic matter content by loss on ignition (LOI) and specific gravity.

Results

All the sampled marshes at Tollesbury, Northey Island and North Fambridge consist predominantly of finely laminated to structureless, fine grained sediments. Modal size generally ranges from 8–10 microns and the mean size from 7–16 microns (Table 1). The major minerals present are

Table 1. *Average grain size characteristics of relatively muddy active saltmarshes of southern Essex and the Severn estuary*

Marsh	Mean (μm)	Mode (μm)	Sand (%)	Silt (%)	Clay (%)	<20 μm (%)	N
Essex							
Old Hall	7.8	8.5	7.6	77.2	15.2	79.4	5
Northey Island	15.7	9.7	17.9	71.9	10.2	59.3	4
N. Fambridge	10.6	8.0	9.1	73.5	17.4	70.7	5
Severn estuary							
Northwick Fmn.	14.6	13.6	4.5	73.1	22.4	75.7	8
Rumney Fmn.	7.2	13.1	5.6	73.6	20.8	75.3	8
Wentlooge Fmn.	5.9	13.8	2.3	74.3	23.4	81.0	6

Table 2. *Clay mineralogy (<2 μm fraction) of saltmarsh sediments from southern Essex and Severn estuary sites, determined by x-ray diffraction (approximate accuracy is ±5%)*

	Clay mineral abundance (%)				
Region	Smectite	Illite	Kaolinite	Chlorite	N
Southern Essex	41	41	14	4	11
Severn estuary	32	52	8	8	12

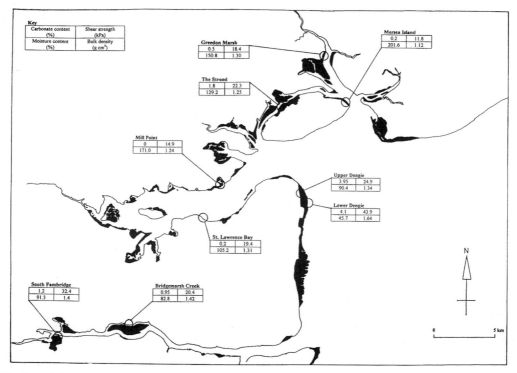

Fig. 8. Relationship between carbonate content, moisture content, bulk density and shear strength on marshes between the Colne Estuary and the Crouch estuary.

quartz and the clay minerals illite and smectite (including some mixed-layer clay); feldspar, kaolinite and chlorite are also important subsidiary constituents (Table 2). Calcium carbonate content was generally undetectable in all of the cores from Tollesbury, Northey Island and North Fambridge with the exception of a small amount (c. 3%) at the surface in the North Fambridge cores. Elsewhere, carbonate content was generally found to be low (<2%) everywhere except at Sayles Point on the Dengie Peninsula, where shell ridges (cheniers) are well-developed (Fig. 8).

All the actively accreting marshes were found to be very poorly consolidated with low bulk densities, extremely high moisture contents, which approached extremely high liquid limits, and thus possessed low undrained shear strengths (13–20 kPa; Table 3) compared, for example, with three active marshes at Littleton Warth in the Severn estuary (Table 4).

By comparison with the active marsh sediments, the reclaimed and former reclaimed marsh sediments at Tollesbury, Northey Island and North Fambridge have much higher values

of shear strength and bulk density. Values for porosity, moisture content, liquid limit, plastic limit and liquidity index are correspondingly lower (Table 5). Comparisons with data for three reclaimed marshes of different age at Slimbridge Warth, Severn estuary (Table 6) indicate that the Essex reclaimed marsh sediments have comparable values for shear strength but slightly lower values for bulk density and dry density. On average, moisture content, porosity, Liquid Limit and Plastic Limit are higher in the Essex reclaimed marshes. Loss on Ignition values are also slightly higher at the Essex sites, but calcium carbonate content is much lower.

At Old Hall Marsh, which is at least several hundred years old, shear strength decreased slightly with depth in the upper 55 cm, mainly reflecting mainly the binding effect of live and recently live roots near the surface (Fig. 9). Below 55 cm the shear strength increased again from c. 20–90 kPa. Bulk density and dry density are both relatively low but increase slightly with depth. Moisture content near the surface is extremely high (>100%) and approaches the

Table 3. *Geotechnical properties of active saltmarsh sediments in Essex*

Property	N. Fambridge	N	Northey Island	N	Old Hall	N
Shear strength (kPa)	13.8 (10.5; 17.5)	5	15.6 (11.6; 20.0)	3	19.5 (14.7; 27.8)	3
Moisture content (%)	93.9 (56.8; 117.5)	5	130.4 (116.1; 147.1)	15	84.2 (64.0; 136.9)	17
Bulk density (gcm^{-3})	1.35 (1.32; 1.40)	5	1.27 (1.22; 1.36)	15	1.45 (1.24; 1.51)	17
Dry density (gcm^{-3})	0.65 (0.65; 0.65)	2	0.55 (0.48; 0.60)	15	0.88 (0.55; 0.92)	17
Porosity (%)	75.7 (75.7; 75.7)	2	79.2 (77.4; 80.7)	15	66.9 (65.2; 79.1)	17
Liquid limit (%)	128.8 (125.3; 135.1)	5	138.8 (128.5; 149.0)	2	117.0 (99.5; 134.5)	2
Plastic limit (%)	42.1 (37.4; 46.9)	5	64.5 (61.0; 68.0)	2	65.0 (61.0; 66.0)	2
Plasticity index	84.4 (80.6; 90.2)	3	73.9 (60.5; 87.2)	2	52.0 (35.5; 68.5)	2
Liquidity index	0.43 (0.12; 0.66)	3	0.97 (0.88; 1.05)	2	0.64 (0.57; 0.71)	2
Carbonate content (%)	0.94 (0; 3.17)	5	Not detected	6	Not detected	6
Loss on ignition (%)	8.27 (7.78; 9.3)	5	9.16 (7.48; 11.1)	5	6.81 (1.69; 12.7)	6

Average (minimum; maximum).

Table 4. *Geotechnical properties of active marsh sediments at Littleton Warth, Severn Estuary*

Property	L.L.M.	N	L.I.M.	N	L.U.M.	N
Shear strength (kPa)	41.5 (23.0; 76.1)	5	95.4 (75.1; 109.4)	4	83.9 (57.9; 106.2)	4
Moisture content (%)	47.6 (35.0; 64.4)	13	34.6 (31.3; 37.7)	9	40.7 (27.1; 78.9)	14
Bulk density (gcm^{-3})	1.65 (1.53; 1.76)	12	1.72 (1.57; 1.93)	10	1.71 (1.25; 2.09)	14
Dry density (gcm^{-3})	1.12 (1.00; 1.28)	12	1.25 (1.15; 1.37)	10	1.26 (0.70; 1.64)	14
Porosity (%)	56.8 (50.6; 61.4)	12	51.9 (48.1; 55.6)	10	51.7 (36.7; 73.1)	14
Liquid limit (%)	67.5 (57.3; 75.4)	7	56.4 (52.4; 59.3)	6	61.8 (50.6; 93.3)	7
Plastic limit (%)	39.4 (36.1; 47.0)	4	32.3 (27.1; 36.8)	4	34.8 (27.1; 53.2)	4
Plasticity index	27.1 (22.6; 34.0)	4	23.0 (19.3; 27.5)	4	28.0 (22.2; 40.1)	4
Liquidity index	0.24 (-0.04; 0.39)	4	0.09 (−0.12; 0.37)	4	0.24 (0.07; 0.52)	4
Carbonate content (%)	12.1 (10.0; 14.3)	8	12.49 (6.19; 15.9)	8	2.98 (0.23; 7.13)	8
Loss on ignition (%)	7.84 (7.12; 8.53)	8	5.99 (2.00; 10.6)	8	3.09 (1.19; 5.16)	8

LLM = Lower Marsh, LIM = Intermediate Marsh, LUM = Upper Marsh; Average (minimum; maximum).

Table 5. *Geotechnical properties of reclaimed marsh sediments at Tollesbury, and former reclaimed marsh sediments at Northey Island and North Fambridge, Essex*

Property	Tollesbury	N	Northey Island	N	N. Fambridge	N
Shear strength (kPa)	116.8 (57.5; 186.3)	5	78.5 (77.5; 79.6)	2	71.3 (65.0; 77.3)	5
Moisture content (%)	34.3 (24.0; 48.3)	23	47.6 (44.8; 52.3)	7	50.3 (41.1; 56.8)	5
Bulk density (gcm^3)	1.65 (1.59; 1.73)*	3	1.62 (1.45; 1.67)	7	1.63 (1.51–1.70)	5
Dry density (gcm^{-3})	1.15 (1.09; 1.24)*	3	1.10 (1.00; 1.17)	7	1.09 (1.05; 1.13)	2
Porosity (%)	56.7 (53.5; 59.3)*	3	59.0 (56.4; 62.6)	7	60.6 (59.2; 60.0)	2
Liquid limit (%)	74.1 (69.5; 77.3)	4	87.5 (86.5; 88.5)	2	88.6 (78.9; 99.1)	4
Plastic limit (%)	35.8 (35.0; 37.0)	4	39.0 (37.5; 40.5)	2	39.7 (26.1; 53.3)	4
Plasticity index	38.4 (33.5; 40.5)	4	50.5 (46.0; 55.0)	2	48.9 (37.9; 60.6)	4
Liquidity index	0.08 (0.007; 0.21)	4	0.19 (0.12; 0.26)	2	0.24 (0.13; 0.29)	4
Carbonate content(%)	Not detected	9	Not detected	3	Not detected	4
Loss on ignition (%)	3.66 (1.94; 8.47)	9	4.49 (4.06; 4.18)	3	5.21 (3.32; 6.49)	3

Average (minimum; maximum); * based on only 3 values from near base of core.

Table 6. *Geotechnical properties of reclaimed marsh sediments at Slimbridge Warth, Severn Estuary*

	Age of Reclamation					
Property	14th Century	N	18th Century	N	19th Century	N
Shear strength (kPa)	65.9 (58.4; 70.0)	4	89.2(71.2; 109.7)	4	99.8(66.4; 122.4)	5
Moisture content (%)	37.2 (31.0; 58.6)	17	38.2 (25.3; 65.2)	17	32.8 (24.9; 59.3)	21
Bulk density (gcm^{-3})	1.73 (1.58; 1.83)	17	1.73 (1.36; 1.89)	17	1.70 (1.17; 1.93)	21
Dry density (gcm^{-3})	1.36 (1.11; 1.43)	16	1.27 (0.62; 1.44)	17	1.30 (0.74; 1.53)	21
Porosity (%)	46.6 (43.9; 56.3)	16	51.7 (45.4; 76.6)	17	49.8 (40.8; 71.5)	21
Liquid limit (%)	56.1 (50.1; 68.5)	4	54.2 (50.1; 65.3)	3	46.9 (42.6; 53.7)	4
Plastic limit (%)	25.4 (18.5; 32.0)	4	29.2 (25.2; 33.5)	3	24.5 (22.5; 28.5)	4
Plasticity index	26.2 (17.6; 36.5)	4	25.0 (21.1; 31.8)	3	22.4 (20.0; 25.2)	4
Liquidity index	0.40 (0.21; 0.64)	4	0.28 (0.05; 0.51)	3	0.27 (0.15; 0.45)	4
Carbonate content (%)	4.57 (0.06; 10.7)	7	7.77 (0.57; 12.6)	7	9.80 (2.98; 12.9)	9
Loss on ignition (%)	2.31 (0.9; 12.47)	7	3.86 (1.12; 1.12)	7	3.46 (1.64; 9.97)	9

Average (minimum; maximum).

liquid limit, decreasing to *c.* 60% at 80 cm depth. A discontinuity is present at 80 cm depth; below this level the sediment is coarser grained, has a higher density, lower porosity, lower moisture content and higher shear strength. It is interpreted to represent either an older, possibly reclaimed marsh surface (although no traces of former seabanks are visible on aerial photographs), or the weathered surface of the underlying London Clay.

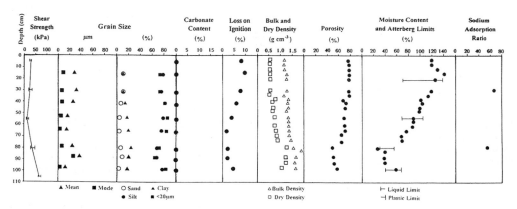

Fig. 9. Sedimentological and geotechnical characteristics of the profile from Old Hall active marsh, Tollesbury.

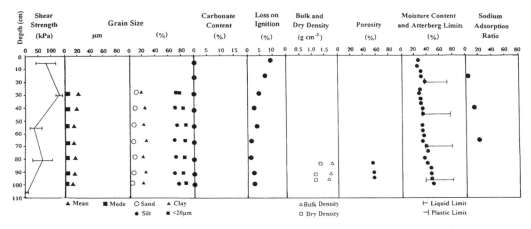

Fig. 10. Sedimentological and geotechnical charcteristics of the profile from the reclaimed marsh at Tollesbury (now the MAFF experimental managed retreat site).

SEM analysis of the pore structure of the mud in the upper 80 cm showed the fabric to be very open with large pore spaces, depicting a high degree of edge-to-edge contact, consistent with the high porosity and high moisture content.

By contrast, the reclaimed marsh at Tollesbury (now within the MAFF set-back site) was well consolidated and SEM investigation found evidence of destructuring of the fabric and dispersion of clay particles. Vane shear strength near the surface was relatively high (70–140 kPa), decreasing with depth to <50 kPa (Fig. 10). Moisture content was low throughout, ranging from 25% at the surface to c. 40% at 100 cm depth. No systematic variation in grain size with depth is evident, reflecting a continuous sequence of former marsh sediments to the base of the core. The

observed differences compared with the active Tollesbury marsh core clearly reflect the effects of dewatering and consolidation.

The sediments in the naturally regenerated marsh at Northey Island, which have accumulated since 1897, are characterized by very low vane shear strength (<20 kPa), low bulk and dry density, high porosity and very high moisture content, again approaching the liquid limit (Fig. 11). There is a marked discontinuity at c. 70 cm depth which corresponds to the pre-breach reclaimed marsh surface. Below this level the shear strength is much higher (c. 90 kPa), the bulk and dry densities higher, the porosity and moisture content lower. Grain size, carbonate content and sodium adsorption ratio vary little with depth. The differences between the

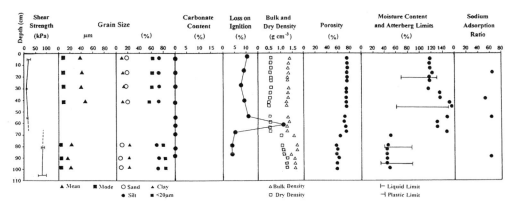

Fig. 11. Sedimentological and geotechnical characteristics of the profile from the naturally regenerated marsh on Northey Island.

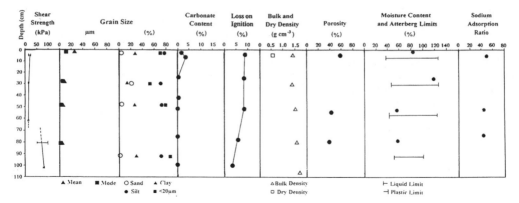

Fig. 12. Sedimentological and geotechnical characteristics of the profile from the naturally regenerated marsh (area with dendritic creek system) at North Fambridge.

sediments in the upper 70 cm and those beneath are attributable mainly to the effects of dewatering and consolidation.

At North Fambridge, the uppermost 70 cm of sediments in the core taken from the naturally regenerated marsh with dendritic creek system displayed low vane shear strength (<20 kPa). Below a clear colour and textural discontinuity at 70 cm depth, which represents the pre-breach surface, the shear strength rises to 80–100 kPa (Fig. 12). The bulk density of the upper 70 cm of sediments is low, the porosity moderate to high (40–60%) and the moisture content moderate to high, especially in the upper 40 cm where it approaches the liquid limit.

The North Fambridge core taken from the area with a reticulate creek system, closer to the landward edge of the marsh, showed a marked discontinuity at c. 45 cm depth. Above this level, vane shear strength, bulk density and dry den-

sity are again low, while moisture content is high (>100%), approaching or in excess of the liquid limit (Fig. 13). Below 45 cm the fomer reclaimed marsh sediments have a shear strength of 60–80 kPa and the moisture content is below 60%. As at other sites, there is little variation in grain size, carbonate content or sodium adsorption ratio with depth, indicating that the observed variations in shear strength primarily reflect the effects of de-watering and consolidation.

Discussion

Active marshes

The shear strength of muddy marshes is determined primarily by factors which affect the rate of consolidation and dewatering of the sediment. Root binding aids stabilization of the marsh surface but in muddy marshes its influence on

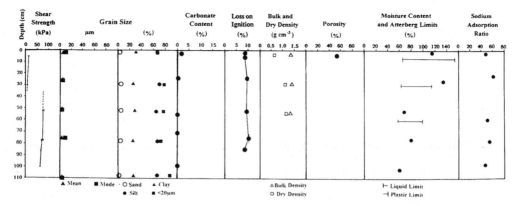

Fig. 13. Sedimentological and geotechnical characteristics of the profile from the naturally regenerated marsh (area with reticulate creek system) at North Fambridge.

shear strength and marsh erosion is less significant than in sandy marshes. Comparing data from several different muddy marshes, it is clear that the Essex marsh sediments have much higher moisture contents, liquid limits, lower bulk densities and lower undrained shear strengths than marshes in many other parts of Britain, including the Severn estuary (compare Tables 3 & 4). Other muddy marsh sites, such as Warham marshes in North Norfolk, are intermediate between Essex and the Severn estuary in this respect (data in Crooks 1996).

These geotechnical differences clearly influence the erodibility of the sediments and, through interactions with the hydrodynamic forces, the morphology of the saltmarshes. The relatively high density and shear strength of the surface active marsh sediments in the Severn estuary offers comparatively high resistance to tidal flows and wave action compared with the active marsh sediments in Essex.

Although the Severn estuary marshes are slightly coarser grained than those in Essex (modal size typically in the range 12–20 microns, Table 1), this factor cannot account for the differences in shear strength. Differences in clay mineral composition may play a role; average content of smectite, which is well-known for its water retentive and swelling properties, is, on average, higher in the Essex marshes than in the Severn estuary marshes (Table 2). This reflects the importance of the smectite-rich London Clay as a source of fine sediment in SE England. However, a further factor appears to play a more important role.

Previous work on other sediments and soils has shown that geotechnical properties and erosion resistance are strongly dependent on the cohesion/dispersion behaviour of the sediment (Renasamy 1983; Dexter & Chan 1991; Bell & Maud 1994; Anson & Hawkins 1998). Dispersive soils present a widespread problem because their colloidal clay particles enter suspension even at very low flow velocities. Dispersion occurs when the repulsive forces between clay particles exceed the attractive forces, thus causing deflocculation and reducing resistance to erosion. Dispersive soils in terrestrial environments are highly prone to gullying, piping and sheet erosion (Bell & Maud 1994).

The tendency for dispersion is dependent on the nature of the interaction between the clay particles and the surrounding pore fluid. Clay particles adsorb cations onto their surfaces in order to satisfy electrical charges which result from broken ionic bonds and missing interlayer cations. The adsorbed cations, in turn, attract a film of water molecules which surrounds the clay particles. The thickness of the water film is dependent on the number and nature of the adsorbed cations, and on the osmotic potential between the fluid at the clay platelet surface and the bathing pore fluid. If the concentration of cations in the bathing solution is lower than that of the water film, water molecules will migrate from the former to the latter, causing it to become thicker. If the film of bound water is thick enough, the inter-particle attractive bonds become so weak that the clay platelets are effectively dispersed.

Smectite clays generally have the highest cation exchange capacity (CEC), followed by mixed layer clays, illite and kaolinite. Calcium, being a divalent cation, has a high ionic charge and approximately half as many calcium ions as monvalent sodium ions are required to satisfy the cation exchange capacity of the clay. Since the attraction of water molecules to sodium is very similar to that of divalent calcium ions, a greater quantity of water molecules migrate into the film when sodium dominates the exchange sites. The high ionic charge of calcium ions is sufficient to prevent the water film expanding beyond a thickness of 0.9 nm, and so a calcium-saturated clay will remain flocculated even when placed in almost pure water. The weaker charge on sodium is insufficient to prevent the water film expanding to a much larger extent unless the concentration of dissolved salts in the bathing fluid is sufficiently high to prevent an osmotic gradient developing. Owing to the high salinity of seawater, sodium-saturated clays remain flocculated in marine environments, but they may become dispersed if the pore fluid salinity is subsequently reduced (e.g. following reclamation and lowering of a saline groundwater table). In saline waters the relatively thick water film surrounding clay particles maintains a more open fabric than is the case with calcium saturated clays, but the presence of even a very modest amount of divalent cations is often sufficient to cause flocculation by reducing the dimensions of the water films.

The presence of exchangeable sodium, which is the main factor influencing the degree of dispersive behaviour, can be expressed in terms of the exchangeable sodium percentage (ESP):

$$\text{ESP} = (\text{exchangeable sodium}/ \\ \text{cation exchange/capacity})$$

$$\times 100 \text{ (in meq/100 g of dry sediment).}$$

Terrestrial soils with ESP values >15% show a tendency to be highly dispersive. Soils with low CEC values (<15 meq/100 g of clay) have been found to be completely non-dispersive at ESP values <6%. Soils with high CEC values but with a plasticity index (PI) >35% have also been found to swell to such an extent that dispersion is not significant (Bell & Maud 1994).

The sodium adsorption ration (SAR) can be be used to quantify the role of sodium where free salts are present in the porewater. The SAR is defined by:

$$SAR = \frac{[Na]}{([Ca] = [Mg])^{0.5}}$$

Although there is variation with pH and clay mineral type, terrestrial soils with SAR values >2 are likely to be dispersive (Bell & Maud 1994).

In saline systems, such as active saltmarshes, the pore waters are normally dominated by sodium and have a high ionic concentration. Divalent cations are present in low concentrations (relative to sodium) within sea-water and so sodium initially dominates the exchange sites of the clay particles accreting on saltmarsh surfaces. However, following sedimentation, calcium concentrations are determined primarily by the availability and solubility of detrital calcium present in the sediment. Potential sources include detrital geological material (e.g. chalk or limestone), and recent biogenic material (forams, shell debris etc.) which begins to dissolve following deposition.

In the Severn estuary, the saltmarshes contain 5–15% calcium carbonate derived mainly from the bedrocks around the estuary and in the Severn catchment. In Essex, many of the saltmarshes are underlain and surrounded by Eocene London Clay which typically is low in calcium carbonate (<1%). Mineralogical and geochemical evidence clearly indicates that a high proportion of the fine sediment found in the saltmarshes of SE England is derived from the London Clay. At the present time, the main sources of calcium carbonate are biogenic; shell material reworked from intertidal flats is an important source but is largely restricted to more exposed, open coast areas with significant wave action, such as the Dengie Peninsula, Mersea Island and Foulness.

Sodium adsorption ratios for the active marshes at Old Hall and Northey Island ranged from 53–67, compared with values of less than 40 for the younger active marsh formations at Littleton Warth in the Severn estuary (Tables 7 & 8). Values for the reclaimed marsh at Tollesbury ranged from 4–21, compared with values of 1–11 for reclaimed marshes at Slimbridge Warth, Severn estuary. This is

Table 7. *Sodium adsorption ratio (SAR) and electrical conductivity EC) of active (A) and reclaimed (R) marsh sediments in Essex*

Marsh	SAR	EC (dS m^{-1})	N
A – Old Hall	53.4–66.9	22.3–45.60	2
A – Northey Island	53.9–64.4	23.9–50.50	4
R – Tollesbury	4.4–20.6	1.01–6.49	3

Table 8. *Sodium adsorption ratio (SAR) and electrical conductivity (EC) of active (A) and reclaimed (R) marsh sediments in the Severn estuary*

Marsh	SAR	EC (dS m^{-1})	N
A – Northwick Fmn.	36.0–39.40	15.5–15.9	3
A – Rumney Fmn.	35.0–36.00	9.8–17.8	4
A – Wentlooge Fmn.	1.99–7.38	0.67–1.48	4
R – 14th century	0.93–4.19	0.42–0.62	3
R – 18th century	3.55–11.35	0.66–0.96	3
R – 19th century	1.99–7.38	0.67–1.48	4

consistent with the hypothesis that the higher carbonate content of the Severn estuary marshes is linked to lower sodium adsorption ratios in both active and reclaimed marshes.

The majority of sheltered estuarine marshes in Essex are carbonate-deficient, possess extremely high moisture contents, and have low bulk densities and low undrained shear strengths (Fig. 8). Carbonate-bearing (up to 4%) marsh sediments are generally restricted to more open coast sites in Essex and Kent, as on the Dengie Peninsula. Such sites typically are characterized by signficantly lower moisture contents, higher bulk densities and higher shear strengths than the sheltered estuarine marshes. Even though wave activity appears to have been the main driving force behind the recent regional erosion in SE England (Pye 2000), the Dengie Peninsula marshes have experienced the lowest proportion of marsh loss of all areas in SE England since 1973 (Burd 1992; Pye & French 1993. This may be related, at least in part, to the higher shear strength of the sediments.

Reclaimed marshes

It is well known that terrestrial sodic soils are highly susceptible to dispersion which causes a loss of soil structure and reduction in hydraulic conductivity. In north Kent and Essex, dispersion has been shown to occur following drainage of reclaimed carbonate-deficient saltmarsh soils, but not on drained carbonate-bearing soils or undrained soils (Hazelden *et al.* 1986). Carbonate-bearing drained saltmarshes soils in the Severn estuary region do not appear to be prone to dispersion in the same way.

The implications of drainage induced dispersion for subsequent saltmarsh regeneration are twofold. Firstly, the dewatering and consolidation of high moisture content saltmarsh sediments, such as those in Essex, results in a marked drop in the elevation of the surface. While this occurs to some degree in all marshes, the process is more marked in sodium-dominated marshes with a high moisture content and in which the soil fabric totally collapses following de-sodification. This, coupled with continuing sea-level rise, may mean that a former reclaimed surface at the time of marsh re-inundation is too low in the tidal frame for halophyte colonization. Secondly, once soil peds have deflocculated the soil structure is permanently altered and reintroduction of a saline water table will not re-establish a more open fabric. Following renewed tidal flooding, the former-reclaimed surface is likely to act as an impermeable aquaclude, maintaining a high water table in the overlying regenerated marsh. Such a situation was found within the profile of the regenerated marsh at Northey Island, where highest moisture contents occurred immediately above the former reclaimed surface (Crooks 1996). At the MAFF experimental managed retreat site at Tollesbury, poor drainage of the site has led to surface waterlogging which favours algal growth over the establishment of higher plants, and large areas of higher parts of the site remain essentially unvegetated some five years after the breach.

A further consequence of the high water table, and the high rates of sedimentation on a surface low in the intertidal frame, is that regenerated marshes possess lower undrained shear strengths than active marshes (Table 3) and as such will offer lower resistance to erosion. On managed retreat or natural set back sites the breached sea-embankment may protect the regenerating marsh from externally generated waves, but it does not protect the sediments from erosion by tidal currents.

Conclusions

The morphology of intertidal sediments, including saltmarshes, reflects interactions between hydrodynamic forces and the geotechnical properties of the sediments which act to resist change. Geotechnical properties are, to a large extent, sedimentologically controlled.

Estuarine marshes in SE England are less well consolidated and have lower undrained shear strength than those of comparable age in many other parts of England and Wales, including the Severn estuary. This low shear strength, particularly in near-surface sediments, is reflected in high rates of marsh retreat, internal dissection and high density creek systems. These geotechnical characteristics are apparently related to source sediment control, notably a high smectite content in the clay fraction and sodium-domination of ion exchange sites on the surfaces of clays due to calcium-deficiency in the sediments and marsh pore waters.

Reclamation and drainage of carbonate-depleted fine-grained saltmarsh deposits in this region, without careful land management, results in dispersion of the clays and the formation of a low permeability, over-consolidated surface. Following marsh regeneration, the former reclaimed surface acts as an aquaclude which helps maintain a high water table in the overlying sediment column, so hindering halophyte colonization and reducing the shear strength of the accumulating sediment. De-watering and consolidation of the newly accumulating mud is also hampered by the sodium-dominated, open nature of the clay fabric. Low rates of consolidation and shear strength gain increase the likelihood of erosion by tidal currents and even quite small waves, producing a dissected marsh topography with a high ratio of bare mud to vegetated surface. While this may not necessarily be serious from an ecological point of view, the flood defence value of the newly recreated marshes is significantly reduced.

The possibilities of using chemical treatments to modify the geotechnical properties and consolidation behaviour of muds within managed realignment areas warrant further investigation. Such techniques have previously been used to stabilize low strength marine clays in other contexts (e.g. Rajasekaran *et al.* 1997).

This work was supported by NERC (Research Studentship to S. Crooks) and the Leverhulme Trust (Grant and Senior Research Fellowship to K. Pye). We thank D. Thornley and D. Rowell for technical assistance and Cambridge University Committee for Air Photography for permission to reproduce air photographs of selected marsh localities.

References

Anson, R. W. W. & Hawkins, A. B. 1998. The effect of calcium ions in pore water on the residual shear strength of kaolinite and sodium montmorillonite. *Geotechnique*, **48**, 787–800.

Bell, F. G. & Maud, R. R. 1994. Dispersive soils: a review from a South African perspective. *Quarterly Journal of Engineering Geology*, **27**, 195–210.

BRITISH STANDARDS INSTITUTION 1990. BS1377. *Methods of Testing Soils for Civil Engineering Purposes*. Part 1. British Standards Institution, Milton Keynes.

BURD, F. 1992. *Erosion and vegetation change on the saltmarshes of Essex and North Kent between 1973 and 1988*. Research & Survey in Nature Conservation 42, Nature Conservancy Council, Peterborough.

CARPENTER, K. E. & PYE, K. 1997. *Saltmarsh Change in England and Wales – Its History and Causes*. R & D. Report W12, The Environment Agency, Bristol.

CROOKS, S. 1996. *Sedimentological Controls on the Geotechnical Properties of Intertidal Saltmarsh and Mudflat Sediments*. PhD Thesis, University of Reading.

DEXTER, A. R. & CHAN, K. Y. 1991. Soil mechanical properties as influenced by exchangeable cations. *Journal of Soil Science*, **42**, 219–226.

HAZELDEN, J., LOVELEAND, P. J. & STURDY, R. G. 1986. *Saline soils in North Kent*. Soil Survey of England and Wales, Special Survey No. 14, Harpenden.

PYE, K. 2000. Saltmarsh erosion in southeast England: mechanisms, causes and implications. *In*: SHERWOOD, B. R., GARDINER, B. G. & HARRIS, T. (eds) *British Saltmarshes*. Westbury Publishing, Yorkshire (in press).

—— & FRENCH, P. W. 1992. *Targets for Coastal habitat Recreation*. English Nature Science Series 17, English Nature, Peterborough.

—— & —— 1993. *Erosion and Accretion Processes on British Saltmarshes*. 5 Volumes. CERC Ltd., Cambridge.

RAJASEKARAN, G., MURALI, K. & SRINIVASARAGHAVAN, R. 1997. Fabric and mineralogical studies on lime treated marine clays. *Ocean Engineering*, **24**, 227–234.

RENASAMY, P. 1983. Clay dispersion in relation to chnages in electrolyte composition of dialysed red-brown earths. *Journal of Soil Science*, **34**, 723–732.

STEEL, T. & PYE, K. 1997. *The development of saltmarsh tidal creek networks; evidence from the UK*. Proceedings of the Canadian Coastal Conference, University of Guelph, 22–25 May 1997, 267–280.

Vertical accretion versus elevational adjustment in UK saltmarshes: an evaluation of alternative methodologies

DONALD R. CAHOON[1], JONATHAN R. FRENCH[2], THOMAS SPENCER[3], DENISE REED[4] & IRIS MÖLLER[3]

[1] *U.S. Geological Survey, National Wetlands Research Center, 700 Cajundome Blvd., Lafayette, Louisiana 70506 USA (e-mail: don_cahoon@usgs.gov)*

[2] *Coastal & Estuarine Research Unit, Department of Geography, University College London, Chandler House, 2 Wakefield Street, London WC1N 1PF, UK (e-mail:jfrench@geog.ucl.ac.uk)*

[3] *Cambridge Coastal Research Unit, Department of Geography, University of Cambridge, Downing Place, Cambridge CB2 3EN UK (e-mail: ts111@hermes.cam.ac.uk)*

[4] *Department of Geology and Geophysics, University of New Orleans, New Orleans, LA 70148, USA (e-mail: djreed@uno.edu)*

Abstract: Simultaneous measurements of vertical accretion from marker horizons and marsh-elevation change from sedimentation-erosion tables (SET) were made in selected marshes along the East Anglian coast of the UK in order to address the following objectives:

(1) to ascertain the validity of treating accretion measurements obtained within tidally dominated, minerogenic saltmarshes as equivalent to surface elevation changes;
(2) to explore the implications, in terms of physical and biological processes, of discrepancies between separately measured vertical accretion and elevation change within contrasting marsh types.

Data were collected from several marsh environments at Scolt Head Island and Stiffkey on the North Norfolk coast and at an experimental managed realignment project near Tollesbury, Essex. Scolt Head Island was selected for its long-term datasets of marsh accretion, Stiffkey for its contrasting open coast-back barrier settings, and Tollesbury for its experimental management, in order to illustrate the potential application of the SET method and evaluate the relationship between vertical accretion and elevation change in a variety of marsh settings.

The relationship between vertical accretion and elevation change varied widely among marsh settings of different age and height (within the tidal frame) at Scolt Head Island and Stiffkey. Rates of vertical accretion and elevation change were similar in the older and mid-height settings on Scolt Head Island, indicating control of elevation change by surface accretionary processes (e.g. sediment deposition). However, subsurface processes controlled elevation at three of the marsh sites. Spartina Marsh, the youngest and lowest of the back barrier settings at Scolt Head Island, exhibited continuous shallow subsidence (vertical accretion greater than elevation change) over a 4-year period, implying that compaction controls elevation change. In the upper part of Hut Marsh and the interior of the Stiffkey marshes, elevation change exceeded vertical accretion suggesting that subsurface processes (e.g. organic accumulation) controlled elevation in these settings. Surface accretionary processes control elevation change in both the highly dynamic, outer marsh at Stiffkey and the low, restored marsh at Tollesbury. Despite the occurrence of shallow subsidence, all sites gained elevation at an annual rate comparable to that of sea-level rise. In summary, the SET provides the means to critically evaluate the influence of vertical accretion measures on elevation and represents an improved method by which to evaluate the vulnerability of a marsh to sea-level rise.

From: PYE, K. & ALLEN, J. R. L. (eds). *Coastal and Estuarine Environments: sedimentology, geomorphology and geoarchaeology*. Geological Society, London, Special Publications, **175**, 223–238. 0305-8719/00/$15.00 © The Geological Society of London 2000.

UK saltmarshes have long been valued as wildlife habitats and as an important component of coastal and estuarine ecosystems. The last decade has witnessed further recognition of their engineering significance as a natural component of sea defences, especially in estuaries bounded by extensive areas of reclaimed land at risk of tidal flooding (Allen & Pye 1992; National Rivers Authority 1995; Halcrow & Partners 1996). At the same time, historically high rates of saltmarsh erosion have caused more focused attention on the fate of remaining saltmarsh resources under the influence of anthropogenically enhanced relative sea-level rise (Boorman *et al.* 1989; French 1994). Management of saltmarsh for flood defence, and for conservation, depends, *inter alia*, on accurate quantification of the mass balance of saltmarshes as the intertidal zone undergoes adjustment to changes in tidal levels, inundation regime and wave energy distribution (see for example, Pethick 1998). Of equal importance for the viability of plant and invertebrate communities (Boorman *et al.* 1989), and for the attenuation of wave and tidal energy (Möller *et al.* 1996, 1999) is the vertical stability of marsh *elevations* in relation to upward movement of the tidal frame. Improved understanding of both sedimentary and elevational adjustments has recently assumed a higher priority, as a result of the renewed emphasis placed upon the managed realignment of sea defences and on the restoration of saltmarsh and tidal flat as part of a fundamental reappraisal of the UK's coastal and estuarine flood defence infrastructure (Agriculture Select Committee 1998).

For much of the UK, aerial photographic cover is of sufficient quality to permit detailed inventories of changing saltmarsh horizontal extent from the 1940s to the 1960s (see for example, Burd 1992; Pye & French 1993). These surveys need to be combined with information on the rate and distribution of vertical adjustment in order to determine the fate of material eroded from the saltmarsh edge and to assess the stability of surface elevations in relation to the upward migration of the tidal frame. Technological advances in airborne remote sensing, particularly the development of scanning LiDAR altimetry (Environment Agency 1997), have the potential to facilitate volumetric surveys which, in time, can be expected to revolutionize the geomorphological monitoring of the intertidal zone. However, vertical accuracies attainable with current remote sensing technologies are, at best, an order of magnitude below those required for resolution of saltmarsh elevational adjustment at anything shorter than

a decadal timescale. This limitation implies a continued reliance on inferences from existing sedimentation rate studies and from additional field monitoring at locations chosen to represent various combinations of sea-level rise, geomorphological setting and ecosystem structure.

An extensive research literature addresses the geomorphological development of saltmarshes in terms of the controls on their establishment and the dynamics of sedimentation. In both Europe and North America, much has been made of the role of sea-level rise as a trigger for marsh initiation (Pethick 1980; Gehrels & Leatherman 1989) and as a determinant of subsequent elevational adjustment within the tidal frame (Streif 1989; Allen 1990*a, b*; French 1991, 1993). Recent studies have placed considerable emphasis on the comparison of rates of sedimentation (i.e. vertical accretion) with local and regional trends in mean sea-level. Within the microtidal environments of the southeastern United States, an imbalance between vertical accretion and high rates of subsidence-driven relative sea-level rise has been highlighted as a cause of widespread deterioration of marsh interior areas (DeLaune *et al.* 1983; Templet & Meyer-Arendt 1988). Similar comparisons within tidally dominated saltmarshes reveal no evidence for such 'accretionary deficits' (Stevenson *et al.* 1986; French 1994), but indicate, instead, a tendency for sedimentation to keep pace with modest rates of sea-level rise, even where erosional adjustments are reducing the areal extent of saltmarsh (see for example, Reed 1988).

Results from short-term (<10 years) sedimentation monitoring must be considered in the light of conceptual models of marsh development under specific combinations of tidal range, biological productivity and sediment supply. In their geographical inventory of saltmarshes along the east coast of the United States, Stevenson *et al.* (1986) observed a strong linear relation between marsh accretionary balance (defined as the difference between the rates of vertical accretion and relative sea-level rise) and mean tidal range. This relationship is explained by reference to the importance of tidal energy in 'subsidizing' biological productivity (Odum 1980) and facilitating the introduction of inorganic sediment. Additional variability arises from differences in marsh sedimentary fabric, notably between *organogenic* marshes formed by the accumulation of (primarily belowground) plant production and *minerogenic* marshes formed chiefly through the introduction of externally-derived inorganic sediments (Allen 1990*a, b*). As envisaged by Stevenson *et al.*

(1986), organogenic marshes depend for their stability on the rate of carbon burial and thus are more susceptible to more rapid sea-level rise, especially when this feeds back (through an increase in hydroperiod) into reduced productivity (Reed & Cahoon 1992). French (1994) has drawn attention to the nature of the linkage between sedimentation and sea-level rise in the predominantly minerogenic marshes of NW Europe, in which physical processes are dominated by strong tidal exchanges of water and materials. Vertical adjustment in these systems is mediated by a strong 'form-process' feedback between elevation (via its control on the frequency of inundation) and the rate of inorganic sedimentation (Pethick 1981). Tidally dominated marshes thus tend towards a sedimentary balance with background sea-level rise: in the case of eastern England, this 'equilibrium time' is probably of the order of hundreds of years for historical rates of sea-level rise in the region of $1–2\,mm\,a^{-1}$ (French 1993; see also Allen 1990b). Importantly, this model predicts that (in the absence of external sediment supply limitation) well-established marshes should exhibit rates of elevational change that are comparable to local relative sea-level rise. Large accretionary surpluses should, therefore, be rare.

Such interpretations are fundamentally dependent upon the assumption that the rate of vertical accretion caused by sedimentation is closely comparable to surface elevation change. In fact, as Kaye & Barghoorn (1964) observed more than three decades ago, marsh sedimentary sequences undergo post-depositional autocompaction which negates the elevational effect of a proportion of surface sedimentation. Few studies have attempted to quantify the significance of this set of processes. Cahoon et al. (1995) introduced the term 'shallow subsidence' to describe the component of surface settlement affecting the upper few metres of the sedimentary sequence, as distinct from 'deep subsidence' caused by geological processes operating at a regional scale. Under this conceptualization, the thickness of new sediment (both inorganic and organic) laid down in a time increment must equal the total subsidence (i.e. shallow plus deep) in order for the marsh surface to remain stable at the same level. Sedimentation and elevation change are not, therefore, the same thing: the magnitude of the discrepancy will depend upon the extent of post-depositional autocompaction as well as other processes, such as the rate and fate of above- and below-ground plant production (Reed & Cahoon 1993). In a comparative study of salt marshes in Louisiana,

Florida & North Carolina, Cahoon et al., (1995) showed that sedimentation determined from the burial of artificial feldspar marker horizons provides a poor approximation to actual elevation change as recorded by a 'sedimentation-erosion table' (SET, see below).

Further consideration must be given to these issues before meaningful assessments can be made of the vulnerability of UK saltmarshes to the effects of accelerated sea-level rise. Of particular importance is the implication from North American studies (Reed & Cahoon 1993; Cahoon et al. 1995) that vertical accretion (as determined by measurement of sedimentation thickness above a marker horizon) is a poor surrogate for the elevational adjustments which are of great physical and ecological significance. Within a UK context, the purpose of the present paper is twofold:

(1) to ascertain the validity of treating accretion measurements obtained within tidally dominated, minerogenic saltmarshes as equivalent to surface elevation changes.

(2) to explore the implications, in terms of physical and biological processes, of discrepancies between separately measured vertical accretion and elevation change within contrasting marsh types.

Research design and environmental setting

Three contrasting locations in eastern England were selected in 1994 and 1995 as a basis for a comparison of vertical accretion and elevation change measurement (Figs. 1a, b & 2a). These comprise a range of marsh environments as follows:

(i) Scolt Head Island, Norfolk – back barrier marshes of different age, elevation and vegetation cover (Fig. 1c)

(ii) Stiffkey, Norfolk – an eroding outer marsh exposed to wave action, and an inner marsh protected by a low shingle barrier (Fig. 1d)

(iii) Tollesbury, Essex – an experimental, managed, realignment trial on the Blackwater estuary, including eroding estuarine marsh and an area of formerly reclaimed land subjected to tidal action since 1995 (Fig. 2b).

East Anglian saltmarshes cover 13 000 ha, around 30% of the total UK resource (National Rivers Authority 1995). Whilst marsh areas appear to have been stable in the period from

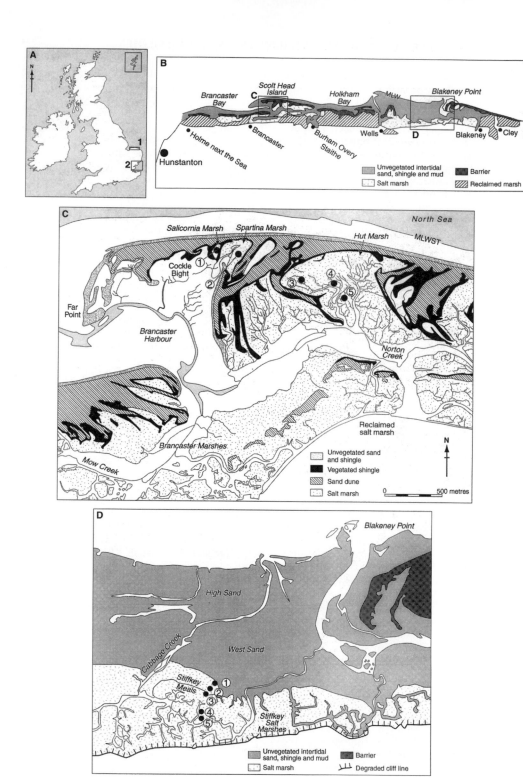

Fig. 1. (**A**) Site map of southeastern England showing the location of Scolt Head Island, Stiffkey and Tollesbury marshes in East Anglia. (**B**) Site map showing the North Norfolk coast, including Scolt Head Island and Stiffkey. (**C**) Site map showing the marsh environments at Scolt Head Island and the location of sampling plots. (**D**) Site map showing the marsh environments at Stiffkey and the location of sampling plots.

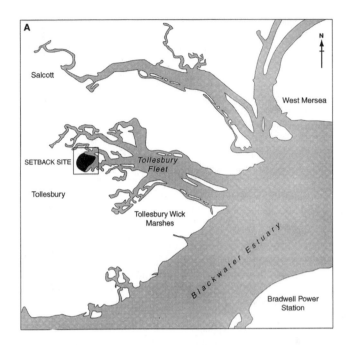

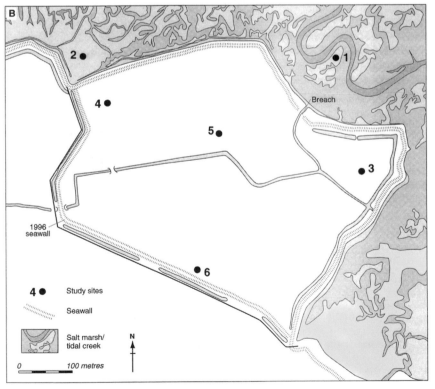

Fig. 2. Site map showing (**A**) the location of the managed realignment project near Tollesbury and (**B**) the location of sampling plots.

1900 to 1960, erosion accelerated locally in the 1960s (see for example, Harmsworth & Long 1986) and more widely in the 1970s (Burd 1992; Carpenter & Pye 1996). The predominant source of sediments appears to be the erosion of cliffs containing 40–60% fine material: fluvial inputs are considered insignificant (McCave 1987). Regional subsidence in East Anglia is estimated at $1–2\,mm\,a^{-1}$ (Shennan 1989); over the last century or so this subsidence has been supplemented by additional eustatic sea-level rise estimated at $0.9\,mm\,a^{-1}$ (Pirazzoli 1989). Tide gauges within the region indicate relative sea-level trends that are broadly consistent with this picture. Since 1953, mean annual levels have increased at $1.6\,mm\,a^{-1}$ at Lowestoft and $2.1\,mm\,a^{-1}$ at Sheerness (UK Permanent Service for Mean Sea-level data).

Study Sites

North Norfolk. The 40 km of coastline between Holme-next-the-Sea in the west and Salthouse in the east (Fig. 1b) is characterized by extensive intertidal sands and muds, shingle spits and barrier islands developed seaward of a pre-Glacial coastline. Salt marshes have developed both in the lee of the shingle barriers and on the open coast. Development of back-barrier salt marsh has been strongly related to historical barrier dynamics: periodic marsh development has been associated with the episodic westward extension of the main barrier, with individual marshes being enclosed by landward-curving shingle 'laterals' which indicate periods of barrier stasis and consolidation. On open coasts, periods of marsh development and degradation appear linked to the dynamics of seaward intertidal sand bars.

The saltmarshes at both Scolt Head Island and Stiffkey (Fig. 1c, d) have been subject to intensive investigations of the physical processes associated with tidal exchange, sedimentation and wave action (French & Stoddart 1992, French & Spencer 1993, Möller *et al.* 1996). Both sites are characterized by a variety of marsh surfaces of different ages, morphologies and vegetation communities.

At Scolt Head Island (Fig. 1c), a sequence of marshes increases in age and elevation from west to eastward in the lee of the protective barrier. Hut Marsh, around 100 years in age, has an area of approximately $0.54\,km^2$ and is connected to the tidal inlet by two major channel networks. The highest surfaces (0.8 m below HAT) support a diverse 'General Salt Marsh' plant community (after Chapman 1960). Channel margins are dominated by dense growths of *Atriplex portulacoides*, which, in places, have coalesced to cover extensive interior areas. *Salicornia* spp. and *Suaeda maritima* are the main pioneer species. Marsh sediments here, and elsewhere in Norfolk, are predominantly inorganic: organic contents are typically less than 15% by weight (French & Spencer 1993). Three SET plots were established in 1994: on a creek margin, in mid-marsh interior, and in high marsh interior. Sand marker horizons were established adjacent to the elevation plots 1 year later in 1995.

Salicornia Marsh is a much smaller unit $(0.02\,km^2)$ formed during the last 50 years within two enclosing shingle ridges on the margin of the large tidal flat (Cockle Bight) at the western end of the island. The marsh is drained by a single channel system. Although lower than Hut Marsh (the mean elevation is inundated by less than 50% of tides compared to around 30% for Hut Marsh), Salicornia Marsh supports a similar range of plant communities. A single SET plot was established in the centre of the marsh in 1994 and a sand marker established 1 year later.

Spartina Marsh is a slightly younger and larger unit, developed since the 1960s also within the confines of shingle ridges on the northern margin of Cockle Bight. It is slightly lower than Salicornia Marsh and is inundated by more than 60% of tides. The marsh is distinctive in that it has been subject to vigorous colonization by *Spartina anglica* which, with *Aster tripolium*, dominates all but a narrow high marsh community similar to that found elsewhere. Although highly inorganic, the sediments accumulate at a much lower density than is the case for the other marshes at Scolt. A single SET plot and marker horizon were established in the centre of the marsh in 1994.

At Stiffkey (Fig. 1d), a stretch of mainland saltmarshes has developed landward of wide intertidal flats characterized by migratory bars and tidal channels. The saltmarshes are up to 1 km wide and make up a lower outer marsh (surfaces 1.0–1.3 m below HAT), separated by a low shingle ridge from a more extensive inner marsh (surfaces around 0.8 m below HAT). The low outer marsh is believed to have formed since the 1950s–1960s, but it has been eroding since the late 1970s (Möller *et al.* 1996); its current seaward margin is degraded into a hummocky 'mudmound' topography, drained by poorly defined anastamosing channels. The inorganic marsh muds incorporate discontinuous horizons of sand, apparently derived from the fronting tidal flats. Dominant plant species are *Salicornia* spp., *Spartina* spp., and *Aster tripolium*; occasional clumps of *Atriplex portulacoides* occur on the high surfaces. The inner marsh is higher and characterized by diverse plant communities similar to those found at Scolt Head Island. In 1995, three SET plots were established across the outer marsh in a transect from the seaward edge to the marsh adjacent to the ridge. This transect was laid out parallel to a transect of accretion plots uniformly spaced from the seaward edge to the base of the ridge which was established by Möller (1997) the previous year. The accretionary environment of the back barrier marsh at Stiffkey was characterized in the vicinity of a second order creek draining the high marsh. Möller (1997) established accretion plots at the head and mid portions of the creek (locations were approximately 125 m apart), both adjacent to the creek margin and in the interior marsh a few metres from the creek. Two SET plots (sites 4 and 5 in Fig. 1d), one on the creek margin and one in the interior marsh, were established between Möller's sampling locations.

Blackwater estuary, Essex: The macrotidal Blackwater estuary extends for 20 km from the town of Maldon, Essex, to the island of west Mersea (northern shore) and St Peter's Point, Dengie Peninsula (southern shore). Saltmarshes account for some 13% of the total tidal area, a tiny fraction of their extent before long-continued land claim (Burd 1992). The remaining saltmarsh area underwent erosion from 1870 to 1935, followed by a period of stability until the 1970s when renewed and rapid areal loss occurred (Carpenter & Pye 1996). Pioneer marsh in the Blackwater estuary is colonized by *Spartina anglica*, *Aster tripolium* and *Salicornia* spp.; low marsh above it is dominated by the grass *Puccinellia maritima* and, at higher levels, *Atriplex portulacoides*, *Puccinellia maritima*, *Aster tripolium*, *Limonium vulgare* and *Elymus* spp. (Burd 1992).

An experimental 'managed realignment' of the sea defences is being conducted at Tollesbury Fleet (Fig. 2) under the auspices of the Ministry of Agriculture Food and Fisheries (MAFF). The Tollesbury realignment comprises 0.21 km^2 of formerly reclaimed agricultural land allowed to revert to tidal action in August 1995, following breaching of the old seawall. Since the breaching, a fringe of pioneer *Salicornia* spp. and *Suaeda maritima* has developed in front of the new seawall constructed along the landward margin. The remainder of the site remains unvegetated mud. Six SET sites were established in 1995, including two on higher mud surfaces now colonized by pioneer plants, two on lower surfaces nearer the breach, and two on the higher 'natural' saltmarsh outside the experimental site (Fig. 2b). Feldspar marker horizons were established 14 months later in 1996.

Methods

Vertical accretion

Following Reed & Cahoon (1993), marsh accretion is defined as the vertical dimension of marsh substrate development as determined relative to a subsurface marker horizon. The present study utilizes accretion data obtained by using three types of near-surface marker material. At Scolt Head Island, over 100 patches of medium sand (area ≈ 1m^2), were laid between 1983 and 1986 at Hut Marsh. Accretion rates have been subsequently determined by the extraction of annual (latterly bi-annual) microcores (Stoddart *et al.* 1989; French & Spencer 1993). In 1995, additional sand patches were deployed within the nearby Spartina Marsh and Salicornia Marsh, as well as in the high marsh plot at Hut Marsh. At Stiffkey (Fig. 1d), a series of perforated aluminium plates was installed in 1994 to provide accretion measurements in support of an investigation of wave attenuation processes (Möller 1997). The 20 cm × 20 cm plates were pushed horizontally into the undisturbed marsh immediately adjacent to the removed section at depths of approximately 0.1 m. Despite the initial disturbance, this method had the advantage that subsequent determination of the depth of burial can be easily accomplished by using a graduated metal pin pushed through the soil. The plots were allowed to recover for 2 months before measurements were commenced and 14 pin readings were made of each plate during each sampling. Sampling was conducted every 3 to 6 months from 1994 to 1998. At Tollesbury (Fig. 2), surface patches of white feldspar were laid adjacent to each of the elevation change monitoring sites. Depth of burial at subsequent intervals was recorded, as at Scolt Head Island, by the extraction of microcores.

Elevation change

Far fewer studies of saltmarsh sedimentation have recorded surface elevation change. In the UK, electronic theodolites equipped with distance measuring capability (electronic 'total stations') have been used to detect seasonal fluctuations (Carr & Blackley 1986) in the level of both vegetated and unvegetated surfaces. More recently, Pethick & Burd (1996) have presented elevation change data covering the period of saltmarsh reestablishment for a small experimental managed realignment site at Northey Island, Blackwater estuary. Most saltmarshes exhibit annual rates of surface elevation change which are too low to resolve accurately by using sequential theodolite surveys of this kind.

There have been a few attempts to obtain high resolution measurements of saltmarsh microrelief in the UK. At New Marsh at Gibraltar Point, Lincolnshire,

Hartnall (1984) measured surface elevation in relation to a reference frame (i.e. bedstead) which was attached to fixed points anchored to a depth of 80 cm. Hazelden & Boorman (1999) measured changes in saltmarsh surface level (*sensu* Hartnall 1984) in relation to an aluminum bar placed across pairs of fixed points (anchored to a depth of 80 cm) at Stiffkey and Tollesbury (outside the experimental managed realignment site). Although suitable for shallow saltmarsh soils, the large size and weight of the reference frame limit its usefulness in thicker wetland soils because of the potential for the shallow anchoring pipes to sink.

The SET works on the same principle of the reference frame, but is smaller and can be attached to deeper benchmarks (up to 6 m), and has been used successfully in a number of tidal and riverine marsh environments in the southeastern United States (Reed & Cahoon 1993; Cahoon *et al.* 1995; Cahoon & Lynch 1997; Cahoon *et al.* 1999). The SET was originally developed in the Netherlands for the monitoring of tidal flats (van Erdt 1985) and subsequently was adapted for saltmarsh use by John Day and colleagues at Louisiana State University (Boumans & Day 1993). The essential features of the SET and its method of deployment are summarized in Fig. 3. A 7.5 cm internal-diameter aluminium benchmark pipe is driven into the substrate to the limit of penetration and is trimmed to within 30 cm of the marsh surface. A smaller pipe, notched at the four

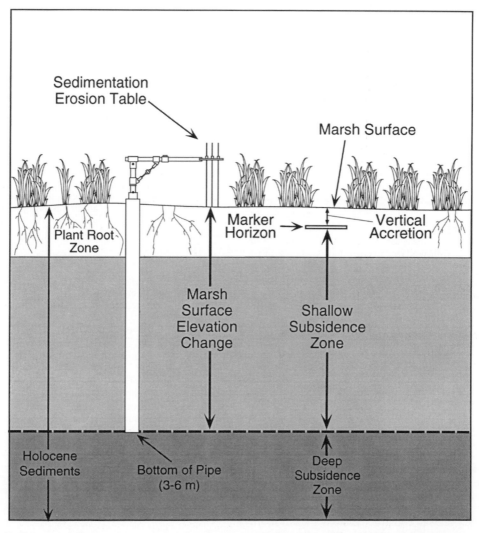

Fig. 3. Conceptual diagram (not to scale) showing those portions of the soil profile being measured by the sedimentation-erosion table (SET), sand/feldspar soil markers and the accretion plate methods. The boundary separating the shallow and deep subsidence zones is defined operationally by the bottom of the SET pipe. Adapted from Cahoon *et al.* (1995).

cardinal points, is cemented into the outer pipe to receive the SET. The SET deploys nine measuring pins mounted at the end of a 1.4 m long arm which can be accurately levelled by using adjusting screws and a built-in bubble level. Together with the notches in the receiving pipe, these levelling devices are used to precisely align the array of nine measuring pins in each of the four quadrants. Surface elevation changes are determined at each of 4×9 locations by carefully placing the pins at the sediment surface, and measuring their protrusion through the mounting plate (Fig. 3).

The SET instrument offers superior accuracy and statistical precision (± 1.5 mm, Boumans & Day 1993) to sequential theodolite survey, albeit at the expense of the initial overheads incurred in installing the benchmark pipes and of more limited spatial coverage. It is assumed that the benchmark pipe provides a stable datum throughout the monitoring campaign (Childers *et al.* 1993); this stability can be checked through carefully levelling to a network of local benchmarks located in stable substrates beyond the tidal influence. Typically, benchmark pipes are several metres long, ensuring that the surface elevation determinations are effectively decoupled from all but regional-scale subsidence (to which all adjacent benchmarks are also subject).

In the present study, SET benchmark pipes were driven to the limit of penetration with a heavy sledgehammer, typically to about 2 m. Slightly shorter pipes were sufficient in some cases, at Tollesbury and at Scolt Head Island, where they reached impenetrable sands and gravels. In contrast, both the outer salt marsh sites at Tollesbury received 3 m pipes.

Statistical analyses

Annual rates of vertical accretion and elevation change were calculated by using sample means by simple linear regression (intercept through zero; Zar 1984) using PROC REG in SAS (1989, p. 1351–1456). Rates

were compared to one another by using the multiple regression technique in PROC REG in SAS (1991). All comparisons were tested at the $p = 0.05$ level unless otherwise noted.

Results and discussion

Accretion vs. elevation change

Scolt Head Island. Over the period of this study, measures of vertical accretion provided a reasonable estimate of elevation change for the creek margin and interior marsh sites at Hut Marsh, but not for the high marsh site (Fig. 4). In the creek margin and interior marsh sites, there were some annual variations in the relationship between vertical accretion and marsh elevation change (Fig. 4a, b), but the overall trend for each variable, based on comparison of annual rates calculated from regression analyses (Table 1), was similar. Although the rates of accretion and elevation change were statistically significantly different for the interior marsh site (Table 1), the small difference between the rates coupled with the close similarity of the curves in Fig. 4b suggest that this statistical difference has little biological or geological significance. Such is not the case for the high marsh site, however, where elevation change was consistently and significantly greater than vertical accretion (Fig. 4c). The annual rate of elevation change was nearly twice as great as the annual rate of vertical accretion (Table 1), indicating that subsurface processes exerted as great a control over elevation as did sediment deposition at this site.

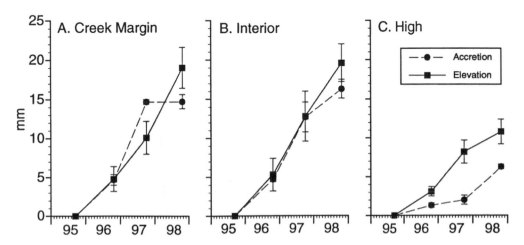

Fig. 4. Vertical accretion and elevation data for three environments at Hut Marsh on Scolt Head Island: (**a**) creek margin, (**b**) interior middle marsh, and (**c**) interior high marsh. See Fig. 1c for location of sampling plots.

Table 1. *Rates of vertical accretion, elevation change, and shallow subsidence* $(mm\,a^{-1})$ *calculated by regression analysis for five marsh sites on Scolt Head Island, North Norfolk, UK**

Marsh site	Vertical accretion	Elevation change	Shallow subsidence	Probability > F
Hut Marsh				
Creek Margin	5.4 (0.5)	6.4 (0.3)	ns	0.128
Interior	5.5 (0.2)	6.2 (0.2)	−0.7	0.029
High	1.7 (0.3)	2.9 (0.2)	−1.2	0.007
Spartina Marsh	10.9 (0.3)	7.0 (0.3)	3.9	0.0001
Salicornia Marsh	5.2 (0.4)	5.4 (0.3)	ns	0.59

* Rates were calculated by regression analyses with intercept forced through zero for data from 1995–1998 for all sites. Values are means with 1 SE in parentheses.

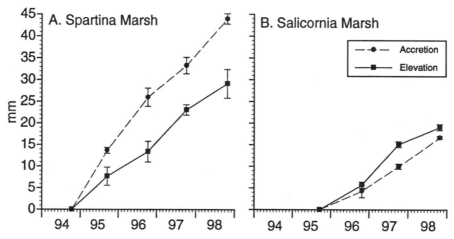

Fig. 5. Vertical accretion and elevation data from Scolt Head Island for (**a**) Spartina Marsh and (**b**) Salicornia Marsh. See Fig. 1c for location of sampling plots.

Measures of vertical accretion did not provide a reasonable estimate of elevation change in Spartina Marsh on Scolt Head Island (Fig. 5a) because elevation change consistently lagged behind vertical accretion, indicating a rate of shallow subsidence of nearly $4\,mm\,a^{-1}$ (Table 1). The occurrence of shallow subsidence in low Spartina Marsh is not without precedent. Cahoon *et al.* (1999) reported rates of shallow subsidence of 12.2 and $22.5\,mm\,a^{-1}$ for two salt marshes dominated by *Spartina alterniflora* in the United States. In contrast, vertical accretion was a reasonable surrogate for elevation change in Salicornia Marsh (Fig. 5b & Table 1) during the course of the study.

Stiffkey – outer marsh. Vertical accretion was characterized across the outer marsh at Stiffkey by calculating annual rates for each of the 11 sampling plots. Annual rates were fairly consistent for most of the plots, varying between 1.7 and $8.5\,mm\,a^{-1}$. Rates were lower and more variable at 2 plots on the seaward margin of the marsh (-5.8 and $1.2\,mm\,a^{-1}$) because of the highly dynamic and eroding nature of the marsh-sand flat ecotone. The rate was also low for the most landward plot ($0.8\,mm\,a^{-1}$) located in the marsh-ridge ecotone at an elevation significantly higher than the adjacent marsh. Consequently, data from these three marginal plots were dropped from the analysis and the data from the remaining eight plots were combined to calculate, by regression, an annual mean accretion rate representative of the vegetated surface of the outer marsh. This rate was $5.5\,(0.3)\,mm\,a^{-1}$ (mean with 1 SE). Annual variation in marsh elevation change measured from SET plots located adjacent to three plots on the outer marsh is presented in Fig. 6. In order to characterize elevation change across this portion of the marsh, the data from the SET plots were combined to calculate by regression (n = 12) an annual mean elevation change rate. This rate was $6.5\,(0.6)\,mm\,a^{-1}$. The rates of vertical accretion

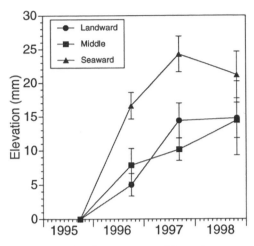

Fig. 6. Elevation change measured from three sampling locations in the outer marsh at Stiffkey.

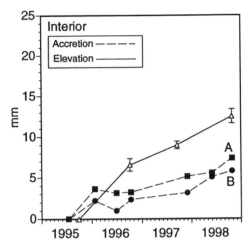

Fig. 8. Vertical accretion and elevation change measured in the interior marsh environment in the back marsh at Stiffkey. Line A represents accretion at the head of the creek while Line B represents accretion from the mid creek plot. The error bars for the accretion data are smaller than the symbols.

and elevation change were not significantly different (p = 0.42), indicating that vertical accretion was a reasonable predictor of elevation change in this marsh environment.

Stiffkey – back marsh. The accretionary and elevational responses of the creek margin environment between 1995 and 1998 are presented in Fig. 7. In order to quantitatively evaluate the relationship between accretion and elevation

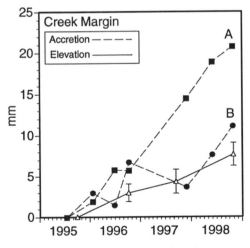

Fig. 7. Vertical accretion and elevation change measured in the creek margin environment in the back marsh at Stiffkey. Line A represents accretion at the head of the creek and Line B represents accretion from the mid creek plot. The error bars for the accretion data are smaller than the symbols.

in the creek margin environment, the accretion data from the head and mid creek sites were combined and an annual mean rate was calculated by regression analysis. This rate was 4.6 (0.5) mm a^{-1} (mean with 1 SE). Similarly, an annual mean rate of elevation change was calculated by regression analysis. This rate was 2.4 (0.5) mm a^{-1}. The two rates are not significantly different at the 5% level (p = 0.0831), indicating that accretion measures provided a reasonable estimate of elevation change during this time period. However, the low p-value, coupled with the trend for a high rate of accretion as shown in Fig. 7 suggests there may be a subsurface process influencing elevation which may become statistically meaningful if the current trends continue.

The accretionary and elevational responses of the interior marsh environment between 1995 and 1998 are presented in Fig. 8. For the creek margin environment, the accretion data from the head and mid creek were combined and an annual mean rate calculated by regression analysis. This rate was 1.9 (0.1) mm a^{-1} (mean with 1 SE). In contrast, the mean rate of elevation change calculated by regression analysis was 4.4 (0.4) mm a^{-1}, which was significantly greater than the rate of accretion (p = 0.0001). This finding suggests that subsurface processes exerted as great an influence on elevation as did sediment deposition at this site.

The annual rates of elevation change for the creek margin (2.4 mm) and the interior marsh

(4.4 mm) are comparable to the annual rates of elevation change (3.08 mm) reported by Hazelden & Boorman (1999) for the back marsh at Stiffkey from 1993 to 1995. Hazelden & Boorman (1999) did not indicate, however, if their measurements were made in the creek margin or interior marsh. Also, since Hazelden & Boorman (1999) did not make simultaneous measurements

of vertical accretion, shallow subsidence rates occurring over the 80 cm depth of the reference frame cannot be calculated from their data.

Tollesbury managed realignment. Accretionary and elevational responses were strongly influenced by hydrologic restoration at the managed realignment project at Tollesbury. Vertical

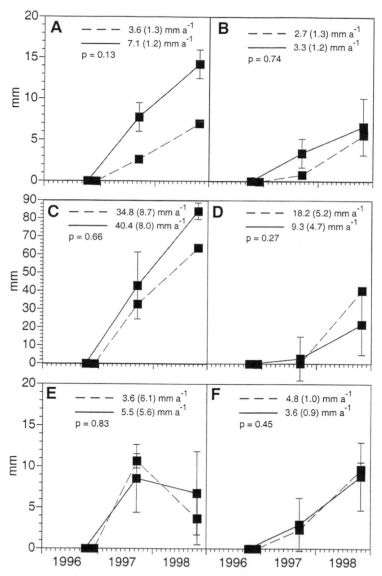

Fig. 9. Vertical accretion (dashed line) and elevation change (solid line) measured at six sampling locations at Tollesbury; numerical values are mean annual rates with one standard error. (**A**) Plot 1 streamside natural marsh, (**B**) Plot 2 interior natural marsh, (**C**) Plot 3 lower elevation restored marsh, (**D**) Plot 5 lower elevation restored marsh, (**E**) Plot 4 higher elevation restored marsh, and (**F**) Plot 6 higher elevation restored marsh. See Fig. 2b for location of sampling plots. Note the difference in the scale for 9C and 9D.

accretion and elevation change were greatest at the plots with the lowest elevation relative to the restored tidal regime (Fig. 9c, d). This finding probably reflects both the increased frequency of tidal flooding and the proximity to the seawall breach as a sediment source. Annual rates of accretion and elevation change were approximately one order of magnitude greater in this area than for higher elevations in the restored marsh and for the natural marsh outside the seawall (Fig. 9). Rates of accretion and elevation change were similar for the natural marsh and the higher elevations of the restored marsh. Interestingly, there was no measurable amount of shallow subsidence at any of the six sampling plots (Fig. 9), indicating that neither tidal restoration nor elevation within the restored marsh influenced the relationship between vertical accretion and elevation change.

Hazelden & Boorman (1999) reported an annual rate of elevation change for the saltmarsh outside the experimental managed realignment site at Tollesbury of 4.27 mm from 1993 to 1995. This is similar to the rate we measured for the interior marsh (3.3 ± 1.2 mm a^{-1}) but lower than the rate we measured for the creek margin (7.1 ± 1.2 mm a^{-1}) (see Fig. 9). Shallow subsidence rates occurring over the 80 cm depth of the reference frame cannot be calculated from the data of Hazelden & Boorman (1999), however, because they made no simultaneous measures of vertical accretion.

Processes controlling elevation

The approach used in this study of simultaneously measuring, with a high degree of resolution (≈ 1 mm), vertical accretion at the marsh surface and elevation change integrated over the top few metres of the marsh substrate (Fig. 3) allowed, not only direct comparison of these two variables (and calculation of the amount of shallow subsidence), but also separation of the effects of surface and subsurface processes on elevation change (Cahoon et al. 1995; Cahoon et al. 1999). Since the occurrence of shallow subsidence signifies that subsurface processes are exerting significant control over elevation, knowledge of the pattern of shallow subsidence coupled with an understanding of the local environmental setting can be used to infer which subsurface processes most likely influenced elevation (e.g. biological vs. geological processes). Therefore, this approach allowed us to address our second objective, which was to explore the implications of the discrepancies between separately measured vertical accretion and elevation change within contrasting marsh types.

The back barrier marsh sites at Scolt Head Island and Stiffkey vary in age and elevation, from youngest/lowest to oldest/highest, as follows: Spartina Marsh/Salicornia Marsh/Hut Marsh/Stiffkey. The youngest/lowest environment, Spartina Marsh, was the only one to exhibit a significant rate of shallow subsidence. Vertical accretion was not a good predictor of elevation change in this environment, as has been reported in other low *Spartina* marshes (Cahoon et al. 1999), apparently because of compaction of unconsolidated clay sediments. The older back barrier marshes located higher in the tidal range, where soil consolidation rates are lower and where high marsh plant community types dominate, did not exhibit shallow subsidence. Indeed, elevation gain was significantly greater than vertical accretion at the high marsh site on Hut Marsh and the interior site of the inner marsh at Stiffkey, indicating that subsurface processes exert a strong positive influence on elevation. We believe that the cause of this response is the belowground accumulation of organic matter through root growth and not the swelling of the substrate by porewater storage, because these sites are well drained. Experimental research is needed to confirm this inference.

The outer marsh environment at Stiffkey differs greatly from the back barrier marsh environments described above. This marsh is located between a large tidal sand flat and a barrier shingle ridge and hence is exposed to high energy wave and wind events in addition to large daily tidal influences. This dynamic marsh setting provides a highly stressed environment for plants where the typical growth form is small and stunted. The substrate is sandy, well-drained and prone to erosion on the seaward edge. Historical aerial photographs show that this site is aggrading onto the sand flat and has a fluctuating shoreline. The similarity between accretion and elevation change of the marsh surface, coupled with the dynamic, aggrading setting, indicates that elevation change in this environment is being driven by surface depositional processes.

The restored, estuarine-type marsh environment at Tollesbury differs importantly from both the back barrier and outer marsh settings described above. The site is in a sheltered location several kilometres up the estuary from the coast. The interior portions were embanked for nearly 200 years and experienced more than 1 m of subsidence under agricultural usage. Since restoration, only the higher sites have developed any vegetative cover. Elevation change is, presently at least, dominated by inorganic sediment deposition.

Implications for marsh submergence

The ability of a wetland to build vertically at a pace equal to sea-level rise was traditionally determined by comparing rates of vertical accretion with sea-level rise and calculating an 'accretion deficit' (Stevenson *et al.* 1986). Our approach of simultaneously measuring accretion and elevation means that both 'accretion deficits' and 'elevation deficits' can be calculated in order to determine the potential for submergence of a marsh. For those sites in this study where no shallow subsidence was measured, the accretion deficit approach can be used to accurately estimate the potential for submergence of the marsh. The regional rate of relative sea-level rise for the East Anglia coast is about $2 \, \mathrm{mm \, a^{-1}}$ ($1 \, \mathrm{mm \, a^{-1}}$ from regional subsidence and $1 \, \mathrm{mm \, a^{-1}}$ from eustatic sea-level rise; Shennan 1989; Pirazzoli 1989). Given that the accretion rates for those sites with no shallow subsidence were equal to or greater than the rate of sea-level rise, the potential for submergence of these marshes at the present time is low.

When collected in conjunction with vertical accretion data, elevation change data can help clarify the processes maintaining surface elevation. For example, vertical accretion at the high marsh site at Hut Marsh ($1.7 \, \mathrm{mm \, a^{-1}}$) appears to be barely keeping pace with sea-level rise. In reality, however, the potential for submergence of this site is low because elevation change ($2.9 \, \mathrm{mm \, a^{-1}}$) was greater than accretion. Another example of how elevation data can be used to clarify the role of sedimentation is found at Spartina Marsh on Scolt Head Island. This young, low, marsh had the only significant amount of shallow subsidence of all the sites studied. But accretion and elevation change both greatly exceeded the local sea-level rise, so there was no threat of submergence and there appeared to be a 'surplus of accretion'. It must be noted, however, that the local sea-level rise rate does not include any shallow subsidence since it is based on regional subsidence estimates. Consequently, the sea-level rise experienced by Spartina Marsh is about $6 \, \mathrm{mm \, a^{-1}}$ (about $2 \, \mathrm{mm \, a^{-1}}$ sea-level rise + about $4 \, \mathrm{mm \, a^{-1}}$ shallow subsidence). This marsh is just keeping pace with this adjusted sea-level rise (elevation change about $7 \, \mathrm{mm \, a^{-1}}$) and it must accrete about $11 \, \mathrm{mm \, a^{-1}}$ to do so.

The findings at the Tollesbury managed realignment project suggest that, so long as sediment supply does not become limiting, the very low surface of the restored marsh should continue to accrete rapidly and increase its elevation within the tidal frame. As the tidal frame fills, the 'form-process' feedback model predicts that the rate of accretion will slow. It will be interesting to see how much shallow subsidence occurs, if any, as the marsh accumulates more than $1 \, \mathrm{m}$ of sediment during this process and eventually becomes vegetated.

Lastly, it should be noted that there are constraints to determining the potential for wetland submergence using this approach. Care must be taken in extrapolating results from a few years of data collection to projections of sea-level rise over the next century because of the long-term response of elevation to compaction and the effects of feedback mechanisms on the processes which control elevation. Models have recently been developed (Rybczyk *et al.* 1998) which can simulate sediment processes over decades and incorporate feedback mechanisms. These models are a potentially powerful tool for examining the response of wetlands to increasing rates of sea-level rise during the next century.

Conclusions

Measures of vertical accretion provided not only reasonable estimates but also, in some cases, overestimates and underestimates of the amount of elevation change occurring in the selected marshes in eastern and southeastern England. Hence, the assumption that near-surface vertical accretion measures provide a good analogue for elevation change in all tidally dominated, minerogenic saltmarsh settings is not valid. Vertical accretion measures were equivalent to elevation change (i.e. surface accretionary processes controlled elevation) in the highly subsided, restored marsh site at Tollesbury, the highly dynamic, exposed outer marsh at Stiffkey, and, most of the back barrier settings on the North Norfolk coast. However, the low *Spartina*-dominated saltmarsh at Scolt Head Island exhibited significant shallow subsidence (accretion > elevation), while at some interior high marsh settings at Scolt Head Island and Stiffkey, the rate of elevation gain was greater than the rate of accretion. For these sites, subsurface processes occurring in the top 1 to 2 m of the substrate were as equally important as surface accretionary processes in determining elevation change.

Simultaneous measurement of accretion and elevation change allowed greater insight into processes of marsh maintenance than either method alone. Compaction of unconsolidated clay sediments was apparently a controlling factor in elevation change of Spartina Marsh while biological processes (e.g. accumulation of belowground organic matter) apparently contributed significantly to elevation change in some high marsh environments. Overall, the processes controlling marsh elevation were site specific and dependent on the environmental setting and marsh type. Thus, caution should be used when extrapolating results among and within marsh settings. All of these findings indicate the need to reinterpret assessments of the vulnerability of marshes in this region to present and predicted future rates of sea-level rise, and also the effectiveness of management and restoration practices. The key to assessing vulnerability and management effectiveness is an understanding of the processes controlling elevation change.

We are grateful to The National Trust and English Nature for permission to work at Scolt Head Island and Stiffkey and to the Ministry of Agriculture Food and Fisheries for permission to work at Tollesbury. This work has been carried out with support from the Jackson Environment Institute (UCL), Natural Environment Research Council (NERC Research Studentship No. GT4/93/7/P to IM), and the National Rivers Authority (Anglian Region Operational Investigation 569). We thank C. Watson, B. Adams, C. French, and E. Czyzowska for their assistance with the SET measurements.

References

AGRICULTURE SELECT COMMITTEE 1998. *Sixth report: Flood and coastal defence*. London, House of Commons.

ALLEN, J. R. L . 1990a. Constraints on measurement of sea level movements from salt-marsh accretion rates. *Journal of the Geological Society, London*, **147**, 5–7.

——1990b. Salt-marsh growth and stratification: a numerical model with special reference to the Severn Estuary, southwest Britain. *Marine Geology*, **95**, 77–96.

—— & PYE, K. (eds) 1992. *Saltmarshes: morphodynamics, conservation and engineering significance*. Cambridge, Cambridge University Press.

BOORMAN, L. A., GOSS-CUSTARD, J. & MCGRORTY, S. 1989. *Climate change, rising sea level and the British coast*. Institute of Terrestrial Ecology Research Publication 1, HMSO.

BOUMANS, R. M. J. & DAY, J. W. 1993. High precision measurements of sediment elevation in shallow coastal areas using a sedimentation-erosion table. *Estuaries*, **16**, 375–380.

BURD, F. 1992. *Erosion and vegetation change on the salt marshes of Essex and North Kent between 1973 and 1988*. Research & Survey in Nature Conservation **42**, Peterborough, Nature Conservancy Council.

CAHOON, D. R. & LYNCH, J. C. 1997. Vertical accretion and shallow subsidence in a mangrove forest of southwestern Florida, USA. *Mangroves and Salt Marshes*, **1**, 173–186.

——, REED, D. J. & DAY, J. W. 1995. Estimating shallow subsidence in microtidal saltmarshes of the southeastern United States: Kaye and Barghoorn revisited. *Marine Geology*, **128**, 1–9.

——, DAY, J. W. JR. & REED, D. J. 1999. The influence of surface and shallow subsurface soil processes on wetland elevation: a synthesis. *Current Topics in Wetland Biogeochemistry*, **3**, 72–88

CARPENTER, K. E. & PYE, K. 1996. *Saltmarsh change in England and Wales – its history and causes*. Environment Agency R&D Technical Report W12, 1–158.

CARR, A. P. & BLACKLEY, M. W. L. 1986. Seasonal changes in surface level of a salt marsh creek. *Earth Surface Processes and Landforms*, **11**, 427–439.

CHAPMAN, V. J. 1960. The plant ecology of Scolt Head Island. *In*: STEERS, J. A. (ed.) *Scolt Head Island*. Cambridge, Heffer, 85–163.

CHILDERS, D. L., SKLAR, F. H., DRAKE, B. & JORDAN, T. 1993. Seasonal measurements of sediment elevation in three mid-Atlantic estuaries. *Journal of Coastal Research Special Issue*, **18**, 280–294.

DeLAUNE, R. D., BAUMANN, R. H. & GOSSELINK, J. G. 1983. Relationship among vertical accretion, coastal submergence, and erosion in a Louisiana Gulf Coast marsh. *Journal of Sedimentary Petrology*, **53**, 147–157.

ENVIRONMENT AGENCY 1997. *Evaluation of the LIDAR technique to produce elevation data for use within the Agency*. Bath, National Centre for Environmental Data and Surveillance.

FRENCH, J. R. 1991. Eustatic and neotectonic controls on salt marsh sedimentation. *In:*, N. C. KRAUS, K. J. GINGERICH & D. L. KRIEBEL (eds) *Coastal Sediments '91*. New York, American Society of Civil Engineers, 1223–1236.

——1993. Numerical modelling of vertical marsh growth and response to rising sea-level, Norfolk, UK *Earth Surface Processes & Landforms*, **18**, 63–81.

——1994. Tide-dominated coastal wetlands and accelerated sea-level rise: a northwestern European perspective. *Journal of Coastal Research Special Issue*, **12**, 91–101.

—— & STODDART, D. R. 1992. Hydrodynamics of salt-marsh creek systems: implications for marsh morphological development and material exchange. *Earth Surface Processes & Landforms*, **17**, 235–252.

—— & SPENCER, T. 1993. Dynamics of sedimentation in a tide-dominated backbarrier saltmarsh, Norfolk, UK. *Marine Geology*, **110**, 315–331.

GEHRELS, W. R. & LEATHERMAN, S. P. 1989. *Sea-level rise animator and terminator of coastal marshes: an annotated bibliography on U.S. coastal marshes and sea-level rise*. Public Administration Series Bibliography P2634, Monticello, Illinois, Vance Bibliographies.

HALCROW, SIR W. & PARTNERS (ed.) 1996. *Saltmarsh management for flood defence: research seminar proceedings.* Bristol, National Rivers Authority.

HARMSWORTH, G. C. & LONG, S. P. 1986. An assessment of saltmarsh erosion in Essex, England, with reference to the Dengie Peninsula. *Biological Conservation*, **35**, 377–387.

HARTNALL, T. J. 1984. Salt-marsh vegetation and micro-relief development on the New Marsh at Gibraltar Point, Lincolnshire. *In*: CLARK, M. (ed.) *Coastal research: UK perspective.* Norwich, UK, GeoBooks, 37–58.

HAZELDEN, J. & BOORMAN, L. A. 1999. The role of soil and vegetation processes in the control of organic and mineral fluxes in some western European salt marshes. *Journal of Coastal Research*, **15**, 15–31.

KAYE, C. A. & BARGHOORN, E. S. 1964. Late Quaternary sea-level change and crustal rise at Boston, Massachusetts, with notes on the auto-compaction of peat. *Geological Society of America Bulletin*, **75**, 63–80.

McCAVE, I. N. 1987. Fine sediment sources and sinks around the East Anglian coast, UK. *Journal of the Geological Society, London*, **144**, 149–152.

MÖLLER, I. 1997. *Wave attenuation over saltmarsh surfaces.* PhD thesis, University of Cambridge.

——, SPENCER, T. & FRENCH, J. R. 1996. Wave attenuation over salt marsh surfaces. *Journal of Coastal Research*, **12**, 1009–1016.

——, SPENCER, T., FRENCH, J. R., LEGGETT, D. J. & DIXON, M. 1999. Wave transformation over salt marshes: a field and numerical modelling study from North Norfolk, England. *Estuarine Coastal and Shelf Science*, **49**, 411–426.

NATIONAL RIVERS AUTHORITY 1995. *A guide to the understanding and management of saltmarshes.* Summary of R&D Note 324. Bristol, National Rivers Authority.

ODUM, E. P. 1980. The status of three ecosystem-level hypotheses regarding saltmarsh estuaries: tidal subsidy, outwelling, and detritus-based food chains. *In*:, KENNEDY, V. S. (ed.) *Estuarine perspectives.* New York, Academic Press, 485–495.

PETHICK, J. S. 1980. Salt marsh initiation during the Holocene transgression: the example of the north Norfolk marshes. *Journal of Biogeography*, **7**, 1–9.

——1981. Long-term accretion rates on tidal marshes. *Journal of Sedimentary Petrology*, **61**, 571–577.

——1998. Coastal management and sea level rise: a morphological approach. *In*: LANE, S. N., RICHARDS, K. S. & CHANDLER, J. (eds) *Landform monitoring, modelling and analysis.* Chichester, John Wiley and Sons, 405–419.

—— & BURD, F. 1996. Sedimentary processes under managed retreat. *In*: HALCROW, SIR W. & PARTNERS (ed.) *Saltmarsh management for flood defence: research seminar proceedings.* Bristol, National Rivers Authority, 14–26.

PIRAZZOLI, P. A. 1989. Present and near-future global sea-level changes. *Palaeogeography, Palaeoclimatology and Palaeoecology*, **75**, 241–258.

PYE, K. & FRENCH, P. W. 1993. *Erosion and accretion processes in British saltmarshes.* Final Report to MAFF. 5 volumes, Cambridge, Cambridge Environmental Research Consultants Ltd.

REED, D. J. 1988. Sediment dynamics and deposition in a retreating coastal salt marsh. *Estuarine and Coastal Shelf Science*, **26**, 67–79.

—— & CAHOON, D. R. (1992) The relationship between marsh surface topography, hydroperiod and growth of *Spartina alterniflora* in a deteriorating Louisiana salt marsh. *Journal of Coastal Research*, **8**, 77–87.

—— & CAHOON, D. R. 1993. *Marsh submergence vs. marsh accretion: interpreting accretion deficit data in coastal Louisiana.* Proceedings Coastal Zone 93, 8th Symposium on Coastal and Ocean Management, 243–256.

RYBCZYK, J. M., CALLAWAY, J. & DAY, J. W. JR. 1998. A relative elevation model (REM) for a subsiding coastal forested wetland receiving wastewater effluent. *Ecological Modelling*, **112**, 23–44.

SAS INSTITUTE, INC. 1989. *SAS/STAT^R User's Guide*, Version 6, 4th ed., Volume 2, Cary, North Carolina, USA.

——1991. *SAS^R System for Linear Models.* 3rd ed., Cary, North Carolina, USA.

SHENNAN, I. 1989. Holocene crustal movements and sea-level changes in Great Britain. *Journal of Quaternary Science*, **4**, 77–89.

STEVENSON, J. C., WARD, L. G. & KEARNEY, M. S. 1986. Vertical accretion in marshes with varying rates of sea level rise. *In*: WOLFE, D. A. (ed.) *Estuarine variability.* Orlando, Academic Press, 241–260.

STODDART, D. R., REED, D. J. & FRENCH, J. R. 1989. Understanding salt marsh accretion, Scolt Head Island, Norfolk, England. *Estuaries*, **12**, 228–236.

STREIF, H. 1989. Barrier islands, tidal flats and coastal marshes resulting from a rise in relative sea-level in East Frizzy on the German North Sea coast. *In*: VAN DER LINDEN, W. J. M. (ed.) *Coastal lowlands: geology and geotechnology.* Dordrecht, Kluwer, 213–223.

TEMPLET, P. H. & MEYER-ARENDT, K. J. 1988. Louisiana wetland loss: a regional water management approach to the problem. *Environmental Management*, **12**, 181–191.

VAN ERDT, M. 1985. The influence of vegetation on erosion and accretion in saltmarshes of the Oosterschelde, The Netherlands. *Vegetatio*, **62**, 367–373.

ZAR, J. H. 1984. *Biostatistical Analysis.* Prentice-Hall, Inc., Englewood Cliffs, New Jersey, USA.

Holocene coastal lowlands in NW Europe:
autocompaction and the uncertain ground

J. R. L. ALLEN

*Postgraduate Research Institute for Sedimentology and Department of Archaeology,
University of Reading, Reading RG6 6AB, UK (e-mail: j.r.l.allen@reading.ac.uk)*

Abstract: The continuous, progressive, irreversible and asymptotic processes of sediment autocompaction play a significant but so far largely neglected role in determining the co-evolving character of Holocene landscapes and sedimentary sequences formed in coastal marshlands. Autocompaction ensures that actual total sediment deposition rates are always greater than the rate at which sea-level rise creates accommodation space. High rates of autocompaction help to foster resource-rich, mineralogenic tidal marshes that can be readily exploited by humans from neighbouring higher ground, for example, dryland areas, or locations within the marshland where peat formation had persisted sufficiently late that domal, raised bogs had not yet completely collapsed. Subsequent autocompaction may bring about a significant inversion of relief. The general effects of autocompaction are a high degree of vertical stratigraphic distortion and displacement amounting to as much as a few metres, depending on the depth to 'basement', the lithologies present, and their order of deposition. Autocompaction results in inaccurate sea-level curves when based on inter-calated peats, inaccurate rates of sea-level change when calculated on a bed-averaged basis, and inconsistent age-altitude relationships among archaeological sites preserved in coastal deposits. The challenge is to predict/retrodict autocompaction in Holocene coastal lowlands, in order to better understand sequence development, the evolution of surface environments, topography and landscape, and the constraints placed upon (and opportunities presented to) human communities living in these contexts.

The ground that conceals a growing sequence of Holocene sediments in a coastal lowland may be described as uncertain for two reasons. Firstly, the subtle processes of sediment autocompaction are insidiously, continuously and irreversibly lowering the level of the surface, especially where the sequence beneath is rich in silts and peats, as is the case in many NW European coastal areas. Secondly, despite the significant effects which it can be shown are attributable to autocompaction, and the long acknowledgement of auto-compaction as a geological process, the topic in practice has generally been set aside in Holocene stratigraphic and geoarchaeological work in NW Europe. Autocompaction is, and will for some time remain, a difficult field, but there is no longer any justification for ignoring its role and effects at the quantitative level. This set of processes has profound implications for salt-marsh morphodynamics, sea-level studies, Holocene stratigraphy and geoarchaeology (including land scape reconstruction), and coastal land-claim and management. Broadly, autocompaction is the group of interlinked processes whereby the sediment within a growing stratigraphic column diminishes in volume, on account of burial and self-weight, leading to rearrangement of the mineral skeleton and, in the case of vegetable matter, a loss of mass as the result of biological and chemical decay. On the Holocene time scale, some mineral matter may be gained as the result of early diagenetic processes (e.g. Pye *et al.* 1990), but processes such as clay dehydration and silica solution, with their vastly greater thickness and time scales (e.g. Audet 1995), can safely be ignored.

The aim of this paper is to describe and use a simplified, semi-empirical model for autocompaction, calibrated against stratigraphic field data, in order to demonstrate in a general way some of the more important of these implications and effects. The model is, therefore, exploratory and generic rather than site-specific, although it may yield tolerably accurate predictions in the region from which its parameters take their particular numerical values.

Previous work

Early interest focused on decompacting (back-stripping) buried coastal peats, a very variable

From: PYE, K. & ALLEN, J. R. L. (eds). *Coastal and Estuarine Environments: sedimentology, geomorphology and geoarchaeology*. Geological Society, London, Special Publications, **175**, 239–252. 0305-8719/00/$15.00 © The Geological Society of London 2000.

lithology but generally an order of magnitude more compressible than intertidal silt (Knott et al. 1987).

Kaye & Barghoorn (1964) estimated peat compaction from the distortion of tree trunks and boughs assumed to have been originally circular in cross section. A different geometrical approach is followed by Bloom (1964), Belknap & Kraft (1977), Allen (1996a) and Haslett et al. (1998), depending on the measurement of the changing altitude of the top of a concealed peat bed known, or assumed to be, effectively isochronous. Most recently, Shaw & Ceman (1999) have described in considerable detail the differential compaction of a sequence which includes organic beds with well-dated, effectively isochronous boundaries. A similar approach, but using salt-marsh facies (also a palaeotidal indicator), is used at a Dutch archaeological site by Roep & van Regteren Altena (1988). However, van de Plassche (1991) concluded that, in a New England marsh sequence, diachroneity as well as autocompaction influenced the present altitude of lithostratigraphic boundaries.

A fundamentally different attack is pursued by Kidson & Heyworth (1973), Devoy (1982) and Smith (1985), who used simple consolidation theory and geotechnical tests to decompact Holocene peats. Although limited by the fact that the lithology comes in many facies and is geotechnically anaomalous, this work suggests that buried Holocene peats may have lost up to 80–90% of their thickness at deposition.

More recently, descretized consolidation equations combined with data from index tests were used by Pizzuto & Schwendt (1997) to model a stratigraphically proven and dated Holocene marshland sequence, and by Paul & Barras (1998) to decompact a Holocene subtidal succession. Callaway et al. (1996) and Rybcyzk et al. (1996a, b, 1998) recently developed 1D models with explicit autocompaction for the build-up of very short thicknesses of Holocene marshland and related sequences.

The very few direct measurements of current rates of autocompaction that have been published come exclusively from North America. Organic-rich marshlands in San Francisco Bay gave rates upward from about 4 mm annually (Patrick & DeLaune 1990). Cahoon et al. (1995) found the rate in four plant-dominated marshes in the southeastern United States to vary between 4.5 and 49 mm over two years. High subsidence rates are also claimed from Mississippi Delta marshlands on the basis of tide gauge records (Boesch et al. 1983; Penland et al. 1994). All of these values substantially exceed the generally accepted rate of global sea-level rise (Gornitz

1995). Modelling the response of non-coastal peatlands in the northern Netherlands to changes in artificial drainage, Niewenhuis & Schokking (1997) estimated that a lowering of the groundwater table by a matter of decimetres caused over a 50-year period an almost equal amount of land subsidence.

A model for sequence growth and autocompaction

The role of autocompaction in the vertical build-up of sedimentary sequences in coastal marshlands and genetically-related intertidal flats is best seen in the context of a general 1D growth model embracing all forcing factors.

The models proposed by Randerson (1979), Krone (1987), Allen (1990, 1995) and French (1993) effectively reduce for a steady tidal regime to the form

$$\Delta E = \Delta S_{min} + \Delta S_{org} - \Delta M - \Delta P \qquad (1)$$

in which ΔE is the change in the level of the sediment surface relative to the tidal frame, ΔS_{min} the added thickness of tidally imported mineralogenic sediment, ΔS_{org} the thickness of indigenous organogenic sedimentary material (chiefly below-ground root biomass), ΔM the change in relative mean sea level, and ΔP the amount by which autocompaction lowers the surface. Essentially, the third and fourth terms to the right combine to give the total rate at which accommodation space is made available, whereas the first and second terms combine to describe the total rate at which sediment is introduced to fill it. Because of a feedback effect, the mineralogenic term is a very steeply declining, non-linear function of height in the tidal frame (Pethick 1981; Allen 1990; French 1993). Hence, inspecting the equation, an increase in the rates of sea-level rise and autocompaction will have the effect of depressing the sedimentary surface, favouring a mudflat or a mineralogenic rather than organogenic marsh. A stable or falling sea level favours peat formation, but the organogenic term can in principle be so large that the environment remains supratidal (terrestrial) even when sea-level is rising.

Rearranging Eqn (1), and dividing by ΔM, we have

$$\frac{\Delta S_{min} + \Delta S_{org}}{\Delta M} = 1 + \frac{\Delta P + \Delta E}{\Delta M} \qquad (2)$$

where the term on the left may be called the deposition-rate enhancement factor (DEF). This factor, the inverse of the so-called 'submergence index' of Nydick et al. (1995), measures the rate at which sediment fills the accommodation space relative to the rate at which sea-level change – the more fundamental influence – contributes to accommodation space. For a 'mature' mudflat or marsh, that is, one in a state of stable dynamic equilibrium, $\Delta E = 0$ and the DEF is a direct measure of the extent to which auto-compaction secondarily creates space for sedimentation, over and above the fundamental provision by sea-level change. However, a value $\Delta E > 0$ enters into the relationship in the case of youthful marshes and mudflats, which have not yet gained equilibrium. The magnitude of the DEF necessarily is always in excess of one.

Autocompaction is a set of continuous, progressive, asymptotic and irreversible processes which can be modelled analytically only under the most restricted and idealised of circumstances (e.g. Gibson et al. 1967, 1981). Although Holocene coastal successions are comparatively thin (10–20 m), this approach to them is far from appropriate, for vertical and lateral lithological change is rapid and substantial, geotechnically anomalous peats of varied facies are almost invariably present, many beds accumulated under the influence of atmospheric processes (seasonal drying, soil formation), and a variable unsaturated zone occurs naturally in the uppermost part of the sequence. The enclosure and drainage of coastal marshes by humans, a process almost 2000 years old in parts of NW Europe, has the effect of deepening this zone and rendering it even more unpredictable. Under these circumstances, and for exploratory purposes where insight rather than accuracy is desired, a simplified, semi-empirical approach is both practical and useful. Given Skempton's (1970) empirical findings, we may to a rough approximation over Holocene time and thickness scales write

$$T = (T_0 - T_{min}) - \exp(kH) + T_{min} \qquad (3)$$

where T is the final thickness of a sediment layer, T_0 the thickness at the time of deposition, T_{min} the limiting thickness ('zero' porosity), k (m^{-1}) an empirical coefficient describing the compressibility of the layer, and H the overburden thickness, assumed in the particular environment to fill the accommodation space to the height determined by sea level at the time. It will be apparent from the equation that the effects of autocompaction will depend critically on

(1) the thickness of the compacted sequence above the 'basement' (assumed stable and incompressible)
(2) the range of lithologies present in the sequence (from gravel/sand, silt, peat in order of increasing compressibility) and

(3) the vertical order in which the lithologies were deposited.

Autocompaction is usually formulated in terms of effective stress rather than sediment thickness, but under the assumption of full saturation. We then have for a layer of sediment experiencing compaction the relationships

$$T = T_0 \frac{(1 + e)}{(1 + e_0)} \qquad (4)$$

where e_0 and e are the initial and final void ratios, and

$$\gamma = \sigma \left(1 - \frac{e}{(1 + e)}\right) \qquad (5)$$

where γ and σ are, respectively, the bulk density of the compacted layer and the mineral density (assumed constant). Under the assumption of full saturation, the effective stress P on the layer at a depth H below the surface is

$$P = \int_0^H \gamma \cdot dH - \rho H \qquad (6)$$

where ρ the density of water. The corresponding compressibility is now in units of m^2 kg^{-1}. Referring back to Eqn (3), the extent to which autocompaction is underestimated by using over-burden thickness rather than effective stress depends on the strength of $\gamma(H)$. For exploratory calculations, however, when full saturation cannot be assumed and the proportion of the column that is saturated is unknown but variable, the substitution is acceptable for thicknesses of silt of up to a few tens of metres and for peats up to a few metres. The use of a constant compressibility for silts is also acceptable but is a more severe assumption in the case of peat. The engineer's compressibility coefficient for this material in laboratory tests varies with, among other factors, the void ratio, but the dependence is strong only at very high values (MacFarlane 1969; Hobbs 1986). Moreover, whereas a thin peat bed may be composed of a single, highly compressible facies, for example, reed peat, a thick one is likely to consist of a sequence of facies (e.g. reed swamp, carr, raised bog, reed swamp), some less compressible than others.

Equations (1) and (3) were used to synthesize numerically a range of stratigraphic cross sections composed of alternating silts (mudflats/mineralogenic marshes) and peats (organogenic marshes), examples of which are discussed below (Figs 2, 3, 5, 7). These cross sections were built on stable, incompressible 'basement' landscapes of arbitrary form. They have no explicit horizontal scale, but range from the local (10s–100s m) to that of the district (1–10 km) or even the region (10–100 km). The field relationships of Holocene peats at two widely separated localities in the Severn Estuary Levels yielded a working value of $k = 0.537\,\text{m}^{-1}$ for this lithology (Haslett *et al.* 1998 fig. 6; Bell 1995 fig. 61). The compressibility $k = 0.0361\,\text{m}^{-1}$ for silt was derived from profiles of bulk density in silt sequences in these Levels (Hawkins *et al.* 1989 fig. 9). It was assumed that T_{min}/T_0 is respectively 0.22 for peat (DeLaune *et al.* 1983) and 0.65 for silt. All the experiments assumed a dynamically stable sedimentary surface and a steady sea-level rise of $1.5\,\text{mm a}^{-1}$, a fair average for the mid and late Holocene in most of NW Europe. The stratigraphic cross-sections are illustrated with time-lines (isochrones) at a uniform interval of 667 years (called a period), equivalent in the experiments to the provision of 1 m of accommodation space by sea-level rise and the accumulation of 1 m of *uncompacted* sediment. Because environmental gradients operate within salt marshes, the isochrones are coincident with lithostratigraphic boundaries only in cross sections that are parallel with the depositional strike. In transverse stratigraphic profiles, that is, 'dip' sections, the lithostratigraphic boundaries are made diachronous.

Stratigraphic distortion and displacement

All of the simulations demonstrate that the beds experience, because of autocompaction, a progressive vertical stratigraphic displacement and

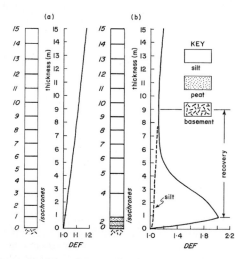

Fig. 1. Experimental autocompaction in (**a**) a silt sequence formed over 15 periods, and (**b**) a sequence with a basal peat (three periods) followed by silt (12 periods). *DEF* – deposition-rate enhancement factor.

distortion, whereby altitude-age relationships conferred at deposition are subsequently lost. Implicitly, each element in a bed may in principle experience in total a combination of body translation and rotation, combined with pure shear and simple shear (Ramsay & Huber 1983). In real Holocene sequences, this deformation may locally be sufficiently marked as to find some kind of physical expression as a small-scale structural feature (e.g. joints, extension faults, pull-aparts, silt injections into peat, peat diapers). Places where the basement is of bold relief, or where there are buried sand/gravel barriers or channel fills, are the most likely to see the production of such features.

The development of stratigraphic displacement and distortion is bound up with the operation of the deposition rate enhancement factor (*DEF*), Eqn (2). Its value increases monotonically but only very gradually upward through a thick sequence of relatively incompressible silts, with isochrones not much further apart at the top of the column than at the more compressed base (Fig. 1a). Behaviour changes considerably, however, with the inclusion of a basal (Fig. 1b) or intercalated peat. The *DEF* increases steeply through the compressible peat but, because of continuing peat compaction, the value for the subsequently deposited silts recovers approximately to the silt curve of Fig. 1a only after about twice the interval of time represented by the peat. Had the peat been intercalated, but of the previous depositional thickness, the interval required for recovery would merely have been shifted higher up the stratigraphic column. The peat phase could have been made so recent that the sedimentary surface at the final isochrone was still significantly affected by compaction of the concealed organic bed.

Figures 2 & 3 depict the compaction on a local scale of a silt-peat sequence in a concealed valley and over a buried hill or ridge. The peat is basal on the sides of each feature and here it has experienced strong rotation. Where it is intercalated, in the axis of the valley and away from the hill, the peat is not significantly rotated but has experienced considerable displacement. The base, which may be considered as a regressive overlap in Tooley's (1982) terms, is not much affected, but the top – a transgressive overlap – lies some 2.5 m below its altitude at deposition. Base and top, also isochrones in this example, are roughly parallel and weakly concave-up, reflecting the form of the basement below. Isochrones in the silt overlying the peat also mimic the basement form, but their relief is more subdued. Compaction over the hill shown in Fig. 3 parallels almost exactly the distortion of a basal

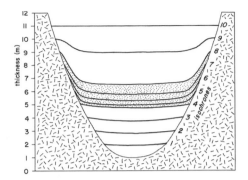

Fig. 2. Differential autocompaction in a silt-peat sequence infilling a symmetrical valley (local scale). See Fig. 1 for symbols.

peat with isochronous top over a bedrock feature as described by Haslett *et al.* (1998) from the Severn Estuary Levels (Fig. 4). As in the simulation, the top of this peat varies in altitude by more than 2 m on a horizontal scale of tens of metres. With the help of considerable dating evidence, Shaw & Ceman (1999) describe the similar, progressive distortion of a sequence of silt and peats deposited against a rising basement below a Nova Scotian marsh.

These effects are seen again in a simulated regional 'strike' section across a varied basement landscape (Fig. 5a). The form of the isochrones mimics that of the concealed features, but more and more faintly with declining age. The *DEF* increases upward overall, but in detail in a series of jumps as peat conditions come and go and recovery follows. Recovery was not complete by the time the last silts were deposited at isochrone 12. Because a number of intercalated peats are present, regressive contacts are also severely displaced, although not as much as transgressive ones. This bed profile is similar to

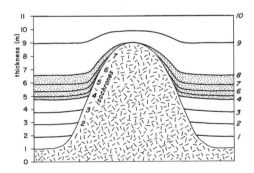

Fig. 3. Differential autocompaction in a silt-peat sequence burying a symmetrical hill (local scale). Symbols as in Fig. 1.

many stratigraphic cross sections on a district scale described from the Holocene of NW Europe, of which Streif's (1971) example from the Krummhörn in the Ems-Dollart region (Dutch–German North Sea coast) is typical (Fig. 6). Here localized palaeochannels filled with relatively incompressible sands help along with the form of the basement (Pleistocene deposits, river sediments) to shape the eventual configuration of the beds. In the Krummhörn autocompaction causes the same lithostratigraphic boundaries to vary in altitude by up to about 4 m. Individual peat beds have, however, upper and lower contacts that seem to be only weakly to moderately diachronous, the top of the uppermost peat, for example, ranging in age

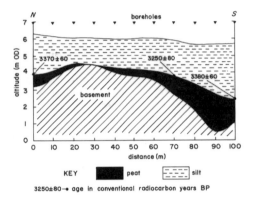

Fig. 4. Observed differential autocompaction in a Holocene peat-silt sequence overlying a basement ridge/hill, Nyland Hill, Axe Valley, Somerset Levels, Southwest England (after Haslett *et al.* 1998). Note the isochronous top of the peat unit.

between 2925 ± 75 in the south and 2305 ± 65 radiocarbon years BP in the north (a thin transgressive silt may locally split the top into two levels). Similar geometrical effects and degrees of displacement are also seen at the regional scale. In geologically complex Zeeland (Vos & van Heeringen 1997) buried channel-fills make a particularly strong contribution to the observed stratigraphic displacement and distortion. The basement is the chief contributor in the Holocene infill of the Thames Estuary (Devoy 1979).

Typically, in NW European Holocene coastal lowlands peats grow in total thickness, but first increase and then decline in number, from the seaward to the landward edge of the outcrop (e.g. Morzadec 1974). This is a response to a number of environmental gradients evident in coastal marshlands, including the advection of tidal silt from the general direction of the

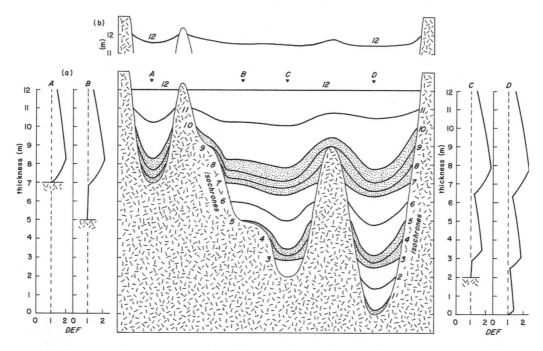

Fig. 5. Experimental autocompaction, together with profiles of the deposition-rate enhancement factor (*DEF*), in a silt-peat sequence deposited on a basement of varied relief (strike section, district-regional scale), (**a**) after 10 periods, and (**b**) the ground surface at a time after land-claim equivalent to two further periods of sedimentation. See Fig. 1 for symbols.

seaward edge. The effects of autocompaction in the presence of lateral facies change and diachroneity are, therefore, best dealt with in terms of simulated district or regional 'dip' sections. Figure 7a illustrates such a section containing two intercalated peats constructed above a concave-up basement. Although its top

in particular is significantly displaced, the lower intercalated peat shows comparatively little distortion because it overlies silt in a basal context. Overall, the main peat bed is concave-up and exhibits strong distortion as well as displacement. Across the inner part of the profile, the diachronous base of this bed rises

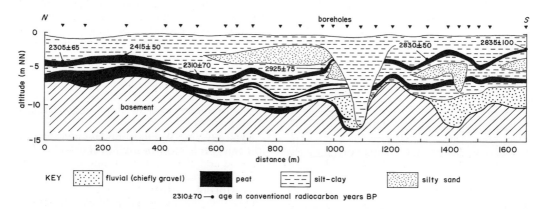

Fig. 6. Stratigraphic cross-section of the Holocene coastal deposits in the Krummhörn, Ems-Dollart region, East Friesland, Germany. After Streif (1971 fig. 2 & table 6).

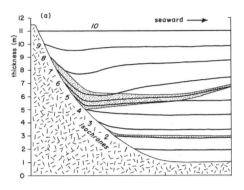

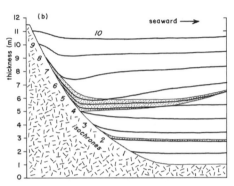

Fig. 7. Experimental autocompaction in a district-scale 'dip' section composed of intercalated peats and silts deposited on a concave-up basement, (**a**) after 10 periods, and (**b**) the topography of the ground surface after land-claim equivalent to four further periods of sedimentation. The main peat is diachronous, with accretion ranging over four periods at the landward end of the section. Symbols as in Fig. 1.

only gradually seaward where it is intercalated among the silts, in spite of an age range of one period. The diachronous top in mid-section is depressed by about 3 m relative to its younger counterpart at the landward extremity and by about 0.75 m relative to its older, seaward equivalent.

Sea level and its change

Curves of Holocene sea level have been drawn up for many parts of NW Europe on the basis of radiocarbon-dated peats and other organic materials (Pirazzoli & Pluet 1991; Pirazzoli 1996). Typically, the dated materials, like the peats in the simulated sections above, are intercalated within sequences dominated by mineral sediments. While it is recognized that autocompaction will have contributed to the blurring of these

curves (e.g. Kidson 1982, 1986; van de Plassche 1986), the effect has either been left unquantified or 'corrected' only in some arbitrary way.

The simulations described above, together with local to regional stratigraphic cross sections revealing displacement and distortion such as those of Streif (1971), Baeteman (1991), Devoy (1979), Vos & van Heeringen (1997), Haslett *et al.* (1998) and Shaw & Ceman (1999), among many others, suggest that sea-level curves based on intercalated peats are likely to be substantially in error, even when the database includes equal numbers of regressive (the least affected) and transgressive (the most affected) overlaps. As an example, Fig. 8 compares sea-level index points derived from the autocompaction experiments outlined above with the single, true sea-level curve for the set of simulations. Similar plots derived from real Holocene sequences will be most in error in terms of the vertical positions of the curves in the time-altitude frame, as Haslett *et al.* (1998) suggested. As both the experimental and the field data show, index points can be displaced vertically by as much as 3–4 m from their true positions. Furthermore, some systematic error may be expected in the underlying *rates* of sea-level change implied by these curves, since the older beds, lower in the sequences to which they contribute, will have experienced more compaction and, consequently, displacement, than younger ones at higher stratigraphic levels. Hence it may become necessary to revise shoreline positions modelled on the basis of conventionally handled sea-level index points (Lambeck 1995). The sea-level curves constructed using basal peats (e.g. Gehrels 1999) are the least likely to be affected by significant compactional errors, but even these are not above suspicion, especially where the deposits are thick and the dated materials did not come from the very base.

Because of the long-ranging influence of the *DEF* (Figs 1b & 5a), caution is also necessary in approaching short and medium term rates of sea-level rise calculated from Holocene borehole profiles made up of compacted clastic units (chiefly silts) and peats (basal and/or intercalated) that had been dated at their bases and tops. Shennan (1995) derived such rates by dividing the present stratigraphic thickness of each kind of unit by its age range. He found a good positive correlation between the derived rate of sea-level change and bed thickness. The peats, however, occuring in relatively thin beds, gave low rates of sea-level rise, whereas the generally much thicker clastic units yielded rates up to several times greater. It was suggested that these rates might define a geomorphic threshold requiring a change in coastal character and

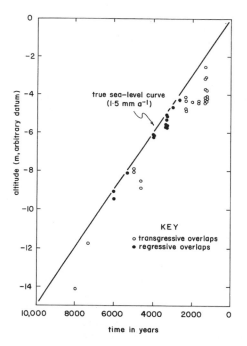

Fig. 8. A set of sea-level index points (sea-level curve) read from sequences generated during the autocompaction experiments, compared to the true sea-level curve based on the assumed steady rate of rise of 1.5 mm a^{-1}. Twenty-four transgressive overlaps are represented, including nine from basal peats. There are 15 regressive overlaps from intercalated peats.

behaviour. But the trends and patterns Shennan noted are also found in the simulated stratigraphic profiles described above, all of which were built under the same conditions of steady sea-level rise (1.5 mm a^{-1}). The model silt beds are comparatively thick and, except where they lie in a basal context, yield apparent rates of sea-level rise up to two-and-a-half times the applied rate (Fig. 9a). By contrast, the simulated basal and intercalated peats are relatively thin and yield apparent rates of rise invariably smaller than the rate actually applied (Fig. 9b, c).

An environmental factor may also contribute along with autocompaction to the total effect apparent to Shennan (1995) from his analysis of field data. The silt-peat couplets widely observed in the mid and late Holocene of NW Europe may record district- to regional-scale fluctuations of water level, with many possible causes, of the order of decimetres to a few metres. Theoretical considerations (Allen 1990, 1995), which led to stratigraphic simulations with autocompaction neglected (Allen 1995), link

the silt units with the higher bed thicknesses and the higher bed-averaged rates of deposition and sea-level change. A positive trend like Shennan's (1995) is again obtained. Hence the environmental effect, should it be real, will add to that shown to be due to autocompaction.

Human activities

Over time humans have exploited the coastal lowlands of NW Europe in a wide variety of ways. One of these is the rather drastic process of landscape transformation through land-claim – the enclosing of an area of salt marsh by an engineered embankment and the insertion of drains and outfalls – practised in Britain from Roman times and in mainland NW Europe chiefly from around the beginning of the present millennium (Allen 1998). As the result of embanking, the enclosed area is denied further supplies of tidal silt, although plant matter may continue to accumulate. In the context of a rising relative sea level, a difference of elevation gradually develops across the seabank as the remaining active marsh continues to build up. Autocompaction will, however, continue and is likely to be accelerated by the improvements to drainage, which further lower the water table. The effect is significantly to increase the various

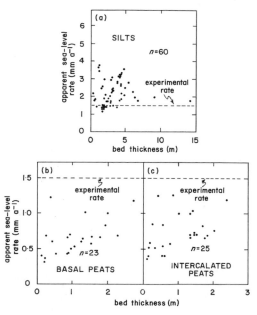

Fig. 9. Randomly selected experimental bed-averaged rates of sea-level change. (**a**) Silt units. (**b**) Basal peats. (**c**) Intercalated peats.

stresses effective in the upper part of the sediment column and to expose any buried peats in addition to renewed decay and to oxidation. By way of illustration, Vranken *et al.* (1990) observed that the mineralogenic salt marshes of the inner Oosterscheldt experienced an irreversible fall in level and increase in sediment bulk density when the completion of barrages led to a reduction in the local tidal range. The consequences of draining peatlands can be profound, as Hutchinson (1980) demonstrates from the East Anglian Fenland, and as Niewenhuis & Schokking (1997) predict from Friesland.

An attempt was made in some of the simulations described above to reproduce the effects of embanking. Autocompaction was in these experiments allowed to continue for a small number of further periods, but without any actual sediment being added to the cross sections. Figure 5b shows the effect on the final landscape developed above a basement with mainly concealed hills and valleys. Generalizing, the surface topography takes the form of two unequal, concave-up segments. It has a maximum relief of about 0.6 m and mimics, but in a subdued form, the configuration of the basement below. In the 'dip' section of Fig. 7b the ground surface becomes concave-up overall, because of a differential response between the silt-dominated seaward part of the sequence and the landward section with its thick basal-intercalated main peat. The additional periods of autocompaction serve only to strengthen the effects earlier described that had been achieved by the end of period 10. In particular, the base of the main peat has now become almost horizontal.

These simulated effects are not unrealistic in form and magnitude. The ground surface in Streif's (1971) Krummhörn profile (Fig. 6) tends to mimic the concealed basement and has a relief of about 1 m. Dengie Marsh (Fig. 10), in the approaches to the Thames Estuary, has a markedly concave-up surface between the seabank and rising dryland (Wilkinson & Murphy 1995). The surfaces of the two parts of the Gwent Levels on the Severn Estuary (Rippon 1996) are both concave up, although the pattern of the Wentlooge Level, with a relief in excess of 2 m is only partly preserved because of massive coastal erosion and deep set-back occurring very late after the initial Roman embanking (Allen 1997).

Autocompaction is likely to have more subtle effects in actively accreting high intertidal areas, as a consideration of Eqn (1) suggested. Suppose that an area has achieved a dynamically stable state ($\Delta E = 0$) under the influence of a uniform, steady rate of sea-level rise ΔM. Let there be a difference in the value of ΔP between two points some distance apart on the surface, perhaps because the sequence of sediments is thicker beneath the one station than the other, or there is a difference in the compressibility of the beds between the two points. Eqn (1) then demands that the total deposition rate is the greater at the point where ΔP is the larger. If there is no difference between the points in the contribution ΔS_{org} from plant material, the surface at the point of greater ΔP will necessarily be the lower relative to the tidal frame, in view of the strongly non-linear, inverse relationship between ΔS_{min} and relative height (Allen 1990). Hence, lateral facies variations in the prior sediment sequence,

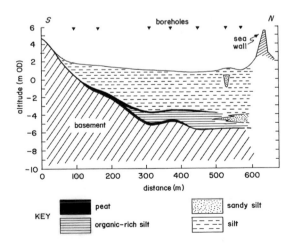

Fig. 10. Observed 'dip' section in Holocene sediments underlying part of Dengie Marsh, Bradwell-on-Sea, Essex, Southeast England. After Wilkinson & Murphy (1995 fig. 22).

together with basement features and buried channel-fills, can through autocompaction influence the co-evolving surface topography and environmental pattern at any given time, and so help shape the availability of natural resources and the way in which these can be exploited. Attempts to characterize such landscapes through environmental studies using, for example, foraminiferal or diatom assemblages do not lead to topographical accuracy. Firstly, because of scale and geographical boundary effects, tidal planes generally deviate significantly from the horizontal, even along open coasts. Secondly, the assemblages merely reveal the position of the sedimentary surface relative to the *local* tidal frame, which is generally undefined quantitatively.

It is also evident from Eqn (1) that if circumstances create a sufficiently large value of ΔS_{org}, the sedimentary surface, even when $\Delta M > 0$, can 'escape' upward from within the tidal frame into the supratidal (terrestrial) zone. Freshwater peats and, especially, patterned, domal raised bogs (Godwin 1981; Hobbs 1986; Clymo 1987, 1991; Winston 1994) may well result. In Zeeland (Vos & van Heeringen 1997) and the Severn Estuary Levels (Bell & Neumann 1997), as well as in coastal lowlands elsewhere in NW Europe, a strong association between human activity and the tops of thick peat beds, especially where there is some diachroneity, is clearly evident. In the Severn Estuary Levels there is a clear link with places where raised bogs had been developed.

Vos & van Heeringen (1997) tabulate data showing that the top of the 'main' Holland peat – a mildly diachronous lithostratigraphic unit found throughout the region – is very variable in present altitude (Fig. 11) on account of the stratigraphic displacement and distortion simulated above (e.g. Fig. 5a). Not only do bed tops of about the same date range widely in height, but the youngest tops now overlap in altitude with some of the oldest. Human activity/occupation sites of a number of periods are associated with the upper surface of this peat, and occasional sites are found in the context of salt-marsh silts. The peat-related Iron Age site is interpreted as a permanent settlement. Two peat-related sites of the Roman period are also considered to be permanent settlements and at three others some kind of industrial activity occurred. It would appear from Fig. 11 that the sites were established shortly after or perhaps even while the last peat was forming in each locality. No embankment would have been necessary to protect these sites from marine inundation if the peat top had been supratidal. However, once peat formation ceased and the

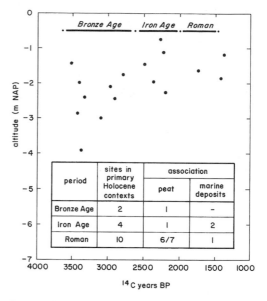

Fig. 11. The age and present altitude of the top of the 'main' Holland peat in Zeeland, southwestern Netherlands, together with the numbers by archaeological period of activity/occupation sites in primary Holocene contexts associated with the peat top. Data of Vos & van Heeringen (1997).

superficial part of the deposit began to dry out, autocompaction would have begun to lower the surface, eventually forcing either site abandonment or the engineering of a protective bank in the face of the increasing inundation.

The behaviour of the thick 'main' peat and the archaeological sites associated with its top in the Welsh portion of the Severn Estuary Levels (Allen 1996b; Bell & Neumann 1997) demonstrates particularly well the important role of autocompaction (Fig. 12). In this case the effects are severe, for the later Iron Age buildings were erected on a peat top that is now 2–3 m lower in altitude than the peat top that had supported the preceding activities of the later Bronze Age. The extent to which the configuration of the basement in the area may contribute to this age-altitude inversion is not known, but it seems clear from the regional development of peat that the rapid compaction of the various beds of this lithology strongly influenced sequence development. A substantial development of raised-bog peat as well as other peat facies underlies the Iron Age buildings, which were used to house cattle, probably seasonally. It is tempting to see these structures when in use as situated on one or more of the last, relatively uncollapsed peat domes in the area, overlooking extensive but lower-lying, mineralogenic, tidal

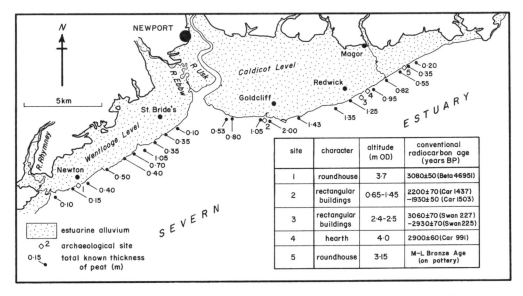

Fig. 12. The age and altitude of archaeological features and structures associated with the top of the 'main' peat exposed intertidally in the Gwent Levels (part of Severn Estuary Levels), SE Wales, together with the regional variation in the known total thickness of Holocene peat as exposed in intertidal sections. Archaeological data from Allen (1996*b*) and Bell & Neumann (1997).

marshes with creeks that provided rich spring-summer grazing and opportunities for wild-fowling and fishing, as well as other resources. The progressive collapse of the domes, combined with the rising sea level, would have led to their recorded increasing inundation, at first during storm surges (1–2 m above normal levels (Lennon 1963)), and eventual abandonment.

A final but more recent example of associated relief inversion and human activity comes from the extensive Holocene outcrop of Romney Marsh on the English Channel coast (Green 1968). At The Cheyne a late Holocene peat accumulated thickly up to about 900 years ago, to include a final substantial development of raised bog (Long *et al.* 1998; Waller *et al.* 1999). At about that time the locality, probably elevated slightly above its surroundings as a kind of island or dome, seems to have been enclosed within an encircling, engineered embankment remote from other land-claims in the area (Allen 1996*a*). Subsequent peat collapse has brought the enclosure to its present altitude of about 2 m OD, making the site today one of the lowest-lying places in the whole of Romney Marsh.

Conclusions

Autocompaction is a continous, progressive, irreversible and asymptotic process affecting the co-evolution of Holocene coastal sequences and landscapes at every stage of development.

The process can be roughly predicted/retrodicted for exploratory purposes using a simple formula and generic/site specific empirical coefficients.

Autocompaction affects instantaneous surface sedimentation rates, even under conditions of stable dynamic equilibrium, increasing them often considerably above the rates at which accommodation space is provided by sea-level rise.

Even though Holocene coastal sequences in NW Europe are typically no more than 10–20 m thick, autocompaction significantly displaces and distorts beds in their vertical sequence, especially where the pre-Holocene basement is uneven or there are concealed, effectively incompressible channel/barrier deposits. Vertical displacements of up to a few metres are both predicted and observed. Sea level curves based on intercalated peats, and related estimates of rates of sea-level rise, are unreliable when not corrected for autocompaction.

Autocompaction has influenced, and continues to influence, the human exploitation of coastal wetlands. The most instructive interpretations of past activity in these zones and guides to future behaviour will result from the combination of environmental analyses with models of surface behaviour, topography and relief based on an understanding of sequence autocompaction.

References

ALLEN, J. R. L. 1990. Salt-marsh growth and stratification: a numerical model with special reference to the Severn Estuary, southwest Britain. *Marine Geology*, **95**, 77–96.

——1995. Salt-marsh growth and fluctuating sea level: implications of a simulation model for Flandrian coastal stratigraphy and peat-based sea-level curves. *Sedimentary Geology*, **100**, 21–45.

——1996a. The sequence of early land-claims on the Walland and Romney Marshes, southern Britain: a preliminary hypothesis and some implications. *Proceedings of the Geologists' Association*, **107**, 271–280.

——1996b. Three final Bronze Age occupations at Rumney Great Wharf on the Wentlodge Level, Gwent. *Studia Celtica*, **30**, 1–16.

——1997. The seabank on the Wentlooge Level: date of set-back from documentary and pottery evidence. *Archaeology in the Severn Estuary*, **7**, 67–84.

——1998. The geoarchaeology of land-claim in coastal wetlands: a sketch from Britain and the northwest European Atlantic and North Sea coasts. *Archaeological Journal*, **154**, 1–54.

AUDET, D. M. 1995. Mathematical modelling of gravitational compaction and clay dehydration in thick sediment layers. *Geophysical Journal International*, **122**, 283–298.

BAETEMAN, C. 1991. Chronology of coastal plain development during the Holocene in west Belgium. *Quaternaire*, **2**, 116–125.

BELKNAP, D. F. & KRAFT, J. C. 1977. Holocene relative sea level and coastal stratigraphic units on the north flank of the Baltimore Canyon trough geosyncline. *Journal of Sedimentary Petrology*, **47**, 610–629.

BELL, M. 1995. Field survey and excavation at Goldcliff, Gwent 1994. *Archaeology in the Severn Estuary*, **6**, 115–144, 157–165.

—— & NEUMANN, H. 1997. Prehistoric intertidal archaeology and environments in the Severn Estuary, Wales. *World Archaeology*, **29**, 95–113.

BLOOM, A. L. 1964. Peat accumulation and compaction in a Connecticut salt marsh. *Journal of Sedimentary Petrology*, **34**, 599–603.

BOESCH, D. F., LEVIN, D., NUMMEDAL, D. & BOWLES, K. 1983. *Subsidence in Coastal Louisiana: Causes, Rates and Effects on Wetlands*. U.S. Fish and Wildlife Service, Divisional Biological Service Report No. FWS/OBS-83/26, Washington, DC.

CAHOON, D. R., REED, D. J. & DAY, J. W. 1995. Estimating shallow subsidence in microtidal salt marshes of the southeastern United States: Kaye and Barghoorn revisited. *Marine Geology*, **128**, 1–9.

CALLAWAY, J. C., NYMAN, J. A. & DeLAUNE, R. D. 1996. Sediment accretion in coastal wetlands: a review and simulation model of processes. *Current Topics in Wetland Biogeochemistry*, **2**, 2–23.

CLYMO, R. S. 1987. The ecology of peatlands. *Science Progress*, **71**, 593–614.

——1991. Peat growth. *In*: SHANE, L. C. K. & CUSHING, E. J. (eds) *Quaternary Landscapes*. University of Minnesota Press, Minneapolis, 76–112.

DELAUNE, R. D., BAUMANN, R. H. & GOSSELINK, J. G. 1983. Relationship among vertical accretion, coastal submergence, and erosion in a Louisiana Gulf Coast marsh. *Journal of Sedimentary Petrology*, **53**, 147–157.

DEVOY, R. J. N. 1979. Flandrian sea level changes and vegetational history of the lower Thames Estuary. *Philosophical Transactions of the Royal Society*, **B285**, 355–407.

——1982. Analysis of the geological evidence for sea level movements in South East England. *Proceedings of the Geologists' Association*, **93**, 65–90.

FRENCH, J. R. 1993. Numerical simulation of vertical marsh growth and adjustment to accelerated sea-level rise, North Norfolk, U.K. *Earth Surface Processes and Landforms*, **18**, 63–81.

GEHRELS, W. R. 1999. Middle and Late Holocene sea-level changes in eastern Maine reconstructed from foraminiferal saltmarsh stratigraphy and AMS ^{14}C dates on basal peat. *Quaternary Research*, **52**, 350–359.

GODWIN, H. 1981. *The Archives of the Peat Bogs*. Cambridge University Press, Cambridge.

GIBSON, R. E., ENGLAND, G. L. & HUSSEY, M. J. L. 1967. The theory of one- dimensional consolidation of saturated clays. *Géotechnique*, **17**, 261–273.

——, SCHIFFMAN, R. L. & CARGILL, K. W. 1981. The theory of one-dimensional consolidation of saturated clays. II. Finite nonlinear consolidation of thick homogeneous clays. *Canadian Geotechnical Journal*, **18**, 280–293.

GORNITZ, V. 1995. Sea-level rise: a review of recent past and near-future trends. *Earth Surface Processes and Landforms*, **20**, 7–20.

GREEN, R. D. 1968. *Soils of Romney Marsh*. Soil Survey of Great Britain, Harpenden.

HASLETT, S. K., DAVIES, P., CURR, R. F., DAVIES, C. F. C., KENNINGTON, K., KING, C. P. & MARGETTS, A. J. 1998. Evaluating relative sea-level change in the Somerset Levels, southwest Britain. *The Holocene*, **8**, 197–207.

HAWKINS, A. B., LARNACH, W. J., LLOYD, I. M. & NASH, D. F. T. 1989. Selecting the location, and the initial investigation of the SERC soft clay test bed site. *Quarterly Journal of Engineering Gelogy*, **22**, 281–317.

HOBBS, N. B. 1986. Mire morphology and the properties and behaviour of some British and foreign peats. *Quarterly Journal of Engineering Geology*, **19**, 7–80.

HUTCHINSON, J. N. 1980. The record of peat wastage in the East Anglian Fenlands at Holme Post, 1848–1978, A.D. *Journal of Ecology*, **68**, 229–249.

KAYE, C. A. & BARGHOORN, E. S. 1964, Late Quaternary sea-level change and crustal rise at Bostom, Masachusetts, with notes on the autocompaction of peat. *Geological Society of America Bulletin*, **75**, 63–80.

KIDSON, C. 1982. Sea-level change in the Holocene. *Quaternary Science Reviews*, **1**, 121–151.
——1986. Sea-level changes in the Holocene. *In*: VAN DE PLASSCHE, O. (ed.) *Sea Level Research: a Manual for the Collection and Evaluation of Data*. Geo Books, Norwich, 27–64.
—— & HEYWORTH, A. 1973. The Flandrian sea-level rise in the Bristol Channel. *Proceedings of the Ussher Society*, **2**, 565–584.
KNOTT, J. F., NUTTLE, W. K. & HEMOND, H. F. 1987. Hydrologic parameters of salt marsh peat. *Hydrological Processes*, **1**, 211–220.
KRONE, R. B. 1987. A method for simulating historic marsh elevations. *In*: KRAUS, N. C. (ed.) *Coastal Sediments '87*. American Society of Civil Engineers, New York, 316–323.
LAMBECK, K. 1995. Late Devensian and Holocene shorelines of the British Isles and North Sea from models of glacio-hydro- isostatic rebound. *Journal of the Geological Society, London*, **152**, 437–448.
LENNON, G. W. 1963. A frequency investigation of abnormally high tidal levels at certain west coast ports. *Proceedings of the Institution of Civil Engineers*, **25**, 451–484.
LONG, A. J., WALLER, M., HUGHES, P. & SPENCER, C. 1998. The Holocene depositional history of Romney Marsh proper. *In*: EDDISON, J., GARDINER, M. & LONG, A. (eds) *Romney Marsh. Environmental Change and Human Occupation in a Coastal Lowland*. Oxford University Committee for Archaeology, Oxford, 45–63.
MACFARLANE, I. C. 1969. Engineering characteristics of peat. *In*: MACFARLANE, I. C. (ed.) *Muskeg Engineering Handbook*, University of Toronto Press, Toronto, 78–126.
MORZADEC, M. T. 1974. Variations de la ligne de rivage armoricaine au Quaternaire. Analyse pollinique de dépôts organique littoraux. *Mémoires Societé Géologique Mineralogique Bretagne*, **7**, 1–208.
NIEWENHUIS, H. S. & SCHOKKING, F. 1997. Land subsidence in drained peat areas of the Province of Friesland, The Netherlands. *Quarterly Journal of Engineering Geology*, **30**, 37–48.
NYDICK, K. R., BIDWELL, A. B., THOMAS, E. & VAREKAMP, J. C. 1995. A sea- level rise curve from Guilford, Connecticut, U.S.A. *Marine Geology*, **124**, 137–159.
PATRICK, W. H. & DELAUNE, R. D. 1990. Subsidence, accretion and sea level rise in San Francisco Bay. *Limnology and Oceanography*, **35**, 1389–1395.
PAUL, M. A. & BARRAS, B. F. 1998. A geotechnical correction for post- depositional sediment compression: examples from the Forth Valley, Scotland. *Journal of Quaternary Science*, **13**, 171–176.
PENLAND, S., ROBERTS, H. H., BAILEY, A., KUESCHER, G. J., SUHAYDA, J. N., CONNOR, P. C. & RAMSEY, K. E. 1994. Gelogic framework, processes and rates of subsidence in the Missisippi River delta plain. *In*: ROBERTS, H. H. (ed.) *Critical Physical Processes of Wetland Loss*. United States Geological Survey Open File Report, Washington DC, 7.1.1–7.1.51.

PETHICK, J. S. 1981. Long-term accretion rates on tidal salt marshes. *Journal of Sedimentary Petrology*, **51**, 571–577.
PIRAZZOLI, P. A. 1996. *Sea level Changes: the Last 20,000 Years*. Wiley, Chichester.
—— & PLUET, J. 1991. *World Atlas of Holocene Sea-level Changes*. Elsevier, Amsterdam.
PIZZUTO, J. E. & SCHWENDT, A. E. 1997. Mathematical modeling of autocompaction of a Holocene transgressive valley-fill deposit, Wolfe Glade, Delaware. *Geology*, **25**, 57–60.
PYE, K., DICKSON, J. A. D., SCHIAVON, N., COLEMAN, M. L. & COX, M. 1990. Formation of siderite-Mg-calcite-iron sulphide concretions in intertidal marsh and mudflat sediments, Norfolk, England. *Sedimentology*, **37**, 325–343.
RAMSAY, J. G. & HUBER, M. L. 1983. *The Techniques of Modern Structural Geology. Volume I: Strain Analysis*. Academic Press, London.
RANDERSON, P. F. 1979. A simulation model of salt-marsh development and plant ecology. *In*: KNIGHTS, B. & PHILLIPS, A. J. (eds) *Estuarine and Coastal Land Reclamation and Water Storage*. Saxon House, Farnborough, 48–67.
RIPPON, S. J. 1996. *Gwent Levels: the Evolution of a Wetland Landscape*. Council for British Archaeology, York.
ROEP, T. B. & VAN REGTEREN ALTENA, J. F. 1988. Paleotidal levels in tidal sediments (3800–3635 BP); compaction, sea level rise and human occupation (3275–2620 BP) at Bovenkarspel, NW Netherlands. *In*: DE BOER, P. L., VAN GELDER, A. & NIO, S. D. (eds) *Tide-influenced Sedimentary Environments and Facies*. Reidel, Dordrecht, 215–231.
RYBCZYK, J. M., DAY, J. W., RISMOND, A., SCARTON, F. & ARE, D. 1996a. In integrated wetland elevation model for the Po Delta, Italy. *In*: *Impact of Climatic Change on Northwestern Mediterranean Deltas. Final Workshop. Vol. II – The Present and the Future*. Commissions of the European Community, Directorate-General XII, Science, Research and Development, Venice, 1.17–1.31.
——, IBAÑEZ, C., CURCO, A., CANICO, A., PRAT, N. & DAY, J. 1996b. An integrated wetland elevation model for the Ebre delta. *In*: *Impacts of Climatic Change on Northwestern Mediterranean Deltas. Final Workshop. Vol. II. – The Present and the Future*. Commissions of the European Community, Directorate-General XII, Science, Research and Development, Venice, 1.1–1.16.
——, CALLAWAY, J. & DAY, J. W. 1998. A relative elevation model (REM) for a subsiding coastal forested wetland receiving wastewater effluent. *Ecological Modelling*, **112**, 23–44.
SHAW, J. & CEMAN, J. 1999. Salt-marsh aggradation in response to late-Holocene sea-level rise at Amherst Point, Nova Scotia, Canada. *The Holocene*, **9**, 439–451.
SHENNAN, I. 1995. Sea-level and coastal evolution: Holocene analogues for future changes. *Coastal Zone Topics: Process, Ecology and Management*, **1**, 1–9.

SKEMPTON, A. W. 1970. The consolidation of clays by gravitational compaction. *Quarterly Journal of the Geological Society*, **125**, 373–411.

SMITH, M. V. 1985. The compressibility of sediments and its importance on Flandrian Fenland deposits. *Boreas*, **14**, 1–28.

STREIF, H. 1971. Stratigraphie und Fazies entwicklung im Küstengebiet van Woltzeten in Ostfriesland. *Beihefte Geologisches Jarhbuch*, **119**, 1–61.

TOOLEY, M. J. 1982. Sea-level changes in northern England. *Proceedings of the Geologists' Association*, **93**, 43–51.

VAN DE PLASSCHE, O. 1986. Introduction. *In*: VAN DE PLASSCHE, O. (ed.) *Sea Level Research: a Manual for the Collection and Evaluation of Data*. Geo Books, Norwich, 1–26.

——1991. Late Holocene sea-level fluctuations on the shore of Connecticut inferred from transgressive and regressive overlap boundaries in salt marsh deposits. *Journal of Coastal Research*, **11** (Special Issue), 159–180.

VOS, P. C. & VAN HEERINGEN, R. M. 1997. Holocene geology and occupation history of the Province of Zeeland. *Mededelingen Nederlands Instituut voor Toegepaste Geowetenschappen TNO*, **59**, 5–109.

VRANKEN, M., OENEMA, O. & MULDER, J. 1990. Effects of tide range alterations on salt marsh sediments in the eastern Scheldt, S.W. Netherlands. *In*: MCLUSKY, D. S., DE JONGE, V. N. & POMFRET, J. (eds) *North Sea-Estuaries Interactions*. Kluwer, Dordrecht, 13–20.

WALLER, M. P., LONG, A. J., LONG, D. & INNES, J. B. 1999. Patterns and processes in the development of coastal mire vegetation: multi-site investigations from Walland Marsh, southeast England. *Quaternary Science Reviews*, **18**, 1419–1444.

WILKINSON, T. J. & MURPHY, P. L. 1995. *The Archaeology of the Essex Coast. Volume I: the Hullbridge Survey*. Essex County Council, Chelmsford.

WINSTON, R. B. 1994. Models of the geomorphology, hydrology and development of domed peat bodies. *Geological Society of America Bulletin*, **106**, 1594–1604.

Stratigraphic architecture, relative sea-level, and models of estuary development in southern England: new data from Southampton Water

A. J. LONG[1], R. G. SCAIFE[2] & R. J. EDWARDS[1]*

[1] *Environmental Research Centre, Department of Geography, University of Durham, South Road, Durham DH1 3LE, UK*
[2] *Department of Geography, University of Southampton, Highfield, Southampton SO17 1BJ, UK*
* Present address: Faculteit der Aardwetenschappen, Vrije Universiteit, De Boelelaan 1085, 1081 HV Amsterdam, Netherlands*

Abstract: This paper presents the results of an investigation into the Holocene depositional history of Southampton Water, southern England. A three phase history of estuary development is proposed. Between *c.* 7500 and 5000 BP (8200 to 5700 cal. a BP), mean sea-level rose rapidly from *c.* −9 m to −4 m OD. During this interval thin basal peats which developed in present outer estuary locations were inundated and the area of intertidal and subtidal environments within the estuary expanded. Relative sea-level (RSL) rise began to slow between 5000 and 3000 BP (5700 and 3200 cal. a BP) and a phase of saltmarsh and freshwater peat accumulation occurred. In this interval freshwater peat-forming communities extended outwards and seawards across former saltmarsh and mudflat environments and caused a reduction in the extent of the intertidal area within the estuary. During the late Holocene there was a switch to renewed minerogenic sedimentation as most of the freshwater coastal wetlands of Southampton Water were inundated. This tripartite model is broadly applicable to the Thames and the Severn estuaries, suggesting that regional processes have controlled their macroscale evolution. RSL change and variations in sediment supply emerge as key controls during the first two phases of estuary development. The late Holocene demise of the estuary wetlands probably reflects a propensity for increased sediment reworking and unfavourable conditions for the accumulation and preservation of organogenic deposits due to reduced rates of long-term RSL and watertable rise.

Estuaries are traditionally viewed as strong-holds for Holocene relative sea-level (RSL) research, occupying a pivotal position between terrestrial and oceanic sediment stores and processes and often containing a rich record of human activity from the prehistoric to the present. Despite their obvious attractions to coastal scientists, most previous studies in the UK have tended to be estuary specific and, whilst offering explanations for some aspects of the stratigraphic sequences recorded, tend not to develop more general models applicable beyond the confines of a single estuary. This situation contrasts with that in the USA, Canada, and Australia, where models of estuary facies distribution and estuary development abound (e.g. Roy & Thom 1981; Woodroffe *et al.* 1985, 1993; Fletcher *et al.* 1990; Dalrymple *et al.* 1992; Dalrymple & Zaitlin 1994).

Facies distributions within estuaries reflect variations in the influence of tidal, wind/wave and fluvial processes, as well as sediment supply (Dalrymple *et al.* 1992). Two models for estuary development, common to literature from the USA, Canada and Australia, are termed here the 'transgressive' and 'highstand' models. The former model is often applied to wind/wave (micro or mesotidal) and tidal (macrotidal) systems which have experienced RSL rise throughout the Holocene, including many estuaries in eastern North America and Canada (e.g. Belknap & Kraft 1981; Frey & Howard 1986; Nichols *et al.* 1991; Boyd *et al.* 1992; Carter *et al.* 1992). In contrast, the 'highstand' model is common to estuaries that experienced a mid Holocene RSL maximum, such as those in North Australia (e.g. Woodroffe *et al.* 1993). Estuaries in southern England have experienced RSL rise throughout the Holocene which amounts to at least 30 m and, therefore, the highstand model is not considered further here. However, application of the 'transgressive' model to the estuaries

From: PYE, K. & ALLEN, J. R. L. (eds). *Coastal and Estuarine Environments: sedimentology, geomorphology and geoarchaeology*. Geological Society, London, Special Publications, **175**, 253–279. 0305-8719/00/$15.00 © The Geological Society of London 2000.

in southern England is valid, although other factors such as human impact on the estuaries (and associated changes in catchment sediment delivery, for example) will obviously differ between these and their North American and Canadian counterparts.

At its simplest, the 'transgressive' model involves the upward and landward translation

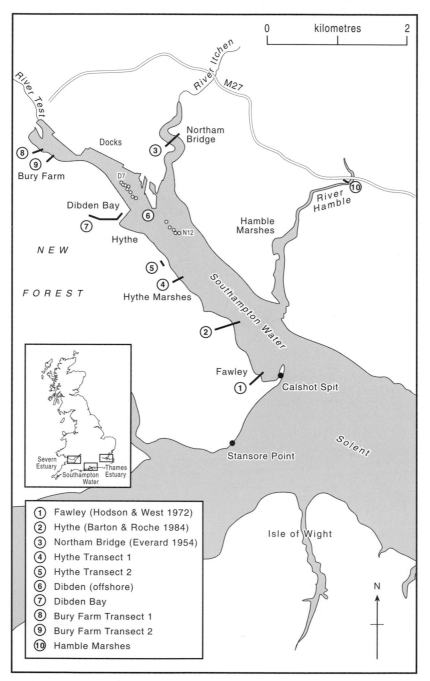

Fig. 1. Southampton Water location map, showing place names mentioned in the text as well as the position of stratigraphic transects.

of estuarine facies, driven by RSL rise. Vertical stacking of facies varies in detail between and within estuaries depending on sediment supply, the degree of erosion and sediment reworking, variations in the rate of RSL rise, as well as the range of depositional environments present in any system (e.g. Allen & Posamentier 1993; Fenster & FitzGerald 1996). For example, the energy characteristics (wind/wave and tidal) of a 'transgressive' estuary frequently vary as it widens under the early rapid phase of the transgression and subsequently infills. Hence, over Holocene timescales an estuary may switch from a tide to a wind/wave dominated system. A good example of this, and of transgressive estuary behaviour in general, is provided by the microtidal Delaware Bay estuary in Eastern North America (Fletcher et al. 1990). During the early stages of Holocene transgression, sedimentation here was dominated by tidal processes and the location of the turbidity maximum depocentre. As the Holocene transgression continued, so the estuary enlarged, the depocentre moved landward and an increase in wind/wave energy occurred. This switch from tide to wind/wave dominated processes led to the development of coarse-grained barrier-spit lithofacies, behind which accumulated mid and late Holocene salt and freshwater marshes (e.g. Fletcher 1993; Fletcher et al. 1990, 1993). Sediment for these barriers and marshes, and the landward transgressing estuary as a whole, is provided by erosional truncation and re-working of older Holocene sediments, as well as by planation of remnant highland areas in the estuary.

Aspects of this 'transgressive' model have been applied by Allen (1990) to the Severn Estuary, southern England, specifically in relation to its development during the late Holocene when minerogenic sedimentation persisted. Using sediment budget calculations, Allen (1990) has argued that the estuary is 'about full' with sediment and, under the upward trend in RSL of the last 2000 years or so, has migrated up-estuary by perhaps as much as 20 km via a process described as 'stratigraphical roll-over'. However, this 'transgressive' model cannot explain other characteristics of the Holocene depositional history of the Severn Estuary, most notably the alternating organic and minerogenic sediments which characterize the mid-Holocene depositional record in this estuary. The preferred explanation for these, and similar sequences observed in the Thames Estuary (Devoy 1979), is that they reflect oscillations in RSL (Allen 1995).

This paper presents new stratigraphic and RSL data from Southampton Water, a large but previously little studied estuary in southern England. These data are compared with previously published results from the Severn and the Thames Estuary in an effort to examine large scale patterns of estuary development. Of particular interest is the extent to which the 'transgressive' model of estuary development is applicable to Southampton Water and other estuaries in southern England. This paper is not concerned with detailed correlations between individual sites within or between each estuary, nor with the long-standing debate which surrounds the origin of the multiple intercalated peats that are a common element of the stratigraphic record of coastal lowlands in NW Europe. Whilst not down-playing the importance of these local variations, this paper adopts a more holistic perspective to address a different set of questions relating to the large scale development of the estuaries in southern England.

Southampton Water

Southampton Water is situated on the central English Channel coast in the shelter of the Isle of Wight, and drains the combined waters of the Hampshire Basin via the rivers Test, Itchen and Hamble (Fig. 1). Tidal conditions in Southampton Water, and the Solent as a whole, are complicated with a double peak on the flood tide and a double high water at spring tides. Present mean high water spring tides (MHWST) varies between 1.66 m OD and 1.86 m OD and the tidal range is 3 m. Southampton Water is a partially mixed estuary and the tidal prism of the estuary is 1.03×10^8 m^3 and 5.31×10^7 m^3 for spring and neap tides respectively (Westwood 1982). Salinity stratification occurs in the upper reaches of the Rivers Itchen, Test and Hamble, with mean surface salinities in Southampton Water being slightly less than 34‰ and falling below 30‰ in its upper reaches (Phillips 1980). The seabed sediments in the main body of the estuary comprise silty clays, with slighter coarser deposits (sandy clay and sand) in the upstream portions of the Rivers Test, Itchen and Hamble. However, the majority of this fine-grained sediment is derived from marine sources and only limited terrigenous sediment enters Southampton Water (Dyer 1980). Although today much of the estuary is reclaimed for port facilities, industrial activities and marinas, unreclaimed saltmarshes still occur locally on the west side of Southampton Water and in the Hamble Estuary.

Systematic investigations of the Holocene deposits of Southampton Water are limited and much previous work has occurred as and when sections and boreholes have become available during the excavation and development of the estuary and docks (e.g. Shore & Elwes 1889; Hooley 1905; Shore 1905; Godwin & Godwin 1940; Oakley 1943; Everard 1954; Hodson & West 1972; Barton 1979). The only outer estuary site studied previously is at Fawley (Fig. 1), where excavations associated with the development of a power station in the 1960s revealed up to 21 m of Holocene sediments. One prominent peat bed exists between $c. -5$ m OD and 0 m OD (Fig. 2a) and two samples of inwashed peat and wood from a small channel at -7.63 m and -7.33 m OD are dated to 6366 ± 124 BP (7511–6997 cal. a BP) and 6318 ± 134 BP (7424–6887 cal. a BP) (Table 1). The main peat bed towards the top of the sequence is described as a *Betula-Phragmites* fen-wood peat and attains a maximum thickness of 3.55 m. Its lower and upper contact (at -4.19 m and -2.75 m OD) is dated to 3563 ± 96 BP (4080–3560 cal. a BP) and 3689 ± 120 BP (4407–3692 cal. a BP) respectively. The discordance between these dates suggests that one of them is suspect (Godwin & Switsur 1966).

Hythe Marshes form a significant expanse of saltmarsh on the south bank of the estuary (Fig. 1) and Hodson & West (1972) and Barton & Roche (1984) have described a series of organic and minerogenic sediments from borehole transects in the area. The stratigraphy presented by the latter authors shows a basal peat in the landward cores which, towards the main channel of the estuary, becomes intercalated within silts and clays. The intercalated peat lies at a similar elevation to the prominent peat at Fawley, between -3 m and 0 m OD (Fig. 2b). No radiocarbon dates are available from this site.

Previous investigations within the inner estuary relate almost exclusively to the construction of the docks on the north bank of Southampton Water. In most cases the stratigraphy comprises gravels overlain by a basal peat and then estuarine silts and clays which extend to the present surface. For example, Shore & Elwes (1889) describe 3 m to 4 m thick beds of peat at the Eastern Docks, which underlie about 4.5 m of estuarine sediment containing Roman pottery. Within the peat are abundant remains of *in situ* freshwater shell marl, typically in discrete pockets up to 6 m in diameter. Hooley (1905) also recorded a single bed of peat containing *Pinus* and *Quercus* macrofossils from the Electric Light Works on the south side of the estuary opposite the Docks. This deposit is overlain by sand-rich sediments and then mud which contains the remains of a small sheep of suggested Roman age. Further to the east, the first (and only) published pollen diagram from Southampton Water is based on an exposure of these peats at George V Graving Dock (Godwin & Godwin 1940). *Betula* and *Pinus* pollen occur in the basal layers of the peat (at $c. -6$ m OD), while higher up in the profile, pollen from these taxa are replaced with that from *Quercus*, *Corylus* type, *Tilia* and then *Alnus*. Godwin & Godwin (1940) suggest that the base of the peat began accumulation on the waterlogged floor of the river valley between $c. 9500$ BP (10 500 cal. a BP) and 9000 BP (10 000 cal. a BP), and that the end of peat formation occurred sometime after $c. 6000$ BP (6800 cal. a BP). Estuarine silts and clays overlie the peat at -1.3 m OD and extend to the surface. Lastly, Everard (1954) describes the lithostratigraphy of the River Itchen, an important tributary to Southampton Water. His stratigraphic data from Northam Bridge (Fig. 1) show a 1 m to 3 m thick peat bed overlying gravel which extends part or whole of the way across the valley between $c. -6$ m OD and 0 m OD (Fig. 2c).

Relative sea-level changes

Long & Tooley (1995) proposed a provisional RSL graph for the Solent using six radiocarbon dates collected from close to Stansore Point, 2 km west of Calshot Spit on the north shores of the Solent (Fig. 1). Their study suggested that mean sea-level (MSL) rose rapidly from $c. -10$ m OD at 7000 cal. a BP to -2.5 m OD by $c. 3000$ cal. a BP, after which the rate of rise fell. Data from the late Holocene are limited but indicate a rise in RSL since 2000 cal. a BP of $c. 1.5$ m.

Site selection

The sampling strategy in this study was designed to provide information from sites in the mid estuary (Hythe Marshes and Dibden Bay), the inner estuary (Bury Farm), and a tributary (Hamble Marshes) (Fig. 1). Data from these sites complement the work undertaken by Hodson & West (1972) from the outer estuary (Fawley), and that associated with the Dock construction, detailed above. Together with offshore borehole data from the centre of Southampton Water and the River Itchen (Everard 1954), these sites provide a good coverage of the estuary.

Techniques

Most stratigraphic data were collected using a hand-operated gouge auger. Sample cores for laboratory analysis were retrieved using a 'Russian'-type sampler with undisturbed sediment samples from Dibden Bay collected using a percussion drilling rig. All cores are levelled to the UK Ordnance Datum (OD = mean sea level, Newlyn).

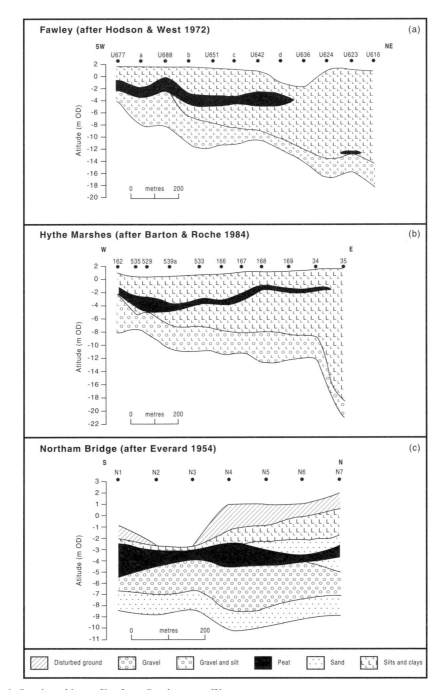

Fig. 2a–j. Stratigraphic profiles from Southampton Water.

Standard techniques were used for the extraction of sub-fossil pollen and spores from the sample cores (Moore *et al.* 1991). Samples were deflocculated using NaOH and then sieved (150 μm) to remove coarse organic and inor-ganic debris. Micromesh sieving (10 μm) was used on those samples containing significant quantities of clay and all samples required treatment with hydrofluoric acid (40% vol.). The concentrated pollen was stained using

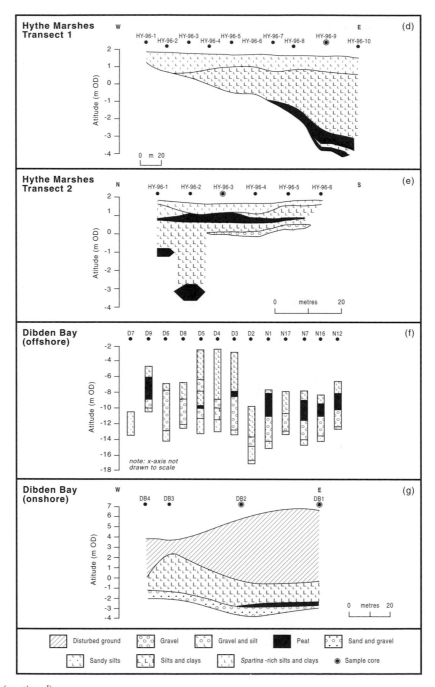

Fig. 2. (*continued*)

safranine and mounted in glycerol jelly for counting. Minimum pollen sums of 300 land pollen grains were made where possible and pollen frequencies are calculated as a percentage of total land pollen (%TLP), and for marsh and spores as a percentage of these categories respectively. Samples for foraminifera analysis were washed through 500 μm and 63 μm mesh sieves (Scott & Medioli 1980) and the residue stored in buffered formalin. This material was

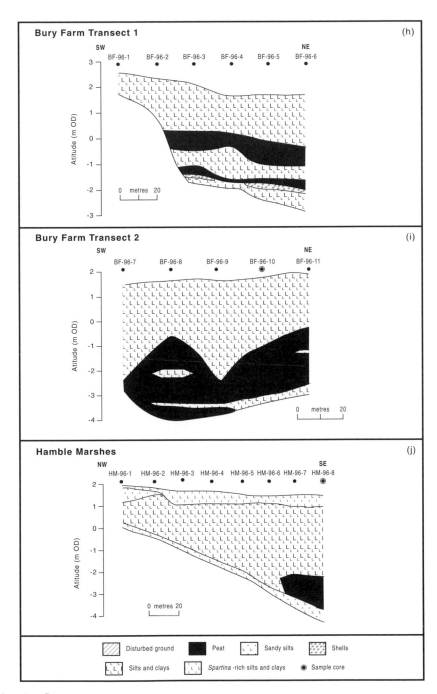

Fig. 2. (*continued*)

Table 1. *Radiocarbon dates from Southampton Water*

Site	Source	Grid reference	Age (^{14}C a BP ± 1σ)	Calibrated age (cal. a BP ± 2σ) max (mid) min	Lab. code	Altitude (m OD)	Tendency	Stratigraphic context	Sediment description
Fawley	1	SU 4740 0235	3689 ± 120	4407 (4040) 3692	Q831	−2.75	+ve	Transgressive contact	*Phragmites* peat
Fawley	1	SU 4740 0235	3563 ± 96	4124 (3840) 3624	Q832	−1.19	−ve	Regressive contact	*Betula* wood from *Betula-Phragmites* fen-wood peat
Fawley	1	SU 4740 0235	6366 ± 124	7511 (7230) 6997	Q834	−7.33	None	Towards base of channel	Silty *Phragmites* peat with fragments of charcoal
Fawley	1	SU 4740 0235	6318 ± 134	7424 (7210) 6887	Q835	−7.63	None	Base of channel	*Quercus* wood from sand overlying gravel
Stansore Point	2	SZ 4627 9872	5565 ± 130	6664 (6380) 6038	Hv.17322	−4.63 to −4.58	−ve	Regressive contact	Dark brown well-laminated herbaceous detritus in a matrix of humous material, with rare sand and gravel Dh2, Sh2, Ga$^+$, Gg(maj.)$^+$
Stansore Point	2	SZ 4627 9872	5600 ± 180	6841 (6360) 5952	Hv.17323	−4.17 to −4.13	+ve	Transgressive contact	Dark brown well-laminated herbaceous detritus in a matrix of humous material, with rare silt and sand Dh2, Sh2, Ga^{++}, Ag$^+$
Stansore Point	2	SZ 4627 9872	5320 ± 200	6490 (6100) 5648	Hv.17324	−3.77 to −3.74	−ve	Regressive contact	Brown, well-laminated humous material with herbaceous detritus Sh2, Dh2
Stansore Point	2	SZ 4627 9872	3570 ± 105	4143 (3840) 3583	Hv.17325	−1.55 to −1.50	+ve	Transgressive contact	Dark brown, well-humified and well-laminated monocotyledonous peat with humous material Th^{3}3, Sh1, Dl$^+$

Site	No.	Grid reference	Date ±	Calibrated date	Lab code	Altitude range (m OD)		Contact	Sediment description
Stansore Point	2	SZ 4627 9872	2350±110	2740 (2350) 2114	Hv.17326	−0.68 to −0.64	−ve	Regressive contact	Dark brown, well-humified, laminated monocotyledonous peat with humous material Th³3, Sh1
Stansore Point	2	SZ 4627 9872	2480±75	2753 (2640) 2343	Hv.17327	−0.56 to −0.52	+ve	Transgressive contact	Dark brown, well-humified, laminated monocotyledonous peat with humous material and rare detritus Th³3, Sh1, Dl⁺, Dh⁺
Hythe Marshes Transect 1	3	SU 4445 0601	5320±60	6278 (6100) 5935	Beta-93198	−3.15 to −3.10	−ve	Regressive contact	Dark brown woody humified *turfa.* Sh2, Dl1, Th²1
Hythe Marshes Transect 2	3	SU 4350 0670	1250±50	1284 (1171) 1059	Beta-93196	+0.82 to +0.87	+ve	Transgressive contact	Dark brown *turfa.* Th²3, Sh1
Hamble Marshes	3	SU 4955 1002	4410±70	5289 (4980) 4837	Beta-93197	−2.33 to −2.38	+ve	Transgressive contact	Brown woody humified peat with some clay and *turfa.* Abrupt upper contact. Sh2, Dl1, As1, Th²⁺
Dibden Bay	3	SU 4195 0860	5040±60	5919 (5830) 5648	Beta-106550	−2.66 to −2.64	+ve	Base of basal peat	Dark brown/black organic sand with some silt and gravel up to 15mm. Rare detrital wood. Ga2, Sh2, Ag⁺, Gg(maj)⁺, Dl⁺
Dibden Bay	3	SU 4195 0860	4650±70	5579 (5430) 5059	Beta-106551	−2.47 to −2.44	+ve	Transgressive contact	Dark brown/grey humified peat with rare silt clay lenses. Abrupt upper contact. Sh3, Ag1, As⁺
Bury Farm	3	SU 3820 1140	3080±60	3394 (3290) 3083	Beta-93195	−0.16 to −0.11	+ve	Transgressive contact	Dark brown humified peat with some *turfa.* Sh4, Th²⁺

Those dates from Fawley and Stansore Point are from Hodson and West (1972) and Long and Tooley (1995) respectively. All remaining dates are from this paper. Sediment descriptions according to Troels-Smith (1955) are given where available.

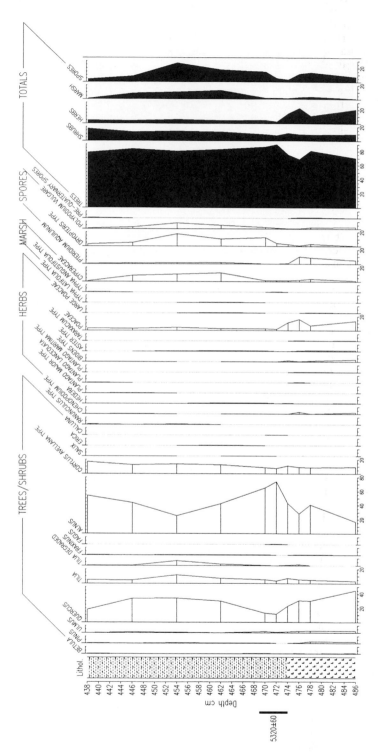

Fig. 3. Selected pollen diagram from Hythe Marshes Transect 1 HY-96-10. Pollen are expressed as a percentage of total land pollen, and for marsh and spores as a percentage of these categories respectively. Stratigraphic symbols are modified from Troels-Smith (1955).

divided into eighths using a wet-splitter and counted wet using a binocular microscope. Foraminifera counts are expressed as a percentage of total foraminifera tests.

Samples for conventional and AMS radiocarbon dating were analysed by Beta Analytic. All ages are quoted in calendar years before present (cal. a BP) with a two sigma age range (Table 1). All dates are calibrated using the intercept method and the bidecadal terrestrial dataset of Stuiver & Reimer (1993).

Results

The middle estuary

As part of the current study, a stratigraphic survey was undertaken c. 1 km NW of the Barton & Roche (1984) transect at Hythe. Transect 1 comprises 8 boreholes, each of which extended to an impenetrable deposit of either gravel or coarse sand and silt (Fig. 2d). A sample core was collected from HY-96-10 for pollen analysis and radiocarbon dating. A humified peat with some detrital herbaceous plant remains occurs where the subcrop of these impenetrable sediments is below c. −1 m OD. Interleaved within the base of this peat is a 0.20 m thick grey-brown organic silt with some woody *detritus*. Barton & Roche (1984) (Fig. 2b) also observe traces of silt clay within the equivalent peat in their transect. Low frequencies of saltmarsh pollen taxa occur within this organic silt in the sample core. These include *Chenopodium* type and *Aster* type (Fig. 3), suggesting that the sediments accumulated in a saltmarsh environment. A sharp rise in the frequency of *Alnus* pollen at 474 cm coincides with the stratigraphic transition to a brown woody peat. These changes, together with a rise in frequencies of Cyperaceae pollen and the increase in spore frequencies, indicate the replacement of saltmarsh by semi-terrestrial damp alder/oak woodland. A sample from the base of the peat is dated to 5320 ± 60 (Beta-93198, 6278–5935 cal. a BP) (Table 1). The upper contact of the peat is in all cases abrupt and shows signs of reworking with clasts of peat in the overlying minerogenic sediment, whilst in core HM-96-8, a 0.12 m thick unit of sand silt caps the peat. This upper contact was not sampled for analysis. Above c. 1 m OD, the stratigraphy consists of soft silt clays which, in the uppermost metre or so of sediment, are enriched with the remains of *Spartina anglica*.

To identify suitable material for radiocarbon dating in the uppermost sediments of the Hythe Marshes, a further stratigraphic investigation was completed in a narrow (70 m) infilled valley which enters Southampton Water approximately 300 m SW of the Hythe coast road (Fig. 1).

The stratigraphy here consists of a shallow (2–3 m) sequence of silts and clays, with a thin near-surface peat which in places overlies a coarse deposit of gravel and silt (Fig. 2e). Above this peat is an organic silt clay with *turfa* which extends to the marsh surface. The coarse deposit beneath the upper peat was penetrated in two cores and a deeper sequence of minerogenic and organic sediments encountered. Additional cores (not shown here) were completed at c. 20 m intervals across the width of the valley entrance, some 50 m seaward of a gravel ridge which separates the valley from the main expanse of saltmarsh. In all cases, an impenetrable deposit of gravel occurs at a depth of approximately 0.8–1.0 m below marsh surface.

A sample of the near surface peat and its overlying minerogenic sediments was collected from the location of HB-96-3 for laboratory analysis. High frequencies of Cyperaceae occur in the lower part of the peat, with lesser frequencies of saltmarsh pollen, notably *Chenopodium* type and *Plantago maritima*. This assemblage indicates a sedge reedswamp environment with a brackish water influence (Fig. 4). The organic content increases above 96 cm and accompanying this stratigraphic change is a rise in values of Poaceae pollen and a fall in those of Cyperaceae. Frequencies of aquatic pollen taxa also fall as drier conditions develop. The end of peat formation at 75 cm is sudden, with a sharp rise in pollen types indicative of saltmarsh conditions in the base of the overlying minerogenic sediment. The end of peat formation is dated to 1250 ± 50 BP (Beta-93196, 1284–1059 cal. a BP) (Table 1). Pollen data extend through the overlying mineral sediment to the present marsh surface. A rise in the curve of large Poaceae occurs above 45 cm, which we here attribute to *S. anglica* but which may also include the pollen of *Glyceria* spp. and *Elymus arenarius*. *S. anglica* was established on the Hythe Marshes at c. AD 1870 (Goodman *et al.* 1959), and the occurrence of *S. anglica* pollen dates these uppermost sediments with reasonable accuracy. From their maximum values at 30 cm, frequencies of *S. anglica* begin to gradually decline and are replaced by those of other saltmarsh pollen types (notably *Aster* type and *Chenopodium* type). These changes in pollen assemblage probably record the widely observed decline in *S. anglica* in Southampton Water and elsewhere in the Solent region from the 1950s onward (Goodman *et al.* 1959).

Dibden Bay is located on the south bank of Southampton Water, directly opposite the

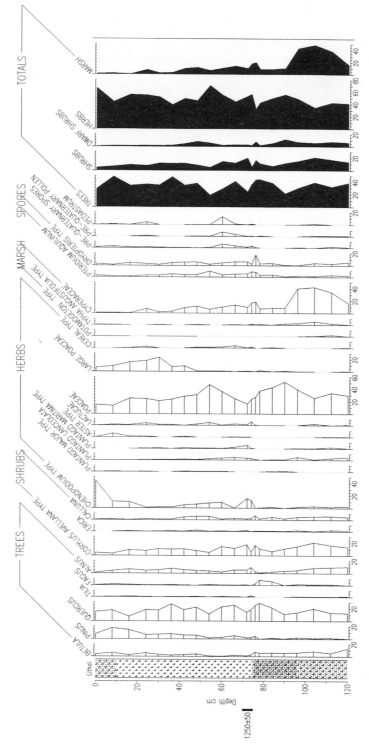

Fig. 4. Selected pollen diagram from Hythe Marshes Transect 2 HB-96-3. Pollen are expressed as a percentage of total land pollen, and for marsh and spores as a percentage of these categories respectively. Stratigraphic symbols are modified from Troels-Smith (1955).

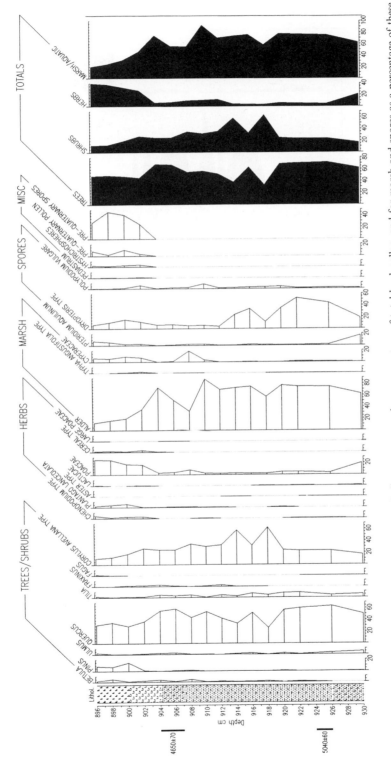

Fig. 5. Selected pollen diagram from Dibden Bay DB-1. Pollen are expressed as a percentage of total land pollen, and for marsh and spores as a percentage of these categories respectively. Stratigraphic symbols are modified from Troels-Smith (1955).

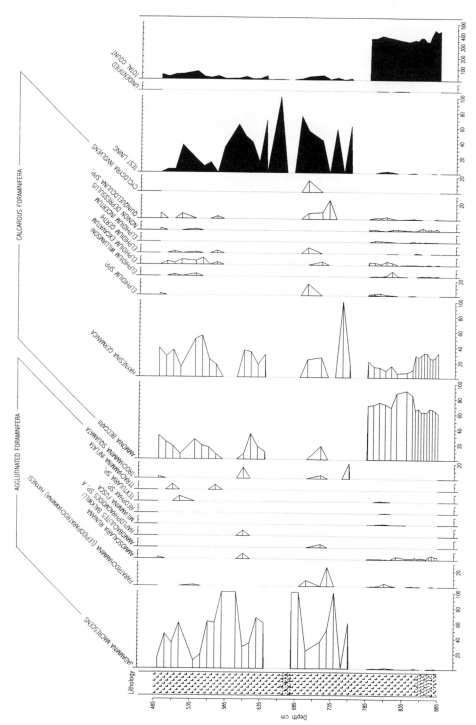

Fig. 6. Foraminiferal diagram from Dibden Bay DB-2. Foraminifera are expressed as a percentage of total foraminifera counted. Stratigraphic symbols are modified from Troels-Smith (1955).

confluence of the rivers Test and Itchen (Fig. 1). Formerly supporting saltmarsh and intertidal mudflats, the bay was reclaimed between AD 1930 and 1960. The offshore stratigraphy in this part of the estuary is shown by a 4 km transect of 14 cores which extends along the long-axis of the estuary (Fig. 2f). Pleistocene gravels overlie Eocene strata in the base of most cores. Overlying these gravels between c. −6 m and −12 m OD is a 1–2 m thick bed of peat, which is in turn overlain by silts and clays that extend to the sea bed surface. These upper sediments may have been truncated by recent dredging.

Four cores were recovered from the reclaimed saltmarsh of Dibden Bay (DB1 to DB4, Fig. 2g). A peat bed overlies sand and gravel in the base of two of these cores at c. −2.75 m OD. In borehole DB1, the peat comprises a humified sandy *turfa* with some woody *detritus*. This peat is abruptly overlain by a 0.04 m thick bed of whole and broken shells, including abundant specimens of *Mytilus*, *Cerastoderma* and *Hydrobia* spp. Above this shell-rich unit is a grey silt clay which extends to the present surface. Pollen in the basal peat in DB-1 are dominated by *Alnus*, indicating the on-site development of alder carr (Fig. 5). Lesser frequencies of *Quercus* and *Corylus avellana* type also occur, and the assemblage is very similar to that observed from the peat analysed at Hythe Transect 1 and the Hamble Marshes (see below). High frequencies of spores from *Dryopteris* type in the base of the peat suggest accumulation under relatively dry conditions. In the central part of the diagram, small fluctuations in frequencies of *Hedera*, *Plantago lanceolata* and Cyperaceae may record temporary opening of the forest. The base of the peat at (−2.66) 2.66 m OD is dated to 5040 ± 60 BP (Beta-106550, 5919–5648 cal. a BP) (Table 1). An abrupt change in pollen stratigraphy occurs at 902 cm where frequencies of tree pollen fall and those of herbs (notably Poaceae) and marsh taxa rise. The rise in saltmarsh pollen values, notably *Chenopodium* type, as well as frequencies of *Pinus* and pre-Quaternary pollen and spores, confirm the intertidal origin (probably mudflat) of the overlying shell-rich minerogenic sediments. The upper contact of the peat at −2.44 m OD is dated to 4650 ± 70 BP (Beta-106551, 5579–5059 cal. a BP) (Table 1).

Samples of peat from both DB-1 and DB-2 contain no foraminifera. However, their frequencies increase immediately above the peat in both cores, as an assemblage dominated by the calcareous foraminifera *Ammonia beccarii* and *Haynesina germanica* becomes established with a lesser abundance of agglutinated foraminifera. This assemblage is similar to that recorded in the contemporary intertidal mudflats of the neighbouring Hamble Estuary (Alve & Murray 1994). The lack of a gradational change from the peat to the overlying minerogenic sediments suggests an abrupt rise in RSL or an erosional hiatus. In DB-2, the assemblage described above persists from 885–773 cm, before frequencies of foraminifera fall (Fig. 6). Those forminifera present above this level include a mixture of agglutinated and calcareous tests. This abrupt change in biostratigraphy is interpreted as the change from natural to artificial sediment associated with the reclamation of Dibden Bay.

The inner estuary

The largest remaining saltmarsh in the inner estuary occurs on the south bank of the estuary below Bury Farm (Fig. 1). The marsh edge here is currently eroding between 0.5 m and 1 m per annum probably as a result of the over-steepened gradient of the subtidal area, which is dredged to form a swinging ground for container vessels (Barton 1979). Two short borehole transects were completed at the site.

Transect 1 is located to the east of the marsh. Bedrock (commonly stiff silts and sands) was recorded in the base of each of the six cores between c. −2.8 m and 2 m OD (Fig. 2h). The stratigraphy is very varied, with alternating deposits of humified peat, organic clays and silts, as well as *turfa*. Two organic-rich units occur, each separated by organic clays and silts. The base of the lower of these units contains abundant deposits of turfaceous marl. Throughout the sediments are small lenses of coarser material, typically of sand and fine gravel. This material was probably washed onto the site following disturbance of the neighbouring slopes or from the estuary under storms. Due to the sediment inwashing and the overall complexity of the stratigraphy, a second transect of cores was completed c. 500 m SW of Transect 1.

Five boreholes in transect 2 located a single prominent peat bed above impenetrable sediments between c. −4 m and −0.5 m OD (Fig. 2i). Thin layers of organic-rich clays are common throughout the peat, which consists of a humified organic matrix with variable quantities of detrital wood as well as the roots and stems of herbaceous plants. A 0.1 m thick peat bed occurs within the overlying minerogenic sediments at a depth of c. 0.8 m below the present marsh surface. Two closely spaced sample cores were collected for pollen and foraminiferal analyses from the position of core BF-96-11, where there is minimal evidence of disturbance in the stratigraphy.

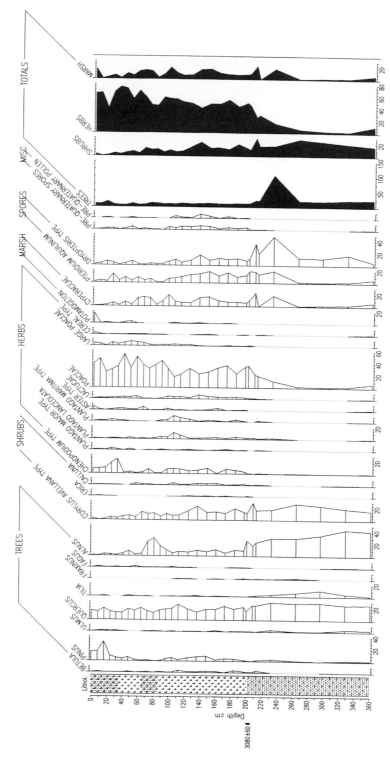

Fig. 7. Selected pollen diagram from Bury Farm BF-96-11. Pollen are expressed as a percentage of total land pollen, and for marsh and spores as a percentage of these categories respectively. Stratigraphic symbols are modified from Troels-Smith (1955).

Pollen from *Quercus*, *Alnus* and *Corylus avellana* type pollen grains are common in the upper levels of the deeper peat (Fig. 7) and suggest sediment accumulation under a relatively dry oak-alder woodland with hazel. Towards the top of the peat, above 225 cm, frequencies of Poaceae begin to rise, as do those of some salt-marsh types including *Chenopodium* type and *Plantago maritima* type. These changes probably reflect the approach of marine conditions to the site. The peat is overlain by silts and clays at 201 cm. Immediately above the transgressive contact in BF-96–11a, the foraminiferal assemblage (Fig. 8) is dominated by a combination of agglutinated (*Milliamina fusca*) and calcareous taxa (e.g. *Ammonia beccarii*, *Haynesina germanica*, *Nonion depressulus* and *Elphidium williamsoni*). Comparison with contemporary foraminiferal distributions at Bury Farm (Edwards 1998) suggests deposition in a low marsh or mudflat environment. The transgressive contact here is dated to 3080 ± 60 BP (Beta-93195, 3394–3083 cal. a BP) (Table 1). The abrupt change in foraminifera and pollen across the contact suggests either rapid inundation or some erosion.

Pollen in the upper silts and clays of core BF-96-11 are dominated by Poaceae, which rise to approximately 40% of the pollen count. Salt-marsh conditions at, or close to the site, are indicated by the increase in values of *Chenopodium* type, *Plantago maritima* type and *Aster* type pollen. A rise in *Alnus* pollen frequencies between *c.* 90 cm and 75 cm suggests a temporary expansion of coastal woodland near to the site and coincides with an increase in organic material in the sample core and a fall in frequencies of agglutinated foraminifera. Frequencies of *Pinus* pollen increase in the uppermost minerogenic sediments above *c.* 20 cm and probably relate to the expansion of coniferous

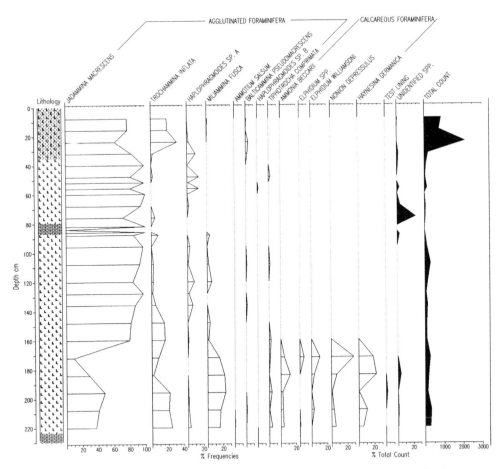

Fig. 8. Foraminiferal diagram from Bury Farm BF-96-11a. Stratigraphic symbols are modified from Troels-Smith (1955). Foraminifera are expressed as a percentage of total foraminifera counted.

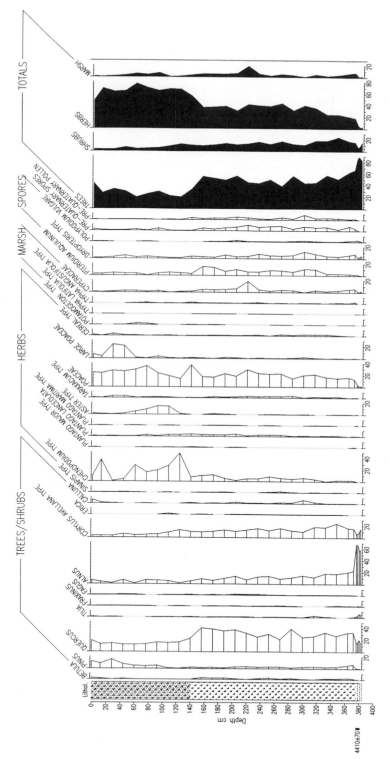

Fig. 9. Selected pollen diagram from Hamble Marshes HM-96-8. Pollen are expressed as a percentage of total land pollen, and for marsh and spores as a percentage of these categories respectively. Stratigraphic symbols are modified from Troels-Smith (1955).

plantations in the region during the 19th Century (Long *et al.* 1999).

The tributaries

Further stratigraphic data were collected from the Hamble Estuary, where a small marsh was sampled immediately downstream of the M27 crossing (Fig. 1). The stratigraphy at the sample site was described with eight boreholes, each of which extended to compacted minerogenic sediments of presumed pre-Holocene age (Fig. 2j). A single mineral-rich peat with some woody and herbaceous *detritus* occurs in the base of the most seaward cores below an altitude of *c.* −2 m OD (HM-96-7 and HM-96-8). The peat has an abrupt upper contact and is overlain by a thin (2–5 cm) lense of mixed and finely comminuted shells and sand which grades into clays and silts. These become progressively enriched with organic matter towards the present marsh surface. A sample core of the top peat contact and the overlying silts and clays was collected from the location of core HM-96-8 for analysis.

The peat is characterized by very high frequencies of *Alnus* pollen which indicate the on-site presence of alder carr (Fig. 9). Despite the close sampling interval there is little evidence immediately below the upper peat contact of impending site inundation, and the abrupt and irregular contact between the peat and the overlying shell-rich unit suggests that some erosion has occurred at this boundary. The radiocarbon date from the top of the peat (4410 ± 70 BP (Beta-93197, 5289–4837 cal. a BP)) provides a minimum age estimate for the date of site inundation.

Alnus pollen frequencies fall above the upper peat contact, whilst those of other tree pollen rise, such as *Quercus* and *Corylus avellana* type. These changes reflect the varying proportion of pollen reaching the site from local and regional sources, as the alder woodland was inundated and more open intertidal environments developed. Towards the top of the sequence, frequencies of *Chenopodium* type pollen increase sharply above 135 cm. This rise heralds the beginning of a phase of saltmarsh development at the site, indicated by the rise in values of first *Aster* type, and then, above 52 cm, large Poaceae. As at Hythe Marshes, the increase in frequencies of large Poaceae probably relates to the establishment of *S. anglica* which, in the Hamble Marshes, is dated to *c.* AD 1907 (Goodman *et al.* 1959). This most recent phase of saltmarsh development appears to have begun sometime before *c.* AD 1800, since it occurs 48 cm below the clear rise in frequencies of *Pinus* pollen which is seen at 100 cm.

Discussion

Holocene sea-level changes in Southampton Water

Nearly all of the radiocarbon dates from Southampton Water are problematic in one way or another. For example, most of the transgressive contacts are abrupt and show signs of erosion and, despite extensive sampling, only one gradational regressive contact was sampled and dated (from Hythe Transect 1). In some instances a hiatus may have occurred between site inundation and deposition of the overlying minerogenic sediments. Given these problems, each index point is plotted with a conservative y-axis range equal to ±0.5 m and an x-axis range equal to the calibrated two sigma age range of each radiocarbon date (Fig. 10). A more quantifiable estimate would be possible (e.g. Long *et al.* 1998), but this erosion, the as yet unquantified effects of sediment compaction, and the long-term focus of this study, render such analysis inappropriate here.

Holocene estuary development in Southampton Water and the Solent

Surface contours of the Pleistocene gravels (Dyer 1975) suggest that the early Holocene shoreline lay in the eastern Solent, beyond the outer limits of Southampton Water which, during the early Holocene, was entirely freshwater. However, as RSL rose, the Solent and then the outer portions of Southampton Water were flooded. Thin basal peats at *c.* −12 m OD occur at Calshot and Fawley which, although not dated, probably record the earliest inundation of the estuary at about 7500 BP (8200 cal. a BP). These may be remnants of a once more extensive deposit which was eroded by the early Holocene transgression. Elsewhere within the middle and inner portions of Southampton Water, thicker basal peats overlie Pleistocene gravels at between −12 m and −6 m OD (e.g. offshore at Dibden, Fig. 2f) and these indicate that freshwater conditions persisted in these areas, as well as in the adjoining tributaries, during the early Holocene (Godwin & Godwin 1940). There are presently no dates for the drowning of the peats recorded offshore in Southampton Water, but altitudinal comparison with deposits from the Isle of Wight suggest their inundation occurred at

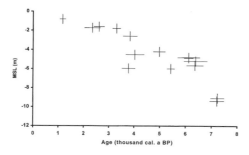

Fig. 10. Graph depicting changes in mean sea level using index points from Southampton Water. See Table 1 for sources and additional details.

or shortly after *c.* 7500 BP (8200 cal. a BP) and 7000 BP (7800 cal. a BP). For example, tree boles rooted at −12 m OD at the foot of Bouldnor Cliff, off the north shores of the Isle of Wight, are dated to 7440 ± 60 BP (8343–8016 cal. a BP) (Tomalin *et al.* in press).

Continued upwards and lateral expansion of intertidal and subtidal environments within Southampton Water was interrupted in the mid Holocene by an important episode of shoreline advance, which is registered by the widespread expansion of freshwater peats across areas of former intertidal saltmarsh and mudflat. This is seen most clearly in the stratigraphy at Fawley and Hythe (Figs 2a, b). A minimum age of peat inception at Fawley is *c.* 3600 BP (3900 cal. a BP) (Hodson & West 1972); in the more protected site at Hythe (Transect 1) the regressive contact to the peat is dated to *c.* 5500 BP (6300 cal. a BP) (Table 1). At both these sites, freshwater environments migrated over former saltmarsh and mudflat sediments for a horizontal distance of at least 800 m and was associated with a significant reduction in the extent of intertidal environments at this time. Outside of Southampton Water, a major period of freshwater peat accumulation also began at Stansore Point, dated here to 5320 ± 200 BP (6490–5648 cal. a BP) (Long & Tooley 1995), whilst in the smaller estuaries of the Isle of Wight a period of freshwater peat development and associated reduction in intertidal area commenced at Ranelagh Spit and Yarmouth at 4340 ± 60 BP (5045–4738 cal. a BP) and 5680 ± 100 BP (6726–6289 cal. a BP) respectively (Tomalin *et al.* in press).

This phase was followed by renewed expansion of saltmarsh and mudflat environments after *c.* 4500 BP (5200 cal. a BP). This phase saw the tidal inundation of basal freshwater peats within parts of the mid and inner estuary which had previously lain above MHWST. The timing of this transition appears diachronous (see also

Hodson & West 1972) and, although occurring over a height range of several metres, is not well dated due to the near-ubiquitous erosion of the upper peat contact. Maximum ages for the end of peat accumulation (Table 1) indicate that most freshwater peat-forming communities in Southampton Water were inundated by *c.* 3200 BP (3000 cal. a BP) and thereafter only localized peats developed. For example, the end of peat formation is dated in the Hamble, at Dibden Bay and at Bury Farm at 4410 ± 70 BP (5289–3211 cal. a BP), 4650 ± 70 BP (5579–5059 cal. a BP) and 3080 ± 60 BP (3394–3083 cal. a BP) respectively. Similar widespread inundation of coastal freshwater and saltmarsh peats is recorded throughout the Solent region during the late Holocene; indeed virtually all the significant coastal organic forming communities were submerged by *c.* 3000 BP (3200 cal. a BP). Thus, the main period of organic accumulation at Stansore Point ended at 3570 ± 105 (4143–3583 cal. a BP), whilst on the Isle of Wight coastal peats were inundated at Yarmouth (4730 ± 50 BP, 5589–5315 cal. a BP) and Ranelagh Spit (3120 ± 50 BP, 3457–3211 cal. a BP).

Models of estuary development in southern England

The data from Southampton Water suggest a tripartite model of Holocene estuary development characterized by an early and late Holocene phase of lateral and vertical expansion, separated by a significant phase of estuary contraction during the mid Holocene when the lateral extent of intertidal environments reduced significantly. In this section this three phase model is compared with data previously presented from the Severn and the Thames estuaries to determine whether similar sequences are also present in these estuaries. The implications of this analysis for the 'transgressive' model of estuary development are then considered.

Early Holocene estuary expansion in southern England

The early Holocene sediment sequences of the Thames and the Severn estuaries are superficially similar and show evidence of lateral and vertical estuary expansion driven by rising sea-level. During this period, elevated groundwater levels induced by this RSL rise resulted in the widespread formation of basal peat. For example, in the outer reaches of the lower Thames Estuary, these deposits (termed Tilbury I by Devoy (1979)) occur between −25.53 m and −13.23 m OD and

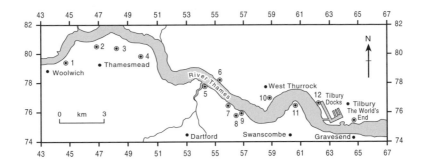

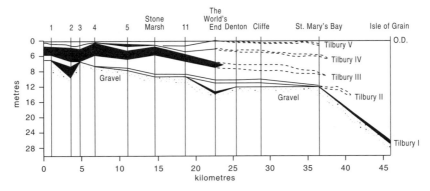

Fig. 11. The stratigraphy of the lower Thames Estuary (from Devoy 1979).

date from 8510 ± 110 BP (9818–9253 cal. a BP) to 7830 ± 110 BP (8981–8371 cal. a BP) (Fig. 11). Basal peats also occur in the Severn Estuary beneath the Gwent Levels (Allen 1987; Allen & Rae 1987), and in Bridgwater Bay where they are dated at $c. -20$ m OD to $c.$ 8400 BP (9400 cal. a BP) (Kidson & Heyworth 1973).

Basal peats in the current outer and mid parts of the Thames and the Severn estuaries are succeeded by thick deposits of estuarine sediments containing thin peat beds that accumulated during periods of typically 500 to 1000 radiocarbon years. One example of this is the Tilbury II deposit of the Thames Estuary where six radiocarbon dates indicate accumulation between $c.$ 7050 ± 100 BP (8054–7634 cal. a BP) and 6575 ± 90 BP (7549–7265 cal. a BP) (Devoy 1979).

Mid Holocene estuary contraction in southern England

A significant contraction in the area of intertidal (and perhaps subtidal) environments in the mid Holocene is demonstrated in both the Thames and the Severn estuaries by a major phase of peat accumulation which involved coastal advance over former mudflat deposits for distances of kilometres to tens of kilometres. As in Southampton Water, the physical impact of these changes must have been significant through a restriction of the intertidal area, concentrating flow of tidal waters and reducing the effects of wind and wave action due to a fall in fetch. In the Thames Estuary this contraction is registered by the accumulation of the peat deposit, Tilbury III, which overlies intertidal and subtidal sediments (Thames II) along a 20 km E–W transect between Gravesend and Woolwich (Devoy 1979) (Fig. 11). Boreholes extending across the estuary at Crossness indicate a reduction in the width of mudflat and sandflat environments here from a minimum of 4700 m to 670 m during this period. Radiocarbon ages date this episode to between 6200 ± 90 BP (7239–6864 cal. a BP) and 3850 ± 80 BP (4503–3988 cal. a BP) (Devoy 1979).

An equivalent event in the Severn Estuary is recorded on the Gwent Levels where a substantial peat bed can be traced outcropping in intertidal cliff sections for over 30 km (Allen

1987; Smith & Morgan 1989). Locally two or more peat beds occur but for the most part a single deposit is present (Locke 1971; Allen & Rae 1987; Smith & Morgan 1989; Scaife 1995; Walker & James 1993; Scaife & Long 1995; Walker *et al.* 1998). Radiocarbon analyses date this phase of sedimentation to between *c.* 6900 and 2500 BP (7700–2600 cal. a BP) (Smith & Morgan 1989; Walker *et al.* 1998). An expansion of freshwater peat-forming communities is also apparent in both the Somerset Levels and Bridgwater Bay where a widespread freshwater peat bed overlying estuarine silts and clays thins toward the coast and is finally divided by two or more brackish water minerogenic deposits (Kidson & Heyworth 1973, 1976). Radiocarbon determinations date the beginning of this phase in the Somerset Levels to between *c.* 5600 and 5400 BP (6400–6200 cal. a BP) (Beckett & Hibbert 1979), whilst Kidson & Heyworth (1976) suggest a date of *c.* 6000 BP (6800 cal. a BP) in Bridgwater Bay.

Late Holocene estuary expansion in southern England

The extensive areas of freshwater and saltmarsh communities present during the mid Holocene began to be inundated after about 4000 BP (4400 cal. a BP). In the Severn Estuary, Smith & Morgan (1989) propose that the peatlands were 'virtually obliterated' by a late Holocene marine transgression which is recorded on both the Gwent Levels and on the seaward side of the Somerset Levels. Radiocarbon dates from the Gwent Levels suggest an age of between *c.* 3100 and 2100 BP (3300–2100 cal. a BP) for this event (Smith & Morgan 1989), whilst in the Somerset Levels the return of intertidal sedimentation has recently been dated by Haslett *et al.* (1998) to 3250 ± 80 BP (3640–3330 cal. a BP). In the lower Thames Estuary, the end of TIII is dated to between 4195 ± 70 BP (4866–4459 cal. a BP) (Crossness) and 3850 ± 80 BP (4503–3988 cal. a BP) (Tilbury) (Devoy 1979). Further upstream, at Silvertown, a protracted phase of freshwater peat accumulation ended with the deposition of saltmarsh and mudflat sediments at approximately 2500 BP (2600 cal. a BP) (Wilkinson *et al.* 2000). The end of peat formation varies in timing, no doubt reflecting local factors such as differences in site elevation, estuary response time to external forcing by RSL, exposure, sediment supply and freshwater inputs, which individually or in combination moderated any regional process responsible for the inundation observed. Moreover, as in Southampton Water,

erosion of the upper peat contacts complicates the establishment of a reliable chronology during the late Holocene period and at present there are insufficient data to discriminate separate phases of inundation common to each estuary. Until more precise information is available the data simply indicate a general reduction in coastal wetlands which by *c.* 3000–2000 BP (3200–1900 cal. a BP) were almost absent from the three estuaries.

Minerogenic sedimentation dominated the late Holocene in each of the three estuaries until reclamation. In the Severn Estuary, the Upper Wentlooge Formation comprising estuarine silt clay with sand and gravel was accumulating (Allen 1987; Allen & Rae 1987). At least four oscillations in shoreline position during this period are attributed to changes in wind/wave climate rather than oscillations in RSL and no organic sediments are recorded (Allen 1987). In the Thames Estuary short-lived episodes of silt rich organic sedimentation (termed TIV and TV by Devoy (1979)) are present although the dominant sediment deposited is minerogenic. In Southampton Water, thin peats also accumulated in protected locations (e.g. at Hythe Marshes Transect 2), but minerogenic sedimentation was prevalent here and at many other sites in the Solent (Godwin & Godwin 1940; Devoy 1987; Nicholls & Webber 1987; Long & Tooley 1995; Long & Scaife in press; Long *et al.* 1999).

Models of estuary development

As noted above, the 'transgressive' model of estuary development has been used by Allen (1990) to explain the late Holocene changes in estuary sedimentation and morphology recorded in the Severn Estuary, when the predominantly minerogenic Upper Wentlooge Formation accumulated. Elements of the 'transgressive' model can also be applied to the longer term Holocene evolution of each of the three estuaries studied here. For example, the early Holocene phase of estuary development in all three was accompanied by the upward and landward migration of freshwater, saltmarsh and intertidal environments, as predicted by the 'transgressive' model. These processes are seen by the initiation and subsequent inundation of basal peats in the now lower reaches of each estuary. Subsequently, during the late Holocene, estuary infilling and a switch from tidal to wind/wave dominated processes is well documented in the Severn Estuary (Allen 1990). This switch in dominant process is similar to changes recorded in other 'transgressive' estuaries such as the

Delaware in North America (Fletcher *et al.* 1990). The stratigraphy of the inner Thames also records evidence for the late Holocene landward transgression of intertidal environments; Tyers (1988) interprets the presence of the peat Tilbury IV in Southwark and Lambeth as evidence for a 25 km upstream transgression of the tidal head between *c.* 3800 BP (4100 cal. a BP) (the end of TIII) and the onset of TIV, dated in central London to between *c.* 3000 and 2500 BP (3200–2600 cal. a BP).

Despite these observations, the 'transgressive' model fails to explain adequately the tripartite stratigraphic sequence proposed above (Fig. 12). Most significantly, the model is not compatible with the widespread lateral contraction of the intertidal area of these estuaries during the mid Holocene, a change in estuary morphology and sedimentation which, despite its diachroneity, must reflect the operation of regional and not local processes. The most likely cause of this contraction, which in some instances is associated with several oscillations in shoreline position, is that it records a significant reduction in the rate of RSL rise during the mid Holocene. Certainly the RSL curves from each of these estuaries show a pronounced inflexion during the mid Holocene (Devoy 1979; Heyworth & Kidson 1982), the exact timing of which varies slightly from estuary to estuary. Although the transgressive behaviour of these estuaries was severely curtailed for several thousand years during this interval, vertical accretion continued since the long-term trend in RSL during the mid Holocene was upward and the accumulating peat deposits attained thickness of several metres. The pattern observed is, therefore, of an upward but seaward migration of intertidal and subtidal depositional environments and sediments which is clearly contrary to the upward and landward pattern predicted by the 'transgressive' model.

The late Holocene inundation of coastal wetlands is a defining characteristic of each of the estuaries studied here. Similar changes from organic to minerogenic-dominated sedimentation are recorded in the back-barrier environments of southern England (Long & Innes 1995) and also in Belgium (Baeteman 1998) and Holland (Beets *et al.* 1992). Three hypotheses are proposed to explain this phenomenon:

(1) *An increase in the rate of RSL.* There is no clear evidence to indicate an increase in the rate of RSL rise at this time. The age-altitude data from the late Holocene (e.g. Fig. 10) are typified by considerable vertical scatter whilst interpretation of these data is complicated by the prevalence of eroded transgressive contacts, such as those described above from Southampton Water. Furthermore, there is no obvious way of accounting for an acceleration when set against the prevailing linear trend of crustal subsidence in southern Britain and the widely documented deterioration in northern Hemisphere climate from the mid-Holocene onwards (e.g. Dahl-Jensen *et al.* 1998).

(2) *A decrease in organic preservation.* It is possible that the absence of peats in the late Holocene sequences from southern England reflects poor conditions for organic

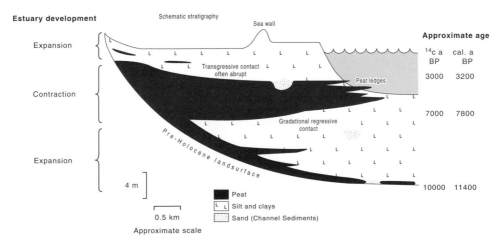

Fig. 12. A simplified stratigraphic section typical of the estuarine sequences recorded in southern England, showing sediments recorded, their ages and the three main phases of estuary evolution.

sediment preservation. For example, various authors (e.g. Allen 1995) have demonstrated that intercalated minerogenic and organogenic sequences can be generated and preserved under conditions of a steadily rising RSL upon which an oscillating component is superimposed. However, Holocene RSL rise in southern England reached its lowest rate during the last 3000 years. During this interval, sequences that formed in response to such secondary oscillations would have been susceptible to erosion and reworking, or to non-preservation due to enhanced aerobic conditions, since the tendency for sediment waterlogging, preservation and burial by RSL rise was much reduced.

(3) *A change in minerogenic sediment supply.* A reduction in sediment supply may also have been responsible for the end of peat formation (e.g. Beets *et al.* 1992) by promoting increased lateral erosion of mudflat and saltmarsh environments, ultimately leading to a loss of freshwater organogenic environments and deposits. However, this hypothesis fails to explain why minerogenic sediments, sometimes attaining several meters in thickness, dominate the late Holocene stratigraphy of the three estuaries studied here.

The opposite of the above, namely an increase in minerogenic sediment input, is widely documented during the late Holocene as a result of human activities within the catchments of each of the three estuaries. Recent research in the Tees Estuary (Plater *et al.* 2000) and the Humber (Long *et al.* 1998; Rees *et al.* 2000; Ridgway *et al.* 2000; Metcalfe *et al.* 2000) demonstrate the importance of terrigenous sediment influx from the Bronze Age onwards, whilst longer-term studies in the Sussex valleys also point to the importance of minerogenic sediment sources for coastal lowlands during earlier periods (Burrin & Scaife 1982; Scaife & Burrin 1992). Given this probable increase in sediment supply one might expect the late Holocene mudflats and saltmarshes to have accreted more rapidly creating, with time, conditions conducive to high marsh and freshwater peat formation. However, as noted above, the preservation of organic deposits requires an upward moving watertable to produce and maintain anaerobic conditions, something which the slow rate of late Holocene RSL rise would not have encouraged. So, whilst an increase in minerogenic sediment supply

due to human activity no doubt occurred, this was probably not, in itself, sufficient to promote an increase in the extent of freshwater peat-forming communities and organogenic saltmarshes.

Conclusions

In North America and Canada, large scale seismic and lithostratigraphic surveys employing the principles of sequence stratigraphy have been used to investigate general patterns of Holocene coastal evolution (e.g. Walker 1992; Dalrymple *et al.* 1992). The resulting models are, through their emphasis on the minerogenic component of the sedimentary sequences, poorly equipped to explain the coastal stratigraphic sequences observed in NW Europe where early and mid Holocene organic sediments are widespread. This scale of data collection and analysis contrasts much previous RSL research in the UK where detailed site and estuary specific studies have focussed on producing high resolution records of local RSL change. Where regional comparisons have been attempted, these have tended to focus on resolving the relative importance of isostatic and 'eustatic' processes (e.g. Shennan 1989). A consequence of this emphasis is that no coherent model has been proposed to explain the Holocene stratigraphic architecture of the three major estuaries in southern England. New data presented from sites in Southampton Water suggest a tripartite stratigraphic model which has many gross parallels with changes recorded in the Thames and the Severn Estuary, despite the obvious and significant differences in the physical attributes of these estuaries. These can be summarized as follows:

(1) Basal freshwater peats accumulated during the early Holocene in the now outer portions of these estuaries as RSL rose between c. 10 000–7000 BP (11400–7800 cal. a BP), only to be inundated by the continuing upwards trend. Once inundated, temporary fluctuations between freshwater, saltmarsh, mud and sandflat conditions occurred but poor age control means it is presently difficult to correlate these events between estuaries.

(2) A widespread reduction in the extent of intertidal mudflat environments followed which persisted from c. 7000–3000 BP (7800–3200 cal. a BP). This is well recorded in sites within the present mid and outer portions of these estuaries, whilst freshwater peat accumulation persisted during this period in the

inner parts of the systems. At the end of this phase the extent of intertidal minerogenic sedimentation increased once more.

(3) Much of the late Holocene (c. 3000 BP (3200 cal. a BP) to present) has been characterized by a predominance of minerogenic sedimentation in all three estuaries and by their continued vertical and landward expansion.

A simple 'transgressive' model of estuary development fails to explain the significant phase of freshwater peat formation which is a defining characteristic of the mid Holocene evolution of these estuaries. The scale of this change suggests the operation of a regional process, with the most likely contender being a slow-down in the rate of RSL rise. During this period all three estuaries examined continued to infill vertically but environments and associated sedimentary facies also migrated seaward, contrary to the preceeding trend observed in the early Holocene, and the subsequent minerogenic phase during the late Holocene. The preferred hypothesis to explain the deposition of minerogenic sediments during this final phase is an increase in minerogenic sediment supply caused by human activity, coupled with a deterioration in organic preservation potential due to a reduction in the rate of RSL rise.

We thank Dr D. Roberts for his assistance in the field. Parts of this work was supported by Associated British Ports Research and Consultancy Ltd (Southampton), and we appreciate the support and interest in this project provided by Dr I. Townend and Dr T. Wells, including granting us access to unpublished borehole logs from several sites within the estuary. Dr A. Plater and J. Sidell made helpful comments on a draft of this paper and we thank Professors J. Allen and K. Pye for their constructive suggestions. We also are grateful to the various landowners who allowed access to the sites described in this paper. Lastly, thanks to W. Scaife for assistance in preparing the pollen diagrams.

References

ALVE, E. & MURRAY, J. W. 1994. Ecology and taphonomy of benthic foraminifera in a temperate mesotidal inlet. *Journal of Foraminiferal Research*, **24**, 18–27

ALLEN, J. R. L. 1987. Late Flandrian shoreline oscillations in the Severn Estuary: the Rumney Formation at its typesite (Cardiff area). *Philosophical Transactions of the Royal Society of London*, **B315**, 157–184.

——1990. The Severn Estuary in southwest Britain: its retreat under marine transgression, and fine-sediment regime. *Sedimentary Geology*, **66**, 13–28.

——1995. Salt-marsh growth and fluctuating sea level: implications of a simulation model for Flandrian coastal stratigraphy and peat-based sea-level curves. *Sedimentary Geology*, **100**, 21–45.

—— & RAE, J. E. 1987. Late Flandrian shoreline oscillations in the Severn Estuary: a geomorphological and stratigraphical reconnaissance. *Philosophical Transactions of the Royal Society of London*, **B315**, 188–230.

ALLEN, G. P. & POSAMENTIER, H. W. 1993. Sequence stratigraphy and facies models of an incised valley fill – the Gionde Estuary, France. *Journal of Sedimentary Petrology*, **63**, 378–391.

BAETEMAN, C. 1998. Factors controlling the depositional history of estuarine infill during the Holocene. *In*: *Actas do 1° Simpósio Interdisciplinar de Processos Estuarinos*, Universidade do Algarve, Faro.

BARTON, M. E. 1979. Engineering geological aspects of dock and harbour engineering in Southampton Water. *Quarterly Journal of Engineering Geology*, **12**, 243–255.

—— & ROCHE, M. H. 1984. A geological appraisal of the foundation failure of the giant oil tanks at Fawley, Hampshire. *Quarterly Journal of Engineering Geology*, **17**, 307–318.

BECKETT, S. C. & HIBBERT, F. A. 1979. Vegetational changes and the influence of prehistoric man in the Somerset Levels. *New Phytologist*, **83**, 577–600.

BEETS, D. J., VAN DER VALK, L. & STIVE, M. J. F. 1992. Holocene evolution of the coast of Holland. *Marine Geology*, **103**, 423–443.

BELKNAP, D. F. & KRAFT, J. C. 1981. Preservation potential of transgressive coastal lithosomes on the, U.S. Atlantic shelf. *Marine Geology*, **42**, 429 442.

BOYD, R., DALRYMPLE, R. & ZAITLIN, B. A. 1992. Classification of clastic coastal depositional environments. *Sedimentary Geology*, 80, 139–150.

BURRIN, P. & SCAIFE, R. G. 1984. Aspects of Holocene valley sedimentation and floodplain development in southern England. *Proceedings of the Geologists' Association*, **95**, 81–86.

CARTER, R. W. G., ORFORD, J. D., JENNINGS, S., SHAW, J. & SMITH, J. P. 1992. Recent evolution of a paraglacial estuary under conditions of rapid sea-level rise: Chezzetcook Inlet, Nova Scotia. *Proceedings of the Geologists' Association*, **103**, 167–185.

DAHL-JENSEN, D., MOSEGAARD, K., GUNDESTRUP, N., CLOW, G. D., JOHNSEN, S. J., HANSEN, A. W. & BALLING, N. 1998. Past temperatures directly from the Greenland Ice Sheet. *Science*, **282**, 268–271.

DALRYMPLE, R. W. & ZAITLIN, B. A. 1994. High resolution sequence stratigraphy of a complex, incised valley succession, Cobequid Bay – Salmon River Estuary Bay of Fundy, Canada. *Sedimentology*, **41**, 1069–1091.

——, ZAITLIN, B. A. & BOYD, R. 1992. Estuarine facies models: conceptual basis and stratigraphic implications. *Journal of Sedimentary Petrology*, **62**, 1130–1146.

DEVOY, R. J. N. 1979. Flandrian sea level changes and vegetational history of the lower Thames estuary. *Philosophical Transactions of the Royal Society of London*, **B285**, 355–410.

——1987. The estuary of the Western Yar, Isle of Wight: sea-level changes in the Solent region. *In*: BARBER, K. E. (ed.) *Wessex and the Isle of Wight*, Quaternary Research Association Field Guide, Cambridge, 115–122.

DYER, K. R. 1975. The buried channels of the 'Solent River', southern England. *Proceedings of the Geologists' Association*, **86**, 239–245.

——1980. *Sedimentation and sediment transport*. NERC Publications, Series C, **22**, 20–24.

EDWARDS, R. J. 1998. *Late Holocene sea-level change and climate in Southern Britain*. PhD Thesis, University of Durham.

EVERARD, C. E. 1954. The Solent River: a geomorphological study. *Transactions of the Institute of British Geographers*, **20**, 41–58.

FENSTER, M. S. & FITZGERALD, D. M. 1996. Morphodynamics, stratigraphy, and sediment transport patterns in the Kenneber River estuary, Maine, USA. *Sedimentary Geology*, **107**, 99–120.

FLETCHER, C. H. 1993. Sea-level rise acceleration and the drowning of the Delaware Bay coast at 1.8Ka. *Geology*, **21**, 121–124.

——, KNEBEL, H. J.& KRAFT, J. C. 1990. Holocene evolution of an estuarine coast and tidal wetlands. *Geological Society of America Bulletin*, **102**, 283–297.

——, VAN PELT, J. E., BRUSH, G. S. & SHERMAN, J. 1993. Tidal wetland record of Holocene sea-level movements and climate history. *Palaeogeography, Palaeoclimatology, Palaeoecology*, **102**, 177–213.

FREY, R. W. & HOWARD, J. D. 1986. Mesotidal estuarine sequences: a perspective from the Georgia Bight. *Journal of Sedimentary Petrology*, **56**, 911–924.

GODWIN, H. & GODWIN, M. E. 1940. Submerged peat at Southampton; data for the study of Postglacial history. *New Phytologist*, **39**, 303–307.

—— & SWITSUR, V. R. 1966. Cambridge University natural radiocarbon measurements VIII. *Radiocarbon*, **8**, 390–400.

GOODMAN, P. J., BRAYBROOKS, E. M. & LAMBERT, J. M. 1959. Investigations into die-back of *Spartina townsendii* agg. I. The present status of *Spartina townsendii* in Britain. *Journal of Ecology*, **47**, 651–677.

HASLETT, S. K., DAVIES, P., CURR, R. H. F., DAVIES, C. F. C., KENNINGTON, K., KING, C. P. & MARGARETTS, A. J. 1998. Evaluating late-Holocene relative sea-level change in the Somerset Levels, southwest Britain. *The Holocene*, **8**, 197–207.

HEYWORTH, A. & KIDSON, C. 1982. Sea-level changes in southwest England and Wales. *Proceedings of the Geologists' Association*, **93**, 91–112.

HODSON, F. & WEST, I. M. 1972. Holocene deposits at Fawley, Hampshire and the development of Southampton Water. *Proceedings of the Geologists' Association*, **83**, 421–444.

HOOLEY, R. W. 1905. Excavations on the site of the Electric Light Works, Southampton, May 1903. *Proceedings of the Hampshire Field Club*, **5**, 47–52.

KIDSON, C. & HEYWORTH, A. 1973. The Flandrian sea-level rise in the Bristol Channel. *Proceedings of the Ussher Society*, **2**, 565–584.

—— & ——1976. The Quaternary deposits of the Somerset Levels. *Quarterly Journal of Engineering Geology*, **9**, 217–235.

LOCKE, S. 1971. The post glacial deposits of the Caldicot Level and some associated archaeological discoveries. *The Monmouthshire Antiquary*, **III**, 1–16.

LONG, A. J. & INNES, J. B. 1995. The back-barrier and barrier depositional history of Romney Marsh and Dungeness, Kent, UK. *Journal of Quaternary Science*, **10**, 267–283.

—— & TOOLEY, M. J. 1995. Holocene sea-level and crustal movements in Hampshire and Southeast England, United Kingdom. *Journal of Coastal Research Special Issue*, **17**, 299–310.

——, INNES, J. B., KIRBY, J. R., LLOYD, J. M., RUTHERFORD, M. M. SHENNAN, I. & TOOLEY, M. J. 1998. Holocene sea-level change and coastal evolution in the Humber Estuary, eastern England: an assessment of rapid coastal change. *The Holocene*, **8**, 229–247.

——, SCAIFE, R. G. & EDWARDS, R. G. 1999. Pine pollen in intertidal sediments from Poole Harbour, U.K.; implications for late-Holocene sediment accretion rates and sea-level rise. *Quaternary International*, **55**, 3–16.

—— & SCAIFE, R. G. In press. Solent sea-level record. *In*: TOMALINSON, D. SCAIFE, R. G. & LOADER, R. (eds) *The Wootton-Quarr Survey*, Isle of Wight County Council, Newport.

METCALFE, S. E. ELLIS, S., HORTON, B. P. *ET AL*. 2000. The Holocene evolution of the Humber Estuary: reconstructing change in a dynamic environment. *In*: SHENNAN, I. & ANDREWS, J. T. (eds) *Holocene land-ocean interaction and environmental change around the North Sea*. Geological Society, London, Special Publications, **166**, p.97–118.

MOORE, P. D., WEBB, J. A. & COLLINSON, M. E. 1991. *Pollen Analysis*. Blackwell, London.

NICHOLS, M. N., JOHNSON, G. H. & PEEBLES, P. A. 1991. Modern sediments and facies models for a microtidal coastal plain estuary, the James Estuary, Virginia. *Journal of Sedimentary Petrology*, **61**, 883–899.

NICHOLLS, R. J. & WEBBER, N. B. 1987. The past, present and future evolution of Hurst Castle Spit, Hampshire. *Progress in Oceanography*, **18**, 119–137.

OAKLEY, K. P. 1943. A note on the postglacial submergence of the Solent margin. *Proceedings of the Prehistoric Society New Series*, **9**, 56–59.

PHILLIPS, A. J. 1980. *Distribution of chemical species*. NERC Publications, Series C, **22**, 44–59.

PLATER, A. J., RIDGWAY, J., RAYNER, B., SHENNAN, I., HORTON, B. P., HAWORTH, M. R., WRIGHT, M. R., RUTHERFORD, M. M. & WINTLE, A. G. 2000. Sediment provenance and flux in the Tees Estuary: the record from the Late Devensian to the present. *In*: SHENNAN, I. & ANDREWS, J. (eds) *Holocene Land-Ocean Interaction and Environmental Change around the North Sea*. Geological Society, London, Special Publications, **166**, 171–195.

REES, J. G., RIDGWAY, J., KNOX, O'B., ELLIS, S., NEWSHAM, R. & PARKES, A. 2000. Holocene sediment storage in the Humber Estuary. *In*: SHENNAN, I. & ANDREWS, J. (eds) *Holocene Land-Ocean Interaction and Environmental Change around the North Sea*. Geological Society, London, Special Publications, **166**, 119–143.

RIDGWAY, J., ANDREWS, J. E., ELLIS, S. *ET AL*. 2000. Analysis and interpretation of Holocene sedimentary sequences in the Humber Estuary. *In*: SHENNAN, I. & ANDREWS, J. (eds) *Holocene Land-Ocean Interaction and Environmental Change around the North Sea*. Geological Society, London, Special Publications, **166**, 9–39.

ROY, P. S. & THOM, B. G. 1981. Coastal Quaternary deposits of New South Wales: a model for development in the Late Quaternary. *Journal of the Geological Society of Australia*, **28**, 471–489.

SCAIFE, R. G. 1995. Pollen analysis and radiocarbon dating of the intertidal peats at Caldicot Pill. *In*: BELL, M. (ed.) *Archaeology in the Severn estuary 1994*. Annual report of the Severn Estuary Levels Research Committee, 67–80.

—— & BURRIN, P. J. 1992. Archaeological inferences from alluvial sediments: some findings from southern England. *In*: NEEDHAM, S. & MACKLIN, M. G. (eds) *Alluvial archaeology in Britain*. Oxbow Monograph **27**, 75–91.

—— & LONG, A. J. 1995. Evidence for Holocene sea-level changes at Caldicot Pill, the Severn Estuary. *In*: BELL, M. (ed.) *Archaeology in the Severn estuary 1994*. Annual report of the Severn Estuary Levels Research Committee, 81–86.

SCOTT, D. B. & MEDIOLI, F. S. 1980. *Quantitative studies of marsh foraminiferal distributions in Nova Scotia; implications for sea level studies*. Cushman Foundation for Foraminiferal Research Special Publication, **17**.

SHENNAN, I. 1989. Holocene crustal movements and sea-level changes in Great Britain. *Journal of Quaternary Science*, **4**, 77–89.

SHORE, T. W. 1905. The origin of Southampton Water. *Proceedings of the Hampshire Field Club*, **5**, 1–25.

—— & ELWES, J. W. 1889. The New Dock excavations at Southampton. *Proceedings of the Hampshire Field Club*, **1**, 43–56.

SMITH, A. G. & MORGAN, L. A. 1989. A succession to ombrotrophic bog in the Gwent Levels, and its demise: a Welsh parallel to the peats of the Somerset Levels. *New Phytologist*, **112**, 145–167.

STUIVER, M. & REIMER, J. 1993. Extended ^{14}C data base and revised CALIB 3.0 ^{14}C age calibration program. *Radiocarbon*, **35**, 215–230.

TOMALIN, D. J., SCAIFE, R. G. & LOADER, R. (eds) 2000. *The Wootton-Quarr Survey*, Isle of Wight County Council, Newport.

TROELS-SMITH, J. 1955. Karakterisaring af Lose jordarter (Characterisation of Unconsolidated Sediments). *Danmarks Geologiske Undersogelse*, **IV/3**, 10, 73.

TYERS, I. 1988. The prehistoric peat layers (Tilbury IV). *In*: HINTON, P. (ed.) *Excavations in Southwark 1973–76 and Lambeth 1973–79*. Museum of London Department of Greater London Archaeology, 5–12.

WALKER, R. G. 1992. Facies, facies models and modern stratigraphic concepts. *In*: WALKER, R. G. & JAMES, N. P. (eds) *Facies models: response to sea level change*. Geological Association of Canada, Ontario, 1–14.

WALKER, M. J. C. & JAMES, J. H. 1993. A radiocarbon-dated pollen record from Vurlong Reen, South Wales. *In*: BELL, M. (ed.) *Archaeology in the Severn Estuary 1993*. Severn Estuary Levels Research Committee, Annual Report, Lampeter, 65–70.

——, BELL, M., CASELDINE, A. E., CAMERON, N. G., HUNTER, K. L., JAMES, J. H., JOHNSON, S. & SMITH, D. N. 1998. Palaeoecological investigations of middle and late Flandrian buried peats on the Caldicot Levels, Severn Estuary, Wales. *Proceedings of the Geologists' Association*, **109**, 51–78.

WESTWOOD, I. J. 1982. *Mixing and dispersion in Southampton Water*. PhD Thesis, Department of Civil Engineering, Southampton University.

WILKINSON, K. N., SCAIFE, R. G. & SIDELL, E. J. In press. Environmental and sea-level changes in London from 10 500 BP to the present: a case study from Silvertown. *Proceedings of the Geologists' Association*, **111**, 41–54.

WOODROFFE, C. D., THOM, B. G. & CHAPPELL, J. 1985. Development of widespread mangrove swamps in mid-Holocene times in northern Australia. *Nature*, **317**, 711–713.

——, MULRENNAN, M. E. & CHAPPELL, J. 1993. Estuarine infill and coastal progradation, southern van Diemen Gulf, northern Australia. *Sedimentary Geology*, **83**, 257–275.

Recent geological evolution and human impact: Fraser Delta, Canada

J. VAUGHN BARRIE

Geological Survey of Canada, Pacific Geoscience Centre, P.O. Box 6000, Sidney, British Columbia V8L 4B2 Canada (e-mail: barrie@pgc.nrcan.gc.ca)

Abstract: Throughout the Holocene, the river dominated Fraser Delta on the Pacific coast of Canada has prograded by continuous channel switching and avulsion into a deep (>300 m) basin. However, at the beginning of the 20th century the delta was modified to provide a navigable channel and port facilities for the city of Vancouver. Now most of the sand brought down by the river (35% of the sediment load) is removed from the system by dredging. The remaining fine-grained sediment is transported in a plume past the intertidal estuary within the distributary channels then deflected northwards by the dominant flood tidal flow into the basin. Two causeways to the south of the main channel and one to the north that cross the intertidal zone to the delta foreslope act as barriers to the dominant northward sediment transport causing estuarine and localized seabed erosion. An eroded distributary channel failure complex has been exposed on the delta foreslope, off the southern causeways, by flood tidal flows that scour the seabed and form northward migrating subaqueous dunes, further increasing the delta slope. This, combined with slow sea-level rise and seismicity, intensifies the risk of further erosion and instability of the delta, particularly along the subaqueous delta front and the intertidal estuaries.

Marine deltas develop from the interaction of natural processes such as the grain size of sediment delivered by the river (Orton & Reading 1993), local conditions, such as bathymetry and oceanographic conditions of the receiving basin, and human interference. Delta progradation typically prevails during construction phases when fluvial processes dominate at the mouth of a river, while destruction phases occur when marine coastal processes dominate (Stanley & Warne 1998). Deltas such as the Nile (Stanley & Warne 1993, 1998), Mississippi (Coleman et al. 1988) and Po (Cencini 1998) have passed from a constructive phase to destructive phase due to human interference over several hundred to thousands of years. The river dominated Fraser Delta on the Pacific coast of Canada (Fig. 1) has also been impacted by human interference in recent years such that it may be changing from a constructive phase to a destructive phase. Hart et al. (1998) suggest that approximately half of the modern marine delta is presently non-depositional, based on core lithofacies and ^{137}Cs fallout stratigraphy, and most of this area is erosional (Kostaschuk et al. 1995). Further, evidence suggests that the erosion and lack of deposition is a result of engineering development on the delta and dredging within the river (Barrie & Currie 2000).

The Fraser River has built its delta throughout the Holocene by continual, lateral channel migration across the subaqueous delta front (wave influenced portion of the delta) as each distributary channel aggraded with the deposition of the sediment load (Johnston 1921; Clague et al. 1983). Extensive distributary channel migration for the Fraser River is interpreted to be due to the interaction of tidal and fluvial processes and the high proportion of sand in the sediment load (Monahan et al. 1993). Similar channel switching is a well-known occurrence in deltaic settings and has been documented in the Nile Delta (Sestini 1989), Yellow River Delta (Xue 1993) and Ganges/Brahmaputra Delta (Coleman 1969). Channel migration and avulsion is more typical of sand-dominated distributary systems with erratic fluvial discharges such as the Fraser Delta (Hart 1995) and Mahakam Delta (Allen et al. 1979). Indeed Monahan et al. (1993) demonstrated that migration of the distributaries of the Fraser Delta has led to the generation of a nearly continuous sheet sand beneath the delta plain. Consequently, the topset of the delta is dominated by a diachronous and continuous massive sand facies. The upper foreset deposits can be broadly subdivided into inter-laminated sediment facies and sharp-based sands (Monahan 1999). The laminated sediments represent

From: PYE, K. & ALLEN, J. R. L. (eds). *Coastal and Estuarine Environments: sedimentology, geomorphology and geoarchaeology.* Geological Society, London, Special Publications, **175**, 281–292. 0305-8719/00/$15.00 © The Geological Society of London 2000.

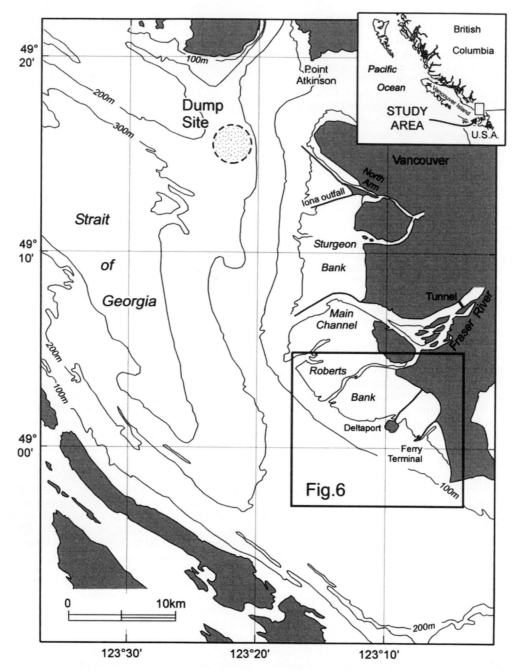

Fig. 1. The Fraser Delta, British Columbia, Canada.

suspension deposits derived from the plume, regulated by tidal and fluvial cycles, whereas the sharp-based sands represent sediment gravity flow deposits. These facies represent a continuum from finer to coarser sediments, from dominantly suspension to dominantly sediment gravity flow deposits, and reflect increasing proximity to active distributary mouths.

In the last 100 years the Fraser Delta has undergone development as a result of being adjacent to the fast growing city of Vancouver (1998 population 1.9 million). The city has grown out onto the dyked delta plain, an area that is bounded on the north by the Coast Mountains and on the south by the Cascade Mountains. The inevitable consequence is exploitation of the river, estuarine and nearshore areas for various purposes including navigation (jetties and break-waters), port facilities, sewage disposal, build-ing aggregates, dredge spoil dumping, fishing and the laying of submarine cables (electrical transmission, telecommunications). This paper examines recent delta evolution and the impact resulting from human development. The research approach used here, of undertaking a case study of the complex interactions between fluvial, oceanographic, morphologic and human factors and their affect on submarine sediment dynamics, has application to studies of other large deltas and subaqueous environments.

Geology and setting of the present delta

The Fraser River, with its source in the Rocky Mountains, is the largest river draining the Pacific margin of Canada (mean annual flow of $3.5 \times 10^3\,\mathrm{m}^3\,\mathrm{s}^{-1}$). It has produced a delta which is prograding into the Strait of Georgia, a semi-enclosed 300 m deep basin separating the British Columbia mainland from Vancouver Island (Fig. 1). The delta is a Holocene feature that developed after the end of the late-Wisconsin glaciation (Clague et al. 1983). The annual river load (approximately 17.3×10^6 tonnes) is 50% silt, 35% sand and 15% clay, transported pri-marily during the spring and summer freshet (Stewart & Tassone 1989). Of this about 80% of the sediment (and all of the sand) discharges through the main channel. The peak in sediment load precedes the peak in river flow by a month or more (Kostaschuk et al. 1989, 1992). Fine sand is transported in suspension with the mud fraction while coarser sand (transported as bedload) is deposited near the river mouth during freshet discharges and ebbing tides when the entire thickness of the water column in the channel is flowing seaward (Milliman 1980). At other times (including high tide during freshet) a salt wedge penetrates into the channel beneath the seaward flowing surface waters and bedload material is trapped in the estuary (Kostaschuk et al. 1989, 1992). The sand which reaches the river mouth is transported downslope in a submarine channel to the base of the slope reaching a zone of debris flow deposits and turbidites (Hart et al. 1992; Evoy et al. 1993).

The Strait of Georgia has mixed, semi-diurnal tides with a mean range of 2.6 m and maximum range of 5.4 m (Thomson 1981). Tides are recti-linear along the delta slope with the flood towards the NW and ebb to the SE. Flood currents are both stronger and of greater dura-tion than the ebb currents. The sediment-laden plume that extends into the Strait of Georgia from the mouth of the main channel is pulled north towards the Sturgeon Bank (Fig. 1) slope by the effects of Coriolis on the dominant flood tide. During the ebb tide much, but not all, of the fine sediment is also transported northward as the southeasterly ebb tidal drag on the plume is balanced by the Coriolis effect (Thomson 1981).

Anthropogenic alteration of the delta

Prior to 1912, the charted water depth across the intertidal delta front was 2.5 m and no navigable access was available to the Fraser River. The main river channel occupied six different chan-nels between 1827 and 1912 (Clague et al. 1983). By 1932 a jetty was completed along the 10 km stretch of the main channel of the river that crossed the delta front, similar to that con-structed on the north arm of the river in 1925 (Fig. 1). After 1912 and up until present, the principal river channel has been dredged to create water depths of 12 m or greater for navi-gation. Dredging has increased in recent years to supply aggregate to the domestic market resulting in at least 50% (approximately 6×10^6 tonnes) of the sediment load coarser than 0.18 mm being taken from the river before reaching the delta (McLean & Tassone 1990).

Three causeways have been built across the extensive intertidal estuary of the delta in the last 40 years. Two of the facilities are critical to the region's economy. A ferry terminal which has the world's largest flow of traffic (8.8 million passengers and 2.8 million cars in 1996) and the Roberts Bank Deltaport, Canada's largest coal and container export facility, both extend across the delta front to the delta foreslope (Fig 2). These features create permanent barriers to sediment transport and tidal flow across and along the delta front and upper delta foreslope. The economic risk associated with alteration or removal of these facilities to other locations is significant in terms of cost and economic disruption. In addition, a tunnel constructed in 1954 beneath the main channel near the mouth of the river (Fig. 3) is the primary transportation link across the delta into the city of Vancouver.

Patterns of sedimentation and erosion

Several anomalies exist in the sediment dis-tribution pattern that do not correspond to

(a)

(b)

Fig. 2. The Deltaport (**a**) and ferry terminals (**b**) located on the intertidal and delta foreslope of southern Roberts Bank (Fig. 1).

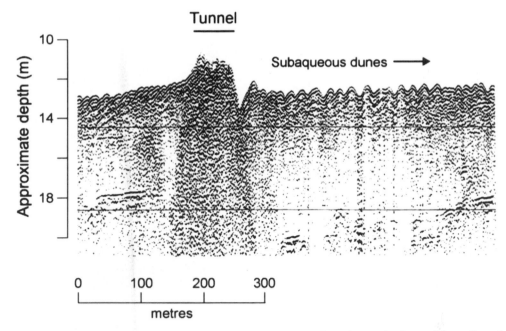

Fig. 3. Seistec high resolution sub-bottom profile of the main river channel over the George Massey Tunnel (Fig. 1). The asymmetry of the dunes indicates upstream sediment transport. The profile was collected in November 1992 when discharge was low.

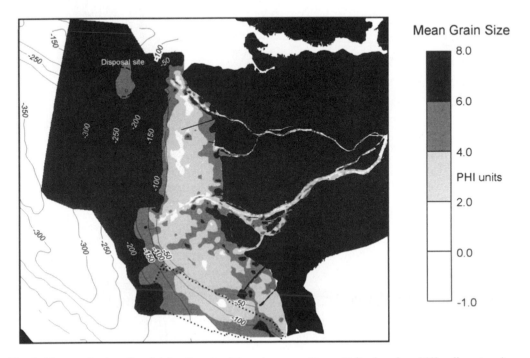

Fig. 4. Mean grain size of surficial sediments of the subaqueous Fraser Delta, based on 1650 sediment grab samples (Barrie & Currie 2000).

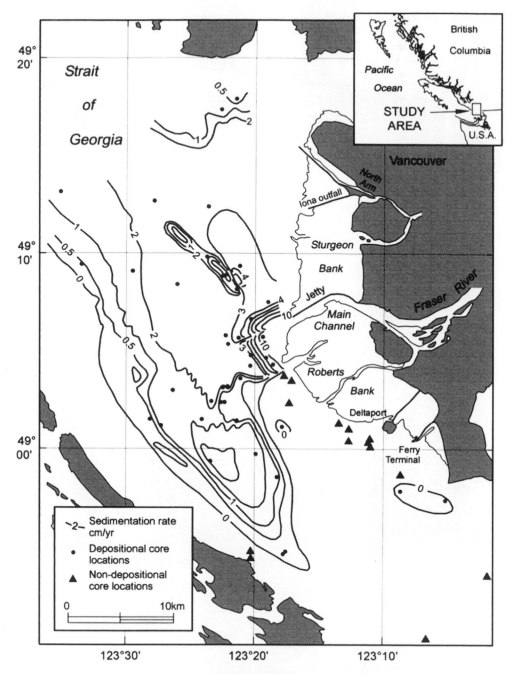

Fig. 5. Distribution of sedimentation rates for the Fraser River Delta slope and prodelta based on the depth of the 1964 ^{137}Cs fallout record, after Hart *et al.* (1998).

typical delta sedimentation patterns of a river-dominated system. The first apparent anomaly is that the sediment distribution pattern across the tidal flats adjacent to the main distributary channel of the river is distinctly different on either side of the river channel (Fig. 4). The channel jetty is on the north side of the river while the south side of the channel is not constrained. Just north of the channel wall the surficial sediments are well-sorted medium sands but south of the channel a mixture of sands and silts exists (Fig. 4). Hart *et al.* (1998) conclude that there is an asymmetry in accumulation rates near the river mouth, with higher rates extending farther away from the mouth to the south, rather than to the north as would be expected (Fig. 5). Rates of $10 \, \text{cm} \, \text{a}^{-1}$ occur near the mouth of the main channel and to the south on the foreslope, but these drop to less than $3 \, \text{cm} \, \text{a}^{-1}$ 4 km offshore (Fig. 5).

Secondly, a linear region of fine grained sediment (silt) that extends in a E–W orientation for 6.0 km totally surrounded by moderately-well sorted fine to medium sands (Fig. 4) is an anomaly in the delta sedimentation pattern. This sediment facies does not conform to bathymetry. The silts occur in water depths from less than 10 m on the delta front to greater than 50 m on the delta slope, centered on the Deltaport. This area of silt is surrounded by fine to medium

sands (Fig. 4). Sediment samples collected in 1970 (Pharo & Barnes 1976), before the Deltaport was completed do not show this pattern, though their sampling only covered the seaward end of this anomaly. This zone of finer-grained deposition on Roberts Bank would appear to be an area of deposition, a result of flow separation of the main northwestward tidal current and formation of back eddies (McLaren & Ren 1995; Barrie & Currie 2000). This is the result of the building of the causeways crossing the intertidal zone to the delta foreslope.

Finally, the most striking feature of the sediment distribution pattern on the present Fraser Delta is the difference between the delta front and slopes of Sturgeon Bank to the north and Roberts Bank to the south of the main channel (Fig. 4). Sturgeon Bank has a medium to fine-grained sandy delta front that changes into a muddy facies on the western edge before

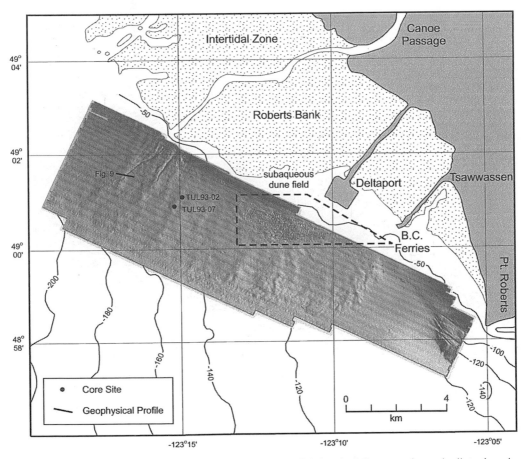

Fig. 6. Multi-beam bathymetry of southern Roberts Bank highlighting the failure complex and relict submarine distributary channels.

the break in slope (Fig. 4). The slope consists entirely of muds becoming increasingly finer downslope from primarily silts to a mixture of silt and clay, except in the area of the offshore dumpsite (Fig. 1) where a mixed sediment distribution occurs. Only the outer delta front and delta slope of Sturgeon Bank are prograding with the deposition of mud from the plume that is deflected north, based on ^{137}Cs fallout stratigraphy (Fig. 5). Roberts Bank, however, has a more variable sediment pattern on the delta front with predominantly fine sand, changing progressively to silt towards the intertidal estuary (Fig. 4). On the delta slope of Roberts Bank the surficial sediments become progressively finer (silts) except for southern Roberts Bank where the dominant sandy delta front continues and coarsens well onto the delta slope, becoming finer-grained at the base (Fig. 4). There is no evidence for present day sedimentation occurring on the southern delta foreslope of Roberts Bank (Fig. 5).

Southern Roberts Bank is defined acoustically by discontinuous wavy reflectors, buried channels and transparent mounds that consist primarily of fine sands and silts (Hart & Barrie 1995). The slope here is made up of relict distributary channels and channel failures as seen in the multi-beam bathymetry data (Fig. 6). The nature of the gullies and failures highlighted by the image (Fig. 6) are similar to those found on

present submarine distributary channels elsewhere on the delta (Hart et al. 1992). High-resolution sub-bottom profiles collected within the complex illustrate the existence of palaeochannels and adjacent failed sediments (Figs 7 & 8). For example, at least two generations of channels can be seen in Fig. 8 and the relict morphology of the channels is seen in the swath image (Fig. 6). The sediment facies identified from a core collected at the edge of the palaeochannel includes a variety of silty, very fine to fine sand units with up to 25% mud content, normal grading, parallel laminations marked by silty clay and an upper unit of massive fine sand containing rip-up clasts (Fig. 8). These facies are characteristic of high-energy turbidity currrents and debris flows where depositional processes including subaqueous channel migration, avulsion and abandonment have occurred (Evoy et al. 1994).

As the river mouth changed location across the delta front, the associated distributary channels migrated, resulting in a failure complex being built up over a period of time on southern Roberts Bank. A similar situation would likely exist at the present river mouth if the channel had not been confined and no dredging was occurring. Radiocarbon dates taken on wood fragments from sediments collected in vibrocores on Roberts Bank that intersect different submarine distributary channels suggest that these

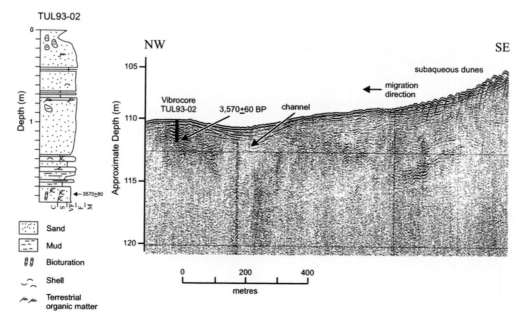

Fig. 7. Seistec high resolution sub-bottom profile and vibrocore (TUL93-02) from southern Roberts Bank. Location of vibrocore shown in Fig. 6.

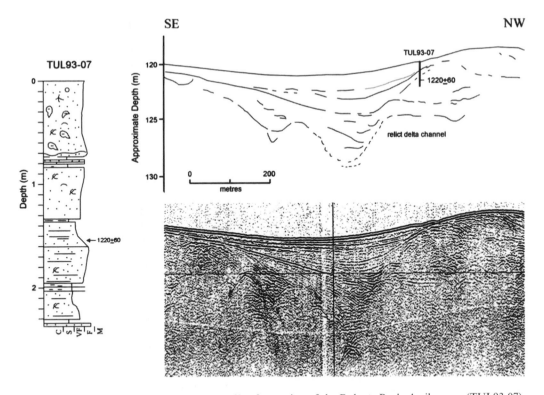

Fig. 8. Seistec high resolution sub-bottom profile of a portion of the Roberts Bank. A vibrocore (TUL93-07) demonstrates the facies stratigraphy within and overlying a buried submarine palaeo-channel. Index of stratigraphic symbols is shown in Fig. 7 and the location of the vibrocore is shown in Fig. 6.

were active anywhere from 3570–1220 C^{14} a BP (Barrie & Currie 2000). These dates suggest that the river mouth was in this area of Roberts Bank from the later part of the Holocene up to historic times as suggested by Clague *et al.* (1991). The last active channel that enters southern Roberts Bank from Canoe Pass can be seen in the northwestern portion of the multi-beam bathymetric survey (Figs 6 & 9).

The Fraser Delta appears not only to have been non-progradational for at least the past 100 years on most of southern Roberts Bank but also erosional. An erosional unconformity exists at the seafloor truncating some of the relict distributary channels with superimposed subaqueous dunes transporting eroded sand to the NW with the flood dominated flood currents (Fig. 7). A large area of the Roberts Bank has a superimposed subaqueous dune field (Fig. 6), with the dunes migrating in a northwesterly transport direction (Kostaschuk *et al.* 1995). This suggests significant transfer of sand with the only source of sediment being the underlying seabed and local dredge dumping. Indeed, delta slope appears to be greatest along the break in slope (exceeding 10°) at the shallow end of the

subaqueous dune field adjacent to the causeways and flattens to less than 1° at the base of the foreslope (Christian *et al.* 1997).

Clearly, there is ample evidence that the amount of sand sized material now entering the delta is negligible, except at the mouth of the main channel where it enters the delta slope and primarily the prodelta (Evoy *et al.* 1997). Fine-grained deposition does occur to the north of the main channel on the delta slope and prodelta of Sturgeon Bank but little sediment gets onto the delta front or south of the river mouth except from the area immediately south of the river channel. Even within the river at the site of the tunnel (Fig. 3) erosion is occurring adjacent to the tunnel.

Relative sea-level rise

Geodetic Survey of Canada levelling surveys were conducted during the period 1914–1924 and again between 1958–1967 in the area of the delta. Comparison of data sets indicates subsidence of the delta between 0.5 mm a^{-1} to greater than 3.0 mm a^{-1} (Mathews *et al.* 1970). Rate

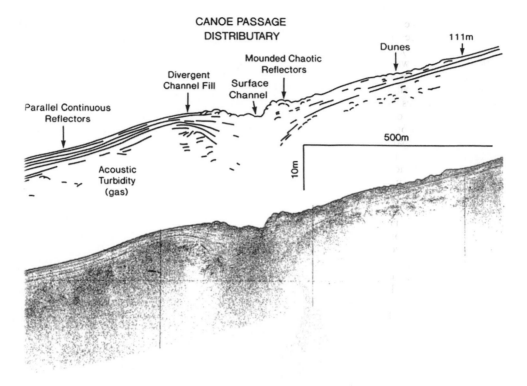

Fig. 9. Huntec DTS high resolution sub-bottom profile of the abandoned distributary channel off Canoe Passage. Location of the seismic profile shown in Fig 6.

variation may reflect the differences in thickness of delta sediments. In addition sea-level rose approximately 8 cm between 1914 and 1984 at the Point Atkinson tide gauge (Fig. 1), just north of the delta, giving a predicted sea-level rise rate of $1.2\,\mathrm{mm\,a}^{-1}$. Though these rates are uncertain, some relative sea-level rise is occurring (between approximately 1.7 and $4.2\,\mathrm{mm\,a}^{-1}$) by a combination of subsidence, compaction and possibly tectonics. In comparison to other deltas such as the Mississippi and Po these rates of relative sea level rise are low. Regardless, relative sea-level rise on the delta slope will enhance the risk of erosion and instability of the delta over time, particularly along the delta front and the intertidal estuaries.

Future implications of human impact to the delta

Disruption of the natural dispersal of sediment reaching the delta front marshes has already resulted in increased variability in sediment accretion and localized erosion. For example,

net erosion of the marsh on Sturgeon Bank has been attributed to the lack of sediment reaching the delta front from the river (Williams & Hamilton 1994). Using $^{137}\mathrm{Cs}$ it was determined that sedimentation rates were lower by an average of 51% in the period 1964–1981 compared to 1954–1964. These marshes are important environments to migratory birds, fish and the local estuarine ecosystem as well as a coastal defense to flooding.

Moreover, the Fraser Delta is situated in an area of high seismic risk, where considerable damage is likely to result from ground motion amplification, liquefaction, and landslides (Clague 1997). If the delta foreslope of southern Roberts Bank is being eroded with no new sediment input, then the impact of an earthquake on the stability of the delta and the structures built on it could well be great. For example, the loss the the electrical transmission cables to Vancouver Island would leave the city of Victoria and surrounding municipalities (1 million people) without power for several months and any loss or damage to the ferry terminal would disrupt the principal transportation link to the Island. The eroding delta foreslope sediments also overlie a geotechnically sensitive marine silt and clay unit (Christian *et al.* 1997), further increasing the risk. This combined with a rising sea-level, a result of delta subsidence and the tectonic setting, suggests the risk will increase in the decades to follow if no measures for mitigation are taken.

Any consideration of mitigation measures would require a rigorous determination of the sediment transport pathways and rates of erosion for the delta front and delta slope, particularly south of the river mouth. This will be the direction of future research. Only after this can an evaluation be made of impacts the causeways and facilities crossing the intertidal zone have in accelerating the erosion process. Engineering modifications to these structures could then be considered. The sediment transport model would also provide the necessary information regarding the level of river dredging that can be tolerated, and in the case of dredging for navigation, provide an understanding of what locations would be most suitable for dredge spoil dumping.

We like to thank the Captains and crews of CSS *John P. Tully* and CSS *Parizeau* for their support in the collection of the data in the southern Strait of Georgia and the participants of cruises PGC91-04, PGC92-06 and PGC93-10. R. Kung was instrumental in the production of the GIS maps used for this publication. K. Conway, W. Hill and R. Macdonald provided technical support and D. Mosher provided the aerial photographs. Earlier drafts of the manuscript were improved based on the excellent suggestions of J. R. L. Allen, K. Pye, R. Currie and one anonymous reviewer. This is Geological Survey of Canada Publication 1998190.

References

ALLEN, G. P., LAURIER, D. & THOUVENIN, J. 1979. *Etude Sedimentologique du Delta de la Mahakam.* Compagnie Francaise des Petroles, Notes et Memoires, 15.

BARRIE, J. V. & CURRIE, R. G. 2000. Human impact on the sedimentary regime of the Fraser River Delta, Canada. *Journal of Coastal Research*, **16**, 747–755.

CENCINI, C. 1998. Physical processes and human activities in the evolution of the Po Delta, Italy. *Journal of Coastal Research*, **14**, 774–793.

CHRISTIAN, H. A., MOSHER, D. C., MULDER, T., BARRIE, J. V. & COURTNEY, R. C. 1997. Geomorphology and potential slope instability of the Fraser River delta foreslope, Vancouver, British Columbia. *Canadian Geotechnical Journal*, **34**, 432–446.

CLAGUE, J. J. 1997. Earthquake hazard in the Greater Vancouver area. *In*: EYLES, N. (ed.) *Environmental Geology of Urban Areas.* Geological Society of Canada, St. John's, Newfoundland, 423–437.

———, LUTERNAUER, J. L. & HEBDA, R. J. 1983. Sedimentary environments and postglacial history of the Fraser River Delta and lower Fraser Valley, British Columbia. *Canadian Journal of Earth Sciences*, **20**, 1314–1326.

———, ——, PULLEN, S. E. & HUNTER, J. A. 1991. Postglacial deltaic sediments, southern Fraser Delta, British Columbia. *Canadian Journal of Earth Sciences*, **28**, 1386–1393.

COLEMAN, J. M. 1969. Brahmaputra River: channel processes and sedimentation. *Sedimentary Geology*, **3**, 131–239.

———, ROBERTS, H. H. & STONE, G. W. 1998. Mississippi River Delta: An overview. *Journal of Coastal Research*, **14**, 698–717.

EVOY, R. W., MOSLOW, T. F., PATTERSON, R. T. & LUTERNAUER, J. L. 1993. Patterns and variability in sediment accumulation rates, Fraser River delta foreslope, British Columbia, Canada. *Geo-Marine Letters*, **13**, 212–218.

———, ——, KOSTASCHUK, R. A. & LUTERNAUER, J. L. 1994. Origin and variability of sedimentary facies of the Fraser River delta foreslope, British Columbia. *Marine Geology*, **118**, 49–60.

———, —— & ——1997. Grain size distribution patterns supporting sediment bypassing on the Fraser River delta foreslope, British Columbia, Canada. *Journal of Coastal Research*, **13**, 842–853.

HART, B. S. 1995. Delta front estuaries. *In*: PERILLO, G. M. E. (ed.) *Geomorphology and Sedimentology of Estuaries.* Developments in Sedimentology **53**, Amsterdam, Elsevier Science, 207–226.

—— & BARRIE, J. V. 1995. Environmental Geology of the Fraser Delta, Vancouver. *Geoscience Canada*, **22**, 172–183.

———, PRIOR, D. B., BARRIE, J. V., CURRIE, R. G. & LUTERNAUER, J. L. 1992. A river mouth submarine landslide and channel complex, Fraser Delta, Canada. *Sedimentary Geology*, **81**, 73–87.

———, HAMILTON, T. S. & BARRIE, J. V. 1998. Sedimentation on the Fraser Delta slope and prodelta, Canada, based on high-resolution seismic stratigraphy, lithofacies and ^{137}Cs fallout stratigraphy. *Journal of Sedimentary Research*, **68**, 556–568.

JOHNSTON, W. A. 1921. *Sedimentation of the Fraser River delta.* Geological Survey of Canada, Memoir 125.

KOSTASCHUK, R. A., CHURCH, M. A. & LUTERNAUER, J. L. 1989. Bedforms, bed material, and bedload transport in a salt-wedge estuary: Fraser River, British Columbia. *Canadian Journal of Earth Sciences*, **26**, 1440–1452.

———, —— & ——1992. Sediment transport over salt-wedge intrusions: Fraser River estuary, Canada. *Sedimentology*, **39**, 305–317.

———, LUTERNAUER, J. L., BARRIE, J. V., LEBLOND, P. H. & WERTH VON DEICHMANN, L. 1995. Sediment transport by tidal currents and implications for slope stability: Fraser River delta, British Columbia. *Canadian Journal of Earth Sciences*, **32**, 852–859.

MATHEWS, W. H., FYLES, J. G. & NASMITH, H. W. 1970. Postgalcial crustal movements in southwestern British Columbia and adjacent Washington state. *Canadian Journal of Earth Sciences*, **7**, 690–702.

MCLAREN, P. & REN, P. 1995. *Sediment transport and its environmental implications in the lower Fraser River and Fraser delta*. Environment Canada, DOE FRAP 1995-03.

MCLEAN, D. G. & TASSONE, B. L. 1990. *A sediment budget of the lower Fraser River*. Environment Canada Report.

MILLIMAN, J. D. 1980. Sedimentation in the Fraser River and its estuary, southwestern British Columbia (Canada). *Estuarine and Coastal Marine Science*, **10**, 609–633.

MONAHAN, P. A. 1999. *The Application of Cone Penetration Test Data to Facies Analysis of the Fraser River Delta, British Columbia*. PhD Thesis, University of Victoria.

——, LUTERNAUER, J. L. & BARRIE, J. V. 1993. A delta plain sheet sand in the Fraser River delta, British Columbia, Canada. *Quaternary International*, **20**, 27–38.

ORTON, G. J. & READING, H. G. 1993. Variability of deltaic processes in terms of sediment supply, with particular emphasis on grain size. *Sedimentology*, **40**, 475–512.

PHARO, C. H. & BARNES, W. C. 1976. Distribution of surficial sediments of the central and southern Strait of Georgia, British Columbia. *Canadian Journal of Earth Sciences*, **13**, 684–696.

SESTINI, G. 1989. Nile Delta: a review of depositional environments and geological history. *In*: WHATELEY, M. K. G. & PICKERING, K. T. (eds) *Deltas, Sites and Traps for Fossil Fuels*. Geological Society, London, Special Publications, **41**, 99–127.

STANLEY, D. J. & WARNE, A. G. 1993. Nile Delta: Recent geological evolution and human impact. *Science*, **260**, 628–634.

—— & ——1998. Nile Delta in its destruction phase. *Journal of Coastal Research*, **14**, 794–825.

STEWART, I. & TASSONE, B. 1989. *The Fraser River delta: A review of historic sounding charts*. Environment Canada, Inland Waters Directorate, Pacific and Yukon Region, Vancouver, British Columbia.

THOMSON, R. E. 1981. *Oceanography of the British Columbia Coast*. Canada Special Publication of Fisheries and Aquatic Sciences, No. 56.

WILLIAMS, H. F. L. & HAMILTON, T. S. 1994. Sedimentary dynamics of an eroding tidal marsh derived from stratigraphic records of ^{137}Cs fall-out, Fraser Delta, British Columbia, Canada. *Journal of Coastal Research*, **11**, 1145–1156.

XUE, C. 1993. Historical changes in the Yellow River delta, China. *Marine Geology*, **113**, 321–329.

How anthropogenic factors in the back-barrier area influence tidal inlet stability: examples from the Gulf Coast of Florida, USA

RICHARD A. DAVIS, JR. & PATRICK L. BARNARD[1]

[1] *Present address: Department of Earth Sciences, University of California – Riverside, Riverside, California 92521–0423, USA (e-mail: rdavis@chuma.cas.usf.edu)*
Coastal Research Laboratory, Department of Geology, University of South Florida, Tampa, Florida 33620, USA

Abstract: Human development along the coast of the world has caused important changes to coastal morphodynamics. The barrier-inlet system of Florida, especially the tidal inlets, has been severely impacted by this development. Beginning in the 1920s and continuing through the 1960s there was: (1) extensive construction of fill-type causeways connecting the mainland to the barrier islands, (2) widespread dredge-and-fill construction along the backbarrier and mainland, and (3) dredging of the Intracoastal Waterway (ICW) in the back-barrier area.

The primary effect of these various types of construction and development was to cause instability of many inlets by diminishing the tidal flux through them. In some cases there was a combination of human and natural causes that resulted in the inlet degradation or closure such as at Dunedin Pass and Blind Pass, whereas at others this instability was almost exclusively the result of human activity such as at Midnight Pass. Although these detrimental development practices have been stopped, a large amount of irreparable damage has been done.

The Gulf Coast of the Florida peninsula is a very complex and fragile system of open coast marshes on the north, a barrier-inlet system in the middle, and an open coast mangrove mangle system on the south (Fig. 1). This is a low-energy coast with a maximum mean wave height at the shore of about 40 cm, and a mean tidal range of a metre or less. The adjacent inner continental shelf gradient ranges from about 1:400 to 1:3000. The barrier islands that protect this entire estuarine coast are served by 30 tidal inlets with tidal prisms that range across four orders of magnitude (Fig. 2). Numerous previous investigations have documented that rates of change along this coast are quite high, even with low tidal ranges and wave energy, and in the absence of severe storms (e.g. Hine *et al.* 1987; Davis 1989; Davis & Hine 1989).

The first major construction practices that impacted on the coastal environments were the causeways constructed beginning in the early 1920s between the mainland and some of the barriers. In the next decade tidal inlets began to be stabilized by hard construction in the form of jetties. Rates of development increased greatly after World War II, and in the 1950s and 1960s there was extensive dredge-and-fill construction for purposes of adding land which would support house and would be on the waterfront.

The last major project in the back-barrier area was the dredging of the Intracoastal Waterway (ICW) along the entire Gulf Coast. In the study area this took place in 1963–64.

Causes and effects

Coastal systems, especially barrier-inlet systems, are quite dynamic. Changes that take place in one element of this system will nearly always bring about a response in the form of a change in another of the elements. Because tidal inlets are dependent upon the flux of tidal water through them for their existence, they represent one of the most fragile elements of a barrier-inlet system. Any changes in the coastal zone that result in some modification of this tidal flux or tidal prism will bring about a change in the inlet; typically one that is detrimental.

Sometimes these changes are the result of natural processes. One of the best examples occurs when a storm breaches a barrier island forming an opening through which there is tidal flux. The continuation of the existence of this opening, i.e. the formation of a tidal inlet, is dependent on having enough tidal flux to prevent the accumulation of sediment in the channel from littoral drift on the open-coast

From: PYE, K. & ALLEN, J. R. L. (eds). *Coastal and Estuarine Environments: sedimentology, geomorphology and geoarchaeology*. Geological Society, London, Special Publications, **175**, 293–303. 0305-8719/$15.00 © The Geological Society of London 2000.

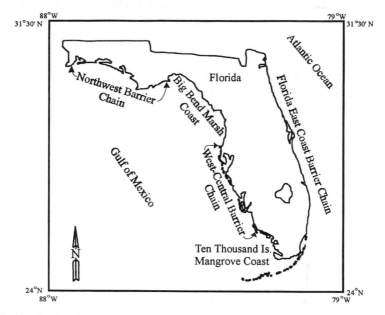

Fig. 1. Map of Florida showing the major coastal segments.

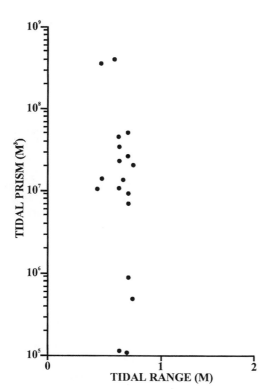

Fig. 2. Diagram showing the relationship of tidal prism and tidal range for many inlets along the west-central coast of Florida.

side. This may or may not happen. If it does, that means that an adjacent tidal inlet in the system has experienced a decrease in tidal prism which can cause instability, and eventually, closure of that inlet.

Various types of human activities in the back-barrier area of the coastal system can result in the same situation, i.e. decease in tidal prism leading to instability. As pressure is exerted for development of the coastal zone for housing, tourism, and industrialization, various construction activities come into play, and some result in problems for tidal inlets.

Causeway construction

As people began to live and recreate on the open coast, there was increasing pressure to provide a rapid and easy means for transporting them to the barriers. This was best and most economically done by dredging material from the estuaries and bays landward of the barrier, and using the borrow material for constructing roads from the mainland to the barrier islands. Care was taken to provide for boat traffic by including openings with lift bridges. No attention was paid to the circulation behind the barrier or between the open coast and the back-barrier bays. Beginning in the early 1920s these causeways were constructed so that within a couple of decades,

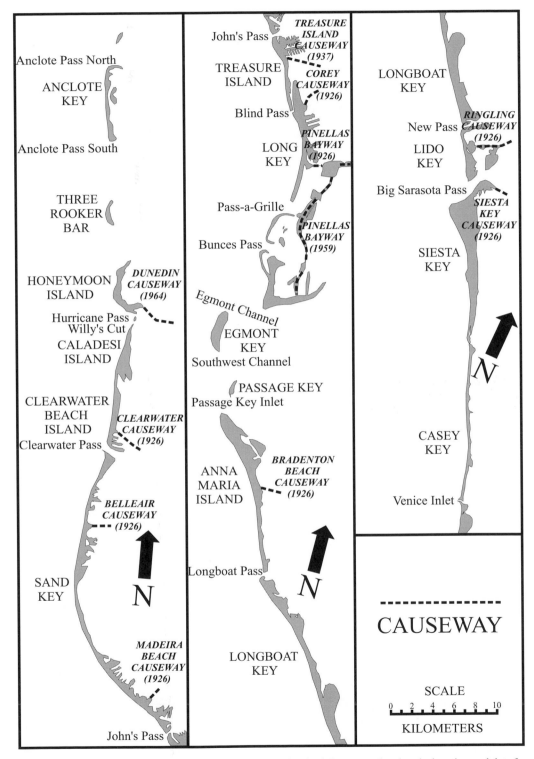

Fig. 3. Map of the northern half of the west-central Florida barrier-inlet system showing the location and date for the construction of the fill-type causeways that connect the barrier islands to the mainland.

nearly all barrier islands had at least one such thoroughfare connecting it with the mainland (Fig. 3).

These causeways were, in effect, dams across the back-barrier areas that partitioned the open water, severely limiting the tidal flux that could pass through them. As a consequence, the tidal prism of various inlets was changed dramatically. Typically it was reduced which means that the inlet being served is likely to become unstable. This instability will result in migration of the inlet along the open coast and/or closure of the inlet by littoral sediment which cannot be flushed by the reduced tidal prism. In some cases, the inlets were stabilized by hard structures, e.g. jetties, which cause downdrift erosion by inhibiting littoral drift across the inlet mouth.

Dredge and fill

As the barrier islands became completely developed there was pressure for more space to place homes and commercial properties. The solution of the time (1950s) was to dredge from one area and fill in another, thereby creating buildable upland in areas that were originally intertidal or subtidal environments. The typical result was a series of elongate upland areas separated by finger canals (Fig. 4) which were produced from what was originally mangrove communities and/or seagrass beds. In this way, developers could expand their opportunities and many people could live on waterfront property.

In most cases, this type of development took place at the expense of the important intertidal communities that fringed both the back-barrier and the mainland. Destruction of these environments was a major blow to the coastal ecosystem. Some of the upland areas were developed on shallow subtidal environments which are extremely productive and are also important to the ecosystem. The other major problem for the ecosystem is the deterioration of water quality due to poor circulation in the finger canals, and from runoff of nutrients from the developed uplands. All of these factors have caused great deterioration to the coastal ecosystem.

There was also a major negative impact of the dredge-and-fill practice on the tidal inlets in the coastal system. Because one of the two variables controlling tidal prism is the area of the back-barrier system that is served by the inlet, and because the dredge and fill practice caused major reduction in the water area of the backbarrier, there was also a major reduction in the tidal prism flowing through individual inlets. This also leads to inlet instability and potential for migration and/or closure.

Fig. 4. Oblique aerial photograph of a typical back-barrier area in this part of Florida showing the result of dredge-and-fill development.

In Boca Ciega Bay, one of the most highly developed back-barrier areas along this part of the Florida coast, there was a reduction in surface area of 28% (Mehta *et al.* 1976). This can be seen well from the comparison of the first accurate map of the area in 1883 with that from just over a century later in 1997 which shows the striking changes in this bay (Fig. 5).

Intracoastal waterway

Commercial boat traffic is an important part of the commerce along most coasts and is especially so for the Gulf of Mexico in the United States. The need for a protected waterway and the presence of the extensive barrier island system along this coast led to a fairly natural decision to dredge and maintain an inland waterway (ICW) along this part of Florida. The design for the channel was a depth of 8 feet (2.45 m) and a width of 50 feet (15.3 m). Dredging was primarily by suction dredge with sidecast disposal of spoil along the margins of the channel. This created small spoil islands which became places for fisherman, birds, etc.

The ICW channel was, and is, a huge success for inland waterway transportation, both commercial and recreational. The channel did, however, have some negative effects. Production of the spoil islands further decreased the tidal prism by decreasing the water area of the back-barrier but this effect was very small. The more problematic impact was the channelization of tidal flow along the path of the waterway, particularly in narrow back-barrier bays. This condition has the effect of robbing tidal prism from some inlets in favor of others. Especially affected were small inlets that did not have a natural or dredged channel connecting it to the ICW. The problem

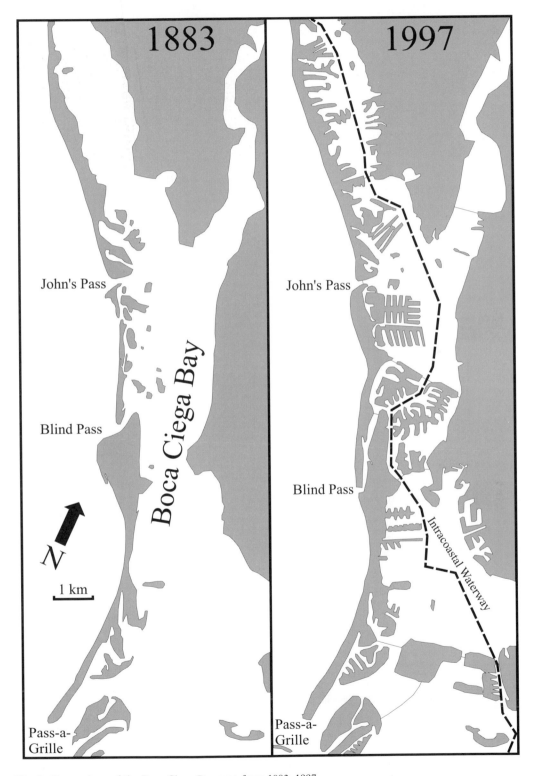

Fig. 5. Comparison of the Boca Ciega Bay area from 1883–1997.

was slightly increased by the presence of spoil islands or spoil levees along the channel which further enhanced the channelization of flow.

Case histories

Some specific examples of significant change caused, at least in part, by human activity can demonstrate how each of the three factors discussed have contributed to inlet deterioration along this part of the Florida Gulf Coast. In some situations there has been a combination of both natural processes and anthropogenic influences, and in others, the human activities are the primary responsible contributor

Dunedin Pass

At about the turn of the century, Dunedin Pass (Fig. 6) was a large inlet called Big Pass with a cross sectional area of 1200 m^2 (Lynch-Blosse & Davis 1977). In 1921, a hurricane with a storm surge of about 3 m caused a breach in what was Hog Island, forming Hurricane Pass, only 3.5 km north of Dunedin Pass. This new inlet rapidly became a fairly stable inlet, and it has persisted since its formation (Lynch-Blosse & Davis 1977). Only five years later, in 1926, the causeway between the city of Clearwater and Clearwater Beach Island was completed (Fig. 3). Both of these events, one natural and one human-induced, caused changes to the tidal prism of Dunedin Pass (Big Pass). The opening of an inlet only a few kilometres away captured some of the tidal prism of Dunedin Pass. The prism was further reduced at nearly the same time by the construction of the causeway which partitioned the coastal bay serving Dunedin Pass. As a result, there was a rapid reduction in the cross sectional area of the inlet (Fig. 7).

About 40 years later, in 1964, another causeway was completed connecting the mainland at the city of Dunedin to Honeymoon Island (Fig. 3). This further compartmentalized the back-barrier bay and further reduced the tidal prism available to Dunedin Pass. The reduction in cross sectional area was accelerated (Fig. 7) so that by 1975, the inlet had been reduced to only about 10% of its size from 100 years previous.

The final event that led to the closure of Dunedin Pass was the passage of Hurricane Elena in 1985. Although this storm did not have landfall near the inlet in question, it did create enough wave energy to remove the ebb-tidal delta that existed in the mouth of the inlet. By this time, the inlet channel was only about 50 m

wide and 1.5 m deep with a very small tidal flux. After removal of the ebb delta, the northward moving littoral drift along Clearwater Beach Island caused the channel to fill within three years (Fig. 8). The absence of severe storms and associated surge inbetween removal of the ebb delta and final closure, aided the cause. The inlet has remained closed for the past decade with sediment being added regularly through washover during the passage of winter cold fronts.

This is an excellent example of how both human activities landward of the barrier system coupled with natural phenomena have caused the demise of a once large tidal inlet.

Blind Pass

Blind Pass is located on the SW-facing portion of the barrier island system in Pinellas County where it separates the barriers of Treasure Island and Long Key (Fig. 6). In the middle of the 19th century this tidal inlet was fairly large and was immediately Gulfward of its flood-tidal delta. After the hurricane of 1848 formed Johns Pass 5 km to the north there was a marked reduction in the size and stability of Blind Pass because the new inlet had captured a large amount of the tidal prism. As a result, the inlet began to migrate rapidly to the south so that by 1926, the time of construction of the nearby causeway (Fig. 3), the mouth had moved more than 2 km. The causeway to the south was constructed in 1926 and the one to the north of the inlet was finished in 1937. By that time (1937) the decision was made by the US Army Corps of Engineers to stabilize the inlet, and they constructed a rubble jetty on the south side of the channel (Mehta et al. 1976).

Within a short time there was extensive dredge-and-fill construction landward of the barrier islands adjacent to Blind Pass (Fig. 5). The large decrease in surface area of Boca Ciega Bay caused by this type of construction resulted in a further decrease in tidal prism at Blind Pass. During most of the time that Blind Pass was experiencing a decease in tidal prism and therefore, cross sectional area, Johns Pass was becoming larger at its expense (Fig. 9). It can be seen from the time-series of inlet size, that there has been little change in the area of the combined inlets.

After stabilization of Blind Pass and continued dredge-and-fill construction, the inlet had such a small tidal prism that littoral drift from the north accumulated in the channel threatening closure. A north jetty was added in 1968 but the fillet exceeded its length in only a few years thereby requiring an extension of the north jetty which was added in the late 1970s. There is still

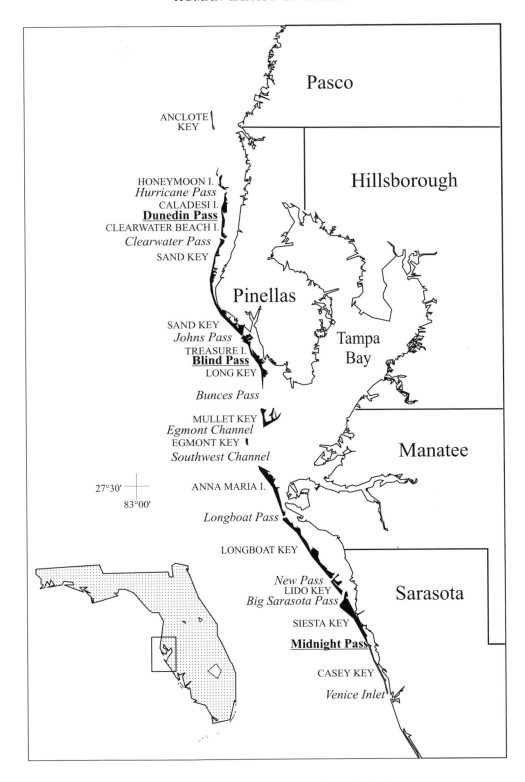

Fig. 6. Map showing the study area with inlets used as examples being underlined.

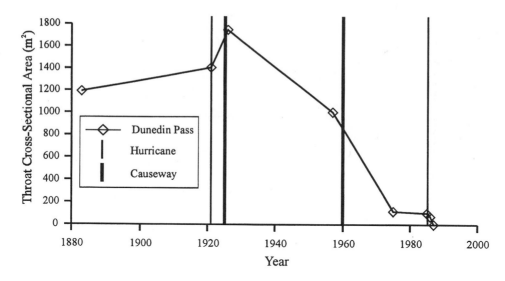

Fig. 7. Changes over time for the cross sectional area of Dunedin Pass.

considerable infilling of the inlet because its small tidal flux cannot keep the channel free of sediment accumulation from the southerly-moving littoral transport. The downdrift effects of the extensive stabilization are severe, and require nourishment of the beaches every few years. Much of that nourishment is obtained from the accumulated sediment in the mouth of the inlet.

Here again, there have been both natural and anthropogenic factors that have constributed to the instability of the inlet. Stabilizing it has not really solved the problem and has resulted in tremendous chronic downdrift erosion that is very expensive to mitigate.

Midnight Pass

Historically, a small inlet has separated Siesta Key on the north from Casey Key on the south in Sarasota County (Fig. 6). This inlet, Midnight Pass, had a history of being unstable, and it displayed lengthy migration to the north during the early 20th century (Davis *et al.* 1987). The tidal flux was typically modest at best because the inlet served only Little Sarasota Bay (Fig. 6). This narrow and shallow bay had several oyster reef complexes along its length whose orientation and configuration indicated that at least some tidal flux moved along the length of the bay, not simply in and out of Midnight Pass. The elongate

Fig. 8. Oblique aerial photographs of Dunedin Pass taken in 1979 (left) when the ebb-tidal was present and in 1989 (right) after closure.

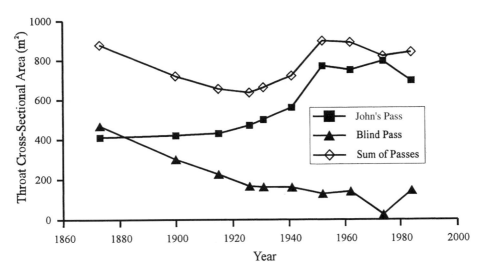

Fig. 9. Time-series showing the changes in inlet cross-sectional area for Johns Pass and Blind Pass (after Mehta *et al*. 1976).

orientation of the reefs (Fig. 10a) is the result of tidal flux moving perpendicular to the reefs. The oysters receive their nourishment from suspension feeding which means that the most efficient organization is across the currents that are carrying the suspended nutrient material.

In the early 1960s some dredge and fill construction took place associated with the oyster reefs. Sediment was dredged from the floor of the bay and filled over the oyster reefs creating small peninsulas extending into the bay and oriented perpendicular to the adjacent shoreline both on the mainland and on the landward side of the barrier islands (Fig. 10b). At this time (1954), Midnight Pass was at its maximum size in recorded history with a width of 130 m and a maximum depth of 4 m. A modest sized ebb-tidal delta was also present indicating that the inlet had a tidal prism sufficient to keep the channel open and in fairly stable position (Davis and Gibeaut 1990).

In 1963–64 the Intracoastal Waterway (ICW) was constructed along this part of the Florida Gulf Coast. This inland channel extended the length of Little Sarasota Bay and was dredged between the small dredge-and-fill peninsulas. It enhanced tidal circulation along the length of the bay by providing a pathway that captured tidal flux from Midnight Pass. Flooding tides entered the bay but exited at either end through the ICW. Because most inlets have stronger ebb currents than flood currents (Hayes 1975, 1979), the channel was not able to flush out sediment

that was accumulating as the result of the northerly littoral drift in this area. Within a decade or so, there was significant reduction in the size of the inlet channel and there was considerable migration of the channel to the north. The inlet eventually was closed in 1984.

The combination of the dredge-and-fill construction over pre-existing oyster reefs with the dredging of the ICW captured most of the tidal prism of Midnight Pass and eventually closed it as it remains today. In this situation, virtually all of the cause can be attributed to anthropogenic activities in the back-barrier area.

Conclusions

Barrier-inlet systems are quite fragile and very important elements of the coastal zone. The maintenance of the inlets that connect open marine with protected bays and estuaries must be managed very carefully and with consideration for the long-term future of the coastal system. This has not been done properly along most of the developed coast of Florida. Huge pressures for development have led to the redesign and construction of the back-barrier environments with dramatic consequences to the inlet.

Practices such as causeway construction, dredge-and-fill construction, and dredging of channels have combined to reduce tidal prism at many inlets. The result has been a decrease in inlet size which is nearly always accompanied by

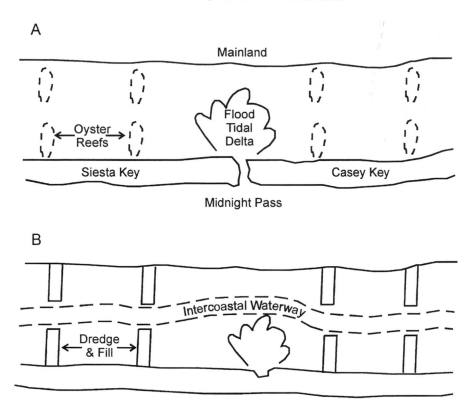

Fig. 10. Diagrammatic sketchshowing the Little Sarasota Bay area (**a**) in its natural condition and (**b**) after closure of the inlet, dredge-and-fill construction over the oyster reefs, and dredging of the Intracoastal Waterway.

instability. This instability requires stabilization which further complicates the situation. The end result has been closure of some inlets, and erosion of downdrift areas of those that have been stabilized. In some cases, natural phenomena, such as storms opening inlets, have also contributed to the problem.

Although construction of such causeways and dredge-and-fill development have been stopped, the damage has already been done and it will not be repaired in the future. At the present time, there is considerable discussion about the merits of maintenance dredging of the ICW because of its effects on the back-barrier environment.

This paper benefited from support of the cooperative program between the US Geological Survey and the University of South Florida, and the Florida Sea Grant Program. Numerous students at USF have assisted in the collection of the data that contributed to the project. T. Hepner helped with the illustrations. The manuscript was prepared while the senior author was visiting professor at the University of Utrecht in The Netherlands.

References

DAVIS, R. A. 1989. Morphology of the west-central Florida barrier system: the delicate balance between wave- and tide-domination. *In*: VAN DER LINDEN, W. J. M. *ET AL.* (eds) *Coastal Lowlands, Geology and Geotechnology*, Kluwer, Dordneckt, 225–235.

—— & GIBEAUT, J. C. 1990. *Historical Morphodynamics of Inlets in Florida: Models for Coastal Zone Planning*. Florida Sea Grant College, Technical Report No. 55.

—— & HINE, A. C. 1989. *Quaternary Geology and Sedimentology of the Barrier Island and Marshy Coast, West-central Florida*. International Geological Congress Guidebook #375, American Geophysical Union, WASHINGTON, D.C.

——, —— & BLAND, M. J. 1987. Midnight Pass, Florida: inlet instability due to man-related activities in Little Sarasota Bay. *In*: *Coastal Sediments '87*, American Society of Civil Engineers, New York, 2062–2077.

HAYES, M. O. 1975. Morphology and sand accumulation in estuaries: an introduction to the symposium. *In*: CRONIN, L. E. (ed.) *Estuarine Research*, Academic Press, New York, **2**, 3–22.

——1979. Barrier island morphology as a function of tidal and wave regime. *In:* LEATHERMAN, S. P. (ed) *Barrier Islands*, Academic Press, New York, 1–27.

HINE, A. C., EVANS, M. W., DAVIS, R. A. & BELKNAP, D. F. 1987. Depositional response to seagrass mortality along a low-energy, barrier-island coast: west-central Florida. *Journal of Sedimentary Petrology*, **57**, 431–439.

LYNCH-BLOSSE, M. A. & DAVIS, R. A. 1977. Stability of Dunedin and Hurricane Passes, Pinellas County, Florida. *In: Coastal Sediments '77*, American Society of Civil Engineers, New York, 774–789.

MEHTA, A. H., JONES, C. P. & ADAMS, W. D. 1976. *Johns Pass and Blind Pass*. Glossary of Inlets Repot, Florida Sea Grant Program, Rept. No. 18.

Shoreline change and fine-grained sediment input: Isle of Sheppey Coast, Thames Estuary, UK

ROBERT J. NICHOLLS, ANDREW DREDGE & THERESA WILSON

Flood Hazard Research Centre, Middlesex University, Enfield EN3 4SF, UK
(e-mail: R.Nicholls@Mdx.ac.uk)

Abstract: The northern coast of the Isle of Sheppey comprises actively-eroding cliffs up to 50 m high cut into the London Clay. From 1867 to 1998 the average cliff-top recession was about $1 \, \mathrm{m \, a^{-1}}$, while the maximum recession was $1.9 \pm 0.08 \, \mathrm{m \, a^{-1}}$. From 1897 to 1998, this provided at least $4.5 \times 10^5 \, \mathrm{t \, a^{-1}}$ of fine-grained sediment to the Thames Estuary system and southern North Sea. This sediment input due to erosion is comparable in magnitude with fluvial sediment input from the Thames. The sinks for this material are unclear, but it is likely that the Essex and Kent estuaries and marshes have historically been important in this regard. Given climate change and accelerated sea-level rise, estuaries will again act as sinks, and it is prudent to maintain these supplies of sediment so that these estuarine systems can adjust to this forcing. To maintain sediment supply, shoreline management and estuary management needs to recognize more explicitly the importance and scale of fine-grained sediment supply and transport, including any implications for statutory land use planning.

Coastal cells are defined based on units of the coast which contain all the sources, pathways, stores and sinks for beach-sized material (sand and shingle). In Britain, the primary source of new sediment is cliff erosion. This sediment input has progressively declined over the last century due to increasing hard stabilization of the coast with consequent downdrift problems of increased erosion. Over the last 10 years, the application of the cell concept to coastal management and planning has made this problem increasingly apparent (e.g. Bray *et al.* 1995; French 1997). The UK Ministry of Agriculture, Fisheries and Food (MAFF) have defined 11 coastal cells and more than 40 sub-cells around the coastline of England and Wales (MAFF *et al.* 1995). These cells and sub-cells are the basis for about 40 shoreline management plans which collectively cover the entire coast of England and Wales.

While this approach broadly defines the transport pathways for sand and shingle it is less applicable to silt and clay which moves in suspension and hence circulates over much larger distances. Erosion on the East Coast provides large supplies of silt and clay (McCave 1987; Odd & Murphy 1992; Balson *et al.* 1998) some of which is transported across the North Sea to the German Bight and beyond (Eisma 1981; Dyer & Moffat 1998). These supplies of sediment are of importance to estuarine areas which have acted as sediment traps over the

Holocene. However, as with sand and shingle, these inputs have tended to decline due to increasing cliff protection.

In the outer Thames estuary, the northern shoreline of the Isle of Sheppey comprises cliffs up to 50 m in height. These cliffs are retreating rapidly and given their fine-grained composition (dominantly London Clay), they provide a large source of fine-grained sediment to the overall Thames estuary and its tributary estuaries in north Kent and Essex (henceforth the Thames Estuary System) and more broadly the southern North Sea. The sinks for this sediment are unclear, but it is likely that the estuaries and marshes in the Thames Estuary System are important in this regard over the long-term.

This paper evaluates the historical evolution of this coast from 1867 to 1998, including fine-grained sediment input. Future changes are considered in the light of accelerated sea-level rise. Lastly, the relationship of estuary management planning, shoreline management planning and land use planning are considered. It is argued that we must allow erosion to continue via statutory land use planning to maximize the benefits of fine-grained sediment inputs through the 21st century.

Study area

From Minster to Leysdown, on the northern shoreline of the Isle of Sheppey (Fig. 1), the

From: PYE, K. & ALLEN, J. R. L. (eds). *Coastal and Estuarine Environments: sedimentology, geomorphology and geoarchaeology*. Geological Society, London, Special Publications, **175**, 305–315. 0305-8719/00/$15.00 © The Geological Society of London 2000.

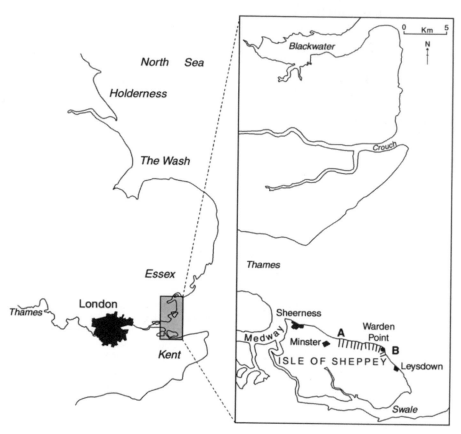

Fig. 1. The study area. The actively eroding cliffs are located between A and B.

coast comprises cliffs cut in Palaeogene deposits. The cliffs are composed almost entirely of London Clay overlain by more localized out-crops of the Claygate and Bagshot Beds (Dines *et al.* 1954; Holmes 1981). Quaternary gravels and brickearth are also locally developed. The intertidal zone comprises a variable coarse-grained beach above a wide (100–500 m), low gradient (0.5°–2°) shore platform cut into the London Clay. There is a littoral drift divide at Warden Point. The surface of the platform is actively degrading under present conditions. Sea-ward of low water is a wide shallow platform covered in sand (British Geological Survey 1997). The 2 m and 5 m depth contours (below chart datum) occur 2 km and 4–6 km seaward of chart datum, respectively.

The rapid recession of these cliffs is well documented (Steers 1964; Holmes 1981; Jones 1981), producing relatively large quantities of fine-grained sediments and relatively small amounts of sand and shingle. Steers reports an average annual recession rate (AAER) for the cliff-top of $1.2\,\mathrm{m\,a^{-1}}$ from 1865 to 1908, with a maximum loss of $3\,\mathrm{m\,a^{-1}}$ at Warden Point. However, the cliff recession does not occur continuously: rather there is periodic failure of the cliff-top by slumping (Hutchinson 1968; Bromhead 1979). After a slump occurs, marine toe erosion removes material and other degrada-tional processes occur on the undercliff until the cliff is steepened sufficiently for slumping to occur again. The length of this cycle at Warden Point is about 30–40 years. In addition, the shore platform, beach and cliffs were stripped for septaria and pyrite from the London Clay up to about 1914 when the trade ceased to be profit-able (Davis 1936; Holmes 1981). This would have increased recession rates in this period compared to natural conditions. Therefore, in addition to marine and slope processes, direct anthropogenic influence needs to be considered when evaluating cliff retreat.

The spring tidal range is about 5 m. The dominant direction of wave approach is from the NE with a fetch into the North Sea. However, the local wave height is controlled by the shallow water depths (see below) and hence, the biggest waves occur at high tides and/or surge conditions. Sheerness on the Isle of Sheppey has mean sea level data starting in 1834 which shows a long-term acceleration in sea-level rise (Woodworth 1990). During the 19th century (1834–1900) sea-level rise averaged about $0.4 \, \mathrm{mm \, a^{-1}}$, while during the 20th century (1900–1993) sea-level rise averaged $2.2 \, \mathrm{mm \, a^{-1}}$.

The eroding cliffs have been stabilized at their eastern and western limits to protect the towns of Leysdown and Minster, respectively, leaving about 7 km of actively eroding cliffs today (Fig. 1). (South of Warden Point the beach has groynes, but the cliff continues to retreat). The land use above the eroding cliffs mainly comprises agriculture and recreation based on caravans and holiday camps. This land use is largely compatible with continued erosion as the recreational structures are usually mobile. There are scattered permanent residences and some losses due to cliff retreat are occurring. The eroding cliffs near Warden Point are designated as a Site of Special Scientific Interest (SSSI).

Cartographic analysis

While maps of the British coast have been made for hundreds of years, the first maps that are both cartographically accurate and of sufficient scale to accurately measure coastal change are the 1:2500 County Series of the Ordnance Survey (OS) (Carr 1980). Three shoreline indicators: mean low water, the cliff base/mean high water and the cliff-top were all digitized from OS 1:2500 maps for 1867, 1897 and 1966 and then imported into a common grid within a geographic information system (GIS). The resulting errors are similar to those reported by Crowell *et al.* (1991) and the uncertainty when comparing any feature is about 10 m (i.e. change less than 10 m is no evidence of change). In addition, a differential global positioning system was used in kinematic mode to survey the cliff base and cliff-top in July 1998. This data was also imported into the GIS.

The results show that on average, the cliff-top has retreated $1.02 \pm 0.08 \, \mathrm{m \, a^{-1}}$ since 1867 (Fig. 2). The maximum recession of 250 m (at an average rate of $1.93 \pm 0.08 \, \mathrm{m \, a^{-1}}$) has been at Warden Point and in the long-term (centuries), it would appear that the coastline is rotating from north-facing towards the dominant fetch. Two local irregularities in the cliff-top recession are associated with two small, steep-sided valleys (or 'chines') that are moving landward in tandem with the eroding cliff. The base of the

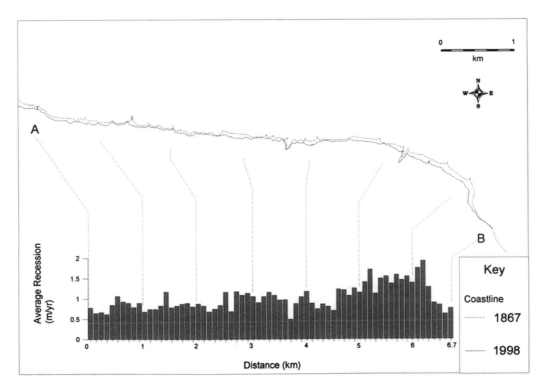

Fig. 2. Average annual recession rate for the cliff-top between A and B (Fig. 1) from 1867 to 1998.

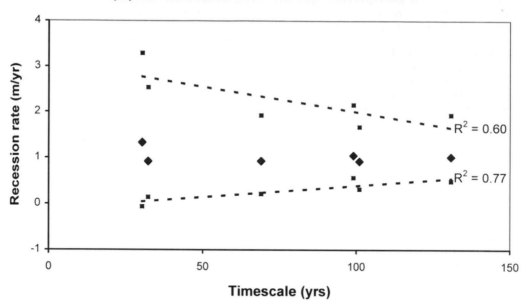

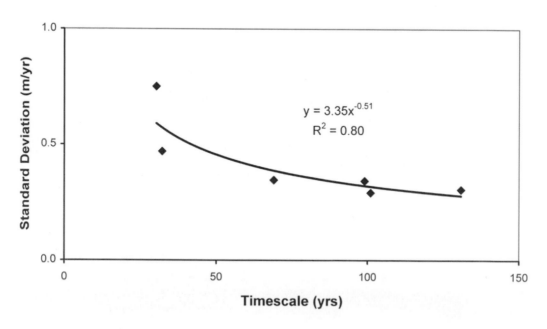

Fig. 3. (a) Minimum and maximum annual recession rates (shown with squares) and average annual recession rates (shown with diamonds) for the cliff-top as a function of time interval between surveys. The linear trend for the minimum and maximum rates is also shown. (b) Longshore standard deviation of average annual recession rates as a function of time interval between surveys.

cliff has moved onshore at a similar rate to the cliff-top showing that the broad cliff form has been conserved over time. However, mean low water appears to have moved 370 m shoreward from 1867 to 1897, and a further 150 m shoreward from 1897 to 1966. This suggests a steepening of the shore platform. However, mean low water is the least reliable of the three shoreline indicators used given both the methods used to measure mean low water before the advent of aerial photographs, the low slopes which characterize the shore platform, and changes in vertical datum. Therefore, the changes in low water are not analysed further.

Figures 3a & 3b show the minimum, maximum and average annual cliff-top recession and the longshore standard deviation as a function of time interval between surveys. Broadly, the average recession rate is constant, independent of time interval, but the maximum recession rate and the standard deviation declines, and the minimum recession rate increases. This probably reflects that measurements over several decades

(<30–40 years) do not include a complete geomorphic cycle and hence cliff-top retreat will not have occurred at all points along the frontage. At longer timescales (≥60 years) the shoreline change statistics are more stable, and the average retreat rates are meaningful estimates for these time scales. This suggests that the smaller scale processes involved with the degradation of the cliff can be ignored as residual effects that average to noise at these longer time scales (cf. Stive *et al.* 1990; DeVriend 1991). Similar results have been found for shoreline recession on sandy coasts (Crowell *et al.* 1993).

Following this rationale, the best data that has been generated covers the longest period (1867–1998). However, stripping of the cliffs, beach and shore platform for septaria and pyrite up to 1914 has already been noted. This would be expected to increase the removal of material from the base of the cliff and hence accelerate cliff retreat in general. Table 1 shows that the period 1867 to 1897 was characterized by the most rapid recession rate, and this influences the recession

Table 1. *Summary Statistics for Cliff-Top Average Annual Recession Rate (AAER)*

	Period	1867–			1897–		1966–
		1897	1966	1998	1966	1998	1998
AAER (m a^{-1})	Average	1.33	1.05	1.02	0.93	0.92	0.92
	Maximum	3.29	2.15	1.93	1.92	1.67	2.53
	Minimum	−0.06	0.57	0.49	0.22	0.32	0.14
	Standard Deviation	0.75	0.34	0.31	0.35	0.29	0.47

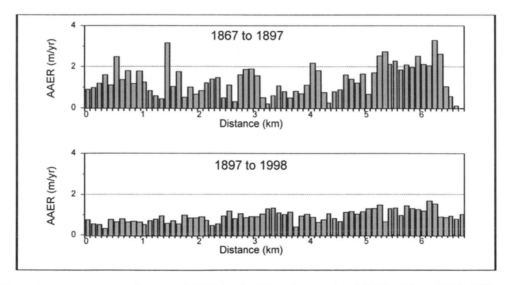

Fig. 4. Average annual recession rates (AAER) for the cliff top between A and B (Fig. 1) from 1867 to 1897 and 1897 to 1998, respectively.

rates in all the periods beginning with 1867. Figure 4 contrasts the recession from 1867 to 1897 with 1897 to 1998. In general, the 1867–1897 period shows larger rates of recession with a maximum retreat of $3.29 \pm 0.33 \, \mathrm{m \, a^{-1}}$, combined with a large alongshore variability. This is similar to the rates of retreat reported by Steers (1964). In contrast, 1897–1998 shows much less long-shore variation and a maximum retreat of $1.67 \pm 0.10 \, \mathrm{m \, a^{-1}}$. Therefore, it seems that the period 1867–1898 experienced untypically high rates of cliff retreat due to human influence. To understand this effect more completely, data at decadal intervals is required but this is simply not available. Pragmatically, the data for the period 1897–1998 seems the best data set available to this study, given the need for data length exceeding at least one geomorphic cycle. However, it must be acknowledged that it includes some human influence prior to 1914, plus any readjustment that occurred subsequent to this human interference.

Sediment input

Sediment input can be quantified by applying mass continuity to two consecutive profiles. In the case of cartographic data, only one or two points on the profile are known such as the cliff-top and cliff base and we need to assume that the rest of the profile moves with these indicators. In the case of Sheppey, the near-constant cliff width over time suggests that this is a reasonable assumption. Following Harlow (1979), the coast can be divided into a number of transects and the annual silt/clay input ($Q_{silt/clay}$) is:

$$Q_{silt/clay} = b \sum H A_c K_{silt/clay} \qquad (1)$$

where:

b is the longshore spacing between transects (in this case 100 m);
H is the height of the eroding cliff, including the submerged portion;
A_c is the average annual erosion rate of the cliff-top;
$K_{silt/clay}$ is the percentage of eroded material which is silt and clay.

The cliff height relative to Ordnance Datum is taken directly from the GPS survey in 1998. Based on the submarine contours it appears that wave erosion is only having a significant influence down to about 2 m below chart datum, and this is added to the cliff height. This means that most of the sediment is being produced from the sub-aerial cliff which contrasts with the

situation on more open coast settings such as Holderness where the eroding shoreface supplies significant quantities of sediment (Balson *et al.* 1998). The recession rates have already been discussed. $K_{silt/clay}$ depends on the geological composition of the eroded material which is dominantly London Clay. Based on Dines *et al.* (1954) and Holmes (1981) allowance was made for the presence of Claygate Beds and Bagshot beds at the top of some cliffs with a lower $K_{silt/clay}$ of 0.5 and 0.0, respectively. For the rest of the material eroded a range of $K_{silt/clay}$ values from 0.95 to 0.85 was considered. These values include any Quaternary deposits at the top of the cliff, and an allowance for septarian nodules and pyrite in the London Clay. Based on London Clay outcrops in Essex, the work of James & Lewis (1996) suggests that the most appropriate value of $K_{silt/clay}$ may be 0.85. The bulk density is assumed to be $2 \, \mathrm{tonnes \, m^{-3}}$.

The results show that from 1867–1897 the input of fine-grained sediment was about 660 000 to $740 000 \, \mathrm{t \, a^{-1}}$, falling by about one third to 450 000 to $500 000 \, \mathrm{t \, a^{-1}}$ from 1897 to 1998. If the frontages at Minster and Leysdown that were eroding from 1867 to 1897 are included, the supply was even larger at about 730 000 to $820 000 \, \mathrm{t \, a^{-1}}$ and the present supply is only about 60% of those values. This conclusion is reinforced by the possibility of cliff height decline over time, particularly near Warden Point where the most rapid changes have occurred (Brom-head 1979).

Future changes

Climate change is expected to occur in the 21st century and this will have important implications for coastal change. While there is significant uncertainty, sea-level rise is expected to accelerate significantly. Under a greenhouse gas emissions scenario of business-as-usual (no mitigation) and constant aerosols, the low, mid and high estimate for global rise is 0.23 m 0.55 and 0.96 cm from 1990 to 2100, respectively (Warrick *et al.* 1996). If we assume a global rise in sea level of 18 cm/century during the 20th century (Douglas 1991, 1997), then relative sea-level rise by 2100 will be about 4 cm higher than the global rise at Sheppey. These scenarios are shown in Fig. 5. It is worth noting that there are many uncertainties in transforming global scenarios to relative (or local) scenarios (see Titus & Narayanan 1996).

Given that the waves at the base of the cliff are depth limited, any rise in sea level would be expected to cause increased basal erosion and

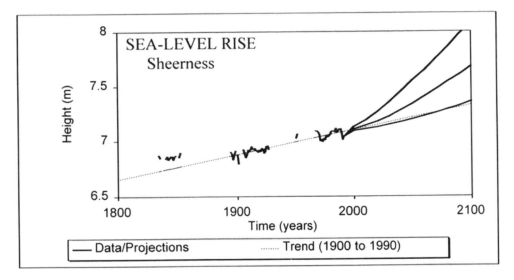

Fig. 5. Relative sea-level rise for Sheerness from 1800 to 2100, comprising observations to 1993 from the Permanent Service for Sea-Level, and the sea-level rise scenarios of Warrick *et al.* (1996) thereafter.

ultimately increased cliff-top recession (cf. Bray & Hooke 1997). However, the observations at this site show that a significant acceleration in sea-level rise (4 cm/century to 22 cm/century) was associated with a *decline* in recession rates. This is not to say that sea-level rise does not enhance recession, but rather that the cessation of mining activities on the cliff was a more important factor than the acceleration of sea-level rise. This suggests that while sea-level rise may accelerate cliff recession, the response may not be as dramatic as some models would suggest.

Bray & Hooke (1997) examined a range of simple geometric models to explore changes in rates of cliff recession as sea levels rise. They conclude that cliffs composed of large amounts of fine-grained sediment, like those at Sheppey, will be most sensitive to sea-level rise. Given an average rise in sea level of 0.55 m/century, which corresponds to the mid estimate of Warrick *et al.* (1996) for the 21st Century, all the models predict at least a twofold increase in cliff recession rates. While these projections are probably overestimates as they assume an instantaneous equilibrium response to the forcing, they suggest that the observed rates of cliff-top retreat observed from 1897 to 1998 provide good estimates of the *minimum* recession of the cliff-top in the 21st century.

Other aspects of climate change may affect recession rates and the overall cliff morphology. Changes in rainfall and storm frequency and intensity are particularly relevant. Based on

Hulme & Jenkins (1998), these factors may change (e.g. increased winter rainfall), but their influence on long-term recession rates is probably secondary compared to sea-level rise.

If sea-level rise causes increased recession, this will provide an increased input of fine-grained sediment to the Thames estuary system. The sinks for this sediment are not well understood, but the estuaries in Kent and Essex are likely to be one important long-term depositional site (see Prentice 1972). Despite widespread losses of saltmarsh and intertidal habitat from 1973 to 1988 (Burd 1992), the Blackwater is reported to be importing large quantities of sediment (Pethick 1993). Therefore, increased cliff erosion due to sea-level rise provides a beneficial negative feedback against the impacts of sea-level rise within the neighbouring estuaries (cf. Nicholls & Branson 1998).

Coastal management implications

The cliff erosion on Sheppey is an important natural process which is providing a significant and arguably important source of fine-grained sediment to the Thames estuary system and the southern North Sea. This section examines how existing coastal management considers this process.

The Isle of Sheppey coast is included in the Shoreline Management Plan (SMP) from the Isle of Grain to North Foreland (Halcrow 1996). Each SMP defines a number of management units and then selects one of four strategic responses for each unit (MAFF *et al.* 1995; Leafe *et al.* 1998):

- hold the line
- retreat the line
- advance the line
- do nothing

On the Sheppey coast, hold the line has been selected for Minister and Leysdown, while for the eroding cliffs, the response is do nothing, except south of Warden Point where the policy is hold the line. On this 500 m length of coast the beach already has groynes, but the cliff is presently retreating and properties will soon be threatened. Transition zones between the two policies about 500–600 m long have been defined at both boundaries (Fig. 6). At the western boundary the transitional zone fronts defended coast, but at the eastern boundary, the transitional zone includes Warden Point and areas which presently provide significant inputs of sediment. Therefore, if the chosen SMP strategic responses are fully implemented, the sediment supply is likely to decline.

As part of an initiative by English Nature (1993*a*, *b*), Estuary Management Plans (EMPs) have also been developed for parts of the Thames Estuary system. This includes the inner Thames estuary (Thames Estuary Project 1996, 1999), the Medway/Swale (North Kent Marshes Initiative 1997) and the Blackwater (Maldon District Council *et al.* 1996). One of the goals of these plans is to avoid disruption of natural sedimentary processes. However, the current plans emphasize an individual estuary perspective of the problem and do not explicitly acknowledge their relationship with the Thames Estuary System, or the wider North Sea. This omission includes potential sediment exchanges, including sources such as cliff erosion on Sheppey. These exchanges might be important to sustain intertidal areas and hence their associated ecological vales, particularly under scenarios of rising sea-level. The need to define such boundary conditions is explicit in emerging generic estuarine management frameworks (e.g. Pontee & Townend 1999). Given that both SMPs and EMPs are envisaged as living plans, these issues should be addressed in future revisions. In particular, the implications of exchanges of fine-grained sediments across cell boundaries for SMP purposes (e.g. Sheppey to Essex) need more consideration.

An important point is that both SMPs and EMPs are non-statutory plans. To be most effective they need to inform statutory plans such as land use and zoning within Town and Country Planning. Following local restrictions on cliff-top development in the urban areas of

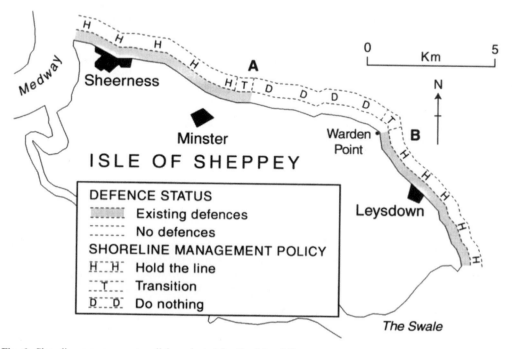

Fig. 6. Shoreline management policies selected for the Isle of Sheppey.

Minster and Leysdown (Department of Environment 1995, p. 18), a statutory building setback has recently been established along the entire eroding cliff-top of Sheppey (cf. Kay 1990; Owens & Cope 1992). This is to be commended. However, the setback is not explicitly linked to the SMP process, which is something that could be considered in future revisions.

The relative size of a building setback should reflect the cliff-top recession observations and hence in Sheppey would vary along the coast with the largest setback at Warden Point. The local effects on cliff-top retreat adjacent to the two valleys also need to be included. The absolute size of the setback depends on the appropriate timescale selected by the planning authorities: this is often based on building life and set at 60–100 years. An additional allowance for the effects of accelerated sea-level rise would be prudent, although difficult to quantify in detail. The goal of a setback is to minimize the human assets that would be threatened by coastal recession so that natural processes can continue unhindered. Therefore, permanent buildings would be precluded within the setback. However, a setback need not preclude all human development. As many recreational structures are mobile, they could continue to be located within a setback and moved landward as the cliff-top retreats (such land uses within a setback need to make such mobility an explicit requirement). This is the present policy in Sheppey.

Establishing setbacks on eroding coasts seems prudent even if the natural processes have no explicit value. In the case of Sheppey, the sediment supply has a value and this can be considered as a benefit of erosion (Department of Environment 1995), even though this is not yet formalised in benefit-cost analysis. This stresses that the Do Nothing option within SMPs is a No Engineering option, rather than a No Action option.

Discussion

The eroding cliffs at Sheppey provide large quantities of fine-grained sediment to the Thames Estuary system, although this source has declined due to coastal protection. Historically there were other areas of eroding London Clay such as Clacton to Frinton, Essex and parts of Whitstable to Herne Bay, Kent. Before large-scale coastal defences were built, this source of fine-grained sediment must have significantly exceeded fluvial supply from the Thames which is estimated at $7 \times 10^5\,\mathrm{t\,a^{-1}}$ (Odd & Murphy 1992). Even today, production of sediment on

Sheppey is at least $4.5 \times 10^5\,\mathrm{t\,a^{-1}}$. Therefore, cliff erosion remains an important source of fine-grained sediment within the Thames Estuary system.

The transport and deposition of this sediment is less clear, but several scales must exist. Locally there is exchange with estuaries like the Blackwater, Medway and the inner Thames, although the net fluxes are uncertain. At larger scales, some sediment must contribute to the large-scale exchanges of fine-grained sediment within the North Sea (Eisma 1981; Dyer & Moffat 1998). Large-scale exchanges may also import sediment into the Thames estuary system from external sources and pathways such as the English Channel.

While the sediment budget of both the Thames estuary system and more broadly the North Sea remains imperfectly understood, these balances are critical to the strategic management of estuaries under rising sea level (e.g. Thames Estuary Project 1996). In the absence of detailed understanding, a precautionary approach suggests that sediment supplies should not be interrupted. Coastal management is evolving in this direction, but maintaining and reinforcing the existing statutory building setbacks for the Sheppey coast would facilitate this goal. In parallel, further research is required to better quantify the long-term budget of sediment supply, transport and deposition within the Thames estuary system, including historical and possible future changes for different climate and management scenarios. This will improve estuary management and will further understanding of the North Sea sediment budget.

Conclusions

The Isle of Sheppey cliffs are an important source of fine-grained sediment input to the Thames Estuary system due to their height, composition and rapid retreat. While the pathways and sinks for this sediment are uncertain, any resulting accretion in the estuaries and marshes within the system is an important benefit in a situation of rising sea-levels. Therefore, we can apply the precautionary principle to manage the coastal system such that we sustain this supply of sediment as much as possible. Maintaining and enhancing the existing statutory building setbacks is essential for this goal. At the same time, there is a need to develop a better understanding of sediment supply, transport and deposition within the Thames estuary system and its relationship to the North Sea.

The authors would like to thank A. Moon and S. Chilton of Middlesex University for technical and field assistance. P. Joyce drew some of the diagrams. G. Thomas of Swale Borough Council kindly provided information on land use planning on the Isle of Sheppey.

References

BALSON, P. TRAGHEIM, D. & NEWSHAM, R. 1998. *Determination and prediction of sediment yields from recession of the Holderness coast, eastern England.* Proceedings of the 33rd MAFF Conference of River and Coastal Engineers, Keele University, 1 to 3 July 1998, 4.5.1–4.5.11.

BRAY, M. J. & HOOKE, J. 1997. Prediction of soft-cliff retreat with accelerating sea-level rise. *Journal of Coastal Research*, **13**, 453–467.

——, CARTER, D. J. & HOOKE, J. M. 1995. Littoral Cell Definition and Budgets for Central Southern England. *Journal of Coastal Research*, **11**, 381–400.

BRITISH GEOLOGICAL SURVEY 1997. *Inner Thames Estuary. England and Wales.* Part of Sheets 257, 258, 259, 271,272, 273. Pre-Quaternary Geology and Quaternary Geology. 1: 50 000. Keyworth, Nottingham.

BROMHEAD, E. N. 1979. Factors affecting the transition between the various types of mass movement in coastal cliffs consisting largely of overconsolidated clay with special reference to southern England. *Quarterly Journal of Engineering Geology*, **12**, 291–300.

BURD, F. H. 1992. *Erosion and vegetation change on the saltmarshes of Essex and North Kent between 1973 and 1988.* Research Survey in Nature Conservation No. 42. Nature Conservancy Council.

CARR, A. P. 1980. The significance of cartographic sources in determining coastal change. *In*: CULLINGFORD, R. A., DAVIDSON, D. A. & LEWIN, J. (eds) *Timescales in Geomorphology*, John Wiley, Chichester, pp. 67–78.

CROWELL, M., LEATHERMAN, S. P. & BUCKLEY, M. K. 1991. Historical shoreline change: error analysis and mapping accuracy. *Journal of Coastal Research*, 7 839–852.·

——, —— & ——1993. Erosion rate analysis: Longterm versus short-term data. *Shore and Beach*, **61**, 13–20.

DAVIES, A. G. 1936. The London Clay of Sheppey and the location of its fossils. *Proceedings of the Geologists Association*, **47**, 328–345.

DEPARTMENT OF THE ENVIRONMENT 1995. *Coastal Planning and Management: A Review of Earth Science Information Needs*, HMSO, London.

DEVRIEND, H. J. 1991. Mathematical modelling and large-scale coastal behaviour, Part I: Physical Processes. *Journal of Hydraulic Research*, **29**, 727–740.

DINES, H. G., HOLMES, S. C. A. & ROBBIE, J. A. 1954. *Geology of the country around Chatham.* Memoir of the Geological Survey, Great Britain, HMSO, London.

DOUGLAS, B. C. 1991. Global Sea Level Rise. *Journal of Geophysical Research*, **96**(C4), 6981–6992.

——1997. Global Sea Rise: A Redetermination. *Surveys in Geophysics*, **18**, 279–292.

DYER, K. R. & MOFFAT, T. J. 1998. Fluxes of suspended matter in the East Anglian plume, Southern North Sea. *Continental Shelf Research*, **18**, 1311–1331.

EISMA, D. 1981. Supply and deposition of suspended matter in the North Sea. *In*: NIO, S. D., SCHUTTENHELM, R. T. E., VAN WEERING, T. C. E. (eds) *Holocene Marine Sedimentation in the North Sea Basin*. International Association of Sedimentologists, Special Publication, No. **5**, Blackwells, Oxford, 415–428.

ENGLISH NATURE 1993a. *Strategy for the sustainable use of England's estuaries*, English Nature, Peterborough.

——1993b. *Estuary Management Plans – A Coordinators Guide*, English Nature, Peterborough.

FRENCH, P. W. 1997. *Coastal and Estuarine Management*, Routledge, London.

HALCROW, W. 1996. *Shoreline Management Plan for Sub-Cells 4a and 4b.* Sir William Halcrow & Partners, Swindon.

HARLOW, D. A. 1979. The Littoral Sediment Budget Between Selsey Bill and Gilkicker Point, and its Relevance to Coast Protection Works on Hayling Island, *Quarterly Journal of Engineering Geology*, **12**, 257–265.

HOLMES, S. C. A. 1981. *Geology of the country around Faversham.* Memoir of the Geological Survey, Great Britain, Sheet 273, HMSO, London.

HULME, M. & JENKINS, G. 1998. *Climate Change Scenarios for the United Kingdom*. UKCIP Technical Report No. 1, Climatic Research Unit, University of East Anglia, Norwich.

HUTCHINSON, J. N. 1968. Field meeting on the coastal landslides of Kent. *Proceedings of the Geologists Association*, **79**, 227–237.

JAMES, J. W. C. & LEWIS, P. M. 1996. *Sediment input from coastal cliff recession*, Environment Agency, Technical Unit 577, Peterborough.

JONES, D. K. C. 1981. *Southeast and Southern England.* Methuen, London.

KAY, R. 1990. Development controls on eroding coastlines: reducing the future impact of greenhouse-induced sea-level rise. *Land Use Policy*, 7 169–172.

LEAFE, R., PETHICK, J. & TOWNEND, I. 1998. Realising the Benefits of Shoreline Management. *Geographical Journal*, **164**, 282–290.

MALDON DISTRICT COUNCIL, COLCHESTER BOROUGH COUNCIL, ENGLISH NATURE & ESSEX COUNTY COUNCIL 1996. *The Blackwater Estuary Management Plan*, Maldon District Council and Colchester Borough Council, Maldon.

MINISTRY OF AGRICULTURE, FISHERIES & FOOD (MAFF), Welsh Office, Association of District Councils, English Nature & National Rivers Authority 1995. *Shoreline Management Plans: A guide for coastal defence authorities*. Ministry of Agriculture Fisheries & Food, London.

McCAVE, I. N. 1987. Fine sediment sources and sinks around the East Anglian Coast (UK). *Journal of Geological Society, London*, **144**, 149–152.

NICHOLLS, R. J. & BRANSON, J. 1998. Coastal Resilience and Planning for an Uncertain Future: An Introduction. *Geographical Journal*, **164**, 255–259.

NORTH KENT MARSHES INITIATIVE 1997. *Medway Estuary & Swale Management Plan.* (Consultation Draft).

ODD, N. V. M. & MURPHY, D. C. 1992. *Particle pollutants in the North Sea.* Report SR 292, Hydraulics Research, Wallingford.

OWENS, S. & COPE, D. 1992. *Land use planning policy and climate change*, Department of the Environment, London, HMSO.

PETHICK, J. 1993. Shoreline adjustment and coastal management: physical and biological processes under accelerated sea-level rise. *Geographical Journal*, **159**, 162–168.

PONTEE, N. I. & TOWNEND, I. H. 1999. *An estuary cause-consequence model.* Proceedings of the 34th MAFF Conference of River and Coastal Engineers, Keele University, 30 June to 2 July 1999, 5.2.1–5.2.17.

PRENTICE, J. E. 1972. Sedimentation in the inner estuary of the Thames and its relation to the regional subsidence. *Philosophical Transactions of the Royal Society*, **A272**, 115–119.

STEERS, J. A. 1964. *The coastline of England and Wales*, 2nd edn. Cambridge University Press, Cambridge.

STIVE, M. J. F., ROELVINK, J. A. & DEVRIEND, H. J. 1990. *Large Scale Coastal Evolution Concept.* Proceedings 22nd Coastal Engineering Conference, ASCE, New York, 1962–1974.

THAMES ESTUARY PROJECT 1996. *Thames Estuary Management Plan.* (Draft for consultation), Thames Estuary Project, English Nature, London.

——1999. *Management Guidance for the Thames Estuary: Principles for Action.* Thames Estuary Partnership, Institute for Environmental Policy, University College, London (see also http://www.thamesweb.com//).

TITUS, J. G. & NARAYANAN, V. 1996. The risk of sea-level rise: A Delphic Monte Carlo analysis in which twenty researchers specify subjective probability distributions for model coefficients within their respective areas of expertise. *Climatic Change*, **33**, 151–212.

WARRICK, R. A., OERLEMANS, J., WOODWORTH, P. L., MEIER, M. F. & LE PROVOST, C. 1996. *Changes in sea level. In*: HOUGHTON, J. T., MEIRA FILHO, L. G. & CALLANDER, B. A. (eds) *Climate Change 1995: The Science of Climate Change*, Cambridge University Press, Cambridge, 359–405.

WOODWORTH, P. 1990. A search for acceleration in records of European mean sea level. *International Journal of Climatology*, **10**, 129–143.

Holocene development of the east bank of the Gironde Estuary: geoarchaeological investigation of the Saint Ciers-sur-Gironde marsh

SIMEON J. MELLALIEU[1], LAURENT MASSÉ[1], DIDIER COQUILLAS[2], STÉPHANIE ALFONSO[1] & JEAN-PIERRE TASTET[1]

[1] *DGO, UMR CNRS 5805 'EPOC', Université Bordeaux I Avenue des Facultés, 33405 Talence cedex, France (e-mail: masse@geocean.u-bordeaux.fr)*
[2] *IRAM, Maison de l'Archéologie, Université de Bordeaux III, Esplanade des Antilles, 33405 Talence cedex, France*

Abstract: The nature of postglacial sea-level change and sediment infilling of the Gironde Estuary, SW France, has previously been reconstructed using a sequence stratigraphic model. This paper examines specifically the development of the St Ciers-sur-Gironde marsh during the late Holocene. The study area forms the largest expanse of coastal wetlands on the east bank of the Gironde. A geoarchaeological approach is used incorporating borehole survey, sedimentological and diatom analysis, radiocarbon dating, archaeological, documentary and cartographic evidence, which aims to test and refine the previous model of estuarine development.

The later Holocene sequence is characterized by alternating clay-silt and peat facies. Diatom evidence indicates that clay-silt units represent sedimentation under marine-brackish estuarine conditions in intertidal mudflat, and potentially saltmarsh, environments. The palaeoenvironmental conditions represented by the main upper peat unit, dated to 5600–2600 BP, are currently unknown due to the absence of diatom evidence from these levels. Within an overlying trend of rising relative sea-level over the past 6000 years, 3 negative sea-level tendencies appear to have occurred. There is insufficient resolution in the present data set to determine the exact nature of each or their duration.

Sea-level reconstruction based on the large scale studies of entire coastlines has long since been abandoned. In their place small-scale regional studies are now preferred (Kidson 1982). Studies of the French coastline are no exception to this shift in approach. Early models combining data from the Atlantic and English Channel seaboards (Ters 1973; Verger 1968) have been superceded following this trend (e.g. Clet-Pellerin *et al.* 1981; Labeyrie *et al.* 1976; Van de Plassche 1991) and the impact of differential rates of glaciohydroisostasy upon the north and west coasts of France has recently been emphasized, clearly illustrating the need for small-scale approaches (Lambeck 1997). Studies thus far all show common agreement of a phase of rapid sea-level rise between 15 000 and 7000 BP at which point a slow gradual rise to the present datum occurred (Pirazzoli 1991). However, data derived from SW France has made little contribution to such regional comparisons as the area has passed largely unstudied.

The Gironde Estuary is the largest estuary in Europe (Jouanneau & Latouche 1981) and is located on the Atlantic coast of SW France. The estuary has been the focus for a large number of sedimentological and facies based studies (e.g. Allen 1972; Assor 1972; Feral 1970; Migniot 1971; Pontee *et al.* 1998), but as yet there is only a rudimentary model for sea-level change in the area (Allen & Posamentier 1993; Feral 1970). This model is the result of over 20 years of research which has largely focused upon Holocene sequences from the west bank of the estuary. As yet there has been no attempt to produce a holistic interpretation of estuarine development using data from the east and west banks, both of which are bounded by marshes with ample potential for sampling.

This study examines the development of the St Ciers-sur-Gironde Marsh, an extensive wetland area which borders the east bank of the Gironde estuary. In addition to the traditional methods of palaeoenvironmental reconstruction, such as litho-, bio- and chronostratigraphic evidence, archaeological site distributions are also used to provide palaeogeographical evidence for estuarine infilling.

From: PYE, K. & ALLEN, J. R. L. (eds). *Coastal and Estuarine Environments: sedimentology, geomorphology and geoarchaeology*. Geological Society, London, Special Publications, **175**, 317–341. 0305-8719/00/$15.00 © The Geological Society of London 2000.

Archaeological evidence has proved to be a useful tool in the reconstruction of coastal wetland areas in the past (e.g. Allen & Fulford 1986; Simmons 1980; Wilkinson & Murphy 1986). Site distributions are better suited to palaeogeographical, rather than sea-level, modelling as it is frequently difficult to relate an archaeological structure/feature to contemporary sea-level with any degree of precision. Along the Mediterranean coast archaeological indicators have been used to define contemporary sea-levels to precision of up to ±0.15 m (Flemming 1979–80). However, precision is effected by the type of archaeological indicator used, their frequency in an area and tidal range so that often, such narrow error margins are not possible to predict. Therefore, sea-level curves utilizing purely archaeological data are rare (e.g. Louwe Kooijmans 1980; Scarre 1984) and no attempt to produce such a curve is made here.

The geoarchaeological study models marsh evolution over the past 6000 years. The approach can be subdivided into three fields of investigation: palaeoenvironmental change, marsh palaeogeography, and marsh chronology. Evidence of palaeoenvironmental change is derived from sedimentological and diatom analysis. Archaeological evidence and cartographic sources are combined with lithostratigraphic data to reconstruct the pattern of marsh expansion over time. Both absolute and relative dating methods are used in establishing a chronology of marsh development in the form of radiocarbon age estimates and archaeological evidence respectively. The pattern of past human activity on the marsh has implications for sea-level change within the estuary and the combined data set will be used to refine the previous model for the Gironde.

The study area

The Gironde Estuary

The Gironde is formed by the confluence of the Garonne and Dordogne rivers. The estuary is strictly defined as the region between the river confluence at Bec d'Ambès and the Atlantic Ocean and measures 76 km in length (Fig. 1). However, the tidal current penetrates beyond the river confluence to a maximum 130 km from the estuary mouth (Jouanneau & Latouche 1981). The Gironde is macrotidal with a spring tidal range of 5.5 m. The estuary is funnel-shaped, 11 km wide at its mouth, tapering to 2 km at Bec d'Ambès, as is the typical form of estuaries in macrotidal environments.

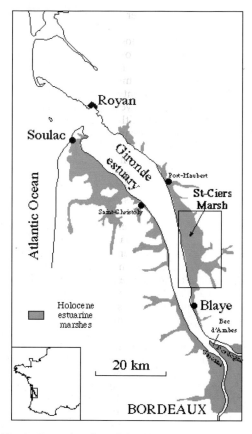

Fig. 1. General setting of the Gironde estuary and location of the study area.

The estuary occupies a flooded valley incized into Tertiary limestone during Pleistocene sea-level low-stands. The modern estuary can be subdivided into three zones based upon morphology and dynamic processes (Allen 1972). The upper estuary is characterized by meandering channels, sand and mud point bars and back barrier marshes. The middle estuary has a complex morphology of anastamosing channels between longitudinal bars and is bounded by mudflats and saltmarshes. The outer estuary is a more simplified two channel system, a deeply scoured tidal inlet with sandy shoals and well developed mudflats and saltmarshes (Allen 1972). Of fluvial sediment, all sand sized particles and 40% of silts and clays are deposited in the estuary. The remaining sediment is deposited on the continental shelf as mud patches. Up to 1.5×10^6 t. yr^{-1} of sediment is delivered to the Atlantic coast (Castaing & Jouanneau 1987). This depositional pattern has not been constant over the Holocene (Lesueur *et al.* 1996).

The most recent model of sea-level change and estuarine infilling of the Gironde is that of Allen & Posamentier (1993) derived from a sequence stratigraphic model of the estuary. The Holocene sequence is interpreted as representing a transgressive-regressive sediment wedge within which three major lithofacies types can be identified. Tidal estuarine sands and muds (representing estuarine point bars, tidal sand bars, tidal flat and marsh deposits) dominate the sequence. A tidal inlet unit composed of massive marine sands occurs at the estuary mouth. Massive fluvial coarse sands and gravels occupy the base of the sequence.

From these facies Allen & Posamentier (1993) defined three major phases of sea-level change and associated sedimentation which can be further elaborated upon by the incorporation of additional recent evidence. Rapid sea-level rise at the start of the Holocene flooded the incized valley and the lowstand systems tract of Pleistocene fluvial gravels was submerged. A transgressive systems tract was deposited during this phase composed of estuarine sands and muds and tidal inlet sands onlapping fluvial facies. Sediment supply could not keep pace with the the new accommodation space created and a ria type estuary was formed (Diot & Tastet 1995; Klingebiel & Tastet 1995). Sea-level attained its present position around 6000 BP (Lambeck 1997) thereby limiting sediment accommodation space. The sedimentation pattern shifted from a transgressive systems tract to a highstand systems tract (Allen & Posamentier 1993). At this stage all fluvial sediment was being deposited within the estuary. A regressive bayhead delta composed of tidal bars and flats prograded into the head of the middle estuary whilst saltmarshes and mudflats accumulated and prograded in channels and embayments at estuarine margins (Pontee *et al.* 1998; Massé *et al.* in press *a, b*). This sedimentation pattern continued to close to the present day, although the quantities of fluvial sediment reaching the continental shelf has increased since 2000 BP (Lesueur *et al.* 1996). Comparison of bathymetric charts dating back to the 18th century indicate that by this time the estuary had reached equilibrium (Migniot 1971).

As this model is derived solely from lithostratigraphic evidence a large amount of detail is lacking. There is at present no indication of whether sea-level rise occurred in a smooth or spasmodic fashion (Kidson 1982) or any data pertaining to the amount or rate of sea-level rise since 6000 BP. In addition, the model does not incorporate data from the east bank of the estuary and thus may not be truely representative of the estuary as a whole.

The Saint Ciers-sur-Gironde marsh

The St Ciers-sur-Gironde marsh forms 40 000 ha of reclaimed coastal marshes on the east bank of the middle estuary extending 30 km from Port-Maubert in the north to Blaye in the south (Fig. 1). It is bounded on its western estuarine margin by sea defences first constructed in 296 BP (1654 AD). Low hills, which attain a maximum elevation of 75 m NGF (Nivellement General de la France, the French levelling system), form the eastern landward boundary of the marsh. The Tertiary carbonate substratum of the region can be sub-divided into the Cretaceous limestones to the north and Eocene sands and clays to the south. The modern marsh surface lies between +0.5 and +2.5 m NGF and is dissected by a complex system of drainage channels. Twelve different soil types can be identified on the marsh with profiles extending through the upper 2 m of Holocene stratigraphy (Blondy 1987). Hydromorphic gleys and pseudogleys predominate although all soil types are poorly developed. Current landuse is a mixture of pasture and arable (Blondy 1987). A number of archaeological sites, largely dating to the Iron Age to Gallo-Roman periods (Coquillas 1993, 2001), are known both on the present marsh surface and upon its landward margins (Fig. 2b). These will be discussed in greater detail below.

Stratigraphic studies of the St Ciers marsh focus upon a central zone delimited by St Bonnet-sur-Gironde in the north and Le Canal Saint-Georges in the south (Fig. 2a). A chronology of marsh development is presented concentrating specifically within this zone and considering the study area in its wider context.

Methods

Lithostratigraphic interpretation is based upon 12 boreholes which form two transects running across the marsh perpendicular to the sea-defences. Seven boreholes were made using a mechanical percussion auger which provided uncontaminated samples for laboratory sedimentological and diatom analysis. In addition, a manual gouge auger was used to produce five additional lithostratigraphic records at selected intermediate points between percussion boreholes. The upper part of the Holocene sequence was targeted for sampling as this relates to sediment accumulation since

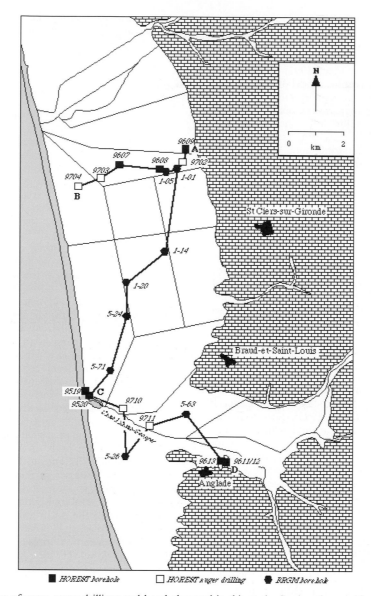

Fig. 2a. Location of cores, auger drillings and boreholes used in this study. See location on Fig. 1.

6000 BP after sea-level rise slowed (Allen & Posamentier 1993; Bertero 1993) and also to the period during which the marshes were exploited by human activity. Where possible, boreholes (percussion and gouge augers) were placed directly over archaeological sites in order that archaeological horizons could be placed in their lithostratigraphic context. The deepest boreholes were drilled using the percussion auger and a maximum depth of 8 m below the present marsh surface was obtained.

These lithostratigraphic records were supplemented by eight additional borehole logs made by the Bureau de Recherches Géologiques et Minières (B.R.G.M – French Geological Survey) which allows more widespread lithostratigraphic correlation across the marsh along additional transects. The borehole records provided by the B.R.G.M survey have been summarized by Bertero (1993) which provides the first lithostratigraphic model for the St Ciers-sur-Gironde marsh. The spatial distribution of the boreholes is shown in Fig. 2a and Table 1.

Continuous samples made by percussion auger from 8 boreholes were analysed in the laboratories of the Departement de Géologie et Océanographie,

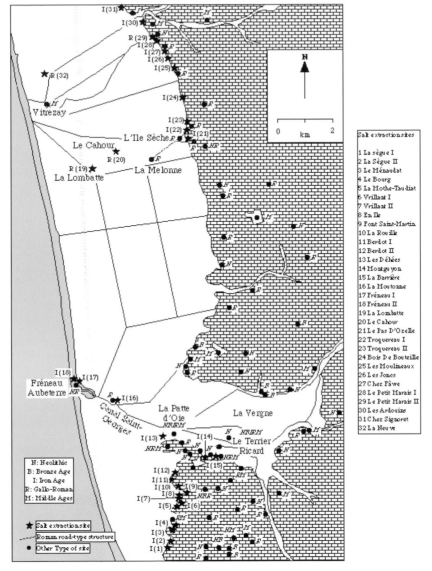

Fig. 2b. Location and nature of archaeological sites in the St-Ciers marsh area.

Université Bordeaux I. The sediments were first described in detail incorporating colour, compositional and structural properties. Sub-samples were taken every 10 cm for particle size analysis and diatom analysis. Particle size data was produced using a Malvern 3600e laser particle size analyser. All organic material was removed using hydrogen peroxide prior to analysis. Diatom slides were prepared using standard organic digestion and centrifugation methods described by Battarbee (1986) and the resulting suspensions mounted using Naphrax. Counts of 200 valves per slide were made using phase contrast microscopy

at ×400 magnification. Diatom species were identified with reference to Germain (1981) and assemblages interpreted following the Vos and De Wolf (1993) method. This method draws upon both lithostratigraphic and diatom evidence to derive an interpretation of sedimentary environment and therefore provides and excellent link between the different approaches employed in this study.

The current known archaeological site distribution for the St Ciers-sur-Gironde marsh has also been integrated with stratigraphic data to reconstruct the spatial extent of marsh development during specific

Table 1. *Location of HOREST cores and BRGM boreholes used in this study. Italics indicate auger drillings*

Borehole	LIII X	LIII Y	Z m NGF	Latitude	Longitude
HOREST 9519	362.19	330.77	2.08	45° 14′ 18.50″	0° 41′ 28.61″
HOREST 9520	362.28	330.73	1.56	45° 14′ 17.32″	0° 41′ 24.42″
HOREST 9607	363.40	338.09	1.60	45° 18′ 16.86″	0° 40′ 45.47″
HOREST 9608	365.28	338.73	1.70	45° 18′ 39.80″	0° 39′ 20.31″
HOREST 9609	366.33	339.29	1.30	45° 18′ 59.16″	0° 38′ 33.08″
HOREST 9611/12	367.38	330.77	2.00	45° 13′ 02.72″	0° 37′ 26.67″
HOREST 9613	367.22	328.30	2.00	45° 13′ 04.48″	0° 37′ 34.10″
HOREST 9702	366.05	338.76	1.10	45° 18′ 41.68″	0° 38′ 45.04″
HOREST 9703	363.00	338.20	2.50	45° 18′ 19.95″	0° 41′ 04.00″
HOREST 9704	362.20	338.05	2.30	45° 18′ 14.14″	0° 41′ 40.44″
HOREST 9710	363.62	330.12	2.50	45° 13′ 59.16″	0° 40′ 22.01″
HOREST 9711	364.50	329.42	2.50	45° 13′ 37.55″	0° 40′ 21.13″
BRGM 755-1-01	365.90	338.81	2.00	45° 18′ 43.12″	0° 38′ 52.01″
BRGM 755-1-05	365.36	338.51	1.00	45° 18′ 32.78″	0° 39′ 16.28″
BRGM 755-1-14	365.30	335.88	1.10	45° 17′ 07.58″	0° 39′ 14.65″
BRGM 755-1-20	363.72	334.86	1.00	45° 16′ 32.70″	0° 40′ 25.38″
BRGM 755-5-24	363.78	333.62	0.75	45° 15′ 52.64″	0° 40′ 20.55″
BRGM 755-5-26	363.58	328.50	2.52	45° 13′ 06.68″	0° 40′ 21.13″
BRGM 755-5-71	362.69	331.52	2.00	45° 14′ 43.37″	0° 41′ 06.97″
BRGM 755-5-63	365.80	328.66	0.89	45° 13′ 14.48″	0° 38′ 39.73″

time periods. The site listing from the St Ciers-sur-Gironde, Braud-et-Saint-Louis and Anglade regions has been utilized (Coquillas 1990, 2001). A total of 96 sites are known including those both on the marsh and on its continental margins. From this number, all sites represented by only a single find, hoards and dolmens have been excluded from analysis along with all sites located at datums >15 m NGF. In this way only long-term occupation sites are considered which are more reliable for the aims of this study. The number of sites remaining after screening is also sufficient for marsh occupation to be considered in the wider context of the total settlement distribution of the region. Cartographic evidence has been utilized to determine the nature of marsh development over the past 300 years (Migniot 1971).

A minimum occupiable datum (MOD) has been defined for successive archaeological periods to provide a preliminary indication of the maximum upper limit for the position of past sea-levels (Fig. 8). The definition of the MOD is based upon the premise that a permanently occupied site would not have been established upon a landsurface prone to regular flooding e.g. due to the daily tidal cycle or through a fluctuating ground water table. The relationship between the MOD and contemporary tidal levels will be dependent upon the type of site from which it comes as for functional reasons sites are established either on dry land, or partly or completely submerged by the sea (Flemming 1979–1980). Where sites are present in a distribution which is known to have had a strong maritime association, a closer association can be made between the MOD and tidal levels. All of the archaeological sites in the

St Ciers region are of a dry land setting but many demand a coastal location. Mean high water spring tide (MHWST) is therefore used as the tidal reference point for former sea-levels throughout.

Due to the general unreliability of archaeological sites as sea-level indicators (Akeroyd 1972), the site distribution is used largely to infer patterns of vertical/horizontal marsh development. However, the nature of human occupation on the St Ciers marsh does have significant implications for sea-level change in the Gironde Estuary. Where evidence for a fluctuation in relative sea-level rise does occur, greater emphasis is placed upon the timing of the event rather than the inferred height sea-level had attained. Thus, MOD's are provided merely as a guide at this stage.

The Holocene sequence

The fourteen boreholes taken across the marsh show a sequence of massive clay-silts with intercalated peat units overlying sandy muds (Figs 3a, b & c). This sequence correlates well with that derived from B.R.G.M boreholes (Bertero 1993). The Holocene units vary in depth from 3 m at the landward margin to >20 m at the estuarine channel (Bertero 1993). Combining the two sets of boreholes the sequence can be described, from bottom to top, as follows:

- Sand – interbedded sands and sandy silts with occasional gravels.
- Lower clay-silt – generally massive with occasional tidal bedding, frequent plant

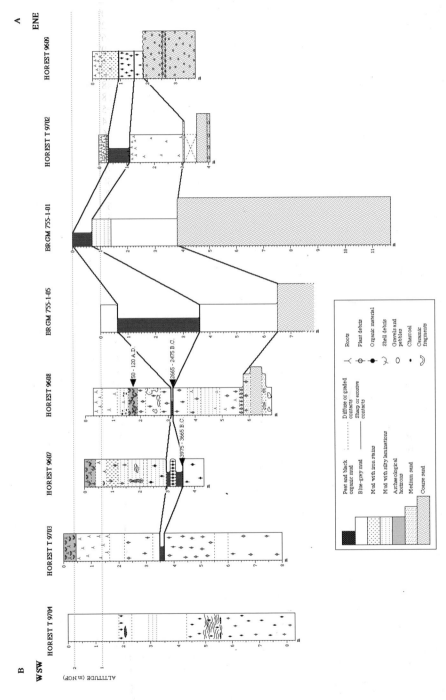

Fig. 3a. Fence diagram of the northernmost core transect (see Fig. 2a for location).

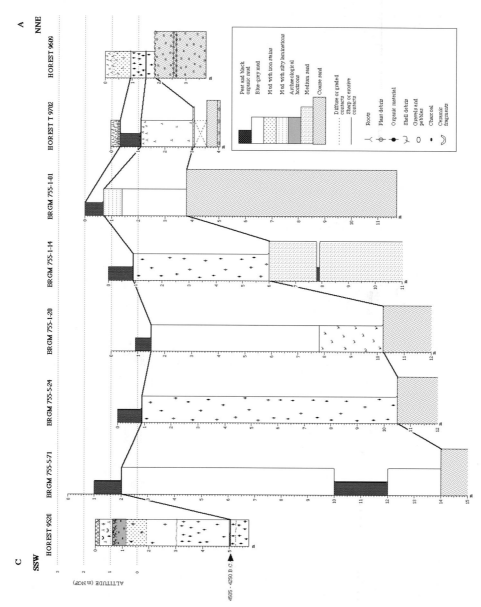

Fig. 3b. Fence diagram of the median core transect (see Fig. 2a for location).

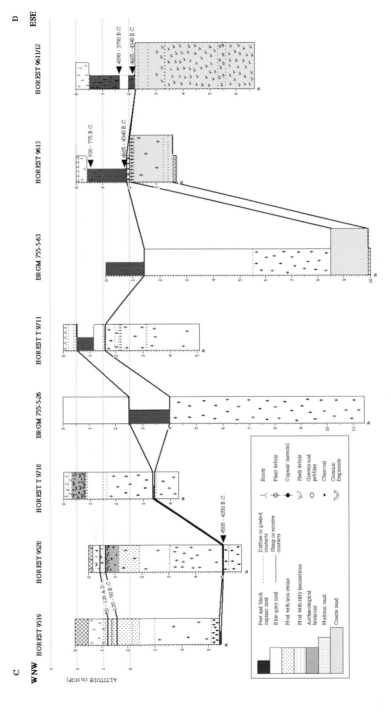

Fig. 3c. Fence diagram of the southernmost core transect (see Fig. 2a for location).

debris and *in situ Scrobicularia* shells in some boreholes.
- Peat – well humified peat bounded by sharp contacts with organic mud intercalations; often containing woody roots.
- Upper clay-silt – massive clay-silt over-printed by pedogenesis. Absent in some boreholes.

Borehole evidence and local knowledge of the sequence derived through well digging (R. Goyon pers. comm.) indicates that the principle litho-stratigraphic units are laterally extensive at least through the central section of the marsh.

The particle size properties of each stratigraphic unit are shown in Table 2. An overlap in size parameters is shown by fine grained units in all boreholes. Little variation is shown down-core, although grading trends are apparent (Fig. 4). The absence of sand units in the upper part of the sequence marks a significant shift in the depositional regime of the marsh. This shift can be attributed to two factors. Firstly, the shift from a transgressive phase to a regressive phase as the rate of sea-level rise slowed (Allen & Postmentier 1993) and secondly to the decreasing competence of water flow to transport coarse grained sediments as the infilling of the estuary progressed (Jouanneau & Latouche 1981).

Given the homogeneity of sedimentary characteristics within the upper and lower clay-silt units, the distribution of plant rooting is one of the few criteria which can be used in stratigraphic differentiation. The modern saltmarsh sediments of St Christoly on the west bank of the Gironde provide a perfect modern analogue for the massive, rooted clay-silts. The high sediment load of the estuary is presumably the reason for the low organic content of the salt-marsh sediments bordering the Gironde in comparison to those of other estuaries (Mellalieu 1997). The frequent alternation of rooted and unrooted clay-silt beds is suggestive of a dynamic intertidal environment showing continuous shifts in the distribution of facies.

Diatom valves were only found to be present in the lower clay-silt units (Fig. 4). Preservation is not continuous either down through the sequence or at comparable datums across the marsh. It would appear that all assemblages have been subject to differential dissolution of diatom valves. This is suggested firstly by the low species diversity shown in each assemblage counted (12–20 species) and secondly by the high preservation potential of the species present (as recorded by Denys 1991).

Benthic and planktonic species across a salinity spectrum ranging from marine to fresh-water are present in all assemblages counted. Marine/brackish epipelic species dominated throughout (Fig. 4), *Nitzschia navicularis* and *Diploneis didyma* being particularly abundant. Using the Vos & De Wolf (1993) method, all assemblages are interpreted as those of intertidal mudflats and is supported by the fine grained, and generally massive nature of the deposits to which they relate (Evans 1965; Larsonneur 1975; Reineck & Singh 1980). However, given the absence of many genera, particularly *Navicularis*, it is possible that other intertidal depositional environments present in the sequence may be unrecognizable due to the effects of differential dissolution upon less robust indicator species. This is particularly the case for salt-marsh units, the presence of which is suggested by frequent beds of rooted massive clay-silts described above.

Two peat beds are present in the sequence. The first, lower, peat bed is deeply buried and its development appears to have had a restricted and irregular distribution (Fig. 3b). This unit is only recorded in B.R.G.M. boreholes and there are no ^{14}C assays available with which to date its formation. The second, upper, peat bed is far more extensive and has been recorded throughout the marsh interior up to the continental margin. In the interior of the marsh the upper peat bed varies between 1–3 m in thickness and occurs across a datum range of +2.0 m to −3.5 m NGF. The peat bed thins considerably

Table 2. *Mean values of grain-size in the lithologic units (in μm)*

Borehole	Upper Clay-Silt	Peat	Lower Clay-Silt	Sand
HOREST 9519	10.3	8.6	absent	absent
HOREST 9520	11.5	no data	11.2	absent
HOREST 9607	14.0	23.5	8.6	absent
HOREST 9608	12.4	no data	11.0	284.3
HOREST 9609	10.2	13.0	absent	no data
HOREST 9611/12	absent	no data	absent	204.4

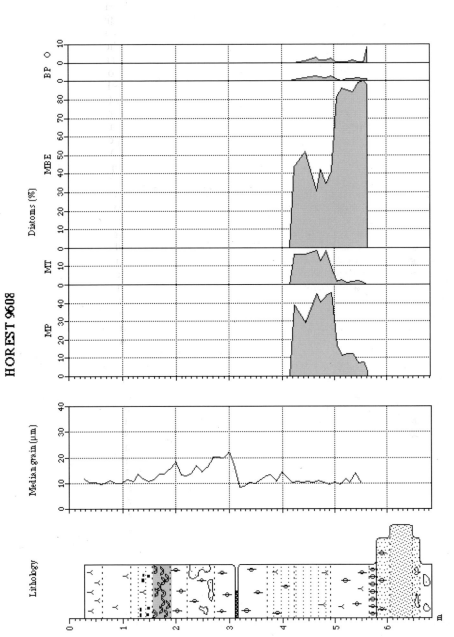

Fig. 4. Lithology, median grain and diatom distribution in core HOREST 9608 (see Fig. 2a for location). MP: marine plankton; MT: marine tychoplankton; MBE: marine/brackish epipelon; BP: brackish plankton; O: others.

Table 3. *¹⁴C age estimates have obtained from the upper peat unit*

Borehole	Depth (cm)	Age (BP)	Cal. BC	Material	Sample ref.	Measurement type
HO 9520	500–503	5540 ± 70	4505–4250	Peat	Beta 95392	Traditional
HO 9607	350–355	5030 ± 70	3975–3665	Peat	Beta 99067	Traditional
HO 9608	311–316	4120 ± 40	2665–2475	Peat	Beta 99068	AMS
HO 9611/12	210–215	5630 ± 70	4605–4340	Peat	Beta 104801	Traditional
HO 9611/12	160–165	5160 ± 70	4090–3790	Peat	Beta 104802	Traditional
HO 9613	50–55	2670 ± 70	930–775	Peat	Beta 104803	Traditional
HO 9613	180–184	5630 ± 70	4605–4340	Peat	Beta 104804	Traditional

towards its western estuarine margin. In some cases the reduced thickness of the unit may also be due to erosion of the upper contact. The upper clay-silt unit overlies the upper peat in a number of boreholes (Fig. 3a, b & c). This indicates that in marginal areas peat development was arrested by tidal inundation whereas in more sheltered/protected areas peat continued to accumulate until the marsh was reclaimed.

Seven ¹⁴C age estimates have been obtained from the upper peat unit (Table 3). The base of the peat at its landward margin at Anglade (HO 9611/12, HO 9613) is dated consistently at 5630 ± 70 BP (4605–4340 cal. BC) Two radiocarbon dates of 5030 ± 70 BP (3975–3665 cal. BC; HO 9607) and 4120 ± 40 BP (2665–2475 cal. BC; HO 9608) from the centre of the marsh indicate that the peat unit prograded towards the estuary over time. An age estimate of 2670 ± 70 BP (930–775 cal. BC; HO 9613) is, at present, the only assay available for the transgressive contact between peat and the overlying upper clay-silt unit. This age estimate is derived from the continental margin of the more sheltered La Vergne marsh, making it possible that the transgressive event commenced earlier in more open areas closer to the estuarine channel.

The environmental conditions under which the peat units accumulated are currently unknown due to the absence of diatom data. This is disappointing in that the extent of peat development marks the major difference between lithostratigraphic evidence from the St Ciers marsh and the Allen & Posamentier (1993) model for estuarine infilling (peat lenses only being noted as occurring in the previous model). Freshwater conditions at the start of peat development are indicated by the presence of wood fragments at the base of the unit. This evidence is supported by the presence of a submerged forest which is known to occur in the region of l'Ile Sèche at approximately 0 m NGF (R. Goyon pers. comm.) which correlates with peat datums. The migration of channels across the marsh surface would seem to be a likely cause of erosion due to the irregular lateral distribution of the erosion surface. Minerogenic horizons within the peat unit suggest both the proximity of channels and a surface prone to flooding.

From the present lithostratigraphic data it would appear that a relative sea-level change of around 4.5 m has occurred since the onset of peat formation around 5600 BP. However, all stratigraphic contacts would have been subject to datum changes since deposition through compaction, subsidence and land shrinkage. Therefore the actual relative sea-level rise is likely to be less than that apparent. Clay-silt units and peat beds will have undergone the greatest compaction although the actual amount is difficult to establish due to the combined effects of variable lithology and variable depth of the succession (Greensmith & Tucker 1986). However, where a peat overlies a basal sand unit, as occurs in boreholes HO 9612 and HO 9613 (Fig. 3b), the lower contact is expected to be closer to its original datum. The effects of land shrinkage due to oxidation and desiccation are obvious on the present marsh surface. Topographic lows, forming a surface relief of 2 m, correlate with the distribution of peat at the surface. The degree of tectonic subsidence in the Gironde region is currently unknown but is thought to be lower than subsidence rates for the area immediately to the south of the Gironde around Arcachon Bay which vary between 0.0–0.7 mm a^{-1} (Klingebiel & Gayet 1995). These figures cannot be expected to have remained constant over the course of the Holocene as contributions from sediment loading and hydro-isostacy will have varied (Lambeck 1997). A constant rate of 0.7 mm a^{-1} since the onset of peat formation is sufficient to account for almost all of the apparent relative sea-level rise observed using lithostratigraphic data (3.92 m). Therefore a considerable difference between recorded datum and datum at the time of deposition is anticipated but cannot be quantifed at present. These processes will also effect the values for MOD quoted below.

Archaeology of the St. Ciers-sur-Gironde marsh

From the original archaeological distribution, a list of 63 sites remain after the screening process. Sites covering an archaeological time span from the Neolithic through to the Medieval Period are represented (8000–500 BP). Iron Age and Gallo-Roman remains predominate but older remains are worthy of comment.

Neolithic and Bronze Age

Sites relating to Neolithic (8000–3750 BP; 6000–1800 cal. BC) and succeeding Bronze Age (3750–2675 BP; 1800–725 cal. BC) periods are distributed along the landward marsh margins and surrounding uplands, but within the marsh are rare. This is to be expected as chronological horizons relating to the Neolithic and Bronze Age periods in marsh areas will be more deeply buried within the estuary fill and therefore are generally invisible to surface survey. Neolithic sites are more numerous than those of the succeeding Bronze Age in accordance with evidence from the west bank of the estuary (Coquillas 2001). The apparent occupation pattern is surprising as the low density of Bronze Age sites contrasts with archaeological evidence from the British Isles, for example, which shows that Bronze Age peoples actively exploited wetland areas (Wilkinson & Murphy 1986), and that site numbers often exceed those from other time periods (Wilkinson 1989).

Iron Age

From the Iron Age (2675–2000 BP; 725–50 BC) onwards archaeological evidence shows that the St Ciers region was an important area for local industry and trade/sea-transport. More than 25 Iron Age salt production sites are known within and around the St Ciers marsh (Coquillas 1993). The salt industry flourished in the region between 2100–2000 BP (1st to 2nd centuries BC) and has parallels throughout France and western Europe. Salt production is the only evidence of Iron Age activity in the study area. Identification of such sites is indisputable through the recovery of briquetage fragments, a ceramic fabric type specific to the salt production industry. The greatest concentration of salt production sites occurs along the border of the southern sector of the marsh in the environs of Braud-et-St.-Louis, Anglade and St Androny (Fig. 2b) although a small number of sites are known on the marsh surface itself.

Four of the cores described in this study were placed directly upon such sites: La Lombatte (HO 9703), Le Cahour (HO 9607), La Moutonne (HO 9710) and Fréneau-Aubeterre (HO 9520). The latter is the best known example in the area. It is located on the estuarine edge of the marsh and has been particularly well exposed on erosion cliffs during recent years. The outcrops reveal two phases of salt production separated by a thin mud layer (Fig. 5). Although poorly preserved, all of the material currently found on briquetage sites has been described, along with domestic warehouse indicating a temporary settlement. The date of this occupation is La Tène III (120–80 cal. BC).

The precise relationship of salt production sites to the intertidal zone is often unclear as sites may be found located upon both marsh and dryland surfaces, as is also the case in the St Ciers region. Current thinking favours a supratidal, rather than an intertidal, position for site location (e.g. Fawn *et al.* 1990; Perrichet-Thomas, 1986) and is also assumed here. The presence of sites on the present marsh surface suggests that at least part of the current marsh area may have been above MHWST during the Iron Age period. However, the variability in the location of salt production sites prevents a consistent relationship to contemporary tidal levels being identified. Therefore, datums derived from salt production sites only provide a maximum upper level for the position of contemporary MHWST.

Gallo-Roman period

Whilst there is no evidence for the continuation of the salt industry in the area after 2000 BP (50 cal. BC) during the succeeding Gallo-Roman period, there is evidence to suggest that Iron Age sites continued to be occupied or were re-occupied. A number of further Gallo-Roman sites are known, many of which consist of settlements/villas and again occur on the marsh margins and further inland (indicating a wider range of activities), but more significantly, also on the outer marsh surface towards the estuary channel (Fig. 2b). This occupation pattern occurs without any indication of the construction of a drainage system or sea-defences during this period as exists, for example, in the Severn Estuary marshes, UK (Allen & Fulford 1986). The three most important sites are clearly related to warehouse/ceramic industry and trade/sea-transport.

(A)

(B)

Fig. 5. General (**A**) and close-up (**B**) views of the La Tène III salt production layers in Fréneau-Aubeterre.

(A)

(B)

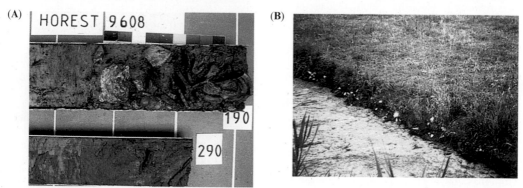

Fig. 6. The Gallo-Roman road-type structure in core HOREST 9608 (**A**) between 1.92 and 1.67 m depth in core 9608 (La Melonne) and (**B**) in a ditch near l'Ile Sèche, 0.7 m below the surface.

Fig. 7. Wooden pieces of the Gallo-Roman jetty in La Patte d'Oie.

A road-type structure (Fig. 6), extending 1.2 km southwestwards on the marsh surface from l'Ile Sèche to La Melonne (Fig. 2b) has been described as early as 1856. It consists of numerous rocks, tiles and warehouse/ceramic debris (over 4000 m³) spread over the marsh surface with occasional wooden posts for stabilization. The highly homogeneous material essentially originates from the South Saintonge production sites, located some 50 km to the northeast, and was produced there between 50 and 120 AD. The 'road' ends abruptly in the vicinity of La Melonne, where it was sampled as a 35 cm thick layer of highly compacted ceramic fragments in core HO 9608. Apparently, the main function of this rudimentary structure was to board and export the ceramic production of the South Saintonge, and it was built with the artifacts which had been broken during the land transportation.

The second warehouse site is located in La Patte d'Oie near Anglade (Fig. 2b) which bears thick deposits of tiles and ceramics with occasional domestic waste and human bones, as well as a a large paved surface (20 m wide and over 25 m length) built on a complex piled wooden structure located close to a creek, which may have been used as a jetty for the exportation of the South Saintonge ceramic production towards the estuary (Fig. 7).

The third site is located in Freneau-Aubeterre (Fig. 2b) where large amounts of tiles and intact ceramic were recovered during the last thirty years. Some of these were still perfectly lined up in a possible wreck. Most of the site has presently been destroyed by the erosion of the marsh edge, but a circulation surface is still observed 30 cm above the Iron age briquetage layers. This place was apparently the last stocking/transit point of the South Saintonge ceramic production before definitive exportation towards the estuary.

The function of these sites as distribution centre implies occupation of a landsurface above MHWST located at, or at least very close to, a tidal creek system to facilitate the loading of goods onto vessels for transport. This interpretation makes warehouse sites very attractive as supportive indicators of sea-level position. However, their precision as such in the macrotidal environment is low as their relationship to water level at various stages of the tidal cycle will change markedly and a sufficient water depth to allow constant access by boat cannot be assumed. The datum of the jetty surface (where known) is therefore used as the maximum upper level of MHWST as with salt production sites.

Middle Ages

Evidence of occupation becomes less clear after 1750 BP (3rd century AD). Only two mainland sites show occupation until the end of the Gallo-Roman period (1474 BP, 476 AD Bastisse & Picotin 1978). There then follows a complete absence of archaeological evidence until 950 BP (11th century AD). Documentary evidence from the Abbaye de St Etienne de Baignes testifies the presence of a farm at Vitrezay which it acquired around 950 BP (end of the 10th century AD) indicating that some form of agriculture or stock rearing was possible on certain parts of the marsh at this time.

Implications for sea-level reconstruction

Given the nature of archaeological remains known on the St Ciers marsh, the site distribution, particularly of the Iron Age and Gallo-Roman periods, has important implications for marsh development described below. There is no trend of decreasing site age across the marsh. This suggests the development of a broad marsh area by at least the late La Tène period of the Iron Age (2200–2000 BP, 120–50 cal. BC). A complex marsh topography is also indicated by archaeological datums from which no common occupation level can be identified.

The datums of archaeological sites in the St Ciers region used to derive figures for MOD are shown in Fig. 8. MOD's for the Iron Age

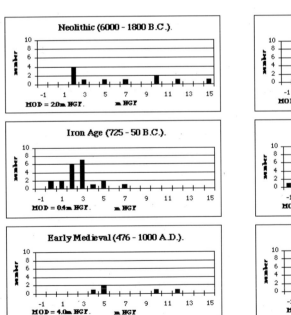
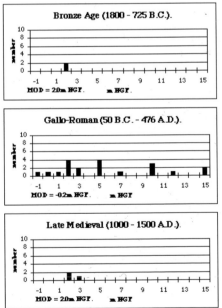

Fig. 8. Altitudinal distribution of archaeological sites across the St-Ciers sur Gironde marsh and its hinterland. Sites are presented by chronological period. Minimum occupiable datum (MOD) is calculated from each distribution.

and Gallo-Roman period are expected to be more accurate due to the maritime association of sites described above. The Iron Age MOD's is +0.4 m NGF and is derived from the salt production site of Fréneau-Aubeterre (Fig. 2b). As mentioned above, the archaeological horizons are separated by clay-silt beds representing phases of inundation by tidal waters which suggests that contemporary MHWST could have been located as close as 50 cm below the MOD. The Gallo-Roman MOD is +0.6/+1.19 m NGF but the relationship between this level and contemporary MHWST cannot be accurately determined due to the nature of the lowest known site (L'Ile Sèche). Gallo-Roman horizons are known below this level but are considered to represent dump units rather than actual occupation levels. The metalled road which crosses the marsh between l'Ile Sèche and La Melonne provides supporting evidence for a supratidal marsh during the Gallo-Roman period. Whilst roads have absolutely no relationship to contemporary sea-level, its presence does suggest that at least the landward marsh area was not prone to flooding at the time of its construction (1950–1850 BP, 1st century AD).

Chronology of marsh development

An interpretation of marsh development is described below using the current available lithostratigraphic and archaeological evidence. Documentary and cartographic sources have also been incorporated to reconstruct the final phases of development during the post-Medieval Period.

Pre-6000 BP (Fig. 9)

The present study adds no additional evidence to the model of morphosedimentary change in the estuary of Allen & Posamentier (1993) during this time period. Only the uppermost units of the transgressive systems tract were sampled and often in marsh marginal situations where they occur close to the present ground surface. It is impossible to derive any palaeogeographical inferences from the data sets due to the absence of the early Holocene sediments in many boreholes and a corresponding lack of archaeological remains of equal age known within the marsh.

6000–2200 BP (Fig. 10)

Sea-level attained a level close to present at/around 6000 BP (Pontee *et al.* 1998). Fluvial sediments began to infill the now delimited estuarine volume causing a negative sea-level tendency. A phase of prograding tidal flats and salt-marshes ensued corresponding to the highstand systems tract of Allen & Posamentier (1993) and the upper Holocene units of Bertero (1993). A restricted phase of peat development may have occurred at or before this date as indicated by deeply buried thin peat units (Fig. 3b). A final extensive phase of peat formation then occurred over clay-silt sediments across the marsh. This period of peat formation was prolonged, spanning minimally 5600–2600 BP. From the available assays (Table 3) it appears that peat accumulation commenced at the continental marsh margins and gradually extended towards the estuary, possibly keeping pace with the progradation of mudflats and saltmarshes, and causing a negative sea-level tendency. At present there is no palaeoecological data to indicate what relative sea-level conditions promoted peat development. However, the peat does appear to have been prone to flooding and accumulated contemporarily with woodland extension along the landward margins of the marsh.

2200–1800 BP (Fig. 11)

Peat development was terminated by tidal inundation and clay-silt deposition during a positive sea-level tendency at some point prior to 2200 BP This date is derived from a ^{14}C assay of 2670 ± 70 BP from the upper contact of the peat bed in the south of the marsh near Anglade and from the Iron Age horizons associated with the overlying upper clay-silt unit. It remains possible that the timing of this event was earlier along the outer marsh margins. The transgressive phase had a complicated effect on marsh geography as a mosaic of different environments evolved. Lowering of the peat surface through tidal erosion led to the landward extension of mudflat and saltmarsh units particularly in the regions of Vitrezay and Canal St Georges. In the central sector of the marsh, peat accumulation survived this inundation and persisted until the area was reclaimed.

The presence of Iron Age and Gallo-Roman sites on the marsh, without any evidence for the construction of sea-defences, indicates that at least part of the marsh was situated at or slightly above MHWST during this time period. This would imply that following a period of accretion of intertidal environments, a short phase of marsh stabilization ensued, possibly during a negative sea-level tendency, lasting approximately 150–200 years from the current available relative dating evidence. The distribution of

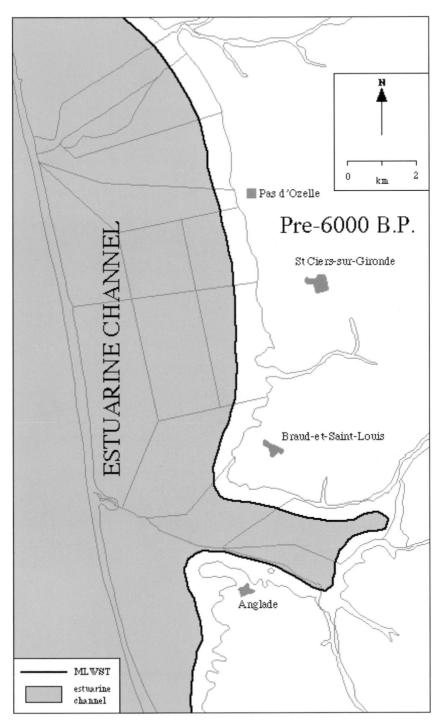

Fig. 9. Palaeogeography of the Saint-Ciers sur Gironde marsh pre-6000 BP.

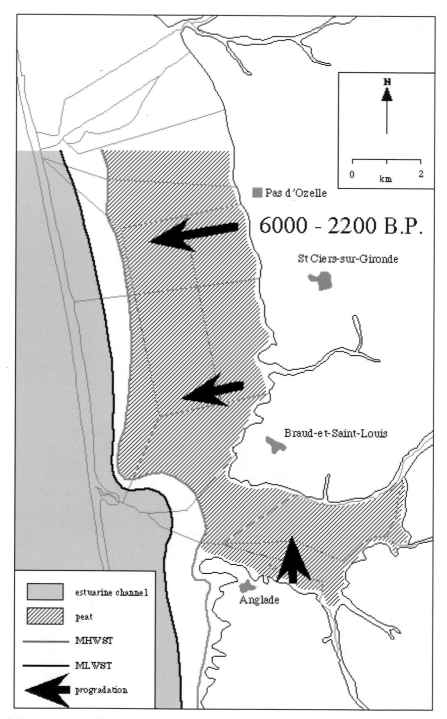

Fig. 10. Palaeogeography of the Saint-Ciers sur Gironde marsh 6000–2200 BP.

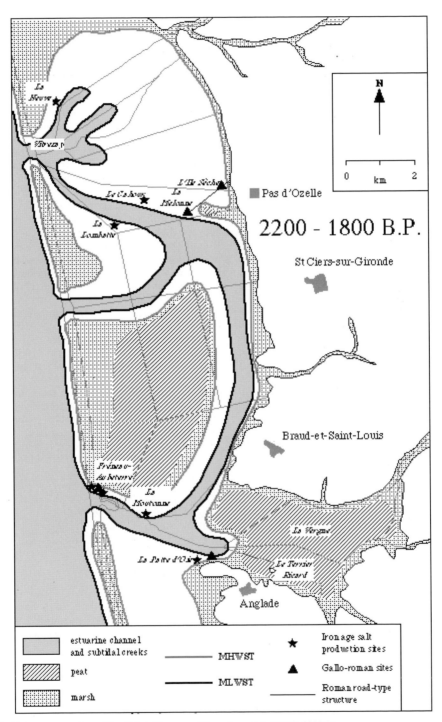

Fig. 11. Palaeogeography of the Saint-Ciers sur Gironde marsh 22000–1800 BP.

facies would, therefore, have remained essentially similar to that at the end of the preceding time period. However, this interpretation is derived solely from archaeological evidence due to the absence of primary lithostratigraphic and biostratigraphic data.

No palaeosols have been identified in association with any archaeological site to suggest the stability of the marsh surface at this time. Soil formation may not be expected given the relatively short duration of inferred stability and the assumed hydromorphic nature of the ground conditions. If sites were situated on poorly developed soils it is possible that these horizons have been masked from detection using the analytical techniques applied by pedogenesis which has occurred since marsh reclamation; a process which has also destroyed primary lithostratigraphic evidence from the upper clay-silt. A buried landsurface has been recorded in the Anglade–St. Androny sector of the marsh (Blondy 1987) but the lack of dating evidence does not allow it to be definitely attributed to this time frame.

The archaeological sites cannot in any case be considered as being established in a completely dryland setting as the ground water table beneath the marsh at this time would have had to have been high in order to maintain peat growth. Indeed, the presence of 2 inundation horizons during the Iron Age occupation, and separating the Iron Age and Gallo-Roman occupations, of Fréneau-Aubeterre indicates that this site was situated in a highly marginal location. This is the only site on the marsh which shows any evidence of flooding and the majority of sites are located in more landward, and presumably more protected, locations. The distribution of archaeological sites shows a clear preference for surfaces on the upper clay-silt unit, avoiding areas of continuing peat growth. Areas of minerogenic sedimentation would probably also have been in close association with tidal channels penetrating the marsh which would certainly have been an additional factor in site selection for the foundation of warehouse sites. High level inter-creek areas and creek levees, or possibly supratidal coastal reed-swamp areas, as defined by Shennan (1986), are possible environments for the human occupation of the marsh during this time frame.

There is no evidence in our lithostratigraphic data set for the existence of a system of barrier islands and a channel/creek between l'Ile Sèche/La Melonne and La Patte d'Oie. This pattern is solely inferred from archaeological evidence, and especially from the distribution of Gallo-Roman ceramic handling sites within the marsh.

From available evidence, the South Saintonge productions were transported on land to l'Ile Sèche, where the road-type structure may have served as a jetty to reach a place near La Melonne where boats could access. The ceramics were then transferred to La Patte d'Oie, probably via a channel/creek running along the landward margin of the marsh, and finally reached the estuary in Freneau-Aubeterre. The existence of other creeks running through the possible system of barrier islands is very likely, especially near Vitrezay which is presently the most important harbour in the marsh; however, the choice of Freneau-Aubeterre as the main transit zone seems to indicate that the other channels were not sufficiently deep to allow boat circulation.

The trend of sea-level change during this period is difficult to elucidate. The difference between MOD's for the Iron Age and Gallo-Roman periods (+0.4m and +0.6m NGF respectively) does not reliably indicate a relative sea-level rise. Significant overlap occurs between the datum distribution of both periods (Fig. 8) and both MOD's merely represent the maximum upper limit for the position of contemporary MHWST rather than a fixed datum. Evidence of flooding at Fréneau-Aubeterre cannot be taken to indicate relative sea-level rise as the site is situated in a very exposed position directly on the banks of the estuary and shows persistent re-occupation. Further, the abandonment of marsh sites following 1900 BP after only a short period of occupation (around 60 years) cannot be attributed to rising relative sea-level. Archaeological sites across the region, including those located on dryland in the continental interior, were also abandoned at the same time. This indicates that a cultural factor or some other environmental variable was affecting human activity in the region and resulting in depopulation. A static sea-level or negative sea-level tendency is inferred only through the absence of definitive evidence for a positive tendency. The duration of these assumed conditions is difficult to determine as there is little archaeological dating evidence after 1750 BP However, the MOD's do show that there has been a relative sea-level change of around 2.0 m since the latter date (using MHWST as the tidal reference point).

1800 BP to Present (Fig. 12)

The burial of archaeological horizons by overlying clay-silt units presumably reflects continued intertidal mudflat and saltmarsh development from 1750 BP onwards or possibly as a result of a continuing positive sea-level tendency since

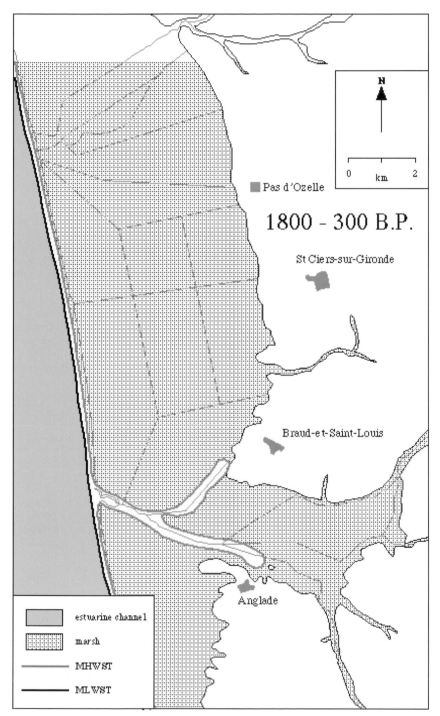

Figure 12. Palaeogeography of the Saint-Ciers sur Gironde marsh 1800–300 BP.

around 2500 BP. The datum of the archaeological horizon at La Melonne (−0.2 m NGF) shows that up to 2 m of stratigraphy has accumulated since this time although comparison of archaeological datums shows that this rate of accumulation is not continuous across the marsh e.g. the Gallo-Roman horizon at Ile Sèche is buried beneath 0.7 m of clay-silt; at Le Cahour and La Lombatte archaeological material occurs at the present ground surface. Infilling of a complex marsh topography to a common datum is therefore inferred.

Evidence from 1000 BP to 350 BP (10th to 16th centuries AD) is complex. Documentary evidence recording the presence of a farmstead at Vitrezay around 950 BP suggests that at least part of the marsh surface was stable during the Medieval Period. A negative sea-level tendency may be inferred although this interpretation is based upon a single piece of evidence and should be treated with caution, particularly as the activities on the farmstead are unknown. It is possible that the settlement was used purely for summer grazing on the saltmarsh surface rather than year round stock rearing and/or arable farming which would require land less prone to tidal inundation. All sites of similar age are found above the present marsh surface and therefore cannot be used to support a negative tendency. In the absence of archaeological and litho-/biostratigraphic data, the available documentary evidence is not sufficient to resolve whether a positive sea-level tendency post-1800 BP was interupted by a negative tendency around 950 BP.

Documentary evidence covering the period from 750 BP to 350 BP (13th to 16th centuries AD) suggests that a positive sea-level tendency ensued. At this time the marsh is described as being covered by reed beds and fens inaccessible for the greater part of the year due to tidal inudation (Blondy 1987). Documents relating to 550 BP to 450 BP (15th century AD) also describe deep tidal channels extending from the estuary to ports at Braud-et-St Louis and Anglade, showing that the communication at Freneau-Aubeterre was still sufficiently deep to allow navigation. A palaeochannel system is still visible today on the marsh surface at St Thomas de Conac (Blondy 1987). Extensive tidal inundation and continued minerogenic deposition is therefore indicated for this time period.

Cartographic evidence provides little additional information in the developement of the marsh. The earliest available maps date to the 16th century (Migniot 1971) and are not of sufficient scale, and provide insufficient anchor points, to reliably compare the shape and form of the relevant sections of the coastline. The next major phase in the history of the marsh was the reclamation of the area between Blaye and St Bonnet in 1654 AD, and of the remaining northern marsh sector a little later (Blondy 1987). A map of the reclaimed marshes from 1677 AD clearly shows the main channels of the drainage system employed which can still be traced today (Migniot 1971). There have been no subsequent marsh innings since this date. Intertidal mudflats and saltmarshes continue to accumulate on the seaward side of the sea defences to a datum slightly higher than the reclaimed marsh surface.

Discussion

The St Ciers marsh differs from many other marsh systems in the Gironde Estuary in terms of its size. Palaeoenvironmental studies thus far have concentrated upon narrow embayments formed between the well developed Pleistocene fluvial terraces and tributary systems of the Medoc peninsula (Diot & Tastet 1995; Massé *et al.* in press a; Pontee *et al.* 1998). Within the paradigm of an infilling ria type estuary (Allen & Postementier 1993) such shallow restricted embayments can be expected to be infilled relatively rapidly promoting the advanced formation of peat units. In contrast, the St Ciers marsh system forms a much deeper and larger embayment which would have been open and susceptible to estuarine influences for a longer period of time and thus present a more complex Holocene succession. Differences in sea-level tendencies are therefore to be expected (Long 1992) and points of comparison are at this stage limited.

Peat formation post-6000 BP is the only estuary wide event which can be recognized on both sides of the estuary thus far (no peat units are known in the estuary with which to correlate the older more deeply buried peats of the St Ciers marsh). West bank peat beds occur at similar datums to the primary upper peat unit of the St Ciers marsh (−1 m to +2 m NGF) and age estimates indicate that peat formation commenced slightly earlier around 6000 BP (Massé *et al.* in press a; Pontee *et al.* 1998). The conditions in the estuary at this time were optimum for the formation of peat. Relative sea-level rise had slowed but not actually stopped maintaining high water tables in marginal zones. Sedimentation rate exceeded the rate of sea-level rise allowing the rapid accretion and progradation of intertidal environments behind which would have followed peat accumulation in backwaters and supratidal areas where minerogenic sediment delivery was restricted.

Peat accumulation in the St Ciers marsh may have been terminated through either autocompaction and/or an increasing rate of relative sea-level rise. Supporting evidence for this rise in relative sea-level, which commenced around 2600 BP, can be found in the form of various local scale events recorded at different points in the estuary. At Monards Marsh, Barzan, on the NE bank of the estuary a sea-level index point for a positive sea-level tendency is recorded at a comparable datum and dated to 2840 ± 70 BP (Massé *et al.* in press *b*). On the west bank of the estuary, the timing of this event correlates to the formation of a chenier ridge known as the Cordon de Richard. Two radiocarbon age estimations have been obtained from the chenier of 2575 ± 120 BP and 1421 ± 162 BP although it must be stated that rising relative sea-level is not the only possible process leading to its formation (Pontee *et al.* 1998). Following the formation of this ridge sediment supply was still sufficiently high to allow marsh progradation to continue (Pontee *et al.* 1998) as inferred for the same time period in the St Ciers marsh up until its reclamation.

Whilst the development of the west bank marshes are well known (Diot & Tastet 1995; Massé *et al.* in press *a*; Pontee *et al.* 1998), there is little comparative evidence with which to reconstruct a coherent history on the east bank. There remain extensive areas of east bank marshes which require examination; even within the St Ciers marsh itself where little is known e.g. La Vergne and the area north of St Bonnet-sur-Gironde. Biostratigraphic approaches are much needed. Lithostratigraphic evidence for significant shifts in depositional environment occur in all of the marshes described but as yet biostratigraphic data with which to interpret the cause of these changes is virtually absent.

Conclusions

A geoarchaeological approach has been applied in the examination of the development of the St Ciers-sur-Gironde marsh, the first such examination of the east Gironde marshes. The model has been produced using lithostratigraphic borehole records in combination with diatom, archaeological, documentary and cartographic sources. The combination of data sets has proved advantageous, especially over timescales covering the past 2000 years, where litho- and biostratigraphic evidence is lacking.

The data available at present suggests that by around 5000 BP a broad area of saltmarshes and intertidal mudflats had accumulated to around -2.5 m NGF in the St Ciers region. Upon this surface a peat unit developed. The peat surface was subsequently modified by erosion, presumably through channel migration. Clay-silt deposition later continued and upon this surface human occupation occurred during the Iron Age to Gallo-Roman periods (2100–1750 BP), possibly due to a reduced rate of sea-level rise. A maximum height for MHWST during the Gallo-Roman period has been estimated from archaeological datums at $+0.6$ m NGF. Clay-silt deposition recommenced (if not previously interrupted) in the region during the 3rd century AD (1750 BP) at the earliest and continued until the reclamation of the marsh in the 17th century AD (200 BP) by which time the elevation of the marshes had attained their present datum. All inferred datums are subject to error through a combination of compaction and subsidence, the effects of both being currently unknown in this area. Further modifications to this model may be anticipated in future as new borehole and archaeological evidence comes to light.

This study develops the previous model of estuarine infilling and sea-level change developed by Allen & Posamentier (1993). The identification of a thick and laterally extensive peat unit between $+2.0$ m to -3.5 m NGF introduces a significant additional facies type to the Holocene sequence. A gradual and continual rise in relative sea-level is described. There is insufficient resolution in the data set at present to identify any fluctuations with certainty although two or possibly three points in the combined Holocene record may represent deviations about the overall trend which were not taken into account in the previous model. The first is characterized by the upper peat unit, dated to 5600–2600 BP, which represents a negative tendency during a period when sediment accumulation rate exceeded the rate of relative sea-level rise. The second occurs during the Gallo-Roman period (2000–1750 BP) during which time human occupation of the marsh surface suggests, at best, a slowing in the rate of sea-level rise. A third potential negative tendency may have occurred during the Medieval period around 950 BP, although evidence for this is almost completely lacking. Pollen analysis may help elucidate these palaeoenvironmental changes in the marsh in future to a greater degree than the diatom evidence presented here.

This research was supported by the C.N.R.S. programme 'Morphogenèse, paysages et peuplements holo-cènes en Aquitaine', by the E.C. funded Human Capital and Mobility Network (CHRX-CT94–0541), Coastal Environments and by the E.C. LIFE program

340 S. J. MELLALIEU *ET AL.*

'Coastal Change, Climate and Instability' (97ENU/UK/000510). This work is UMR 5805 EPOC contribution no. 1281.

References

AKEROYD, A. 1972. Archaeological and historical evidence for subsidence in southern Britain. *Philosophical Transactions of the Royal Society of London*, **A272**, 151–169.

ALLEN, G. P. 1972. *Etude des processus sédimentaire dans l'estuaire de la Gironde*. Thèse doctorate de l'Université de Bordeaux I no. 369.

—— & POSAMENTIER, H. W. 1993. Sequence stratigraphy and facies model of an incised valley fill: the Gironde Estuary, France. *Journal of Sedimentary Petrology*, **63**, 378–391.

ALLEN, J. R. L. & FULFORD, M. 1986. The Wentlooge Level: a Romano-British saltmarsh reclamation in southeast Wales. *Britannia*, **17**, 91–117.

ASSOR, R. 1972. *Interpretation paleogéographique des terrains sedimentaires de la presqu'ile du Médoc (zone du Verdon) son interet dans le cadre d'une etude géotechnique*. Thèse de 3e cycle, Université de Bordeaux I no. 1021.

BASTISSE, C. & PICOTIN, D. 1978. *Essai sur l'histoire et l'archéologie du canton de Saint Ciers-sur-Gironde*, Saint-Ciers.

BATTARBEE, R. W. 1986. Diatom Analysis. *In*: BERGLUND, B. E. (ed.) *Handbook of Holocene Palaeoecology and Palaeohydrology*. John Wiley, Chichester, 527–570.

BERTERO, J. P. 1993. *L'Holocène de Remplissage Estuarien du Marais de St Ciers-sur-Gironde*. Rapport de Stage, Maitrise d'Oceanographie, Université de Bordeaux I.

BLONDY, F. 1987. *Le marais de la rive droite de la Gironde*. Memoire de Maitrise. Université de Bordeaux I.

CASTAING, P. & JOUANNEAU, J. M. 1987. Les apports sédimentaires actuels d'origine continentale aux océans. *Bulletin de l'Institute de Géologie du Bassin d'Aquitaine, Bordeaux*, **41**, 53–65.

CLET-PELLERIN, M., LAUTRIDOU, J. P. & DELIBRIAS, G. 1981. Les formations holocènes et pléistocènes de la partie oriental de la baie du Mont-Saint-Michel. *Bulletin de la Société Linnéenne de Normandie*, **109**, 3–20.

COQUILLAS, D. 1990. *Etude sur l'occupation du sol en Blayais-Bourgeais*. T.E.R. Maîtrise. Université Michel de Montaigne, Bordeaux III.

——1993. *L'exploitation du sel en Blayais a la fin de l'Age du Fer*. L'Estuaire de la Gironde de Pauillac à Blaye. Fédération Historique du Sud-Ouest, 41–60.

——2001. *Les rivages d'estuaires de la Gironde du Néolithique au Moyen Age*. Thése de Université Michel de Montaigne, Bordeaux III.

DENYS, L. 1991. *A Check-List of Diatoms in the Holocene Deposits of the Western Belgian Coastal Plain with a Survey of Their Apparent Ecological Requirements*. I. Introduction, Ecological Code and Complete List. Belgische Geologische Dienst, Professional Paper 1991/1992 – No 246.

DIOT, M-F. & TASTET, J-P. 1995. Paleoenvironnements holocène et limites chronoclimatiques enregistrés dans un marais estuarien de la Gironde (France). *Quaternaire*, **6**, 85–94.

EVANS, G. 1965. Inter-tidal flat sediments and their environment of deposition in the Wash. *Quarterly Journal of the Geological Society, London*, **121**, 209–245.

FAWN, A. J., EVANS, K. A., MCMASTER, I. & DAVIES, G. M. R. 1990. *The Red Hills of Essex*. Colchester Archaeological Group, Colchester.

FERAL, A. 1970. *Interpretation Sedimentologique et Palaeogeographique des Formations Alluviales Flandriennes de l'Estuaire de la Gironde et de ses Dependances Marines*. Thèse de 3eme cycle no. 806. Université de Bordeaux I.

FLEMMING, N. C. 1979–1980. Archaeological indicators of sea-level. *Oceanis*, **5**, 149–166.

GERMAIN, H. 1981. *Flore des Diatomées (Diatomophycées) Eaux Douces et Saumâtres du Massif Armoricain et des Contrées Voisines d'Europe Occidentale*. Société Nouvelle des Editions Boubée, Paris.

GREENSMITH, J. T. & TUCKER, E. V. 1986. Compaction and Consolidation. *In*: VAN DE PLASSCHE, O. (ed.) *Sea-Level Research: a manual for the collection and evaluation of data*. Geo Books, Norwich, 591–306.

JOUANNEAU, J. M. & LATOUCHE, C. 1981. The Gironde Estuary. *In*: FÜCHTBAUER, M., LISITZYN, A. P., MILLIMAN, J. D. & SEIBOLD, E. (eds) *Contributions to Sedimentology*, Stuttgart.

KIDSON, C. 1982. Sea-level changes in the Holocene. *Quaternary Science Reviews*, **1**, 121–151.

KLINGEBIEL, A. & GAYET, J. 1995. Fluvio-lagoonal sedimentary sequences in Leyre Delta and Arcachon Bay, and Holocene sea-level variations, along the Aquitaine coast (France). *Quaternary International*, **29/30**, 111–117.

—— & TASTET, J-P. 1995. *Histoire géolgique de l'embouchure de l'estuaire de la Gironde*. Actes du colloque de Conservatoire de l'estuaire de la Gironde, Les Cahiers no. 2 Saint-Georges de Didonne, 9–24.

LABEYRIE, M. J., LALOU, C., MONACO, A. & THOMMERET, J. 1976. Chronologie des niveaux eustatiques sur la côte du Roussillon de 33 000 ans B.P. à nos jours. C. *Rapport Academie des Sciences de Paris*, **282** Serie D, 349–352.

LAMBECK, K. 1997. Sea-level change along the French Atlantic and Channel coasts since the time of the Last Glacial Maximum. *Palaeogeography, Palaeoclimatology and Palaeoecology*, **129**, 1–22.

LARSONNEUR, C. 1975. Tidal Deposits, Mont St Michel Bay, France. *In*: GINSBURG, R. N. (ed.) *Tidal Deposits: A Casebook of Recent Examples and Fossil Counterparts*. Springer Verlag, New York, 21–30.

LESUEUR, P., TASTET, J-P. & MARAMBAT, L. 1996. Shelf mud field formation within historical times: examples from offshore the Gironde Estuary, France. *Continental Shelf Research*, **16**, 1849–1870.

LONG, A. J. 1992. Coastal responses to changes in sea-level in the East Kent Fens and southeast England, UK, over the last 7500 years. *Proceedings of the Geologists' Association*, **103**, 187–199.

LOUWE KOOIJMANS, L. P. 1980. Archaeology and coastal change in the Netherlands. *In*: THOMPSON, F. H. (ed.) *Archaeology and Coastal Change*. The Society of Antiquaries of London. Occasional Paper (New Series) I, 106–133.

MASŚE, L., DIOT, M. F., MCMILLEN, T., TASTET, J. P., CAPDEVILLE, J. P., LAPEYRE, R. & LESUEUR, P. in press *a*. Holocene palaeoenvironments of the Reysson Marsh on the western bank of the Gironde Estuary, S.W. France. *Quaternary International*, in press.

——, WANG, J. & TASTET, J-P. in press *b*. Vertical accretion of the Holocene infill of the Monards Marsh (Barzan, Gironde Estuary, France). *Quaternary International*, in press.

MELLALIEU, S. J. 1997. *Archaeology in the inter-tidal zone: models of lithostratigraphic resolution in relation to site preservation*. PhD Thesis. University of London.

MIGNIOT, C. 1971. L'evolution de la Gironde au cours des temps. *Bulletin de l'Institut de Géologie du Bassin d'Aquitaine*, **11**(ii), 221–279.

PERRICHET-THOMAS, C. 1986. Les sites à sel en Aunis et Saintonge: présentation et problématique. Actes du VIIIe Colloque sur les Ages du Fer. *Revue Aquitania*, Supplement **1**, 167–171.

PIRAZZOLI, P. A. 1991. *World Atlas of Holocene Sea-Level Changes*. Elsevier Oceanography Series, 58. Elsevier, Amsterdam.

PONTEE, N. I., TASTET, J-P. & MASSE, L. 1998. Morpho-sedimentary evidence of Holocene coastal changes near the mouth of the Gironde and on the Medoc Peninsula, SW France. *Oceanologica Acta*, **21**(2), 243–261.

REINECK, H. E. & SINGH, I. B. 1980. *Depositional Sedimentary Environments*. Springer Verlag, Berlin.

SCARRE, C. 1984. Archaeology and sea-level in west-central France. *World Archaeology*, **16**, 98–107.

SHENNAN, I. 1986. Flandrian sea-level changes in the Fenland II: tendencies of sea-level movement, altitudinal changes and local and regional factors. *Journal of Quaternary Science*, **1**, 155–179.

SIMMONS, B. B. 1980. Iron Age and Roman coasts around The Wash. *In*: THOMPSON, F. H. (ed.) *Archaeology and Coastal Change*. The Society of Antiquaries London. Occasional Paper (New Series) **1**, 56–73.

TERS, M. 1973. *Les variations du niveau marin depuis 10 000 ans, le long du littoral Atlantique Francais*. Le Quaternaire: Travaux français récents; 9eme congrès International INQUA, Christchurch, New Zealand, 114–135.

VAN DE PLASSCHE, O. 1991. Coastal submergence of the Netherlands, northwest Brittany (France), Delmarva Peninsula (VA, USA), and Connecticut (USA) during the last 5500 to 7500 sidereal years. *In*: SABADINI *ET AL.* (eds) *Glacial Isostacy, Sea-Level and Mantle Rheology*. Kluwer, Dordrecht, 285–300.

VERGER, F. 1968. *Marais et waddens du littoral Français*. Biscaye Frères, Bordeaux.

VOS, P. C. & DE WOLF, H. 1993. Diatoms as a tool for reconstructing sedimentary environments in coastal wetlands; methodological aspects. *Hydrobiologia*, **269/270**, 285–296.

WILKINSON, T. J. 1989. The archaeological survey of coastal and estuarine wetlands. *In*: COLES, J. M. & COLES, B. J. (eds) *The Archaeology of Rural Wetlands*. W.A.R.P. Occasional Paper No. 2. University of Exeter, 23–26.

—— & MURPHY, P. 1986. Archaeological survey of an inter-tidal zone: the submerged landscape of the Essex coast, England. *Journal of Field Archaeology*, **13**, 177–194.

Holocene coastal change in the north of the Isle of Man: stratigraphy, palaeoenvironment and archaeological evidence

SILVIA GONZALEZ[1], JIM INNES[2], DAVID HUDDART[3],
PETER DAVEY[4] & ANDREW PLATER[5]

[1] School of Biological and Earth Sciences, Liverpool John Moores University, Byrom Street,
Liverpool L3 3AF, UK (e-mail: bessgonz@livjm.ac.uk)
[2] Department of Geography, Science Laboratories, The University of Durham, South Road,
Durham DH1 3LE, UK
[3] School of Education, Community and Social Science, Liverpool John Moores University,
I. M. Marsh Campus, Liverpool L17 6BD, UK
[4] Centre for Manx Studies, 6 Kingswood Grove, Douglas, Isle of Man IM1 3LX, UK
[5] Department of Geography, The University of Liverpool, P.O. Box 147,
Liverpool L69 3BX, UK

Abstract: New multidisciplinary work at Phurt in the north of the Isle of Man using stratigraphy, radiocarbon dating, pollen, diatoms, foraminifera and archaeology has re-evaluated the sedimentological and archaeological sequence located in a series of basins containing organic peats, silts and sands at the south end of the Flandrian Ayres raised beach succession. From this work it is clear that all the Mesolithic finds from the beach have been reworked and are not significant in terms of human occupation in this area and there is no evidence for human modification of the Mesolithic vegetation from Phurt. The radiocarbon dates for the middle peat fit into the Neolithic phase and although all the *in situ* artifacts are from layers above the peat from a sandy palaeosol, these layers are likely to have been deposited rapidly after the peat formation. Although the artifacts are Middle Neolithic in typology it is considered that the dates from the peat are not inconsistent with the archaeological dating framework.

The pollen indicates an early woodland phase but there are indicators of the close proximity of the sea from coastal pollen taxa, foram test linings in the upper peat layer and diatoms. In the middle peat tree pollen was much less frequent, there was a wide range of open ground herb taxa, mainly of freshwater type but again there were salt marsh taxa present, indicating the close proximity of the sea. In the upper organic horizon and the burnt mound profiles the lack of coastal pollen must indicate a relative sea-level drop. The depositional environment envisaged to account for the litho- and pollen stratigraphy in these small basins is predominantly a freshwater lake behind shingle bars, with the close proximity to seaward of a saltmarsh. On occasions there must have been brackish water in these lagoons and a marine connection through the shingle barrier based on the diatom evidence, which is similar to the interpretation at nearby Lough Cranstal. This is in contrast with the Liverpool Bay sequences where there is evidence for several marine transgressions, but in both areas the coastal or near coastal environments indicate much well preserved evidence for Neolithic and Bronze Age occupation and vegetational alteration by these populations.

The Isle of Man is situated in the middle of the northern Irish Sea Basin within 60 km of the coasts of North Wales, Cumbria, Galloway and Northern Ireland (Fig. 1a). The northern plain of this island (Fig. 1b) is dominated by the Ayres raised beach ridge complex, beyond the complex, glacitectonized Bride Hills moraine and the raised Flandrian cliff line which is cut into the northern flank of this moraine (Lamplugh 1903; Ward 1970; Thomas 1971, 1977, 1984, 1985; Dackombe & Thomas 1985, 1991). However, only two sites at Loch Cranstal and Phurt have provided some information with regard to changing Flandrian palaeoenvironmental climatic, floral, sea-level and archaeological conditions (Phillips 1967; Thomas 1971; Mitchell 1971;

From: PYE, K. & ALLEN, J. R. L. (eds). *Coastal and Estuarine Environments: sedimentology, geomorphology and geoarchaeology*. Geological Society, London, Special Publications, **175**, 343–363. 0305-8719/00/$15.00 © The Geological Society of London 2000.

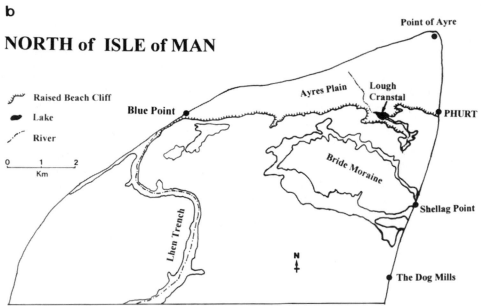

Fig. 1. (**a**) Location of the Isle of Man in the middle of the Irish Sea Basin. (**b**) Geomorphological map of the North of the Isle of Man, showing the location of Phurt and the Ayres Plain.

Carter 1977; Tooley 1977, 1978; Dackombe & Thomas 1985; McCarroll *et al.* 1990). This previous work is summarized below and some problems identified with the interpretations. New exposures at Phurt have provided an opportunity to reinvestigate this site using multidisciplinary techniques to provide detailed palaeoenvironmental interpretation. This new work is presented here and the conclusions include a brief summary of how this work fits into the sea-level and environmental history of adjacent coastal lowlands in the eastern Irish Sea basin.

Previous work at Lough Cranstal and Phurt

Lough Cranstal. This site is composed of two separate basins (Carter 1977; Tooley 1978). The shallower southern basin contains terrestrial peats and detritus suggesting fen conditions, whereas the larger basin to the north is more complex. The lower part of the sequence has a freshwater diatom assemblage (Mitchell 1971; Carter 1977), together with significant washed-in mineral material. Above is a tenacious, grey clay beginning at +1.53 m OD which has halophytic diatoms (93% brackish water) and the remains of *Ruppia*, a plant of brackish water ditches and salt marsh pools, which suggests some form of marine influence. The beginning of this phase has been dated to 7825 ± 120 BP. A return to freshwater diatoms, including *Fragillaria construens*, *F. brevistriata* and *Amphora ovalis* suggests that the basin developed as a lagoon, separated from the sea by the early ridges of the Ayres raised beach. By +2.21 m OD most salt water indicators had been removed from the flora and marine-influenced deposition ceased by 7370 ± 110 BP. The marine event correlates closely both in age and elevation with the Lytham III transgression in the Fylde (Tooley 1974). The brackish sedimentation was succeeded by lake-mud deposition, which contains a mixed oak woodland pollen spectra. This in turn is succeeded by terrestrial sediments in which cereals enter the flora in consistent frequencies. These cereals can be linked with late Neolithic (Ronaldsway) artifacts that have been found on the lough edge, or the middle Neolithic finds at Phurt.

Phurt. On the east coast the Bride Hills glacial sediments pass beneath the beach and are replaced by basins of lagoonal sediments and peats. Ward (1970) recognized three such basins above beach level, the southernmost one being located at Phurt. Below beach level there is an earlier basin which is only rarely exposed but which is cut into a reddish-brown sandy till (suggested as the Ballaquark Till by Dackombe & Thomas 1985). The basin flanks showed evidence of a periglacial climate, with a polygonal crack pattern and frequent shattered stones and a former soil. The evidence for the latter are deeply etched limestone cobbles and bleached granite erratics in the top of the till which suggests that these higher parts of the till were once covered by a palaeosol.

The basin is filled with a sand and laminated, clayey silts sequence which has an abundance of carbonized wood, including birch. Above the clayey silts is a thin but extensive peaty clay,

with compressed wood pieces, pine cones, *in situ* pine stumps and large trunks of pine. This 'forest bed' (Phillips 1967) includes oak wood and together with the pollen assemblage suggested a discontinuous coastal woodland, with a freshwater marsh or lake nearby. The presence of seablite (*Suaeda maritima*) and other chenopods which favour such coastal habitats throughout the Flandrian and the water germander (*Teucrium*), which typically favours dune slacks and calcareous soils, suggest this and the presence of horsetail spores and common waterweed suggest the lake. Phillips (1967) suggests that the bed represents Pollen Zone VIa (Boreal). It is overlain by laminated muds and sands deposited in a freshwater environment with a maritime influence.

The upper basins, exposed above the modern beach, Phillips (1967) thought represented shifting lagoons amongst encroaching sand dunes. The dunes are represented by a variable thickness of generally well-sorted, bleached coarse to medium sands. Only the southernmost basin has been investigated in detail but it consists of a suite of silty sands and clayey silts which show marked lateral facies change from the basin centre to the margins. The approach of a marine environment is indicated by the occurrence of the alga, *Pediastrum boryanum*, which is characteristic of salt-laden sands. These sandy clays are not true marine clays but a salt-marsh environment was envisaged by Phillips (1967), although the large amount of bog myrtle (*Myrica*) indicated adjacent boggy fen conditions. No indications of a marine transgression could be seen but the water table remained high (in the Atlantic period). Above, the freshwater muds represent a drop in sea-level and lower water table and these sediments grade laterally into a silty detritus peat and, to the north, into a palaeosol. Towards the basin margin this unit yields charcoal and a range of Mesolithic and Neolithic artifacts similar to those found around Lough Cranstal.

Above the northern bank of the basin and laterally continuous with the artifact-bearing layer of the southern basin is a layer of dark grey to blackish sand, which is heavily cemented and contains abundant artifacts. This has been interpreted as an occupation layer (Dackombe & Thomas 1985), delimited to the south by the peaty mud and to the north by a series of wedges, interpreted as post-holes. Pits, containing much charcoal, extend beneath this horizon. To the north this horizon shows what might be ghosts of tree roots, suggesting that the occupation level was a clearing in a woodland. The Ayres throughout this period would have been prograding to the north as successive shingle ridges were added.

Summary of previous work at these locations. The evidence from these sites allows a reconstruction of the evolution of the Ayres Plain, although there is still uncertainty about the absolute dating of events and the precise interpretation of the pollen record at Phurt (McCarroll *et al.* 1990). Initially the raised cliff line between Phurt and Blue Point was eroded. This must have preceded the initiation of the shingle spit growth from Blue Point by a significant interval. The lower parts of the Lough Cranstal and Phurt sequences appear to have been deposited in lagoons in which there was some salt-water influence. This suggests the development of a shingle barrier through which seepage occurred in the case of Lough Cranstal. The sea was at about -0.6 and $+2.2$ m OD at the beginning and end of this phase. At Phurt the age of the lower biogenic sequence is similar to the basal peat at Lough Cranstal but the contact with the overlying clays and sands is at an altitude of *c.* 5 m OD which places the transgression facies at this location in a completely different altitudinal category (Tooley 1978). Since Phillips (1967) notes a depositional hiatus above the biogenic horizon, it is possible that this transgression is a more recent event than the transgression recorded at Lough Cranstal (Tooley, 1978). However, it has been suggested that this high sea-level at Lough Cranstal coincided with the timing of a high sea level in Wigtown Bay which Jardine (1975)

dates at between 6600–7200 BP. Hence there is some uncertainty not only as to the position of sea-level during this period but also in the evidence for the marine conditions and the exact age of such evidence. McCarroll *et al.* (1990) also suggest that the pollen data provided by Phillips (1967) might require some reinterpretation and it could be that too much weight has been given to the presence of salt-tolerant and salt-loving species in his reconstructions. With this background of uncertainty, the Phurt location was reinvestigated, although the sections referred to by Phillips (1967) have all been eroded by the sea. By using a range of multidisciplinary techniques the aim of the current work was to identify the sequence of environmental changes, to date these changes, to evaluate the evidence for associated contemporary sea-levels and to evaluate the influence of such changes on the archaeological record.

Phurt stratigraphy

One of the main characteristics of the coast north of Shellag Point to Phurt is the large rate of coastal erosion, with a loss of approximately 30 m in the period from 1869 to 1976. This fact is important in understanding the apparent discrepancies between the descriptions of the stratigraphy of the post-glacial deposits by different authors (Phillips 1967; Ward 1970; Dackombe & Thomas 1985), which have occurred simply because they were describing different sections exposed on the beach as erosion proceeded. This is important as well in the interpretation of the

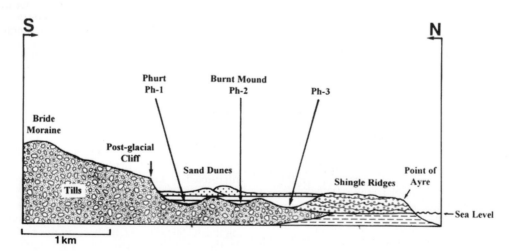

Fig. 2. Diagrammatic section from the coastal cliffs north of the Bride Moraine to the Point of Ayre, showing the three basins infilled with post-glacial deposits exposed at beach level, together with the position of the sections studied in each basin (Ph-1, Ph-2 Burnt Mount and Ph-3).

PHURT (Ph-1)

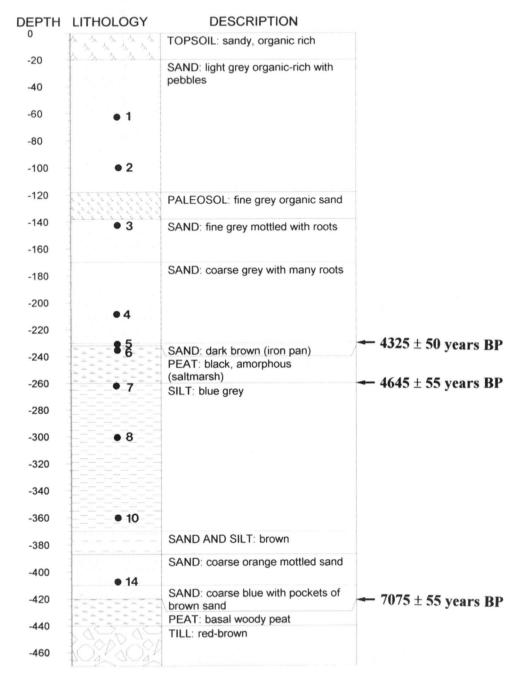

Fig. 3. Stratigraphic section at Phurt (site Ph-1). The black dots indicate samples taken through the section. The radiocarbon dates are uncalibrated: basal woody peat with 7075 ± 55 years BP (Lab. No. AA-28384, $\delta13 = -27.5$), bottom black amorphous peat with 4645 ± 55 years BP (Lab. No. AA-29333, $\delta13 = -28.5$), top black amorphous peat with 4325 ± 50 years BP (Lab. No. AA-28380, $\delta13 = -29.2$).

archaeological artefacts which have been found on this beach during the last forty years.

The work in this paper describes the sections exposed at beach level from Phurt to the Point of Ayre in October 1997 and January 1998. Three small basins, approximately 40 m long and 2–5 m in thickness were well exposed. In each basin a section was studied in detail (Phurt Ph-1, Ph-2 and Ph-3, see Fig. 2). On top of the basins a well developed 'occupation horizon' or cultural soil, consisting mainly of organic-rich sand, with artifacts and post-holes, indicates that humans were living in this area at the time. The sequence is finally capped by a series of sand dunes.

Each basin has different types of sediment infill which show rapid, distinctive vertical and lateral changes in sedimentary facies during the Holocene for this area. The sections studied in detail in each basin (Figs 3, 4 & 5) are described below.

Phurt (Ph-1)

This is the southerly basin and it is the only place in which it is possible to see red-brown, sandy till well exposed at beach level forming the base of the basin. The top part of the till shows a palaeosol with evidence of deep frost action developing a polygonal crack pattern, together with roots and tree stumps growing on this palaeo-surface (Fig. 6). An age of 7075 ± 55 years BP was obtained for a tree root found at this stratigraphic level during January 1998, when the base of the basin was well exposed. During the first visit in October 1997 the beach was completely covered with shingle and it was impossible to see the bottom of the basin.

The basal peat has a variable thickness, with the maximum value in the middle of the basin (15–20 cm), thinning towards the sides of the basin, where it is only a few cm thick. The peat is

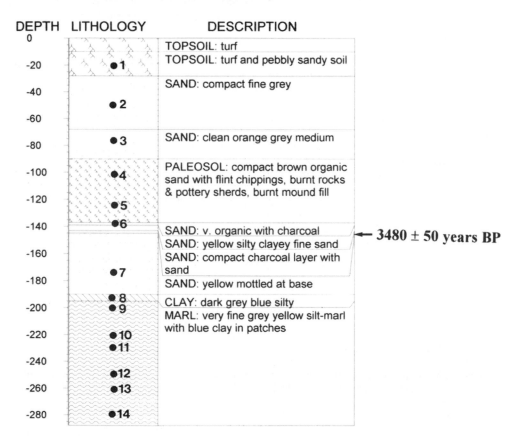

Fig. 4. Stratigraphy at the Burnt Mound (site Ph-2). The radiocarbon date is uncalibrated, from charcoal at the bottom of the burnt mount with 3480 ± 50 years BP (Lab. No. AA-29331, $\delta13 = -25.8$).

PHURT (Ph-3)

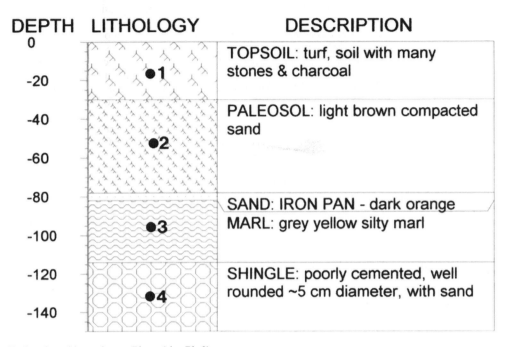

Fig. 5. Stratigraphic section at Phurt (site Ph-3).

dark brown, generally amorphous, with wood and *Phragmites*. On top of the peat there is a sequence of thin layers of sands and blue silts at a depth of 420–370 cm. From 370 to 260 cm there is a blue-grey, silty clay, followed by a 30 cm thick mid-profile, silty detrital peat, with wood and other plant macrofossils, described by Dackombe & Smith (1985) as an extension of the thin organic clay noted by Phillips (1967) in his original section. This peat was well exposed in October 1997. Above it a sand dune sequence was deposited, which persisted to the present day surface sandy soil. This upper sand facies contained a layer of highly organic sand from a depth of 140–120 cm, which represents a palaeosol and an old ground surface. In places this contains archaeological material, including Neolithic pottery (Davey *et al.* 1985) and represents an 'occupation horizon' (see Archaeology section later). This sequence is analogous to the most recently reported Phurt lithology (Dackombe & Smith 1985; McCarroll *et al.*, 1990). The middle section peat attenuates and becomes much less organic towards the basin sides where the till surface rises, until it merges into a clayey, organic paleosol. The upper organic-rich, sandy,

cultural soil is a laterally-persistent horizon, almost one hundred metres to the north of Ph-1 section, where it becomes very heavily indurated, capping the second basin in which the Ph-2 succession is found. Here it overlies a silty-sandy sequence within which the Ph-1 mid-profile peat is represented only by a thin, organic clay.

Phurt (Ph-1A)

Severe storms during the winter months in 1997 greatly lowered the beach level and exposed till in several places along this coast. Close to Ph-1 a thin, well humified, compact basal peat lay on the till surface and incorporated abundant *Phragmites* macrofossils and wood remains, some carbonized, including large branches and stumps which were rooted *in situ* in the till below. This section was called Ph-1A. This basal peat was overlain by a silty sand which is the same unit as the lower sand recorded at Ph-1, and then by the rest of the Ph-1 succession, although both the mid-profile peat unit and the cultural soil were poorly developed.

Fig. 6. Roots growing on top of the till (paleosol) at site Ph-1. This basal woody peat was radiocarbon dated to 7075 ± 55 BP.

Burnt Mound (Ph-2)

This section is included in the middle basin exposed along the beach (Fig. 2). In this case the base of the basin was not exposed. The lower part of the succession is represented by a 90 cm thick, marl unit, the top 5 cm of which is represented by grey-blue silt, with a high organic content (Figs. 7, 8). The upper part of the succession consisting of sands, including the cultural soil horizon described previously, is cut by an archaeological structure with a fill of organic sand and burnt stones, with a basal charcoal layer (Fig. 7). It is interpreted as a 'burnt mound' of which there are many on the island (Woodcock 1995; Garrad 1999).

Phurt (Ph-3)

The base of this section in the most northern basin, started with 40 cm of poorly cemented, well rounded shingle, with a 5 cm diameter maximum and a sandy matrix. This was followed by 32 cm of grey-yellow, silty marl. This is covered by an iron pan (5 cm thick) which is developed at the base of a layer of light brown, compacted sand in which the present sandy soil is developed which has many stones and charcoal. Just a few tens of metres from Ph-3 it is possible to see how the small basin wedges out (Fig. 9). From this location to the Point of Ayre, the Ayres Plain consists only of well rounded, shingle ridges.

Fig. 7. Burnt mound exposed at site Ph-2. These archaeological features have been associated with cooking using hot stones and are common in the Isle of Man.

Fig. 8. Detail of the sediments at the bottom of the burnt mount, site Ph-2 showing the marl sediments (*A*) and the layer of blue silt (*B*).

Pollen analysis

The two organic layers at Phurt Ph-1 and the basal peat at Phurt Ph-1a were sampled for pollen analysis at close intervals and pollen and spores were prepared and identified following the methods outlined in Moore *et al.* (1991). A total of at least 300 land pollen grains, excluding aquatics and spores, was completed at each counted level. The Phurt Ph-1a section was close to that of Phurt 1 and the cliff top altitude was found hardly to vary at and between the sites. For ease of presentation the litho- and pollen-stratigraphic results from the two profiles are combined in a single composite diagram (Fig. 10a), which gives an accurate conspectus of this part of the Phurt coastal sequence.

The basal woody peat resting on till at Phurt Ph-1a was sampled for pollen throughout, but pollen was only preserved in the upper two levels. These contained high percentages of *Pinus* and *Corylus*, with lesser frequencies of *Betula*, *Quercus* and *Ulmus*. *Alnus* percentages are very low. Herb pollen frequencies are low, with *Graminae* (*Poaceae*) the main type. Other herbs present are mainly of probable coastal type, including *Chenopodiaceae*, *Artemisia* and *Cruciferae*. Foraminifera test linings occur in the upper peat layers. Well preserved pollen assemblages were recovered from throughout the higher, mid-profile, silty, detrital peat at Phurt 1 but were quite different to the basal peat data. Tree pollen accounted for much less of the total count, and was dominated by *Alnus*. *Quercus* frequencies were about the same as in the basal peat, but all other trees, as well as *Corylus*, were greatly reduced. *Graminae* and *Cyperaceae* frequencies were high, and a wide range of open ground herb taxa occurred. These were of mainly freshwater marsh type, with *Typha angustifolia* increasingly important. Consistent curves for likely coastal type *Chenopodiaceae*, *Plantago maritima* and *Taraxacum*-type are characteristic, among a group which includes *Armeria*, *Artemisia*, *Spergularia*, *Aster*-type,

Fig. 9. Detail showing the middle basin 'wedging out'. The sediments consist mainly of fine layers of marl (A), the bottom of the basin is on gravels.

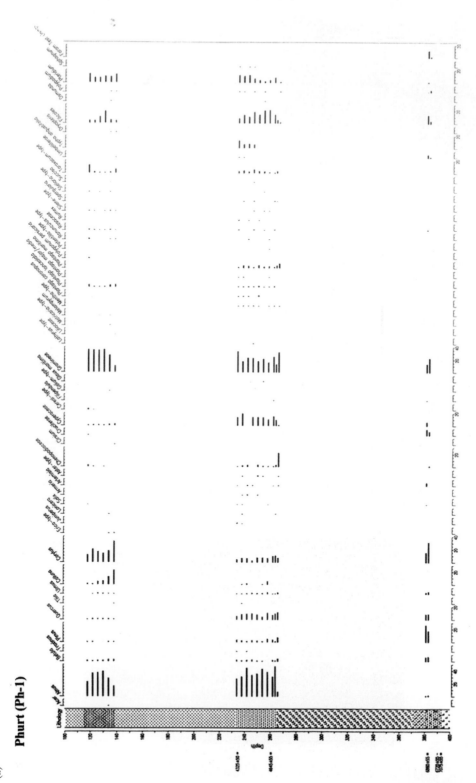

Phurt (Ph-1)

(a)

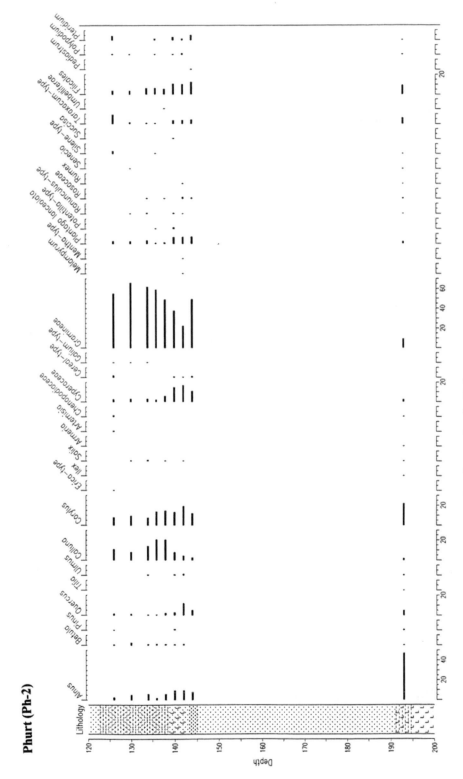

Fig. 10. (a) Pollen composite diagram for site Ph-1. (b) Pollen diagram for site Ph-2.

Glaux maritima, Plantago coronopus and *Silene*-type. Plants which suggest disturbed or open and more dryland conditions also occur, including *Plantago lanceolata, Pteridium and Calluna.* The third organic horizon, the cultural soil high in the Phurt 1 section, contained well preserved pollen throughout, despite being much less organic than the lower units. Few forest trees are present and shrubs such as *Alnus, Corylus* and *Calluna* show high percentages. *Graminae* frequencies are very high and open ground taxa such as *Pteridium, Plantago lanceolata* and *Taraxacum*-type are prominent. Grass grains of cereal type appear in the upper part of the horizon.

A pollen diagram through the profile containing the burnt mound at Phurt Ph-2 is presented in Fig. 10b. A thin, silty, organic unit occurs beneath the sand body into which the burnt mound is cut, and it forms a lateral extension of the mid-profile, silty peat at Phurt Ph-1. Its pollen profile is similar, dominated by *Alnus*, with some *Corylus* and coastal type herbs, *Chenopodiaceae* and *Armeria.* All other taxa are very poorly represented. The burnt mound fill contained well preserved pollen. The lower fill, including the primary charcoal-rich layer, contained significant *Alnus, Quercus* and *Corylus* with high *Graminae* frequencies and those of open ground taxa like *Plantago lanceolata, Taraxacum*-type and *Pteridium*, as well as grass grains of cereal type. The upper fill is dominated by *Calluna* and *Graminae* pollen, with all other types much diminished, although open ground taxa do rise again in the uppermost level.

Interpretation of the pollen data

The pollen data from the basal peat at Phurt Ph-1a suggest a date before the *Alnus* rise and decline of *Pinus* which define the end of the Flandrian 1 chronozone dated around 7000 BP in areas near the east coast of the Irish Sea (Hibbert *et al.* 1971), although there is considerable local variation in the age of this feature. Radiocarbon dates on the upper contact of this peat of 6860 ± 55 BP and on a carbonized *in situ* tree root of 7075 ± 55 BP support the pollen evidence and suggest deposition immediately pre-*Alnus* rise. Foraminifera test linings and saltmarsh pollen taxa in the upper layers of this peat might initially suggest that the clayey sand overlying the peat is of marine origin but because there are no *in situ* foraminifera in these layers it is much more likely that the upper peat formed very close to a salt marsh but was freshwater. The sand fines upwards into the

blue-grey, sandy clay and then the mid-profile, silty peat. The upper level of the blue grey clay is again very close to a salt marsh as it has very high *Chenopodiaceae* values and the peat also shows saltmarsh pollen throughout so must be either very close to a saltmarsh or of upper saltmarsh origin. However, again there are no marsh foraminifera present in these levels. The low *Ulmus* and high values for other trees suggest an age early in Flandrian III, after the *Ulmus* decline dated regionally after about 5000 BP (Hibbert *et al.* 1971). The dates of 4645 ± 55 BP and 4325 ± 50 BP for the lower and upper peat contacts agrees well with this. The fining-upward sequence and the reduction in coastal indicators through the peat suggest a negative sea-level tendency and a progressive relative fall in sea-level and withdrawal of marine influence. Although the local vegetation was mostly oak-alder-hazel woodland, the presence of open dryland indicators points to some limited early Neolithic forest clearance.

The pollen data from the organic cultural soil horizon at Phurt Ph-1 shows significant evidence of woodland clearance and agriculture, which can be attributed to the later Neolithic period by the cultural material stratified within it. The pollen changes indicate the replacement of oakwoods by heather and hazel scrub heath with open grassland, with local alder carr woods untouched. The evidence of cultivation from cereal pollen only appears late in this land-use history. The absence of key indicators like *Plantago maritima* suggest that marine influence was now absent from the site, either due to relative sea-level fall, or the presence of a coastal dune barrier. The low levels of *Chenopodiaceae* and other possible coastal taxa are associated with the cultivation phase and are probably derived from agricultural activity.

Further agricultural land-use activity within a near-coastal environment is recorded by the burnt mound sequence at Phurt Ph-2. The lower, thin, organic clay, as an extension of the mid-profile peat at Phurt Ph-1, has not been dated but must approximate to the date of its upper contact at *c.* 4235 BP. The sediments of the burnt mound itself contained well preserved pollen. The charcoal-rich primary silt of the feature is dated to the Bronze age at 3480 ± 50 BP and the pollen data record a phase of clearance of already light oak-alder-hazel woodland during which cereal cultivation and pastoralism led to the creation of grassland, with the occupation of some areas by *Calluna* heath after the cessation of active agricultural activity. A second phase of land-use begins near the top of the sediment fill, truncated by the modern, sandy, aeolian, soil development. The coastal plain around Phurt seems to have been almost entirely deforested at this time. There are no pollen indicators of any marine influence, although the shoreline was presumably not far away.

Diatom analysis

Approximately 0.5 ml of sediment was sampled from selected stratigraphic units in sections Ph-1 and Ph-2. These aliquots were digested in 70–100 ml volume H_2O_2 by heating gently for up to 24 hours. Single drops of the digested samples were pipetted onto glass cover slips and dried on a warm hot plate. The cover slips were then inverted and placed onto a glass slide, using Naphrax as the mountant. After further gentle heating and cooling, the diatoms preserved in each sample were identified at ×630 magnification using the identification keys of Hendey (1964) and Van de Werff & Huls (1958–66), with nomenclature following Hartley (1986). Palaeoenvironmental interpretation was undertaken using the model of Vos & deWolf (1993).

Diatom results and interpretation

A summary table listing the relative abundance of the different diatom ecological groupings and the interpreted palaeoenvironment is presented in Table 1. A full diatom species listing is given in Appendix 1 from which it is clear that diatom preservation was rather poor (a low number of of assigned valves compared with total valve count) and, hence, the number of diatoms identifed in each sample was low. Only the count from sample Ph1-8 can be regarded as statistically robust, although this is dominated by an almost monospecific assemblage of *Paralia sulcata*. Consequently, the interpreted environments should be considered as tentative

assessments and are only made in the absence of other palaeoecological data.

In section Ph-1, the diatom assemblage in the lower of the two samples with any notable degree of preservation (Ph1-8) is dominated by marine planktonic species with a subordinate marine/brackish aerophilous component. The environment of deposition is interpreted as an open marine tidal channel, perhaps with marginal mudflats. The overlying sample (Ph1-7) from the transition between the blue silt and the overlying peat exhibits a more varied diatom assemblage with roughly equal contributions from marine planktonic, marine/brackish epipelon and marine/brackish aerophilous species, and a minor input from marine tychoplankton. This combination would appear to represent deposition in a saltmarsh setting around the height of mean high water, although perhaps the brackish/freshwater aerophilous species are under-represented when compared with the ranges quoted in Vos & deWolf (1993). The environmental change illustrated by the transition from the diatom assemblage in Ph1–8 to that preserved in Ph1-7 is indicative of a regression brought about by a fall in relative sea-level or coastal sedimentation.

The diatom assemblage preserved in sample Ph2-8 is perhaps the most tentative of the palaeoenvironmental reconstructions due to the low number of assigned diatom valves and the poor degree of preservation. However, *Navicula pusilla* is a brackish/freshwater aerophilous diatom species (Vos & deWolf 1993) which, in combination with the single valve of *Paralia sulcata*, would suggest deposition above the height of mean high water on a saltmarsh.

Archaeological finds at Phurt

Since 1959 the Phurt eroding cliffs have produced along 500 m of their length a wide range

Table 1. *Relative abundance of ecological groupings for assigned diatoms valves*

Ecological groupings	Ph1-7	Ph1-8	Ph1-10	Ph2-8	Ph2-9
Marine plankton	36%	97%	–	25%	–
Marine tychoplankton	9%	0%	–	0%	–
Marine/brackish epipelon	27%	3%	–	0%	–
Marine/brackish aerophilous	27%	0%	–	0%	–
Brackish/Fresh aerophilous	0%	0%	–	75%	–
Total valves	62	329	2	31	0
Total assigned valves	11	326	0	4	0
Interpreted environment	Saltmarsh c. MHW	Tidal Channel		Saltmarsh above MHW	

of prehistoric artifacts. These consist mainly of Middle and Late Neolithic and Early Bronze Age pottery, together with contemporary lithics. However, over a forty year period, with artifact collection by many individuals, the standard of recording of findspots and stratigraphy has been variable in quality and often confusing. Although a majority of the finds are in the Manx Museum collections, many key pieces remain in private hands (Davey *et al.* 1995, 1999). Recent research at the site and on the Manx and Irish Sea context of the artifact types represented has enabled this present analysis to be proposed. The resulting synthesis provides further chronological and geographical evidence for the understanding of the physical development of the land north of the Flandrian cliff-line.

The Neolithic period in the Isle of Man has recently been the subject of intense study, including a programme of radiocarbon dating (Burrow 1997; Burrow & Darvill 1997) and an equivalent study of the Bronze Age is far

advanced. However, the overwhelming majority of the finds at Phurt are of Middle Neolithic type. Burrow (1997) illustrated 106 rim sherds and diagnostic carinated, or decorated body sherds from the site. He did not find any of the Late Neolithic (Ronaldsway) pottery. Woodcock (in prep.) has located in the museum collections four decorated sherds which are clearly of Early Bronze Age type, together with eight fragments in private hands. There are also quantities of undiagnostic 'prehistoric' pottery from this site.

The lithics have not been the subject of recent study but the assemblage includes a fragment of a Group VI Langdale polished axe of Middle Neolithic type and a good deal of 'Neolithic' debitage, little of which is diagnostically Late Neolithic or Early Bronze Age. A few late Mesolithic flakes have also been recovered (McCartan 1990).

Many of these artifacts were eroded from the cliffs, recovered from the beach and are

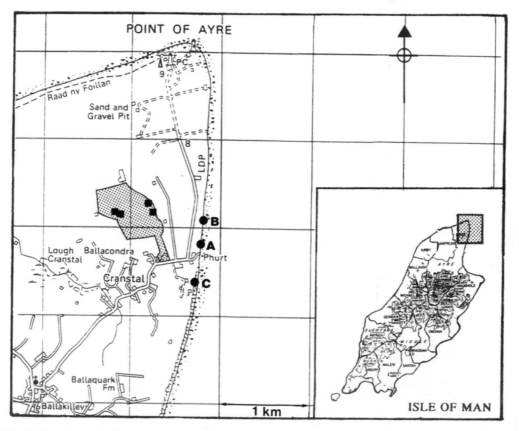

Fig. 11. Location of archaeological sites on the coast around Phurt (black dots). Locality 'A' is equivalent to Ph-1, locality 'B' is equivalent to Ph-2. The black squares represent other burnt mounds in the area. The stippled area correspond to the Kerrowdhoo Survey 1992–1994. (After Davey *et al.*1995 with modifications).

therefore unstratified. All of the finds which have been excavated from undisturbed sediment have been derived from a buried soil near the cliff top, separated from the modern ploughsoil by a varying thickness of blown sand. There have been no clear finds from the lower peat or the middle peat at Phurt. Recent fieldwork, together with a detailed study of the museum records, has therefore concentrated on the need to establish more precisely the location of the artifacts of differing periods and their types. From this work it is clear the finds are not evenly distributed over the 500 m stretch of coastline from which they derive. There appear to be three concentrations of artifacts (Sites A–C), with a very low find density between them (Fig. 11). Site A is located between *c*. 20 m and 120 m north of the exposed road section at Phurt (the latter at [NX 4675 0272], Fig. 11) and is equivalent to the Ph-1 section. With the exception of two probable Late Mesolithic flint flakes, all of the finds from this section are of Middle Neolithic date (Fig. 12). The concentration of finds, the nature of the lithics and the presence

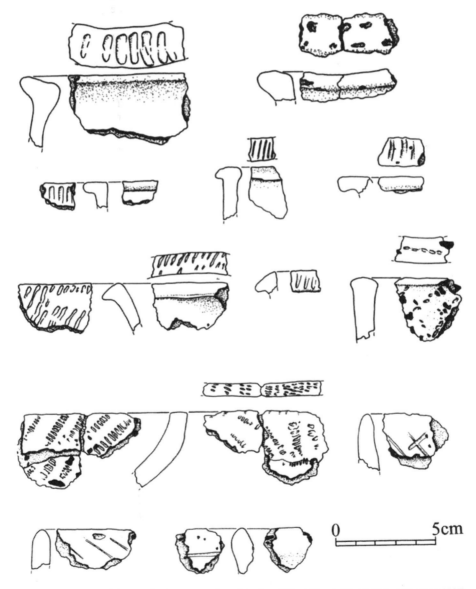

Fig. 12. Examples of Middle Neolithic pottery found in the cliffs at Phurt (Ph-1) (After Burrow 1997).

of post-features and wicker-lined storage pits in the section from time to time, strongly suggests the presence of a significant farming settlement, one of only twelve so far identified in the Isle of Man during this period (Burrow, pers. comm.). Site B some 350 m north of the road, is the source of the identifiable Bronze Age pottery (Fig. 13) and a handful of poor quality, later Neolithic, or Bronze Age lithics. At its focus, there is the substantial sub-surface remains of a burnt mound (site Ph-2) for which an Early Bronze Age date has been obtained (3480 ± 50 BP). Site C, 170 m south of the road, has produced a small quantity of Later Mesolithic material.

Archaeological interpretation

During the Middle Neolithic an area of sand dunes, just to the north of the Flandrian cliff-line, was occupied by an agricultural settlement for long enough, probably a number of centuries, for a substantial soil profile to be developed. This settlement was buried by blown sand. At the end of the Neolithic and the beginning of the Bronze Age, land some 400 m to the north, was occupied for a relatively short time before it, in turn, was buried by dunes.

The area to the north of the Flandrian cliff-line did not experience the rapid extension of human activity which occurred in the area between the uplands and the Bride Moraine between the early and later Mesolithic period (McCartan 1990, 1999) despite the presence of a significant Middle Neolithic settlement at Phurt, the equivalent Late Neolithic expansion of agricultural settlement did not take place there (Burrow, pers. comm.).

A convenient comparison and control for the Phurt sequence is provided by Kerrowdhoo, a site some 350 m inland from the Phurt road section (Fig. 11). Here trial excavations and fieldwork established a settlement sequence running from the farm to the boundary of modern cultivation, almost 1 km to the north (Davey 1995; Johnson 1995). There is a marl pit cut into till at the farm and test pits excavated in the drive showed clay at the surface. The farmhouse itself was constructed on blown sand and sealed a large Neolithic rubbish pit (Higgins 1995). The farmyard was built directly onto thin plough-soils of Neolithic date. The two ploughed fields to the north of the farm produced during fieldwalking a wide range of flint from later Mesolithic onwards, together with medieval and post-medieval pottery. Beyond the boundary of medieval cultivation a group of fields which were enclosed in the early 19th century were walked and a number of test and trial pits were exca-

vated. Mesolithic material only occurred on the southern boundary of these fields and was rare. The very large flint assemblage recovered in this study (over 3000 artifacts) was of Late Neolithic and Early Bronze Age types (McCartan 1995). Four burnt mounds were investigated (Fig. 11), at least one of which was of Iron Age date (Woodcock 1995). The finds were contained in very shallow sand-ranker type prehistoric soils, based on blown sand over gravels, which had been completely destroyed by ploughing at the time of enclosure. At the northern end of the field system rolled Mesolithic flints, presumed to derive from earlier land surfaces and deposited in storm beaches, were recovered. Thus, the Kerrowdhoo data tends to confirm that the first occupation of the area to the north of the Flandrian cliff-line took place during the Neolithic period and that occupation of sand dunes moved progressively northwards reaching its maximum extent in the Iron Age.

Discussion and conclusions

The main discussion points and conclusions from this work relate to the following: the dating of the sediments and related archaeological finds; the palaeoenvironments from the pollen and diatom records with regard to the proximity of sea-level; the modification of the vegetation by human activity.

(1) Dating: A new synthesis of the Neolithic settlement of the Isle of Man and its absolute chronology, based partly on a detailed radiocarbon study of the Late Neolithic (Burrow & Darvill 1997) has recently been completed. All of the existing radiocarbon dates for the Isle of Man have also been subject of a detailed review (Chiverrell *et al.* 1999). It is clear that some Mesolithic finds have been located on the beach but they are reworked and not significant in terms of human occupation at Phurt. There is no evidence at Phurt for human modification of the vegetation in the Mesolithic. The radiocarbon dates for the middle peat fit into the Neolithic phase, and although all the *in situ* artifacts are from layers above the peat from the sandy palaeosol, these layers could have been deposited rapidly after the peat formation. Although the artifacts are Middle Neolithic it is considered that the dates from the peat are not inconsistent with this dating framework.

(2) Palaeoenvironments with regard to proximity of sea-level: The pollen record indicates an early woodland phase, although

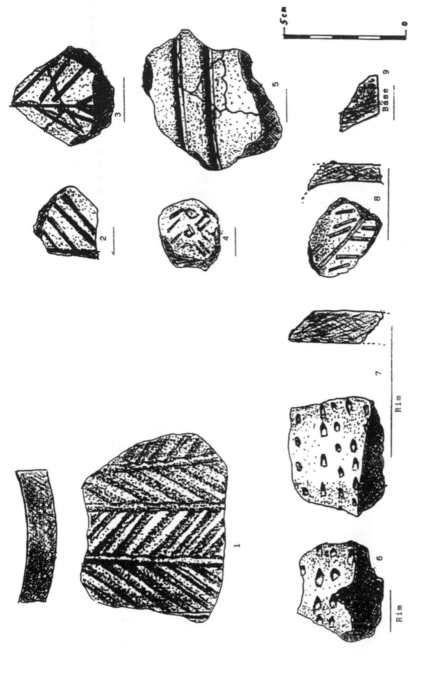

Fig. 13. Examples of Bronze Age pottery found at site Ph-2 (Drawing by A. Skillan).

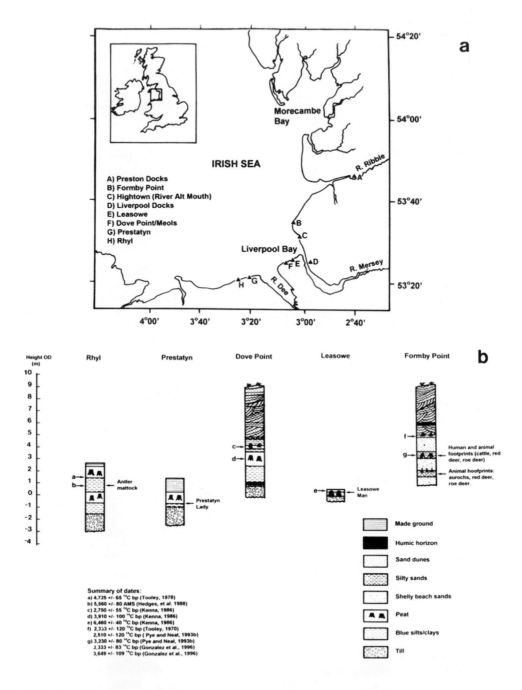

Fig. 14. (**a**) Localities in the intertidal zone of NW England in which human remains, mammalian remains and prehistoric artefacts have been found in post-glacial sequences (peats, silts, gravels and sand dunes). (**b**) Stratigraphy and radiocarbon dates from some important intertidal zone localities around Liverpool Bay, equivalent in age to the Phurt sequences.

there are indicators of the close proximity of the sea from coastal pollen taxa and diatom assemblages. This close marine environment is also indicated by the foram test linings in the upper peat layers and the single test of *Trochammina inflata* in the sands immediately above. This is an upper salt marsh foramininferid which must have either lived in that environment or have been wind blown a short distance. In the middle peat tree pollen was much less frequent, there was a wide range of open ground herb taxa mainly of freshwater type but again there were coastal, salt marsh taxa present, indicating the close proximity of the sea. In the upper organic horizon and the burnt mound profiles the lack of coastal pollen must indicate a relative drop in sea-level. The depositional environment envisaged to account for the litho- and pollen stratigraphy in these small basins is predominantly freshwater lake basins behind shingle bars, with the close proximity to seaward of salt marsh. On occasions there must have been brackish water in these lagoons and a marine connection through the shingle barrier. This environment is similar to the chronologically earlier succession at Loch Cranstal discussed in the section on previous work. The post-glacial sediments found north of Phurt do not have a direct marine influence. This is in strong contrast to the sequences preserved on the coast of Liverpool Bay (Gonzalez *et al.*

1998; Huddart *et al.* 1999a, b; Roberts *et al.* 1996; Figs 14a & b), where there is clear evidence for at least three marine transgressions occurring during the Holocene. The archaeological evidence preserved in the intertidal zone of the eastern part of the northern Irish Sea basin indicates much human activity in coastal or near coastal environments during the Neolithic and Bronze ages. This evidence is normally very well preserved and the well developed 'occupation horizon' at Phurt is a good example of human presence at these prehistoric periods and in a near coastal environment.

(3) Modification of the vegetation by human activity: The pollen record reinforces the archaeological evidence of woodland clearance and agriculture that is associated with the organic cultural horizon at Phurt 1 which seems to be associated with the Middle Neolithic finds. Further agricultural land use is associated with the later Early Bronze Age burnt mound sequence and the coastal plain in this area seems to have been almost completely deforested during this period.

We thank N. Johnson and R. Moore for assistance in the field and surveying work. P. Davey is grateful to A. Skillan for information and drawings about his most recent finds from the Phurt cliff-sections and to J. Woodcock for details of the Bronze Age material from the site in advance of the publication of her definitive study of the Manx Bronze Age.

Appendix I: Diatom species listing for Phurt samples

Diatom species	Ph1-7	Ph1-8	Ph1-10	Ph2-8	Ph2-9
Coscinodiscus sp.	3	1	–	–	–
Diatom sp.	37	2	2	25	–
Diploneis sp.	1	–	–	–	–
Diploneis interrupta	1	–	–	–	–
Diploneis ovalis	2	–	–	–	–
Diploneis smithii	2	–	–	–	–
Mastogloia sp.	1	–	–	–	–
Navicula sp.	1	–	–	–	–
Navicula pusilla	–	–	–	3	–
Nitzschia sp.	–	–	–	1	–
Nitzschia navicularis	1	8	–	–	–
Paralia sulcata	4	310	–	1	–
Pinnularia sp.	9	–	–	1	–
Podosira stelligera	–	2	–	–	–
Pseudopodosira westii	1	–	–	–	–
Scoliopleura tumida	–	1	–	–	–
Thalassiosira eccentrica	–	5	–	–	–
Total valves	62	329	2	31	0
Total assigned valves	11	326	0	4	0

References

BURROW, S. 1997. *The Neolithic culture of the Isle of Man.* British Archaeological Reports, British Series, **263**.

—— & DARVILL, T. 1997. AMS dating of the Manx Ronaldsway Neolithic. *Antiquity*, **71**, 412–419.

CARTER, P. A. C. 1977. Lough Cranstal. *In*: TOOLEY, M. J. (ed.) *The Isle of Man, Lancashire Coast and Lake District.* Guidebook for Excursion A4, X INQUA Congress, GeoAbstracts, Norwich, 28–29.

CHIVERRELL, R. C., DAVEY, P. J., GOWLETT, J. A. J. & WOODCOCK, J. J. 1999. Radiocarbon dates for the Isle of Man, *In*: DAVEY, P. J. (ed.) *Recent Archaeological Research on the Isle of Man.* British Archaeological Reports, British Series, **278**, 321–336.

DACKOMBE, R. V. & THOMAS, G. S. P. 1985. *Field Guide to the Quaternary of the Isle of Man.* Quaternary Research Association, Cambridge.

—— & ——1991. Glacial deposits and Quaternary stratigraphy of the Isle of Man. *In*: EHLERS, J., GIBBARD, P. L. & ROSE, J. (eds) *Glacial Deposits in Great Britain and Ireland.* Balkema, Rotterdam, 333–344.

DAVEY, P. J. 1995. The fieldwalking programme at Kerrowdhoo, May 1992 to March 1994, 21–36. *In*: DAVEY, P. J. *ET AL.* (eds) *Kerrowdhoo, Bride, Isle of Man: fieldwork and excavations 1992–1994.* Centre for Manx Studies Research Report, **4**, Douglas.

——1999 (ed.) *Recent Archaeological Research in the Isle of Man.* British Archaeological Reports, British Series, **278**.

——, HIGGINS, D. A., JOHNSON, N. C., McCARTAN, S. B. & WOODCOCK, J. J. 1995. *Kerrowdhoo, Bride, Isle of Man: fieldwork and excavations 1992–1994.* Centre for Manx Studies Research Report, **4**, Douglas.

——, FOXON, A. D., PALMER, S., SIMONS, H. & WOODCOCK, J. J. 1999. Recent archaeological accessions into the Manx Museum, *In*: DAVEY, P. J. (ed.) *Recent Archaeological Research in the Isle of Man.* British Archaeological Reports, British Series, **278**, 337–368.

GARRAD, L. S. 1999. Field walkers' records of burnt mounds in the Isle of Man, *In*: DAVEY, P. J. (ed.) *Recent Archaeological Research in the Isle of Man.* British Archaeological Reports, **278**, British Series, 75–80.

GONZALEZ, S., ROBERTS, G. & HUDDART, D. 1998. Holocene palaeoenvironmental reconstruction on the Sefton coast: a multidisciplinary approach. *In*: SINCLAIR, A., SLATER, E. & GOWLETT, J. (eds) *Archaeological Science 1995*, Oxbow Press, Oxford, 277–287.

HARTLEY, B. 1986. A check-list of the freshwater, brackish and marine diatoms of the British Isles and adjoining coastal waters. *Journal of the Marine Biological Association, UK*, **66**, 531–610.

HENDEY, N. I. 1964. *An Introductory Account of the Smaller Algae of British Coastal Waters. Bacillariophycaeae (Diatoms).* Fishery Investigation Series N, HMSO, London.

HIBBERT, F. A., SWITSUR, V. R. & WEST, R. G. 1971. Radiocarbon dating of Flandrian pollen zones at Red Moss, Lancashire. *Proceedings of the Royal Society of London*, B **177**, 161–176.

HIGGINS, D. A. 1995. Excavations at Kerrowdhoo farm, April 1993, *In*: DAVEY, P. J. *ET AL.* (eds) *Kerrowdhoo, Bride, Isle of Man: fieldwork and excavations 1992–1994*, Centre for Manx Studies Research Report, **4**, Douglas, 45–62.

HUDDART, D., ROBERTS, G. & GONZALEZ, S. 1999*a*. Holocene human and animal footprints and their relationships with coastal environmental change, Formby Point, NW England. *Quaternary International*, **55**, 29–41.

——, GONZALEZ, S., & ROBERTS, G. 1999*b*. The archaeological record and Mid-Holocene marginal coastal palaeoenvironments around Liverpool Bay. *Quaternary Proceedings*, **7**, 563–574.

JARDINE, W. G. 1975. Chronology of Holocene marine transgression and regression in in south-western Scotland. *Boreas*, **4**, 173–196.

JOHNSON, N. C. 1995. Sampling excavations at Kerrowdhoo, Fields 1 to 4 April 1993, *In*: DAVEY, P. J. *ET AL.* (eds) *Kerrowdhoo, Isle of Man: fieldwork and excavations 1992–1994*, Centre for Manx Studies Research Report, **4**, Douglas, 37–44.

LAMPLUGH, G. W. 1903. *The Geology of the Isle of Man*, Memoir of the Geological Survey of Great Britain, HMSO, London.

McCARROLL, D., GARRAD, L. & DACKOMBE, R. V. 1990. Lateglacial and Postglacial environmental history. *In*: ROBINSON, V. & McCARROLL, D. (eds) *The Isle of Man. Celebrating a Sense of Place.* Liverpool University Press, Liverpool, 55–76.

McCARTAN, S. B. 1990. The early prehistoric colonisation of the Isle of Man: Mesolithic hunter-gatherers. *Proceedings of the Isle of Man Natural History and Antiquarian Society*, **IX**(4), 517–534.

——1995. Kerrowdhoo lithic analysis: summary and conclusions, *In:* DAVEY, P. J. *ET AL.* (eds) *Kerowdhoo, Bride, Isle of Man: fieldwork and excavations 1992–1994.* Centre for Manx Studies Research Report, **4**, Douglas, 62–64.

——1999. The Manx Mesolithic: a story in stone, *In*: DAVEY, P. J. *ET AL.* (eds) *Recent Archaeological Research on the Isle of Man*, British Archaeological Reports, **278**, British Series, 5–11.

MITCHELL, G. F. 1971. Lough Cranstal. *In*: THOMAS, G. S. P. (ed.) *Isle of Man Field Guide*, Quaternary Research Association, Liverpool.

MOORE, P. D., WEBB, J. A. & COLLINSON, M. E. 1991. *An Illustrated Guide to Pollen Analysis*, 2nd edn, Blackwell Scientific, Oxford.

PHILLIPS, B. A. M. 1967. The Post-Glacial Raised Shoreline around the Northern Plain, Isle of Man. *Northern Universities Geographical Journal*, **8**, 43–48.

ROBERTS, G., GONZALEZ, S. & HUDDART, D. 1996. Intertidal Holocene footprints and their archaeological significance. *Antiquity*, **70**, 647–651.

THOMAS, G. S. P. 1971. (ed.) *Isle of Man Field Guide*, Quaternary Research Association, Liverpool.

——1977. The Quaternary of the Isle of Man. *In*: KIDSON, C. & TOOLEY, M. J. (eds) *The Quaternary History of the Irish Sea*, Geological Journal Special Issue 7, Seel House Press, Liverpool, 155–178.

——1984. On the glacio-dynamic structure of the Bride Moraine, Isle of Man. *Boreas*, **13**, 355–364.

——1985. The Quaternary of the Northern Irish Sea basin. *In*: JOHNSON, R. H. (ed.) *The Geomorphology of North-west England*. Manchester University Press, Manchester, 143–158

TOOLEY, M. J. 1974. Sea-level changes in the last 9000 years in north-west England. *Geographical Journal*, **11**, 37–52.

——(ed.) 1977. *The Isle of Man, Lancashire and Lake District*. Field Guide for Excursion A4, X INQUA Congress, GeoAbstracts, Norwich.

——1978. Flandrian Sea-Level Changes and Vegetational History of the Isle of Man: A Review. *In*:

DAVEY, P. (ed.) *Man and Environment in the Isle of Man*. British Archaeological Reports, **54**, Oxford, 15–24.

VAN DER WERFF, H. & HULS, H. 1958–1966. *Diatomeeënflora van Nederland*. 8 parts, published privately by van der Werff, De Hoef (U), The Netherlands.

VOS, P. C. & DEWOLF, H. 1993. Diatoms as a tool for reconstructing sedimentary environments in coastal wetlands; methodological aspects. *Hydrobiologia*, **269/270**, 285–296.

WARD, C. 1970. The Ayres raised beach, Isle of Man. *Geological Journal*, **7**, 217–220.

WOODCOCK, J. J. 1995. The excavation of a burnt mound at Kerrowdhoo, July 1992. *In*: DAVEY, P. J. *ET AL*. (eds) *Kerrowdhoo, Bride, Isle of Man: fieldwork and excavations 1992–1994*. Centre for Manx Studies Research Report, **4**, 11–20.

Coastal development and human activities in NW Germany

BIANKA E. M. PETZELBERGER

*Lower Saxony Institute for Historical Coastal Research, Postfach 2062, D-26360
Wilhelmshaven, Germany (e-mail: bianka.petzelberger@nihk.terramare.de)*

Abstract: The flat coastal region of NW Germany is constructed of siliciclastic and organic sediments which were deposited during the Holocene sea level rise. By 7500 BP the marine transgression had reached the present coastal area which is proved by brackish-marine sediments. Nearly coinciding with this there was an evident deceleration of the sea-level rise. A reconstruction of the coast-line for the last 2000 years on the basis of the sediment and settlement distribution shows that the coast remained more or less in the same position during this period of time. However this does not apply to certain regions. Thus, bays which existed around the time 0 AD, gradually became mainland. In other areas late Medieval and early Modern storm floods were responsible for great losses of mainland, such as the Jade Bay. These losses of mainland are especially noteworthy, because these area had been protected with dykes. Until the beginning of dyke building the settlers of the flat coastal region raised their dwelling areas artificially and built dwelling mounds (so-called Wurten) in order to be protected against flooding. By doing this men reacted to the influences of their environment, but by building dykes they started to shape their environment actively.

The Holocene sediments of the NW German coastal region are composed of a basal peat and clay, silt and fine sand. They were deposited from about 7500BP onwards, the time at which the marine transgression reached today's coastal region (Behre 1987; Streif 1989, 1990). Around the same time the rate of the sea level rise decreased (Fig. 1). In the lower parts of the coastal profile the different sediments reflect sensitive changes in the rate of sea-level rise. Whereas in the upper part the nature of human occupation shows even more sensitive changes in sea-level rise, specially in storm flood level, but only until the beginning of dyke building.

Coastal sediments and their interpretation

The basal peat was produced due to the rising ground water level which, on flat coasts like the German North Sea Coast, is dependent on sea-level. Due to rising ground water level before the marine transgression, these areas became wet and supported the growth of bog formation in the coastal region. At first the clastic material was deposited in lagoonal environments, later mainly in tidal flats and salt marshes (Fig. 2); during this process the salinity increased slowly, as can be concluded from the preserved plant material (Streif 1989). These deposition areas are now to be found exclusively in front of the

dykes, which draw a sharp boundary between sedimentation areas which were originally connected. Before dykes were built there was a multitude of transition zones from salt marsh to coastal marsh and the marshes were flooded in winter and during certain wind conditions. These temporary floodings brought new nutrients and sediment to the soils.

There may be up to three peat layers intercalated in the clastic Holocene sequence, which show sensitive changes in the rates of sea-level rise. Even in these cases the interdependence of ground water level and sea-level in the flat coastal regions is of high importance. During a rapid sea-level rise clastic sediments are deposited on the peat which had developed previously (Streif 1986). During a deceleration of the rate of sea-level rise the ground water table reacts in the same way. If the rate of ground water rise drops below the rate of bog growth, the bog can expand over the marine sediments to seaward (Fig. 2). If the rate of sea-level rise and thus the rate of ground water rise once again increases over the rate of bog growth, the bog is in a way 'drowned' and covered by clastic sediments. As terrestrial deposits within a mainly marine sequence, the intercalated peats indicate regressive phases. This is not a real regression, as the sea level was still rising, but at a lower rate than the rate of bog growth.

From: PYE, K. & ALLEN, J. R. L. (eds). *Coastal and Estuarine Environments: sedimentology, geomorphology and geoarchaeology*. Geological Society, London, Special Publications, **175**, 365–376. 0305-8719/00/$15.00 © The Geological Society of London 2000.

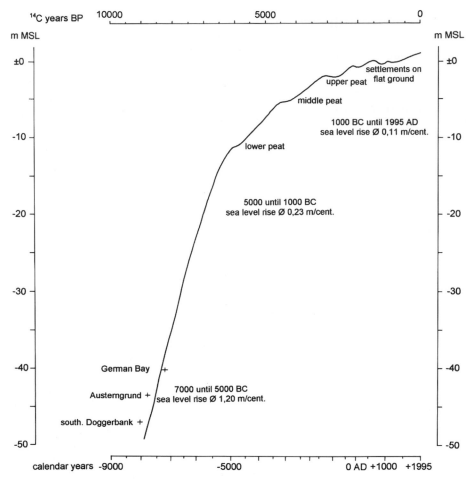

Fig. 1. Sea-level curve for NW Germany indicating the mean high water level (MHW). The three mentioned peat layers occur in the area of Wilhelmshaven (after Behre & Schmid 1998).

A regression is documented by a fossil soil horizon (Figs 2 & 3). Unlike peat formation, for soil formation the ground water level has to be clearly below the ground surface. As in the flat coastal regions the ground water level is dependent on the height of sea-level, we can see from soil formation that the ground water level – and thus also the sea-level – was clearly lower at the time of soil formation. The ground surface became dry which led to the start of soil formation. Such a regression is substantiated by a supra-regionally proved fossil soil horizon for the time 100 BC until 100 AD (Behre & Streif 1980). Parallel to soil formation in fens near the coast a change to raised bog growth could be noticed (Fig. 3). As raised bogs grow only outside the ground water range, this is also proof of the

evident drop in the ground water level. A part of these bogs was flooded during the next transgression and covered with sediments, whereas in other areas the raised bogs continued to grow.

Due to the existence of intercalated peats and soil formation it is possible to reconstruct in detail the curve of sea-level rise for the last approx. 5000 years (Fig. 4). For this reconstruction not only geological and pedological information was used, but also archaeological results, especially from the most recent period from about 1000 BC. From this period settlements on the German North Sea Coast are known. In this connection the different levels on which these settlements are situated are of particular importance, as it can be assumed that the founders settled on dry land.

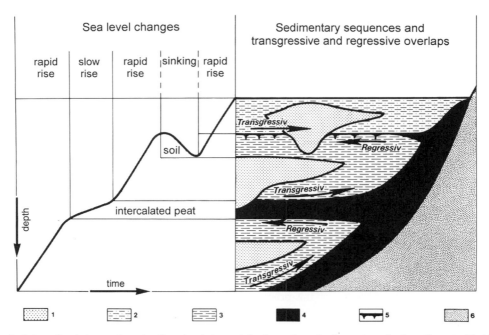

Fig. 2. Interaction between the rate of sea-level rise and the formation of soils, peat or clastic sediments. (1) tidal channel infill; (2) tidal flat deposits; (3) brackish and lagoonal deposits; (4) peat; (5) soil; (6) Pleistocene deposits (from Streif 1989).

Human settlements and their evidence for sea-level rise

The oldest settlements from the last millenium BC, as well as what is the oldest known settlement in the German marsh district from the late Bronze Age at Rodenkirchen, which is situated on the western bank of the river Weser, were built on river banks along the river marshes (Fig. 5). The natural levees may be as large as up to two kilometres wide and were formed by floodings (Fig. 6). During these flooding events the

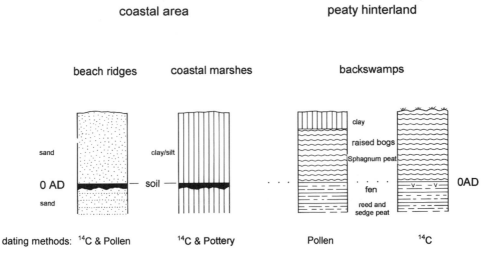

Fig. 3. Schematic diagram indicating regressive horizons in different parts of the German coastal region (from Behre 1987).

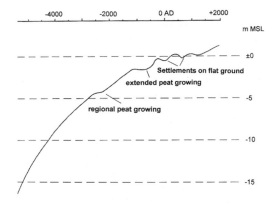

Fig. 4. Sea-level rise and its effect on the German coastal area (time scale in radiocarbon years) (after Behre 1994).

sediment, which was transported by the river, was deposited in the area of the levees; this process was favoured by the vegetation, acting as some kind of a filter. In the course of time the accumulation of the sediment led to the rise of the levees above the level of the hinterland, were no sedimentation was possible. Due to the rising sea-level and the connected rise of the ground water and the river level, there was comparatively continuous sedimentation and thus a continuous raising of the levees, which, on the other hand, led to a sediment deficit in the hinterland (Fig. 6). As a result of flooding and the rising ground water level these areas remained wet and growth of fens started (Behre 1985, 1987). In this back-swamp area (so-called Sietland) no forests grew and it was not suitable as settlement ground due to the high ground water level in the fens. How-

ever, the naturally raised backs of the levees offered relatively dry areas for settlement on the one hand, and on the other the levees were originally covered with river bank forests and thus provided the building material for settlements. The composition of the river bank forests can be determined with the help of the wood which was used for settlements and is found in archaeological excavations (Fig. 7). The discovery of a stump horizon in such a settlement shows that in that case the wood was cut on the spot (Behre 1986). This conclusion can be made by comparing the wood of the stumps and the wood found in the remnants of house constructions in archaeological excavation sites. The preservation of wood in the coastal marshes is not always good enough to determine working marks on the wood.

The settlements on the natural levees were eventually abandoned. It is not clear whether increasing wetness was the reason for this, but the settlements were covered with sediments. After a break in habitation new settlements in the coastal marsh on flat ground are known from about 50 BC (Fig. 5). In this connection it is of importance that the settlements were built on flat ground, so-called 'Flachsiedlungen' (settlements on flat ground). At this time flooding seemed to be no menace for men, as otherwise naturally raised areas of the land would have been preferentially settled (Behre 1987). This period of settlement on flat ground developed in parallel with the above mentioned soil formation. Thus, the archaeological results and the scientific studies are complementary. The short regression, which led to the formation of soil caused by a lower ground water level, was also a precondition that men could settle on flat ground due to the evident reduced threat of flooding.

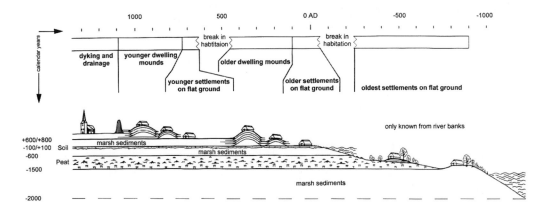

Fig. 5. Schematic diagram showing the geological coastal development and human occupation in the German coastal marsh area (after Behre 1995).

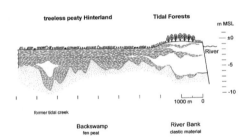

Fig. 6. Schematic cross section through a river marsh. Example from the lower Ems area at about 500 BC (western Germany). Dotted area, Pleistocene; no signature, clastic sediments; broken lines, fen peat (after Behre 1987).

Only in the 2nd century AD the settlers of the coastal region were apparently menaced again by storm floods. The settlements on flat ground were abandoned, or the settling grounds were raised artificially (Fig. 5). The thickness of the different strata is very different, but it is very probable that the height was dependent on the last storm flood. If the settling ground was flooded by approx. 50 cm, the next artificially raised layer was at least 60 cm thick, in order not to be flooded during the next storm flood. Thus, dwelling mounds (so-called 'Wurten') gradually came into existence; these dwelling mounds may be up to 5 m high and can contain up to seven occupation levels (Figs 8 & 9). Dung and other organic materials were originally used for the strata. Through botanical studies of this material it is possible to reconstruct the close environment of the dwelling mounds (Behre 1976; Behre & Jacomet 1991). In this connection, above all the tolerance of the plants against salt is of high importance, in order to be able to work out even the slightest level differences of the salt marshes (Fig. 10). These studies also proved the considerably greater biodiversity in former times of the area from the tidal flat across the salt marshes to the fresh marshes, which was typical for the coastal area. Today the dykes form a fixed border at which the tidal flat or the salt marshes end. From organic material, as well as from phytogenic remains of the different occupation levels, conclusions can be drawn about agricultural practice and human diet.

After a new break in habitation at the end of the 5th century and in the 6th century AD, a short settlement period on flat ground is evident (Fig. 5). A demonstrably supra-regional fossil soil horizon is not known from this time. Therefore it cannot be proved for certain, whether there was a new regression, which was too short for soil formation, or whether there were no storm floods which menaced the land over a longer period of time. This younger period of 'Flachsiedlungen' lasted less than 100 a. Then men were forced to leave their settlement areas again, or to raise them artificially, in order to be protected against higher and higher storm floods. The dwelling mounds of the Middle Ages, contrary to the older dwelling mounds from Roman Iron Age, were only in the early stages built from dung and other organic material. Later people began to use the available sediment in the surroundings for the formation of the mounds. Unfortunately the preservation conditions of the organic material in these dwelling mounds were not very favourable due to better

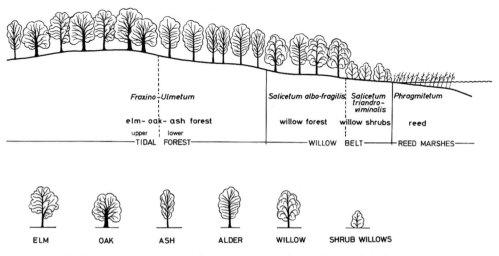

Fig. 7. The subdivision of former river bank forests (Auenwälder) according to their elevation above water level (from Behre 1986).

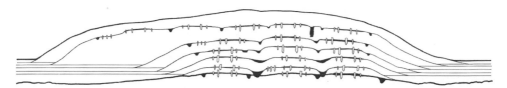

Fig. 8. Schematic section of a dwelling mound (Wurt) from the times of the older dwelling mounds starting with a settlement on flat ground of Roman Iron Age. The layers above this show different dwelling horizons with ground plans as well as organic material (from Behre 1987).

Fig. 9. Archaeological excavation of a dwelling mound. At first view the stratigraphy of a dwelling mound is not always as simple as shown in Fig. 8.

aeration. Nevertheless it is possible to find botanical remains in these dwelling mounds, e.g. in burnt occupation levels, which make it possible to reconstruct the environment and human diet. The horse bean *Ficia faba* seems to have been a basic food, before the appearance of the potatoe, which supplied the necessary starch, in the coastal marsh of the Middle Ages (Ey 1995a; Lempiäinen & Behre 1997). *Ficia faba* has been cultivated on the coastal marsh in

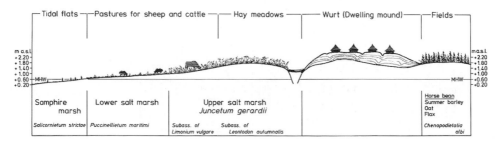

Fig. 10. Schematic cross section through a medieval dwelling mound (Wurt) and its environment. Example from Elisenhof, Schleswig-Holstein (from Behre & Jacomet 1991).

the Middle Ages, based on evidence from different archaeological excavations where it was found in great amounts.

Dykes and their impact on coastal evolution

As long as there were no winterproofed dykes to protect the settlements against storm floods, it was necessary to raise the dwelling mounds. But the first dykes were merely summer dykes, which were built in a ring round the arable land to protect it against storm floods in summer. These oldest dykes, which due to their structure are also called ring dykes, first appeared in the 11th century (Ey 1996a, 1997). Parallel to this the dwelling mounds had to be raised further, as the summer dykes, as the name already indicates, were only a protection against the summer floods, and not against the winter floods with their considerably higher levels. The ring dykes were enlarged little by little and more and more arable land was gradually surrounded with dykes and several ring dykes were connected with each other (Ey 1996b). Their heights vary between 1 m and 1.5 m above the former ground level (Ey 1992, 1995b)

From the 13th century the first winterproofed dykes are known (Ey 1995b), built along nearly all of the NW coast of Germany, and behind which people believed themselves to be secure. If we compare reconstructions of the coast-line in Lower Saxony from the time around 0 AD and about 800 AD (Fig. 11a, b), on one hand some land losses through creation of new sea bays are obvious, but on the other hand many former bays became smaller, or disappeared completely. In addition to this it has to be taken into consideration that the time around 0 AD coincides with the above mentioned regression, whereas for the time around 800 AD (the younger dwelling mound period) a rising storm flood level is documented. The next reconstruction shows the position of the coastline at about 1500 AD (Fig. 11c). In comparison to the map of 800 AD great land losses are evident. Considerable ingressions of the sea along the North Sea Coast of Lower Saxony are especially noteable in the late Middle Ages (Behre 1987). The question is, what was the reason for these great land losses even though men had started to build dykes in the Middle Ages?

The different factors which are important in this connection are nearly all dependent on the dyke building procedure itself. During storm floods the dykes increase the destructive energy of the rising water. The risk of dyke bursts was clearly increased by this. If a dyke broke it was generally very difficult to remove the ingressed sea water from the flooded areas due to the low topographic height of the dyked land. The topographic level of the dyked land was, and even is today, nearly always under the level of the land in front of the dykes. This is because the land on the interior side of the dyke has been cut off from sedimentation and has experienced consolidation. As the land is no longer flooded, no new material can be deposited there, but the

(a)

Fig. 11. Reconstruction of the NW German coast-line. (**a**) around the Birth of Christ, (**b**) around 800 AD and (**c**) around 1500 AD (from Behre 1987).

(b)

(c)

Fig. 11. (*Continued*)

areas in front of the dyke are still exposed to flooding, sedimentation and heightening (Behre 1987). In coastal areas, dykes of different ages lie one behind the other, a flat scarped table-land can develop (Fig. 12), which is also called polder stairs (Poldertreppe). The oldest dyked areas are the lowest ones and the nearer to the present dyke line the younger and higher is the land. Such polder stairs differ in height dependent on their geographical situation. The height of the first winterproofed dykes is about 2 m above the former ground (Hallewas 1984,

Ey 1997). Today the height of the dykes is 8.5 m or 9.2 m dependent on their position at the coast.

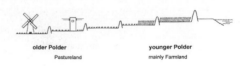

Fig. 12. Schematic transect across polders of different age (the coast is on the right side) (after Behre 1987).

The nutrient content and supply of the soil also depended on flooding. Thus, agriculture was possible on the younger polders due to the better nutrient content of the soil, whereas on older polders stock-farming predominated, due to nutrient diminution as well as the effects of compaction of the soil during soil formation. In the marshes even today this division between pasture- and agricultural land may be observed. In the flat coastal region the topographic level differences of the polder stairs (Poldertreppe) are not very striking, but they are noticeable with the naked eye.

Another factor in the considerable land losses of the late Middle Ages was the cutting of salt peat (Bantelmann 1966; Marschalleck 1973) (Fig. 13 & 14). Due to the repeated floodings during the following transgressions the upper layer of the peat was enriched with salt from the sea water and finally covered with clastic sediment (Fig. 3). For the exploitation of salt peat the sediment cover was removed by cutting blocks which were turned upside down (Fig. 13), in order to win the peat which was enriched with salt. The peat was burnt, the ashes were repeatedly washed and little by little a brine was con-centrated. By evaporating that brine salt could be won. This salt production method was common along the Frisian coast from the Netherlands to Denmark and the so-called Frisian salt was traded during medieval and early modern times (Marschallek 1973). Due to peat cutting the land was lowered by the thickness of the peat that was exploited. If, in the course of a storm flood, a dyke broke, this had a catastrophic effect for the land which had been lowered by salt peat cutting. The cutting of salt peat happened mainly in front of the dykes, but there also exists evidence of salt peat cutting in a landward direction far behind the former coastline, for example south of the Jade Bay at Diekmannshausen (Behre 1987, Krämer 1991). Here was found a situation like that shown in Fig. 14. The clods of the sediment that covered the peat before being turned up side down have been eroded to a certain horizon but are still visible in the profile. It is assumed that the enormous size of the Jade Bay was, among other things, caused by the salt peat cutting (Krämer 1991).

A further factor which contributed to the great losses of land was the drainage of the land. With dyke building drainage of the land had to

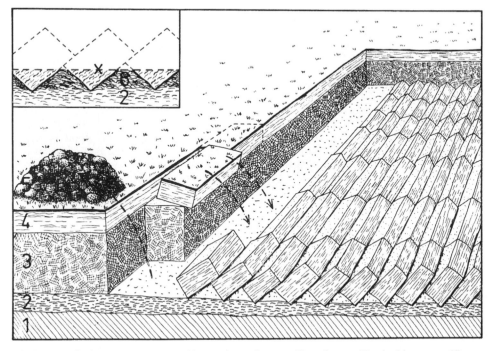

Fig. 13. System of salt peat cutting. (1) Older marine sediments; (2) reed peat; (3) raised bog peat; (4) younger marine sediments; (5) dug salt peat; (6) mixture of peat and sediment between the clods. On top left: During a new transgression the upper part of the clods has been eroded to the marked horizon (×), representing the situation as it can be seen today in the tidal flats and in Fig. 14 (after Overbeck 1975).

Fig. 14. Cross section in a tidal flat showing long clods of younger marine sediments (Fig. 13) thrown upside down. This proves salt peat cutting activities in that area. (Photo Bantelmann 1954).

Fig. 15. Profile of the archaeological excavation at Rodenkirchen. Two fossil soils can be seen clearly in the profile. The lower one represents the marine regression between 100 BC and 100 AD. The upper soil is of medieval age. More than 1 m of sediment occurs on top of this soil, deposited after a flood as a result of a breach in a dyke, giving evidence of the anthropogenic induced drainage of the land.

be undertaken otherwise the land would be saturated from the impounded ground water. However the artificial drainage accelerated soil consolidate and with this sinking of the land (Allen 1999). Especially in those areas with many and/or thick peat layers, which obviously have a higher compaction potential intercalated in the Holocene clastic sedimentary sequence, the subsidence may be considerable. Thus, for example a 2 m thick peat occurs within a 10 m thick Holocene sediment sequence under the late Bronze Age settlement at Rodenkirchen on the western bank of the river Weser. In the excavation profile there could be noticed a soil horizon from the Middle Ages under a sediment cover of about 1 m (Fig. 15). In addition to this in the excavation there could be noticed a drainage ditch, which had been excavated down into the medieval soil horizon (Fig. 16). The length and the straight passage of the ditch are unmistakable indications that this ditch had been built artificially. The excavation lies in an area, which, due to a dyke burst, was flooded during the Marcellus Storm Flood in 1362 (Ey 1995b, 1997). The burst happened in the eastern part of the present Jade Bay. The flooding reached up to the river Weser. Presumably the erosive force of the water decreased very quickly after the actual dyke burst. Thus, an erosion within the area of the archaeological excavations may be excluded, as the medieval soil in the excavation profile shows no signs of reworking or erosion. As the drained land had subsided so much, among other things because of the peat in

the subsoil, large areas were flooded by the ingressing sea water. With flooding new sediment was delivered. In the area of the excavation the exposed sediment above the medieval soil is 1 m or more thick. This is especially remarkable, if we take into consideration that only about 150 years later this area was cut off again from further flooding by new dykes (Ey 1997). A considerable amount of sediment was deposited within a relatively short time. One reason for this may be the low level of the medieval soil, so that the area acted as a kind of sedimentary trap. The grain size of the sediment, mainly clay and silt, is indicative of low transport energy. Due to the sedimentary structure it is presumed that a salt marsh facies developed in a comparatively short time after the first flooding; this salt marsh facies was flooded quite often. This is the only explanation for the large sediment thickness, despite the small grain size, in this short period of time.

Fig. 16. Plan view of the archaeological excavation of Rodenkirchen showing a former ditch in the medieval soil constructed to drain the land.

The beginning of dyke building led to different effects. The land was cut off from the supply of new sediments, and the areas which were first surrounded by dykes have a lower topographic level than the areas around which the dykes were built later. The drainage of the land following dyke building caused increased soil subsidence; this led to a considerable down sinking of the land, especially in areas with peat in the subsoil. In addition to these factors depending on dyke building, in some areas man aggravated the problems connected with dyke burst, by salt peat cutting. All these factors resulted in a lowering of the topographic level of the dyked land. In all probability these effects are cumulative. If, in early periods of dyke building, when the techniques were not fully developed, a dyke broke under these conditions, this led to major losses of land and significant mortality (Behre 1987). Only with progressive knowledge in dyke building was it gradually possible to regain parts of the land which had been lost by dyke bursts.

Conclusions

In NW Germany the Holocene sedimentary sequence sensitively reflects changes in the rate of sea-level rise. Intercalated peat layers in the clastic marine sediments represent phases with a low rate of sea-level rise, land fossil soil horizons provide evidence of regressions. Since the human occupation of the coastal landscape man has reacted to natural forces. For example, the selection and cultivation of plants for human diet and house building were a very early intervention in the natural competition behaviour of the plants. In times before dykes were built man had shaped the coastal landscape already e.g. by building dwelling mounds (Wurten). However only with dyke building did man significantly intervene in the natural equilibrium of water- and sediment balance on the North Sea Coast and thus aggravate the problem of storm floods. There is no doubt that there were storm floods, but the question is whether the damage inflicted by medieval storm floods would have assumed such grave proportions without dyke building and the resulting soil subsidence. It appears that the disastrous effects of storm floods of the late Middle Ages are mainly due to the massive human intervention.

All these developments can be compared with those in the Netherlands (van Es *et al.* 1988; Hallewas *et al.* 1997) and Ribe, southwestern Denmark (Jensen 1998). But even in this coastal lowlands there are differences in the geological evolution. For example in the Netherlands regional subsidence and a microtidal range exist. On salt marshes the first human settlements are known from late Neolithic times (Louwe Kooijmans 1993) and the first dwelling mounds are already known from 500 BC in the Netherlands. During the migration period a break of habitation can be recognized in the Netherlands as well as in Germany, but not in Britain because men migrated from the continent to Britain. It may be assumed that the knowledge of building dwelling mounds existed in Britain but there was no need for this great effort because of the different coastal landscape.

References

ALLEN, J. R. L. 1999. Geological impacts on coastal wetland landscapes: some general effects of sediment autocompaction in the Holocene of northwest Europe. *The Holocene*, **9**, 1–12.

BANTELMANN, A. 1966. Die Landschaftsentwicklung an der Schleswig-Holsteinischen Westküste, dargestellt am Beispiel Nordfriesland. *Die Küste, Heide in Holstein*, **14**, 5–99.

BEHRE, K.-E. 1976. Die Pflanzenreste aus der frühgeschichtlichen Wurt Elisenhof. *Studien zur Küstenarchäologie Schleswig-Holsteins*, **A2**, Bern und Frankfurt/M.

——1985. Die ursprüngliche Vegetation in den deutschen Marschgebieten und deren Veränderung durch prähistorische Besiedlung und Meeresspiegelbewegungen. *In*: WEIDEMANN, G. (ed.) *Verhandlungen Gesellschaft für Ökologie*, Bremen, **XIII**, 85–96.

——1986. Analysis of botanical macro-remains. *In*: VAN DE PLASSCHE, O. (ed.) *Sea-level Research: a manual for the collection and evaluation of data*. Norwich, 413–433.

——1987. *Meeresspiegelbewegungen und Siedlungsgeschichte in den Nordseemarschen*. Vortrag vor der 20. Landschaftsversammlung der Oldenburgischen Landschaft am 13. März 1987 in Wilhelmshaven, Oldenburg.

——1994. Kleine historische Landeskunde des Elbe-Weser-Raumes. *In*: DANNENBERG, H.-E. & SCHULZE, H.-J. (eds) *Geschichte des Landes zwischen Elbe und Weser, I Vor- und Frühgeschichte*. Stade, 3–63.

——1995. Die Entstehung und Entwicklung der Natur- und Kulturlandschaft der ostfriesischen Halbinsel. *In*: BEHRE, K.-E. & VAN LENGEN, H. (eds) *Ostfriesland – Geschichte und Gestalt einer Kulturlandschaft*, Wilhelmshaven, 5–37.

—— & JACOMET, S. 1991. The ecological interpretation of archaeobotanical data. *In*: VAN ZEIST, W., WASYLIKOWA, K. & BEHRE, K.-E. (eds) *Progress in Old World Palaeoethnobotany*. Balkema, Rotterdam, 81–108.

—— & SCHMID, P. 1998. *Das Niedersächsische Institut für historische Küstenforschung – 60 Jahre Forschungstätigkeit im Küstengebiet*, Wilhelmshaven.

—— & STREIF, H. 1980. Kriterien zu Meeresspiegel- und darauf bezogene Grundwasserabsenkungen. *Eiszeitalter und Gegenwart*, **30**, 153–160.

EY, J. 1992. Früher Deichbau und Sturmfluten im östlichen Friesland. *In*: STEENSEN, Th. (ed.) *Deichbau und strumfluten in Friesland*, Bredstedt, 32–36.

——1995a. Die mittelalterliche Wurt Neuwarfen, Gde, Wangerland, Ldkr. Friesland – Die Ergebnisse der Grabungen 1991 und 1992. *Probleme der Küstenforschung im südlichen Nordseegebiet*, **23**, 265–315.

——1995b. *Der Sachsenspiegel als Quelle zum frühen Deichbau*. Der Sachsenspiegel. Sachsenspiegel – Recht – Alltag. Oldenburg, 203–205.

——1996a. Deichverlauf. *In*: LINDGREN, U. (ed.) *Europäische Technik im Mittelalter 800 bis 1400*. Tradition und Innovation, Berlin, 101–104.

——1996b. Siedlungssysteme des mittelalterlichen und frühneuzeitlichen Landesausbaus im Küstengebiet des östlichen Frieslandes. *Siedlungsforschung, Archäologie-Geschichte-Geographie*, **14**, 237–244.

——1997. Aufbau und Profile früherer Deiche – kritische Betrachtung einer neuen Sichtweise. *Oldenburger Jahrbuch*, Oldenburg, **97**, 1–9.

HALLEWAS, D. P. 1984. Mittelalterliche Seedeiche im Holländischen Küstengebiet. *Probleme der Küstenforschung im südlichen Nordseegebiet*, **15**, 9–27.

——, SCHEEPSTRA, G. H. & WOLTERING, P. J. (eds) 1997. *Archeologie en geologie van het Nederlandse kustgebied*. Amersfoort.

JENSEN, S. (ed) 1998. *Marsk, land og bebyggelse. Ribeegnen gennem 10.000 år*. Århus.

KRÄMER, R. 1991. Mittelalterliche Salztorfgewinnung im Gebiet des Jadebusens. *Archäologische Mitteilungen aus Nordwestdeutschland*, **5**, 99–108.

LEMPIÄINEN, T. & BEHRE, K.-E. 1997. Zur Umwelt und Ernährung einiger hochmittelalterlicher Wurtsiedlungen in der Marsch des Landes Wursten, Ldkr. Cuxhaven (Niedersachsen), nach archäobotanischen Untersuchungen. *Probleme der Küstenforschung im südlichen Nordseegebiet*, **24**, 275–300.

LOUWE KOOIJMANS, L. P. 1993. Wetland exploitation and upland relations of prehistoric communities in the Netherlands. *In*: GARDINER, J. (ed.) *Flatlands and Wetlands: Current Themes in East Anglian Archaeology*. East Anglian Archaeology Report No. **50**.

MARSCHALLECK, K. H. 1973. Die Salzgewinnung an der friesischen Nordseeküste. *Probleme der Küstenforschung im südlichen Nordseegebiet*, **10**, 127–150.

OVERBECK, F. 1975. *Botanisch-geologische Moorkunde*. Wachholtz, Neumünster.

STREIF, H. 1986. Zur Altersstellung und Entwicklung der Ostfriesischen Inseln. *Offa*, **43**, 29–44.

——1989. Barrier islands, tidal flats, and coastal marshes resulting from a relative rise of sea level in East Frisia on the German North Sea coast. *Proceedings KNGMG Symposium 'Coastal Lowlands, Geology and Geotechnology'*, 1987, 213–223.

——1990. Das ostfriesische Küstengebiet. *Sammlung geologischer Führer*, **57**, 1–376.

VAN ES, W. A., SARFATIJ, H. & WOLTERING, P. J. 1988. *Archeologie in Nederland*. Amsterdam.

Intertidal peats and the archaeology of coastal change in the Severn Estuary, Bristol Channel and Pembrokeshire

MARTIN BELL

Department of Archaeology, University of Reading, Whiteknights, PO Box 218, Reading, RG6 6AA, UK (e-mail: m.g.bell@reading.ac.uk)

Abstract: Dates for the beginning and end of intertidal and coastal peat formation are reviewed in the Severn Estuary, Bristol Channel and Pembrokeshire. Peat formation at many sites started between *c.* 6000–4000 Cal BC and in the Severn Estuary continued until *c.* 200 Cal BC. Archaeological evidence is concentrated at two main stages within the coastal sequences. Throughout the area Mesolithic sites underlie the earliest peat and relate to coastal exploitation just prior to the transgression represented by peat formation. During the main period of peat formation from the later Mesolithic to the early Bronze Age there is only small-scale human activity within the coastal peats. A second episode of concentrated human activity is confined to the Severn Estuary and occurs in the middle Bronze Age and Iron Age. Round and rectangular buildings and trackways are associated with the initial stages of marine transgressions which led to the burial of a coastal bog by minerogenic silts. A transgression in the middle Bronze Age *c.* 1400 Cal BC was followed by a regression phase, the main period of human activity at Goldcliff, this ended with a widespread transgression centred on in the third century BC. The factors which attracted human activity at particular stages within the coastal sequence are considered, as is the relative visibility of human activity during each sedimentary stage. The contribution which archaeological evidence, particularly dendrochronological dating of wooden structures, can make to the dating of coastal change is emphasized.

Submerged forests and intertidal peats have puzzled and excited antiquarians and geologists for generations and the Bristol Channel region (Fig. 1) has figured prominently in the history of their study. Accounts include the earliest observation by Geraldus Cambrensis (1191, 1908 edn) of a submerged forest exposed by a storm at Newgale in AD 1172 'cut down perhaps at the time of the deluge'. There also are accounts by prominent thinkers, topographers and polymathic scientists of the 18th and 19th centuries including John Wesley, Philip Gosse, Thomas Huxley, and William Pengelly. The first archaeological discovery was of flint artifacts at Westward Ho! (Ellis 1866). Major dock excavations in the later 19th century up to the First World War revealed fine exposures of Holocene stratigraphy, peats and archaeological finds. For Britain as a whole information on these early discoveries is contained in the Geological Survey Memoirs and was synthesized by Reid (1913). Interest in these finds in the 18th and 19th centuries was partly because intertidal peats were thought to imply catastrophic environmental change and contained the bones of extinct animals and people. Such discoveries were relevant to contemporary debates within

geology and the emergence of archaeology, indeed Keith (1925) entitled a chapter in his book *The Antiquity of Man* 'The people of the submerged forest'.

During the 20th century, archaeological finds have continued to be made in intertidal contexts although detailed investigations have been surprisingly limited by comparison with those in land areas which have good Holocene sequences. The palaeoenvironmental evidence from submerged forests and intertidal peats, and their potential for further work, has recently been reviewed (Bell 1997). The present paper examines the relationship between the intertidal peats and prehistoric human activity in the Bristol Channel, Pembrokeshire and Severn Estuary (Fig. 1). Peats in the Severn Estuary figured little in archaeological literature prior to a perceptive paper by Locke (1971). However, as a result of detailed investigation from the mid-1980s this area now provides what may be the greatest concentration of intertidal archaeology in Britain. The completion of a recent survey of prehistoric aspects of this sequence in the Welsh Severn Estuary (Bell *et al.* 2000) provides the opportunity for comparison with sites in a wider area, including the English side of the Severn Estuary, the Bristol

From: PYE, K. & ALLEN, J. R. L. (eds). *Coastal and Estuarine Environments: sedimentology, geomorphology and geoarchaeology.* Geological Society, London, Special Publications, **175**, 377–392. 0305-8719/00/$15.00 © The Geological Society of London 2000.

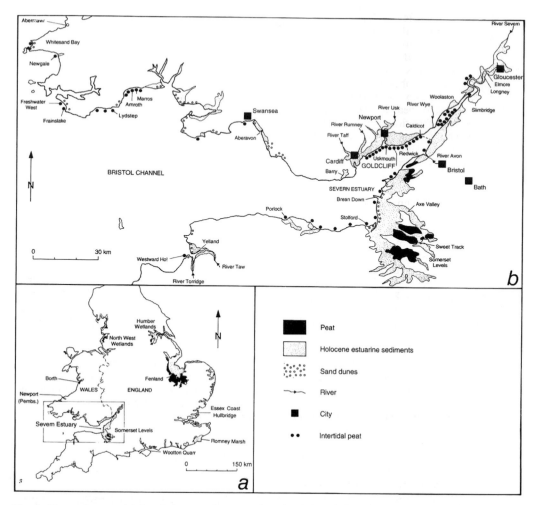

Fig. 1. The study area: (**a**) In relation to other coastal wetlands in Britain; (**b**) Showing the location of the sites discussed in relation to the distribution of Holocene coastal sediments (sources Bell 1997; Lewis 1992).

Channel and Pembrokeshire. This draws on the results of observations over 187 years at Westward Ho! (synthesized in Balaam *et al.* 1987), and on a long history of discoveries in Pembrokeshire, summarized as part of new palaeoenvironmental research by Lewis (1992).

Archaeological sites, particularly those which are dendrochronologically dated, can contribute significantly to an understanding of the chronology of coastal change. This requires comparison of dendrochronological and radiocarbon dates, for this reason dates are generally quoted in both uncalibrated and calibrated form.

Topographic context

Intertidal peats have formed in the context of the overall rising trend of sea-level during the Holo-

cene. This has been successively documented in this study area by the sea-level curves of Hawkins (e.g. 1973) and Heyworth & Kidson (e.g. 1982), studies recently critiqued and refined as a result of detailed site specific studies by Jennings *et al.* (1998) at Porlock, and Haslett *et al.* (1998) in the Axe Valley. Sea-level rise resulted in the flooding of extensive areas of coastal lowland which in the later Mesolithic represented a highly indented coast with marine influence extending well inland as shown by the shaded areas of Holocene stratigraphy on Fig. 1. These areas were subject to progressive Holocene sedimentation. With the reduction in the rate of Holocene sea-level rise around 6000 BP (4800 Cal BC) peats began to form. Long *et al.* (2000) note a broadly coeval episode of mid-Holocene estuary contraction from *c.* 6000 BP (4800 Cal BC) – *c.* 3000 BP (*c*. 1000 Cal BC) in the Severn, Thames and Solent Estuaries. Although the mid-Holocene peats typically begin to form in the later Mesolithic and continue until the Bronze Age, the pattern at individual sites varies and at many sites is interrupted by several phases of marine innundation giving rise to alternating peat-clay sequences. Phases of peat formation are shorter to seaward and duration varies according to topographic context. Intertidal peats are essentially sections of Holocene coastal wetland stratigraphy which have been exposed on the foreshore by later erosion.

Most of the sites in the western part of the area, the Bristol Channel and Pembrokeshire, outcrop at the base of substantial sand and shingle bars which form spits partly closing estuaries (e.g. Westward Ho!, Newport, Pembrokeshire, and Borth), or forming complete barriers across valleys, or more extensive wetlands (e.g. Porlock, Brean Down, Freshwater West, and Whitesands Bay). At least some of the coastal barriers are clearly of antiquity. At Porlock the existence of a barrier from *c*. 5850 Cal BC has been inferred from stratigraphic evidence (Jennings *et al.* 1998), there is similar evidence of an earlier barrier at Stolford (Kidson & Heyworth 1976). The dune system running south of Brean Down was in existence by *c*. 1800 Cal BC (Bell 1990) and at Westward Ho! there are traces of undated earlier pebble ridges in the intertidal zone. In most cases where there is an existing substantial barrier it is probable that peat formation occurred behind a barrier and that phases when a barrier was less extensive, or breached, are represented by minerogenic bands within the peat. Continuing Holocene sea-level rise has led to the landward migration of barriers by 'roll over' and the erosion in the intertidal zone of the wetland stratigraphy which formerly lay behind the barrier. Thus exposures on the foreshore are often the basal part of a much longer wetland sequence extending landward behind the bar. Abermawr, Pembrokeshire (Lewis 1992) is an example where the foreshore peat exposure is 2 m thick, and covers about the first 2000 years of a sequence which, behind the large shingle barrier, is 8 m thick and spans the period from 7640 ± 150 BP (OxA-1411; 6650–6260 Cal BC) to the present. Abermawr is a small valley bog fronted by a shingle barrier 500 m long. The mouth of the Dovey Estuary at Borth/Ynyslas represents a similar phenomenon on a much larger scale: an estuary *c*. 7.5 km wide only partly closed by a major dune and shingle bar. Here, seaward of the bar, one of the most impressive submerged forests in Britain dates to around 5300 BP (4100 Cal BC) (Heyworth 1978; Heyworth & Kidson 1982) and represents the basal portion of the second largest raised bog in Britain where peats continue to form to the present day. In situations such as Borth and Abermawr, peat inception clearly relates to sea-level rise but the date of the latest peat exposed on the foreshore is a function of the pattern of erosion, although on some sites this picks out estuarine clay horizons within the peats.

A contrasting topographic context is represented by the Welsh Severn Estuary where there is no evidence that a coastal barrier ever existed. Here Holocene sea-level rise has been accompanied by the upstream migration of the estuary leading to exposure of long Holocene sequences in the intertidal area. The prehistoric part of this sequence has been divided by Allen & Rae (1987) into three units: at the base silty clays of the lower Wentlooge Formation; a sequence of peats and clays of the middle Wentlooge Formation; silty clays of the upper Wentlooge Formation. We are principally concerned here with the middle Wentlooge peats, which started to form between *c*. 5600 and 4400 Cal BC (Fig. 2). Peat formation was interrupted by varying numbers of minerogenic episodes, peat ceased forming and was succeeded by upper Wentlooge clays at varying dates between *c*. 1500 and 300 Cal BC. What appears on initial examination to be a simple sequence has been shown by detailed investigation of the succession associated with archaeological sites at Goldcliff to be of some complexity.

Mesolithic activity below intertidal peats

Within the Holocene sedimentary sequence, prehistoric archaeological evidence is particularly concentrated in specific horizons. The earliest of these is a basal soil often developed on head, or as in some of the Pembrokeshire sites, on till; these basal horizons contain Mesolithic flints. The most fully investigated site of this type is on the edge of the former Goldcliff island; a extensive charcoal scatter with flint debitage, a few tools and many bones. Four of the five radiocarbon dates for this site indicate occupation between *c*. 5250–5700 Cal BC with one date suggesting activity continued to *c*. 4050–4400 Cal BC. Mesolithic artifacts are also reported on head below the submerged forest at Porlock (Boyd-Dawkins 1870), where we now know that a series of five peat bands date between 8300–5500 Cal BP (Jennings *et al.* 1998), and at Whitesand Bay (Lewis 1992) on till below peat dated 5250 ± 80 BP (CAR-1176; 3970–4230 Cal BC).

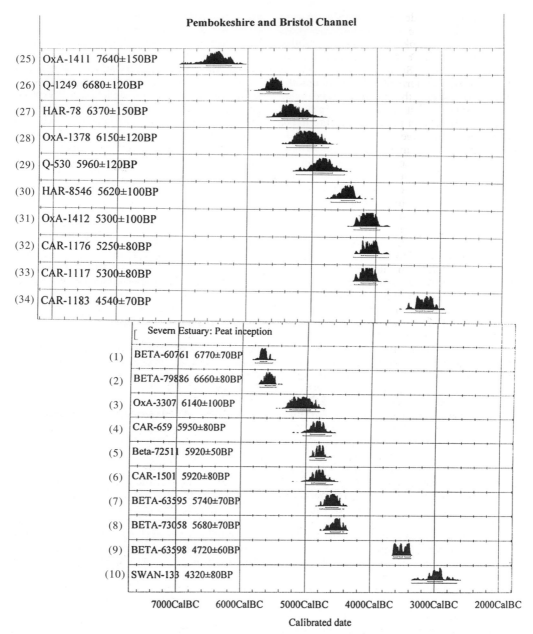

Fig. 2. Calibrated radiocarbon dates for peat inception in the Severn Estuary and inception, and in some cases the early stages of peat growth and associated animal bones, in Pembrokeshire and the Bristol Channel. Each graph shows the distribution of the probability of the calibrated date; the horizontal line below each graph represents 1 standard deviation, the bar below that two standard deviations. Calibration follows Stuiver *et al.* 1998; Graphs produced using OxCal v3. For further details of dates see Table 1.

A number of the Mesolithic sites occur, not on head, but on an overlying clay for which an estuarine origin has been inferred. This appears to be the case at Westward Ho! where the Mesolithic shell midden dated *c.* 5450 Cal BC

(Balaam *et al.* 1987) and a much more extensive artifact and charcoal scatter overlies silty clay which, on account of its very low pH, seems likely to be of marine origin, although macrofossil evidence as to its mode of deposition was lacking. Similar silty deposits were reported by Lewis (1992) below the artifact and/or charcoal scatters at the Pembrokeshire sites of Amroth, Frainslake, Freshwater West and Lydstep and Penybont, Newport. Such deposits could, as Lewis suggests, have formed in lagoons behind a coastal barrier. Given the significant tidal range of the study area, it is also possible that minerogenic deposition took place at the upper limit of the tidal range in advance of tidally related water table changes reaching a level at which peat inception occurred.

Some sites were above the water table at the time of occupation. Biota were not generally preserved in the Goldcliff Mesolithic site; however, the more decay-resistant seeds did survive, showing that waterlogging of that site occurred within a few years of the deposition of these seeds. At Westward Ho! the site was waterlogged at the time of occupation and a wide range of biota survived. Extensive evidence for the footprints of wild animals in the lower Wentlooge Formation of the Severn Estuary (Allen 1997) and Mesolithic human footprints at Uskmouth and Magor (Aldhouse-Green et al. 1992) emphasize the rich faunal resources which were available in the coastal wetland. At Goldcliff the vertebrates, in order of abundance, were red deer, pig, otter, roe deer, wolf and birds. Fish exploited were eel, smelt, goby, stickleback and flatfish, fish sizes suggesting the use of traps. At Westward Ho! the vertebrates exploited were aurochsen, red deer, roe deer, pig and fish. The midden comprised molluscan evidence for the exploitation of rocky, sandy and muddy coast. The fauna as a whole emphasizes the range of resources which could be exploited from this ecotonal situation.

Each of these Mesolithic sites seems to have been close to the shore, in some cases around the limits of Highest Astronomical Tide minerogenic sedimentation. In the case of Westward Ho!, where our environmental evidence is most precise, occupation was within wildwood back from the shore. At Goldcliff occupation is contemporary with a regression phase during which a extensive *Phragmites* swamp developed across the saltmarsh. Welinder (1978) has shown that the growing over stage of wetland represents the episode of greatest ecological productivity.

A notable aspect of Mesolithic sites below the basal peats is the occurrence of charcoal horizons which are widespread at the two broadly contemporary sites of Goldcliff and Westward Ho! The presence of charcoal is also recorded at a number of Leach's (1918) Pembrokeshire sites. This could derive from camp fires close to the shore, but the extent of the Westward Ho! and

Goldcliff charcoal scatters suggest the possibility of deliberate modification at the coastal woodland edge, as is widely attested in the upland woodland edge of England and Wales (Simmons 1996). This possibility cannot yet be confirmed by the palaeoenvironmental evidence. At Westward Ho! the proportions of birch and hazel and the presence of some open ground indicators could relate to human activity, but not on the scale suggested by the charcoal scatter. Unfortunately, at Goldcliff the pollen sequences examined so far began shortly after the period of the main charcoal scatter. Clearer palynological evidence of Mesolithic impact comes from the edge of the Welsh Severn Estuary at Vurlong Reen, between 5250–5500 radiocarbon years BP (c. 4000–4400 Cal BC) (Walker et al. 1998), and Abermawr, Pembrokeshire where increased grasses and herbs indicate possible clearance around 5520 ± 150 BP (OxA-1377; c. 4375 Cal BC). Both sites have produced flints below the peats. It is probable that the concentration of human activity along the shores of the Bristol Channel/Severn Estuary during the later Mesolithic had an impact on the local vegetation communities and that burning helped to increase the ecological diversity of the coastal zone.

Mesolithic to Bronze Age activity within coastal peats

Human activity occurred, but apparently on a reduced scale, following peat inception. Most evocative of the way the wetland was being used is the skeleton of a pig at Lydstep associated with two microliths showing it was a wounded animal which escaped to the fen wood to die. This old discovery reported by Leach (1918) has now been radiocarbon dated with the result 5300 ± 100 BP (OxA-1412; 4250–3990 Cal BC); at this site the peat base has yielded 6150 ± 120 BP (OxA-1378; c. 5260–4940 Cal BC; Lewis 1992). The only site on which Mesolithic human activity is attested actually on the peat is at Frainslake, Pembrokeshire where Gordon-Williams (1926) recorded a charcoal and flint scatter associated with a wood structure which he interpreted as a possible windbreak. At Goldcliff there is some evidence of continued activity at the island edge in the form of a solitary flint flake and patches of charcoal dated around 5820 ± 50 BP (GrN-24143; 4790–4540 Cal BC).

At Westward Ho! peat formation ceased around 5000BP (c 3900 Cal BC). Elsewhere on the coast it is clear that peat formation continued later: at Marros there is a date of 4640 ± 70BP

(CAR-1116; 3505–3395 Cal BC) 55 cm from the peat top and at Whitesands Bay one of two aurochs skulls in the peat is dated 4540 ± 70 BP (CAR-1183; 3370–3100 Cal BC). In the valleys extending inland, and separated, at least partly, from the coast by barrier beaches, peat formation continued very much later as at Penybont, Newport; Abermawr and Castlemartin (inland of Freshwater West) all in Pembrokeshire (Lewis 1992). Pollen spectra from these peats demonstrate that clearance of the coastal lowlands in the Neolithic was generally small-scale and temporary, not perhaps very different from what is indicated during the Mesolithic. That the exploitation of coastal resources, attested by the Mesolithic sites, continued to be significant into the Neolithic is indicated by the coastal distribution of Neolithic tombs, which in West Wales is similar to that both of Mesolithic sites and those topographic contexts in which submerged forests are preserved. The importance of such areas is highlighted by continued use of some coastal sites, such as Newport, Pembrokeshire where a Neolithic tomb overlies a Mesolithic site, the downslope part of which is buried by estuarine peat, or Yelland where an intertidal site with evidence of Mesolithic and Neolithic flint scatters was elaborated as a stone row (Rogers 1946).

Evidence of human activity associated with post-Mesolithic peats is limited: a double line of stakes at Westward Ho! is dated 4840 ± 70 BP

Table 1. *Radiocarbon dates for peats, and two Pembrokeshire finds of animal skeletons within peats in the Severn Estuary, Bristol Channel and Pembrokeshire. For details of calibration see Fig. 2*

	Site name	14 C BP	Lab no	Cal BC	Reference
Severn Estuary					
1	Goldcliff Island	6770 ± 70	Beta-60761	5740–5490	Allen 2000
2	Caldicot Pill	6660 ± 80	Beta-79886	5670–5430	Scaife 1995
3	Uskmouth	6140 ± 100	Oxa-3307	5270–4830	Aldhouse-Green *et al.* 1992
4	Goldcliff East S1	5950 ± 80	CAR-659	4950–4720	Smith & Morgan 1989
5	Barlands Farm	5920 ± 50	Beta-72511	4919–4710	Walker *et al.* 1998
6	Goldcliff Pit 15	5920 ± 80	CAR-1501	5060–4660	Bell *et al.* 2000
7	Vurlong Reen 1	5740 ± 70	Beta-63595	4776–4406	Walker *et al.* 1998
8	Magor	5680 ± 70	Beta-73058	4720–4360	Allen & Rippon 1997
9	Vurlong Reen 2	4720 ± 60	Beta-63598	3642–3356	Walker *et al.* 1998
10	Goldcliff Pond	4320 ± 80	SWAN-133	3350–2650	Bell *et al.* 2000
11	Goldcliff East S2	4390 ± 80	CAR-773	3340–2890	Smith & Morgan 1989
12	Goldcliff Pit 15	3640 ± 60	CAR-1499	2200–1880	Bell *et al.* 2000
13	Goldcliff Pond	3180 ± 70	SWAN-104	1640–1300	Bell *et al.* 2000
14	Goldcliff East S1	3130 ± 70	CAR-644	1610–1210	Smith & Morgan 1989
15	Barlands Farm	2900 ± 60	Beta-72506	1263–909	Walker *et al.* 1998
16	Llanwern	2660 ± 100	Q-691	1100–400	Godwin & Willis 1964
17	Vurlong Reen	2470 ± 60	Beta-63590	795–397	Walker *et al.* 1998
18	Goldcliff B6	2460 ± 35	GrN-24149	770–410	Bell *et al.* 2000
19	Magor	2430 ± 70	Beta-73059	770–400	Allen & Rippon 1997
20	Goldcliff B2	2270 ± 70	CAR-1351	520–110	Bell *et al.* 2000
21	Rumney	2180 ± 50	SRR-2678	380–110	Allen & Fulford 1986
Inner Severn Estuary					
22	Slimbridge	3110 ± 50	Beta-80696	1520–1220	Hewlett & Birnie 1996
23	Elmore	2360 ± 60	Beta-81686	800–200	Hewlett & Birnie 1996
24	Longley	2340 ± 60	Beta-80693	800–200	Hewlett & Birnie 1996
Pembrokeshire and Bristol Channel					
25	Aber Mawr	7640 ± 150	OzA-1411	6500–6405	Lewis 1992
26	Westward Ho!	6680 ± 120	Q-1249	5810–5370	Balaam *et al.* 1987
27	Newport Sands, Pembs	6370 ± 120	HAR-78	5650–4950	Lewis 1992
28	Lydstep	6150 ± 120	OxA-1378	5210–5200	Lewis 1992
29	Freshwater West	5960 ± 120	Q530	4900–4810	Godwin & Willis 1964
30	Brean Down	5620 ± 100	HAR-8546	4720–4250	Bell 1990
31	Lydstep pig	5300 ± 100	OxA-1412	4230–4040	Lewis 1992
32	Whitesands Bay	5250 ± 80	CAR-1176	4225–4035	Lewis 1992
33	Marros	5300 ± 80	CAR-1117	4230–4040	Lewis 1992
34	Whitesands Bay Aurochs	4540 ± 70	CAR-1183	3340–3150	Lewis 1992

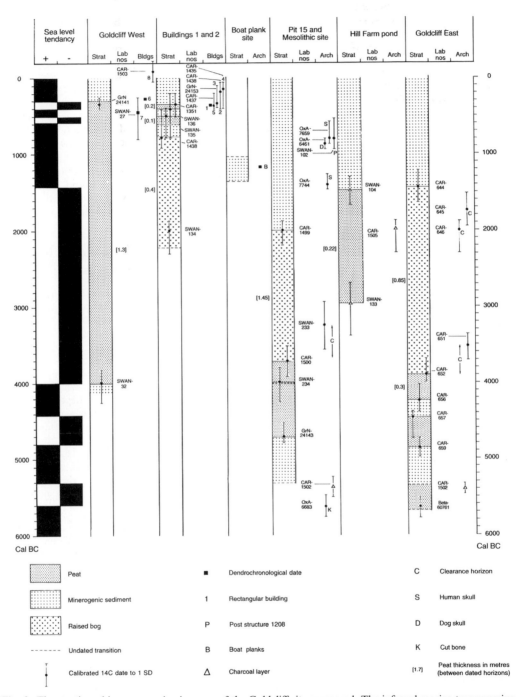

Fig. 3. The stratigraphic sequence in six areas of the Goldcliff site compared. The inferred marine transgressive and regressive phases are shown on the left. For full details of the radiocarbon dates shown see Bell *et al.* 2000, appendix 2.

(HAR-5642; 3790–3370 Cal BC) and is likely to represent a trackway or other structure within the peat since it antedates the latest peat date for the site which is 5004 ± 105 BP (IGS-42). In Pembrokeshire and the Bristol Channel intertidal peats have only been dated to the post-Neolithic in the estuary of the Nevern at Newport, Pembrokeshire dated 3650 ± 80 BP (Car-1142; 2300–1750 Cal BC; Lewis 1992). A lack of exposures probably accounts for the absence of later prehistoric intertidal archaeology beyond the Severn Estuary. However, sites must exist as illustrated by an earlier find of a Neolithic axe in its shaft from Aberavon near Swansea (Savory 1980), and discoveries of prehistoric artifacts during dock construction at Barry (Wheeler 1925). At Westward Ho! wooden stakes, perhaps representing a fishing structure, are dated 1600 ± 80 BP (HAR-6440; c. Cal AD 430) confirming that there is later intertidal archaeology of this area.

Up estuary in the Somerset peat levels (Coles & Coles 1986) Neolithic and Bronze Age activity is well represented but mainly takes the specialist form of trackways and artifacts associated with the use of the wetlands for hunting and gathering activities. These trackways occur within peat, from the early *Phragmites* swamp and fen wood stages in the Neolithic, there are fewer during the main period of raised bog formation but trackways increase again in the later Bronze Age from c. 1400 Cal BC.

The dates for peat inception in the Welsh Severn Estuary are summarized in Table 1 and Fig. 2 and the Goldcliff sequence is outlined in Fig. 3. Between c. 5600 and 5000 Cal BC reed peats started to form at Caldicot Pill and Uskmouth. On the edge of the former island at Goldcliff an oak on peat is of similar date and here auger survey has traced an extensive reed peat at a similar OD height. This regression phase with reed peat formed the context of the main activity on the Goldcliff Mesolithic site. That initial phase of peat formation was, on each site investigated, followed by renewed minerogenic sedimentation. Widespread peat formation occurred around 4800 Cal BC (Fig. 2) and at Barland's Farm and Vurlong Reen was continuous. At Goldcliff peat formation was interrupted by a short-lived transgression around 4400–4000 Cal BC. This was followed by continuous peat development for a period which ranged from 2.5–3.5 millennia. Later dates for peat inception at Goldcliff Hill Farm and Vurlong Reen II (Fig. 2) occur at higher OD levels on the margins of bedrock outcrops. On the Welsh side of the Severn Estuary the middle Wentlooge peats exposed in the intertidal area formed from late Mesolithic to Iron Age but in the Neolithic and early Bronze Age human activity seems to have been limited. There are individual artifacts such as polished Neolithic axes and bronze tools (Green 1989). Only one structure of this period has so far been recorded. At Peterstone one of several wooden posts driven into the side of a palaeochannel has been dated 3910 ± 60 BP (GrN-24149, 2580–2200 Cal BC). This is below a thin peat and the line of posts probably points to fishing activity to seaward of the peats in the very late Neolithic, or early Bronze Age. That find serves to remind us that, even if there is little evidence of activity on the peat at this time, other areas of the coastal wetland, which may have been largely eroded, or are still buried, could have been subject to exploitation.

Bronze Age and Iron Age sites on intertidal peats in the Welsh Severn Estuary

The final stages of peat formation in the Severn Estuary are marked by a concentration of archaeological sites on a peat surface, making it particularly important to establish the date of the transgression associated with minerogenic sedimentation which overlies the peat. The episode is also relevant to wider issues concerning the date of transgressions, the extent to which episodes are coeval between sites and the contribution which archaeological structures can make to chronological precision in a coastal context.

Radiocarbon dates are available for wooden structures and occupation horizons on the peat surface. In cases where the peat surface has not been directly dated, the dates are those of post structures apparently emplaced from that surface. The sites are roundhouses at Rumney 3, (3080 ± 50, Beta-46951; 1460–1210 Cal BC), Chapel Tump 1 (2910 ± 70 BP, CAR-402; 1320–920 Cal BC) and Collister Pill, the last not radiocarbon dated but with middle Bronze Age pottery. Of similar date is a group of four rectangular buildings at Redwick which have radiocarbon dates between 3060 ± 70 (SWAN-227; 1510–1100 Cal BC) and 2930 ± 70 (SWAN-225; 1390–930 Cal BC). We can be confident in dating this transgression on the basis of structures at the interface since the structures are associated with occupation horizons comprising peaty clay deposits, charcoal, burnt stone and in some cases pottery, the context of which indicates that activity occurred in the early stages of the transgressive phase. In the case of these Bronze Age archaeological sites the palaeoenvironmental record across the transition has not yet been investigated.

Detailed stratigraphic dating and palaeoenvironmental investigation has been carried out at Goldcliff, a study area comprising 3 km of shore to east and west of a former bedrock island, the Quaternary history of which has been investigated by Allen (2000a). A summary of the stratigraphic sequence is shown in Fig. 3. Peat formation began, as already noted, around 4800 Cal BC and continued in places until c. 300 Cal BC. Even within this small study area there is significant variation in the extent and thickness of peats, as the bracketed figures for peat thickness beside the columns in Fig. 3 show. Here the maximum thickness at Goldcliff West is 1.3 m, which formed over 3700 calendar years, elsewhere in the study area thicknesses up to 1.8 m have been recorded. It is important to appreciate that prior to compaction these peats would have been very much thicker. A single peat surface, with many wood structures all with closely similar radiocarbon dates c. 300 Cal BC, occurs at steadily decreasing OD height west of the former bedrock island. From this difference in height it can be calculated that the original peat thickness prior to compaction was c. 5.5 m. This is likely to be an underestimate because it assumes an originally level peat surface, whereas

for much of its life this was a raised bog which has a domed profile (Godwin 1981). The domed nature of the raised bog probably explains how peat growth continued for thousands of years of rising sea-level with few major innundations. A domed profile also helps to explain the complex history of innundations of this bog in the later Bronze Age and Iron Age. The latest dates for peats and wood structures on the peat surface are summarized in Fig. 5. On the flanks of the island there are 4 sites where the main phase of peat formation has been dated and pollen sequences are available. Two of these are manifestly truncated: Smith and Morgan's site 2 (Goldcliff East) where the last peat is 4390 ± 80 BP (CAR-773; 3340–2890 Cal BC) and Pit 15 where the last peat is 3640 ± 60 BP (CAR-1499; 2200–1880 Cal BC) and there is evidence of a palaeochannel cutting the peat surface. The probable date of the transgression is indicated by two apparently untruncated sequences with very similar dates on opposite sides of the former island: to the east Smith and Morgan's Site 1 where the latest peat is 3130 ± 70 BP (CAR-644; 1610–1210 Cal BC) and to the west Hill Farm Pond 3180 ± 70 BP (SWAN-104; 1640–1300 Cal BC).

Fig. 4. Goldcliff, Iron Age rectangular Building 6 (photograph by Lesley Boulton).

Confirmatory evidence that the bog was innundated during the middle Bronze Age comes from a site 350 m west of the island where, in minerogenic sediments overlying peat, a small trackway included reused planks from a sewn boat with a dendrochronological date of 1170 BC, a *terminus post quem* since sapwood is missing. The transgression onto raised bog was not, however, everywhere of similar date; 800 m west of the former island the raised bog was innundated at 2580 ± 70 BP (CAR-1438; 910–410 Cal BC) and 1.2 km west of the island the raised bog continued to form until at least the third century BC.

Further evidence of the extent of the transgression in the Bronze Age comes from Barland's Farm where the latest peat is dated 2900 ± 60 BP (BETA-72506; 1263–909 Cal BC), and in the inner Severn Estuary at Slimbridge where the latest peat is 3110 ± 50 BP (1520–1220 Cal BC; Hewlett & Birnie 1996). In the Axe valley a marine incursion has been dated by Housley (1988) between 850 and 550 BC. It has been suggested that landscape changes associated with that incursion may have led to the abandonment of the estuary edge settlement site at Brean Down (Bell 1990).

At Goldcliff the transgressive phase following the raised bog was interrupted by a number of episodes of peat formation. Very thin peat bands above, and below, the structure with boat planks indicate shortlived regressive phases at around that time which have not been more precisely dated. Around 2360 ± 70 BP (SWAN-136; 800–200 Cal BC) peat formation once again occurred west of the former island. These peats represented three distinct contemporary plant communities from east to west: *Phragmites* reedswamp, fen woodland and then the surviving raised bog which had not been innundated during the Bronze Age transgression. The surface of this peat is dated 2270 ± 70 BP (CAR-1351; 520–110 Cal BC) and that date is broadly confirmed by a whole series of dates for archaeological structures. These include 18 trackways and 8 rectangular buildings. In addition to radiocarbon dates there are more precise dendrochronological dates (Hillam 1999) for three buildings and one trackway. Of these the most precise is Building 6 (Fig. 4) the oak planks for which were cut in April–May 273 BC, with wood for repairs being cut in the same months 271 BC. Building 1 has dendrochronological dates within the period 382–342 BC and Building 2 was constructed after 454 BC, a *terminus ante quem* because sapwood is lacking. Trackway 1108 had wood, which, allowing for sapwood estimates, is likely to have been cut in the period 336–318 BC.

From these dendrochronological date ranges we know that wood was being cut for the buildings over a period of 70–100 years, which is the probable timescale of the innundation of the fen wood at Goldcliff. This transgression, like that in the later Bronze Age, seems from the dating evidence to have progressed from east to west. A radiocarbon date for the most westerly Building 8 of 1930 ± 50 BP (CAR-1503; 50 BC-220 AD) could indicate that the final innundation of the raised bog to the west may not have taken place until the late Iron Age, or early Romano-British period, but that rests on a single radiocarbon date.

Trackway surfaces and the floors of rectangular buildings, where they survive, show that occupation occurred at a time when marine influence was beginning to encroach onto the peat. There are thin lenses of clay within the peat of the occupation horizons, cattle footprints associated with occupations are at the peat/clay interface and biological data of pollen, plant macrofossils, beetles and diatoms all show clear evidence of increasing marine influence within the upper few centimetres of the peat during the period of occupation. Thus activity was concentrated during the initial stages of a marine transgression, a somewhat surprising conclusion which is likely to be explained by evidence that activity was seasonal. It seems to have been concentrated in spring and summer and associated with cattle husbandry exploiting the rich grazing offered by the minerogenic marsh to seaward and the bog margins. Confirmatory evidence comes from the wood of Building 6 which was cut in April/May and the presence of neonatal cattle, suggestive of spring and summer activity. Thus occupation is likely to have taken place just above HAT at sites subject to occasional innundation during the winter period of increased tidal extremes. Although occupation seems to have been concentrated in the spring and summer, the wetland resources were apparently also exploited at other times of year, most of the wood for trackways being cut during the winter.

At Goldcliff we have identified two main transgression phases in later prehistory, the earlier during the middle Bronze Age, the other more precisely dated by dendrochronology in the period between a *terminus ante quem* of 454 BC and a precise date of 271 BC. The dating evidence for both transgressions shows they are earlier in the east and transgress westwards. The likely explanation is that the transgressions were onto the margins of raised bog which, to the west, had not been innundated at the time of the middle Bronze Age transgression. Raised bogs, being

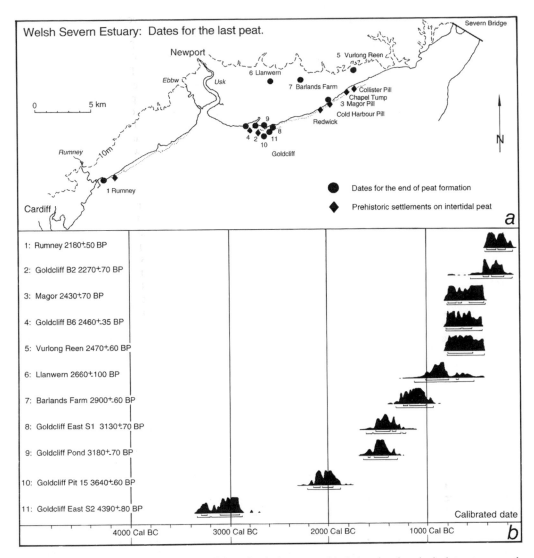

Fig. 5. Severn Estuary (**a**) the distribution of dates for the latest peat (circles) and archaeological structures on the peat surface (diamonds). (**b**) Calibrated ranges of the latest peats, for further information on Calibration Fig. 2. For full details of the dates see Table 1.

rain rather than groundwater fed, adopt a domed profile with the bog centre being several metres higher than its margin (Godwin 1981) which in a transgression is likely to be innundated earlier.

In addition to raised bog formation, the Goldcliff sequence points to other factors which may have contributed to the development of topographic contrasts in coastal wetlands and which are therefore relevant to an understanding of the effects of transgressive and regressive tendencies. In this area raised bogs were clearly subject to marine influence at their margins. Phases of increased marine influence, whether

related to higher sea-level or increased storminess, would have led to innundations onto the bog and the development of drainage, which in some cases is likely to have led to erosion gullies on the bog surface. One substantial erosion gully runs part way round Goldcliff Building 6 (Fig. 4). Where a positive marine tendency was strong, or sustained, it is probable that substantial areas of former bog would have been eroded. Gullying of the margins, and larger scale erosion to seaward, are both likely to have disrupted the hydrological balance of the bog, causing it to lose water leading to a reduction in the height of the bog, an increased area of which then becomes subject to innundation. The effects of dewatering due to the development of drainage might be expected to be particularly marked in the Severn Estuary with the second highest tidal range in the world (14.5 m at Avonmouth). Drainage and erosion will have particularly pronounced effects in areas of raised bog; similar, but lesser, effects may occur in thick wood or reed peats where gullying could also lead to a drier surface and ultimately perhaps to a reduction of peat thickness. This hypothetical model would allow innundation of bog by minerogenic sediments to occur as the result of increased erosion of the bog margin, independent of any absolute rise of sea-level. In this instance, however, there are indications that sea-level changes were a factor, since both the middle Bronze Age and the later Iron Age transgressions are equally marked in areas of former raised bog and in other peat types.

The transgression affecting the Iron Age occupation site at Goldcliff, at one time appeared anomalously late in the Severn Estuary chronology. The main innundation was thought to be middle to late Bronze Age, the period suggested by Fig. 5 Sites 7–9. It now appears that late innundations, comparable to Goldcliff, occur on several geographically widespread sites (Fig. 5). In addition to Goldcliff other areas which had been innundated by the Bronze Age transgression were subject to a subsequent regression marked by a thin upper peat. This is present in the Redwick area, where it has not yet been directly dated. At Rumney 1 (Allen 1996) an upper organic horizon separate from the main peat is dated 2250 ± 60 BP (BETA-39437; 410–160 Cal BC); that date, which once seemed anomalous, can now be seen as very close to the main concentration of dates for activity at Goldcliff. In many areas of the estuary, beyond the limits of the Bronze Age transgression, the peat was not innundated until the more extensive transgression of the Iron Age as the range of dates for the latest peat in Fig. 5 and Table 1 shows. Spatially separated sites from the west at Rumney to Llanwern and Magor and Vurlong Reen in the east produce dates for the latest peat which are close to those obtained from Goldcliff. This transgression apparently also extended to the Inner Severn Estuary (upstream of Sudbrook) where peat formation ended at Elmore (2360 ± 60 BP; 800–200 Cal BC) and Longney (2340 ± 60 BP; 800–200 Cal BC). On the Somerset Levels innundations are indicated by the Meare Heath pollen diagram where raised bog peats were subject to flooding by base rich waters which ended around 2252 ± 45 BP (SRR-913;

$c.$ 235 Cal BC), with a later flooding episode centering on 2062 ± 45 BP (SRR-912; $c.$ 5 Cal BC) (Hibbert 1980).

A date as late as the third century BC for extensive innundation of the Severn Levels peats has significant implications for the development of the overlying upper Wentlooge Formation. At Goldcliff the main peat horizon on which Iron Age archaeology is concentrated has a whole series of closely similar radiocarbon dates around 2200 BP. That peat has a gradually decreasing OD height away from the former bedrock island: 400 m from the island it is at 3 m OD, 900 m from the island at 0.2 m OD. This is explained by the increased effects of post depositional compaction in areas of thicker Holocene stratigraphy as discussed by Allen (2000b). Thus at Goldcliff the highest Iron Age peat is shown to occur at heights varying from just above OD to $c.$ 4 m OD. The present ground surface is at 6 m OD. Thus the upper Wentlooge formation is of variable thickness between 4 and 6 m. At a depth of about 0.8 m below the present surface there is a stabilization horizon with Romano–British pottery associated with drainage ditches also containing Romano–British pottery (Bell 1995). This indicates the deposition of between 3.2 and 5.2 m of upper Wentlooge Formation between the transgression in the third century BC and the period of Romano–British drainage around the second century AD. Thus sedimentation over this period was exceptionally rapid; this can be explained by the evidence presented by Allen (1999, 2000b) for the post depositional compaction of sediments which, as the differences in peat height quoted above indicate, would have had the effect of greatly increasing accommodation space for sediment deposition.

It is notable that a period of rapid sedimentation in the later Iron Age also occurs in the inner Severn Estuary on sites not directly subject to marine influence but affected by sea-level related water table rises of the perimarine zone (Hewlett & Birnie 1996). In the River Severn catchment there is also increased sedimentation in the Iron Age which has been correlated with extensive evidence for increased clearance during this period (Brown 1987). Given the scale of upper Wentlooge sediment deposition in the Severn Estuary it seems improbable that this was directly related to land-use caused increases of sediment supply from the riverine catchment. The similar dates for major sedimentary changes in the Severn river catchment and its estuary, may, however, cause us to rethink whether there are climate, or weather, related factors which may have had a significant effect on both the river and estuarine systems during the first millennium BC.

It would be a mistake to assume that during transgressive phases of minerogenic sedimentation human activity was no longer possible on the wetland, although the character of activity may well have changed. There is evidence of some activity associated with minerogenic sediments in both the later Bronze Age and Iron Age, particularly in palaeochannels which cut the peat and contain wood structures. Dated examples are a basket-like wood structure at Cold Harbour, probably associated with fishing, and dated 2520 ± 60 BP (SWAN-241; 790–530 Cal BC); a trackway at Collister Pill 2 dated 3050 ± 65 BP (GrN-24152; 1450–1100 Cal BC) and a wood structure at Collister Pill 3 dated 2390 ± 60 BP (GrN-24151; 770–380 Cal BC). Activity during the minerogenic phase was not apparently restricted to trackways and fishing. Cattle footprints are present near the base of the upper Wentlooge Formation showing the continuance of grazing. Furthermore, Iron Age pottery in palaeochannels at Magor Pill (Allen & Rippon 1997) and Collister Pill 3 is likely to have reached the channels from eroded occupation sites. Activity was clearly taking place during the minerogenic phase, although its extent and intensity remains unclear.

Conclusions

The two main phases of activity identified in the intertidal archaeology of this area are the later Mesolithic and the middle Bronze Age to middle Iron Age. During those periods the strip of coastal wetland which is now exposed intertidally offered particular opportunities to human communities and that led to a concentration of activity. These were also periods when the sedimentary environment favoured site preservation. It is possible that there may have been other periods of equally intensive activity from which the evidence has not been so well preserved, or when activity was concentrated in those parts of the wetland which are now eroded away, or buried inland.

The concentration of well-preserved archaeology in the upper part of the middle Wentlooge peat, and the more limited evidence for activity at the time of the upper Wentlooge minerogenic sediments, accords in broad stratigraphic terms with Louwe-Kooijmans (1993) view that archaeological sites will be better preserved in regressive than transgressive phases. However, in this case the associated palaeoenvironmental evidence demonstrates that activity was occurring, not during the main period of regression, but in the early stages of the subsequent transgression. Many of the Mesolithic sites were also buried and preserved during a transgression. This emphasizes that contrasting opportunities for archaeological preservation occur during specific stages of both transgressions and regressions.

Although the stratigraphic sequence points to alternating periods of organic and minerogenic sedimentation (Fig. 3), it is clear from Goldcliff, where we have a spatial picture derived from 68 cores and extensive excavation, that from 1400 Cal BC peats and minerogenic sediments were being laid down at the same time in different parts of this study area (Bell et al. 2000, fig 17.4). It is considered probable that such circumstances obtained throughout the period of peat formation with minerogenic saltmarsh thickening seaward of the bog and around the margins of palaeochannels. This would have contributed to the insulation of the bog from marine influence. On a regional scale such a model is in line with the thin peats of short duration to seaward, where there is greater minerogenic sedimentation, and thicker peats to landward.

Despite such spatial complexity there are coastal changes which appear to be coeval. For instance the regressions associated with the Mesolithic activity at Westward Ho! and Goldcliff are broadly contemporary. The problem is that the level of precision provided by radiocarbon dates is seldom sufficient to provide convincing evidence that events are coeval at different sites. This is particularly apparent given the complex sequence of transgressive and regressive phases represented for instance in the Goldcliff sequence between c. 5800 and 4000 Cal BC and between 700 and 300 Cal BC (Fig. 3). The increasing availability of dendrochronological dates in prehistory offers great opportunities for accurate correlation between sites. This is particularly the case in coastal situations with submerged forests. Tree-ring sequences have been established at Stolford from 4052–3779 BC and Wollaston from 4096–3869 BC and 2843–2692 BC (Hillam et al. 1990). The demise of the Stolford and earlier Wollaston Forest is close in time to the construction of the Sweet Track in 3807/6 BC, which was associated with a period of flooding. There are hints here of a period of dramatic coastal change which may have been more widespread if Heyworth's (1978) evidence of apparent matches between floating chronologies at Stolford, Alt Mouth, Lancashire and Borth, Wales, could be substantiated by the absolute dating of the other sites.

The innundation of the Welsh Severn Estuary peat, which took place between 1500 and 200 Cal BC, is echoed in the innundations of mid-Holocene peats in the Thames and Solent as already noted (Long *et al.* 2000). Particular stages in this change may be related to the abrupt climate change and pronounced rise in the radiocarbon content of the atmosphere between 850 and 760 Cal BC which has been documented in the Netherlands and worldwide (van Geel *et al.* 1996). In the Netherlands these changes have been associated with the abandonment of sites on peat but settlement colonization of saltmarsh at a time of lower sea-level. That phase is broadly contemporary with the initial stages of the Iron Age regression in the Severn Estuary, although the latter clearly continued later because some of the buildings are of the third century BC. There is an interesting similarity with the sequence in Romney Marsh where peats formed from *c.* 4000 Cal BC but were subject to the most widespread period of marine innundation around 350 Cal BC (Long *et al.* 1998, fig 4.7). At Romney, as in the Severn, some earlier dates for the latest peat are manifestly the result of erosion and truncation of the peat for which there is widespread evidence following the marine incursion.

Notwithstanding the possibility of these wider connections it is clear from the level of chronological precision we have at Goldcliff that the later prehistoric transgression here was a complex process extending over about a millennium and interrupted by two or three brief regressions. The more precisely dated part of this sequence, innundation of the Iron Age peats, seems to have taken place from east to west over perhaps a century. Thus, it represents a gradual process rather than a sudden event. The level of complexity revealed by detailed investigation in this case highlights the problematic nature of interpretations of coastal sequences based on small numbers of dates for sites where stratigraphic investigation and palaeoenvironmental analyses have been limited.

Research at Goldcliff also highlights the contribution which archaeological structures can make to the precise dating of coastal change. Such structures are frequently made of oak and often occur in situations, which lack natural timbers, such as the western raised bog part of the Goldcliff site. Structures are also sometimes associated with distinct floors, or activity surfaces, which may be related to palaeoenvironmental evidence for particular stages of coastal change. For instance the dendrochronologically dated Goldcliff Structures 1, 2 and 6 can be shown to be in use during the stage when the peat was subject to the initial stages of, probably seasonal, minerogenic sedimentation.

Human activity at the time of the peats and the reduced activity at the time of minerogenic sedimentation can be described as mainly opportunistic: it is concentrated at times and places where appropriate environmental conditions obtained, particularly at the margins of marine influence. Human manipulation of the wetland environment seems during prehistory to have been limited. It was most extensive perhaps at the time of the hypothesized Mesolithic burning of coastal woods. During the Iron Age there is evidence for the cutting of fen wood to make buildings and trackways. The trackways themselves can, to some extent, also be seen as transformations of the environment, in that some helped to maintain networks of social communication in a situation where the environmental evidence shows the peat was increasingly subject to marine innundation. The greatest effect of human activity on the wetland in prehistory is likely to have been indirect, associated with the large numbers of grazing cattle represented by footprints. Grazing pressure, where it was concentrated, is likely to have led to vegetation changes, even perhaps to erosion and gullying, which could conceivably have set in train progressive drying and shrinkage of the peat surface like that suggested above as a possible consequence of marine erosion of the bog margins. There is no evidence, however, that during the period of Iron Age activity associated with the peats, these communities made any attempt to modify their environment by the digging of ditches, nor was there any attempt to create artificial mounds for building construction, although the buildings were positioned on areas of peat which were slightly raised and in some cases separated by encircling depressions.

The pattern of opportunistic prehistoric activity described, is in marked contrast to that which has been identified in the Severn Estuary during the Romano–British period, when there is extensive evidence of drainage and the making of seawalls can be inferred (Allen & Fulford 1986; Fulford *et al.* 1994; Rippon 1997). Thus, there is a great deal of evidence for human activity in the Holocene sediments of the Severn Estuary and Bristol Channel and that evidence contributes significantly to dating the sequence and understanding the nature of the environments represented. It is only, however, from the Romano–Britsh period onwards in the Severn Estuary, and later elsewhere in the study area, that human activity and land claim became a very significant influence on the sedimentary history itself.

Many of the Severn Estuary sites were discovered by D. Upton who is thanked for his help and companionship in the field. The contribution of H. Neumann in the study of these sites is acknowledged as is the collaboration of the team of specialists involved in the Goldcliff project, results from which have been included in this article, particularly botanical work by A. Caseldine and dendrochronological dating by J. Hillam. Funding for aspects of the Severn Estuary research was provided by Cadw and the Board of Celtic Studies of the University of Wales. Particular acknowledgement is due to M. Lewis for permission to refer to the radiocarbon dates and other evidence from his unpublished thesis on the Pembrokeshire sites. Collaboration is also acknowledged with N. Balaam, who led the investigation of Westward Ho!, M. J. C. Walker and J. R. L. Allen.

References

ALDHOUSE-GREEN, S. H. R., WHITTLE, A. W. R., ALLEN, J. R. L., CASELDINE, A. E., CULVER, S. J., DAY, H., LUNDQUIST, J. & UPTON, D. 1992. Prehistoric human footprints from the Severn Estuary at Uskmouth and Magor Pill, Gwent, Wales. *Archaeologia Cambrensis*, **141**, 14–55.

ALLEN, J. R. L. 1996. Three Final Bronze Age occupations at Rumney Great Wharf on the Wentlooge Level, Gwent. *Studia Celtica*, **XXX**, 1–16.

——1997. Subfossil mammalian tracks (Flandrian) in the Severn Estuary, SW Britain: mechanics of formation, preservation and distribution. *Philosophical Transactions of the Royal Society of London*, **B352**, 481–518.

——1999. Geological impacts on coastal wetland landscapes: some general effects of sediment autocompaction in the Holocene of northwest Europe. *The Holocene*, **9.1**, 1–12.

——2000a. Goldcliff Island: geological and sedimentological background. *In*: BELL, M. G., CASELDINE, A. & NEUMANN, H. (eds) *Prehistoric Intertidal Archaeology in the Welsh Severn Estuary*, Council for British Archaeology Research Report 120, 12–18.

——2000b. Holocene coastal lowlands in NW Europe: autocompaction and the uncertain ground. *This volume*.

—— & FULFORD, M. G. 1986. The Wentlooge Level: A Romano-British saltmarsh reclamation in southeast Wales. *Britannia*, **17**, 91–117.

—— & RAE, J. E. 1987. Late-Flandrian shoreline oscillations in the Severn Estuary. *Philosophical Transactions of the Royal Society of London B*, **315**, 185–230.

—— & RIPPON, S. J. 1997. Iron Age to Modern activity and palaeochannels at Magor Pill, Gwent: an exercise on lowland coastal-zone geoarchaeology. *Antiquaries Journal*, **77**, 127–170.

BALAAM, N. D., BELL, M. G., DAVID, A. E. U., LEVITAN, B., MACPHAIL, R. I., ROBINSON, M. & SCAIFE, R. G. 1987. Prehistoric and Romano-British sites at Westward Ho! Devon: archaeology and palaeoeconomy and environment in southwest England 1983 and 1984. *In*: BALAAM, N. D., LEVITAN, B. & STRAKER, V. (eds) *Studies in palaeoeconomy and environment in southwest England*. Oxford. Oxbow, British Archaeological Reports British Series **181**, 163–264.

BELL, M. G. 1990. *Brean Down Excavations 1983–1987*. English Heritage, London.

——1995. Field survey and excavation at Goldcliff, Gwent 1994. *Archaeology in the Severn Estuary*, **5**, 115–144.

——1997. Environmental Archaeology in the coastal zone. *In*: FULFORD, M., CHAMPION, T. & LONG, A. (eds) *England's Coastal Heritage*. English Heritage, London, 56–73.

——, CASELDINE, A. & NEUMANN, H. 2000. *Prehistoric Intertidal Archaeology in the Welsh Severn Estuary*, Council for British Archaeology Research Report 120.

BOYD-DAWKINS, W. 1870. On the discovery of flint and chert under a submerged forest in West Somerset. *Journal of the Ethnographic Society of London*, **2**, 141–145.

BROWN, A. G. 1987. Holocene flood-plain sedimentation and chemical response of the lower River Severn, UK. *Zeitschrift für Geomorphologie*, **31**, 293–310.

COLES, B. & COLES, J. 1986. *Sweet Track to Glastonbury*. Thames & Hudson, London.

ELLIS, H. S. 1866. On a flint-find in a submerged forest of Barnstaple Bay, near Westward Ho! *Report and Transactions of the Devon Association*, **I**(v), 80–1.

FULFORD, M. G., ALLEN, J. R. L. & RIPPON, S. J. 1994. The settlement and drainage of the Wentlooge Level, Gwent: excavation and survey at Rumney Great Wharf 1992. *Britannia*, **25**, 175–211.

GIRALDUS CAMBRENSIS (TRANS) 1908. *The itinerary through Wales: descriptions of Wales*, Dent, Everyman, London.

GODWIN, H. 1981. *The archives of the peat bogs*. Cambridge University Press, Cambridge.

—— & WILLIS, E. H. 1964. Cambridge University natural radiocarbon measurements VI. *Radiocarbon*, **6**, 116–137.

GORDON-WILLIAMS, J. P. 1926. The Nab Head chipping floor. *Archaeologia Cambrensis*, **81**, 86–111.

GREEN, S. 1989. Some recent archaeological and faunal discoveries from the Severn Estuary Levels. *Bulletin of the Board of Celtic Studies*, **XXXVI**, 187–99.

HASLETT, S. K., DAVIES, P. & STRAWBRIDGE, F. 1998. Reconstructing Holocene sea-level change in the Severn Estuary and Somerset Levels: the Foraminifera connection. *Archaeology in the Severn Estuary*, **8**, 24–48.

HAWKINS, A. B. 1973. Sea-level changes around South-West England. *In*: BLACKMAN, D. J. (ed.) *Marine Archaeology*. Butterworths, London, 67–87.

HEWLETT, R. & BIRNIE, J. 1996. Holocene environmental change in the Inner Severn Estuary, UK: an example of the response of estuarine sedimentation to relative sealevel change. *The Holocene*, **6**(1), 49–61.

HEYWORTH, A. 1978. Submerged forests around the British Isles: their dating and relevance as indicators of post-glacial land and sea-level changes. *In:* FLETCHER, J. (ed.) *Dendrochronology in Europe.* British Archaeological Reports, Oxford, International Series **56**, 279–88.

—— & KIDSON, C. 1982. Sea-level Changes in Southwest England and Wales. *Proceedings of the Geologists Association*, **93**(1), 91–111.

HIBBERT, F. A. 1980. Possible evidence for sea-level change in the Somerset Levels. *In:* THOMPSON, F. H. (ed.) *Archaeology and Coastal Change.* Society of Antiquaries, London, 103–5.

HILLAM, J. 1999. *Tree-ring analysis of oak timbers from the excavations at Goldcliff, Gwent.* English Heritage, London: English Heritage Ancient Monuments Laboratory Report.

——, GROVES, C. M., BROWN, D. M., BAILLIE, M. G. L., COLES, J. M. & COLES, B. J. 1990. Dendrochronology of the English Neolithic. *Antiquity*, **64**, 210–20.

HOUSLEY, R. A. 1988. The environmental context of Glastonbury Lake Village. *Somerset Levels Proceedings*, **14**, 63–82.

JENNINGS, S., ORFORD, J. D., CANTI, M., DEVOY, R. J. N. & STRAKER, V. 1998. The role of relative sea-level rise and changing sediment supply on Holocene gravel barrier development: the example of Porlock, Somerset, UK. *The Holocene*, **8:2**, 165–81.

KEITH, A. 1925. *The Antiquity of Man.* William and Northgate, London.

KIDSON, C. & HEYWORTH, A. 1976. The Quaternary deposits of the Somerset Levels. *Quarterly Journal of Engineering Geology*, **9**, 217–235.

LEACH, A. L. 1918. Flint working sites on the submerged land (submerged forest) bordering the Pembrokeshire coast. *Proceedings of the Geologists Association*, **XXIX**, 46–64.

LEWIS, M. P. 1992. *The prehistory of coastal south-west Wales.* PhD thesis, University of Wales, St Davids University College, Lampeter.

LOCKE, S. 1971. The post-glacial deposits of the Caldicot Level and some associated archaeological discoveries. *Monmouthshire Antiquary*, **3**(1), 1–17.

LONG, A., WALLER, M. & MCCARTHY, P. 1998. The Holocene depositional history of Romney Marsh proper. *In:* EDDISON, J., GARDINER, M. & LONG, A. (eds) *Romney Marsh: Environmental change and human occupation in a coastal lowland.* University Committee for Archaeology, Oxford, Monograph **46**, 45–64.

LONG, A. J., SCAIFE, R. G. & EDWARDS, R. J. 2000. Stratigraphic architecture, relative sea-level and models of estuary development in southern England: new data from Southampton Water. *This volume.*

LOUWE-KOOIJMANNS, L. P. 1993. Wetland exploration and upland relations of prehistoric communities in the Netherlands. *East Anglian Archaeology*, **50**, 71–116.

REID, C. 1913. *Submerged Forests.* Cambridge University Press, London.

RIPPON, S. 1997. *The Severn Estuary: Landscape Evolution and Wetland Reclamation.* Leicester University Press, London.

ROGERS, E. H. 1946. The raised beach, submerged forest and kitchen midden of Westward Ho! and the submerged stone row of Yelland. *Proceedings of the Devon Archaeological Exploration Society*, **3**, 109–135.

SAVORY, H. N. 1980. The Neolithic in Wales. *In:* TAYLOR, J. A. (eds) *Culture and environment in Prehistoric Wales.* British Archaeological Reports, British Series, **76**, 207–231.

SCAIFE, R. 1995. Pollen analysis and radiocarbon dating of the intertidal peats at Caldicot Pill. *Archaeology in the Severn Estuary*, 67–80.

SIMMONS, I. G. 1996. *The Environmental Impact of later mesolithic cultures.* Edinburgh University Press.

SMITH, A. G. & MORGAN, S. 1989. A succession to ombrotrophic bog in the Gwent Levels and its demise: a Welsh parallel to the peats of the Somerset Levels. *New Phytologist*, **112**, 145–67.

STUIVER, M. REIMER, P. J. BARD, E. BECK, J. W. BURR, G. S. HUGHEN, K. A. KROMER, B. MCCORMAC, F. G., PLICHT, J. & SPURK, M. 1998. Radiocarbon age calibration 24 000–0 cal BP. *Radiocarbon*, **40**, 1041–1083.

VAN GEEL, B. BUURMAN, J. & WATERBOLK, H. T. 1996. Archaeological and palaeoecological indications of an abrupt climate change in the Netherlands and evidence of climatological teleconnections around 2650 BP. *Journal of Quaternary Science*, **11**(6), 45–460.

WALKER, M. J. C., BELL, M., CASELDINE, A. E., CAMERON, N. G., HUNTER, K. L., JAMES, J. H., JOHNSON, S. & SMITH, D. N. 1998. Palaeoecological investigations of middle and late Flandrian buried peats on the Caldicot Levels, Severn Estuary, Wales. *Proceedings of the Geologists' Association*, **109**, 51–78.

WELINDER, S. 1978. The concept of 'ecology' in Mesolithic research. *In:* MELLARS, P. (ed.) *The early Postglacial settlement of northern Europe: an ecological perspective.* Duckworth, London, 11–26.

WHEELER, R. E. M. 1925. *Prehistoric and Roman Wales.* Clarendon Press: Oxford.

Doggerland: the cultural dynamics of a shifting coastline

BRYONY J. COLES

Department of Archaeology, School of Geography and Archaeology, The University, Exeter, UK (e-mail: B.J.Coles@exeter.ac.uk)

Abstract: The landmass now covered by the North Sea, here referred to as Doggerland, has had an important but neglected influence on the course of prehistory in northwestern Europe. The physical character of Doggerland in the Late Glacial and earlier Holocene is assessed, together with its re-colonization by humans after the Last Glacial Maximum. The development of a maritime-based society along the northern coast of Doggerland is postulated, and it is argued that the coastal inhabitants, with their specialized adaptation to this zone, will have moved with the coast as relative sea-levels changed. The interactions of coastal and inland populations are considered, including the probable influence of the coastal groups in delaying the spread of farming into the region.

In northwestern Europe, from Ireland to southern Scandinavia, there is an absence of archaeological evidence dated to the Last Glacial (Devensian/Weichselian) Maximum. Conditions approximating those of an arctic desert pertained in front of the British and Scandinavian ice sheets, and it is generally accepted that the lack of evidence for human occupation is due, quite simply, to the absence of humans. For 10 000 years, from about 23 000 BP to about 13 500 BP (radiocarbon years), the region was uninhabited (Housley *et al.* 1997). As conditions ameliorated, people began to explore the land beyond their glacial refugia; the changing character of the archaeological evidence indicates that, within a few centuries of pioneering visits, permanent human occupation was established. For southern Britain and southern Jutland, the presence of settled groups of people can be dated to about 12 400 BP, i.e. to the earlier part of the Windermere or Bølling interstadial. At this time, land was continuous between the two regions, and it too will have been inhabited.

The land between, subsequently submerged by the North Sea, is here referred to as Doggerland, named after the Dogger Bank which has long been recognized as a former area of dryland and fresh waters (Reid 1913). Although there has as yet been no specifically archaeological survey of the region, something of its character can be gleaned from the results of geological exploration and by extrapolating from the data available for adjacent regions. The evidence for the physical condition of Doggerland in successive periods is discussed in Coles 1998, including that for coastline position and for the major river courses. Sea-level change in northwestern Europe has recently been modelled in a series of papers by Lambeck and colleagues (e.g. Lambeck 1993, Lambeck *et al.* 1998) which should in due course enable greater precision and confidence in coastline reconstruction. The more that is known of the former landmass, the more its relevance to Late Glacial and Postglacial prehistory becomes clear (Coles 1998, 1999). In the present context, the focus will be predominantly on Doggerland's coastal zone, following a brief consideration first of inland conditions at the time of the Windermere/Bølling-Allerød interstadial and then of the initial character of human occupation of the land.

Topography of Doggerland

The combined effects of erosion and siltation, together with the physical difficulties of underwater survey, make it difficult to determine the detailed topography of Doggerland. Occasionally, coring pin-points a former freshwater lake, or commercial survey incidentally provides evidence for former surface features (Firth 2000). Major features, resulting from Quaternary glaciation and its aftermath, can be identified for some locations, and others can be postulated. For example, the exposed land was cut by deep incisions, which had been eroded out as subglacial drainage channels under the outer margin of ice-sheets. When the ice wasted, the channels were exposed as tunnel valleys, long, narrow and steep-sided, sometimes sinuous and often partially filled by a freshwater lake. Tunnel valleys 1–3 km wide, 100 m deep and 25–60 km long were present in the area between what is now northeastern Scotland and what is now the

From: PYE, K. & ALLEN, J. R. L. (eds). *Coastal and Estuarine Environments: sedimentology, geomorphology and geoarchaeology*. Geological Society, London, Special Publications, **175**, 393–401. 0305-8719/00/$15.00 © The Geological Society of London 2000.

Dogger Bank. A further group of valleys, not quite so deep, extended eastwards from the present Humber estuary to the south of Dogger Bank, which itself is likely to have formed a substantial upland mass. At the Weichselian maximum, land beyond the ice-sheet margins is likely to have been uplifted as a glacial fore-bulge, an effect which only slowly dissipated with de-glaciation. The present Dogger Bank may therefore represent former Dogger Hills which extended further and higher than present bathymetry suggests.

Doggerland had three major river networks, two draining to the north and one southwards to the Channel River (Fig. 1) (Coles 1998, p. 54–57). The northeastern network was dominated by the Elbe which flowed to the west of Jutland through the Urstromtal, a vast valley still identifiable on the sea-floor, and on across eastern Doggerland to an estuary opening into the Norwegian Trench. The northwestern network had a smaller catchment, draining the region west of the Dogger Hills together with much of what is now eastern England, and flowing to an estuary

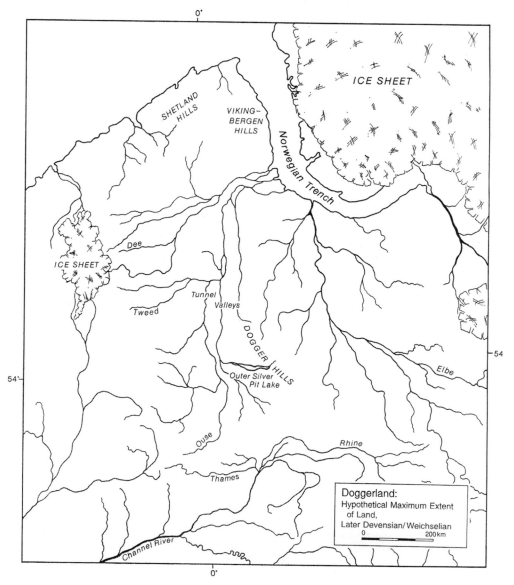

Fig. 1. Doggerland in the Later Devensian/Weichselian, with an indication of the major river systems. The evidence on which Figs 1–4 are based is discussed in Coles 1998.

between the Dogger Hills and the Yorkshire Wolds. South of Doggerland's main watershed, the Rhine and the Thames met to flow south-westwards into the Channel River and out to the Atlantic, with an estuary well to the west.

Flora and fauna

The opening of the Windermere/Bølling-Allerød interstadial (Fig. 2) was marked by a rapid rise in temperature, followed relatively slowly by the development of open grassy parkland vegetation interspersed with patches of light birch wood-land and a few other trees (e.g. Kolstrup 1991; Tipping 1991). There will have been many areas of wetland vegetation fringing shallow lakes and streams and rivers. Herds of grazing and brows-ing mammals colonised the land, accompanied by their predators including humans. Direct evidence for Doggerland's fauna is provided by bones trawled from the North Sea floor, many of them from the vicinity of Brown Bank (van

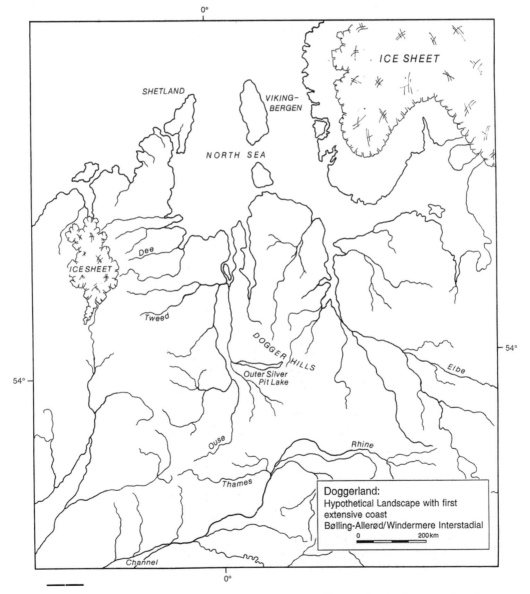

Fig. 2. Doggerland during the Bølling-Allerød/Windermere interstadial, showing development of northern coast and estuaries and presence of Viking-Bergen island.

Kolfschoten & Laban 1995); those bones which, themselves undated, can be attributed to the interstadial by reference to the faunas of adjacent lands, include horse, mammoth and red deer. The open vegetation and frequent expanses of fresh water coupled with warm temperatures, may have attracted many thousands of migrating birds; these too will have attracted human predators.

The people of Doggerland

The Late Glacial hunter-gatherers who explored and then settled Doggerland came from inland Europe (Housley et al. 1997), and as such they will have been familiar with the general conditions that prevailed through the land. Eventually, however, the first exploratory groups reached, what was for them, an entirely new environment: the coast. The location for this encounter will have been along the north coast of Doggerland, both southern Britain and Jutland then being inland regions.

The people who looked out over the cold North Sea faced a double culture shock, not only salt water and an unfamiliar suite of plants and animals which might or might not be exploited using existing skills and equipment, but also an environment which put a halt to the millennia-long process of colonization. An engrained cultural tradition of exploring new lands became in large measure redundant when this particular northwestern frontier was reached.

The coastline of the interstadial and following cold phase may have been relatively stable, for although the British and Scandinavian ice-sheets were reduced, a rapid rise in relative sea-level was only to come with the later wasting of the extensive North American ice-sheets. In places throughout Doggerland, there is evidence for a sea-level standstill, for example along the Norwegian Trench at some stage between 12 500 BP and 10 800 BP (Johnson et al. 1993). Shetland and the Orkneys remained part of mainland Scotland, and a large island existed between their position and Norway, referred to as Viking-Bergen or Frigg island. One small flint flake, probably worked by humans, has been found in a core taken from Viking-Bergen (Long et al. 1986). This raises the possibility that humans reached the island before it was submerged, having therefore developed the boats and the skills required to navigate the North Sea. It is unlikely that people penetrated this far north while Viking-Bergen was still attached to the Dogger mainland, in the light of Housley et al.'s (1997) calculations of the rate at which humans moved into the newly available land as the ice-sheets wasted.

Colonization of western Norway was probably also by boat, given the lack of an ice-free corridor of land around the southwestern margin of the Scandinavian ice sheet at the postulated time of colonization (Anundsen 1996). The first human presence on the Norwegian coast is currently dated to the Allerød, on the basis of indirect evidence in the form of charcoal which is thought to derive from fires that had burned in a context where a natural origin would be unlikely (Bang-Andersen 1996).

From these slight indications, it can be argued that people had developed a way of life adapted to coastal and marine conditions before the opening of the Holocene. The abundance of marine mammals, sea-birds and fish known from Scandinavian coastal sites indicates the attractions of the sea; in cultural terms, the challenge of developing new skills and equipment in order to exploit these marine resources may have taken the place formerly held by land exploration,

Ethnographic studies of coastal hunter-fisher-gatherers indicate potential for the development of complex maritime-orientated societies which, when compared with contemporary inland groups have relatively sedentary settlement patterns and relatively high population densities (e.g. Rousselot et al. 1988). It is unlikely that the first coastal peoples of northwestern Europe will have closely resembled more recent maritime groups, but a relative complexity, density and settled character may have pertained from an early stage vis-a-vis inlanders, in so far as these aspects will have been related to the year-round availability of natural resources along the coast and particularly around estuaries, and to the technological investments related to the exploitation of fish and sea mammals.

Archaeological evidence for Late Glacial maritime hunter-fisher-gatherers is largely absent from northwestern Europe, for the available coastline was that of northern Doggerland, now submerged by the North Sea. From the opening of the Holocene (Fig. 3), evidence is available, from northeastern England and from southern Scandinavia, in those places where the shifting relationship between land and sea levels has left the coastal zone of the earlier Holocene accessible. It appears that from the early Mesolithic onwards, a coastal and an inland way of life can be differentiated, with the coastal peoples exploiting their hinterland as well as the sea, and thereby establishing a broad band of occupied territory along the coast. Inlanders may have exchanged goods with coastal people, and visited the coastal zone, but their own settlement

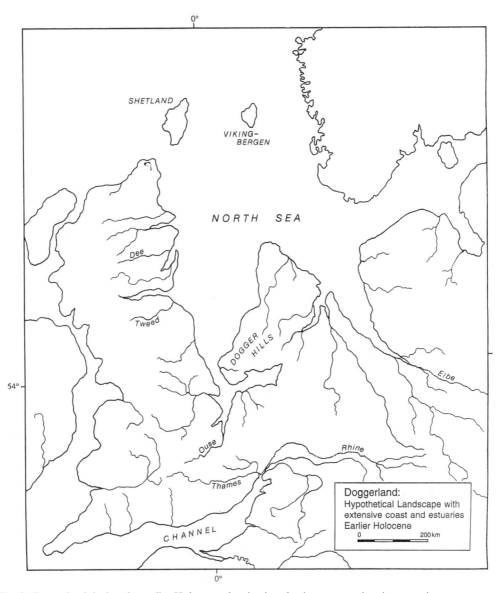

Fig. 3. Doggerland during the earlier Holocene, showing lengthening coast and major estuaries.

pattern did not infringe on the coastal belt. Two strands of evidence support this hypothesis: analysis of stable carbon-isotope ratios in bones from humans and their domestic dogs indicates either a predominantly marine diet or a predominantly inland diet (e.g. Nordqvist 1995), and analysis of material culture shows the development of localized styles within a framework of contacts over long distances. By the Late Mesolithic in southern Scandinavia, three zones can be distinguished, coastal, hinterland and inland, with the hinterland evidence probably left by coastal people during seasonal

visits to the interior of their overall territory (Andersen 1998). For Jutland the inland zone, inhabited by people without access to the coast, extended at least as far west as the present western coast, a reminder of Doggerland's former presence beyond.

Coastal changes

In the time period from the Late Glacial to the Late Mesolithic, approximately 12 000 BP to 6000 cal BP (4000 cal BC) the coastline of Doggerland shifted in response to rising sea-levels

and much of the former landmass became submerged by the North Sea. It has been argued
elsewhere (Coles 1998) that land loss may have
been slower than generally assumed, in part
because Doggerland was not a flat and featureless plain. Figures 1–4 present one possible scenario for land loss, and Shennan *et al.* (2000)
present another. A significant element in the process of land loss, evident from Figs 1–4, was the
increase in the length of coastline and of estuarine
areas, two zones of ecological richness inhabited
by a relatively dense and settled human population adapted to a maritime economy. This, of

course, is an assumption, based on the reasons set
out above. If it is accepted as plausible, it is then
relevant to consider what happened to these
coastal people as sea-level rose.

It is inherently likely that, as the environment
which they knew shifted, the coastal people
moved with it. They will have had the advantage
numerically over inlanders, and they had generations of experience of coastal and estuarine
exploitation. Moreover, their maritime habitat
was expanding, and it will not have stressed
them to absorb formerly inland groups into their
midst. Throughout the millenia of sea-level rise,

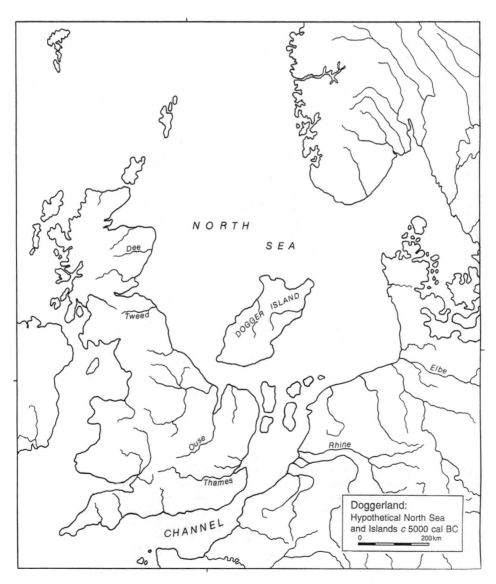

Fig. 4. Doggerland in the later stages of sea-level rise.

the people displaced were not those who saw their familiar beaches and living places lost to the encroaching waves, but the inlanders who yielded to the full package of advancing coastline, complete with flora, fauna and a well-adapted human population.

Almost as soon as the Late Glacial people on Doggerland's coast first developed a maritime-orientated society, the long-term process of moving with the moving coast will have begun. It must have become an entrenched cultural tradition, as was the concomitant absorbtion of inlanders. To call people 'settled' is therefore in one sense misleading, but 'settled' is an apt description of their tenure of the coastal zone and, as suggested by Andersen (1998) for the Late Mesolithic, they probably had tenure of a hinterland belt as well.

At about 6000–5800 cal BC, the watershed between the North Sea drainage systems and the Channel drainage system may have been breached, the event being dated by reference to conditions in the Southern Bight which changed from brackish to marine at about this time (Eisma *et al.* 1981). The Storegga submarine landslide off Norway and the consequent tsunami are possible candidates for natural catastrophic events that hastened the breach. However, sea-level rise continued for a further two millennia, until about 4000 cal BC (Shennan *et al.* 2000; Long *et al.* 2000), and studies of tidal systems off the coast of the Netherlands indicate some impediment to open contact between Channel and North Sea until about 3800 cal BC (B. van der Walk, pers. comm.). Perhaps, therefore, the watershed zone remained as some form of barrier, a series of islands if not continuous land, beyond 6000–5800 cal BC. (For a more detailed discussion of these points, see Coles 1998, p. 66–69).

Effects on people and human economy

The cultural process postulated above, of coastal populations moving with the coastal zone, may therefore have endured until the NW European transition to farming, which took place for what are now the lands bordering the North Sea at about 4200–4000 cal BC. Hypotheses abound as to how farming became established in Europe. The detail of conflicting interpretations need not concern us here, although it is relevant to note the main possibilities:

(a) expansion of farmers together with livestock and crops from southeastern Europe via Danubian and Mediterranean routes;

(b) expansion of the idea of farming and acquisition by indigenous peoples of domestic animals and crops;

(c) local experimentation and development of plant and animal husbandry, with eventual acquisition of non-native species.

Varying combinations of these pathways in different regions and at different times are likely. With farming comes evidence for more substantial and more permanent settlement, for pottery and new lithic technologies, and for changing cultural relations with the land. This last aspect is now seen as the crux of the Neolithic by a number of prehistorians (see Edmonds & Richards 1998 for examples of current concerns).

Neolithic settlement had spread rapidly across Europe from its roots in the Near East, for example along the Danube and its tributaries and down the Rhine, with the earliest farming settlements of the Aegean and Balkans dating to about 6500 cal BC and the earliest of the northwest to about 5400 cal BC (Whittle 1996). The northwestward advance of the Neolithic seems to have met with an invisible barrier some 100–150 km inland of today's coastline: from Ireland, Britain, the Netherlands, North Germany and southern Scandinavia the archaeological evidence at present available indicates the passing of 1200–1400 years before these regions too acquired a neolithic way of life at or shortly before 4000 cal BC.

Prehistorians have suggested various reasons for this lengthy halt to the spread of farming, noting for example the farmers' preference for loess and their slow adaptation to the cultivation of other soils, and the strength of foraging traditions in the lands beyond the loess. In some parts of the farm-free North Sea belt, there is scant archaeological evidence for a late foraging (Mesolithic) population in the 5th millennium cal BC, but in southern Scandinavia in particular a flourishing, culturally rich and innovative foraging population can be documented (e.g. Andersen 1998, Fischer 1995). The evidence comes mainly from what was the coastal zone of the period, from those parts of it which are now accessible to archaeological survey thanks to the interplay of land and sea level change in this particular region. In the Netherlands, the relevant zone is largely blanketed by Holocene sedimentation, but current railroad construction has led to targetted deep archaeological investigations which indicate a similar later Mesolithic potential (e.g. Hardingxveld site, L. P. Louwe Kooijmans, pers. comm.). These flourishing groups were, to take the perspective of this paper, Doggerland's coastal peoples, those who had the advantage over inlanders.

Northwestern Europe in the earlier Holocene can be considered as a land slowly overwhelmed by two advancing waves, farming from the south and the shifting Doggerland coast from the north, Each process, farming as well as the coastal shift, displaced or absorbed inland foragers, in the coastal zone for reasons outlined above, and along the frontier of farming for essentially similar reasons of disparity in population densities and the expansive cultural traditions of the people carried by the wave.

Each people, coastal foragers and inland farmers, will have had a forward zone of contact with inland foragers, and it must have been towards the late 6th millennium cal BC that the unfortunate inland foragers began to find themselves pinched from both sides, between the two waves of advance. In this light, although other factors no doubt contributed, the major force that halted the previously rapid spread of farming can be seen to be Doggerland's coastal population, supported and conditioned by long-term sea-level rise. It has been argued above that the coastal people were more settled than inlanders, their numbers were greater, their economy more diversified, all of which would have put them more on a par with the farmers than their inland neighbours were. And, probably the most significant factor, their cultural outlook was as expansive and tuned to absorbing others, rather than themselves being overwhelmed, as that of the farmers. Moreover, the coastal people had no choice but to move, so long as the coastal zone continued to shift. It was this perhaps which gave the edge to the coastal foragers, and halted the advance of farming 150 km or so inland of the coast, presumably on the outer edge of the coastal zone of exploitation.

In the centuries following their arrival at the invisible barrier at about 5400 cal BC, farming groups can be seen to consolidate and infill their zones of settlement. During this phase, the Linear Bandkeramik or LBK, little cultural change is indicated in the archaeological record. The Rössen period, a time of greater cultural and economic adaptation, followed from about 4800 cal BC. During the Rössen phase in particular, contact is evident with the foragers to the north, traced archaeologically in items such as pottery and stone axe or adze blades of Rössen origin, found on sites beyond the farming frontier (Whittle 1996; Louwe Kooijmans 1998; van Gijn 1998).

For so long as sea-level continued to rise, the buffer zone between the coast and the cultivated lands must have been shrinking. Cultural adjustments will have occured for both farmers and foragers, perhaps even contributing to the LBK-Rössen changes on the farming side and to the development of cemeteries and other indicators of a strengthening hold on the land amongst the coastal foragers. The first archaeological signs of farming settlement in the buffer zone and beyond, in Jutland, south Sweden, Britain and Ireland, date to about 4200–4000 cal BC, at or more probably a little before the standstill in sea-level rise dated by Shennan et al. (2000) and Long (2000) to around 4000 cal BC. Further work on the chronology of both processes might elucidate whether or not there is a link, whether for example marine regression drew with it the coastal people, leaving a belt of relatively unoccupied land soon exploited by farmers. The process of marine regression itself may have sufficiently upset coastal patterns of subsistence and cultural traditions for the system to collapse. Alternatively, 1200 years of contact may have familiarized farmers with the sea, sufficient for their final advance into Britain and Ireland and into southern Scandinavia.

Too often, the long process of sea-level rise has been ignored by prehistorians, and the existence of Doggerland and its people has been neglected. Both were of major importance, exerting an influence on regions beyond the area of the present North Sea, just as the shifting Atlantic coastline and its inhabitants no doubt influenced in some way events further to the west. This paper has been written to draw attention to some of the cultural repercussions of the shifting North Sea coastline, partly in the hope that developments in survey techniques will soon enable a search for evidence to support or refute its arguments.

References

ANDERSEN, S. H. 1998. Ringkloster. Ertebølle trappers and wild boar hunters in eastern Jutland. A survey. *Journal of Danish Archaeology*, **12**, 13–59.

ANUNDSEN, K. 1996. The physical conditions for earliest settlement during the last deglaciation in Norway. *In*: LARSSON, L. (ed.) *The Earliest Settlement of Scandinavia*. Acta Archaeologica Lundensia. Series in 8°, No. **24**, 207–217.

BANG-ANDERSEN, S. 1996. The Colonisation of Southwest Norway. An Ecological Approach. *In*: LARSSON, L. (ed.) *The Earliest Settlement of Scandinavia*. Acta Archaeologica Lundensia, Series in 8°, No. **24**, 219–234.

COLES, B. J. 1998. Doggerland: a speculative survey. *Proceedings of the Prehistoric Society*, **64**, 45–81.

——1999. Doggerland's loss and the Neolithic. *In*: COLES, B. J., COLES, J. M. & SCHOU JØRGENSEN, M. (eds) *Bog Bodies, Sacred Sites and Wetland Archaeology*. WARP Occasional Paper **12**, 51–57.

EDMONDS, M. & RICHARDS, C. (eds) 1998. *Understanding the Neolithic*. Cruithne Press, Edinburgh.

EISMA, D., MOOK, W. G. & LABAN, C. 1981 An early Holocene tidal flat in the Southern Bight. *In*: NIO, S.-D., SCHUTTENHELM, R. T. E. & VAN WEERING, TJ. C. E. (eds) *Holocene Marine Sedimentation in the North Sea Basin*. International Association of Sedimentologists Special Publication **5**, 211–219.

FIRTH, A. 2000. Development-led archaeology in coastal environments: investigations at Queensborough, Motney Hill and Gravesend in Kent, UK. *This volume*.

FISCHER, A. (ed.) 1995 *Man and Sea in the Mesolithic*. Oxbow Monograph 53, Oxford.

VAN GIJN, A. 1998 Craft activities in the Dutch Neolithic: a lithic viewpoint. *In*: EDMONDS, M. & RICHARDS, C. (eds) *Understanding the Neolithic of Northwestern Europe*. Cruithne Press, Edinburgh, 328–350.

HOUSLEY, R. A., GAMBLE, C. S., STREET, M. & PETTITT, P. 1997. Radiocarbon evidence for the Lateglacial Human Recolonisation of Northern Europe. *Proceedings of the Prehistoric Society*, **63**, 25–54.

JOHNSON, H., RICHARDS, P. C., LONG, D. & GRAHAM, C. C. 1993. *The Geology of the Northern North Sea*. Her Majesty's Stationery Office, London.

VAN KOLFSCHOTEN, TH. & LABAN, G. 1995. Pleistocene terrestrial mammal faunas from the North Sea. *Mededelingen Rijks geologische Dienst*, **52**, 135–152.

KOLSTRUP, E. 1991. Palaeoenvironmental developments during the Late Glacial of the Weichselian. *In*: BARTON, N., ROBERTS, A. J. & ROE, D. (eds) *The Late Glacial in North-west Europe*. Council for British Archaeology Research Report **77**, 1–6.

LAMBECK, K. 1993. Glacial rebound of the British Isles – 1. Preliminary model results. *Geophysical Journal International*, **115**, 941–959.

——, SMITHER, C. & JOHNSTON, P. 1998. Sea-level change, glacial rebound and mantle viscosity for northern Europe. *Geophysical Journal International*, **134**, 102–144.

LONG, A, SCAIFE, R. & EDWARDS, R. 2000. Stratigraphic architecture, relative sea-level, and models of estuary development in southern England: new data from Southampton Water. *This volume*.

LONG, D., WICKHAM-JONES, C. R. & RUCKLEY, N. A. 1986. A flint artefact from the northern North Sea. *In*: ROE, D. A. (ed.) *Studies in the Upper Palaeolithic of Britain and Northwest Europe*. British Archaeological Report **S296**, 55–62.

LOUWE KOOIJMANS, L. P. 1998 Understanding the Mesolithic/ Neolithic frontier in the Lower Rhine Basin, 5300–4300 cal BC. *In*: EDMONDS, M. & RICHARDS, C. (eds) *Understanding the Neolithic of Northwestern Europe*. Cruithne Press, Edinburgh, 407–427.

NORDQVIST, B. 1995. The Mesolithic settlements of the west coast of Sweden – with special emphasis on chronology and topography of coastal settlements. *In*: FISCHER, A. (ed.) *Man and Sea in the Mesolithic*. Oxbow Monograph **53**, 185–196.

REID, C. 1913. *Submerged Forests*. Cambridge University Press.

ROUSSELOT, J.-L., FITZHUGH, W. W. & CROWELL, A. 1988. Maritime Economies of the North Pacific Rim. *In*: FITZHUGH, W. W. & CROWELL, A. (eds) *Crossroads of Continents*. Smithsonian Institution Press, Washington DC, 151–172.

SHENNAN, I., LAMBECK, K., FLATHER, R. *ET AL*. 2000. Modelling western North Sea palaeogeographies and tidal changes during Holocene. *In*: SHENNAN, I. & ANDREWS, J. E. (eds) *Holocene Land – Ocean Interaction and Environmental Change around the North Sea*. Geological Society, London, Special publications **166**, 299–319.

TIPPING, R. 1991. Climate change in Scotland during the Devensian Late Glacial: the palynological record. *In*: BARTON, N., ROBERTS, A. J. & ROE, D. *The Late Glacial in North-west Europe*. Council for British Archaeology Research Report **77**, 7–21.

WHITTLE, A. 1996. *Europe in the Neolithic: the creation of new worlds*. Cambridge University Press, Cambridge.

Development-led archaeology in coastal environments: investigations at Queenborough, Motney Hill and Gravesend in Kent, UK

ANTONY FIRTH

Wessex Archaeology, Portway House, Old Sarum Park, Salisbury, UK

Abstract: This paper reviews a series of investigations undertaken by Wessex Archaeology in North Kent in advance of major construction projects. Three sites have been investigated on areas of former saltmarsh at Queenborough, Motney Hill and Gravesend. All three sites currently contain wastewater treatment works (WTW) which are being enhanced in order to meet new water quality standards, involving the construction of new buildings on dense grids of piles driven through the alluvium to more solid strata up to 15 m below ground surface. The paper discusses each investigation in terms of the archaeological and geotechnical background, the evaluation and mitigation strategy adopted, and the contribution that the results may make to our understanding of human activity on the North Kent coast over the past 10 000 years. The paper also looks ahead to development-led investigations at other coastal locations, to show how such work can make a direct contribution to geoarchaeological research while reconciling the objectives of construction and conservation.

Wessex Archaeology has investigated three sites on areas of former saltmarsh at Queenborough, Motney Hill and Gravesend (Fig. 1). All three sites currently contain wastewater treatment works (WTW) which are being enhanced in order to meet new water quality standards, involving the construction of new buildings on dense grids of piles driven through the alluvium to more solid strata up to 15 metres below ground level.

The paper is intended to illustrate three points about development-led archaeology in coastal environments:

(1) Development-led archaeology provides both the opportunities and the means to examine alluvial sequences of considerable archaeological significance;
(2) The investigation of coastal sites requires archaeological curators and contractors to adopt approaches that are innovative in terms of research orientation, field methodology and conservation strategy;
(3) The emerging extension of curatorial control to the sub-tidal zone may – if supported by innovative responses by contractors – promote the investigation of progressively deeper and older coastal environments.

The approach presented here builds on that advocated by Barham *et al.* (1995, p. 349–350; and see Bates & Barham 1995) in encouraging development-led geoarchaeological investigation of deeply buried alluvial sequences, with the eventual aim of investigating submerged alluvial sequences and palaeo-topographies that could illuminate the earliest post-Devensian human occupation of NW Europe.

The development process

The proposals for each of the three wastewater treatment works were subject to receipt of planning permission from Kent County Council, and each planning application was accompanied by an Environmental Statement (see Gill 1995; Champion *et al.* 1997, p. 193–194). Environmental Statements are required to discuss the impact of proposed works on many aspects of the environment, including archaeology. Accordingly, the Environmental Statements for Queenborough, Motney Hill and Gravesend included specific chapters on archaeology and were supported by technical appendices, each in the form of a desk-based study (Wessex Archaeology (WA) 1996*a,d,e*). The Environmental Statements and the accompanying desk studies were subject to the scrutiny and approval of the Archaeological Officers of Kent County Council.

As well as drawing attention to a wide range of conventional archaeological sites and finds,

From: PYE, K. & ALLEN, J. R. L. (eds). *Coastal and Estuarine Environments: sedimentology, geomorphology and geoarchaeology*. Geological Society, London, Special Publications, **175**, 403–417. 0305-8719/00/$15.00 © The Geological Society of London 2000.

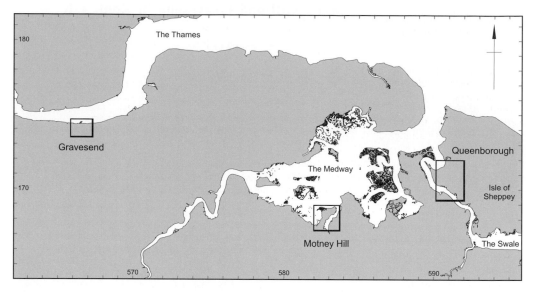

Fig. 1. Location map showing Gravesend, Queenborough and Motney Hill.

each of the three desk-based studies drew attention to the potential for cultural material within the alluvial sequence beneath the sites at Queenborough, Motney Hill and Gravesend, and to the significance of each sequence itself in providing data about the historic environment and sea-level change.

Commitments were made in each Environmental Statement to undertake fieldwork to evaluate these alluvial sequences, and to mitigate the impact of construction on any archaeological material that might be discovered. These relatively open commitments were volunteered by the client in order to secure uncontested acceptance of the planning application. In particular, practical considerations made it desirable to avoid carrying out field evaluation prior to securing planning permission. The commitment to evaluation and mitigation became binding through the inclusion of archaeological conditions on the planning permission for each site.

Conventionally, development sites are evaluated by excavating a series of trenches or test pits to determine whether significant archaeological material is present, and to assess its character, extent and significance. If evaluation demonstrates the presence of significant archaeological material, then mitigation will be required, either by re-designing elements of the proposed scheme, or by recording, analysing and archiving the remains, generally through a programme of open area excavation. If the results of evaluation are inconclusive, then mitigation is more likely to take the form of a watching brief in the course of construction. There are, however, a number of difficulties in applying this conventional approach to the kinds of construction projects envisaged in North Kent:

(1) The horizons in which archaeological deposits are likely to occur are deeply buried, often beyond the depth to which evaluation trenches can be excavated safely and practically.

(2) As the main structures were to be built on piles, then construction would have a relatively limited impact on any archaeological remains that might be present.

(3) On balance it was likely that mitigation would take the form of a cost-ineffective watching brief. Watching briefs can be very expensive – because of the long duration of construction programmes – and archaeologically ineffective – because construction sites are often not conducive to controlled observation and recording.

(4) The greatest archaeological potential at each site rested in the scope to tie discrete archaeological episodes into a sequence of environmental change which would be of general relevance to the history of human occupation of North Kent. As the amounts of artefactual material were likely to be minimal while the cost of environmental

analysis would be quite high, then open area excavation was unlikely to offer optimum results.

Consequently, an unconventional strategy was adopted whereby fieldwork effort was focussed on evaluation, with mitigation pursued off-site through analysis of samples collected during evaluation. In crude terms, the resources that might be applied to an inefficient and unsatisfactory watching brief were redirected to enhanced analysis of an admittedly constrained dataset. Moreover, the emphasis in evaluation was placed not on opening up a representative sample of each site through extensive trenching, but on building up a picture of the alluvial sequence in three dimensions through systematic augering, supplemented by relatively few trenches targeted on specific horizons. Implicit in this strategy was the acceptance that some archaeological material might be missed entirely.

Systematic augering has generally been carried out by a specialist sub-contractor (Geodrive Ltd) under archaeological supervision. At all three sites, at least two transects were logged using a side window corer, with spot samples taken to assist description and comparison. The resulting logs were then used to position two plastic sleeved continuous cores for each site. In each case, one of the continuous cores was split, described and sub-sampled for analysis of pollen and foraminifera, and for radiocarbon dating of suitable horizons. The remaining continuous cores have been retained for posterity.

All of the fieldwork, analysis, reporting and – eventually – publication is being funded by the developer as an integral cost of each construction project. Currently, the evaluation programme has been completed for all three sites, and mitigation proposals have been accepted for Queenborough and Gravesend. Fieldwork at Motney Hill was completed in the summer of 1998; detailed analysis of all three sites will commence upon acceptance of mitigation proposals for Motney Hill.

Sea-level change and archaeological context

Although all three sites occupy a section of the mid-Thames estuary, each has a different relationship to the open coast (Fig. 1). Queenborough WTW is on the shores of The Swale, which is the double-ended channel separating the Isle of Sheppey from the mainland as it passes from the Medway-Thames confluence to Whitstable Bay. Motney Hill WTW is located on a peninsula within the Medway, and Gravesend WTW sits directly on the shores of the Thames within a relatively narrow channel.

These differences in coastal environment militate against simple mapping of regional trends in sea-level change onto the particular WTW sites, as differential crustal movement and changing patterns of coastal sedimentation, erosion and compaction may cause the character and apparent height of successive land surfaces to differ markedly from the regional 'norm' (see Long 1992; Allen 1999). Consequently, any correlation of sea-level changes with episodes of human activity remain tentative, especially when trying to establish patterns that hold true beyond any one particular site. This difficulty has been recognized in preparing 'An Archaeological Research Framework for the Greater Thames Estuary'. Although noting that the Greater Thames estuary is a key area for the study of past environmental change and its relationship with human activity, the absence of a satisfactory regional lithostratigraphic framework is highlighted (Williams & Brown 1999, p. 11–13). Nonetheless, such regional trends as are currently available necessarily form the background to any initial assessment of the threat to potentially significant archaeological and palaeoenvironmental deposits.

The account of sea-level change in the Thames estuary presented by Devoy on the basis of analysis of a sequence from Tilbury offers a framework that is accepted generally despite some reservations (Devoy 1980, 1982; and see Haggart 1995, Long 1995 and Wilkinson & Murphy 1995). Devoy identified five transgressions (Thames I–V) separated by stabilizations (indicated by biogenic deposits) in the early Mesolithic (Tilbury I), later Mesolithic (Tilbury II), the Late Neolithic/Early Bronze Age (Tilbury III), the Late Bronze Age/Early Iron Age (Tilbury IV), and the Roman period (Tilbury V). His figures correspond broadly to Evan's account (Evans 1953) of peat horizons in the North Kent Marshes, which refers to peat levels below Chatham Dockyard at c. 10.5 m below OD (Mesolithic), c. 5.75 m below OD (Late Neolithic/Early Bronze) and at c. 0.2 m above OD (Roman). Investigations associated with construction of the Medway Tunnel near Chatham led to the identification of distinct peat units at c. 7.0–9.0 m below OD and c. 3.0–4.5 m below OD, together with a complex of small peat units and variable thin organic silty-clay beds at c. 2.0 m below to c. 2.0 m above OD. Radiocarbon dating indicated that the lower unit dated to the Mesolithic, the middle unit to the Later Neolithic, and the upper complex from the Early Bronze Age to the Early Iron Age. Artefacts, charcoal and fire-cracked flint were observed in the lower and middle units (Barham *et al.* 1995).

Turning to the archaeological evidence, a series of sites have been found in reclaimed and intertidal coastal wetlands that are not only rich in finds and structures, well-preserved and associated with palaeo-environmental data, but also of crucial importance in trying to understand overall patterns of human activity throughout SE England (Williams & Brown 1999, p. 14–16). The importance of such coastal sites beyond their immediate locale has been emphasized by Coles, making the point that any consideration of the prehistory of north-western Europe should acknowledge the presence of extensive inhabited lands in the southern North Sea (Coles 1998). At present, however, the relatively few sites that have been reported in North Kent indicate rather than demonstrate the contribution of coastal occupation to the region as a whole. Notwithstanding some authors' willingness to presume a more significant role for the coast, the visibility and accessibility of 'dry' sites gives the impression that coastal activity has played only a minor role through the ages.

In their regional synthesis, 'The South East to AD 1000', Drewett *et al.* (1988) highlight the possible significance of coastal sites in earlier prehistoric periods. Although their distribution plot of the main sites of postglacial hunter-gatherer activity shows just three flint scatters on the North Kent coast (Drewett *et al.* 1988, fig. 1.3), in summing up the early Holocene history of south east England, they state:

'the evidence from the marshes of Kent and the Coastal Plain of Sussex suggests low-density activity, probably of a seasonal nature. An ample supply of shellfish and marsh birds during the summer months, together with greater mobility in marshland during dryer times of year, suggests summer utilisation of marsh resources'

In the Neolithic, Drewett *et al.* note that 'the utilization of strand resources, particularly the collection of shell fish, was clearly undertaken from both fortified settlement enclosures and open agricultural settlements' (Drewett *et al.* 1988, p. 45–46). Where the settlement site was located at some distance from the sea 'the establishment of temporary camps for the utilization of strand and salt marsh resources appears probable' (Drewett *et al.* 1988, p. 46). Whilst noting the difficulty of identifying and dating such temporary sites, these authors note the likely survival of specialized flint assemblages such as that found in a low cliff exposure in Chichester Harbour: 'Careful search along the foreshore of North Kent may produce similar flint assemblages, although most may have been submerged through marine transgression...' (Drewett *et al.* 1988, p. 46). In considering estuarine occupation, observations regarding coastal activity mesh with the possible pattern of riverside activity. Drewett *et al.* state that the presence of long barrows and megalithic monuments overlooking the flood plains of main river valleys such as the Medway suggests intense utilization of the river valleys, though later sedimentation has largely masked all traces of settlement (see also Williams & Brown 1999, p. 17).

In the Bronze Age an agricultural site is noted at Gravesend (Drewett *et al.* 1988, fig. 3.1) as well as a scatter of isolated bronzes at various sites along the North Kent Coast (fig. 4.1). A concentration of Bronze Age hoards around the Greater Thames estuary has also been noted (Williams & Brown 1999, p. 17). However, the main concentrations of settled activity in the Bronze Age have been found on the Sussex Coastal Plain, in Thanet and in the valley of the Thames river. Similarly, the focus of interest in Iron Age activity is directed away from the North Kent coast by denser patterns of finds in Thanet, west Kent, on the South Downs and on the coastal plain of West Sussex (Drewett *et al.* 1988, p. 127–145) though there is also a concentration of Iron Age activity on the Thames shore of the Hoo peninsula and Isle of Grain (Williams & Brown 1999, p. 17).

Moving to the Roman period, the Upchurch Marshes to the east of Motney Hill were one of three main groups of potteries in Kent, and kiln sites have also been found in the marshes east of Gravesend (Drewett *et al.* 1988, p. 241, fig. 6.2; Williams & Brown 1999, p. 17). Extensive evidence for the manufacture of salt which may have Iron Age antecedants has been found in the Thames and Medway marshes (see Detsicas 1984) and it seems likely that the estuarine shores would have supported shell- and fin-fish industries (Drewett *et al.* 1988, p. 244–245). Numerous farmsteads and other finds have been found between Watling Street – the major Roman road that runs from Canterbury via Rochester to London – and the Thames (Drewett *et al.* 1988, fig. 6.2).

The Early Medieval period saw an influx of Germanic settlers to the creeks and rivers of the Thames with the importance of marine resources and transport emphasized by the proximity of occupation sites to landing points. The relative importance of Kent and its close links to the Continent is apparent in the richness and content of burials (Drewett *et al.* 1988, p. 254–8). Continued links with the Continent seem to have influenced the location of early churches such as those at Hoo and Minster (Drewett *et al.* 1988, 299, p. 314–315) though religious and secular interest in the coast may also have been prompted by exploitation of the marshes for grazing, fishing and salt production (Williams & Brown 1999, p. 17–18). Such exploitation may have progressed across the marshes hand-in-hand with early reclamation schemes, though it is not clear at what point reclamation finally interrupted the deposition of Holocene alluvium (see Brandon & Short 1990, p. 106–8, 213–215) and provided the apparently featureless surfaces upon which WTW were established at Queenborough, Motney Hill and Gravesend in the twentieth century.

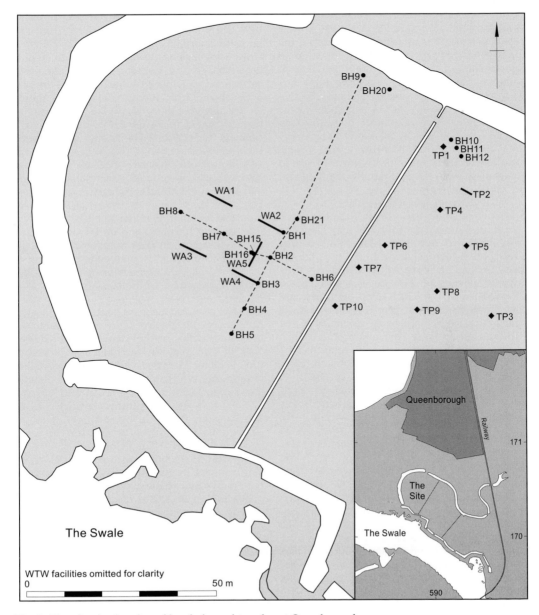

Fig. 2. Plan showing location of boreholes and trenches at Queenborough.

Interim results

Queenborough

The WTW site at Queenborough is located on reclaimed saltmarsh close to The Swale on the southern shore of the Isle of Sheppey [NGR 590800 170500] (see Fig. 2). The underlying geology is of London Clay dipping gently southwards from c. 5 m to c. 15 m below OD, with the top of the alluvium at c. 1 m above OD. There is no recorded evidence of Mesolithic, Neolithic or Bronze Age activity within the area around Queenborough, and although Iron Age pottery production and Roman activity are known from around the Medway and Sheppey, there are no known sites or findspots from these periods within a 1 km study area around the WTW site. The first material evidence of past human activity in the vicinity of Queenborough is the reported remains of a number of salt-making mounds some of which still survive which may date to the Medieval period. Also, some elements of the ditches and seawalls used to reclaim the area may also date to the Medieval period (WA 1996a).

On the basis of geotechnical data and coarse assumptions about the general rate of sea-level rise, it was thought that the site may have first been inundated during the Mesolithic period, with gradual encroachment up the site until the Early Bronze Age when the site would have been entirely submerged. The site was assumed to have formed part of The Swale from the Bronze Age, through the Iron Age, Roman and Early Medieval periods, until being reclaimed in the Medieval period (WA 1996a, para. 2.7).

Two borehole transects were implemented prior to construction, with continuous cores obtained from BH15 and BH16 (see Fig. 2). A series of shallow evaluation trenches was excavated through the post-reclamation sequence in an attempt to locate any remains associated with the reported salt-making mounds (WA 1996b; WA 1997). Consequently, a watching brief was conducted during construction of the WTW enhancements, when additional samples were obtained from the upper horizons (WA 1999a).

London Clay was encountered in boreholes from approximately 2.5 m below OD to 8 m OD, that is 10 m below ground level (see Fig. 3). The principal horizons included organic clay immediately overlying London Clay in the south part of the site at approximately 7–8 m below OD. Grey clay with some organic material (possibly reeds) was observed up to approximately 6.3 m below OD, overlain by organic layers of black silt and greenish brown clay to approximately 5.3 m below OD. The organic layers appear to follow the trend of the underlying London Clay to approximately 1 m below OD to the north. These horizons were all overlain by blue grey sandy silt with a near horizontal surface at approximately 0 m OD, then covered by subsoil and topsoil to current ground level at approximately 1–2 m above OD. No finds were made, and there was no sign of the reported salt-making mounds. Initial interpretation suggests that the organic clay immediately overlying London Clay may correspond to Tilbury II (Later Mesolithic), the organic layers between c. 6.3 and c. 5.3 m below OD to Tilbury III (Later Neolithic) and the horizontal surface at OD to Tilbury V (Roman). Only the organic layers thought to follow the trend of the London Clay to the north correspond to Tilbury IV. Sufficient sub-samples were obtained to attempt radiocarbon dating of organic components of the sedimentary sequence, and to examine the changing environment through analysis of pollen, diatoms and foraminifera.

Although no material evidence of human activity was encountered, the results of dating and palaeo-environmental analysis should shed light on the changing extent of terrestrial, intertidal and marine resources in the prehistoric landscape of Sheppey, and on the development of The Swale as an important waterway in the later prehistoric and Roman periods.

Gravesend

The site at Gravesend is located on Denton Marshes on the fringe of Gravesend, close to the present shoreline of the Thames [NGR 166600 174000] (see Fig. 4). The site itself lies over Flood Plain Gravels, backed by the higher ground of the Upper Chalk to the south. The surface of the gravels is between 9.7 and 11.3 m below OD, with ground level at c. 2–3 m above OD. Geotechnical investigations identified a substantial layer of peat with its top surface at between 3.1 and 3.7 m below OD, a layer of clayey peat in one borehole at c. 0.8 m below OD, and horizons containing black organic matter both above and below (WA 1996e).

Leaving aside the evidence of Palaeolithic activity in the area, Mesolithic material (one tranchet axe) was found in uncertain circumstances on a gasworks adjacent to the site. Neolithic material is entirely unknown in the vicinity, but the higher chalk to the south and SE supports a range of sites and finds from the Bronze Age. Again, Iron Age activity is known to the SE, and Roman sites have also been found on the chalk. Importantly, extensive

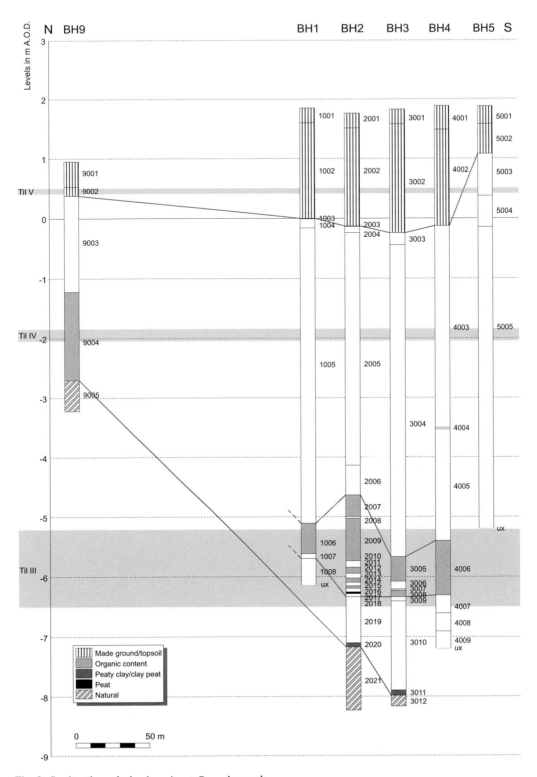

Fig. 3. Section through the deposits at Queenborough.

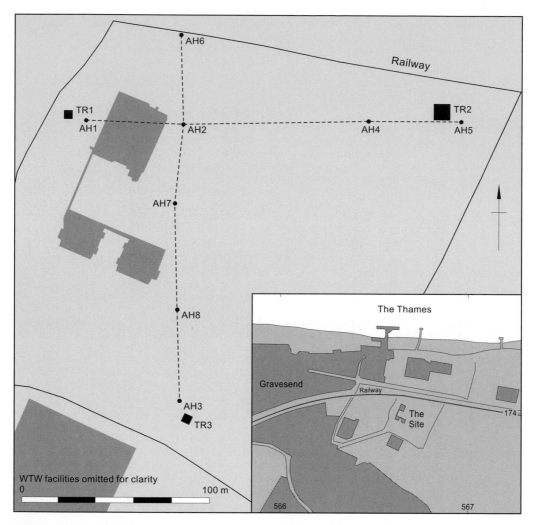

Fig. 4. Plan showing location of boreholes and trenches at Gravesend.

quantities of Roman pottery were found during construction work at Gravesend WTW in 1978, reportedly between a layer of brown silty clay and a layer of soft blue clay. A section through the pottery deposit 'suggested a heap rather than a pit and there was no sign of any adjacent structure' (Harker 1978, p. 7). Archaeological and documentary sources are then silent until the manor of Denton is established, by AD 950, though various sources attest to the Medieval, Post-medieval and Modern history of the area (WA 1996e).

Drawing on the geotechnical data cited above and studies of sea-level change, progress was made on the assumption that the 1.5 m thick layer of peat between *c*. 3.5 and 5 m below OD dated to sea-level stability in the earlier Neo-

lithic, with a layer of clayey peat at approximately 0.8 m below OD being formed during the Late Bronze Age, giving way to sea-level rise thereafter (WA 1996e, para. 2.2.13).

Two intersecting transects were implemented prior to construction, with continuous cores adjacent to AH1 and AH 8 (see Fig. 4). In addition, two stepped trenches were excavated to approximately 2.4 m below ground level, and a third stepped trench was excavated to approximately 3.6 m below ground level. The objective of these trenches was to intercept the source of Roman pottery reported from the 1970s, and possibly the putative Late Bronze Age clayey peat (WA 1998).

The boreholes were driven to the Flood Plain Gravels at approximately 7–8 m below OD.

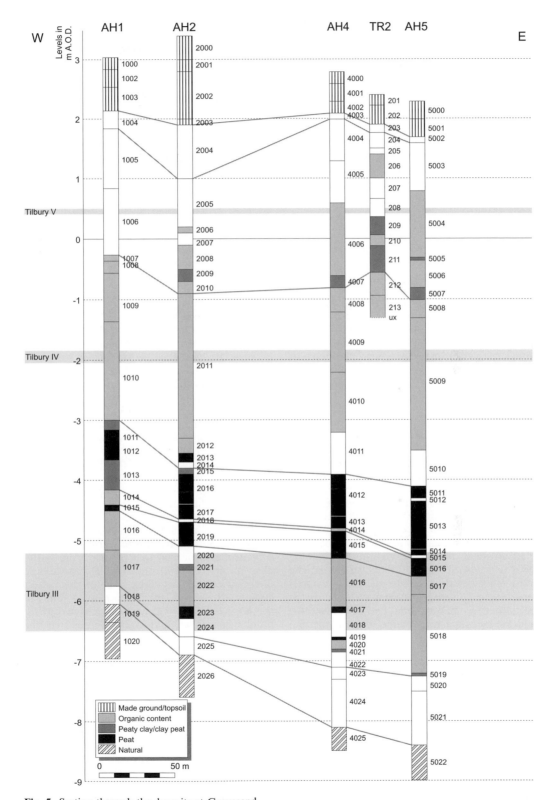

Fig. 5. Section through the deposits at Gravesend.

The presence of a major peat horizon at approximately 3.5–5 m below OD was confirmed, within an overall sequence that included many poorly formed organic deposits (see Fig. 5). Non-organic horizons were observed immediately over the Flood Plain Gravels and at up to approximately 1 m below OD and 1.5 m above OD. Trench 2 revealed organic horizons at c. 0.1 m (211) and 0.4 m (209) above OD. The major peat horizon from 5–3.5 m below OD appears to correspond to Tilbury III (Late Neolithic/Early Bronze Age) and Tilbury IV (Late Bronze Age) may be represented by some of the lower thin, poorly formed peat deposits from 1 m below OD. However, in both cases the horizons at Gravesend are c. 1 m higher than the corresponding Tilbury 'standard'.

The organic horizons in Trench 2 at 0.4 m and 0.1 m above OD seem to correspond to Tilbury V (Early Roman). However, this interpretation is complicated by the discovery of Roman pottery, bone, shell and building material between horizons 205 and 206 at approximately 1.4 m above OD, which may be a further example of the 1 m discrepancy referred to above. The discoveries in Trench 2 generally conform to the description of the finds from 1978, including Samian, possible terra nigra and coarsewares, probably dating to about AD 100. The artefacts and animal bone showed no signs of rolling, comprised relatively large fragments with clean breaks, and were not deposited in any form of cut feature. All-in-all, it appears that the deposit represents dumping of domestic refuse on marshy ground; the source of the refuse may have been some form of settled site nearby but outside the boundaries of WTW, perhaps on slightly higher ground to the south or SW.

Consequent to the evaluation, a watching brief was carried out during construction. The most substantial elements of the enhanced works were generally situated away from the area where Roman material had been identified and the watching brief indicated that construction had not impinged on significant deposits (WA 1999b).

As at Queenborough, the extensive range of samples will undergo detailed analysis for pollen and foraminifera, and radiocarbon dating, in order to clarify our understanding of the developing human environment around Gravesend.

Motney Hill

Motney Hill is a peninsula in the Medway near Lower Rainham [NGR 183000 168500], comprising a low but prominent hill connected to the mainland by a narrow spit (see Fig. 6). The hill, which consists of sands of the Woolwich Beds over Thanet Beds to c. 17 m above OD, tails off on three sides into the surrounding marsh at c. 3–4 m below OD. The surface of the marsh lies at c. 2–3 m above OD (WA 1996d). Geotechnical investigations indicated traces of organic material at depths up to c. 1.6 m below OD (WA 1996d). Monitoring of contamination investigations directed to the upper horizons of the marsh confirmed the presence of organic horizons at levels that could be broadly correlated across the site, the most coherent being a c. 0.2 m layer of peat with its top surface at c. 0.6–0.9 m above OD (WA 1996c). As the contamination investigations did not cover the entire depth of alluvium, the potential for organic horizons below OD – as indicated by earlier geotechnical work – could be assumed but not confirmed.

Large numbers of sites and finds have been reported on and in the immediate vicinity of Motney Hill, covering the Mesolithic, Neolithic, Bronze Age and Roman periods. Of particular note is the large collection of flint artefacts found by a local amateur archaeologist eroding from low cliffs on the west side of Motney Hill, including microliths, blades, scrapers, leaf shaped arrowheads, and a tranchet axe (WA 1996d). Two sites excavated in the 1920s at Lower Halstow, a little to the east of Motney Hill, generated finds of heavy tools, particularly adzes, predominating in an assemblage recovered from sticky clay overlain by peat and 2.1 m of alluvium (Drewett et al. 1988, p. 22). Additionally, evaluation trenching by Wessex Archaeology in advance of enabling works provided evidence of Late Bronze Age settlement on the top of Motney Hill and at the base of the peninsula (including some of the earliest evidence for non-cereal production in Kent, in the form of securely stratified charred peas/beans). Moreover, flint artefacts found on the top of Motney Hill span the Neolithic and Bronze Age and possibly the late Mesolithic (WA 1999c, d). Despite the apparently high level of human activity at Motney Hill throughout prehistory, there is a notable near-absence of Iron Age material (WA 1996d). In the Roman period, however, the area seems to have been quite heavily used. The entire marsh area from Rainham to Lower Halstow was used for the production of blue-black pottery known as Upchurch Ware, and two kilns are recorded from the base of the Motney Hill peninsula. A number of funerary sites and possible dwellings are also recorded (WA 1996d).

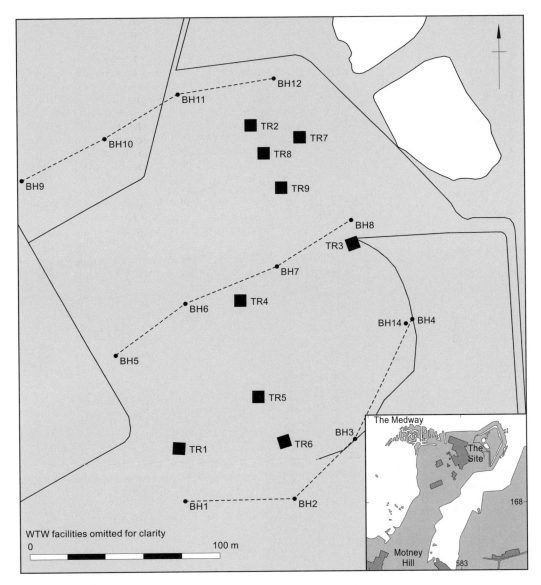

Fig. 6. Plan showing location of boreholes and trenches at Motney Hill.

The geotechnical data cited above and coarse assumptions regarding sea-level rise suggest that the basin surrounding Motney Hill was not inundated until the late Neolithic, with sea-level stability marked by organic horizons in the Bronze Age. Organic deposits at approximately 0.4–0.8 m above OD were thought to indicate further stabilization in the Roman period.

The main elements of the trenching and borehole strategy were a series of 12 side-window and two continuous sleeved cores, and nine trenches excavated to c. 3 m below ground level

(see Fig. 6). The trenches were not intended to examine the entire alluvial sequence, but to examine organic horizons thought to date to the Late Bronze Age and later periods (see WA 1999e).

The boreholes encountered Woolwich Beds at varying depths up to 3–4 m below OD (that is, up to 7 m below ground level) (see Fig. 7). Unexpectedly, several trenches also encountered Woolwich Beds, presenting a plan view of the pre-inundation land surface and an opportunity to examine a complete sequence in section (see

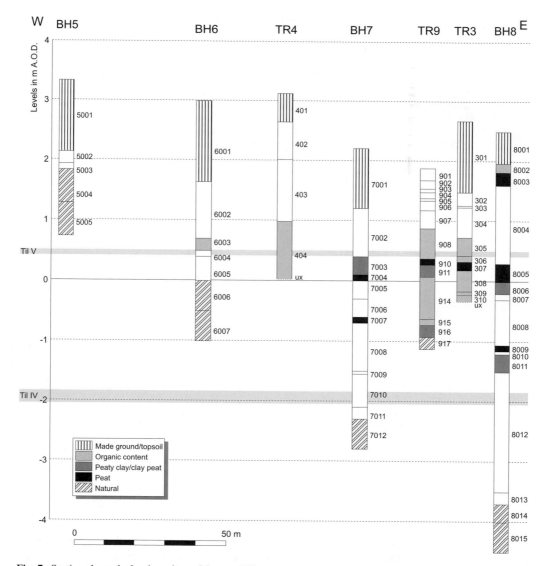

Fig. 7. Section through the deposits at Motney Hill.

Fig. 8). Organic horizons were identified in five discrete ranges that can be correlated across the whole of the survey area. In turn, these ranges can be linked tentatively to the regional framework of sea-level change provided by Devoy. The organic horizons were generally separated by thick horizons of dark grey clay.

Finds were made in trenches 1, 8 and 9 from the surface of the Woolwich Beds sand. The finds included worked flint and a few small crumbs of pottery. The pottery fragments are thought to have come from a single vessel of later Neolithic date. The worked flint has Mesolithic characteristics though these might

extend into the early Neolithic. In addition, a small piece of wood was found in layer 914 (Fig. 8) with tooling marks from a metal blade on two faces. Furthermore, large wood fragments were recovered from various horizons in trenches 3, 8 and 9. Significantly, one piece of tree was clearly *in situ*, with a tap root extending into the Woolwich Beds.

As with the other two sites, detailed analysis has yet to take place, but it appears that the flint, pottery and *in situ* tree all confirm that the Woolwich Beds offered a terrestrial surface through the Mesolithic and into the Neolithic. A basal peat possibly corresponding to Tilbury III (Later

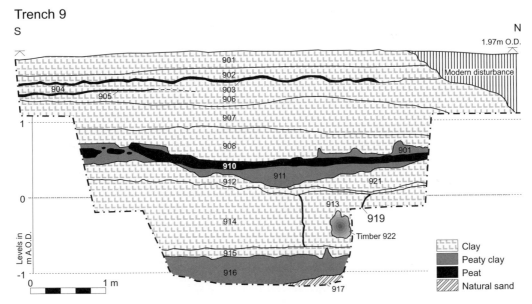

Fig. 8. Section of Trench 9 at Motney Hill.

Neolithic) may have accompanied inundation, with later stability suggested by peat at *c.* 1 m below OD that may correspond to Tilbury IV (Bronze Age). Extensive peat deposits at and a little above OD seem to correspond to Tilbury V (Roman). Further inundation followed, with a number of thin peat horizons perhaps indicating successive episodes of stabilization followed by incursion in post-Roman periods.

Discussion

Discussion of the full archaeological implications of the findings at Queenborough, Gravesend and Motney Hill must await completion of the programme of radiocarbon dating and environmental analysis. However, it is already clear that both the archaeological and palaeo-environmental data acquired from these three sites should facilitate a detailed re-assessment of human activity on the changing coastline of North Kent from the Mesolithic period to the first reclamation. Initial interpretation suggests there is a fair degree of correlation from site-to-site and with the basic framework provided by Devoy. These studies are significant not only to our understanding of the particular sites, or even of the mid-Thames estuary, but to the whole of SE England and the southern North Sea.

With attention drawn to such an extensive scale, it is worth locating such studies in the context of intertidal and subtidal investigations, as well 'dry' investigations with which archaeologists are most familiar. Investigations such as those described above sit uneasily with traditional divisions between and within disciplines. The dependence of archaeologists on input from geologists and environmental scientists should be amply clear from the account above. As far as the discipline of archaeology is concerned, however, prefixes such as 'coastal', 'wetland', 'environmental', 'marine', 'maritime', 'nautical' and 'underwater' become inadequate in the face of circumstance: but for the accident of reclamation, these deposits would lie – like many others whose existence must be presumed – in intertidal or subtidal zones (see Allen 1997). As for the character of the societies whose remains have been located, little can yet be said. So far it can only be assumed that these societies had a maritime dimension due to their proximity to the sea, though open water may have been quite distant until the later Mesolithic (see Wilkinson & Murphy 1995, p. 211–213). Discoveries from other shores imply that in each period these people had access to nautical technologies and would have exploited littoral resources, yet we are still in no position to state how use of the sea impinged on social life. Nonetheless, we should anticipate a point in the near future when the results of particular site investigations, extensive coastal surveys and reappraisal of onshore distributions can be combined in attempts to ascribe specific interpretations to each of the different societies that have inhabited our coasts and estuaries.

As far as archaeological prospection, exploration and mitigation is concerned, the investigations described above point to the value of innovative strategies that focus available resources on the most pressing archaeological issues. The examples above emphasize the usefulness of desk-based assessments that draw together existing archaeological, geotechnical and engineering data in order to gauge the actual impact of the proposed development on potentially significant deposits. The examples also show that integration of archaeological advice within the developer's team can prompt minor alterations to geological or contamination investigations so that they can yield valuable archaeological results at relatively minor additional cost. Gravesend and Motney Hill also demonstrated the use of incremental strategies for intrusive evaluation whereby borehole investigations are used to target relatively small numbers of trenches. Finally, it is hoped that all three investigations achieved a reasonable trade-off between extensive on-site investigations and intensive off-site analysis.

This paper has sought to show how it is possible for development-led archaeology to reconcile the objectives of construction and conservation while making a direct contribution to geoarchaeological research. By way of conclusion, however, it may be appropriate to look ahead to one of the next frontiers of development-led archaeology. It has recently been noted that '... the offshore evidence for RSL change and coastal evolution in southern England has received comparatively little attention' (Dix *et al.* 1998, p. 1), and assumptions regarding the former inhabitants of relatively deeply-submerged landsurfaces are even more tentative than those offered above (see Coles 1998). Nonetheless, the palaeo-coastlines and archaeological sites that they may support are subject to a number of development impacts out to the limits of the UK Continental Shelf.

Wessex Archaeology has been carrying out investigations in intertidal areas for some time and has been developing its approach to shallow subtidal environments through investigations off Plymouth, Southampton and Folkestone, for example. In the last couple of years Wessex Archaeology has also started to address the potential for discoveries of prehistoric material in the deeper waters of the palaeo-channels associated with the course of the former Solent and English Channel River. Preliminary work has all been carried out on behalf of commercial clients who are responding to requests for clarification from curatorial archaeologists of the possible impact of proposed aggregate dredging. Initial work has comprised desk studies that have attempted to overlay coarse details of sea-level change onto elevation models derived from bathymetric and superficial sediment thickness data. Notwithstanding water depths in the 30–40 m range, it would appear that there are palaeo-topographic features that may have offered vantage points to hunter-gatherers in the Late Upper Palaeolithic and Early Mesolithic periods. Moreover, some of these palaeo-topographic features are associated with alluvial sequences containing organic horizons, which may be interrogated for pollen, foraminifera and dating evidence. The conclusions are highly tentative, but they are already serving as working hypotheses to be tested through field evaluation in advance of aggregate production.

Although these are early days, it is evident that the principles of reconciling development and conservation illustrated above could be adopted offshore. In this respect, development-led archaeology may play a key role in clarifying speculation about the character of the earliest human occupation of NW Europe following the last glacial maximum.

The investigations described here are the result of the collective effort of many colleagues and associates at Wessex Archaeology and elsewhere. They have been carried out on behalf of Southern Water in association with their planning consultants (Barton Wilmore Planning Partnership) and main contractors (Birse & Laings). Kent County Council provided curatorial advice. Thanks are offered to everybody that has engaged in or assisted Wessex Archaeology's work on the North Kent WTW projects.

References

ALLEN, J. R. L. 1997. A conceptual model for the archaeology of the English coastal zone. *In*: FULFORD, M., CHAMPION, T. & LONG, A. (eds) *England's Coastal Heritage: a survey for English Heritage and the RCHME*, English Heritage Archaeology Report 15.

——1999. Geological impacts on coastal wetland landscapes: some general effects of sediment auto-compaction in the holocene of northwest Europe. *The Holocene*, **9**, 1–12.

BRANDON, P. & SHORT, B. 1990. *The South East from AD 1000*. Regional History of England, Longman.

BATES, M. & BARHAM, A. J. 1995. Holocene alluvial stratigraphic architecture and archaeology in the Lower Thames. *In*: BRIDGLAND, D. ALLEN, P.

& HAGGART, B. A. (eds) *The Quaternary of the Lower Reaches of the Thames: field guide*, Quaternary Research Association.

BARHAM, A. J., BATES, M., PINE, C. A. & WILLIAMSON, V. D. 1995. Holocene development of the Lower Medway Valley and prehistoric occupation of the floodplain area. *In*: BRIDGLAND, D. ALLEN, P. & HAGGART, B. A. (eds) *The Quaternary of the Lower Reaches of the Thames: field guide*, Quaternary Research Association.

CHAMPION, T., FIRTH, A. & O'REGAN, D. 1997. Managing England's Coastal Heritage. *In*: FULFORD, M., CHAMPION, T. & LONG, A. (eds) *England's Coastal Heritage: a survey for English Heritage and the RCHME*, English Heritage Archaeology Report 15.

COLES, B. J. 1998. Doggerland: a speculative survey. *Proceedings of the Prehistoric Society*, **64**, 45–81.

DETSICAS, A. P. 1984. A salt-panning site at Funton Creek. *Archaeologia Cantiana*, **101**, 165–168.

DEVOY, R. J. 1980. Post-glacial Environmental Change and Man in the Thames Estuary: a synopsis. *In*: THOMPSON, F. S. (ed.) *Archaeology and Coastal Change*, Society of Antiquaries, 134–148.

——1982. Analysis of the geological evidence for Holocene sea-level movements in southeast England. *Proceedings of the Geologists' Association*, **93**(1), 65–90.

DIX, J., LONG, A. & COOKE, R. 1998. The Evolution of Rye Bay and Dungeness Foreland: the offshore seismic record. *In*: EDDISON, J., GARDINER, M. & LONG, A. *Romney marsh: environmental change and human occupation in a coastal lowland*. Oxford University Committee for Archaeology.

DREWITT, P., RUDLING, D. & GARDINER, M. 1988. *The South-East to AD 1000*. Longman.

EVANS, J. H. 1953. Archaeological Horizons in the North Kent Marshes. *Archaeologia Cantiana*, **64**, 103–146.

GILL, G. 1995. *Building on the Past: a guide to the archaeology and development process*. Spon.

HAGGART, B. A. 1995. A re-examination of some data relating to Holocene sea-level changes in the Thames estuary. *In*: BRIDGLAND, D., ALLEN, P. & HAGGART, B. A. (eds) *The Quaternary of the Lower Reaches of the Thames: field guide*, Quaternary Research Association.

HARKER, S. R. 1978. Another Roman site in the North Kent Marshes. *Kent Archaeological Review*, **51**, 7.

LONG, A. J. 1992. Coastal Responses to Changes in Sea-level in the East Kent Fens and Southeast England, UK over the last 7500 years, *Proceedings of the Geologists' Association*, **103**, 187–199.

——1995. Sea-level and crustal movements in the Thames Estuary, Essex and East Kent. *In*:

BRIDGLAND, D., ALLEN, P. & HAGGART, B. A. (eds) *The Quaternary of the Lower Reaches of the Thames: field guide*, Quaternary Research Association.

WESSEX ARCHAEOLOGY 1996a. *Environmental Statement – Queenborough Wastewater Treatment Works Enhancement Scheme: Appendix 9 Archaeology*. Technical Report: archaeology. On behalf of Southern Water.

——1996b. *Queenborough WTW: archaeological field evaluation*. Unpublished client report, August, ref: 41872.

——1996c. *Motney Hill WTW Enhancements: monitoring of contamination investigations (WTW site), monitoring of geotechnical test pits (access road)*. Unpublished client report, August, ref: 41873.

——1996d. *Environmental Statement – Motney Hill Waste-water Treatment Works Enhancement Scheme: Appendix 9 Archaeology*. Technical Report: archaeology. On behalf of Southern Water.

——1996e. *Environmental Statement – Gravesend Wastewater Treatment Works Enhancement Scheme: Appendix 9 Archaeology*. Technical Report: archaeology. On behalf of Southern Water.

——1997. *Queenborough WTW: retained cores and samples – proposal for analysis and publication*. Unpublished client report, January, ref: 41872.

——1998. *Gravesend WTW, Kent: archaeological field evaluation*. Unpublished client report, January, ref: 41876.

——1999a. *Queenborough WTW: archaeological watching brief*. Unpublished client report, January, ref: 41874.

——1999b. *Gravesend WTW, Kent: archaeological watching brief*. Unpublished client report, June, ref: 41876.

——1999c. *Motney Hill WTW Enhancements North Kent: archaeological evaluation – access road*. Unpublished client report, ref: 44355.01.

——1999d. *Motney Hill WTW Enhancements North Kent: archaeological evaluation compound area*. Unpublished client report, ref: 44356.01.

——1999e. *Motney Hill WTW Enhancements North Kent: archaeological evaluation main construction area*. Unpublished client report, ref: 44358.01.

WILKINSON, T. J. & MURPHY, P. L. 1995. *Archaeology of the Essex Coast, Volume 1: the Hullbridge survey*. Essex County Council.

WILLIAMS, J. & BROWN, N. (eds) 1999. *An Archaeological Research Framework for the Greater Thames Estuary*. Essex County Council, Kent County Council, English Heritage, Thames Estuary Partnership.

The Humber estuary: managing the archaeological resource in a dynamic environment

ROBERT VAN DE NOORT[1] & STEPHEN ELLIS[2]

[1] *Department of Archaeology, University of Exeter, Exeter EX4 4QE, UK*
(e-mail: R.van-de-noort@exeter.ac.uk)
[2] *Department of Geography, University of Hull, Hull HU7 6RX, UK*

Abstract: The archaeology of the intertidal wetlands of the Humber estuary is of international importance, and includes prehistoric boats, trackways, fishtraps and platforms, Roman settlements and ports and Post-Medieval fishweirs. This resource is threatened by coastal erosion and flood defence improvement work. This paper outlines a strategic approach to the threatened archaeological resource in the Humber estuary.

As in many other estuaries, the archaeological resource of the Humber estuary is of outstanding quality and importance. This resource is threatened, however, directly or indirectly, by the effects of marine transgressions and the actions required by central and local government agencies to protect the adjacent lowlands from the risk of flooding. In the Humber estuary, we can look back at over six years of meetings, discussions and negotiations and the production of various papers, documents and plans, and although no concrete actions have as yet been taken to protect the estuarine archaeological resource, a consensus is emerging among the agencies and organizations with an interest in the estuary.

This paper addresses two associated issues: first, the archaeological resource of the Humber within a context of the evolving estuary and second, how this resource is and should be managed.

The archaeology of the Humber estuary

Holocene estuarine development

The Humber estuary in its current form comprises around 30 000 ha of water, sandbanks, mudflats, islands, saltmarsh and reedbeds. The estuary forms the centre of the Humber wetlands, a much larger area of some 300 000 ha where tidal activity in the past contributed to the making of the landscape. The Humber estuary commences at Trent Falls at the confluence of the Rivers Ouse and Trent in the west, and flows into the North Sea in between Spurn Point and Donna Nook in the east (Fig. 1). Through its many tributaries, including the Rivers Ouse, Trent, Ancholme and Hull and their tributaries, about 20% of the landmass of England is drained through the Humber (Pethick 1990).

The present shape and character of the Humber estuary is largely a product of Holocene marine transgressions. Its development as a tidal catchment commences from *c.* 8000 cal BC (Berridge & Pattison 1994; J. Reed pers. comm.). Estuarine development is time-transgressive with extensive wetlands developing in the lower estuary well before the upper estuary. Wetland development in the hinterland of the tidal Humber resulted from gradual paludification of the sub-Holocene floor of the lowlands around the Humber, which was a consequence of impeded runoff following sea-level rise, commencing in what is now the lower estuary around 6000 cal BC, and in the upper estuary between 3300 and 1800 cal BC (Gaunt & Tooley 1974; Dinnin & Lillie 1995; Dinnin 1997*a*; Neumann 1998; Long *et al.* 1998). This process created a large diversity of wetlands, including mudflats, saltmarsh, reed swamp, sedge fen, fen carr, and transitional woodland in an area of previously deciduous woodland intersected by relatively steep-sided rivers with narrow floodplains.

Whereas many variations of such a model sequence of vegetation zones could have been encountered in the Humber in the later prehistoric and early historic periods, drainage improvements in the catchment of the Humber and the construction of embankments and sea-defences, land reclamation and warping on the margins of the estuary have resulted in the Humber being a 'highly engineered channel' (Environment Agency 1998). The earliest activities

From: PYE, K. & ALLEN, J. R. L. (eds). *Coastal and Estuarine Environments: sedimentology, geomorphology and geoarchaeology*. Geological Society, London, Special Publications, **175**, 419–427. 0305-8719/00/$15.00 © The Geological Society of London 2000.

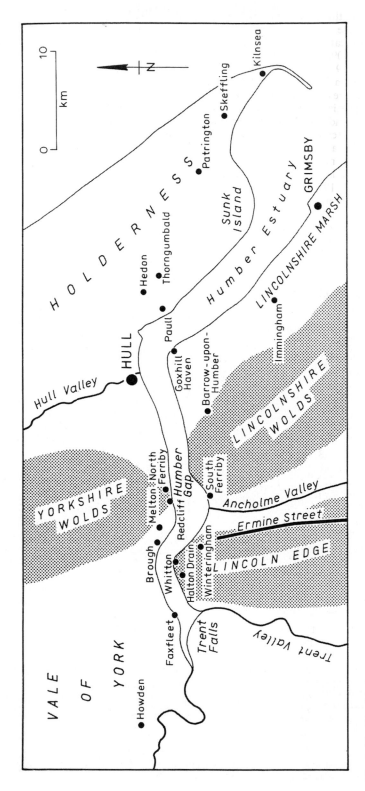

Fig. 1. The Humber Estuary. Main locations mentioned in text.

designed to constrain the sedimentary dynamics within the estuary date to the Middle Ages, but the major schemes date to the 17th century onwards (Dunston 1909; Straw 1955; Sheppard 1956, 1958; Gaunt 1975; Buckland & Sadler 1985; Ellis 1990; Dinnin 1997b; Lillie 1997, 1998, 1999). These activities resulted in the transformation of essentially prehistoric and early historic wetlands into a late- and post-Medieval cultural landscape. The processes involved in this transformation are in general neglected studies of research, although some notable exceptions exist, for example for the reclamation of Sunk Island (Berridge & Pattison 1994). This agricultural lowland landscape, characterized by its sea- and flood-defences, drains, warping drains, windmills and pumping stations, should be regarded as an intrinsic part of the archaeological heritage of the Humber (Pearcey & White 1989).

Archaeology of the Humber estuary in context

The archaeological resource of the intertidal wetlands of the Humber reflects all aspects of past people's activity on the estuary from the later Neolithic through to the present day. Most important of all are the prehistoric plank-built boats, especially from the intertidal zone at North Ferriby, where since 1937 the partial remains of three Bronze Age boats and two Iron Age boats have been discovered (Wright 1990). More recently, an early Bronze Age boat fragment has been discovered from near Kilnsea in the outer estuary (Van de Noort et al. 1999) and boats have been found from the Humber's tributaries, for example at Brigg in the Ancholme valley and at Hasholme in the Foulness valley (McGrail 1998; Millett & McGrail 1987).

During a recent systematic survey of the foreshore as part of the English Heritage funded Humber Wetlands Survey, over 30 sites were discovered from a prehistoric intertidal landscape between Trent Falls and Hull. The majority of sites date to the Bronze Age, but the dates from eight radiocarbon-dated sites ranges from c. 2000 cal BC to c. 400 cal BC (Fletcher et al. 1999). These sites include individual stakes, a platform, post alignments, and clustered stakes that may represent traps for wild fowl and fish (Crowther 1987; Fletcher et al. 1999). The majority of sites were located on peatshelfs which represent recurrence surfaces within the estuary, but a number of sites were identified within alluvium representing deposits of the silted up channels or former creek systems within a saltmarsh environment. These sites included several trackways which were partially excavated during the survey (Fletcher et al. 1999). The trackways were constructed from woven panels or hurdles assembled on dryland from small hazel rods (Fig. 2). The panels were transported to the estuary and placed on unstable ground, across saltmarsh and the tidal creek, and held in place with a series of flanking vertical posts, driven into the mud. They presumably served to provide access to areas of saltmarsh which were exploited as winter pasture. Significantly, waterlogged sites of later prehistoric date are found between the -2–0 m OD. With the exception of the abundance of prehistoric boats, estuaries elsewhere in Britain have produced a similar range of sites and finds, most notably in the Severn, Thames and Solent, illustrating the exploitable resource of estuaries (Bell & Neumann 1997; Fulford et al. 1997).

Other prehistoric landscapes in the Humber estuary include the Kilnsea area, immediately north of Spurn Point, where an extensive prehistoric wetland landscape survives including several barrow and a hengi-form monument, the area around Paull, to the east of Hull, where till outcrops adjacent to the estuary contain cultural debris of Neolithic date, and at Grimsby, at the confluence of the River Freshney, where a Neolithic landscape survives. The survival of Neolithic and Bronze Age wetland landscapes in the Humber estuary is closely associated with the Post-glacial sea-level curve, which reached OD around 2000 cal BC and buried the wetland landscapes of that date (e.g. Long et al. 1998; Neumann 1998).

Post-Bronze Age marine transgression has resulted in a near-absence of archaeological sites of Iron Age date in the Humber estuary, but subsequent marine regression during the Roman period resulted in the location of settlements on alluvial and marine sediments (Neumann 1998). At the confluence of the Rivers Trent and Ouse, for example, a large Roman riverside settlement was found on what was an island in the estuary. This settlement, where further research is ongoing, is at least 8 ha in size, and was ideally placed to function as a transhipment port serving much of northern England, and possibly the continent (Fenwick et al. 1998). Other sites of the Roman period from the Humber estuary include a port and town at Brough, ports at Winteringham and Faxfleet, and a Roman road at South Ferriby, which connected two Roman settlements across the floodplain of the River Ancholme.

Finally, a large number of sites in the Humber estuary are of Post-Medieval date, including V-shaped fishweirs in the areas between Brough

Fig. 2. The excavation of a Bronze Age trackway on the Humber foreshore.

and Hessle, and in the outer estuary at Grimsby (Fletcher *et al.* 1999). These sites survive in the intertidal zone, but have to date not been recorded in any systematic way. Behind the current flood defences, the cultural landscape is the result of centuries of wetland reclamation.

The management of the archaeological resource

The Humber estuary is a focus for much transport activity in the north of England with, for example, *c.* 20% of all British traded goods being conveyed through the Humber (Environment Agency 1998). Associated with this activity is large-scale industrial development, especially in the Immingham region. The estuary is also important for nature conservation and includes extensive areas with Ramsar, Special Protection Area (SPA) and SSSI designation, primarily for the habitats of nine species on the list of Birds of International Significance, and six additional species on the list of Birds of National Significance (HEMS 1997).

Although various industrial developments on the estuary can be identified as posing threats to the archaeological resource, the main threat comes undoubtedly from the effects of accelerated erosion and the proposed updating of sea

defences. The increasing erosion is in part the result of the process of land reclamation combined with the construction of hard defences, resulting in an increased flow rate and tidal range. Sea-level change, and the 'flushing' of precipitation through the network of field drains and drainage channels in the estuary's hinterland have added to the problem, which is know as 'coastal squeeze' (Fig. 3) (Environment Agency 1998; Ellis & Van de Noort 1998)

The need to upgrade the sea-defences is beyond dispute. No less than 500 000 people live and work below mean high tide, protected by defences which were last updated after the 1953 floods in eastern England. Where this upgrading involves the strengthening and increasing the height of the sea defences, the effects on the archaeological resource can be relatively easily identified and are not different from other developments on the estuary. However, where the sea defences are proposed to be upgraded by alternative means, for example by managed retreat or managed re-alignment, the effects on the archaeological resource are much less clear.

Where the threat to the intertidal wetlands comes from various developments, including the upgrading of sea defences and managed retreat, the role of archaeology is governed by the planning process, and a system of assessment and mitigation of the archaeological resource can

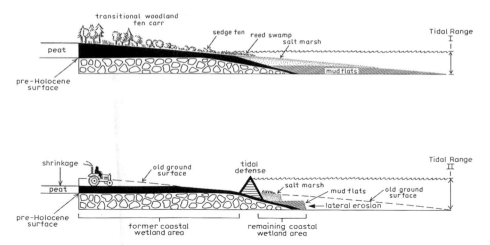

Fig. 3. The 'coastal squeeze' effect, with unconstrained (top) and constrained estuary (bottom).

be undertaken. The mitigation can, as elsewhere, take the form of watching briefs, field based assessments, excavations and *in situ* preservation. PPG 20, 'Coastal Planning' (Department of the Environment 1992), which states as policy objective the conservation of the beauty and amenity of the coast, including the rich cultural heritage of the intertidal zone, offers guidance for the achievement of this objective within the planning process only.

The need for a strategic approach

Examination of recent large-scale coastal and estuarine flood defence schemes in the Humber region can distinguish two main phases. The earlier phase is one wherein archaeology is considered as something with little intrinsic value, and nothing more than a considerations within the planning process. The National Rivers Authority's 'Humber Tidal Defence Strategy' was a clear example of this approach. Archaeologists were consulted on various occasions only shortly before specific reaches of the flood defences in the Humber were to be updated. Desktop studies were hastily undertaken, and the intertidal zone was visited with scant regard for the tidal conditions. The consultant's recommendations for *in situ* preservation of archaeological remains included inappropriate measures, for example the use of geotextile to protect sites from erosion (e.g. Samuels 1994). In an area with a tidal range of up to 7 m and very active erosion, this was simply an unrealistic mitigation.

From 1993 we see the start of a shift in attitudes. The Humber Estuary Management

Strategy (HEMS), must be singled out here. The core of HEMS was formed by English Nature, the National Rivers Authority and since 1996 the Environment Agency, and 22 other organizations including the local authorities, Associated British Ports, local industry and the RSPB. This accepted Archaeology and Cultural Resources as one of eleven areas of concern, alongside, for example, agriculture, industry, flood defences and nature conservation (HEMS 1997). Unfortunately, the archaeological interest was only represented at the level of external consultees, rather than at steering or working group level. Nevertheless, the conservation and enhancements of the estuary's archaeological and cultural heritage was identified as an issue where no dispute existed between the agencies making up HEMS.

More recently, the concept of 'sustainability' has been added to the list of best practice principles. Whatever definition is given to this concept, it can only reinforce the point that the archaeology of the Humber estuary is not to be sacrificed to the demands of industrial development and enhanced sea defences without appropriate mitigation.

While the recognition of the value of the estuary's archaeology is undoubtedly an ongoing process, an additional development is of the greatest importance, that is the desirability by lead agencies in estuarine development to approach the Humber strategically. This may seem all too obvious, but before 1993, the necessity for enhancing the flood defences of a certain area, for example, was considered outside the wider context of sea-level and coastal change, and indeed was undertaken with little regards for adjacent areas. Obviously, the publication of PPG 20 in 1992 set the scene for the change in attitude, and over time this has resulted in more strategic thinking and planning. The strategic principle was also given considerable momentum after the formation of the Environment Agency in 1996, which resulted in outdated working practices of the NRA to be discontinued. Equally, English Heritage expressed in 1996 its more strategically orientated approach to this issue with the publication of 'England's coastal heritage: a statement on the management of coastal archaeology' (English Heritage 1996; also Fulford *et al.* 1997).

The reason why this strategic approach is so important to the estuary's archaeological resource is that only by this approach can the effects of erosion and coastal squeeze on the archaeology of the foreshore be addressed. Without a strategic approach, it may be possible to put constraints and mitigation on industrial developments and sea defence enhancement, but the most important archaeological resource, which is that lying in the intertidal wetlands where waterlogging still preserves both the organic and inorganic remains, is without protection; a strategic approach could look more closely at the *overall* benefits and damage to the archaeology in the estuary.

For example, the effects of managed retreat (cf. Burd 1995) should be considered beyond the site level. Managed retreat may be a mixed blessing for where it is practiced on archaeological remains, but the possibility of reduced erosion and coastal squeeze within the estuary may provide an overwhelmingly positive contribution to *in situ* preservation of archaeological sites in the intertidal wetlands. Furthermore, estuarine management such as managed retreat offers opportunities for enhancing our understanding of past environmental change, as well as providing examples of environments that were common in the past, but no longer exist. This will be of educational interest well beyond the archaeological community.

Designing a strategic approach

An essential first step for a strategic approach is the further enhancement of our understanding of development of the estuary during the Holocene combined with additional archaeological survey work, which includes the assessment of data held by the Sites and Monuments Records, and building on the current work of the Humber Wetlands Survey (cf. Ellis & Van de Noort 1998). Mitigation programmes for tidal defence work and other major developments in the estuary can then be based on this enhanced baseline data. The mitigation should address the Humber estuary as a 'single site', using the principles applied in PPG16, Archaeology and Planning (Department of the Environment 1990).

An understanding of archaeological and palaeo-environmental potential will form a necessary part of the development of a strategic approach to research and archaeological mitigation as part of estuary-wide flood defence schemes, or as part of the production of District or Unitary Authority Development Plans. A map of 'archaeological potential' or 'archaeological constraints' can form the basis for guiding the planning process in order to minimize the possible impact of urban and industrial development on the archaeological resource, or to maximize the outcome of archaeological research in a estuary-wide development scheme.

The ranking of archaeological potential is based on past observations and present understanding of the geomorphological evolution of the Humber estuary and the distribution of known archaeological sites and finds. Ground-truthing of the actual archaeological potential should be an integrated part of any strategic approach to the Humber foreshore; how such ground-truthing may take place has been outlined below.

Although much field survey work remains to be undertaken, within the framework of the Humber Wetlands Survey and beyond, it is possible, on the basis of what is becoming known, to map the archaeological potential of the Humber foreshore and the immediate dryland hinterland, albeit at a limited level of sophistication (Fig. 4). Four mapping categories have been recognized:

(1) Known sites of national archaeological importance
Some of these are included in the Schedule of Ancient Monuments but others are not. They are: the Roman settlement at Kilnsea ('Kilnsea-8' in Van de Noort & Ellis 1995); prehistoric sites on the North Ferriby, Melton and East Clough foreshores; prehistoric and Medieval sites on the Welton Waters foreshore; the Roman harbour at Brough-on-Humber; the Roman settlement at Trent Falls ('Adlingfleet-2' in Van de Noort & Ellis 1998).

(2) Areas of high archaeological potential
These include the following areas from which a multitude of archaeological discoveries have been made and where past and present estuarine erosion is limited: the estuary side of the Kilnsea area; the foreshore and hinterland from North

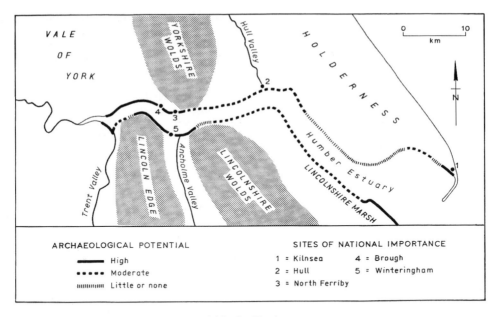

Fig. 4. A global map of archaeological potential in the Humber estuary.

Ferriby to Brough, and from Faxfleet to Trent Falls; the area at Trent Falls west of the Trent and south of the Aire; the area from the Winterton Beck to Ferriby Cliff; the foreshore and hinterland of Grimsby.

(3) Areas of moderate archaeological potential
This category includes areas where limited archaeological discoveries have been made in the past and where estuarine erosion is likely to have destroyed much of the archaeological resource, or where recent sediment accretion is likely to have buried archaeological sites deeply (i.e. beyond the reach of the majority of developments). These areas are: the foreshore and hinterland of the parishes of Patrington and Skeffling; the area around Paull and Hull as far as the Humber Bridge; the Lincolnshire Marsh from Barton-upon-Humber to Cleethorpes.

(4) Areas of little or no archaeological potential
This category includes foreshore and hinterland where past estuarine erosion is presumed to have destroyed the majority of archaeological sites and landscapes. These areas are: southern Holderness between Skeffling and Thorngumbald; the cliffs at Whitton and South Ferriby.

Returning to the map of archaeological potential, work undertaken as part of the planning process or otherwise should be aimed initially at ground-truthing the presumed poten-

tial. The detail and resolution of the work should reflect the presumed archaeological potential (see below). After having confirmed or amended the archaeological potential of an area, the implications for environmental management and planning in the Humber estuary can be considered. The following principles should apply.

(1) Sites of national importance
Whether these are scheduled ancient monuments or not, their protection and *in situ* preservation should be a central consideration in future management and planning. While for some sites of national importance, such as the Roman harbour at Brough, this may be achieved through flood defence works, such works (e.g. provision of toe protection) could have extensive damaging effects at sites on the foreshore, in particular the Bronze Age period 'boatyard' at North Ferriby and sites at Melton. Where *in situ* preservation is not feasible, excavation, recording and publication should be considered for mitigation measures, reflecting the importance of the sites in question.

(2) Areas of high archaeological potential
These should be surveyed three-dimensionally prior to any development. The third dimension is crucial to account for the effects of estuarine sediment accretion and warping. The resolution of the survey in these areas should reflect this high potential. In practice, coring should take

place on a grid-plan of not exceeding 30 by 30 m. Remote sensing (e.g. multi-spectral photography) and geophysical techniques could become suitable for this purpose in the near future. Subsequent work, following initial identification of previously unknown sites, includes the validation of the importance of the site through small scale excavation, and where necessary protection and preservation or alternative mitigation measures, including excavation, analysis and publication. Watching briefs should be held while the development work is in progress.

(3) Areas of medium archaeological potential
These should be assessed in a similar way, although the resolution of the work may be lower, with coring taking place on a grid-plan in the order of 200 by 200 m. Follow-up work should include the validation of the importance of sites through small scale excavation. Watching briefs should be held while the development work is in progress.

(4) Areas with low archaeological potential
The assessment of these areas could be limited to low resolution research aimed at testing the presumed destruction of the archaeological resource by estuarine erosion, with coring taking place on a grid-plan in the order of 1000 by 1000 m. Watching briefs should be held while the development work is in progress. The frequency of visits during watching briefs should reflect the archaeological potential.

Conclusion

The dynamic character of wetlands in general and estuaries wetlands in particular has resulted in a variety of extents of survival of archaeological sites and landscapes. At one extreme the archaeological resource may have been completely destroyed by estuarine and marine erosion, but at the other its preservation may have been greatly enhanced through waterlogging and burial by rapid sediment accretion, as is the case at various sites around the Humber estuary. Archaeological assessment, whether within a planning framework or otherwise, needs to take into account the complex history of wetland landscapes. The use of 'constraint maps', where known archaeology, archaeological potential and landscape development have been combined, may offer opportunities to use resources in a cost-effective manner, guiding research, flood defence schemes and planning processes alike.

For the Humber estuary, enhanced baseline information of archaeological potential is required before estuary-wide mitigation of major developments can be considered. While we do not envisage that all archaeological sites will be preserved *in situ* or excavated before their destruction either by developments or natural forces, it may well be possible to preserve and excavate representative samples of the archaeology of the Humber. This would be a significant step forwards, considering the current rate of erosion of the estuary's intertidal wetlands.

References

BERRIDGE, N. G. & PATTISON, J. 1994. *Geology of the country around Grimsby and Patrington.* Memoir for 1:50,000 sheets 90 and 91 and 81 and 82 (England and Wales). British Geological Survey, HMSO, London.

BELL, M. & NEUMANN, H. 1997. Prehistoric intertidal archaeology and environments in the Severn estuary, Wales. *World Archaeology*, **29**, 95–113.

BUCKLAND, P. C. & SADLER, J. 1985. The nature of late Flandrian alluviation in the Humberhead Levels. *East Midlands Geographer*, **8**, 239–251.

BURD, F. 1995. *Managed retreat: a practical guide.* English Nature, Peterborough.

CROWTHER, D. R. 1987. Sediments and archaeology of the Humber foreshore. *In*: ELLIS, S. (ed.) *East Yorkshire field guide.* Quaternary Research Association, Cambridge, 99–105.

DEPARTMENT OF THE ENVIRONMENT 1990. *Planning policy guidance 16: archaeology and planning.* DoE, London.

——1992. *Planning policy guidance 20: Coastal planning.* DoE, London.

DINNIN, M. 1997a. The palaeoenvironmental survey of the Rivers Idle, Torn and Old River Don. *In*: VAN DE NOORT, R. & ELLIS, S. (eds) *Wetland heritage of the Humberhead Levels: an archaeological survey.* Humber Wetlands Project, University of Hull, Hull, 47–78.

——1997b. The drainage history of the Humberhead Levels. *In*: VAN DE NOORT, R. & ELLIS, S. (eds) *Wetland heritage of the Humberhead Levels: an archaeological survey.* Humber Wetlands Project, University of Hull, Hull, 19–30.

—— & LILLIE, M. 1995a. The palaeoenvironmental survey of southern Holderness and evidence for sea-level change. *In*: VAN DE NOORT, R. & ELLIS, S. (eds) *Wetland heritage of Holderness: an archaeological survey.* Humber Wetlands Project, University of Hull, Hull, 87–120.

DUNSTON, G. 1909. *The rivers of Axholme.* A. Brown and Sons, Hull.

ELLIS, S. 1990. Soils. *In*: ELLIS, S. & CROWTHER, D. R. (eds), *Humber perspectives: a region through the ages.* University Press, Hull, 29–42.

—— & VAN DE NOORT, R. 1998. *Centre for Wetland Archaeology Working paper series: proposals for a strategic approach in environmental management and planning.* Department of Geography, University of Hull, Hull.

ENGLISH HERITAGE 1996. *England's coastal heritage. A statement on the management of coastal archaeology.* English Heritage and the RCHME, London.

ENVIRONMENT AGENCY 1998. *Humber estuary action plan.*

FENWICK, H., CHAPMAN, H., HEAD, R. & LILLIE, M. 1998. The archaeological survey of the lower Trent valley and the Winterton Beck. *In*: VAN DE NOORT, R. & ELLIS, S. (eds) *Wetland heritage of the Ancholme and lower Trent valleys: an archaeological survey.* Humber Wetlands Project, University of Hull, Hull, 143–197.

FLETCHER, W., HEAD, R., CHAPMAN, H., FENWICK, H., VAN DE NOORT, R. & LILLIE, M. (1999). The archaeological survey of the Humber estuary. *In*: VAN DE NOORT, R. & ELLIS, S. (eds) *Wetland heritage of the Vale of York: an archaeological survey.* Humber Wetlands Project, University of Hull, Hull.

FULFORD, M., CHAMPION, T. & LONG, A. 1997. *England's coastal heritage. A survey for English Heritage and the RCHME.* RCHME and English Heritage, London.

GAUNT, G. D. 1975. The artificial nature of the River Don north of Thorne, Yorkshire. *Yorkshire Archaeological Journal*, **47**, 15–21.

—— & TOOLEY, M. J. 1974. Evidence for Flandrian sea-level changes in the Humber estuary and adjacent areas. *Bulletin of the Geological Society of Great Britain*, **48**, 25–41.

HEMS 1997. *Humber Estuary Management Strategy.* English Nature, Wakefield.

LILLIE, M. 1997. Alluvium and warping in the Humberhead Levels: the identification of factors obscuring palaeo-landsurfaces and the archaeological record. *In*: VAN DE NOORT, R. & ELLIS, S. (eds) *Wetland heritage of the Humberhead Levels: an archaeological survey.* Humber Wetlands Project, University of Hull, Hull, 191–218.

——1998. Alluvium and warping in the lower Trent valley. *In*: VAN DE NOORT, R. & ELLIS, S. (eds) *Wetland heritage of the Ancholme and lower Trent valleys: an archaeological survey.* Humber Wetlands Project, University of Hull, Hull, 103–122.

——1999. The palaeoenvironmental survey of the Humber estuary. *In*: VAN DE NOORT, R. & ELLIS, S. (eds) *Wetland heritage of the Vale of York: an archaeological survey.* Humber Wetlands Project, University of Hull, Hull.

LONG, A. J., INNES, J. B., KIRBY, J. R., LLOYD, J. M., RUTHERFORD, M. M., SHENNAN, I. &, TOOLEY, M. J. 1998. Holocene sea-level change and coastal evolution in the Humber estuary, eastern England: an assessment of rapid coastal change. *The Holocene*, **8**, 229–247.

MCGRAIL, S. 1998. Humber wrecks. *In*: DELGADO, J. P. (ed.) *Encyclopaedia of underwater and maritime archaeology.* British Museum Press, London, 199–200.

MILLETT, M. & MCGRAIL, S. 1987. The archaeology of the Hasholme logboat. *Archaeological Journal*, **144**, 69–115.

NEUMANN, H. 1998. The palaeoenvironmental survey of the Ancholme valley. *In*: VAN DE NOORT, R. & ELLIS, S. (eds) *Wetland heritage of the Ancholme and lower Trent valleys: an archaeological survey.* Humber Wetlands Project, University of Hull, Hull, 75–101.

PEARCEY, O. & WHITE, P. 1989. The water heritage. *English Heritage Conservation Bulletin*, **8**, 4–6.

PETHICK, J. S. 1990. The Humber estuary. *In*: ELLIS, S. & CROWTHER, D. R. (eds) *Humber perspectives: a region through the ages.* University Press, Hull, 54–70.

SAMUELS, J. 1994. *Salt End environmental statement.* Archaeological implications addendum. Halcrow, Swindon.

SHEPPARD, J. A. 1956. *The drainage of the marshlands of East Yorkshire.* PhD thesis, University of Hull.

——1958. *The draining of the Hull valley.* East Yorkshire Local History, York.

STRAW, A. 1955. The Ancholme Levels north of Brigg: a history of drainage and its effects on land utilization. *East Midlands Geographer*, **1**, 37–42.

VAN DE NOORT, R. & ELLIS, S. (eds) 1995. *Wetland heritage of Holderness: an archaeological survey.* Humber Wetlands Project, University of Hull, Hull.

—— & ELLIS, S. (eds) 1998. *Wetland heritage of the Ancholme and lower Trent valleys: an archaeological survey.* Humber Wetlands Project, University of Hull, Hull.

——, MIDDLETON, R., FOXON, A. & BAYLISS, A. 1999. The 'Kilnsea boat', and some implications from the discovery of England's oldest boat remain. *Antiquity.*

WRIGHT, E. V. 1990. *The Ferriby boats: seacraft of the Bronze Age.* Routledge, London.

Index